ECONOMETRICS, MACROECONOMICS
AND ECONOMIC POLICY

ECONOMISTS OF THE TWENTIETH CENTURY

General Editors: Mark Perlman, *University Professor of Economics, Emeritus, University of Pittsburgh* and Mark Blaug, *Professor Emeritus, University of London, Professor Emeritus, University of Buckingham* and *Visiting Professor, University of Exeter*

This innovative series comprises specially invited collections of articles and papers by economists whose work has made an important contribution to economics in the late twentieth century.

The proliferation of new journals and the ever-increasing number of new articles make it difficult for even the most assiduous economist to keep track of all the important recent advances. By focusing on those economists whose work is generally recognized to be at the forefront of the discipline, the series will be an essential reference point for the different specialisms included.

A list of published and future titles in this series is printed at the end of this volume.

Econometrics, Macroeconomics and Economic Policy

Selected Papers of Carl F. Christ

Carl F. Christ

Professor of Economics, The Johns Hopkins University, US

ECONOMISTS OF THE TWENTIETH CENTURY

Edward Elgar
Cheltenham, UK • Brookfield, US

Published by
Edward Elgar Publishing Limited
8 Lansdown Place
Cheltenham
Glos GL50 2HU
UK

Edward Elgar Publishing Company
Old Post Road
Brookfield
Vermont 05036
US

HB
119
.C493
A25
1996

British Library Cataloguing in Publication Data
Christ, Carl F.
  Econometrics, Macroeconomics and
  Economic Policy: Selected Papers of Carl
  F. Christ. – (Economists of the Twentieth
  Century Series)
  I. Title II. Series
  330

Library of Congress Cataloguing in Publication Data
Christ, Carl F.
  [Selections. 1996]
  Econometrics, macroeconomics, and economic policy ; selected
papers / of Carl F. Christ.
    p. cm. — (Economists of the twentieth century)
  Includes bibliographical references and index.
    1. Econometrics. 2. Macroeconomics. 3. United States—Economic
policy. I. Title. II. Series.
HB119.C493A25 1996
330'.01'5195—dc20   95–39640
                                                                                        CIP

ISBN 1 85898 135 2

Printed and bound in Great Britain by
Hartnolls Limited, Bodmin, Cornwall

Contents

Acknowledgements

The author and publishers wish to thank the following who have kindly given permission for the use of copyright material.

American Economics Association for articles: 'Early Progress in Estimating Quantitative Economic Relationships in America', *American Economic Review* (December 1985), **75**(6), pp. 39–52; 'The Cowles Commission's Contributions to Econometrics at Chicago, 1939–1955', *Journal of Economic Literature* (March 1994), **32**(1), pp. 30–59; 'A Short-Run Aggregate-Demand Model of the Interdependence and Effects of Monetary and Fiscal Policies with Keynesian and Classical Interest Elasticities', *American Economic Review* (May 1967), **57**(2), pp. 434–43; 'On Fiscal and Monetary Policies and the Government Budget Restraint', *American Economic Review* (September 1979), **69**(4), pp. 526–38.

Bank of Japan for article: 'The Financing of the Government Budget in Japan and its Relation to Macroeconomic Variables', *Bank of Japan Monetary and Economic Studies* (May 1987), **5**(1), pp. 1–32, Appendix II.

Cato Institute for article: 'Rules vs. Discretion in Monetary Policy', *Cato Journal* (Spring 1983), **3**(1), pp. 121–41.

Cowles Commission for Research in Economics for article: 'History of the Cowles Commission 1932–1952', in *Economic Theory and Measurement: A Twenty Year Research Report* (1952), pp. 3–65.

Elsevier Science Publishers B.V. for articles: 'Some Dynamic Theory of Macro-economic Policy Effects on Income and Prices under the Government Budget Restraint', *Journal of Monetary Economics* (January 1978), **4**(1), pp. 45–70; 'Pitfalls in Macroeconomic Model Building', in Tej K. Kaul and Jati K. Sengupta (eds.), *Economic Models, Estimation and Socioeconomic Systems: Essays in Honor of Karl A. Fox. (Contributions to Economic Analysis* No. 186), (1991), pp. 257–89.

Federal Reserve Bank of St. Louis for article: 'Assessing Applied Econometric Results', *Federal Reserve Bank of St. Louis Review* (March/April 1993), **75**(2), pp. 71–94.

Greenwood Press Inc. for paper: 'Economics and Public Policy', in Shripad Pendse (ed.), *Perspectives on an Economic Future: Forms, Reforms and Evaluations (Contributions in Economics and Economic History* No. 116), (1991), pp. 15–29.

Indian Economic Review for article: 'Decomposition of the Expected Squared Error of Forecast from a Linear Forecasting Equation', *Indian Economic Review*, Special number in memory of Sukhamoy Chakravarty (1992 but published in 1994), **27**, pp. 325–8.

International Economic Review for article: 'Judging the Performance of Econometric Models of the U.S. Economy', *International Economic Review* (February 1975), **16**(1), pp. 54–74.

Macmillan Press for paper: 'When is Free Banking More Stable Than Regulated Banking?', in Haim Barkai, Stanley Fischer and Nissan Liviatan (eds.), *Monetary Theory and Thought: Essays in Honour of Don Patinkin* (1993), pp. 185–209.

National Bureau of Economic Research for article: 'A Test of an Econometric Model for the United States, 1921–1947', in Universities–National Bureau Committee, *Conference on Business Cycles* (1951), pp. 35–107.

Ohio State University Press for article: 'Monetary and Fiscal Influences on U.S. Money Income 1891–1970', *Journal of Money, Credit and Banking* (February 1973), **5**(1), pp. 279–300.

University of Chicago Press for article: 'A Simple Macroeconomic Model with a Government Budget Restraint', *Journal of Political Economy* (January/February 1968), **76**(1), pp. 53–67.

Chad Gutstein assisted in preparing the name index.

Dymphna Evans and Jo Perkins ably steered the manuscript through the press.

Introduction

This volume contains a selection of my papers published during my first half century in economics. They span three areas: econometrics, macroeconomics including the government budget restraint, and economic policy. Econometrics, being quantitative and empirical, was a natural point of entry into economics for a former physicist, but my interest in economic policy is also closely related to the reasons for the switch from physics.

From physics to economics

In college I was a physics major, and during World War II I worked on the Manhattan Project (the atom bomb project) in Chicago. After the war I accepted a one-year job teaching freshman physics at Princeton. I had always thought I wanted to be a teacher. The year at Princeton was great fun, and confirmed my desire. But in what subject?

During the war I had lived in an interracial co-op house populated by pacifists and other social activists. Though I was not a pacifist, many of the people I admired were pacifists, ministers, social workers, leaders of the co-op movement, and others who dealt with human problems. I decided that I wanted to switch from physics to something more related to human problems. I looked among the social sciences for a subject where my interest and training in mathematics would be useful. Economics was the obvious choice. While at Princeton I audited an economic theory course given by Oskar Morgenstern, and began to read von Neumann and Morgenstern's *The Theory of Games and Economic Behavior*. I decided to go to graduate school in economics at Chicago. It was a happy choice for me.

The nature of econometrics

At Chicago I encountered the Cowles Commission and econometrics. My initial impression was that the way people do empirical research in econometrics is as follows: first, obtain a complete and correct mathematical model from *a priori* economic theory. Second, assemble data for the model's variables. Third, determine whether or not the model is identifiable with respect to the available type of data, and if not, obtain data of other types, or revise the model (using economic theory), until it is identifiable. At this point one has a maintained hypothesis for use in statistical inference. Fourth, estimate the parameters of the model. Fifth, test hypotheses about the parameters. Then the job is finished. The result is a numerical model that is ready to use to understand economic behaviour from the past, and to predict it in the future.

Experience in research at the Cowles Commission – bolstered by some reflection on the development of physics – soon changed this initial impression. The models we use in econometrics are not correct, they are at best approximations, and at worst they can be quite wrong. They are almost never obtained solely from *a priori* economic theory. They are typically obtained, at least in part, by estimating many different equation forms, and then choosing the set of equations that fits the available data the best – a practice known as data mining.

There is nothing wrong with data mining. It can be a fruitful method of arriving at hypotheses. Indeed, it is essential, because economic theory alone is not powerful enough to specify all the details of an econometric model, such as the form of its equations, the list of variables to be included, the classification of variables as endogenous or exogenous, and especially the dynamic behaviour of the system when it is out of equilibrium (economic theory is more informative about the nature of equilibrium than it is about disequilibrium behaviour).

However, because models chosen in this way are at best not quite correct, statistical estimates and tests using such a model as a maintained hypothesis do not carry the guarantees that are implied in the rigorously derived statistical theorems about unbiasedness, consistency, efficiency and so on. Furthermore, if we use conventional statistical significance tables to test the hypothesis that a coefficient in such a model is zero, we will too often reject it and conclude that the variable in question belongs in the model, because of the screening process that was used to choose the model.

Some method of assessing the validity of a model is needed, so that we may know how much confidence to place in the results of estimates and tests that are based on it. In my view one of the best ways to do this is to see how well the estimated model describes data that were not known to the model builder when the model was chosen. If an estimated model does this as well as a correct and unchanging model could be expected to do, then it tentatively merits some confidence. Otherwise, its usefulness is in question, either for forecasting future behaviour or for explaining a class of behaviour wider than the sample used to estimate it.

The rest of this introduction gives some background about the papers in this volume.

Part I: The history of econometrics
The three papers in Part I of this volume deal with the history of econometrics.

Chapter 1, 'History of the Cowles Commission 1932–1952', was written for the Commission's twentieth anniversary while I was a young research associate there. It lay almost forgotten for rather a long time, but is being referred to more often, now that econometrics is old enough for people to be interested in its history. A part of it, on the founding of the Econometric Society and *Econometrica*, was reprinted in the fiftieth anniversary issue of *Econometrica* in January, 1983. Two of the Cowles Commission's early projects are very interesting, in the light of the recent explosion of research on finance. One was 'Can Stock Market Forecasters Forecast?' by Alfred Cowles, an empirical study that compared actual forecasts with randomly generated forecasts (to the disadvantage of the former) and thus fore-shadowed the efficient markets hypothesis. The other was the Cowles Commission's monograph on common stock indexes, which were the forerunner of the Standard and Poor indexes. See pp. 12, 13 and 18 of Chapter 1.

Chapter 2, 'Early Progress in Estimating Quantitative Economic Relationships in America', was written on the occasion of the hundredth anniversary of the founding of the American Economic Association in 1885. It deals mainly with the pioneering work by Henry Moore in what he called 'statistical economics' and by his student

Henry Schultz in demand analysis, after briefly discussing earlier attempts to estimate demand and supply equations. It ends with the formal solution of the identification problem by Haavelmo and Koopmans in the 1940s.

Chapter 3, 'The Cowles Commission's Contributions to Econometrics at Chicago, 1939–1955', is a retrospective account of the Cowles revolution in econometrics and its place in current practice. The main ingredients were an explicit probability approach, simultaneous equations models, criteria for the identifiability of parameters, and estimation methods suitable for simultaneous equations. The first three are mainstays of present-day econometrics (or should be), but the specific estimation methods developed by the Cowles group have largely been displaced. For example, the limited information method has been displaced by two stage least squares.

Part II: Econometrics and its assessment
The four papers in Part II concern econometrics and the assessment of econometric methods and results.

Chapter 4, 'A Test of an Econometric Model for the United States, 1921–1947', is my dissertation, which was an early attempt to test an econometric model by looking at how well it describes post-sample data. Lawrence Klein (1950) had presented his first major econometric model of the US, formulated after World War II and estimated with data for 1921–41. Andrew Marshall (1950, abstract) had tested Klein's model against 1946 data, and had found that some equations fit the 1946 data well and others didn't. I revised the equations of Klein's model that did poorly in Marshall's test, re-estimated the revised model for 1921–41 and 1946–7, and tested the result against 1948 data. Again some equations did well, and some did not. For some variables the forecast errors were smaller than the year-to-year change in the variable, and for others they were larger.

My debt to my advisers is great, but my debt to Leo Hurwicz is even greater, for he invited me for the weekend to his pre-fab home at the Univeristy of Illinois and went over my draft with me in great detail, pointing out things that should be changed. I was quite depressed when I left him, but after a few days I realized that he had done me an enormous favour which had made a substantial improvement in my dissertation.

It was presented at a National Bureau of Economic Research conference, and was discussed by Friedman and Klein. Friedman (1951) was supportive of its objective and its results, and was sceptical of the usefulness of models of this sort. Klein (1951) approved its methodological account of procedures for testing models, but criticized it vigorously for the choice of data, for the manner of revising equations, and for the forecasting method. My reply is Christ (1951).

Chapter 5, 'Judging the Performance of Econometric Models of the U.S. Economy', is a discussion of methods of forecasting with the aid of econometric models, and my comparison of root mean square errors of post-sample forecasts of GNP and the price level by nine US econometric models for periods between 1969 and 1974, the forecasts and their errors having been computed for each model by its author(s). The root mean square errors of forecasts of real and nominal GNP were 1 per cent or less for forecasts one to two quarters ahead, and less than 3 per cent for forecasts five to six quarters ahead. All of the econometric forecasts were better than ARIMA forecasts. For each variable and each forecasting horizon, the econometric forecast errors varied among models by a factor of about 2, and the best two or three of them (not always by the same model in every case) were better than the average reported in the American Statistical Association–National Bureau of Economic Research survey of judgmental forecasters. In recent years the comparison of forecast errors of different models has been continued by Stephen McNees at the Federal Reserve Bank of Boston and published in the *New England Economic Review* (see Chapter 7).

Some econometric forecasters publish forecasts exactly as they come out of the model, and others make subjective adjustments to try to improve the model's forecasts before publishing them. All practical forecasters must use *ex ante* predictions of their exogenous variables, of course, because the true values are not known until after the forecast period has occurred. To test practical forecasting ability, one wants forecasts that are based on the model proprietor's own *ex ante* forecasts of exogenous variables, and that use any subjective adjustments that the proprietor uses. To test a model as a scientific hypothesis, however, one wants forecasts that are computed using *actual* values of exogenous variables, and *without* any subjective adjustment.

Chapter 5 also presents the time-paths of the multiplier effects of government purchases and of open market operations upon real GNP for each model, for at least 12 quarters after the change, and for as long as 40 quarters in the case of several models. These were also provided by the models' proprietors. The models disagreed so strongly about these time paths that they cannot be considered reliable guides to the effects of fiscal and monetary policies until it can be determined which (if any) was correct.

Chapter 6, 'Decomposition of the Expected Squared Error of Forecast from a Linear Forecasting Equation', is a small piece noting the possible sources of error of forecast (i.e., incorrect choice of variables, changes in parameters after estimation but before forecasting, sampling error of parameter estimates, incorrect forecasts of independent variables, and disturbances during the forecast period) when the correct model is linear, and presenting a decomposition of the expected squared error of a forecast into components related to these sources of error. It is useful as a reminder of possible sources of error and their effects, but it would be difficult to use empirically because the required information is typically not available.

Chapter 7, 'Assessing Applied Econometric Results', is an account of methods and results of assessing econometric output. It is in four parts. The first argues that a good way to test an econometric model is to see how well it forecasts data outside the sample period that was used to estimate it, and explains why the most stringent test is to forecast data that were not available when the model was chosen. The second discusses some recently proposed econometric techniques. The third summarizes McNees's recent comparisons of forecast errors of several macroeconometric models of the US economy. The fourth applies the advice in the first part to a very simple 40-year-old equation that described the behaviour of the Cambridge k (the inverse of monetary velocity) as a linear function of the inverse of a long-term interest rate for 1919–52 with an r square of about 0.75. The result is very unusual in econometric testing: that simple equation, with little change in its parameters, describes the data for 1892–1918 and for 1953–91 about as well as it describes the sample data from which it was first estimated.

Part III: The government budget restraint and its implications

In graduate school at Chicago I was a Keynesian (yes, there were Keynesians there, especially Jacob Marschak and Lloyd Metzler, as well as the more classical Friedman, Knight and Mints; oddly enough the only one who made us actually *read* the *General Theory* was Mints). The Keynesian model used by Klein seemed a natural application for the econometric methods of Koopmans, and I embraced it too, at that time. But something about its treatment of government purchases, taxes, the money stock and the interest rate seemed vaguely unsatisfactory.

Eventually (with some help from Lloyd Metzler (1951) and Don Patinkin (1956); see Chapter 8 for the references) I realized what the problem was: although actual fiscal policy, and good verbal discussions of it, typically involve the government debt, the typical Keynesian mathematical model did not. The natural next step was to take account of the requirement that whatever the Federal government spends must be financed by some combination of revenues, borrowing from the Federal Reserve (i.e., increasing the monetary base), borrowing from others (i.e., increasing the amount of government debt held outside the Federal Reserve), and selling other assets (such as foreign exchange reserves or physical capital). This requirement is the government budget restraint.

For simplicity, the profits of Federal government enterprises and the proceeds of sales of assets can be consolidated with taxes, the losses of Federal government enterprises can be consolidated with subsidies (which are included in transfer payments), taxes minus transfers can be considered as a single variable, and a closed economy can be considered. I shall do that here (but some of my papers consider an open economy). Then the government budget restraint says that the sum of Federal purchases plus transfers less taxes, i.e., the Federal deficit, is equal to the increase in the monetary base plus the increase in Federal debt held by the private sector (which is taken to include state and local governments because unlike the Federal government they cannot create base money).

One of the most important implications is that the Federal government cannot exogenously choose values for all four of the variables, government purchases, taxes less transfer payments, the monetary base, and government debt held by the private sector. Any three can be chosen exogenously, but the remaining one will then be determined endogenously by the joint action of the government budget restraint and the private sector. This means that if any one of the four policy variables is changed exogenously, holding two of the others fixed, the remaining one will respond endogenously along with the system's other endogenous variables: income, the price level, etc. It also means that the effect of an exogenous change in any one of the four policy variables will depend on which of the other three is allowed to respond endogenously. Thus, for example, there are three multiplier effects of government purchases: one if they are financed with a balanced budget by increasing taxes or cutting transfers, one if financed by borrowing from the private sector, and one if financed by issuing base money.

The seven papers in Part III deal with fiscal and monetary policy under the government budget restraint.

Chapter 8, 'A Short-Run Aggregate-Demand Model of the Interdependence and Effects of Monetary and Fiscal Policies with Keynesian and Classical Interest Elasticities', is, to my knowledge, the first systematic treatment of the multiplier effects when each of these four policy variables is changed exogenously, one at a time, while each of the remaining three, one at a time, is allowed to change endogenously. There are thus twelve such policy pairs. The analysis in this paper contains no dynamics: it deals only with equilibrium situations. It contains an error, not noticed until after it went to press, and corrected in my later papers: its government budget restraint incorrectly omits from taxes less transfers the after-tax interest paid by the government to the private sector.

Chapter 9, 'A Simple Macroeconomic Model with a Government Budget Restraint', begins to introduce dynamics, which is proper because introducing the government budget restraint makes a model dynamic even if all its other equations are static. In this paper it is assumed that any government deficit is financed solely by increases in the monetary base: no government bonds are held by the private sector. There are three policy variables: the monetary base or high powered money stock H, real government purchases g, and real autonomous taxes less transfers. Of course there is an induced change in taxes less transfers whenever income changes. Then there are three possible policy pairs: a change in g financed by a change in autonomous and induced taxes less transfers with H fixed, a change in g financed by a change in H (and some induced taxes less transfers) with autonomous taxes less transfers fixed, and a change in autonomous taxes less transfers financed by a change in H (and some induced taxes less transfers) with g fixed. But any two of these policy pairs can be considered as a basic set, for any other policy can be expressed as a linear combination of these two pairs. Thus the third policy pair is the sum of equal-sized but opposite-signed doses of the first two policy pairs, so that g remains fixed. All three policy pairs are dynamically stable under plausible assumptions about the rest of the system and its parameter values.

Chapter 10, 'Monetary and Fiscal Influences on U.S. Money Income, 1891–1970', is an empirical study of the reduced form equation for money income during 1891–1970, taking taxes less transfers as endogenous. The effects of increases in government purchases or in the monetary base were substantial and positive, but not constant from period to period. The effects of increases in Federal debt held by the private sector were positive for recent periods and negative for periods beginning before World War I.

Chapters 11 and 12, 'Some Dynamic Theory of Macroeconomic Policy Effects on Income and Prices under the Government Budget Restraint' and 'On Fiscal and Monetary Policies and the Government Budget Restraint', provide dynamic analysis when the government deficit can be financed by either bonds or money or both, as in Chapter 8. Then we see some striking differences from Chapter 9, which has no bond financing. Under plausible conditions, the assumption that an increase in the monetary base H is inflationary (which is historically and theoretically supported) implies that policy pairs in which government purchases are endogenous are stable, and pairs in which government debt is endogenous are unstable. (Blinder and Solow (1973) arrived at a result that is logically equivalent to the latter, but they interpreted it to imply that an increase in the monetary base is *deflationary*, because they *assumed* stability. Some independent evidence, presented in Chapter 11, supports my interpretation rather than theirs.) Regardless of whether an increase in *H* is inflationary, policy pairs with *H* or autonomous taxes less transfers endogenous are stable.

Chapter 13, 'Changes in the Financing of the Federal Debt and their Impact on the U.S. Economy, 1948–90', is an excerpt from a long paper that consolidates the Flow of Funds data for the US Government sector and the Monetary Authorities sector to express the actual US government budget restraint numerically for 1946 through 1979. It argues that the inflation of the 1970s was unnecessary, and was primarily due to the increases in the monetary base brought about by the Federal Reserve. It predicted (correctly, thus far) that inflation will continue until the Federal Reserve moderates the growth rate of the monetary base.

Chapter 14, 'The Financing of the Government Budget in Japan and its Relation to Macroeconomic Variables', is a discussion of the government budget restraint in Japan, together with pertinent data from the Bank of Japan and the Japanese national accounts, and a model of an open economy with a government budget restraint. An appendix explains why perpetual pure debt finance of government expenditures (including debt interest) is unsustainable.

Part IV: Monetary economics and monetary policy

The two papers in Part IV deal with monetary matters.

Chapter 15, 'Rules vs. Discretion in Monetary Policy', displays data for several money stocks, their growth rates, their velocities and their ratios to the monetary base, as well as the inflation rate and nominal and real interest rates, for several periods between 1929 and 1982. In principle an optimum monetary policy could be deduced from the maximization of an objective function subject to the behaviour of the private sector, but in practice we do not have an agreed-upon objective function in America, and we cannot predict the behaviour of the private sector very well. Even so, it is clear that monetary policy affects output and the price level. Polar opposites for monetary policy are a mechanical rule, and a monetary authority with discretionary power. No simple rule, such as increasing a monetary stock at the constant rate of 3 per cent a year, would be optimal if we knew enough to optimize, but such a rule would have produced better results than the inflation we had during 1961–82. I argue for some discretion, circumscribed by upper and lower limits on the rate of change of a money stock, so that the Federal Reserve will be able to respond to special events, but will not be able to create inflation. The need for discretion is exemplified by the stock market crash of 19 October 1987, when the Federal Reserve wisely announced that the discount window was open for lending to any bank that experienced liquidity difficulties as a result of the crash.

Chapter 16, 'When is Free Banking More Stable Than Regulated Banking?', is directed at the claim, made by some advocates of free banking, that free banking is less prone to inflation, and to bank runs and bank failures, than the regulated banking that most countries have today. Free banking means a system in which there are no bank reserve requirements, and any private bank is free to issue not only deposits but also private bank notes, both being convertible into gold (or, some advocates say, into base money issued by a central bank, possibly with some restrictions). This paper's analysis is conducted with the aid of a nonlinear model of free banking in an open economy in which velocity and the public's holdings of base money are endogenous. Both flexible and fixed exchange rates are considered. An interesting feature of free banking is that the money stock responds positively to changes in productive capacity. The principal conclusion is that the main advantages claimed for free banking are available under regulated banking: if free banking is resistant to inflation, it will be because bank-issued money is convertible into gold (or some other form of base money that cannot be increased at will by a central bank), and not because of the existence of private bank notes. And if free banking is resistant to bank runs and bank failures, it will not be primarily because of the right to issue private bank notes.

Part V: Reflections on macroeconomic modelling and on economic policy

The two papers in Part V are quite different from the rest of this volume, and from each other.

Chapter 17, 'Pitfalls in Macroeconomic Model Building', is a paper I wrote after observing certain types of mistakes in macroeconomic model construction being made repeatedly by successive generations of students (and by authors of many of the papers I have refereed). It contains a number of steps that can be taken to help make a model complete, consistent internally, consistent with what the model builder knows or wants to test about its subject matter, easy for the writer and reader to understand, and ready to analyse mathematically or estimate econometrically. It contains three examples of simple models, showing how these steps work.

Chapter 18, 'Economics and Public Policy', is an attempt to describe what economics can and cannot contribute to the achievement of consensus about public policy. As noted earlier, my interest in human problems was an important reason for switching from physics to economics. Briefly stated, the message of Chapter 18 is that economics in principle can tell us the effects of various policies (and research in economics can increase the range of understanding and agreement about this). But economics cannot always tell us which of two policies is better, because that depends on the objectives to be sought, about which there are sometimes serious conflicting interests.

I hope that you, the reader, will find these papers useful, and that you will have as much enjoyment in reading them as I have had in writing them.

References

The following is a list of references cited in the Introduction, except that it excludes articles reprinted in this volume and references cited in those articles. To locate a reference that is cited in an article in this volume, look up the author in the index.

Christ, Carl (1951), 'Reply' (to Friedman (1951) and Klein (1951)), in Universities–National Bureau Committee for Economic Research, *Conference on Business Cycles*, New York, National Bureau of Economic Research, pp. 123–6.

Christ, Carl (1983), 'The Founding of the Econometric Society and Econometrica', *Econometrica*, **51**(1), (January), pp. 3–6.

Cowles, Alfred, 3rd (1933), 'Can Stock Market Forecasters Forecast?', *Econometrica*, **1**(3), (July), pp. 309–324.

Cowles, Alfred, 3rd and Associates (1939), *Common-Stock Indexes: Cowles Commission Monograph 3*, Bloomington, Indiana, Principia Press.

Friedman, Milton (1951), 'Comment' (on Chapter 4 herein), in Universities–National Bureau Committee for Economic Research, *Conference on Business Cycles*, New York, National Bureau of Economic Research, pp. 107–14.

Keynes, John Maynard (1936), *The General Theory of Employment, Interest, and Money*, London, Harcourt Brace.

Klein, Lawrence R. (1951), 'Comment' (on Chapter 4 herein), in Universities–National Bureau Committee for Economic Research, *Conference on Business Cycles*, New York, National Bureau of Economic Research, pp. 114–23.

Marshall, Andrew W. (1950), 'A Test of Klein's Model III for Changes of Structure' (abstract), *Econometrica*, **18**(3), (July), p. 291.

von Neumann, John and Oskar Morgenstern (1944), *The Theory of Games and Economic Behavior*, Princeton, Princeton University Press.

Errata

There are occasional misprints in some of the papers in this volume. It was not possible to correct them, because of the printing method that was used. Below is a list of corrections for those that might create uncertainty or misunderstanding in the mind of the reader. Page references are not to the page numbers of the original, but to the consecutive page numbers of this volume.

Chapter 6
p. 209:

line 8, end of line: 'minus' should be 'plus'.
line 11: '$= \delta^2 +$' should be '$= \sigma^2 +$'.
line 11: '$\text{cov}(z_{Fi} - z_{Fj})$' should be '$\text{cov}(z_{Fi} - z_i, z_{Fj} - z_j)$'.
line 18, term 2: '$\Sigma\Sigma\delta_j z_i z_j$' should be '$\Sigma\Sigma\delta_i\delta_j z_i z_j$'.
line 22, term 6: '$z_{sub}Ft$' should be 'z_{Fi}'.

Chapter 11
p. 289, line 4: '$\alpha_2 < \alpha_1 \leq 1$' should be '$\alpha_2 \leq \alpha_1 < 1$'.
p. 292, equation (8): '$+H/P$' should be '$+ \dot{H}/P$' and '$/\dot{B}P$' should be '$\dot{B}/P$'.
p. 297, line 4: 'ϕ' should be 'θ'.
p. 305, row (3), column (6): '$1-u - \phi_B$' should be '$1-u - \dfrac{\phi_B}{P'}$'
P'

and row (8), column (5): '$-\Delta_H$' should be '$\dfrac{-\Delta_H}{\Delta_B}$'.

p. 307, last sentence of section A2 should be: 'The discriminant of the characteristic equation is of uncertain sign, so the roots can be real or complex; hence the approach to equilibrium can be monotonic or oscillatory.'
p. 308, last sentence of section A3: 'The' should be 'It is likely that'.

Chapter 14
p. 408:
line 9: 'exceeds' should be 'is less than'.

Chapter 16
p. 434, middle of page, and throughout: whenever the square root symbol '$\sqrt{}$' appears, it applies only to the single letter that follows it. For example, $\sqrt{n}sP$ means $sP\sqrt{n}$, not $\sqrt{nsP}$, and so on.
p. 437, next to last line before section 3: 'rho' should be 'ρ'.
p. 446, Table 9.2, next to last line, column headed '$y\&n$': '$2\sqrt{2}$' should be '$\sqrt{2}$'.

PART I

THE HISTORY OF ECONOMETRICS

[1]

HISTORY OF THE COWLES COMMISSION
1932–1952

BY CARL F. CHRIST*

I. *The founding of the Cowles Commission*

The Cowles Commission for Research in Economics was founded in 1932. Alfred Cowles, president of Cowles and Company, an investment counseling firm in Colorado Springs, Colorado, initiated some inquiries into the accuracy of professional stock market forecasters over the period 1928–1932. This aroused his interest in fundamental economic research, which led him to offer his financial support toward the establishment of the Cowles Commission and to bear a significant share of the burden each year. Fortunately at the outset he encountered Harold T. Davis, a professor of mathematics at Indiana University whose interests included mathematical economics and statistics. Davis was to become an important figure in the

* The source material for this sketch consisted of published and unpublished records of the Cowles Commission, and even more important, the personal recollections of several of its leading members, past and present, with whom I was able to talk. I wish to acknowledge the generous assistance provided by these men. They are Alfred Cowles, Harold T. Davis, Charles F. Roos, Dickson H. Leavens, Theodore O. Yntema, Jacob Marschak, Tjalling C. Koopmans, and William B. Simpson. In addition, Ragnar Frisch gave helpful comments on preliminary drafts.

3

Moffett Photo

ALFRED COWLES

Evanston Photographic Service

HAROLD T. DAVIS

founding of the Cowles Commission and in its progressive development through the years. Also important was the new Econometric Society, not yet two years old, which had been organized in 1930 by Irving Fisher of Yale University, Ragnar Frisch of the University of Oslo, Charles F. Roos of Cornell University, and others.

As early as 1912, while Fisher was vice-president of the American Association for the Advancement of Science, he had attempted to organize a society to promote research in quantitative and mathematical economics. Wesley C. Mitchell, Henry L. Moore, and a few others had been interested but they were too few, and for the time being nothing came of their vision.

In the spring of 1928, Frisch was in the United States under a Rockefeller Foundation grant. At Princeton University he met Roos, then a young mathematician who was a Fellow of the National Research Council and secretary of the rejuvenated Section K (economics, sociology, and statistics) of the American Association for the Advancement of Science. They found themselves in agreement that there was a need for bringing economics, mathematics, and statistics closer together for work in what has come to be called econometrics. Frisch had corresponded with several economists about the possibility of founding a society with this objective. He and Roos decided to solicit Fisher's support in organizing such a society, and Frisch went to see Fisher at Yale. In April, 1928, all three met at Fisher's home in New Haven for a weekend to discuss the idea further. Fisher, mindful of the outcome of his earlier attempt, was pessimistic. At length he said that if Frisch and Roos could name one hundred people in the world who would join a society established for the encouragement of econometric work and the exchange of econometric papers, he would become an enthusiastic partner in organizing such a society. They were very happy with this response, thinking that it would be a simple matter to list a hundred interested people. At first, the list virtually wrote itself, but then the going got harder, and after three days they had to give up with about seventy likely prospects. Fisher looked over their list and suggested about a dozen additional names. He was quite surprised that they had found so many, and he agreed that eighty justified going ahead. The three men drafted a letter of invitation to membership in the proposed society together with a request for the names of others who might be interested. The response to the invitation was excellent and nearly eighty more names were suggested.

The American Economic Association, the American Statistical Association, and Section K of the American Association for the Advancement of Science were to hold their first joint meeting in Cleveland, Ohio in December, 1930. Early in that year Fisher, Frisch (who was again in the United States, this time as a visiting professor at Yale), and Roos issued invitations to an organization meeting of the Econometric Society to be held in Cleveland on December 29, 1930. Twelve Americans and four Europeans attended. Joseph A. Schumpeter, then professor at the University of Bonn, was elected chairman of the meeting, and such was his enthusiasm that he himself made the motion whereby the new society was founded. Fisher was elected the first president and nine others were elected to the Council. A tentative constitution proposed by Frisch was adopted in principle, and was then phrased by a committee consisting of Frisch, Frederick C. Mills, and Roos. The constitution as amended appears with annotations in *Econometrica* for January, 1952, together with the names of those attending the organization meeting and of all officers and Council members since the beginning. The first meeting of the Society after its organization was held in September, 1931, at the University of Lausanne, Switzerland. The second meeting was held in Washington, D. C. in December, 1931, together with the meetings of other social science societies. During the year 1931 the Council elected 173 persons to charter membership, including all those who attended the organization meeting in Cleveland and all who attended the Lausanne meeting.

While the Econometric Society was being formed,

Cowles was publishing the investment service of Cowles and Company in Colorado Springs. He became interested in comparing his forecasts with those of other professional forecasters, and in checking afterwards to see whether an investor would have done well to follow their advice. After the stock market crash in 1929 and the subsequent long decline of security prices amid optimistic predictions by many investment services, he began to feel that most of the forecasters were just guessing, himself included. In fact in 1931, he discontinued his forecasting service, explaining in his investment letter that he did not know enough about the forces that govern the fluctuations of business and the stock market. He further stated that he was going to try to find out more about these matters through research of his own before making any further forecasts.

In the summer of 1931, Cowles discussed his problems with a friend, Charles H. Boissevain, a Dutch biochemist with mathematical training who was head of the Colorado Foundation for Research in Tuberculosis. Boissevain thought that multiple-correlation analysis might be an effective tool for economic research and suggested to Cowles that he consult Davis, professor of mathematics at Indiana University, who spent his summers in Colorado Springs. Shortly thereafter Davis received a telephone call from Cowles, whose first question was whether it was possible to compute the multiple-correlation coefficient in a problem involving twenty-four variables. Davis replied that he didn't know why anyone would want to compute such a correlation coefficient, but a new method of performing such computations with the aid of Hollerith (IBM) punch-card computing machines had recently become available and he thought he could carry out the desired computations. Cowles enlisted Davis' services and acquired a Hollerith computer, and together he and Davis set to work finding correlation coefficients.

On becoming acquainted with the problems on which Cowles was working, Davis suggested to Cowles that he associate himself with the newly-formed Econometric Society because there he would find the men who by training and interest could be most helpful to him. Davis added that Cowles might enlist their aid on a continuing basis and advance his cause still further. He could offer to finance the publication of a journal for them and set up a research organization under their auspices with the resources and freedom for econometric research and publication. Cowles felt that this would be an effective way of securing first-class talent to work on the problems in which he had become interested.

Accordingly he wrote to Fisher, who was president of the Econometric Society and an old friend of his father and uncle from their undergraduate days at Yale, to propose the two projects. Fisher was delighted, for the Econometric Society was severely limited in scope by its poverty. During the first two years of its existence, 1931 and 1932, its activities consisted chiefly of small meetings at which papers were read and discussed. Because dues were very low, the Society simply could not afford more ambitious activities. Against this background, Cowles' proposal seemed like a godsend. In his excitement Fisher telephoned Roos, then permanent Secretary of the American Association for the Advancement of Science, to read him the letter. Roos was equally delighted; it seemed too good to be true. He asked whether Fisher thought it was a crank letter, and Fisher—fortunately—replied that he thought it was not. They invited Cowles to come East to discuss the matter and he accepted their invitation promptly. The three men met at Fisher's home in New Haven on a weekend in October, 1931. Cowles proposed starting with a budget of about $12,000 per year with larger amounts to follow if the venture met with success. Fisher and Roos, having satisfied themselves that Cowles meant what he said and was genuinely interested in econometric research, were enthusiastic about the scheme.

At about the same time Davis arranged with Thornton C. Fry, a mathematician with the Bell Telephone Laboratories and a charter member of the Econometric Society, to acquaint Cowles with several other members of the Society. A few days later, Cowles and Fry met in New York with Donald R. Belcher, chief statistician of the American Telephone and Telegraph Company; J. W. Glover, president of the Teachers' Insurance and Annuity Association of America; Harold Hotelling of Columbia University; and Walter A. Shewhart, statistician of the Bell Telephone Laboratories. Cowles discussed his proposal with them, and they assured him that in their judgment the Society would welcome the support as a ''most fortunate opportunity.''

Fisher and Roos, as president and secretary of the Econometric Society respectively, wrote a letter to the other members of the Council outlining Cowles' proposal and recommending its acceptance. The replies were for the most part favorable. However, some of the members of the Council became alarmed lest the Society's good name be harmed by its implication in a venture with a man who was willing to spend a considerable sum of money in order to accomplish they knew not what purposes of his own. The English and European members held a special meeting to discuss the question. They decided that they could not give their approval until a representative had come to the United States to meet Cowles and find out what his motives were. They chose Frisch as their representative and informed Fisher and Roos of their position. Fisher and Roos wrote as tactfully to Cowles as they could, explaining that his proposal was an important matter that might well have a profound effect on the future of the Society, and that the English and European members of the Council felt they would be able to give fuller support if Frisch were to come as their representative to talk with Cowles about the type of organization he had in mind. Cowles was favorably impressed by this cautious approach and responded by inviting Frisch to come as his guest to Colorado Springs. Frisch came and stayed for a week. As the two discussed the project from every viewpoint, Frisch became perfectly satisfied, as were Fisher and Roos, that Cowles was sincerely interested in econometric research. Before returning to Norway, Frisch met briefly with Fisher and Roos, and the three of them wrote a new letter to the Council of the

Econometric Society, reporting on Frisch's visit with Cowles and recommending that they accept the proposal.

This time, in January, 1932, the Council accepted. The agreement was as follows: Cowles would set up a research organization in Colorado Springs to be known as the Cowles Commission for Research in Economics; the Econometric Society would sponsor the Cowles Commission; the Cowles Commission would be guided by an Advisory Council appointed by and from the Econometric Society; and Cowles would underwrite the cost of publishing a journal for the Society. The earlier apprehensions of some of the Society's Council members, though understandable, turned out to be quite unfounded. Indeed, Cowles' generosity, farsightedness, fairness, and objectivity enabled the Cowles Commission to become established in its first few years as a responsible research organization, and have been among the most important sustaining factors in the achievements of the Cowles Commission ever since. Accordingly the Advisory Council was to play a progressively less active part in its affairs.

At first, however, even before the Cowles Commission was formally founded, the Advisory Council did take an active part in supervising its activities. The members of the Advisory Council, appointed in February of 1932 by the Council of the Society, were Fisher; Frisch; Arthur L. Bowley, professor at the London School of Economics; Mitchell, director of the National Bureau for Economic Research; and Carl Snyder of the Federal Reserve Bank of New York. They held their first meeting with Roos in Syracuse, New York, at the summer sessions of the Econometric Society in 1932; all members were present except Bowley. At this meeting it was decided that the first major project of the Cowles Commission should be the construction of indexes of stock prices, earnings, and dividends in the United States with proper adjustments for stock splits, rights, recapitalizations, etc., since any subsequent analytical work on the security market would require more adequate indexes than were then available.

On the 9th of September, 1932, the Cowles Commission for Research in Economics was formally chartered as a not-for-profit corporation in the State of Colorado. The original Articles of Incorporation contain these words: "The particular purpose and business for which said corporation is formed is to educate and benefit its members and mankind, and to advance the scientific study and development . . . of economic theory in its relation to mathematics and statistics."

Alfred Cowles was elected by the trustees as president of the Cowles Commission. A research laboratory and library were set up in the Mining Exchange Building in Colorado Springs, and good relations were established with the economics department of nearby Colorado College, of which Cowles was a trustee. In addition to Cowles, the initial research staff consisted of Davis, who was in charge of the statistical work; Frisch, who was a nonresident consultant; William F. C. Nelson, who was an economist; and Forrest Danson, who was a statistician. The latter two had been with Cowles in his investment firm before 1932. This group began work on the stock market indexes. Davis and Nelson collaborated in writing a textbook on statistics for economists based on the adaptation of a manuscript previously prepared by Davis. The initial budget was approximately $12,000 per year.

There remains one thread to be picked up. In February of 1932, after the Council of the Society had accepted Cowles' offer to underwrite the founding of a journal, the name *Econometrica* was chosen, Frisch was elected editor-in-chief, Nelson was chosen as assistant editor, and Cowles was chosen as circulation manager and also as treasurer of the Society. Upon its incorporation in September, 1932, the Cowles Commission became host to the archives of the Society, and the offices of the two organizations have been together ever since.

The first issue of *Econometrica* appeared in January, 1933. It contained an editorial by Frisch, an introductory article by Schumpeter, summaries of previous meetings of the

Society, and papers by René Roy, Shewhart, Jan Tinbergen, John B. Canning, and James Harvey Rogers. In introducing Econometrics to the reader, Schumpeter wrote:

"We do not impose any credo—scientific or otherwise—and we *have* no common credo beyond holding: first, that economics is a science, and secondly, that this science has one very important quantitative aspect. . . .

What we want to create is, first, a forum for econometric endeavor of all kinds wide enough to give ample scope to all possible views about our problems. . . . On this forum, which we think of as international, we want secondly to create a spirit and a habit of cooperation among men of different types of mind by means of discussions of concrete problems of a quantitative and, as far as may be, numerical character. . . . Confronted with clear-cut questions, most of us will, we hope, be found to be ready to accept the only competent judgment on, and the only relevant criterion of, scientific method, that is the judgment or criterion of the result. . . . Theoretic and 'factual' research will of themselves find their right proportions, and we may not unreasonably expect to agree in the end on the right kind of theory and the right kind of fact and the methods of treating them, not postulating anything about them by program, but evolving them, let us hope, by positive achievement."

That is the story of the founding of the Cowles Commission, the Econometric Society, and the journal *Econometrica*.

II. *The early years in Colorado: 1932–1937*

The first Cowles Commission product to attract widespread attention, both from businessmen and from professional economists, and still one of the best known of its publications, was a paper by Cowles entitled "Can Stock Market Forecasters Forecast?," published in *Econometrica* in July, 1933. A three-word abstract of this paper runs as follows: "It is doubtful." As mentioned earlier, Cowles had begun to suspect that many forecasters had no real skill and were in effect simply guessing, and he set out to test this hypothesis. He charted the weekly individual stock purchase recommendations of sixteen established financial services from 1928 to 1932, and found that if an investor had followed all of them, with equal initial amounts of capital allotted to each purchase of a stock, he would have come out making about one and a half per cent per year less than if he had invested in the stock market as a whole. He also calculated that if sixteen *random* series of weekly predictions were made, there was at least an even chance that one of them would lead to just as good results as the most profitable service actually did. He then checked the common stock investment records of twenty large fire insurance companies for the same period, and found that on the average they fell behind the market by slightly more than one per cent per year, while the best record among them was only slightly better than that of the best financial service. He then charted the forecasts of stock market level made by twenty-four financial publications from 1928 to 1932 and found that if an investor had followed all of them, again with equal amounts of initial capital allotted to each, he would have fallen behind the market average by about four per cent per year. Finally, he found that when twenty-four series of random forecasts were made by drawing cards from an appropriate deck, the best series of random forecasts was just as good as the best series of actual forecasts, while the worst series of random forecasts was better than any of the six worst series of actual forecasts. Far from refuting the hypothesis that stock market forecasters were operating according to chance rather than skill or insight, these results were quite consistent with it, except that the poorer actual forecasts seemed to be worse than would be expected on the basis of chance alone. The study pointed strongly to the need for more reliable knowledge upon which to base economic forecasts.

In the summer of 1934, Roos was research director of the National Recovery Administration of the United States government. He was beginning to think about where he would go next, for his opinion of the NRA's usefulness was very low, and he was in the process of writing a report for the NRA recommending that the Act under which it was created be allowed quietly to expire without renewal in 1935. He wrote to Cowles for a reference for a prospective new employer, and Cowles replied by offering him a position as the first director of research of the Cowles Commission. Upon hearing of this opportunity, Colorado College offered him a professorship in econometrics. He accepted the two positions, taking up his duties in September, 1934.

During Roos' term as director of research, the Cowles Commission published three volumes, including the first two in its series of monographs. The year 1934 saw the publication of Monograph 1, *Dynamic Economics*, a series of essays by Roos which he had completed before he came to the Cowles Commission. Next, in 1935, was the aforementioned textbook, *Elements of Statistics*, by Davis and Nelson. Third, in 1937, was Monograph 2, *NRA Economic Planning*, by Roos. This was an enlarged version of the adverse NRA report that he had prepared as NRA research director, which the NRA had declined to publish. (Roos writes that in 1935, after the Supreme Court declared the National Industrial Recovery Act unconstitutional, House Speaker Rayburn and Senate President Garner requested and received manuscript copies of the report. Thus, it may well have contributed to the willingness of Congress to let the NRA idea die with no legislative attempt to revive it.) In preparation were three other monographs: the stock market indexes, by Cowles and other members of the staff; a study of the monetary use of silver, by Dickson H. Leavens, a new staff member; and a study of methods of analysis of economic time series, by Davis.

One of the most significant contributions of the Cowles Commission in its early days was made through its summer conferences, of which the first was in 1935. In June of that year, the Econometric Society had held a meeting at Colorado College and for various reasons several economists and statisticians remained in Colorado Springs for the following week, including Davis, Hotelling, August Loesch, Isadore Lubin, Shewhart, and Snyder. Roos suggested that they have a few informal meetings, at which anyone who wished might discuss his current research work and invite help on the problems involved. The others took up the idea and during the week ten informal papers were presented, with considerably more free and substantive discussion than would have been possible in a larger and more formal group listening to finished work. This short session was such a success that Cowles and Roos decided to plan a similar conference for the following summer. They wrote up the proceedings and sent them out as part of an invitation to the second conference to be held at Colorado College in the summer of 1936. They invited thirty-two people to speak, in the hope of getting about ten acceptances, and were surprised when they received twenty, including three from staff members. As a result, the conference was extended to five weeks. The proceedings were written up, and published by Colorado College. Among the participants who were not connected with the Cowles Commission were Irving Fisher, R. A. Fisher of University College, London, Corrado Gini of the University of Rome, Shewhart, and E. J. Working of the University of Illinois.

The setting of Colorado Springs was conducive to a pleasant informality, both in the econometric and recreational aspects of the conferences. Because the group was small and lived in the college dormitories, people had the opportunity to become better acquainted professionally and personally than was possible in the more crowded meetings of the Econometric Society and American Economic and Statistical Associations. There were hikes, drives, and picnics in the inspiring mountains of the Pike's Peak and Cripple Creek regions, and there was even a play, presented by the visitors at a dinner given for the staff, in which some of the more striking characteristics of the staff and speakers came in for some good-natured but pointed and amusing scrutiny.

Four new people joined the staff while Roos was director of research. In the summer of 1935, Herbert E. Jones, a gifted young invalid who was able to work only part time, became a staff member; in 1936 he was appointed as a Fellow of the Cowles Commission. His training was in mathematics and in engineering. He worked on the stock index project and on problems of fitting equations to time series.

CHARLES ROOS

Stone Photo

DICKSON H. LEAVENS

Leavens, a former member of the statistics research staff of the Harvard Business School, first became acquainted with the Cowles Commission through the summer conference of 1936, at which he presented a paper on gold and silver. Nelson, who had been assistant editor of *Econometrica*, had died suddenly in May, 1936, and Cowles was looking for a man to take over the editorial work of the journal and the Cowles Commission, manage the office, and share in the research work. When Leavens was summoned to Cowles' office toward the end of the conference, just after the performance of the play, he must have wondered uneasily whether it had given offense, for he had written it himself. However, if he had any apprehensions they vanished, for what Cowles wanted was to ask whether he knew any graduates of the Harvard Business School who might be interested in the opening at the Cowles Commission, or, for that matter, whether he would be interested in it himself. He was, and accordingly moved to Colorado Springs in September, 1936. His devoted and unceasing attention to the many administrative aspects of the Cowles Commission's activities up to his retirement in 1947, was an essential factor in the Commission's effectiveness.

Gerhard Tintner of Vienna accepted an invitation to become a Fellow of the Cowles Commission in 1936. Edward N. Chapman of Colorado Springs also joined the staff that year.

At the end of January, 1937, Roos resigned as research director of the Cowles Commission to become research director of the Mercer-Allied Corporation in New York. Shortly thereafter he embarked in business for himself with a new economic forecasting agency, The Econometric Institute, which he heads today.

III. *The later years in Colorado: 1937–1939*

Upon Roos' departure, Davis took a leave of absence from Indiana University to become acting director of research of the Cowles Commission. He held this position from February until September, 1937, at which time he left to become professor of mathematics at Northwestern University. He continued to spend his summers with the Cowles Commission for several years.

The summer conference of 1937 was used partly as a recruiting ground for a new director of research, and among the prospects invited were Frisch; Jacob Marschak, then director of the Institute of Statistics at Oxford University; and Theodore O. Yntema, then professor in the School of Business at the University of Chicago. None of them was inclined to accept the position, however, for Colorado Springs was too isolated from the large academic centers to be attractive. For the next two years, until September, 1939, there was no official director of research. However, both Roos and Davis met with Cowles from time to time to advise him on the research program.

During this period, the third and fourth monographs were published, and two more were in process. Monograph 3, *Common-Stock Indexes*, by Cowles and Associates, appeared in August, 1938, and a second edition was published in 1939. It presents the results of the extensive gathering and compiling of data on the stock market, and contains indexes of prices with adjustments for rights, splits, dividends, etc., and of yield expectations, yields, dividends, earnings-price ratios, and earnings for a large group of common stocks comprising ninety to a hundred per cent of the value of all those listed on the New York Stock Exchange, 1871–1939 and for sixty-eight subgroups of these stocks. Monograph 4, *Silver Money*, by Leavens, appeared in March, 1939. It traces the history of the monetary use of silver and analyzes recent developments in some detail. Davis continued to work on his time-series analysis, and Tintner proceeded with another monograph on time series, although he left the Cowles Commission in September, 1937, to join the faculty of Iowa State College.

The summer conferences continued vigorously during the Colorado period. The proceedings after 1936 were published by the Cowles Commission itself, under the editorship of Leavens. Among the participants in 1937–1939 who were not previously connected with the Cowles Commission were R. G. D. Allen of the London School of Economics, Louis Bean and Mordecai Ezekiel of the U. S. Department of Agriculture, Fry, Trygve Haavelmo of the University of Oslo, A. P. Lerner of the London School of Economics, Francis McIntyre of Stanford University, Horst Mendershausen of the University of Geneva, Rogers of Yale University, René Roy of the University of Paris, Henry Schultz of the University of Chicago, Abraham Wald of Vienna, Holbrook Working of Stanford University, and (as already mentioned) Frisch, Marschak, and Yntema. Roy came in 1938 as the official representative of the Government of the French Republic in honor of the one hundredth anniversary of the publication of Cournot's pioneering *Récherches*. Acting on a suggestion by Davis, the Cowles Commission had invited the French Government to send a representative. This invitation was accepted and Roy was designated.

Additional staff changes were as follows. McIntyre came to the Cowles Commission and the faculty of Colorado College in the fall of 1937, by way of the University of Chicago, Stanford University, and the 1937 summer conference. Two new Fellows were appointed for the year 1938–1939, Mendershausen and Wald. Both had contributed to the 1938 summer conference.

IV. The move to Chicago: 1939

Colorado Springs had many advantages as a location for the Cowles Commission, but its geographical position with respect to other centers of economic and statistical research was certainly not one of them. This disadvantage was underlined by the failure to secure as director of research any of the three men who ranked as first choice when Roos departed in 1937. For the next two years, there was continually in the background the question of whether the Cowles Commission ought to move to a more suitable location. Several universities showed interest in providing it with a new home, including California at Los Angeles, Yale, and Northwestern, but no definite arrangements were made. Then in January, 1939, the issue was forced by the death of Cowles' father; as a result it became necessary for Cowles to make his headquarters in Chicago. Northwestern thus became a clear favorite over U. C. L. A. and Yale, but in the end the Cowles Commission did not move to any of these universities.

Schultz had begun to build a strong tradition in mathematical economics and econometrics at the University of Chicago. Then his work was cut short by his death in an automobile accident in November, 1938, and the tradition was left without its most vigorous figure. Thus the University was in a position from which the possibility of adopting a group such as the Cowles Commission appeared particularly attractive. Likewise, the University was an ideal environment for the Cowles Commission, so much so that Cowles decided to see what could be done. Through Laird Bell, his family's attorney and a trustee (now chairman of the trustees) of the University, he met Robert M. Hutchins, then President of the University, and discussed the idea with him. In the early spring of 1939, Cowles and Hutchins worked out a loose and informal relationship between the Cowles Commission and the University, under which the University provided a suite of four offices rent free on the fourth floor of the Social Science Research Building overlooking the Midway; Cowles Commission staff members were granted certain University privileges; Yntema, professor in the School of Business, became director of research of the Cowles Commission; and Jacob Viner, professor of economics, became the sixth member of the Advisory Council of the Cowles Commission. The move was made in September, 1939, the Econometric Society's offices coming along too. On September 29, 1939, the Cowles Commission was chartered as a not-for-profit corporation in the State of Illinois, and the Colorado corporation was dissolved soon afterward.

Several members of the University faculty became part-time staff members of the Cowles Commission when it came to Chicago: Joel Dean of the School of Business, and H. Gregg Lewis, Jacob Mosak, and Oscar Lange of the Economics Department. The Colorado staff came to Chicago with five exceptions: McIntyre took a leave of absence to teach at Stanford and later resigned to accept a position at Indiana; Wald took a position at Columbia where he later became professor of mathematical statistics; Mendershausen joined the faculty of Colorado College; and Chapman and Jones also remained behind in Colorado Springs. Chapman has since devoted himself chiefly to medical research and public health work. Jones died in 1942, when his long illness ended what had promised to be a brilliant career. A memorial note to him in the 1941 Annual Report of the Cowles Commission contains these words:

"During his brief period of active participation in the work of the Cowles Commission, Herbert Jones made a number of significant contributions to statistical and econometric science. Trained in electrical engineering and equipped with an excellent understanding of fundamental mathematics, he brought to bear upon the problems of the Commission a keen and analytical point of view. His breadth of interest is readily observed from the variety and difficulty of the studies which he made. . . .

In all of these studies Herbert Jones proved himself to be a young man with an exceptional imagination and an analytical power far beyond the average. Perhaps there is no higher encomium possible than to repeat what was said about the remarkable English mathematician, W. K. Clifford, who died very young: 'If he had lived we might have known something.' "

V. *The early years at Chicago: 1940–1942*

During 1940–1942, the fifth and sixth monographs were published. Monograph 5, *The Variate Difference Method*, by Tintner, appeared in February, 1940. It analyzes the successive differences of time series, (i.e., the year-to-year differences between adjacent numbers in a series, then the differences between adjacent differences, etc.) and uses them as the basis of a method for deciding whether one should use a straight line, or a quadratic, or a cubic, etc.

for fitting the trend of a particular time series. Monograph 6, *Analysis of Economic Time Series*, by Davis, appeared in December, 1941. It is a survey of many methods available for dealing with time series, with applications to economic situations.

Staff changes during this period were relatively few. John H. Smith, a statistician in the School of Business, joined the staff in September, 1941, and stayed until the summer of 1942 when he went to the Bureau of Labor Statistics. Leonid Hurwicz joined the staff in January, 1942, as an assistant to Lange. Aside from Cowles and Davis, Hurwicz is the only present member of the Cowles Commission staff whose association with it dates back ten years.

A summer conference was held in Colorado Springs in 1940, even though the Cowles Commission had moved to Chicago by then. Among the new participants were W. E. Deming, senior mathematician of the U. S. Census Bureau; E. A. Goldenweiser, chairman of the Board of Governors of the Federal Reserve System; Wassily Leontief of Harvard University; and Paul A. Samuelson of the Massachusetts Institute of Technology. However, with the library and computing equipment no longer available to the participants of the conference, with the added expense of moving the staff to Colorado Springs, and with the interruption of work in the office at Chicago, it was not thought worth while to continue the summer conferences.

The Annual Report of the Cowles Commission for 1940 begins with the words, "Among economic problems none is more important than unemployment of labor and other resources." It continues, "Unless there are compelling reasons for a change of plans, the long-run program of the Commission will be directed to a study of the problems centering in the flow of investment and the incomplete use of resources." There was something almost prophetic in the last statement, for the compelling reasons presented themselves within a year in the form of war. As a result, the Cowles Commission turned early in 1942 to a study of wartime price control and rationing, with a view to appraising the possible policies with respect to them and the administrative devices that might be used for implementing them. Three parts of the study were planned: a theoretical analysis of the problem, an analysis of pertinent available statistical material on prices and wages, and a series of personal interviews with both buyers and sellers to learn about their actual behavior under price controls and rationing. The project was undertaken jointly with the Committee on Price Determination. It was organized under the auspices of the Price Conference of the National Bureau of Economic Research and was under the direction of Yntema and Hurwicz. A monograph was expected to be published by 1944.

Until the Cowles Commission came to Chicago, all of its funds had been provided by Cowles and his family. In 1940, another source of funds made its appearance. The Social Science Research Committee of the University of Chicago made grants so that several members of the Cowles Commission staff might employ research assistants; Melvin Reder, now associate professor of economics at Stanford University, was one of the first of these assistants. In 1942, the Cowles Commission received its first grant from the Rockefeller Foundation, for conducting the price control study. The National Bureau also contributed to the expenses of the price control study.

By 1942, something like half of the staff of the Cowles Commission had been drawn into work directly or indirectly connected with the war effort. Dean was on leave as director of gasoline rationing in the OPA in Washington. Hurwicz was teaching mathematics and statistics in the U. S. Army Signal Corps and Meteorology training programs at the Illinois Institute of Technology and the University of Chicago. Mosak was on leave as head of a section of the research department of the OPA in Washington. Yntema had been on leave in Washington as head of economics and statistics in the division of industrial materials of the Defense Commission in 1940, and was on part-time leave during the spring and summer of 1942 as a consultant to the War Shipping Administration.

Schneider Photo

JACOB MARSCHAK

Moffett Photo

THEODORE O. YNTEMA

LEONID HURWICZ

In November, 1942, Yntema resigned as director of research of the Cowles Commission and took a leave of absence, to become research director of the newly created Committee on Economic Development and organize a study of conditions favorable and unfavorable to full employment after the war.

VI. Simultaneous developments: 1943–1948

In 1939, Marschak left Oxford University to come to the United States as professor of economics at the New School for Social Research in New York. Just before taking up his duties there, he renewed his acquaintance with the Cowles Commission at the summer conference of 1939. In 1942, when Yntema made known his intention to resign, Cowles for the second time offered Marschak the position of director of research of the Cowles Commission.

At the same time, the University of Chicago was again without a senior mathematical economist, for Lange had taken a leave of absence to become visting professor at Columbia for the years 1942–1944 and it was uncertain whether he would return. Accordingly the University offered Marschak a professorship in economics. He accepted, and came to the University and the Cowles Commission at the beginning of 1943.

During Marschak's term as director of research, which extended until July, 1948, the Cowles Commission underwent fundamental changes in several directions. The administrative structure of its relationship to the University of Chicago was reorganized. Its financial support became more extensive and more diversified. There were many changes in its staff, including the arrivals of several of the present staff. The means of making its members and their work known to the University community and to other economists and statisticians were extended. Its research program underwent a major reorientation that determined its essential character for the second ten years of its life. These developments will now be discussed in turn.

The University of Chicago handled its funds for research in the social sciences through its Social Science Research Committee. Applications for funds from outside sources such as the Rockefeller Foundation were also channeled through this committee. In the summer of 1943, to help secure better co-ordination of the research programs and fund-raising activities of the various departments and affiliates of the University, the Cowles Commission replaced the dormant Advisory Council by a new and more active Advisory Committee representing various aspects of the University's interest in the work of the Cowles Commission. The Advisory Committee originally was composed of Walter Bartky (mathematics), Garfield V. Cox (business), Simeon E. Leland (economics, chairman), Theodore W. Schultz and Viner (economics), and Louis Wirth (Social Science Research Committee). Later Neil H. Jacoby (business) and Philip Hauser (Social Science Research Committee) joined it as replacements for some of the others. It periodically received and discussed the progress reports of the research director. It also reviewed the Cowles Commission's applications to the Rockefeller Foundation for grants-in-aid. In addition to grants received from Cowles and his family, the Rockefeller Foundation, and the Social Science Research Committee of the University, the Cowles Commission also received indirect aid through the payment of Marschak's salary (and later Koopmans' as well) by the University, and through grants from the Guggenheim Foundation, the Rockefeller Foundation, and the Social Science Research Council to persons working at the Cowles Commission as guests on problems related to its program.

There were many changes in the staff during the five and a half years from 1943 to the middle of 1948; it is impractical to detail them all here. Those staff members and guests who came during this period and are no longer associated with the Cowles Commission are mentioned in connection with the research program a little further on, or in the biographical sketches.

Haavelmo had been a student and collaborator of Frisch

at the University Institute of Economics in Oslo and the University of Oslo, and had worked at several American universities under fellowships of the American-Scandinavian and Rockefeller Foundations. From 1942 till the end of 1945, he was attached to Norwegian government agencies in New York and Washington. He participated with Marschak, Wald, and others in a small econometrics seminar that met regularly in New York on weekends during 1940–1942. Marschak asked Haavelmo to become a research associate of the Cowles Commission in July, 1943. He accepted although he was not always in residence. He moved to Chicago in January, 1946, where he also became a member of the Agricultural Economics Research Group in the Department of Economics. He has been associated with the Cowles Commission as a research consultant (a new category of staff members, comprising those active but not in residence) ever since his return to Norway in March, 1947. He is now professor of economics at the University of Oslo.

Tjalling C. Koopmans, originally trained as a theoretical physicist, had studied econometrics with Tinbergen at the University of Amsterdam and with Frisch in Oslo. He met Marschak first when he visited Oxford in 1938, and again in New York in 1940 when he became a participant in the above-mentioned seminar. In December, 1943, while he was statistician to the Combined Shipping Adjustment Board in Washington, Koopmans addressed a Cowles Commission seminar. In July, 1944, under a grant of the Rockefeller Foundation, he became a research associate of the Cowles Commission. In the spring of 1946, he was appointed associate professor of economics at the University of Chicago as well.

Herman Rubin joined the staff in July, 1944, as a research assistant. He has been an intermittent staff member ever since, becoming a research associate in 1946 and a research consultant in 1952. His present position is that of assistant professor of statistics at Stanford University. Lawrence R. Klein first became acquainted with the Cowles Commission at a meeting of the Econometric Society in Cleveland in

Sturlason Photo

TRYVE HAAVELMO

LAWRENCE R. KLEIN

September, 1944. He was a research associate from November, 1944, until July, 1947, and has recently become a research consultant. He is at present a research associate both of the National Bureau of Economic Research and of the Survey Research Center at the University of Michigan. Theodore W. Anderson, Jr. was a research associate from November, 1945, to September, 1946, when he became a research consultant. He is now an associate professor of mathematical statistics at Columbia University, and editor of the *Annals of Mathematical Statistics*. Kenneth J. Arrow was a research associate from April, 1947 to July, 1949, and assistant professor of economics at the University of Chicago from October, 1948 to July, 1949. He is now a research consultant, and an associate professor of economics and statistics at Stanford University. Herman Chernoff joined the staff as a research assistant in July, 1947, and was a research associate from the spring of 1948 until September, 1949. Among his other activities was the supervision of the Cowles Commission computing staff. He is at present a research consultant, and an associate professor at Stanford University. Herbert Simon, who is professor of administration and chairman of the Department of Industrial Management at Carnegie Institute of Technology, became a research consultant in April, 1947, while he was professor and chairman of the Department of Political Science at Illinois Institute of Technology.

During the early years, the Cowles Commission made itself known through the summer conferences and through its monographs, of which six had appeared when Marschak became director of research in 1943. With the summer conferences gone, and the publication of a monograph being something less than an everyday event, the output of materials failed signally to indicate the amount or quality of research being performed. From the beginning, the staff members had published numerous articles in professional journals each year, and had presented papers at meetings of the professional societies. Marschak introduced two new devices to help bring the light out from under the bushel. First, beginning in the summer of

1943, was a series of seminars on various topics in econometrics, presented every three or four weeks at the University of Chicago by staff members or by various visitors to the Cowles Commission. The seminars were soon promoted to a regular bi-weekly schedule (except in summer) and are still conducted today.

Second, beginning late in 1943, the Cowles Commission Papers, New Series were initiated. These are reprints of the more important published articles of staff members, bound in paper either singly or in groups of two or three related articles. They are distributed free of charge to a selected list of interested people and to others who write and request individual copies. By the middle of 1948, New Series Papers Nos. 1–27 had been prepared and distributed.

During 1943–1948 the seventh, eighth, and ninth monographs were published. Monograph 7, *General-Equilibrium Theory in International Trade*, by Mosak, appeared in 1944. It extends the modern theory of general equilibrium and comparative statics, as formulated by J. R. Hicks, Allen, and others, to the field of international trade. Monograph 8, *Price Flexibility and Employment*, by Lange, also appeared in 1944. It first extends the modern theory of general equilibrium to treat money as distinct from other goods, and then analyzes the roles of price flexibility and of substitution between money and other goods in the determination of the level of employment. Monograph 9, *Price Control and Business*, describing the results of the price control study initiated in 1942, was published in 1945. Its author was George Katona, whose journalistic and research experience in both economics and psychology well equipped him to write it. He was a research associate of the Cowles Commission and in charge of the study from January, 1943, until it was finished at the end of 1944. He is currently the Program Director of the Survey Research Center and professor of economics and psychology at the University of Michigan.

The reorientation which Marschak and his new staff wrought in the Cowles Commission's research program is sketched in the following passage from the Annual Report for 1943, the first year during which Marschak was director of research (the passage refers to three new studies that were started during the year):

"The method of the studies . . . is conditioned by the following four characteristics of economic data and economic theory: (a) the theory is a system of simultaneous equations, not a single equation; (b) some or all of these equations include "random" terms, reflecting the influence of numerous erratic causes in addition to the few "systematic" ones; (c) many data are given in the form of time series, subsequent events being dependent on preceding ones; (d) many published data refer to aggregates rather than to single individuals. The statistical tools developed for application in the older empirical sciences are not always adequate to meet all these conditions, and much new mathematical work is needed. To develop and improve suitable methods seems, at the present state of our knowledge, at least as important as to obtain immediate results. Accordingly, the Commission has planned the publication of studies on the general theory of economic measurements. . . . It is planned to continue these methodological studies systematically. The available results of mathematical analysis are currently applied and tried out in econometric investigations; conversely, new situations arising in the course of practical work present new problems to the mathematician. It is intended to make this hand-in-hand work the basis of the Commission's activities."

The four characteristics referred to were central to the new program of the Cowles Commission. Accordingly, brief remarks on each one follow.

"The theory is a system of simultaneous equations, not a single equation." Consider for example the theory of the determination of the market price of a commodity. The quantity demanded by buyers depends on the price, rising when the price falls. The quantity offered by sellers also depends on price, falling when price falls. And the price adjusts itself in response to the higgling and bargaining of the market place, being driven up if there is excess demand and down if there is excess supply, until the quantities demanded and supplied are the same. Here is exhibited a system of three equations: the demand equation, the supply equation, and the price adjustment equation. There are three variables: quantity demanded, quantity supplied, and price.

It is important to notice that *none* of the three equations by itself can specify the level of even *one* of the three variables, but together the system specifies the level of all three. It is also important to notice that the number of variables to be explained by the theory is the same as the number of equations, i.e., three. These are called *endogenous* variables. There may be other variables (e.g., an excise tax) whose values are not specified by the theory but are assumed to be determined independently of the relationships described by the theory. Such variables, taken as a starting point of the explanation offered by the theory, are called *exogenous* variables. Exogenous variables are typically used to represent changes in policy or in the underlying economic environment which can effect the operation of the economic relationships described by the theory.

There do exist simple economic theories that consist of one equation only (such as a theory that relates the amount of tax receipts that will be collected under a given revenue act to the national income). But in the most interesting and important problems, the theory that is relevant is typically a system of several simultaneous equations.

"Some or all of these equations contain 'random' terms, reflecting the influence of numerous erratic causes in addition to the few 'systematic' ones." Except for equations expressing definitions, which of course must hold exactly, no one has ever found a numerical theory, i.e. an equation, that fits the relevant facts exactly. Many equations have been found that fit the relevant facts approximately, with errors or deviations that are sometimes positive and sometimes negative. This is true of the "exact" sciences as well as of economics, the chief difference being that in economics the deviations are usually not negligibly small. Accordingly, it is convenient to introduce them explicitly into each equation (except definitions) in the form of an extra term added on at the end, the value of which changes with each observation so that the equation always remains exactly true. It is assumed that the values of the deviations in any equation are determined as if by chance, as if drawn at random from a large jar containing tags with a number stamped on each one, some negative and some positive. Such variables are called "random" or "stochastic" variables. The use of random variables here is quite realistic, even though it may appear to be somewhat artificial. Each of the major factors bearing on a particular economic relationship is presumably accounted for explicitly by a separate variable, so that only the minor factors are left to be thrown into the random term, and the cumulative effect of a large number of small unrelated causes almost always acts as if it really were random.

"Many data are given in the form of time series, subsequent events being dependent on the preceding ones." The vast majority of available statistics on prices, wages, production, income and its components, inventories, etc., are published in chronological series covering successive weeks or months or years; such series are known as time series. They are important because the economy never starts with a clean slate but is always conditioned by what has happened before, and because many theories attempt to explain economic behavior through time. In addition, cross-section data, pertaining to different families, firms, industries, regions, etc. at a single point of time, are provided by surveys and censuses. The methods of treating the two types of data are essentially the same; however, there are some differences which will not be discussed here.

"Many published data refer to aggregates rather than to single individuals." This is clear from an examination of the national income statistics or almost any other familiar economic data. It becomes important when it is realized that most economic theory pertains to individual firms or families, and that there is accordingly a gap to be bridged if the published data are to be used systematically to test economic theory.

It should be noted that all of the four characteristics of economic theory and data were well-known for many years before the Cowles Commission began its research. Walras explicitly introduced systems of simultaneous equations into economics in 1874. Although the concept of a random variable did not appear as such in economic theory until fairly recently, it nevertheless lurks at the base of all attempts to fit equations to data—in fact, the theory of correlation and regression was built upon it in the last quarter of the nineteenth century. Time series and aggregated data have been with us for centuries. It cannot be said that the Cowles Commission contributed to the discovery of any of these important characteristics.

What *can* be said is that the men who were members of the Cowles Commission staff in the early years of Marschak's directorship, realizing that traditional statistical methods are by design unsuited to problems involving systems of simultaneous equations with random components, were among the first to devise new methods that are more suitable. Frisch had published a paper in the *Nordic Statistical Journal* in 1929 entitled "Correlation and Scatter in Statistical Variables" and an amplified version in 1934 entitled *Statistical Confluence Analysis by Means of Complete Regression Systems*, in which he foresaw and dealt with some of the difficulties that arise in regression and correlation analysis where "multicollinearity" exists, i.e., where there are other equations connecting the variables in question, in addition to the equation being studied. Then in January, 1943, in *Econometrica* there appeared Haavelmo's ground-breaking paper, "The Statistical Implications of a System of Simultaneous Equations." Although this paper is scarcely twelve pages long, it contains the beginning of some of the Cowles Commission's most important subsequent research. In particular, Haavelmo considered a three-equation theory of national income, and examined the consequences of fitting one of its equations to observed time-series data by means of the traditional "least-squares" method of regression analysis. (The term "least-squares" is used because this method selects as the best-fitting line the one that produces the smallest sum of squared deviations of the observed points from the line.)

The statistical problem in fitting a line to a set of observed points is that of deriving from observed data estimates of the numerical values of the unknown constants (parameters, as econometricians call them) in the equation of the line. For example, in Haavelmo's consumption equation, the parameters to be estimated are α and β, and the equation is: national consumption expenditure in any year equals α times national income in that year, plus β, plus a random disturbance. Because of the random components, it is impossible to find the *exact* values of the parameters. However, a very powerful general method of estimating unknown parameters, called the maximum-likelihood method, was devised by R. A. Fisher just after the turn of the century. It is difficult to describe clearly in nontechnical language, but it can be likened to the principle of trying to decide a question by considering which alternative, if true, would be most likely to have produced the evidence at hand. If Cassio and Desdemona were not in fact lovers, the chance of her handkerchief coming into his possession would be smaller than if they were; hence on the evidence of the handkerchief, their guilt is more likely than their innocence. (This ironic example illustrates the importance of making sure that the events in question are random and the importance of taking into account all available additional information, such as Desdemona's veracity as opposed to Iago's.) The maximum-likelihood estimate of a parameter is that value of the parameter which, among all possible values, would be most likely to give rise to the data actually observed. The merit of the maximum-likelihood method is that in a wide class of cases, judged by three accepted statistical criteria (known as unbiasedness in large samples, consistency, and efficiency), it yields the best possible large-sample estimates of unknown parameters.

It so happens that if an equation satisfying certain conditions is not a member of a system of equations, the maximum-likelihood estimates of its parameters are identical with the least-squares estimates; thus the least-squares estimates are the best estimates for such an equation. This had been known for a long time before the Cowles Commission came on the scene. Now to return to Haavelmo: he showed how to calculate the maximum-likelihood estimates of the parameters of his consumption equation and showed that they are *different* from the least-squares estimates precisely because the equation *is* a member of a system of simultaneous equations. Thus, the least-squares estimates are not generally the best estimates for an equation that belongs to a system. In fact, Haavelmo showed later that they are biased and inconsistent.

Before one attempts to calculate estimates of the parameters in a system of equations, or in a *model* (as economists say), it is well to pause and ask whether the observed data can really convey any information about the parameters of the model in question. Consider, for example, a two-equation model containing a demand and a supply curve for a commodity, each relating market price to quantity sold, with no other variables. The very best that can be expected from the data here is that they will locate exactly the intersection point of the two curves (random fluctuations would mean that the location could only be estimated). But even if the intersection is exactly located, no light is thrown on the shapes and directions of the curves, because there are infinitely many pairs of curves relating price to quantity that *could* intersect at the observed point. In this case, there is more than one set of parameters consistent with the observations and hence the observations cannot determine the values of the parameters.

This property of a two-variable supply-and-demand model had been commented on by many economists, including E. J. Working, Henry Schultz, and Haavelmo. Koopmans initiated a systematic study of such problems, which he called *identification* problems because the aim is to identify the true values of the parameters among all the possible sets of values consistent with the data and with the known or assumed properties of the model. An equation of a model is declared to be *identifiable* in that model if, given a sufficient (possibly infinite) number of observations of the variables, it would be possible to find one and only one set of parameters for it that are consistent with both the model and the observations. The equations of the simple supply-and-demand model of the preceding paragraph are thus not identifiable.

There are various properties which, if known or assumed a priori about a system, will produce identifiability. For example, if it is known above that the demand curve remains fixed while the supply curve shifts, then all price-quantity observations must lie *on* the demand curve, and the shifts in the supply curve will necessarily trace out the demand curve. Then the demand curve is identifiable, but the supply curve is not. However, for most commodities, the demand curve is not known to be either more or less free from random shifts than the supply curve, so that this kind of a priori information is not typically available.

Information *is* typically available a priori as to what variables appear in each equation; such information is derived from economic theory, from previous observation, or both. For example, we know that most demand curves depend on income as well as price, so that if income rises then larger quantities of goods are demanded at the same price. This is the most frequently available and often the most reliable type of a priori information about theoretical models. Koopmans and Rubin worked out criteria using this type of information to determine the identifiability of equations in linear systems. It is important to note that the determination can be made before any data are observed at all. This is of great importance, for it is futile to try to estimate the parameters in unidentifiable equations. Hurwicz and Wald further clarified the identification problem in logical and mathematical terms.

For several years one part of the Cowles Commission staff, including T. W. Anderson, Meyer A. Girshick, Haavelmo, Hurwicz, Koopmans, R. B. Leipnik, and Rubin, worked on the development of identifiability criteria and of methods for obtaining consistent estimates of the parameters in systems of equations with random elements. In January, 1945, the Cowles Commission held a research conference on the statistical problems arising out of economic theories that are systems of simultaneous equations. The proceedings of this conference were revised and enlarged, becoming Monograph 10, *Statistical Inference in Dynamic Economic Models*, edited by Koopmans.

Contributor revisions, editorial efforts toward uniformity in notation, and exploration of alternative printing techniques all combined to delay the appearance of the monograph until 1950. By that time papers on related topics by several of its contributors had appeared in various journals, and had been included in the Cowles Commission Papers, New Series. It is the most difficult and technical of all the Cowles Commission monographs, but it is one of the most important because it presents the fruits of several years of statistical research in a field where the Cowles Commission has been a pioneer. In reviewing it for the *Review of the International Statistical Institute* in 1950, R. G. D. Allen referred to the 1945 research conference and wrote:

"A comprehensive report of their results has been long promised and eagerly awaited. . . . More than half the volume is taken up with an introductory essay by J. Marschak and the main paper on simultaneous equation systems in dynamic economics, contributed by T. C. Koopmans with the assistance of H. Rubin and R. B. Leipnik. Marschak's introduction leads into the main problems (identification and estimation) of stochastic models by considering the simple case of non-stochastic models, a good expository device. Koopmans' treatment in the main paper, again, is to start with a general survey of problems, before passing to a detailed development, first, of the problem of identification of economic relations and, then, of the derivation of maximum-likelihood estimates of the parameters in the relations. . . . Everyone seriously interested in econometrics should make the effort necessary to read, at least, Marschak's introduction and Koopmans' main contribution. From these, it is evident that the method of simultaneous equations is potentially of great value in dynamic economics, that not all the theoretical problems are yet solved, and that the decisive tests of the method in its applications have still to be made."

While the volume sets a new standard in adapting statistical methods to econometric analysis, further difficulties remain to be overcome in this area. In reviewing it for the *American Economic Review* in 1952, Guy H. Orcutt of Harvard University wrote:

"For all practical purposes, the models dealt with are restricted to linear systems of difference equations. . . . Besides an extensive treatment of the identification problem with respect to such models, estimating their parameters from observational data also represents a problem central to this volume. While greatly impressed with the skill shown in attempting to handle this problem, this reviewer has many misgivings as to the applicability of the results obtained to problems of estimation facing the economist. These misgivings do not stem from any discovery of error in the deductive logical processes carried out, but rather in a failure to accept the premises as being realistic and the large sample characteristics of the estimators as applying to small samples."

In addition to Marschak's introductory survey and the long paper on estimation by Koopmans, Rubin, and Leipnik, there are papers on related problems by R.L. Anderson, T. W. Anderson, Jr., Haavelmo, Hotelling, Hurwicz, Koopmans, H. B. Mann, Rubin, and Wald. T. W. Anderson's contribution is a short summary of a paper by himself and Rubin, published in the *Annals of Mathematical Statistics* in March, 1949, and December, 1950, deriving the so-called "limited-information maximum-likelihood method," a more economical way of obtaining consistent estimates than the "full-information maximum-likelihood method" of Koopmans, Rubin, and Leipnik. It acquired the appellation "limited-information" because it yields estimates of only one or a few of the equations at a time and uses considerably less information (both theoretical and empirical) to get them. It is not as accurate as the full-information method but for reasons of cost it has always been used instead, except in small or simplified systems.

Another part of the staff, including William H. Andrews, Jr., Gershon Cooper, Girshick, Haavelmo, Klein, Marschak, and Don Patinkin, worked on the construction of economic models and the estimation of their parameters by the new methods. The construction of a model, starting from considerations of economic theory, must come before the estimation of its parameters by whatever method: the estimation of the parameters of an equation, i.e., the fitting of a graph to a set of observed points, can only proceed *after* one has decided what variables are to appear in the equation, what the form of the equation is to be (linear, quadratic, exponential, etc.), and what the other equations of the system (if any) are like. Of course the validity of any statistically fitted equation depends heavily on whether the model chosen to begin with is realistic or not (light can be shed on this issue by checking the fitted equation against the same or, even better, against new data). This is why the construction of models is so important in econometrics.

The estimation of the parameters of the models is equally important. Their *numerical* values must be known at least approximately if predictions are to be made about the effects of various possible changes in the economic environment, and such predictions are essential if we are to choose intelligent policies. This applies whether the changes in the economic environment are brought about by deliberate policy action (such as the imposition of an excise tax or a subsidy, or the fixing of quotas on the use of certain materials) or by fortuitous but foreseeable events (examples are shifts in population and the introduction of new products such as nylon and atomic energy). It applies especially if the change, the effect of which is to be predicted, is one with which the economy has had no direct previous experience on which to base predictions. For example, if an excise is applied to a commodity that has previously been tax free, one needs to know certain parameters of both the supply and demand curves for *that commodity* in order to foretell the effect of the tax upon its price and output.

The early results of the Cowles Commission's research in this field appeared in four publications. First was a paper by Marschak and Andrews in *Econometrica* in 1944, estimating the relationship between inputs and outputs in production. Next were two papers in 1947 by Haavelmo and by Girshick and Haavelmo, on the consumption function and the demand for food, published in the *Journal of the American Statistical Association* and *Econometrica*, respectively. Fourth was Monograph 11, *Economic Fluctuations in the United States* by Klein. This was essentially completed in 1948 but additional computational work was undertaken in 1949 and the book did not actually appear until the middle of 1950. It presents three economic models for the American economy, containing from three to fifteen equations, with the estimates of their parameters as obtained by both the least-squares and maximum-likelihood methods. For the large model, the limited-information maximum-likelihood method is used. It represents forward steps in several respects: it contains a good deal of material on the appropriate theoretical procedures for passing from the familiar theory of individual behavior to equations describing entire sectors of the economy; it contains the largest model hitherto fitted by the new techniques; and it presents a statistical test of the hypothesis that the deviations *are* random as assumed, as well as tests of several economic hypotheses.

In 1946, a study of the economic implication of the development of atomic energy was initiated by the Social Science Research Council under the direction of Marschak and Sam H. Schurr. Their coauthors were Simon, who has continued to work on the economic theory of technological change, two economists, E. Boorstein and H. H. Wein, and two engineers, G. Perazich and M. F. Searl. Other research included a study by Koopmans of the optimum use of a transportation system (later to grow into one of the Cowles Commission's major projects), further studies of stock-market forecasting by Cowles, studies of the econometric interpretation of history and politics, and extensive work in preparing and cataloguing mathematical tables by Davis.

Although the informality of the summer conferences was gone, there were still activities on the lighter side at the Cowles Commission. At one party in 1946, a skit was presented portraying the mock trial of Klein on the grave charge of stealing into the Social Science building late at night and finagling with the data for his econometric model. There were many witnesses and clever counsel played by various staff members, and it made delightful entertainment. The record should show, of course, that Klein was acquitted of all wrongdoing.

TJALLING C. KOOPMANS

WILLIAM B. SIMPSON

VII. Economic theory revisited: 1948–1952

In July, 1948, Koopmans and Marschak exchanged places in the Cowles Commission. Koopmans became director of research and also professor of economics in the University of Chicago, while Marschak became the senior research associate and continued as a professor of economics in the University. With the recent growth of the Cowles Commission, which was expected to continue, the sheer weight of administrative work involved in its affairs had become so great that the director of research had relatively little time or energy to devote to the research program and to his own research. Therefore, a new administrative position of assistant director of research was created as part of the arrangement whereby Koopmans became director of research. William B. Simpson, whose acquaintance with the Cowles Commission had begun during his tenure of a Social Science Research Council fellowship for study and research in economics at the University in 1946–1948, was chosen for the new position. He began in May, 1948 and was appointed a research associate at the same time. In September, Simpson was elected secretary of the Econometric Society by its Council. In January, 1949, he became in addition managing editor of *Econometrica*, and then in 1951 co-editor. His great energies in administrative affairs and his dedication to the development of econometrics were to make possible a substantial growth of both the Cowles Commission and the Econometric Society in the subsequent period.

In the fall of 1948, there were further changes in the organizational structure of the Cowles Commission, still preserving its highly valuable academic connection with the University. The Cowles Commission was granted the right to recommend academic rank in the University for its qualified staff members independently of their status in other departments, and thus begin to build up a faculty of its own. This made it easier to attract and hold research workers of high qualifications and attainments. The first appointment was that of Clifford Hildreth, an econometrician, formerly of Iowa State College, who became assistant professsor in the Cowles Commission in January, 1949, and associate professor in July, 1950. Hildreth's appointment was a joint one with the Agricultural Economics Research Group in the Department of Economics in the University where he has the complimentary rank of associate professor. Subsequent appointments went to John Gurland in September, 1949, conferred jointly with the University's Committee on Statistics, Gerard Debreu in June, 1951, and H. S. Houthakker in January, 1952, all as assistant professors. Gurland is a mathematical statistician, formerly an instructor at Harvard. Debreu is a mathematical economist, who joined the Cowles Commission first as research associate in June, 1950, after teaching and doing research at several French institutions and holding a Rockefeller fellowship. Houthakker is an economist, formerly with the Department of Applied Economics, University of Cambridge. Koopmans, Marschak and Simpson (ex officio) are also faculty members of the Cowles Commission. This faculty, now numbering seven men, has gradually emerged as a responsible, self-governing body under the general supervision of the new Executive Committee which was set up in the fall of 1948 in place of the University of Chicago Advisory Committee. The Executive Committee was constituted of the dean of the Division of the Social Sciences (Ralph W. Tyler), the chairman of the Department of Economics (Theodore W. Schultz), the president of the Cowles Commission (Cowles), the director of research (Koopmans), and the assistant director of research (Simpson).

While the Cowles Commission faculty was coming into being, numerous other staff changes took place but they are again too numerous to detail. Hence those who came during this period and are no longer with the Cowles Commission are mentioned later on in connection with the research program, or in the biographical sketches. Franco Modigliani, an erstwhile member of the weekend New York econometrics seminar of 1940–1942, became a research associate in September, 1948, while he held a post-doctoral fellowship from the Department of Economics in the University. Shortly thereafter, he resigned to become associate professor at the University of Illinois and director of a research project on expectations and business fluctuations. He is now a research consultant of the Cowles Commission. Stephen G. Allen joined the staff in January, 1949, as a research assistant. He is now a research consultant and a research associate of the Applied Mathematics and Statistics Laboratory at Stanford University. Carl F. Christ became a research associate in September, 1949, after having been an informal member of the staff for the preceding year while holding a Social Science Research Council fellowship. He is now a research consultant, and an assistant professor of political economy at Johns Hopkins University. In September, 1949, William C. Hood became a research associate and a post-doctoral fellow in the Department of Economics in the University of Chicago. He is now a research consultant and an assistant professor of economics at the University of Toronto. Roy Radner became a research assistant in March, 1951, and a research associate in November, 1951. Martin J. Beckmann, I. N. Herstein, and Daniel Waterman became research associates in July, 1951. Herstein was given the complementary rank of assistant professor as well. William J. Dunaway and C. B. McGuire became research assistants in January, 1952. Aryeh Dvoretzky, professor of mathematical statistics at Hebrew University in Jerusalem, Erich Lehmann, associate professor of mathematics at the University of California in Berkeley, and Robert G. Strotz, assistant professor of economics at Northwestern University, became research consultants during 1951–1952.

Although Abraham Wald was a staff member of the Cowles Commission only briefly in 1938, he subsequently participated in several conferences sponsored by the Cowles Commission and contributed extensively to the literature of econometrics with papers in Monograph 10, *Econometrica*, and elsewhere. Therefore it seems appropriate at this point to pause and recall the high points of his career up to its untimely termination in an airplane crash in southern India on December 13, 1950, in which both he and his wife were killed. He was born in Cluj (also known as Clausenburg), Rumania, in 1902. After overcoming great obstacles to his education, he became associated with the University of Vienna in 1925, where he remained until he was dismissed from his position shortly after Hitler's annexation of Austria early in 1938. In July of that year, at Frisch's suggestion, the Cowles Commission offered him a research fellowship, which he accepted. Soon afterward he moved on to Columbia University where he eventually became professor of mathematical statistics. In his fifteen years there he became one of the most distinguished contributors that mathematical statistics and econometrics have known. He solved many problems of the estimation of parameters in statistical models, and his penetrating decision function analysis (see below) is basic to much of the current research in mathematical statistics. The 1952 volume of the *Annals of Mathematical Statistics* has been dedicated to his memory.

In its new status, the Cowles Commission dealt directly with some of the organizations providing its financial support instead of through the University of Chicago, while of course all contracts and applications for funds were first approved by its Executive Committee. Support continued to come from Cowles and his family, from the University in the form of the salaries of the two senior faculty members and the free use of facilities, and from the Rockefeller Foundation in the form of a grant for the project, "Foundations of Rational Economic Policy." Fellowship aid for persons working in econometrics at the Cowles Commission was provided by the Social Science Research Council, the Rockefeller Foundation, the University of Chicago, and various sponsers in Canada and Europe.

In addition, the Life Insurance Association of America made a grant in 1948 to help finance the study begun in 1946 of the economic implications of the development of atomic energy. The Cowles Commission entered into a contract with the RAND Corporation beginning in January, 1949, for the conduct on a cost basis of a research project called "Theory of Resources Allocation." The Cowles Commission entered into another contract with the U. S. Office of Naval Research beginning in July, 1951, for the conduct of a research project known as "Decision-Making Under Uncertainty," also on a cost basis. For the most part, these grants and contracts are for periods of two or three years, and are subject to renewal.

Concurrent with this growth, the Commission gave thought to adjustments in organizational structure which would recognize formally realignments of functions which had developed since 1948 and which would better prepare the organization to meet the problems of the future. Although the plans outlined in the 1950–1951 Report did not all reach fruition in the current year, an initial step was taken by the appointment of an executive director to serve as the chief executive agent of the Commission. Simpson was named to the new post as of July, 1951. The executive director is responsible to the executive committee (of which he is a member) and to the board of trustees, and together with the director of research is responsible for advising those bodies on matters related to the interests, aims, and policies of the Commission.

From 1948 to the present, the research of the Cowles Commission has proceeded along the lines laid out by Marschak with no fundamental changes in philosophy, but with important amplifications and changes in emphasis. In particular, there was a relative shift toward theoretical work to obtain better models preparatory to another phase of empirical work. There was also more concentration on the proper choice of mathematical methods (see below). The central part of the program, including the four projects mentioned in preceding paragraphs, can be described under the headings *actual behavior* and *rational behavior*. The headings *statistical methods*, *mathematical tools*, and *special studies* include ancillary research on analytical tools and several other studies. "Actual behavior" requires no special definition; it is behavior as it occurs in the real world. "Rational behavior," or as it is sometimes called "optimal behavior,"

is defined as that behavior which best attains the goal
(utility, profit, survival, growth, etc.) of the individual
or group whose behavior is in question. The study of
actual behavior is the attempt to find general laws that
describe behavior as it occurs, or would occur, under
specified circumstances. The study of rational behavior is
the attempt to discover what kind of behavior on the
part of an individual or group in specified circumstances
would most completely achieve the goals pursued; it presupposes that the goals are known and stated in objective
terms, and that their probable achievement or lack of
achievement as a result of following a particular pattern
of behavior can be discovered. Studies of these two types
may be called "descriptive studies" and "prescriptive
studies," respectively.

There is a good deal of overlapping between the descriptive and the prescriptive studies for the following
reasons. First, in setting up models of actual behavior in
a world where monetary and material matters are of great
importance, it is convenient and is often a good approximation to reality to assume, as a basis for such models,
that individuals and firms do behave rationally. Thus, the
assumption of rationality enters into many theories of
actual behavior. Second, in order to prescribe what one
individual or group should do in order to achieve his or
its goals, the economic doctor must know how *other* individuals and/or groups will behave in the future, and in
particular how they will respond to the actions of his
patient. This requires knowledge about the actual behavior of others, whether it is rational or not. Thus prescriptive studies draw on the results of descriptive studies.
Because of this two-way overlapping the distinction must
be regarded as an expository device, and it must be remem-
bered that an accepted description or prescription may become inapt if either the prescriptions or descriptions upon
which it is based turn out to be incorrect.

The five headings mentioned above will now be discussed.

Actual behavior can be investigated by the techniques outlined in the previous section. Several such studies were undertaken. Andrew W. Marshall tested Klein's fifteen-equation model with its estimated parameters, as presented in Monograph II, by checking whether it fitted the data for 1945–1946 as well as it did the 1921–1941 data from which its parameters had been estimated. He found that of the twelve random equations (the other three being definitions), only seven could be considered valid in the postwar period; of the remaining five, two were of doubtful validity and three were clearly contradicted by the postwar data. Christ, starting from Marshall's work, revised those equations of Klein's model which did not pass Marshall's tests. He then re-estimated the parameters of the revised model using data for 1921–1947, omitting the war years 1942–1945, and then tested the results against data of 1948, using tests similar to Marshall's and several other tests. He found that the revised and refitted model performed better on extrapolation to 1948 than Klein's had on extrapolation to 1945 and 1946, but it still was not in itself an accurate instrument for prediction. Christ's work, containing also a summary of Marshall's work, appeared in *Conference on Business Cycles*, published in 1951 by the National Bureau of Economic Research. These two studies were among the first to act on the precept that econometric models, like any other theories, must be tested by their performance in making predictions.

Allen worked on equations describing the inventory behavior of firms in the linseed oil industry. Hildreth has used cross-section data from farms in Iowa to estimate the technological relationship between agricultural inputs and outputs. Together with Frank Jarrett, research associate in agricultural economics at the University of Chicago, he has worked on an econometric study of U. S. livestock production. Arnold C. Harberger, now of Johns Hopkins University, set up import-demand equations for the United States and estimated the elasticities of demand for various types of imports and for imports as a whole.

Harry Markowitz, now of the RAND Corporation, studied the financial behavior patterns of open-ended investment trusts and set up equations to describe them; the statistical results are in preparation. George Borts, now of Brown University, constructed a model of the relations between inputs and outputs in the railroad industry, which is different from most industries in that railroads do not control their own outputs, due to the common carrier law; a part of his work appeared in *Econometrica* in January, 1952.

Rational behavior is typically treated in studies that seek to answer questions like this: given an individual or a group, and given the goals of the individual or the goals of the group or its members, and given some kind of environment in which the individual or group operates, what behavior will lead to the most complete achievement of the goals? The Cowles Commission's work in this field springs from three somewhat related origins.

First, Koopmans had been thinking intermittently, ever since his wartime days with the Combined Shipping Adjustment Board, about a systematic way to find the optimum routing plan for empty ships when there are fixed tonnages of cargo per month to go from each port to other ports. The "optimum" routing plan is the one, among all those that deliver the required fixed amounts of goods, for which the required number of ships in service is smallest. Clearly the optimum routing will not send empty ships to any port which is receiving more goods than it is shipping because such a port is already an exporter of empties and it would be wasteful of ships to send any more empties there. Similarly, if New York and Liverpool are exporters of empties and Philadelphia and le Havre are importers of empties, then it would be silly to send empties from New York to le Havre if empties were also going from Liverpool to Philadelphia, because it would take less time for the empties from New York to go to Philadelphia, and for those from Liverpool to go to le Havre. As a result of this shift less shipping time would be used up in empty voyages, so the number of ships required would be decreased. Considerations of this sort indicate a possible, if unsystematic, approach.

In seeking a systematic approach, Koopmans hit upon the principles of an analytic method that was first known as "linear programming" but has now come to be called more accurately "activity analysis of production." It has grown up from several converging sources, including analyses by Wald and von Neumann of the Walrasian general equilibrium theory, discussions in welfare economics, Leontief's interindustry analyses, and the programming activities of government administrators as studied in the U. S. Air Force by G. B. Dantzig and M. K. Wood. It is *similar* to the traditional economic theory of production in that it seeks first to establish the technological relation between inputs and outputs, i.e., to answer questions like these: if the quantities of all inputs and all outputs but one are held at specified levels, what is the maximum quantity of the remaining output that can be produced? Alternatively, if the quantities of all outputs and all inputs but one are to be held at specified levels, what is the minimum quantity of the remaining input that is required? For example, consider cattle raising, where inputs are grazing land, feed, and labor, and outputs are milk and beef (the cattle themselves are purposely not mentioned, as they are a sort of "intermediate product" that is used up in the process of producing the final outputs of milk and beef). A successful analysis of this industry, or of a firm engaged in it, would be able to tell which combinations of land, feed, labor, milk, and beef are *achievable*, and which are not (i.e., one man using one acre of land and one sack of feed per week cannot produce fifty gallons of milk and fifty pounds of beef every day). Further, it would be able to tell how much milk could be gotten from a given combination of land, feed, and labor if the amount of beef to be produced per week was specified, or how much labor would be required to produce specified amounts of milk and beef per week using a given combination of land and feed, etc. A combination of inputs and outputs is said to be *efficient*, if, when that combination is the status quo, it is impossible to increase the rate of any output without at the same time increasing some input or decreasing some other output. Note that for any inefficient combination, there are efficient combinations that are preferable to it in the sense of producing more outputs with the same inputs, or the same outputs with less inputs. Note also that to move from one efficient combination to another, it is necessary to give up some of one commodity (be it output or input) to get more of another; technological "exchange rates" between commodities can be found showing how much of one can be gained by giving up a unit of another. Note finally that not all efficient combinations are rational or optimal. For example, if we should all become vegetarians, then any combination that produced beef at the expense of milk, even if it did so efficiently, would become irrational. As a more realistic example, suppose that certain amounts per week of milk and beef are being produced efficiently; that to consumers, one gallon of milk is worth one pound of beef; and that the combination of land, feed, and labor actually being used to produce a pound of beef would, if turned to dairy cattle, produce two gallons of milk. To continue in this state of affairs is not rational: if beef-raising were curtailed, and dairying were expanded, then for every pound of beef given up *two* extra gallons of milk could be had, and this would represent a net gain because consumers would have been willing to give up a pound of beef for only one gallon of milk. The rational or optimal combination of milk and beef is obtained by increasing milk production and decreasing beef production to the point where no further gain is obtained by continuing the process. This point may be reached either because consumers find that a pound of beef has become more desirable than a gallon of milk now that they have so little of it and so much milk, or because producers find that they cannot get another two gallons of milk from the resources that are freed by producing one less pound of beef now that they are producing more milk and less beef, or because of both. These developments are related to the economic principles of diminishing utility and diminishing returns to changes in input-proportions, respectively.

Thus in finding the optimal combinations of inputs and outputs, there are three successive winnowings of all the conceivable combinations. First, the achievable ones are selected and the others are discarded. Second, from the achievable combinations the efficient ones are selected and the others are discarded. (These two steps can be accomplished by means of purely technological knowledge, with no notions of which commodities are highly valued and which ones are not.) Third, from the efficient combinations the optimal one(s) is (are) selected, by considering the relative values to producers and consumers of the inputs and outputs. In these respects, activity analysis is like any other good theory of production.

Activity analysis *differs* from the traditional economic theory of production by being more specific about the technology behind the concepts of achievable and efficient combinations and the substitution of one commodity for another. It regards production as resulting from a number of separate activities, each one of which can be operated on a large or small scale, and each one of which uses certain inputs and produces certain outputs in an assumed fixed proportionality to the scale of operation. Thus any possible combination of scales of operation of the respective activities produces an achievable combination of inputs and outputs. If there is to be any substitution of inputs or outputs for one another in production, it cannot be accomplished *within* any one activity, but must come about through changes in the scales of operation of the various activities, resulting in a partial substitution of some activities for others. In the dairy-beef case above, one might substitute the activity of grazing for that of using feed, and thus effect a substitution of land for feed. Or one might substitute the activity of producing a breed of dairy cattle for that of producing a breed of beef cattle, and so substitute milk for beef.

In the shipping problem the outputs are tonnages delivered from each port to each other port, the input is the use of ships, and there are two separate activities corresponding to the dispatching of ships from each port to each other port, i.e. with and without cargo. The original problem of accomplishing a certain pattern of shipping with the smallest number of ships then is seen to be the problem of finding the efficient combination of flows of empty and loaded ships when the tonnages to be shipped (outputs) are given. It is purely a problem of physical efficiency (even if more than one firm is involved) and not a problem of an economic optimum because there is no question of whether the stated pattern of shipping is worth its cost as compared with other possible patterns. But economic optimum problems can also be handled with this analysis: if the relative values placed upon ships and tonnages shipped on different routes are known, then the rational or optimal shipping plan can be found.

In June, 1949, the Cowles Commission sponsored a conference in Chicago on activity analysis, at which papers were presented by economists, mathematicians, statisticians, and administrators. The greater part of the proceedings of the conference were published in 1951 as Cowles Commission Monograph 13, *Activity Analysis of Production and Allocation* edited by Koopmans. (Monograph 12 will be discussed below.) It begins with a long section on the theory of programming and allocation, followed by a section on application of allocation models. The shipping problem appears in a paper by Koopmans and Stanley Reiter (formerly of the Cowles Commission, now of Stanford University) entitled "A Model of Transportation." Other applications appear in "Development of Dynamic Models for Program Planning" by Wood and Murray A. Geisler of the U. S. Air Force, "On the Choice of a Crop Rotation Plan" by Hildreth and Reiter, "Effects of Technological Change in a Linear Model" by Simon, and "Representation in a Linear Model of Nonlinear Growth Curves in the Aircraft Industry" by Wood. In conclusion there are two shorter sections on mathematical properties of convex sets and problems of computation (see below, under the discussion of mathematical tools).

In reviewing the volume for the *American Economic Review* in 1952, Robert Solow of the Massachusetts Institute

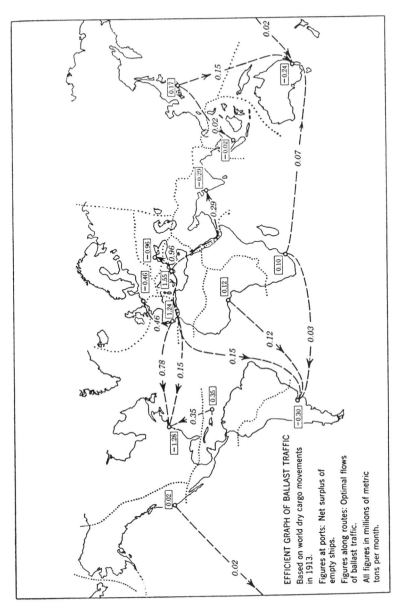

EFFICIENT GRAPH OF BALLAST TRAFFIC

Based on world dry cargo movements in 1913.

Figures at ports: Net surplus of empty ships.

Figures along routes: Optimal flows of ballast traffic.

All figures in millions of metric tons per month.

of Technology wrote as follows:

"Like all things good for body and soul, this book is going to hurt. Nevertheless there is no escaping the fact that everyone seriously interested in economic theory ought to keep a stiff upper lip and attempt to read it. This will be no easy task, since mathematical concepts whose use in economics is relatively new abound; . . . Still, by careful selection and constant attention to the *economics* of what is being said, almost everyone can profit.

It must be said at once that many of the general economic results stated in the book are not new; they are, in other forms, already part of the literature of welfare economics and the theory of production. What the new methods offer are first, a clearer insight into the meaning of some established propositions, such as those concerned with the much more than institutional significance of a set of price ratios in the optimal allocations of resources, and second, a framework for formulating many kinds of optimum-problems in such a way that they lend themselves to systematic computation. . . . In sum, the subject matter of this anthology is one of the frontiers of detailed and aggregative economic theory. It deserves a serious try."

Debreu devised a measure for the extent to which a given allocation of resources is efficient, being the smallest fraction of the given input levels (all reduced proportionally) that permits the community to attain through efficient redistribution of outputs the same standard of living for each member as prevailed under inefficient utilization of resources before the cuts in inputs. It appeared in his paper, "The Coefficient of Resource Utilization" in *Econometrica* in July, 1951. Kirk Fox undertook a study of the routing of railroad boxcars in the United States. Markowitz in his study of the behavior of investment trusts is inquiring whether their portfolios are efficient or not, i.e., whether they achieve a minimum risk for their rate of return.

The second source of the Cowles Commission's work on rational behavior lies in von Neumann and Morgenstern's *Theory of Games*, Wald's *Statistical Decision Functions*, and related work. In their book von Neumann and Morgenstern ask questions like these: given a game and its rules, how should a player behave so as to win as much as possible on the average over a large number of plays of the game, and what is the amount that he will win on the average if he so plays? So far the chief applications of the theory as such have been to games (e.g., chess, poker) and to problems in military strategy and some work in the economics of bilateral monopoly. But it soon became evident that many practical situations calling for decisions are very much like a one-person game in which the winnings depend on the decisions of the "player" and on the (perhaps unknown) "state of nature"; it is as if the player had nondiscriminating "Nature" as his "opponent," instead of another player who is hostile and out to win as much from him as possible. With this realization, the formal apparatus of the theory of games was taken over and applied to decision-making in many familiar situations, with a view to finding out what is the rational behavior appropriate to each. For example, suppose a monetary authority such as the Federal Reserve Board were making an estimate of whether the coming year would bring inflation or deflation if no action were taken in order to decide whether to decrease or increase the money supply. This can be regarded as a game played by the Federal Reserve against an economic "Mother Nature" with the Federal Reserve winning if it makes the right decision and losing if it errs. But since the consequences of deflation are more serious from most viewpoints than those of equally severe inflation (with severity measured let us say by the size of the fiscal deficit or surplus required to maintain stability), the Federal Reserve must regard itself as losing more if it prepares erroneously for inflation than if it prepares erroneously for deflation. Therefore it should be willing to run a bigger risk of predicting deflation incorrectly than of predicting inflation incorrectly. Its rational estimate of what the coming year will bring is not the unbiased estimate, but is instead an estimate *biased* somewhat in favor of preparing for deflation. Furthermore, while the range of uncertainty of the estimate presumably can be reduced up to a point if more resources are invested in the estimation process, the optimal extent to which the Federal Reserve should do this is found by balancing the expense against what the expense buys, namely the resulting reduction in the expected loss due to erroneous decisions. Wald's *Statistical Decision Functions*, published in 1950, is a formalization of this approach.

The accepted theory of the behavior of a business firm under competitive conditions is based on the assumptions that the firm is concerned only with flows of inputs, outputs, and sales, not with stocks of assets and debts, and that the firm knows its cost curves and demand curves exactly so that it can tell just how much profit it will make from any given level of output. For several years Marschak had been interested in making this theory more realistic by introducing the assumption of uncertainty together with the firm's asset and debt structure—particularly its liquid assets and inventories, because as has long been recognized the most compelling reason why these assets are desirable is the fact of uncertainty about future demand, prices, or other economic factors. His paper entitled "The Role of Liquidity under Complete and Incomplete Information," in the *American Economic Review* for May, 1949, and an earlier paper by Hurwicz, "Theory of the Firm and of Investment," in *Econometrica* for April, 1946, present work in this field.

As a different example, suppose that a firm's daily sales are not exactly known in advance, but are determined as if by being drawn at random from a hat containing numbers; that prices are constant; and that there are certain costs of ordering and storing inventories and certain costs of being caught "out of stock." This is similar to a game between the firm and the market; there is an optimal inventory policy for the firm telling, in terms of the numbers that are in the hat and the various costs, how low the firm should let its stocks get before reordering and how much it should order at a time, so as to minimize the total of all three types of cost. Further complications arise if the numbers in the hat are not known, so that the firm does not even know what its sales will be on the average nor how widely they will fluctuate, or if prices are assumed to be random variables and the firm speculates in inventories. Marschak, Arrow, and T. Harris of the RAND Corporation have published a paper on this work, "Optimal Inventory Policy," in *Econometrica*, for July, 1951. Other work in the area of decision-making under uncertainty, much of it using the decision-function approach, has been done by Arrow, Debreu, Hurwicz, Markowitz, Marschak, Radner, and Erling Sverdrup.

The third source of the Cowles Commission's work on rational behavior lies in welfare economics, and the attempt to deduce from the preferences of individuals a concept of social preference or of the general welfare. Monograph 12, *Social Choice and Individual Values* by Arrow, published in 1951, is addressed to this problem. Arrow assumes that each individual has a consistent value scale which ranks all the possible states of society in the order of his preference, and then he uses symbolic logic to try to deduce from this a social preference scale which has certain reasonable properties. He proves that it is impossible to do so, unless the preferences of the individuals are sufficiently in agreement in the beginning. Further work in this area by Hildreth and Markowitz and also by Leo Goodman is described in the reports on research activities for 1951–52 and 1950–51.

Statistical Methods received further attention during this period with concentration in four areas. The first is an expository monograph (No. 14, *Studies in Econometric Method*) being edited by Koopmans and Hood, to accompany Monograph 10 and offer its conclusions and some new results in more accessible and usable form. The second consists of inquiries into the extent and direction of the bias inherent in the least-squares method of estimating the parameters of econometric models, and more generally, into the consequences of using models that are incorrect. This work has been executed chiefly by Allen, Jean Bronfenbrenner (now of the Department of Commerce), Harberger, and Hurwicz. Some of it will appear in Monograph 14. The third is the application of the decision function approach to the problem of finding the best estimates of the parameters of econometric models, along the lines indicated in the monetary policy illustration mentioned earlier. Hildreth, Hurwicz, Radner, and Sverdrup were engaged in this work. The fourth is the theory of statistical procedures to deal with time series where the successive random terms are interdependent, to which Gurland has made several contributions.

Mathematical tools for handling of problems in activity analysis had to be developed or adapted from branches of mathematics that had been little used in economics previously. The essential mathematical concept in activity analysis is the maximization of a function (value or profit) of several variables (inputs and outputs) when certain *inequalities* among the variables must be satisfied (when input levels are given, output cannot be greater than a certain maximum achievable amount). When the relationships in question are linear, the mathematics of such inequalities turns out to be the theory of convex bodies or sets. Murray Gerstenhaber, Koopmans, and Morton Slater have been chiefly responsible for this work, with Slater extending his research to nonlinear relationships as well.

Special studies includes, principally, *Economic Aspects of Atomic Power* by Schurr and Marschak with contributions by Simon and others, published in 1950. It contains the results of the study mentioned at the end of the previous chapter. It attempts to analyze the effects that the peacetime development of atomic energy may be expected to have on particular industries that use large quantities of either heat or electricity, which are the forms that atomic energy is almost sure to take, and on the underdeveloped areas of the world. The method in brief is to consider the probable costs of atomic versus heat and hydroelectric energy in various industries and geographic areas, and also the probable demands for new energy supplies. This work is closely related to the Cowles Commission's research on technological progress pursued by Simon and Debreu. In reviewing the atomic energy study for the *American Scientist* for January, 1951, Kirtley F. Mather wrote:

"This is in many ways an extraordinarily significant book. It undertakes the unprecedented task of assaying the social consequences of the practical application in human affairs of newly discovered scientific knowledge, even before the technologic problems pertaining to that application have been solved. . . . And it accomplishes this extremely difficult project by teamwork organized on a scale rarely observed even in the most complex research enterprises. Its ingenious methodology provides a pattern for procedures that may well be emulated by research groups concerned with many varied problems in quite different aspects of the broad topic of the social implications of science.''

There was levity amid the serious research in this period too. The most notable bit was a skit by some of the junior staff members and others burlesquing the department of economics and its affiliates in songs set to the music of Gilbert and Sullivan's operas and other familiar melodies. The Cowles Commission was featured in this one, to the tune of "The American Patrol" march:

We must be rigorous, we must be rigorous,
We must fulfill our role.
If we hesitate or equivocate,
We won't achieve our goal.
We must investigate our systems complicate
To make our models whole.
Econometrics brings about
Statistical control!

Our esoteric seminars
Bring statisticians by the score.
But try to find economists
Who don't think algebra's a chore.
Oh we must urge you most emphatically
To become inclined mathematically,
So that all that we've developed
May some day be applied!

Its exact authorship is surrounded by a certain degree of obscurity, which perhaps is just as well.

VIII. *Looking back and looking forward*

Since 1932, the motto of the Cowles Commission has been *Science is Measurement*. It was originally suggested by one of Davis' favorite quotations from the British physicist Lord Kelvin, to the effect that when you can measure what you are speaking about, you know something about it, but when you cannot measure it, your knowledge is of a meager and unsatisfactory kind. Although the motto was inspired by a venerable source, it has been criticized several times by social scientists on the ground that not all science is measurement, even if the term "measurement" is given a very broad meaning. While this is admitted, tradition and the ideals of precision and empiricism are on the side of retaining the original motto. However, in 1952 a partial change was suggested by Clifford Hildreth to make the meaning more appropriate and still to preserve some continuity with the original. The suggestion was accepted, and accordingly the new motto of the Cowles Commission is *Theory and Measurement*. It will be inscribed in the emblem that has carried the motto since the beginning.

In twenty years, a characteristic approach to research has grown up at the Cowles Commission. This is true in a methodological sense, as the preceding pages show. It is also true in an operating sense. The work of the Cowles Commission has been characterized from the beginning by a great deal of discussion and cooperation among staff members. The seminars and New Series Papers have been helpful in this activity, but they are rather in the nature of finished products. Far more important in the working stages are the hectographed "Cowles Commission Discussion Papers." As currently stated on the first page of each, these are "preliminary materials circulated privately to stimulate private discussion and are not ready for critical comment or appraisal in publications." Since 1947 the papers have been numbered consecutively in three series, and in the five years down to June 30, 1952, there have been 143 in economics and 74 in statistics. Recently a separate series has been inaugurated for mathematics papers, which formerly were included in the other series. There have been 14 of these to June 30, 1952. Each is circulated to the staff and guests and to a group of other interested persons in the United States and abroad. Each is typically presented by its author or authors at an informal staff meeting, where it gets a thorough going-over by the staff and guests. Following such criticisms, and written comments received from those too far away to attend the meetings, papers commonly undergo several revisions, usually with further discussions and comments on each, before being ready for publication (of course not all are published). In addition to the staff meetings and discussion papers, there is a still more informal level of communication, that of private conferences and correspondence often extending across the seas.

This cooperative approach to work in progress serves several purposes: authors have the benefit of keen criticism of their research while they are working on it; preliminary results are circulated to other workers in the field more quickly than regular channels of publication permit, a larger community than the resident staff of the Cowles Commission is enabled to participate in its work; and the cross-fertilization of ideas that is so important to research is fostered.

The Cowles Commission has always been partly international in character, even while its home was in Colorado Springs. Particularly since the end of World War II this feature has been enhanced by the regular stream of fellows and other visitors from outside the United States who have come as guests for various periods of time. This international flow goes on in both directions. Several Cowles Commission staff members have traveled in other countries as fellows, lecturers, or consultants from time to time, including Anderson, Arrow, Klein, Koopmans, Marschak, Tintner, and Wald. Other present or former staff members are associated with universities in several countries (Dvoretzky, Haavelmo, Hood, Patinkin, Reiersøl, and Sverdrup).

Some members of the Cowles Commission staff offer or have offered courses in the University of Chicago (in the Department of Economics, the Committee on Statistics, the School of Business) and occasionally elsewhere. This has been the case since the Cowles Commission came to the University in 1939.

The ideas and methods developed by the Cowles Commission and by people working in association with it are being taken up, in a number of instances, by economists in other institutions and in government. Several examples follow. Klein is continuing his studies in constructing models of the United States economy at the Survey Research Center of the University of Michigan. T. M. Brown, D. J.

Daly and others in the Canadian Department of Trade and Commerce in Ottawa have been working since 1947 on a systematic program of constructing econometric models of the Klein type and estimating their parameters for purposes of prediction and policy advising. Brown's paper, "Econometric Research and Forecasting" presented before the Econometric Society in Boston in 1951, is a preliminary account of this work. A second paper of his entitled "Habit Persistence and Lags in Consumer Behaviour," in *Econometrica*, for July, 1952, concerns another part of it.

The limited-information method of estimation, described in Section VI, is being used experimentally in several places, including the U. S. Department of Agriculture under the direction of Karl Fox; a U. S. Treasury project under the direction of Francis M. Boddy of Minnesota; at Iowa State College under the direction of Gerhard Tintner and John Nordin; and at the University of California under the direction of George S. Kuznets.

There has been regular cooperation between the Cowles Commission and a research project on expectations and business fluctuations conducted jointly by the Bureau of Business Research of the University of Illinois and the Public Opinion Research Center of the University of Chicago, under the leadership of Franco Modigliani. Arrow's work on social values has been discussed intensively by a joint seminar of social scientists and mathematicians at the University of Michigan early in 1952. Marschak's work on the theory of teams and organizations, described in the report on research activities in 1951–52, was presented at a colloquium on risk and uncertainty organized by the Centre Nationale de la Recherche Scientifique with the aid of the French Government and the Rockefeller Foundation held at the Institut Henri Poincaré in Paris in May, 1952. Other participants in the colloquium associated formally or informally with the Cowles Commission were Arrow and Edmond Malinvaud, who was a guest of the Cowles Commission in Chicago during 1950–1951. A conference on design of experiments on decision processes, organized by the University of Michigan group, is to be held in the summer of 1952 in Santa Monica, California in which Hildreth, Koopmans, Marschak, and Radner will participate.

The joint work of Arrow, Harris, and Marschak on optimal inventory policy has been taken up and given greater mathematical generality by Dvoretzky, Kiefer, and Wolfowitz on a logistics project of the U. S. Office of Naval Research under the direction of Sebastian Littauer of the Department of Industrial Engineering of Columbia University. This work resulted in a long paper, which appeared in *Econometrica* for April and July, 1952.

Activity analysis, developed both at the Cowles Commission and in the U. S. Air Force in Washington, has been a stimulating element in practical programming studies carried on at Carnegie Institute of Technology. "Blending Aviation Gasolines—A Study in Programming Interdependent Activities in an Integrated Oil Company," by W. W. Cooper, A. Charnes, and B. Mellon, in *Econometrica* for April, 1952, presents the results of their application of activity analysis to the problem of gasoline blending. Melvin Salveson of the University of California at Los Angeles is applying programming methods to problems of production scheduling.

This brings up to date the growth and development of the Cowles Commission. In thinking back over the last twenty years as portrayed in these pages, the reader will realize that much of the work of the Cowles Commission is of an abstract nature, and that many of its fruits are not likely to be reaped in the immediate future. Nevertheless, its work is connected in a very real way with the fundamental problems of a free and democratic society. It is by learning to predict in detail the consequences of *general* economic and social policies that we will be best able as a society to achieve desirable objectives without resort to direct controls over individual economic behavior. In the direction of learning to predict, research like that of the Cowles Commission should continue to yield important dividends in the future.

[2]

Early Progress in Estimating
Quantitative Economic Relationships in America

By Carl F. Christ*

Quantitative empirical economics rests on three pillars: economic theory, data, and statistical methods. When the American Economic Association (AEA) was founded in 1885, economics had a good foundation in theory and a modest one in data, but statistical methods were primitive. The story of early progress in learning the shapes and slopes of economic relationships is a dramatic one, full of flashes of insight and moments of blindness, forward steps and false starts. This essay attempts to tell part of that story.

Most of the early estimated relations dealt with demand or supply. Many contained only two variables, quantity and price. The proper inclusion of the prices of related goods, and of income in demand equations and cost conditions in supply equations, came later. For many years, economists were hampered (sometimes unawares) by not knowing whether a curve fitted to price and quantity data was a demand curve, or a supply curve, or some mixture of both. More generally, they did not at first know how to obtain estimates of the parameters of two or more relations that interact. In today's language, they had not solved the problems of identification and estimation of simultaneous equations models.

This essay deals with early empirical economic work related to these problems, mainly work done in America, but also some closely related work done abroad. It ends at the death of Henry Schultz in 1938, with one large exception: Its climax—the solution of the identification problem for the individual equations in a model—did not come until 1945 (though there were two independent correct attacks about 1930 that were not followed up).

After a brief mention of economic theory and data in Section I, and some preliminaries in Section II, we get down to business. Sections III and IV deal with estimation before about 1910. Sections V and VI deal with the two Henrys, Moore and Schultz. Section VII is the climax of the story. Section VIII is a brief conclusion.

I. Early Economic Theory and Data

Augustin Cournot formulated the demand function for a good as a function of its own price. Alfred Marshall gave a careful partial equilibrium analysis of demand and supply, including the effects of income, cost conditions, and the prices of related goods. Leon Walras

included the prices of all other goods in each equation in a general equilibrium analysis. Thus by the time the AEA was founded, a rather sophisticated theoretical apparatus had been constructed on the other side of the Atlantic. Little empirical use was made of it for several decades, perhaps in part because of data limitations.

In the 19th century, even more than today, most economic data were derived from the activities of government: taxing, spending, and regulating. Some of course came from the decennial censuses, and later from the special censuses of agriculture, manufacturing, and so on. The first issue of the *Statistical Abstract of the U. S.*, for 1878, had 157 pages and included headings on government finance, banks, deposits, currency and coinage, gold and silver, imports and exports, production and consumption of goods, immigration, shipping, population, the postal service, railroads, agriculture, and coal mining. The 1889 issue was twice as large, and included data on the telegraph and telephone, pensions, patents, and Indians.

The late 19th and early 20th centuries saw giants making great strides in the collection and systematization of economic data. This essay can only make brief mention of some of them. The work of Wesley Mitchell and Irving Fisher on index numbers made possible the measurement of price levels, and, later, of real income. The National Bureau of Economic Research, founded in 1920, made great contributions: the work of Mitchell and others on business cycles, and of Mitchell, Simon Kuznets, and others in developing the national income and product accounts, were of the highest importance. Wassily Leontief's inter-industry analysis dovetailed with the national accounts, and was a precursor of linear programming.

II. Preliminaries

Much of our story will revolve around two giants, Henry Moore and Henry Schultz. When Moore began to publish empirical work in 1907, the field of statistical economics hardly existed. When Schultz died, it was well developed. Moore and Schultz studied mainly farm products. Apart from them, most of the pioneers of empirical work in demand and supply were agricultural economists. Perhaps this is due to several factors: agriculture was one of the most important sectors of the economy for a long time, farm products are relatively homogeneous, and data on their prices and quantities were available at an early stage.

Empirical economics began slowly in the 19th century, and grew rapidly in the 1920's and 30's. This is vividly indicated by the number of articles listed under selected empirical headings in the first two volumes of

*The Johns Hopkins University. I am happy to acknowledge the assistance of Gabriella Bucci, Shiva Sayeg, and Karlee Gifford, and helpful comments from Moses Abramovitz, David Hendry, Leonld Hurwicz, Charles Kindleberger, Lawrence Klein, Gregg Lewis, Mary Morgan, and George Stigler. I alone am responsible for any inadequacies.

39

the AEA's *Index of Economic Journals.* Table 1 summarizes them for several subperiods, chosen so as to have roughly the same total number of entries in each: see colum (7). Column (8) shows that between 1885 and 1910 the average number of entries per year under the selected empirical headings was only 3. By the 1930's it had reached 40. Index numbers, social accounting and other statistical data accounted for the vast majority of the selected entries until the late 1930's, by which time articles on methods and demand analysis together accounted for about a third. George Stigler (1954) gives an excellent account of early empirical work on consumer behavior.

The antecedents of empirical methods in economics lie in Europe and England, and go back a long way. Probability concepts are very old. The function underlying the normal curve was proposed by Abraham De-Moivre early in the 18th century. The principle of least squares were discovered by Adrien Marie Legendre and Karl Friedrich Gauss before 1800. Nearly a century later, while the AEA was being founded, the methods of correlation and regression so essential to empirical economics were being forged by Francis Galton, Karl Pearson, and Francis Ysidro Edgeworth.

TABLE 1
Number of Articles Listed
Under Selected Empirical Subject Headings
In *Index of Economic Journals,* Volumes I-II

Heading Nos.		8	7.220–7.225	7.230–7.234	2.113 & 16.23		
Topics		Social Acc't'g & Data	Index Numbers	Identification & Estimation	Demand Analysis	Total	Total per Year
Period	Years						
(1)	(2)	(3)	(4)	(5)	(6)	(7)	(8)
1886-1909	24	47	13	2	1	63	3
1910-20	11	45	16	5	5	71	6
1921-24	4	36	21	2	3	62	16
1925-28	4	50	18	4	6	78	20
1929-31	3	42	12	10	5	69	23
1932-33	2	24	17	14	16	71	36
1934-35	2	50	17	12	14	93	46
1936-37	2	40	14	13	5	72	36
1938-39	2	35	23	16	15	89	44
1886-1939	54	369	151	78	70	668	13

Source: American Economic Association, *Index of Economic Journals, Vols. I-II,* Homewood, Illinois: Richard D. Irwin, 1961.

III. The Role of Statistics in American Economics During the AEA's First Quarter Century

At the inception of the AEA in 1885, its members were interested in statistical work, more than in economic theory. The Statement of Principles in the AEA's Constitution (1886, pp. 35-6) said ". . . we look not so much to speculation as to the historical and statistical study of actual conditions of economic life. . ." Many of the AEA's earliest publications dealt with statistics. Its first president was General Francis Amasa Walker, who was already president of the American Statistical Association (ASA).

To most American economists at that time, "statistics" meant the gathering, organizing, and presentation of numerical information, rather than mathematical statistics. Walker was the superintendent of the censuses of 1870 and 1880. His *Statistical Atlas of the U.S.* (1874) introduced colored charts and maps. In "The Study of Statistics in Colleges and Technical Schools" (1890) he wrote that the three uses of statistics were to detect fallacies, to illustrate conclusions, and to find social laws. Davis R. Dewey in "The Study of Statistics" (1889) distinguished three types of statistical method: research and verification, tabulation, and graphical illustration. Richmond Mayo Smith in "Statistics and Economics" (1888) gave an outline of statistics in three parts: statistics of population, of the economy, and of vice and crime. Smith's last section was entitled "The Freedom of the Will." It was a rebuttal of the view expressed by the Belgian astronomer royal, Adolphe Quetelet, that statistical regularities in social phenomena arise from physical laws inherent in the "physique sociale," in which human will has no part. Mayo Smith wrote that statistics had ". . . invaded the domain of the freedom of the will." and replied that "The law of the mass has in itself no power over the individual." (p.126).

Another astronomer, Simon Newcomb of Johns Hopkins, in his *Principles of Political Economy* (1885, pp. 316 and 328) made a careful distinction between stocks ("funds") and flows, and according to Irving Fisher (1909, p. 642) gave the first correct statment of the equation of exchange.

Carroll D. Wright, the first commissioner of the U.S. Bureau of Labor, saw the need for rigorous statistical methods. In "The Study of Statistics in Colleges" (1888, p. 20) he wrote, "The analytical work of statistical science demands the mathematical man." He listed twelve European universities that were giving courses in statistical science, but only three in America.

After this initial burst, there was relatively little material on statistical method in the AEA's publications for the next 20 years. Even the ASA's publications contained little about mathematical methods of statistics before 1910, if the titles of the papers are any guide. Carroll D. Wright again commented favorably on mathematical training in statistics in "The Study of Statistics in Italian Universities" (1890). This is interesting since the earliest use of multiple regression in economics (apart from fitting nonlinear functions to data for two variables) was apparently in *Giornale degli Economisti* (see below). H. S. Pritchett in "A Formula for Predicting the Population of the United States" (1891) offered a cubic function of time, fitted by least squares to data from the censuses of 1790 through 1880. The formula predicts a population of 297 million for 1980, against an actual value of 228 million. (I can imagine him replying today that his equation could not have foreseen the immigration restrictions of the 1920's, so what did I expect?)

An early estimate of demand elasticity is implied in Arthur and Henry Farquhar's *Economic and Industrial Delusions* (1891, pp. 206-8). They computed annual percentage changes in the value and size of the U.S. potato crop per head for 1867-1888, and found that, on the average, for each 1% increase in the size of the crop, the value decreased by 0.3% and hence the price decreased by 1.3%. The implied elasticity is −.77.

IV. Empirical Economic Work Related to Simple Regression and Correlation

Galton proposed the concepts of regression (1885) and correlation (1888). Edgeworth (1892) gave the formula for the multivariate normal density function, and derived the expressions for multiple regression coefficients using determinants (not matrices). Karl Pearson (1896) gave the formula for the product-moment correlation coefficient, and defined the multiple correlation coefficient and showed how it is expressed in terms of simple correlation coefficients. G. Udny Yule (1897) introduced the idea of partial correlation. The use of these concepts in economics followed after about a decade.

The earliest correlations and regressions were bivariate. Aware of more than two variables, many economists adjusted their data to remove the effects of "disturbing influences" that might occur through time. To adjust for population change, amounts per head were used. To adjust for growth in time series, two methods were devised. One was to compute link relatives, that is, the ratio of each period's figure to the preceding one. This is equivalent to computing percentage changes each period. I will use the term "link relatives" for both. The second method was to compute a trend (either some function of time or a moving average of data over a period about as long as one or two business cycles), and then compute trend ratios, that is, the ratio of each period's value to the trend value. This is equivalent to computing percentage deviations from trend. Arithmetic deviations from trend are similar. I will use the term "trend ratios" for all three. In most cases, equations fitted to trend ratios and to link relatives give similar results. However, they can give slopes of opposite sign, as Ferger (1932) demonstrated by means of an especially constructed hypothetical example.

Yule (1907) opined that the earliest use of correlation in economics was his own cross-section study (1895-96) of the relation between pauperism and the method of providing relief. Another early user was R. H. Hooker. In (1901a) he found positive simple correlations of the marriage rate with a number of economic variables, using trend ratios, mostly for 1861-95. He tried various leads and lags to find the highest correlations; as far as I know, he was the first to do this in economics. In (1901b) he correlated the price and output of corn ("maize") in the U.S. for 1870-1899, obtaining $r = -.28$ for raw data and $r = -.84$ for first

differences. He implicitly interpreted this as a demand relation.

The first American economic study to use regression and correlation, to my knowledge, was John Pease Norton's *Statistical Studies in the New York Money Market* (1902), apparently a Yale doctoral dissertation. He graphed the New York Stock Exchange call discount rate D against the reserve ratio R of the New York Associated Banks, using grouped data for 780 weeks from about 1885 to 1900. He noted a curved relation, the discount rate rising more rapidly as the reserve ratio fell toward the required ratio of 25%. A straight line did not fit very well, so he divided the data into two parts at the mean of D, and fitted a straight line to each part, thus obtaining somewhat better fits:

(1)   for the whole sample: D = constant - .3146R, r = −.5231
(2)   for below-average D's: D = constant - 1.1617R, r = −.5920
(3)   for above-average D's: D = constant - .1175R, r = −.5997

He ran a similar regression using trend ratios of R. He also constructed a sort of average seasonal pattern for loans, and one for reserves, and correlated the two with various leads and lags. The best fit (r = .958) occured when loans were correlated with reserves 3 weeks earlier. He interpreted these results in the light of banking theory, which predicts that when the reserve ratio becomes low, bankers raise rates and borrowers soon reduce the amounts of their loans (pp. 80-94).

Stigler (1954) reported that Benini (1907) made the earliest use of multiple regression in economics (not counting least squares fitting of nonlinear equations in two variables). Benini fitted a demand equation for coffee in Italy from 1880-81 to 1905-6 as a function of the prices of coffee and sugar, obtaining negative coefficients for both. In (1908) he also fitted an Engel curve to the log of housing expenditure as a function of income using observations for two cities.

Although Gini (1910) noted that demand depends on price, income, and the prices of related goods, he did not include income in his demand equations for coffee, tea, salt, and other goods. He used the bivariate form

(4) $q = a + b \log p$

where p is either the price of the good in question or an average of that price and the price of a complement. He used a weird estimator of b: minus the ratio of the *average absolute deviations* of q and log p from their means. If q varies, this estimator always gives a negative value of b, even when applied to data where the correlation is zero or positive!

The first article in the ASA publications with a title explicitly dealing with mathematical statistics was Warren M. Persons' "The Correlation of Economic Statistics" (1910). This paper gave a rather complete set of Pearson's formulae for simple regression and correlation, and a rudimentary account of multiple correlation for a three-variable problem.

R. A. Lehfeldt in "The Elasticity of Demand for Wheat" (1914) assumed a constant-elasticity demand equation in output trend ratios and price. He computed a correlation of (minus) .44 between the logarithms of these variables. Then for the absolute elasticity he used an estimator very similar to Gini's and equally weird: the ratio of the *standard deviations* of the logarithms, which was 0.6. If output varies, Lehfeldt's estimator, like Gini's, is always nonzero even when the correlation is zero. It would agree with the regression estimator only if the correlation were perfect.

One of the most famous relations ever estimated by least squares was in "A Theory of Production" by Charles Cobb and Paul Douglas (1928). They proposed their production function bL^kC^{1-k} and estimated k, the labor elasticity of output, at 3/4 for 1899-1922.

V. Henry Moore

Henry Moore is properly recognized as the founder of what he called statistical economics. His student Paul Douglas (1939, p. 104) referred to him as ". . . that lovable and nervous genius. . .". For an excellent study of Moore's work, see Stigler (1962).

Moore took his Ph.D. at Johns Hopkins in 1896. His interest in statistics was not apparent for another decade. His thesis, "von Thunen's Theory of Natural Wages" (1895), had no statistical content. During Moore's student days the *Johns Hopkins University Circular* listed only two course titles under "Economics" that had any mathematical or statistical flavor: the astronomer Simon Newcomb's 10 lectures on "Economics as an Exact Science" in 1893, and Elgin R. L. Gould's 25 lectures on "Statistics" in 1895. Stigler (p. 4) reports that Moore, in a 1901 entry in his journal, listed books in mathematics and physics that he proposed to study, but there is as yet no mention of statistics. In 1903 Moore visited Walras in Europe (Stigler, p. 2). Shortly thereafter Moore published papers (1905, 1908) in which he praised the work of Cournot, William Stanley Jevons, Edgeworth, and Vilfredo Pareto. The second of these makes brief mention of several statistical concepts: the normal curve, the standard deviation of the sum or difference of two means, Pareto's law for income distribution, least squares, and the work to be discussed next.

Moore's first empirical results were published in "The Differential Law of Wages" (1907). He drew a smooth curve to match a frequency distribution of the average wage of workers 16 years old or over in each of 30 manufacturing industries in the U.S., based on data in the 1900 census. He assumed that ability follows the Gaussian distribution, and drew a smooth curve for that. He then compared the two smooth curves, found them similar, and concluded that he had demonstrated that wage differences are due to ability differences. We will return to this conclusion below.

The first of Moore's five books was *Laws of Wages: An Essay in Statistical Economics* (1911). It was dedicated "to John Bates Clark in admiration and affection." It is a rather mixed bag of empirical studies about wages. There is a cross section regression of women's weekly wage y on men's weekly wage x, for states and territories in 1905:

(5) $y = .3829x + 1.504$, $r = .866$

There is a cross section regression of food and fuel expenditure z on the unskilled wage y for 87 departments of France:

(6) $z = .5786y + .2537$, $r = .667$

and a partial correlation holding the price index x constant ($r_{zy.x} = .628$). The near equality of the simple and partial correlations reinforced Moore's view (followed in most of his work) that the simple correlation is adequate.

In Chapter III Moore used annual data for French coal mining for 1847-1899 to establish three empirical propositions: (a) Trend ratios of the wage rate vary with trend ratios of the value of average output per laborer: $r = .843$. (b) Trend ratios of labor's share of output value vary with trend ratios of machine horsepower per laborer: $r = .599$. (c) The trend in labor's share varies with the trend in machine power per laborer: comparing two departments, the one with the faster growth rate of horsepower per laborer for 1880-1902 (5.04% vs. 3.44%) had the faster growth rate of labor's share (0.35% vs. 0.12%); he did not test for statistical significance. He offered these propositions as a test of the marginal productivity theory of wages, but as Stigler (pp. 5-6) noted they do not provide the test he sought. Regarding (a) he was aware that the theory relates the wage to labor's marginal product, but he used average product instead because it is easier to measure. Regarding (b) and (c) he was apparently unaware that the relation of labor's share to the capital/labor ratio depends on the form of the production function (for example it is constant for a linear homogeneous Cobb-Douglas function).

Chapter IV was essentially a repetition of "The Differential Law of Wages" (1907) but with different data, for French male workers in 1893. When Edgeworth (1912) reviewed this book, he praised it highly: ". . . this is the first time, we believe, that the higher statistics, which are founded on the Calculus of Probabilities, have been used on a large scale as a buttress of economic theory." But he attacked this chapter by pointing out that since Moore had no data on ability but simply assumed it normally distributed, and since weight is approximately normally distributed, Moore's result gave just as much support to the theory that weight determines wages as to the theory that ability does.

The last two chapters deal with the relation of wages to strikes and to industrial concentration. They are of limited interest.

Moore pleaded (p. 195) for a combination of economic theory, expressed in a series of simultaneous equations, and "statistical economics." As this book and his later work demonstrate, Moore gave much more attention to statistical economics than to careful economic theory.

Moore's second book was *Economic Cycles: Their Law and Cause* (1914). Its central theme was that "The fundamental, persistent cause of the cycles in the activity of industry and of the cycles of general prices is the cyclical movement of the yield per acre of the crops." which in turn is caused by cycles in rainfall. (pp. 127, 57).

Moore's first step in this argument was his finding of 8 year and 33 year cycles in rainfall in Ohio and Illinois.

The second step was his positive correlations of about .6 between crop yields (trend ratios) and rainfall in certain months (chosen to maximize the correlation) in Illinois from about 1870 to 1910. The third step was his first venture into demand analysis: he regressed price on output for 1886-1911, using link relatives, for each of 4 crops: corn, hay, oats, and potatoes. His correlations were $-.7$ or better, and his elasticities were about -1. He also tried a cubic form of the equation, obtaining a somewhat better fit.

He counseled against multiple correlation for demand equations as follows. To investigate the effect of each factor, caeteris paribus, he wrote, is a ". . . bewildering method. . ." of . . . "vast barrenness. . ." (p. 67). Though he heartily agreed that by using simultaneous equations containing many prices the masters gave the ". . . very best theoretical treatment. . ." of the relation of price to quantity, he regarded it as ". . . hopelessly remote from reality. . .". Instead, he wrote, if this case is typical, ". . . it is unnecessary to face the complex possible interrelation of phenomena contemplated in the theoretical treatment." Happily, ". . . imaginary, theoretical difficulties are dispelled by solving real problems. . ." (pp. 81-82).

Moore's next step was to regress price on yield per acre for each crop; the resulting "yield-price" curves were very similar to his demand curves. He then found that pig iron production (representing industrial output) is positively correlated with the crop yield of the previous year, using trend ratios. Thus his cyclical theory was as follows: a cyclical rise in rainfall raises crop yields, which lowers crop prices this year and raises pig iron output next year, which he expected would lower pig iron prices via a negatively sloping demand curve. But instead he found that pig iron prices *rose* when its output rose. From this he concluded that the idea of universally negative demand slopes was a shibboleth of theory, and that for pig iron he had discovered a new type of demand curve with a positive slope. To confirm this he regressed pig-iron price on pig-iron production using link relatives and found a positive elasticity of .5211 and $r = .537$ (p. 114). He apparently had no idea of the identification problem, and did not consider that his positive elasticity for pig iron was closer to a supply elasticity than to a demand elasticity. Philip Wright (1915) (whom we shall meet again) criticized him for this, as did others. Thereafter Moore stuck to agricultural commodities and discovered no more positive demand elasticities.

Moore's third book, *Forecasting the Yield and Price of Cotton* (1917), was his only work to use multiple regression and correlation. Its theme was that (a) weather data permit better forecasts of cotton yields than do government crop reports, (b) yields and acreage planted influence the cotton crop, and (c) crop forecasts permit price forecasts by means of a demand curve.

After an introductory chapter on the mathematics of bivariate correlation, Moore turned to yield forecasting. The U.S. Department of Agriculture issued yield forecasts each month from May through September, based on reports of the condition of the crop, using trend

ratios. Moore made much better forecasts by regressions of yield on rainfall and temperature for 1892-1914 for Georgia, again using trend ratios. His May forecast equation had a single independent variable, May rainfall. His equation for June and July included also the June temperature. His August equation included a third independent variable, the August temperature, and had a multiple correlation of .732. Each of his equations gave smaller root mean square residuals than did the USDA forecasts made one or two months later. The signs of his coefficients indicated that a dry May, a hot June, and a cool August were favorable for cotton yield. He obtained similar results for Alabama and South Carolina, but not for Texas, where he resorted to first and second differences.

Moore computed simple regressions of cotton acreage planted on six lagged variables, using link relatives. One was the previous year's cotton price. Here the elasticity was positive, with $r = .532$. Though we can now see the germ of the cobweb theorem in this equation, he apparently did not.

He next turned to the law of demand for cotton, using link relatives for 1890-1913. After trying a couple of simple regressions, he chose a multiple regression of cotton price on cotton production and the general price index:

(7) $y = -.97x_1 + 1.60x_2 + $ constant, $R = .859$, $r_{yx1.x2} = -.808$

The implied demand elasticity was -1.03.

He did not use his yield and acreage equations to forecast the crop, nor his demand equation to forecast the price.

He concluded with these comments on research strategy: "When we write the law of demand in the form $x_0 = \phi(x_1, x_2, x_3, \ldots x_n)$, we do not know the form of ϕ nor the types of interrelations of $x_1, x_2, x_3, \ldots, x_n$; but when we are confronted with the practical problem of forecasting x_0, we can find empirical functions that enable us to predict x_0 with a high degree of accuracy." Thus ". . . theoretical difficulties disappear before a practical solution." "When the method of multiple correlation is thus applied to economic data it invests the findings of deductive economics with 'the reality of life and fact'; it is the Statistical Complement of Deductive Economics." (pp. 161, 173). In the light of this last remark it is curious that Moore did not use multiple regression again in his subsequent work.

In "Empirical Laws of Demand and Supply" (1919), Moore defined the flexibility of price as the percent change in price associated with a 1% change in quantity; for a bivariate relation this is the inverse of elasticity. Using link relatives of cotton data he presented a cubic demand equation, and an acreage equation based on the previous year's price similar to the one in his book on cotton.

In "The Elasticity of Demand and the Flexibility of Prices" (1922), Moore expressed the flexibility of prices as a linear function of the quantity demanded,

(8) $\phi = \alpha + \beta x$,

which implies the demand function

(9) $y = Ax^\alpha e^{\beta x}$

where $y = $ price and $x \doteq$ quantity. He said this "may be called the typical equation of the law of demand."

(p. 12). By a suitable choice of units, A can be made equal to $e^{-\beta}$ so that the equation becomes

$$(10) \qquad y = x^a e^{\beta(x-1)}$$

Using trend ratios Y and X for potato price and output for the U.S. for 1881-1913, he estimated the logarithm of equation (10) by least squares, obtaining

$$(11) \qquad Y = X^{0.143} e^{-1.376(X-1)}$$

The implied demand elasticity when output was on its trend (X = 1) was $-.811$.

Moore's fourth book, *Generating Economic Cycles* (1923), was his least successful. He returned to the theme of his earlier book on cycles, and argued that that the probable cause of the cycles in rainfall is the 8-year cycle of Venus in relation to the sun and the earth. This book is best left in the obscurity into which it has settled.

In "A Moving Equilibrium of Demand and Supply" (1925) he reverted to simple demand and supply equations for potatoes for 1900-1913. He computed trend ratios p and x for price and output. He estimated the following pair of linear equations:

$$(12) \qquad \text{demand: } p = -1.425x + 2.425, r = -.95$$
$$(13) \qquad \text{supply: } p_{-1} = 1.222x - .222, r = .80$$

He estimated a second pair having constant elasticities, with units chosen to make the multiplicative constants disappear:

$$(14) \qquad \text{demand: } p = x^{-1.2310}$$
$$(15) \qquad \text{supply: } p_{-1} = x^{1.0828}$$

At last he had found a way to estimate both demand and supply curves from the same price-quantity data. Again he had the ingredients of a cobweb model, and here he realized that it generates a path through time. But he did not investigate its stability.

Moore's last book, and the last work of his that we shall examine, was *Synthetic Economics* (1929). By "synthetic economics" he meant a dynamic theory expressed via simultaneous equations having concrete statistical forms.

He now proposed a more general form of the flexibility of prices than before:

$$(16) \qquad \phi = a + a'D + a''D^2,$$

which implies the demand equation

$$(17) \qquad p = AD^a e^{a'} + (1/2)a''D^2$$

where p = price and D = quantity demanded. He also gave a corresponding form in which elasticity rather than flexibility is set equal to a quadratic function of quantity demanded. For the law of supply he likewise proposed a quadratic function of quantity for the flexibility of price, or alternatively for elasticity, except that here he supposed the relevant price was that of the previous year. He gave no estimates of such equations, but instead reproduced estimates of potato demand and supply from the (1922) and (1925) papers.

He concluded his last book with a long approving discussion of Walrasian equations for factor supply, output demand, and equilibrium conditions, both static and dynamic, but offered no further empirical work.

Moore was a tireless worker in the vineyard of statistical economics, at a time when no one else was doing sustained work of this kind. His methods were exemplary in many ways. He almost always exhibited his data, and he described his procedures clearly. To him

must go the credit for the first concerted effort to give empirical content to the theoretical structure created by Cournot and his successors. Still, as we have seen, his work suffered because he was rather cavalier about the theoretical foundations of his equations, in spite of his brave comments about research strategy.

VI. Henry Schultz

Henry Schultz took his Ph.D. under Henry Moore at Columbia in 1926. He went far beyond his mentor in both theoretical sophistication and empirical thoroughness. His 817-page book, *The Theory and Measurement of Demand* (1938), is by all odds the most complete work in demand analysis published up to that time, and indeed except for its rudimentary treatment of the identification problem it stands up well today. His death in an auto accident in 1938 was a great loss.

In the twenties the level of confusion about correlation was such that the *QJE* saw fit to publish Schultz's first paper (1923), which demonstrated the now obvious fact that there is no necessary connection between the elasticity of demand and the coefficient of correlation obtained in estimating it. His next paper (1924) estimated Moore's demand equation (17) above for beef, using trend ratios.

Schultz's dissertation (1925) dealt with the demand for sugar. He took up the supply in (1927). These papers were incorporated into his book, *Statistical Laws of Demand and Supply with Special Application to Sugar* (1928). The book contains references to Cournot, Walras, Pareto, and Moore, with acknowledgments to Moore, Philip Wright, and Mitchell. Schultz began with a general demand function in terms of n variables and time:

$$(18) \qquad x_0 = F(x_1, x_2, \ldots, x_n, t).$$

He then proposed to remove time as an explicit variable, and instead to adjust each other variable for changes by one or more of several methods such as deflation by population or the price level, or the use of trend ratios or link relatives. He denoted such adjusted variables by $X_0, \ldots, X_n$. This resulted (p.30) in the "dynamic" demand equation

$$(19) \qquad X_0 = \phi(X_1, \ldots, X_n)$$

where X_1 refers to sugar consumption, X_2 to its price, and the other X's to disturbing influences. If the X's are percentage changes, a "static" demand equation can be obtained by putting $X_2, \ldots, X_n = 0$. Schultz acknowledged that the dynamic form is theoretically preferable, but adopted the static one for his empirical work in this book because he believed that the most important disturbing factors could be taken into account by the adjustments for changes mentioned above.

He prepared consumption and price data for 1890-1914 in a 2x2 classification (4 ways): unadjusted data vs. adjusted data (consumption deflated by population, and price deflated by a price index), and trend ratios vs. link relatives. He tried cubic, quadratic, and quintic trends. Some equations were linear and some were like Moore's equation (9) above. When fitting linear equations, he did it three ways: regressions with quantity dependent, regressions with price dependent, and what he called the line of best fit (treating both variables as subject to error and minimizing the sum of squared deviations perpendicular to the fitted line). His correlation coefficients (where he gave them) were between $-.5$ and $-.8$. Most of his elasticity estimates were between $-.4$ and $-.9$ under normal conditions (that is, when the trend ratio was 1 or when the link relative was equal to $1 +$ the normal growth rate). He concluded that the relation was linear, the best trend to use was a cubic, the best fit was obtained from the line of best fit, there was little difference between the estimates using adjusted vs. unadjusted data, or between trend ratios vs. link relatives, and the demand elasticity for sugar was about $-.5$.

Schultz's first estimates of sugar supply were based on the same data and the same 2x2 classification as those for demand, except that he followed Moore's moving equilibrium article (1925) and wrote the quantity consumed as a function of the *previous* year's price. He did this partly because current price always turned out to be negatively related to current consumption (he rejected all negative elasticities as not belonging to supply curves), and partly because of the plausible view that it takes time for sugar producers to respond to changes in price. His elasticities were essentially zero when he used trend ratios, and positive but hardly statistically significant when he used link relatives, no matter whether the data were adjusted or not. He noted that sugar is storable, and hence consumption can differ from production. He decided correctly that production data rather than consumption should be used to estimate the supply curve.

Schultz tried many equations involving production, and presented the results of a few. Some involve world production as well as domestic. Hence he chose for the sample period fiscal years 1904-1914, during which the sugar tariff was constant. He tried simple regressions with link relatives, using four different dependent variables: U.S. production, U.S. duty-free imports (from U.S. possessions), the sum of those two, and world production. He tried sugar price variables from the same year, the previous year, and the succeeding year. For world production he found elasticities of $-.6$ for current price and $.6$ for the previous year's price, corresponding to demand and supply respectively as he expected. But for U.S. production and duty-free imports, separately or together, he found (surprisingly) positive elasticities of about $.6$ to $.9$ using current price, and negative ones using the previous year's price. This led him to some multiple correlations, which he found unsatisfactory. (Curiously, after running the multiple regression of price on X_3 (U.S. production including duty-free imports) and X_w (world production), he interpreted the positive coefficient of X_3 as the inverse of its supply slope, and the negative coefficient of X_w as the inverse of its supply slope. It is possible to construct a model with this property, but it requires very implausible special restrictions on the parameters of several equations). He then abandoned multiple regression for this problem, and reverted to his simple-regression estimates, adopting as supply elasticities

the positive ones mentioned above. Thereafter he avoided supply and concentrated on demand.

In a series of papers from 1930 to 1935 in the *JASA*, the *JFE*, and *Econometrica* Schultz pursued his demand studies with increasing sophistication. He developed a formula for the standard error of a forecast from a curve. (Holbrook Working and Harold Hotelling (1929) had done the same for a straight line.) He introduced time explicitly and nonlinearly into demand functions to measure their rate of shift. He introduced the prices of other goods into demand equations for barley, corn, hay, and oats to see which were substitutes and which were complements. Inspired by the forgotten equations of Eugen Slutsky (1915), which he had helped to unearth, he introduced real income as well as other goods' prices into demand equations for beef, pork, and mutton in (1935). (E. J. Working in (1934) had presented a graph showing that the residuals from a price-quantity equation for pork were correlated with income.)

Schultz's magnum opus was *The Theory and Measurement of Demand* (1938). He dedicated it "to Professor Henry Ludwell Moore: trail blazer in the statistical study of demand." It was an impressive achievement. We look at it next, except that we defer the parts that touch on simultaneous equations bias and the identification problem. It begins with a good theoretical treatment of the derivation of demand curves from indifference curves, after the manner of Slutsky and John R. Hicks and R.G.D. Allen (1934). There follows a discussion of methods of estimating demand curves from time series data and from family budget data, and a description of his time series data. It makes use of the Neyman-Pearson (1928) approach to hypothesis testing.

Schultz summarized the forms of equations to be estimated as follows (pp. 151-2), where x = quantity demanded, y = price, X and Y indicate either link relatives or trend ratios of x and y, t = time, R = income or an index of production, and subscripts denote different commodities:

$$(20) \qquad x = x(y, t) \text{ and } y = y(x, t)$$
$$(21) \qquad x = x(y, R, t) \text{ and } y = y(x, R, t)$$
$$(22) \quad x_i = x_i(y_1, y_2, \ldots, R, t) \text{ and } y_i = y_i(x_1, x_2, \ldots, R, t)$$

Some special cases of the first form in (20) are:

$$(23) \qquad x = a + by + ct$$
$$(24) \qquad x = Ay^\alpha e^{\beta t}$$
$$(25) \qquad X = a + bY$$
$$(26) \qquad X = AY^\alpha$$

He first estimated per capita demand curves for each of ten agricultural commodities: sugar, corn, cotton, hay, wheat, potatoes, oats, barley, rye, and buckwheat. Here he assumed that the demand for each commodity depends on its own price deflated by a price index, but not on other prices. He used equations like (23)-(26). For a few commodities some additional special cases were estimated, including R or t^2 or both, or changing the form slightly. The sample periods were subsets of 1875-1929. All price elasticities were negative, as expected, except for a few of the cotton equations when income was excluded. Most price elasticities were about $-.6$ except that cotton, sugar, barley, rye, and especially wheat were less elastic than that and buckwheat had about a unit elasticity. Most simple correlations were between $-.6$ and -1, and most multiple correlations were at least .8 (pp. 546-53). An appendix shows a few estimates based on data unadjusted for population or price level, with similar results (p. 712).

Several groups of commodities were studied using the prices of related goods. Before presenting results, Schultz called attention (pp. 38-46, 620-22) to the Slutsky (or Hicks-Allen) conditions that must be satisfied by the partial derivatives of the demand functions derived from a consumer's preferences. They say that the *direct* (i.e., income-compensated) effect of a unit price increase of one good upon the quantity demanded of a second good must be equal to the corresponding direct effect of a unit increase in the second good's price upon the demand for the first good. In mathematical terms,

$$(27) \quad \frac{\partial x_i}{\partial y_j} + x_j \frac{\partial x_i}{\partial r} = \frac{\partial x_j}{\partial y_i} + x_i \frac{\partial x_j}{\partial r}$$

where x's are quantities demanded, y's are money prices, r is money income, subscripts denote different goods, and the partial derivatives are from the demand functions $x_i(y_1, y_2, \ldots, y_n, r)$. Schultz recalled that these are general conditions, valid for ordinal utility as well as cardinal, and that in the special case where utility is cardinal and the marginal utility of money is constant (pp. 575-82), the simpler Hotelling (1932) conditions emerge, whereby the *total* effects of the two price increases must be equal:

$$(28) \quad \partial x_i / \partial y_j = \partial x_j / \partial y_i.$$

Schultz estimated the per capita demands for barley, corn, hay, and oats as functions of the real prices of all four goods and time, without an income variable, for 1896-1914, using both linear and log-linear equations. Own price elasticities were all negative, and mostly about the same as in the simpler equations that contained only a single price, discussed above. The adjusted multiple correlations were generally higher than in the simpler one-price equations. The Hotelling requirement (28) was not very well satisfied; indeed, in 4 of the 6 pairs the two cross-derivatives had opposite signs, and in one of those pairs the estimates both had t-ratios greater than 2 (pp. 591-4).

Schultz estimated the total demands for beef and pork for 1922-1930 as functions of money income and both prices. They were found to have respective own-price elasticities of $-.5$ and $-.8$, income elasticities of .4 and .6, and cross-elasticities of about .4. Adjusted multiple correlations were above .95 when each quantity was expressed as a function of both prices, and between .8 and .9 when each price was expressed as a function of both quantitites (p. 584). The Hotelling equality (28) was approximately satisfied (.0637 vs. .0829), and the Slutsky equality (27) was satisfied even more closely (.09444 vs. .10143) (pp. 585 and 633).

The final set of demand equations that Schultz treated was for beef, pork, and mutton for 1922-1933. Per capita quantities were expressed as functions of per capita real income and the real prices of all three

goods. Both linear and log-linear forms were fitted. All own-price elasticities were negative, between $-.6$ and $-.9$ except for mutton's which was about $-.2$. All cross elasticities were positive except for pork's with respect to mutton's price, but it was highly insignificant. All income elasticities were positive, about .5 except that mutton's was .2. The Hotelling and Slutsky effects agreed well with each other, but neither (27) nor (28) was well satisfied by the estimates; indeed, in one of the three pairs the two quantities that are theoretically equal had opposite signs, in (28) as well as in (27) (pp. 639-645).

Schultz concluded with an ambitious program for research in demand as well as in cost and supply. He called for the study of family expenditure and the demand for nonfarm goods and stock-exchange securities. On the supply side he proposed the study of fixed vs. variable factors of production, the marginal productivities of factors, the relation of cost to the scale of enterprises and to the phases of the business cycle, the restatement of supply theory to make it amenable to statistical operations, and the measurement of supply curves for important goods (pp. 661-665).

The book has long appendices giving his data, and setting forth the theory of multiple regression and correlation in mathematical form.

Schultz's work was marked by a thorough command of both the mathematical economic theory and the mathematical statistics methods of his day, and he was knowledgeable and careful about his data. He combined all three components in the best tradition of empirical economics. He presented his basic data and described clearly the transformations he made in them. His tables of results are models of completeness and clarity. Though he had the shoulders of Henry Moore to stand on, and the help of such excellent young research assistants as Milton Friedman, H. Gregg Lewis, and Jacob Mosak, he made an enormous contribution in his own right. His death came as his powers were expanding. Who knows what more he might have done if he had lived a normal life span?

VII. The Solution of the Identification Problem

Throughout the foregoing pages we have repeatedly encountered the question of whether a line (or equation) fitted to data for price and quantity is a demand curve, or a supply curve, or some unknown mixture of both. This is an example of the celebrated identification problem (in the sense in which the term is used in the simultaneous equations literature, not the Box-Jenkins time series literature). We will end this essay with an account of how, after many false starts, this problem was solved for the individual equations in a linear model with any number of equations where we know which variables appear in which equations. The solution falls within our story because it came in America, though its main contributors were from Europe. It makes a natural stopping place, because it resolves a central difficulty that plagued early empirical economists, and because it marks the beginning of a new phase--the consistent empirical treatment of simultaneous economic relationships.

We have noted that Philip Wright (1915) criticized Moore's "new type" of positively sloping demand curve for pig iron. Wright's review contains the earliest recognition I know of in English, in an empirical context as opposed to a theoretical one, of something familiar to every freshman economics student today: If the supply curve shifts in the price-quantity plane while the demand curve does not, as is typical with agricultural products, the data will trace out the demand curve. But in the opposite case, as is typical with industrial products, the data will trace out the supply curve. Since demand and supply diagrams were well established in the theoretical literature decades earlier, it is hard to understand how an economist as able as Moore could have made such an egregious error.

In a remarkable monograph, Marcel Lenoir (1913) presented supply-demand diagrams showing that if supply alone shifts, the curve fitted to the data will be the demand curve, and vice versa, while if both curves shift, then the resulting fitted line will be neither the demand nor the supply curve. Lenoir appears to have been the first to recognize this (see Fox 1968). Then, using French data for 50 to 100 years, he computed simple and multiple regression equations for coal, wheat, oil, cotton, and coffee. The dependent variable was quantity, except for coffee. Based on the direction of the price-quantity slope, he concluded that his equations were more like supply equations for coal and wheat, and more like demand equations for the others.

Wright's and Lenoir's understanding apparently did not spread like wildfire. More than a decade later it was set forth again, with a reference to Wright but not to Lenoir, by Elmer J. Working in "What Do Statistical 'Demand Curves' Show?" (1927), a paper now regarded as a classic.

An important forward step in disentangling supply from demand was Moore's (1925) realization that for many goods, especially in agriculture where planting is generally done once a year, the quantity supplied depends on the previous year's price, while demand depends on the current price. Essentially the same point was made by the biologist Sewall Wright (1925), a son of Philip Wright. He noted that there is approximately a four-year cycle in hog prices and output, and devised a system of nonsimultaneous equations to explain it, using many lagged variables. He analyzed these equations by his method of path coefficients, a way of tracing the effects of independent variables upon dependent variables, in successive stages, which may or may not involve simultaneity. We shall encounter him again.

Mordecai Ezekiel (1928) gave a hypothetical example of a model like Moore's moving equilibrium (without citing Moore), and showed how it can generate cycles in price and quantity, and how it can yield estimates of both supply and demand curves from price-quantity data. He offered it as a solution to the problem posed by Working. Schultz (1928) used a similar model, crediting it to Moore. In (1938, pp. 78-80) he presented an explicit cobweb model, exhibiting both stable and un-

stable cases. He commented that it meant producers do not learn from experience: shades of rational expectations!

Two unsuccessful approaches to the identification problem for supply and demand curves were by Leontief (1929) and by A. C. Pigou (1930). The fact that two such talented economists could stumble over this problem is a testament to its difficulty. Leontief assumed that the elasticities of demand and supply were constant, and that the random disturbances in the demand equation were independent of those in the supply equation. From this, in effect, he cleverly obtained one equation in his two unknowns, the demand and supply elasticities. So far so good. He then decided that if he divided the sample into two parts chronologically, and obtained one equation in the same way from each part, he could solve the resulting two equations for the two elasticities. In fact, as shown by Ragnar Frisch (1933; see below), the resulting estimates are not the required elasticities, but are accidents arising from the disturbances. One way to see the flaw in this proposal is to note that if there are no disturbances, so that the logs of the observed price-quantity data fall exactly on a straight line, then the two equations are identical and cannot reveal either elasticity.

Pigou assumed a constant demand elasticity, and a constant rate of shift of the demand curve over time. He pointed out that if three consecutive observations on price and quantity are available, and if it is known which of the three was the middle one chronologically, then the demand curve can be determined graphically. This is true, but the assumption of a constant rate of demand shift is so unrealistic as to render the method impractical. John M. Cassels (1933) explained the difficulties of this method. Schultz (1938, pp. 83-104) gives a good discussion of both Leontief's and Pigou's proposals.

There were two independent, correct, almost identical, and almost contemporaneous solutions for the simple supply-demand case. Ironically, neither was recognized by the main stream of economics, and the solution had to be found all over again. The two solutions were by Philip Wright (1928) and Jan Tinbergen (1930). (I am indebted to Mary S. Morgan (1981) for leading me to Tinbergen's.)

First-year econometrics students today know that if demand depends linearly on price and a third variable that doesn't affect demand (say, income), while supply depends linearly on price and a fourth variable that doesn't affect demand (say, cost), then the parameters of both equations can be obtained from data on all four variables via the reduced form. This is precisely what both Wright and Tinbergen discovered, each with his own choice of third and fourth variables, and each in his own notation.

In a notation that is today more familiar than theirs, suppose that the model is as follows:

(29)   demand: $q = \alpha p + \beta y \quad + u$
(30)   supply: $q = \gamma p \quad + \delta c + u'$

where q = quantity, p = price, y = income, and c = cost, all measured as deviations from their observed means so that any constant terms in the equations drop out; u and u' are random disturbances with zero means and constant variances and covariance; and Greek letters are parameters to be estimated. Price and quantity are regarded as endogenous variables (to be determined by the model), and income and cost are regarded as exogenous (given by outside forces, not affected by price or quantity, and statistically independent of the disturbances).

The reduced form of a model is obtained by solving its equations algebraically for the endogenous variables, taking the exogenous variables as given. The reduced form of the foregoing model is:

(31) price: $p = \dfrac{\beta}{\gamma - \alpha} y - \dfrac{\delta}{\gamma - \alpha} c + \dfrac{u - u'}{\gamma - \alpha}$

(32) quantity: $q = \dfrac{\gamma\beta}{\gamma - \alpha} y - \dfrac{\alpha\delta}{\gamma - \alpha} c + \dfrac{\gamma u - \alpha u'}{\gamma - \alpha}$

Now, since income and cost are exogenous, and hence independent of the disturbances, ordinary least squares gives unbiased and consistent estimators of the coefficients of y and c in the reduced form equations. Therefore a good estimator of the demand curve's price slope α is obtained by dividing the estimated coefficient of c in (32) by that in (31). Similarly, a good estimate of the supply curve's price slope γ is obtained by dividing the estimated coefficient of y in (32) by that in (31). In symbols, the way to estimate the demand and supply slopes α and γ from the estimated reduced form parameters is as follows:

(33) estimate of $\alpha = \dfrac{\text{estimate of } \alpha\delta/(\gamma - \alpha)}{\text{estimate of } \delta/(\gamma - \alpha)}$

(34) estimate of $\gamma = \dfrac{\text{estimate of } \gamma\beta/(\gamma - \alpha)}{\text{estimate of } \beta/(\gamma - \alpha)}$

In this case we say nowadays that the supply and demand equations are both "just identified", meaning that there is just enough information to estimate them, no more and no less than needed. Neither Wright nor Tinbergen used the modern terms, but their method was the same as that described above, which we use today.

Both saw that if $\beta = 0$ the supply slope γ cannot be discovered, and if $\delta = 0$ the demand slope α cannot. Tinbergen's approach was the more complete of the two, for he explicitly included the random disturbance terms, and also presented stable and unstable cobweb cases, while Wright did not. Tinbergen referred to E. J. Working (1927). Wright gave a brief description of how the method of path coefficients, devised by his son Sewall Wright, helps to understand his result.

Both Wright and Tinbergen gave empirical examples. Both obtained negative price elasticities for their demand curves and positive ones for supply. Wright estimated the demand and supply for butter and for flaxseed. He was not explicit about what variables he treated as exogenous, but it appears that in each case his demand-shift variable was the price of a substitute (flaxseed or butter), and his supply-shift variable was yield per acre (a sort of inverse cost variable). Tinbergen estimated the demand and supply for potato flour in Holland, using potato output of France and Germany as the demand-shifting variable, and production plus

September 1 stocks of potatoes in Holland as the supply-shifting variable.

Neither Wright nor Tinbergen generalized their discovery. Most of the later literature on identification ignores it, and instead traces the beginning of the solution of the problem back to Frisch's monograph, *Pitfalls in the Statistical Determination of Demand and Supply Curves* (1933), which in one sense did not advance matters as far as Wright and Tinbergen did. How could it happen that both of these ingenious and important pieces could have been so neglected? Perhaps it was because Wright's was in an appendix of his book on *The Tariff on Animal and Vegetable Oils*, whose title does not suggest that it contains any methodological econometric nuggets, and Tinbergen's was in German in the *Zeitschrift fur Nationalokonomie*, while most of the progress in statistical and econometric method was being reported in English. Or perhaps their importance was simply not recognized. But it is strange that Schultz did not pick Wright's up, since Schultz was a friend and colleague of Sewall Wright at the University of Chicago, and since his books contain references to Philip Wright's book and to four of Sewall Wright's papers on path coefficients, one of which (1934) even contains a section by Philip and Sewall Wright describing Philip Wright's solution.

Frisch (1933) set forth in different notation the same demand and supply equations given above, except that he did not include any observable variables besides price and quantity. He obtained the reduced form but did not call it that. He used the statistical moments of the demand and supply equations to express the unknown demand and supply slopes in terms of the observable moments of the distribution of price and quantity and the unobservable moments of the random disturbances. From this he showed rigorously that (as Lenoir, Philip Wright, and Working had said without mathematical proof) if the disturbance in the supply equation is zero and the one in the demand equation varies, price and quantity data will reveal the supply slope, and in the opposite case they will reveal the demand slope, while if both disturbances vary then neither the supply nor the demand slope can be discovered without more knowledge. He did not see that knowledge about additional variables that enter into one equation but not the other would be helpful. However, he did assume that the two disturbances u and u' are uncorrelated, and that the ratio of their variances is known, and showed that then the supply and demand slopes can both be obtained from price-quantity data alone. Recall that the first of these two assumptions had been used by Leontief to get one equation in the two slopes. The second assumption yields a second equation.

The next step was an obscure 19-page mimeographed memorandum by Frisch (1938) that was prepared for a conference in Cambridge, England, to discuss a draft of Tinbergen's econometric model of the U.S. (I am indebted to the Cowles Commission Librarian, Karlee Gifford, for making a copy available to me.) Here Frisch reverted to the same road that was chosen by Wright and Tinbergen. That is, he considered a system of simultaneous linear equations where we know which variables appear in each equation and which ones do not. He considered difference equations containing no disturbances and no exogenous variables (that is, all of the explanatory variables were lagged values of the endogenous variables). He noted that such a dynamic equation system generates time paths for all its endogenous variables, if appropriate starting values (initial conditions) are given.

Frisch chose a particular one of the original equations, and considered the question of whether its coefficients can be obtained from a knowledge of the time paths of the variables, that is, in modern terms, whether the chosen equation is identifiable (he used the terms "irreducible" and "coflux equation"). He pointed out that the only equations whose coefficients can be determined empirically are those that are identifiable.

He then found that any such linear equation is unidentifiable if the number of terms in it exceeds $n + 1$, where n is the number of characteristic roots of the dynamic system. Further, if the number of terms in the chosen equation equals $n + 1$, a necessary and sufficient condition for its identifiability is that the rank of a particular n-rowed matrix must be equal to n. The matrix is not the convenient criterion matrix that we use today (see below), but is instead a rather complicated matrix involving the lengths of the lags in the chosen equation and the values of the system's characteristic roots. (A more general necessary and sufficient condition, which he did not give, is that the rank of his matrix be one less than the number of terms in the chosen equation.) Apparently he did not work on the problem after that. His criterion was not adopted by others, probably because of the difficulty of learning the values of the characteristic roots.

Frisch criticized Tinbergen's model of the U.S. on the ground that Tinbergen had not taken care to assure that his equations were identifiable and theoretically meaningful. Tinbergen prepared a mimeographed reply (1938) to Frisch (I am again indebted to Karlee Gifford for a copy). Strangely, this reply did not recognize that Frisch's paper was applicable to Tinbergen's earlier solution of the identification problem for the simple supply-demand case. Perhaps Tinbergen was preoccupied with empirical work on his U.S. model.

The next step was taken by Trygve Haavelmo, a young associate of Frisch, while at Harvard. He prepared a mimeographed study (1941) which was later published as a classic supplement to *Econometrica* under the title *The Probability Approach in Econometrics* (1944). It contains acknowledgements to Abraham Wald, Jacob Marschak, and Leonid Hurwicz. Into Frisch's linear dynamic system Haavelmo introduced exogenous variables (without that name), and normally distributed random disturbances. He used the modern concept of a structure, that is, a model in which numerical values have been assigned to all the parameters, including not only the equations' coefficients but also the parameters of the probability distribution of the disturbances. He presented the system's reduced form, and adopted Frisch's concept of identifiability (without those names). In a quite technical discussion he gave

necessary and sufficient conditions for the identifiability of the entire structure, rather than of one equation as Frisch had done. His conditions hinged on the linear independence of partial derivatives of the joint probability distribution of the endogenous variables. Like Frisch's his approach was difficult to apply and was not used to obtain the solution discussed here.

However, Haavelmo gave an example containing two linear equations for (guess what?) demand and supply (pp. 99-104). He applied his abstract conditions to prove that all the reduced form parameters are identified. He applied the maximum likelihood estimation method, and showed that for the reduced form it yields ordinary least squares estimators. (Here he built on the work of Mann and Wald, to be discussed in a moment.) He then said (p. 102) ". . . it is easy to see . . ." that in this example the structural parameters (i.e., the demand and supply slopes etc.) can be determined from the reduced form parameters, and he did it for the demand slope. The way he did it is identical to the way of Wright and Tinbergen; his supply-demand example is very similar to theirs in that respect. He also showed the inappropriateness of the ordinary least squares estimator of the demand slope, by exhibiting the difference between it and his appropriate estimator.

Haavelmo's paper, "The Statistical Implications of a System of Simultaneous Equations" (1943), is a shorter and simpler version of the study just discussed. Using little abstract mathematics, he made many of the same points, mainly through examples. One of the examples was a simple Keynesian multiplier-accelerator model whose parameters could be got from the reduced form, and whose maximum likelihood estimators he gave. Another example showed a case in which the structural parameters could not be got from the reduced form.

Marschak (1942) gave several examples, showing cases in which one can or cannot obtain the structural parameters from a knowledge of the reduced form.

Henry B. Mann and Abraham Wald in an important paper, "On the Statistical Treatment of Linear Stochastic Difference Equations" (1943), applied the maximum likelihood principle to a general linear system like that considered by Haavelmo (1944) but without exogenous variables. They obtained its reduced form and used that name for it. They proved that the maximum likelihood method yields ordinary least squares estimators of the reduced form, and that they are consistent (this had previously been known for equations containing no lagged values of dependent variables, with or without exogenous variables). They noted that maybe the structural parameters can be got from the reduced form parameters and maybe not, depending on whether we have sufficient theoretical information (of the type used by Wright and Tinbergen) about the structural equations, but they did not say how to tell whether such information is sufficient or not. They showed that if it is sufficient, then maximum likelihood estimators of the structure can be obtained, and are consistent and asymptotically jointly normally distributed. They discussed the same two examples from Haavelmo (1943) that were mentioned above.

In January of 1945 there was a conference at the Cowles Commission in Chicago to discuss the estimation of simultaneous-equations models. Those present included Haavelmo, Marschak, Mann and Wald, Hurwicz, Tjalling Koopmans, Herman Rubin, and Roy Leipnik. Papers were circulated in advance, including part of an extremely technical and difficult one by Koopmans, Rubin, and Leipnik (1950), in which the Wright-Tinbergen solution of the identification problem for a linear demand or supply equation was generalized to individual equations in linear systems with any number of equations, and the term "identification" was used. (The part in question is sections 2.1-2.2, pages 69-85; see pages 4-5 of Marschak's (1950) report on the conference.) In "Identification Problems in Economic Model Construction" (1949) Koopmans gave a simpler and quite accessible statement of the problem and its solution. Neither paper referred to Philip Wright or Sewall Wright or Tinbergen (1930); both acknowledged debts to Frisch (1938) and Haavelmo (1944).

The result, now familiar, is as follows. Consider a system of simultaneous linear stochastic difference equations containing both current and lagged values of endogenous and exogenous variables. Any constant term in any equation is to be regarded as the coefficient of a dummy variable whose value is always equal to 1. Suppose that economic theory tells which variables have zero coefficients in each equation. To decide whether a particular equation (say the nth) is identified or not, on the basis of this information, proceed as follows. Write out the matrix of coefficients of the system, each row representing one equation. Omit every column that does not have a prescribed zero in the row for the nth equation. The resulting matrix is called the criterion matrix for the identifiability of the nth equation. The number of its rows is equal to the number of equations, but its nth row is all zeros. The number of its columns is the number of the system's variables that are excluded by theory from the nth equation (not counting random disturbances). Then the nth equation is indentified if and only if the rank of this criterion matrix is equal to the number of its rows less 1, i.e., to the number of equations less 1. This is called the rank condition, naturally enough. A corollary is that the nth equation cannot be identified (on the basis of this type of information alone) unless the number of the system's variables excluded from it is at least as great as the number of equations less 1. This is called the order condition, because it refers to the order of the criterion matrix.

Consistent methods of estimating the parameters of simultaneous-equations systems, as alternatives to the least squares method which is not consistent for this purpose, were developed hand in hand with the solution of the identification problem. The method of Philip Wright and Tinbergen, given in (33)-(34) above, turns out to be a special case of these consistent methods. Though there have been many extensions and generalizations of these results, we have now come to the end of our story.

VIII. Conclusion

We have come a long way, from primitive estimates of single economic relationships to the identification and consistent estimation of multivariate simultaneous equations. We began by noting that quantitative empirical economics depends on economic theory, data, and statistical methods. It was obvious to the pioneers that data and statistical methods were necessary ingredients of progress. Less obvious at first was the intimate connection, illustrated by the events chronicled here, between statistical methods and economic theory.

REFERENCES

Benini, Rodolfo, (1907) "Sull'uso delle formole empiriche nell'economia applicata," *Giornale degli Economisti*, 2nd ser., November 1907, *25*, 1053-63.

_____, (1908) "Una possibile creazione del metodo statistico: L'economia politica induttiva," *Giornale degli Economisti*, 2d ser., January 1908, *36*, 11-34.

Cassels, John M., "A Critical Consideration of Professor Pigou's Method for Deriving Demand Curves," *Economic Journal*, December, 1933, *43*, 575-87.

Cobb, Charles W., and Douglas, Paul H., "A Theory of Production," *American Economic Review, Supplement*, March 1928, *18*, 139-65.

Dewey, Davis R., "The Study of Statistics," *Publications of the American Economic Association*, September 1889, *4*, 359-76.

Douglas, Paul H., "Henry Schultz as a Colleague," *Econometrica*, April 1939, *7*, 104-6.

Edgeworth, Francis Ysidro, (1892) "Correlated Averages," *Philosophical Magazine*, 5th Ser., August 1892, *34*, 190-204.

_____, (1912) Review of *Laws of Wages* by Henry Moore, *Economic Journal*, March 1912, *22*, 66-71.

Ezekiel, Mordecai, "Statistical Analysis and the 'Laws' of Price," *Quarterly Journal of Economics*, February 1928, *42*, 199-227.

Farquhar, Arthur B. 641-4.

Fox, Karl, "Demand and Supply: Econometric Studies," in *International Encyclopedia of the Social Sciences*, *4*, 104-11, New York: Macmillan, 1968.

Frisch, Ragnar, (1933) *Pitfalls in the Statistical Construction of Demand and Supply Curves*, Veroffentlichungen der Frankfurter Gesellschaft fur Konjunkturforschung, Neue Folge, Heft 5, Leipzig: Hans Buske, 1933.

_____, (1938) "Statistical Versus Theoretical Relations in Economic Macrodynamics," a memorandum prepared for the Business Cycle Conference at Cambridge, England, July 18th-20th, 1938, to discuss Professor J. Tinbergen's publications of 1938 for the League of Nations. Mimeographed, 19 pp.

Galton, Francis, (1885) "Regression Towards Mediocrity in Hereditary Stature," *Journal of the Anthropological Institute*, 1885, *15*, 246-63.

_____, (1888) "Co-relations and Their Measurement, Chiefly from Anthropometric Data," *Proceedings of the Royal Society of London*, December 1888, *45*, 135-45.

Gini, Corrado, "Prezzi e consumi," *Giornale degli Economisti*, 3rd Ser., January and February 1910, *40*, 99-114 and 235-49.

Haavelmo, Trygve, (1941) "On the Theory and Measurement of Economic Relations," Cambridge, Mass.: 1941. Memeographed. This is a preliminary version of Haavelmo (1944).

———, (1943) "The Statistical Implications of a System of Simultaneous Equations," *Econometrica*, January 1943, *11*, 1-12.

———, (1944) *The Probability Approach in Econometrics, Econometrica, Supplement*, July 1944, *12*, pp. viii + 118.

Hicks, John R., and Allen, R. G. D., "A Reconsideration of the Theory of Value," *Economica*, February and May 1934, New Series *1*, 52-76 and 196-219.

Hooker, R. H., (1901a) "Correlation of the Marriage-Rate with Trade," *Journal of the Royal Statistical Society*, September 1901, *64*, 485-92.

———, (1901b), "The Suspension of the Berlin Produce Exchange and its Effect upon Corn Prices," *Journal of the Royal Statistical Society*, December 1901, *64*, 574-604.

Hotelling, Harold, "Edgeworth's Taxation Paradox and the Nature of Demand and Supply Functions," *Journal of Political Economy*, October 1932, *40*, 577-616.

Koopmans, Tjalling C., "Identification Problems in Economic Model Construction," *Econometrica*, April 1949, *17*, 125-44.

———, Rubin, Herman, and Leipnik, Roy B., "Measuring the Equation Systems of Dynamic Economics," pp. 53-237 in Koopmans, Tjalling C., editor, *Statistical Inference in Dynamic Economic Models* (Cowles Commission for Research in Economics Monograph No. 10), New York: John Wiley and Sons, 1950.

Lehfeldt, R. A., "The Elasticity of Demand for Wheat," *Economic Journal*, June 1914, *24*, 212-17.

Lenoir, Marcel, *Etudes sur la Formation et le Mouvement des Prix*, Paris: Giard et Briere, 1913.

Leontief, Wassily, "Ein Versuch zur statistischen Analyse von Angebot und Nachfrage," *Weltwirtschaftliches Archiv*, July 1929, *30*, 1-53.

Mann, Henry B., and Wald, Abraham, "On the Statistical Treatment of Linear Stochastic Difference Equations," *Econometrica*, July-October 1943, *11*, 173-220.

Marschak, Jacob, (1942) "Economic Interdependence and Statistical Analysis," pp. 135-50 in Lange, Oskar, McIntyre, Francis, and Yntema, Theodore O., editors, *Studies in Mathematical Economics and Econometrics in Memory of Henry Schultz*, Chicago: University of Chicago Press, 1942.

———, (1950) "Statistical Inference in Economics: An Introduction," pp. 1-50 in Koopmans, Tjalling C., editor, *Statistical Inference in Dynamic Economic Models* (Cowles Commission for Research in Economics Monograph No. 10), New York: John Wiley and Sons, 1950.

Mayo Smith, Richmond, "Statistics and Economics," *Publications of the American Economic Association*, September and November 1888, *3*, 5-127.

Moore, Henry L., (1895) "Von Thunen's Theory of Natural Wages," *Quarterly Journal of Economics*, April and July 1895, *9*, 291-304 and 388-408.

———, (1905) "The Personality of Antoine Augustin Cournot," *Quarterly Journal of Economics*, May 1905, *19*, 370-99.

———, (1907) "The Differential Law of Wages," *Journal of the Royal Statistical Society*, December 1907, *70*, 638-51.

———, (1908) "The Statistical Complement of Pure Economics," *Quarterly Journal of Economics*, November 1908, *23*, 1-33.

———, (1911) *Laws of Wages: An Essay in Statistical Economics*, New York: Macmillan, 1911.

———, (1914) *Economic Cycles: Their Law and Cause*, New York: Macmillan, 1914.

———, (1917) *Forecasting the Yield and Price of Cotton*, New York: Macmillan, 1917.

———, (1919) "Empirical Laws of Demand and Supply and the Flexibility of Prices," *Political Science Quarterly*, December 1919, *34*, 546-67.

———, (1922) "Elasticity of Demand and Flexibility of Prices," *Journal of the American Statistical Association*, March 1922, *18*, 8-19.

———, (1923) *Generating Economic Cycles*, New York: Macmillan, 1923.

———, (1925) "A Moving Equilibrium of Demand and Supply," *Quarterly Journal of Economics*, May 1925, *39*, 357-71.

———, (1929) *Synthetic Economics*, New York: Macmillan, 1925.

Morgan, Mary S., "Identification and Model Choice Problems in Early Econometric Work on Demand," London School of Economics, 1981 (duplicated). I understand that this is a part of a Ph.D. dissertation (1984) and of a forthcoming book.

Newcomb, Simon, *Principles of Political Economy*, New York: Harper and Brothers, 1885.

Neyman, Jerzy, and Pearson, Egon S., "On the Use and Interpretation of Certain Test Criteria for Purposes of Statistical Inference," *Biometrika*, July and December 1928, *20A*, 175-240 and 263-94.

Norton, John Pease, *Statistical Studies in the New York Money Market*, New York: Macmillan, 1902.

Pearson, Karl, "Regression, Heredity, and Panmixia," *Philosophical Transactions of the Royal Society of London*, Ser. A, 1896, *187*, 253-318.

Persons, Warren M., "The Correlation of Economic Statistics," *Journal of the American Statistical Association*, December 1910, *12*, 287-322.

Pigou, A. C., "The Statistical Derivation of Demand Curves," *Economic Journal*, September 1930, *40*, 384-400.

Pritchett, H. S., "A Formula for Predicting the Population of the United States," *Publications of the American Statistical Association*, June 1891, *2*, 278-86.

Schultz, Henry, (1923) "The Elasticity of Demand and the Coefficient of Correlation," *Quarterly Journal of Economics*, November 1923, *38*, 169-71.

———, (1924) "The Statistical Measurement of

the Elasticity of Demand for Beef," *Journal of Farm Economics*, July 1924, *6*, 254-78.

_____, (1925) "The Statistical Law of Demand as Illustrated by the Demand for Sugar," *Journal of Political Economy*, October and December 1925, *33*, 481-504 and 577-637.

_____, (1927) "Theoretical Considerations Relating to Supply," *Journal of Political Economy*, August 1927, *35*, 437-64.

_____, (1928) *Statistical Laws of Demand and Supply with Special Application to Sugar*, Chicago: University of Chicago Press, 1928.

_____, (1930) "The Standard Error of a Forecast from a Curve," *Journal of the American Statistical Association*, June 1930, *25* 139-85.

_____, (1932) "The Shifting Demand for Selected Agricultural Commodities, 1875-1929," *Journal of Farm Economics*, April 1932, *14*, 201-27.

_____, (1933a) "A Comparison of Elasticities of Demand Obtained by Different Methods," *Econometrica*, July 1933, *1*, 274-308.

_____, (1933b) "Interrelations of Demand," *Journal of Political Economy*, August 1933, *41*, 468-512.

_____, (1935) "Interrelations of Demand, Price, and Income," *Journal of Political Economy*, August 1935, *43*, 433-81.

_____, (1938) *The Theory and Measurement of Demand*, Chicago: University of Chicago Press, 1938.

Slutsky, Eugen, "Sulla teoria del bilancio del consumatore," *Giornale degli Economisti*, 3rd Ser., 1915, *51*, 1-26.

Stigler, George J., (1954) "The Early History of Empirical Studies of Consumer Behavior," *Journal of Political Economy*, April 1954, *62*, 95-113.

_____, (1962) "Henry L. Moore and Statistical Economics," *Econometrica*, January 1962, *30*, 1-21.

Tinbergen, Jan, "Bestimmung und Deutung von Angebotskurven: Ein Beispiel," *Zeitschrift fur Nationalokonomie*, 1929-30, *1*, 669-79.

Walker, Francis Amasa, (1874), editor, *Statistical Atlas of the United States*, Washington: U.S. Census Office, 1874.

_____, (1890) "The Study of Statistics in Colleges and Technical Schools," *Publications of the American Statistical Association*, June 1890, *2*, 83-6.

Working, Elmer J., (1927) "What Do Statistical 'Demand Curves' Show?" *Quarterly Journal of Eco-*

nomics, February 1927, *41*, 212-35.

_____, (1934) "Demand Studies During Times of Rapid Economic Change," *Econometrica*, April 1934, *2*, 140-51.

Working, Holbrook, and Hotelling, Harold, "The Application of the Theory of Error to the Interpretation of Trends," *Journal of the American Statistical Association*, March 1929, *24*, 73-85.

Wright, Carroll D., (1888) "The Study of Statistics in Colleges," *Publications of the American Economic Association*, March 1888, *3*, 5-28.

_____, (1890) "The Study of Statistics in Italian Universities," *Publications of the American Statistical Association*, June 1890, *1*, 41-9.

Wright, Philip G., (1915) Review of *Economic Cycles* by Henry Moore, *Quarterly Journal of Economics*, May 1915, *29*, 631-41.

_____, (1928) *The Tariff on Animal and Vegetable Oils*, New York: Macmillan for The Institute of Economics, 1928.

Wright, Sewall, (1925) *Corn and Hog Correlations, U.S. Department of Agriculture Bulletin No. 1300*, Washington: U.S.G.P.O., 1925.

_____, (1934), with the collaboration of Philip G. Wright, "The Method of Path Coefficients," *Annals of Mathematical Statistics*, 1934, *5*, 161-215.

Yule, George Udny, (1895-6) "On the Correlation of Total Pauperism with Proportion of Out-Relief," *Economic Journal*, December 1895, *5*, 603-11 and December 1896, *6*, 613-23.

_____, (1897) "On the Significance of Bravais' Formulae for Regression &c., in the Case of Skew Correlation," *Proceedings of the Royal Society of London*, February 1897, *60*, 477-89.

_____, (1909) "The Applications of the Method of Correlation to Social and Economic Statistics," *Journal of the Royal Statistical Society*, December 1909, *72*, 721-30. This paper has 39 references in chronological order.

American Economic Association, (1886) "Constitution," *Publications of the American Economic Association*, March 1886, *1*, 35-6.

American Economic Association, (1961) *Index of Economic Journals, Vols. I and II*, Homewood, Illinois: Richard D. Irwin, 1961.

Johns Hopkins University, *Circular*, Baltimore: 1893-4 and 1894-5.

U.S. Department of Commerce, *Statistical Abstract of the United States* for 1878 and 1889, Washington: U.S.G.P.O., 1879 and 1890.

Journal of Economic Literature
Vol. XXXII (March 1994), pp. 30–59

The Cowles Commission's Contributions to Econometrics at Chicago, 1939–1955

By CARL F. CHRIST

The Johns Hopkins University

I wish to acknowledge helpful suggestions from Stephen Blough, Arnold Zellner, and three referees. Philip Gerson assisted in translating the paper from my word processing program to the Journal's. *Remaining inadequacies are my own.*

1. Introduction

THE COWLES COMMISSION for Research in Economics created a revolution in econometric methods and practice during its years at the University of Chicago from 1939 to 1955. This article describes that revolution, together with some of its antecedents, and attempts to put it in perspective today, using simple examples and no matrix algebra.[1]

a. *A Brief Sketch of the Origin of the Cowles Commission*

Alfred Cowles was an investment counselor in Colorado Springs, Colorado. He told me in 1952 that after the stock market crash of 1929, he realized that he did not understand the workings of the economy, and so in 1931 he stopped publishing his market advisory letter, and began research on stock market forecasting.[2] Harold T. Davis, a mathematician who spent summers in Colorado Springs, put him in touch with Irving Fisher at Yale, president of the fledgling Econometric Society. Fisher had known Cowles' father and uncle when all three were undergraduates at Yale. Davis and Fisher proposed an economics research organization and a journal. The idea appealed to Cowles, and he agreed to provide financing. The Cowles Commission was founded in Colorado Springs in 1932, and *Econometrica* began publishing in 1933. The Commission's Articles of In-

---

[1] Two earlier retrospective works on the Cowles Commission are Christ (1952), a nonmathematical history of its first twenty years, and Clifford Hildreth (1986), a detailed and technical account of its work at the University of Chicago from 1939 to 1955. Theodore W. Anderson (1991) and James Heckman (1992) discuss Trygve Haavelmo's contributions. Christ (1985, Section VII), deals with the identification problem. Roy Epstein (1987) and Mary Morgan (1990) discuss the history of econometrics in general, including the Cowles Commission's contributions.

[2] Cowles and his associates generated random stock market advice, and random portfolio choices, and compared them with actual market newsletters and actual fire insurance company portfolios. They found that on the average the actual advice and portfolios were slightly inferior to the random ones. The best actual advice and portfolios were about as good as the best random ones, but the worst actual ones were worse than the worst random ones (Cowles 1933).

30

corporation give its purpose as "to advance the scientific study and development . . . of economic theory in its relation to mathematics and statistics." It moved, with Cowles himself, from Colorado Springs to Chicago in 1939.

Jacob Marschak came to Chicago as professor, and to the Cowles Commission as research director, in 1943. It was he who assembled the staff that created the econometrics revolution. He had organized an informal econometrics seminar that met in New York on weekends during 1940–1942; it included Abraham Wald, Trygve Haavelmo, Tjalling Koopmans, and others. The Cowles theoretical econometric work began in earnest with Marschak's arrival, and continued during the early years of Koopmans' research directorship, which ran from 1948 to 1954.

Seminars at Cowles were lively informal affairs. Students as well as senior members were encouraged to participate in the discussion, and did so with enthusiasm. To maintain a semblance of order, Marschak established the "Cowles Commission rule" under which discussion from the floor was prohibited until after the speaker had finished his or her prepared remarks, except for "clarifying" questions. Members soon learned to preface their interruptions by saying "I have a clarifying question," and the chair for that day had to rule as to whether the interruption was clarifying or not.

In 1955, after James Tobin of Yale had declined to move to the Cowles Commission to become director, the Commission moved to Yale instead, and Tobin became director. As Marschak put it, if Mohammed would not come to the mountain, the mountain had to go to Mohammed. The attractions included faculty appointments in Economics at Yale for Cowles research associates, and the Cowles family's willingness to provide an endowment at Yale (hence the

change in name from "Commission" to "Foundation").

b. *The Main Components*

The two main components of the Cowles econometric revolution at Chicago were

- an explicit probabilistic framework, and
- the concept of a simultaneous equations model.

The Cowles program was intended to combine economic theory, statistical methods, and observed data to construct and estimate a system of simultaneous equations that could describe the workings of the economy. The aim was to learn from such a system of equations how economic policy could improve the performance of the economy.

The program required the development of theoretical methods for solving the *identification problem*, that is, for determining the conditions under which one can be sure that an equation fitted to data is actually the equation one wants, rather than a different equation, or a mixture of the desired equation with other equations. The program also required the development of *methods of estimation and hypothesis testing* suitable for identified equations in simultaneous equations models. In such models the typical equation has more than one dependent variable, so that ordinary least squares regression is biased. In these two tasks the program was enormously influential. However, the implications for applied work are still controversial, as we shall see.

The two chief originators of Cowles' theoretical econometric work were Haavelmo and Koopmans. Both have received Nobel Prizes in economics.[3]

---

[3] Other Nobel Prize recipients associated with the Cowles Commission at Chicago are Kenneth Arrow, Gerard Debreu, Lawrence Klein, Harry Markowitz, Franco Modigliani, and Herbert Simon. Only Klein was closely associated with the Cowles econometric program.

Haavelmo's pioneering contributions are contained in two fundamental papers (1943, 1944).[4] The main body of Cowles theoretical econometric results is contained in two Cowles Commission monographs, Koopmans (1950a) and William C. Hood and Koopmans (1953). Many of the papers in the former were first presented in 1945 at a conference at the University of Chicago.[5]

The rest of this paper is organized as follows. Section 2 gives an overview of the Cowles approach. Section 3 presents a simple two-equation model whose special cases will be used as vehicles to illustrate the Cowles work. Section 4 deals

---

[4] Haavelmo used explicit stochastic simultaneous equations models and applied rigorous statistical inference theory to them. Haavelmo (1943) is a short clear demonstration, by means of simple examples, of why least squares yields biased and inconsistent estimators in simultaneous equations models, and how to get consistent estimators in special cases that we now recognize as just identified. Haavelmo (1944) is a long and rather technical paper that sets forth the approach followed by the Cowles group.

[5] Koopmans' major theoretical econometric contributions are contained in four important papers which are included in these two monographs. The first (1949) is a clear presentation of the solution of the identification problem for linear models. The second (1950b) rigorously defines exogenous and predetermined variables. The third, by Koopmans, Herman Rubin, and Roy B. Leipnik (1950a), is the Cowles Commission's theoretical econometrics magnum opus; it gives the basic Cowles theorems on identification and maximum likelihood estimation of simultaneous equations systems as a whole, in esoteric and difficult mathematical notation. The fourth, Koopmans and Hood (1953), presents some of the Cowles results, including some later ones concerning the estimation of one equation at a time, in a form that is rigorous but less technical and more readable than Koopmans, Rubin, and Leipnik (1950a).

Also important were an early paper by Henry B. Mann and Wald (1943), proving the consistency of maximum likelihood estimators for simultaneous difference equations having no exogenous variables, and three papers on the limited information maximum likelihood method for estimating a single equation in a simultaneous system, one moderately technical by Meyer A. Girshick and Haavelmo (1947), abridged in Hood and Koopmans (1953), and two quite technical by Anderson and Rubin (1949, 1950). Significant theoretical contributions were also made by Marschak, Leonid Hurwicz, and Herman Chernoff and Rubin; see the bibliography.

with the identification problem and its theoretical solution. Section 5 describes simultaneous equations estimation and testing methods and results. Section 6 deals with the Cowles assumptions. Section 7 evaluates the Cowles work in relation to recent developments. Section 8 is a brief summing up.

2. An Overview of the Cowles Approach

a. The Status Quo Ante

Already available before the Cowles Commission came to Chicago were Leon Walras' general equilibrium theory and contemporary business cycle theories, especially J. M. Keynes' *General Theory*. Simon Kuznets, Richard Stone, Raymond Goldsmith, and others were compiling data on national income and wealth, and the U.S. Department of Commerce was soon to begin annual publication of the national accounts.

Attempts to estimate simultaneous supply and demand equations are much older than the Cowles Commission. Marcel Lenoir (1913), Philip Wright (1915), Elmer J. Working (1927), and Ragnar Frisch (1933) understood that if the supply curve alone shifts, then price-quantity data trace out the demand curve, and if the demand curve alone shifts, the data trace out the supply curve. But none of these showed what to do if both curves were shifting.

The ordinary least squares method was well known to economists as a means of estimating and testing a single linear equation having an additive disturbance. Koopmans in his doctoral dissertation (1937) had generalized it by showing rigorously how to estimate a linear equation when all variables are measured with stochastic errors. He specified the joint probability distribution of the observable variables, based on assumptions about the joint distribution of the measurement errors, and obtained estimators by the method of maximum likelihood. Most of the Cowles Commission's work concentrated on models whose stochastic elements were disturbances to equations, rather than errors in variables as in Koopmans' early study. Nevertheless, his explicit treatment of stochastic elements by the method of maximum likelihood was found in all the Commission's theoretical econometric work.

There had been some early successes with estimation methods for simultaneous equations systems, but they had not been generally recognized and accepted by economists. Sewall Wright, a son of Philip Wright, had devised the related method of path analysis (1925, 1934). Further, Philip Wright (1928; possibly with Sewall's help, though the book does not indicate this) and Jan Tinbergen (1929–30) gave the correct solution, apparently independently, to the problem of estimating linear supply and demand curves when both curves shift, for a special case that we now recognize as just identified, but their work was not referred to in Haavelmo's papers or in the Cowles theoretical econometric monographs.

Empirical econometric studies had become more frequent. Henry Schultz at Chicago, in his monumental demand study (1938), went far beyond his teacher Henry Moore. Wesley Mitchell's work (1913, 1927) had provided a great deal of understanding of business cycle behavior, albeit without mathematical models. The famous paper by Charles W. Cobb and Paul H. Douglas (1928) on the aggregate production function had long since appeared. The first macroeconometric models had been prepared by Koopmans' mentor for the Netherlands (Tinbergen 1937, 1959) and for the United States (1939).

Frisch in an unpublished memo (1938) had criticized Tinbergen's models for not attending to the identification problem

(without using that term), and he proposed a sufficient condition for the nonidentifiability of a linear dynamic difference-equation model having no exogenous variables and no disturbances that is similar to the standard condition we use today, but he did not arrive at the definitive solution of the problem. And Milton Friedman (1940) had criticized Tinbergen's U.S. model from a different point of view, urging that it not be accepted unless and until its predictions had been tested successfully against new data.

b. *The Central Idea of the Cowles Econometric Approach, and Some Key Concepts*

The Cowles workers regarded economic behavior as the result of the simultaneous interaction of different agents, as exemplified most simply by the intersection of a supply and a demand curve. For this reason they built their econometric methods around systems of simultaneous equations.

The Cowles view was that to understand a particular aspect of economic behavior, such as the price of food, or aggregate personal consumption, one wanted a system of equations capable of describing it. These equations should contain relevant observable variables, be of known form (e.g., linear, log-linear, quadratic), and have estimatable coefficients. The Cowles program was intended to provide a method for choosing the variables relevant to a particular problem, obtaining a suitable system of equations, and estimating the values of its parameters. Little attention was given to how to choose the variables and the form of the equations; it was thought that economic theory would provide this information in each case. More about this later. The main effort was directed to estimating the equations once they had been formulated.

Experience had shown that except for definitional identities, no equation ever describes observable economic behavior exactly. This may be because of an incorrect mathematical form for the equation; errors of measurement in the data; the presence of variables that are difficult or impossible to observe, or some combination of these. Hence the equations were assumed to contain two types of variables: *systematic observable* variables that are ingredients of economic theory (prices, quantities, government expenditures, tax rates, . . .), and *nonsystematic unobservable* variables that represent random disturbances to equations.[6] The random disturbance in each equation is supposed to account for the discrepancy between the actual observed value of a variable and its theoretical value given by the systematic part of the equation. Assumptions were made about the probability distributions of the random disturbances, in order that the statistical properties of estimators of the parameters of the equations could be deduced by Neyman-Pearson methods.

The observable variables were further classified into two types: *endogenous*, whose behavior is to be explained by the system of equations, and *exogenous*, whose values are assumed to be generated outside of the system of equations and taken as given. Exogenous variables can be stochastic or nonstochastic. Examples of variables often assumed to be endogenous are quantities of inputs demanded and supplied, prices, wages, and interest rates. Examples of variables often assumed to be exogenous are weather, population, and public pol-

icy variables. The Cowles work did not have much to say about the crucial issue of how to decide whether a variable should be treated as endogenous or exogenous, although Koopmans (1950b) had presented rigorous definitions. Of course, if a policy variable is determined by some systematic process that responds to private behavior, then it must be endogenous. More about this later.

The endogenous variables at any time were further classified into two types: the *current* values at that time, and the *lagged* values. The lagged endogenous variables were said to be *predetermined* as of that time, because they are not affected by the current operation of the system. Exogenous variables are also predetermined. The current endogenous variables at any time were said to be *jointly dependent* as of that time.

The end product envisioned by the Cowles strategy for an applied economic problem was thus a system of simultaneous equations that would describe how the jointly dependent variables are determined simultaneously, given the values of the parameters, the predetermined variables, and the disturbances. Because the disturbances are unobservable and assumed to be random, they are typically replaced for forecasting purposes by the expected values of their probability distributions (usually zero).

A song, written by graduate students to the tune of "The American Patrol" march and presented in about 1949 at one of the skits that enlivened parties at the Economics Department, explained the Cowles Commission's objectives to skeptics in the Department (and there were some). Here it is:

We must be rigorous, we must be rigorous,
We must fulfill our role.
If we hesitate or equivocate
We won't achieve our goal.
    We must elaborate our systems complicate

---

[6] Two other types of variables should be considered: systematic unobservable variables representing expectations held by market participants, and random unobservable variables representing errors of measurement of systematic variables. The Cowles Commission did little work on these two, although as noted above Koopmans (1937) had dealt with the latter.

To make our models whole.
Econometrics brings about
Statistical control!
Our esoteric seminars
Bring statisticians by the score.
But try to find economists
Who don't think algebra's a chore.
    Oh we must urge you most emphatically
    To become inclined mathematically
    So that all that we've developed
    May some day be applied.

(Chorus) He read his Marshall so carefully
    That now he is Professor at the U. of C.
Of Keynesians I make mince meat
Their battered arguments now line the street.
I get them in their weakest assumption:
"What do you *mean* by consumption function?"
They never gave an answer that satsifed me
So now I am Professor at the U. of C.
(Chorus) They never gave an answer that satisfied he
So now he is Professor at the U. of C.

The applied econometric work of the Cowles Commission, inspired by Marschak and directed at the improvement of macroeconomic policy, had a definite Keynesian flavor. Friedman was one of the most persistent critics of the Cowles brand of econometrics, not only from the point of view of econometric methods (as exemplified by his critical review of Tinbergen's U.S. model) but also because of his skeptical view of Keynesian models and the Keynesian consumption function.[7] A couple of verses from another song, to the Gilbert and Sullivan tune of "When I Was a Lad," presented at the same party, exemplify this (remember that Friedman had been a student of Arthur F. Burns, and assigned Alfred Marshall's *Principles* to his own students):

When I was a lad I served a term
Under the tutelage of A. F. Burns.
I read my Marshall completely through
From beginning to end and backwards too.
I read my Marshall so carefully
That now I am Professor at the U. of C.

[7] Melvin Reder (1982, p. 10) refers to "a fairly intense struggle" at Chicago in the late 1940s and early 1950s involving Frank Knight and his students, including Friedman, vs. the Cowles Commission and its adherents. Friedman and Gary Becker (1957) argue that the goodness of fit of the least squares estimate of the simple Keynesian consumption function is in part a statistical illusion, because consumption is being regressed on a variable (income) of which consumption is a major part, and they propose a correct approach. Klein (1958) comments that their point deals with least squares bias, and that it had been recognized and made clear by Haavelmo (1943, 1947). Friedman and Becker (1958) reply that Klein may be right about this, but they think not. Friedman (1957) presents his own version of the consumption function.

3. A Simple Illustrative Model and More Key Concepts

a. Model 1: The Generic Version of the Simple Model

To illustrate the econometric methods devised by the Cowles Commission, the problems they solved, and some criticisms of them, we will use a simple two-equation linear model[8] that has two endogenous variables y_1 and y_2, two predetermined variables x_1 and x_2 which may be either exogenous or lagged endogenous, two random disturbances ϵ_1 and ϵ_2, and parameters denoted by β's and γ's with subscripts (the β's go with the y's, and the γ's go with the x's). The subscript t will be used to denote time. For example, if annual data for 1951 through 1990 are used, t could take values from one (for 1951) through 40 (for 1990). The two equations are

$$y_{1t} + \beta_1 y_{2t} = \gamma_1 x_{1t} + \gamma_2 x_{2t} + \epsilon_{1t} \qquad (1)$$

$$\beta_2 y_{1t} + \quad y_{2t} = \gamma_3 x_{1t} \qquad\qquad + \epsilon_{2t}. \qquad (2)$$

This will be called *Model 1*. Though it is simple, it is flexible enough to describe a variety of situations, as we will see.

The equations of Model 1 as written do not appear to contain constant terms. We could include explicit constant terms by adding $+\gamma_4$ to (1), and $+\gamma_5$ to (2).

[8] Sometimes a simple transformation will render an apparently nonlinear equation linear. For example, a Cobb-Douglas production function with a multiplicative disturbance e^u, such as $Y = AK^\alpha L^\beta e^u$, becomes linear with an additive disturbance u upon taking its logarithm.

To keep the ensuing algebra simple we won't do this. However, the equations as written can provide for constant terms, in either of two different ways. First, suppose we had included explicit constant terms as just described. We could subtract from each equation at time t its mean calculated over the sample period (for example, from $t = 1$ to $t = 40$). The constant terms would cancel out, and the equations would appear exactly like (1–2) without an explicit constant term, except that then all the variables would be defined as deviations from their sample means. Second, if one of the x's (say x_1) never varies, but is always equal to one, then the parameters attached to it become explicit constant terms.

The disturbances are assumed to come from a probability distribution, usually with zero mean. If an equation has an unknown constant term, this assumption of a zero mean disturbance imposes no restriction, because if the mean were not zero, but were, say, five, then five could be added to the constant term and subtracted from the disturbance, thus yielding an equivalent equation whose disturbance does have zero mean. But if an equation is specified to have no constant term, then the assumption that its disturbance has zero mean is a real restriction.

Let us suppose that equations (1–2) describe the behavior of two sectors of the economy, perhaps (1) for the suppliers and (2) for the demanders of a product. Such equations were called *structural* by Haavelmo (1944). The idea here is that a change in the form or parameters of one structural equation does not affect other structural equations: in this example a change in the demand equation does not affect the supply equation, and vice versa. Haavelmo used the name *structure* to denote such a system of structural equations when numerical values are specified for all its parameters, including the parameters of the joint distribution of the disturbances as well as the coefficients of the equations.

Marschak (1950) characterized a *model* by means of a set of a priori information (true or false) about the structure, information obtained from economic theory, not from observed values of the variables. Ideally this information tells how many equations there are, what variables appear in each one, which variables are endogenous and which are exogenous, what lagged endogenous variables (if any) appear in the model, what is the form of each equation, and what is the form of the joint distribution of the disturbances (normality is often assumed, for example). Leonid Hurwicz (1950) defined a model as a set of structures that are admissible according to this a priori information. Thus the problem in the Cowles approach is first to construct the model, and second to estimate the structure.

Often one wishes to forecast the future value of an endogenous variable. In general, a structural equation cannot do this, because each structural equation typically includes two or more endogenous variables. To obtain such forecasts, one must solve the system of structural equations algebraically for the endogenous variables. The result is called the *reduced form*. Each of its equations gives the value of one endogenous variable in terms of the predetermined variables, disturbances, and structural parameters.

To solve the system (1–2) for its reduced form, we compute its determinant, which we denote by δ:

$$\delta = 1 - \beta_1\beta_2 \qquad (3)$$

Using this expression, the reduced form of the system (1–2) is

$$y_{1t} = (1/\delta) \, [(\gamma_1 - \beta_1\gamma_3)x_{1t} \\ + \gamma_2 x_{2t} + (\epsilon_{1t} - \beta_1\epsilon_{2t})] \quad (4)$$

$$y_{2t} = (1/\delta) \, [(\gamma_3 - \beta_2\gamma_1)x_{1t} \\ - \beta_2\gamma_2 x_{2t} + (\epsilon_{2t} - \beta_2\epsilon_{1t})]. \quad (5)$$

Sometimes it is convenient to give new names to the parameters and disturbances of the reduced form, and rewrite it thus:

$$y_{1t} = \pi_{11}x_{1t} + \pi_{12}x_{2t} + v_{1t} \qquad (6)$$

$$y_{2t} = \pi_{21}x_{1t} + \pi_{22}x_{2t} + v_{2t}. \qquad (7)$$

Notice that if there is a change in any of the parameters of either one of the structural equation (1) or (2), then the parameters of both of the reduced form equations change, because every one of the β's and γ's appears in both reduced form equations (remember that δ depends on all of the β's). Thus the structural equations can be thought of as the elementary building blocks of the system, while each reduced form equation is a mixture of the structural equations.

To use the reduced form for forecasting future endogenous variables, one obviously needs estimates of its parameters, and forecasts of future values of the predetermined variables and disturbances. Forecasts of exogenous variables must be obtained by some method external to the model. Future values of lagged endogenous variables are obtained either from past data, or from the past operation of the system. The best forecast of a random disturbance is its expected value, typically zero.

The system of equations (1–2) appears to be static, because all the variables are dated at the same time, t. It is indeed static if the y's and x's at time t are four different variables, such as price, quantity sold, income, and production cost, all pertaining to the same period of time. Then we think of the y's as endogenous and the x's as exogenous.

b. *Model 2: A Dynamic Version of Model 1*

However, if either or both of the x's stands for a previous period's value of one of the y's, then the system is dynamic. For example, suppose that by definition

$$x_{2t} = y_{1,t-1}. \qquad (8)$$

This could be because in equation (1) y_1 depends on adaptive expectations about the future value of y_2. Alternatively, it could be because in (1) there is a lag in the response of y_1 to changes in y_2.

The dynamic case of Model 1 obtained by specifying that x_2 is last period's value of y_1, as in (8), will be called *Model 2*. In Model 2 x_2 cannot be exogenous, because it is determined by the past operation of the system. As noted earlier, x_{2t} (that is, $y_{1,t-1}$) is said to be *predetermined at time* t, and y_{1t} and y_{2t} are said to be *jointly dependent at time* t.

The preceding explanations of exogenous and predetermined variables are plausible, but are not suitable for rigorous statistical analysis. Koopmans (1950b) gave rigorous definitions as follows. (i) A variable x (meaning the whole series of values of x for all t) is *exogenous* if and only if the value of x at every time period is statistically independent of all disturbances in the system, past, present, and future. Note that an exogenous variable can be stochastic, or not. (ii) A variable is *endogenous* if it is not exogenous. (iii) A variable x_t is *predetermined at time* t if and only if x_t is statistically independent of all present and future disturbances in the system, but not necessarily of past disturbances. Thus in Model 2, where (8) holds, x_{2t} (that is, $y_{1,t-1}$) will be predetermined at time t if ϵ_1 and ϵ_2 are serially independent, but it cannot be exogenous: it cannot be independent of the previous disturbance $\epsilon_{1,t-1}$ because it is influenced by $\epsilon_{1,t-1}$ through the lagged version of equation (1). Exogenous variables are always predetermined, but the converse is not true. (iv) A variable dated at time t is *jointly dependent at time* t if it is not predetermined at time t. In Model 2, note that $y_{1,t-1}$

is jointly dependent at time $t - 1$, but predetermined at time t or later.

A dynamic system determines the time paths of the endogenous variables from time t onwards, if it is given the values of the parameters, the time paths of the exogenous variables and disturbances, and the initial values of the lagged endogenous variables as of time t. To study the behavior of a dynamic system we assume that the exogenous variables and disturbances are held constant for the future. The system may generate cycles, or not. It may be stable (that is, the endogenous variables may approach equilibrium values), or not. In order to discover the dynamic behavior of a system, we need to find its *final form*, that is, a set of equations similar to the reduced form except that each endogenous variable is expressed in terms of *its own* lagged values (not those of others) and exogenous variables and disturbances (this term is due to Tinbergen 1939).

Let us return to the dynamic Model 2. We can still use the structural system (1–2) and its reduced form (4–5), remembering that x_{2t} is $y_{1,t-1}$ as in (8). In this case the final form equation for y_1 is obtained simply by substituting $y_{1,t-1}$ for x_{2t} in the reduced form equation (4). It expresses y_{1t} as a function of x_{1t} and $y_{1,t-1}$, thus

$$y_{1t} = (1/\delta) \, [(\gamma_1 - \beta_1\gamma_3)x_{1t} + \gamma_2 y_{1,t-1} + (\epsilon_{1t} - \beta_1\epsilon_{2t})]. \quad (9)$$

The final form equation for y_2 is found as follows: first write equation (2) for time $t - 1$; solve the result for $\beta_2 y_{1,t-1}$; then substitute the resulting expression in (5) to get

$$y_{2t} = (1/\delta)$$
$$[(\gamma_3 - \beta_2\gamma_1)x_{1t} + \gamma_2 y_{2,t-1} - \gamma_2\gamma_3 x_{1,t-1} + (\epsilon_{1t} - \beta_2\epsilon_{1t} - \gamma_2\epsilon_{2,t-1})]. \quad (10)$$

Notice that when the exogenous variable x_1 and the disturbances ϵ_1 and ϵ_2 are held constant, the final form equations (9) and (10) are alike except for their constant terms. Each can be written as

$$y_{it} = (\gamma_2/\delta)y_{i,t-1} + \theta_i, \qquad i = 1 \text{ or } 2 \quad (11)$$

where θ_i is a constant depending on the values of x_1 and the parameters and ϵ's. These final form equations are first order linear difference equations. Each has the same characteristic root, γ_2/δ. The system is stable for both y_1 and y_2 if the root is less than one in absolute value, and unstable for both otherwise. Further, it has oscillations for both if the root is negative, and not otherwise. The fact that all endogenous variables in the system have the same dynamic behavior is not an accident; it is typical of linear systems.

The equilibrium values of y_1 and y_2 can be found from (11) by setting the lagged and current values equal; the result is

$$y_{it} = \theta_i/[1 - (\gamma_2/\delta)]. \quad (12)$$

c. *The Recursive Form*

An interesting special case of a structural model occurs when two conditions are met: (i) one of the equations contains only a single jointly dependent variable, another equation contains only two (that one and one other), another contains only three (those two and one other), and so on, until the last equation which contains them all; (ii) the disturbances to all the equations at any time t are statistically independent of each other. Such a model is said to be *recursive*. Model 1 above would be recursive if either β_1 or β_2 were zero (or both) and the disturbances ϵ_{1t} and ϵ_{2t} were independent of each other for all t. In that case, if β_1 were zero, y_{1t} would be predetermined in equation (2); similarly, if β_2 were zero, y_{2t} would be predetermined in equation (1); and if both β_1 and β_2 were zero, the two equations would determine y_{1t} and y_{2t} independently of each other.

The Cowles theoretical results were of course not confined to a two-equation model. They dealt with arbitrary numbers of equations, endogenous variables, exogenous variables, and lags of the endogenous variables. In more general systems, where the number of endogenous variables appearing with a lag is greater than one, and/or where the longest lag of any endogenous variable is greater than one, each final equation is of second or higher order, that is, contains two or more lagged values of its endogenous variable. In that case the characteristic roots can be complex numbers and hence the dynamic path of the system can involve cycles of any length, not merely oscillations up and down in alternate periods as in the case of a first-order final equation such as (9) or (10).

Thus far we have seen how the system of equations (1–2) in Model 1 can handle the presence of constant terms, and how it can describe either a static or a dynamic model. In the next section, by assigning different possible values (sometimes zero) to its parameters, we will obtain and analyze several interesting special cases.

4. *The Identification Problem and Its Theoretical Solution*

a. *Model 3: An Example of the Problem*

As noted in Section 1, econometric equations cannot be estimated unless they are identified. Those who first tried to estimate simultaneous equations models dealt with supply and demand. They stumbled when they came to the identification problem. They used a special case of Model 1 in which equations (1) and (2) are respectively the supply and demand curves for a good, y_1 is quantity, y_2 is price, x_1 is a constant equal to one so that γ_1 and γ_3 are the equations' constant terms, and γ_2 is zero, so that the only systematic variables in the model

are price and quantity. We shall call this special case *Model 3*. It is as follows:

$$y_{1t} + \beta_1 y_{2t} = \gamma_1 + \epsilon_{1t} \quad \text{supply} \quad (13)$$
$$\beta_2 y_{1t} + y_{2t} = \gamma_3 + \epsilon_{2t} \quad \text{demand.} \quad (14)$$

As noted above, they understood that if the supply curve alone shifts (which (13) will if $\gamma_1 + \epsilon_1$ changes but $\gamma_3 + \epsilon_2$ and β_2 do not), the observed price and quantity data trace out the demand curve, and if demand alone shifts, the data trace out the supply curve, but if both curves shift, the data trace out neither curve. Hence if one does not observe when and how the curves shift, one cannot tell whether a curve traced out by the price and quantity data is the supply curve, the demand curve, or neither. They did not know what to do about this.

The Cowles workers called it the problem of the *identification* of structural equations. It is not a problem of uncertainty associated with sampling variation: it does not go away as the sample size becomes infinitely large.

b. *Conditions for Identification*

Koopmans (1949) defined an *identified* equation as one whose parameters can be deduced from observed data, using the a priori information that is incorporated in the model (with no uncertainty except the sampling error that occurs in small samples). He gave necessary and sufficient conditions for the identification of the parameters of an equation in a linear system, based on the knowledge or belief that certain parameters in the equation are zero. His *order condition* is this: if an equation in such a system is to have all its parameters identified, at least $G - 1$ of its parameters must be believed to be zero, where G is the number of equations in the system. The converse is almost always true as well, that is, if an equation satisfies this condition, its parameters are almost certain to be identified. It is called the order condition because it can be expressed by saying that the order (i.e., the number of columns) of a certain matrix[9] must be at least $G - 1$. When we count the number of parameters believed to be zero, it makes no difference whether a parameter is a constant term, or a coefficient of a jointly dependent or a predetermined variable.

There is no identification problem with reduced form equations,[10] because each contains only one dependent variable. The order condition holds automatically for reduced form equations because each is a complete one-equation system, $G = 1$, and each excludes $G - 1 =$ none of its own variables. Because reduced form equations are identified, any structural equation whose parameters can be deduced from a knowledge of the re-

duced form parameters is also identified, and conversely.

The identifiability of structural equations when some parameters are believed to be zero will now be illustrated with several special cases of Model 1. Because there are two equations, $G - 1 = 1$. Hence to be identified a structural equation must have at least one parameter that is believed to be zero, that is, must exclude at least one variable.

c. *Model 3 Again: An Unidentified Model*

Consider Model 3, the one that baffled the early investigators. Its reduced form is as follows, where as before δ is given by (3):

$$y_{1t} = (1/\delta)[(\gamma_1 - \beta_1\gamma_3) + (\epsilon_{1t} - \beta_1\epsilon_{2t})]$$
$$= \pi_{11} + v_{1t} \tag{15}$$

$$y_{2t} = (1/\delta)[(\gamma_3 - \beta_2\gamma_1) + (\epsilon_{2t} - \beta_2\epsilon_{1t})]$$
$$= \pi_{21} + v_{2t}. \tag{16}$$

It is a special case of (4–5) and of (6–7). Here the reduced form parameters π_{11} and π_{21} are automatically identified. The sample mean of the data for y_1 (quantity) is an estimate of the parameter π_{11} in (15), and the sample mean of y_2 (price) is an estimate of π_{21} in (16).

Now consider the structural parameters of Model 3, β_1, β_2, γ_1, and γ_3. The reduced form parameters are functions of them, thus (remember that δ is a function of β_1 and β_2):

$$\pi_{11} = (\gamma_1 - \beta_1\gamma_3)/\delta \tag{17}$$
$$\pi_{21} = (\gamma_3 - \beta_2\gamma_1)/\delta. \tag{18}$$

It is not possible to determine the values of the four unknown structural parameters β_1, β_2, γ_1, and γ_3 from π_{11} and π_{21} and these two equations. Thus in Model 3 the structural parameters are not identified. The order condition confirms this: neither of the equations (13–14) in Model 3 excludes any of the model's variables, whereas identification requires the exclusion of at least one.

---

[9] The matrix in question is obtained by omitting from the matrix of the model's structural coefficients all columns in which the equation does not have a prescribed zero. The so-called rank condition, also set forth by Koopmans (1949), says that, when the a priori information takes the form of such zero restrictions, an equation is identified if and only if the rank of that same matrix is $G - 1$. The rank condition is almost certain to be satisfied if the order condition is, because the parameters in this matrix are very unlikely to have a set of values that will make its columns linearly dependent. However, if a model is segmentable, in the sense that a subset of its equations determine a subset of its dependent variables, the rank condition can fail even if the order condition is met (see Christ 1966, p. 345, ex. 3.10 for an example). Note also that there are other kinds of identifying information besides the requirement that a parameter in an equation be zero. For example, there may be a restriction relating two or more parameters in the same or different equations, or there may be restrictions on the parameters of the probability distribution of disturbances. Identifiability conditions for such information are beyond the scope of this paper (Koopmans, Rubin, and Leipnik 1950; Leon Wegge 1965; Franklin Fisher 1966).

[10] If some of the predetermined variables in a reduced form equation are linearly dependent, then their coefficients are not identified, and cannot be estimated. One remedy for this, if the sample size is large enough, is to omit one (or if necessary more than one) of the predetermined variables, until the remaining ones are linearly independent. Then the least squares estimates can be computed.

d. *Model 4: An Identified Model*

Now consider a case in which all structural parameters are identified. Such a case is obtained from Model 1 by restricting γ_1 to be zero and requiring x_1 to be constant and equal to one. It is similar to Model 3 except that now γ_1 is required to be zero and γ_2 is not. It will be called *Model 4*. It is as follows:

$$y_{1t} + \beta_1 y_{2t} = \gamma_2 x_{2t} + \epsilon_{1t} \text{ supply} \quad (19)$$

$$\beta_2 y_{1t} + \quad y_{2t} = \gamma_3 \quad + \epsilon_{2t} \text{ demand.} \quad (20)$$

Note that each of the equations of Model 4 has one parameter specified to be zero: in (19) it is the constant term (that is, the coefficient of x_1), and in (20) it is the coefficient of x_2. The reduced form of Model 4 is as follows:

$$y_{1t} = (1/\delta) \left[-\beta_1 \gamma_3 + \gamma_2 x_{2t} + (\epsilon_{1t} - \beta_1 \epsilon_{2t}) \right]$$
$$= \pi_{11} + \pi_{12} x_{2t} + v_{1t} \quad (21)$$

$$y_{2t} = (1/\delta) \left[\gamma_3 - \beta_2 \gamma_2 x_{2t} + (\epsilon_{2t} - \beta_2 \epsilon_{1t}) \right]$$
$$= \pi_{21} + \pi_{22} x_{2t} + v_{2t}. \quad (22)$$

(Here the symbols π_{11} and π_{21} are different from those in equations (15–18).) Again the reduced form parameters are automatically identified, and hence can be estimated. They are functions of the structural parameters, thus:

$$\pi_{11} = -\beta_1 \gamma_3 / \delta \quad (23)$$

$$\pi_{21} = \gamma_3 / \delta \quad (24)$$

$$\pi_{12} = \gamma_2 / \delta \quad (25)$$

$$\pi_{22} = -\beta_2 \gamma_2 / \delta. \quad (26)$$

Now the four structural parameters can be deduced from the four equations (23–26) and the values of the reduced form parameters: β_1 is estimated by the ratio of the estimates of $-\pi_{11}$ and π_{21}, β_2 is estimated by the ratio of the estimates of $-\pi_{22}$ and π_{12}, δ is estimated from the estimates of the β's using its definition $\delta = 1 - \beta_1 \beta_2$, γ_2 is estimated by the product of the estimates of δ and π_{12}, and γ_3 is estimated by the product of

the estimates δ of and π_{21}. Thus the structural parameters are identified. The order condition is consistent with this, for the number of variables excluded from each of the structural equations (19–20) is $G - 1 = 1$, as required.

e. *Other Cases*

Now consider Model 1. Equation (1) excludes no variables, and hence is not identified. Equation (2) excludes one variable, x_2, and hence is identified. This result can be verified by comparing the reduced form equations (4–5), and noting that β_2 can be estimated because it is the ratio of $-\pi_{22}$ to π_{12}, as in Model 4, but β_1 cannot be estimated. In Model 2 the situation is the same as in Model 1.

If demand depends only on current price, and supply depends only on last period's price, then the identification problem is solved, because any mixture of the supply and demand curves will contain both current and lagged prices, and hence cannot be mistaken for either demand or supply (Mordecai Ezekiel 1928). This is exemplified by Model 1 if we assume that $\beta_1 = 0$, $x_{2t} =$ last period's price $y_{2,t-1}$, and x_1 is constant and equal to one. Such a model is called the cobweb model, because the dynamic behavior of a graph of price vs. quantity resembles a spider's web. If the disturbances in the two equations are independent at each time t, such a system is recursive.

The order condition says that the number of the model's variables excluded from an identified equation must be *at least* $G - 1$. If it is exactly $G - 1$, the equation is said to be *just identified*. If it is more than $G - 1$, the equation is said to be *overidentified*. Model 4 is just identified. In Model 1, if γ_3 were specified to be zero but γ_1 and γ_2 were not, then equation (2) would be overidentified, because it would exclude two of the model's variables.

When an equation is overidentified,

there are restrictions on the parameters of the reduced form. For example, in the case just mentioned, where equation (2) is overidentified because $\gamma_3 = 0$, a comparison of equations (4) and (5) shows that the ratios π_{21}/π_{11} and π_{22}/π_{12} must be the same, because both must be equal to $-\beta_2$.

5. Simultaneous Equations Estimation and Testing at Cowles

a. Estimation Methods

Under suitable statistical assumptions, least squares yields consistent and asymptotically unbiased estimators of reduced form equations like (6–7), because each of them contains only one dependent variable.[11] However, for simultaneous equations like (1–2), least squares yields biased and inconsistent estimators of structural parameters except in special cases.[12] The problem is that in such a system, even if all structural equations are identified, each equation contains more than one jointly dependent variable.

Hence for simultaneous equations, new estimation methods were needed. These methods, coupled with the solution of the identification problem, constitute the heart of the Cowles revolution in econometric methods.

Using models similar to the just-identified Model 4 in the previous section, Haavelmo (1943) derived estimators of the structural parameters equivalent to those described above for Model 4 and

---

[11] See Section 6. If in addition all predetermined variables are exogenous, least squares estimators of the reduced form become unbiased. If disturbances are normally distributed, least squares estimation of the reduced form is a maximum likelihood method.

[12] This was shown by Haavelmo (1943, 1944). Jean Bronfenbrenner (1953) gives a clear and simple analysis of least squares bias. A recursive model is one special case in which least squares estimation can be unbiased and consistent.

used by Philip Wright (1928) and Tinbergen (1929–30)—but he did not refer to their work. These estimators are now called *indirect least squares* estimators, because the first step is to estimate the reduced form by least squares, and the second step is to deduce estimated values of the structural parameters from the estimated reduced form. He showed that his estimators were consistent.

Haavelmo (1947) used the indirect least squares method to estimate the marginal propensity to consume from annual U.S. data for 1922–1941. His consumption equation was

$$c_t = \alpha y_t + \beta + u_t \qquad (27)$$

where c, y, and u are respectively real per capita consumption, disposable income, and a disturbance. This equation is just identified in his two-equation model, treating consumer saving as the exogenous variable, and also in his three-equation model, treating gross private investment plus the government deficit as the exogenous variable (the estimate in this case was based on data for only 1929–1941 because the Commerce Department investment data did not go back before 1929). The two indirect least squares estimates of α were respectively 0.67 and 0.71. The corresponding least squares estimates for the same two periods were respectively 0.73 and 0.72, larger than the indirect least squares estimates, as predicted by Haavelmo's analysis. These results illustrate a frequent finding: even though least squares estimators are not consistent, they usually turn out in practice to be quite close to consistent estimators. Haavelmo constructed confidence interval estimates for the marginal propensity to consume, based on estimates of the standard deviation of its estimator. He also constructed joint confidence intervals for it and other parameters of the model. When he included lagged income in the equation, he obtained slightly lower estimates for 1922–1941 than without it.

For estimating the parameters of a just-identified structural equation the *instrumental variables* method[13] consists of the following steps: First, using the sample data, form the moment of the equation with each of the predetermined variables in the model (not, as in least squares, with each of the equation's right-hand-side variables), and assign a zero value to the moment of the disturbance with each predetermined variable. The result is a system of equations in which the unknowns are the instrumental variables estimates, and the known quantities are the sample moments of the variables in the equation with the predetermined variables in the model. Then solve this system algebraically for the estimates of the parameters.

For a just-identified equation the instrumental variables method is equivalent to indirect least squares. In this case both methods work because the number of structural parameters to be estimated is just equal to the number of equations to be solved for them: in the case of instrumental variables it is the number of equations relating the structural estimates to moments, and in the case of indirect least squares it is the number of equations relating the structural estimates to the estimated reduced form parameters. In both cases it is the number of parameters that are specified to be zero in the equation. The indirect least squares method is exemplified by the discussion following equations (23–26) for Model 4 above.

For an unidentified equation both methods fail, as they should, because the number of equations to be solved for the estimates of the structural parameters is

too few. For indirect least squares this is exemplified by equation (1) of Model 1: its parameters cannot be got from the estimates of the reduced form (4–5).

For an overidentified equation, the number of equations to be solved is more than needed, and they will contradict each other with probability one if the sample is finite (because the estimated values of the parameters will differ randomly from the true values which satisfy the a priori restrictions exactly). In such a case, if there are n more a priori restrictions than needed, one can ignore n of them (any n of them will do), thus pretending that the equation is just identified. One can then use either indirect least squares or instrumental variables. The disadvantage of this approach is that it wastes some of the a priori information, and gives different results depending on which n restrictions are ignored.

When the method of maximum likelihood is applied to the problem of estimating all the structural parameters of the system at once, using all the a priori restrictions for the entire model, on the assumption that the disturbances are normally distributed, the resulting estimators are called *full information maximum likelihood* estimators, FIML for short, because they use all the available a priori information. Under suitable assumptions FIML estimators of structural parameters are consistent and asymptotically efficient, approximate confidence-region estimators of these parameters can be obtained, and approximate t-tests and F-tests of their statistical significance can be performed (Koopmans, Rubin, and Leipnik 1950).[14]

If the maximum likelihood method is applied to one identified structural equation at a time (whether it is overidentified or not), using only the a priori restrictions

---

[13] The instrumental variables method goes back to Sewall Wright (1925), Olav Reiersøl (1941, 1945), and Robert C. Geary (1949). Reiersøl was a visitor at the Cowles Commission in the summer of 1949.

[14] This is a difficult technical paper. The "suitable conditions" are described in Section 6 below.

that concern that equation, the result is called the *limited information maximum likelihood* method, LIML for short, because it uses only some of the a priori information (Girshick and Haavelmo 1947; Koopmans and Hood 1953). LIML yields the same estimates for an over-identified equation as would be obtained if the reduced form were estimated by least squares subject to the restrictions on the reduced form that are implied by overidentification of the structural equation, and the indirect least squares method were then applied. LIML remains consistent even if the equations are nonlinear, so long as they are linear in unknown parameters and certain moment matrices have appropriate probability limits (Anderson and Rubin 1949, 1950).

For a just-identified equation, LIML reduces to the indirect least squares and instrumental variables methods. For an unidentified equation it fails, as it should. For an overidentified equation, it gives a unique result.[15]

---

[15] The idea behind LIML is this: Each structural equation in a linear system must be a linear combination of just those reduced form equations that concern the jointly dependent variables that are not excluded a priori from the structural equation. The coefficients of the linear combination are the structural equation's coefficients of those jointly dependent variables. An estimate of a *just*-identified equation can be expressed exactly as a linear combination of those estimated reduced form equations; the indirect least squares method finds that linear combination. But this cannot be done with an *over*identified equation, because no linear combination of the least squares estimates of the reduced form equations can exactly satisfy all the a priori restrictions (except in infinite samples). What the LIML method does is to find the linear combination of the estimated reduced form equations that comes closest to satisfying the a priori restrictions, in the sense of making the so-called variance ratio as close to one as possible. The variance ratio is the ratio between two variances, each of which is the variance of the residual of a regression of the jointly dependent component of the equation being estimated (for equation (1) or (2) this is the expression on the left side of the equality sign) on a set of predetermined variables. One of these regressions uses *all* of the model's predetermined vaiables, and the other uses *only* those that are not excluded a priori from the equation. Since the excluded variables are

b. *Applications*

Empirical work in the 1940s and early '50s was done with mechanical desk calculators which, unlike many of today's cheap electronic pocket calculators, couldn't compute square roots or logarithms or exponentials with a single command. The iterative computations for FIML are so complex that the method was never applied by the Cowles workers, except for an illustrative computation for a simplified model containing only three equations. For most of their empirical work, the Cowles workers used LIML, which is also iterative, but much simpler than FIML.[16] Later, with the advent of electronic computers, FIML became a practical method.

The first application of LIML was the estimation of a five-equation model of food demand, using annual U.S. data for 1922–1941 (Girshick and Haavelmo 1947). Some of the equations were just identified, and of course for them the LIML estimates were the same as the indirect least squares estimates. In 1947 it was not yet possible to give confidence interval estimates for the overidentified equations because the standard deviation of the LIML estimator for this case had not yet been derived.

The first macroeconometric model using the new methods was presented in Klein's monograph, *Economic Fluctuations in the United States 1921–1941* (1950). The model has 16 equations, including demand equations for active money balances, idle money balances, consumer goods, owner-occupied hous-

---

supposed to have zero coefficients, the two regressions should be the same except for sampling variation, and so should their residual variances. Hence the LIML estimation procedure was designed to make the ratio of their residual variances as close to one as possible. See also note 25 below.

[16] Chernoff and Nathan Divinsky (1953) described the iterative computation methods for FIML and LIML, and reproduced the actual computations made with desk calculators for one of Klein's simple models.

ing, rental housing, plant and equipment, inventories, and labor; an equilibrium equation for dwelling space; adjustment equations for output, interest rate, and rent; and four definitional equations. Klein checked the identifiability of the equations, and estimated them by the LIML method using U.S. data for 1921–1941. He gave no estimates of the standard deviations of the LIML estimates, because the necessary formula still had not been derived. This model had a clearly Keynesian flavor.

The necessity for testing an econometric model against new data, after it has been constructed and estimated, was not emphasized in the theoretical econometric publications of the Cowles Commission. A simple procedure is to use the estimated model to forecast data that were not used to estimate it, or, even better, were not available when the model was specified, and conclude that something is wrong if the forecast errors are too large. Holbrook Working and Harold Hotelling (1929) and Hotelling (1942) had derived the standard deviation of the error of a post-sample forecast, made from a single equation estimated by least squares, under the hypothesis that the estimated equation still holds during the forecast period, and showed how to use it to test that hypothesis: if the forecast error is too large relative to this standard deviation, the hypothesis is rejected. Rubin (1948, unpublished) showed how to do the same thing with the post-sample residual from a structural equation that has been estimated by LIML. Variants of this test were applied by Andrew Marshall (1949), Christ (1951), Stephen G. Allen (1954), and Hildreth and Francis G. Jarrett (1955) to decide which LIML-estimated structural equations continued to describe data in the post-sample period, and which ones did not.

Andrew Marshall's M.A. thesis at the University of Chicago, entitled "A Test

of Klein's Model III for Changes of Structure" (1949, unpublished), used Klein's model to compute residuals for each equation for 1946 and 1947 (skipping the war years 1942–45 on the ground that normal economic behavior was superseded by wartime regulations),[17] to see which equations held up well and which didn't. Five didn't. This type of test had been proposed, and carried out for one equation, by Friedman in his review (1940) of Tinbergen's model of the U.S. There Friedman pointed out correctly that Tinbergen's procedure (which has become common among model builders) of trying many different forms for each equation, and choosing one with a high correlation coefficient, is appropriate as a way of deriving tentative hypotheses, but does not constitute an empirical test of the equations so chosen. We will expand on this point at the end of this section.

"A Test of an Econometric Model for the United States, 1921–1947" (Christ 1951) built upon Andrew Marshall's results. The five Klein equations that did not hold up well for 1946 and 1947 in Marshall's tests were revised, and the revised model was reestimated by LIML using data for 1921–1941 and 1946–1947. The reduced form of the revised model was then used to compute forecasts for 1948. For six of 13 variables, least squares estimates of the revised model's reduced form made better forecasts for 1948 than the naive methods of assuming no change from the previous year, or no change in the trend from the previous two years, and for seven of 13, worse.[18]

---

[17] An unusual example of a consumption equation successfully fitted right through World War II is Richard E. Brumberg (1956). For consumer durables, he defined and measured consumption not in the usual way as purchases of goods, but as the flow of services represented by interest and depreciation.

[18] Andrew Marshall also used naive model tests, but for structural equations rather than reduced forms.

When a structural equation is over-identified, restrictions on the reduced form are implied (recall the discussion of this point at the end of Section 4e above). A chi-square test of whether the data reject these restrictions was proposed by Anderson and Rubin (1950). The Anderson-Rubin test of overidentifying restrictions was performed by Christ (1951); they were rejected for four of his ten stochastic equations at the 95 percent level, and seven of ten at the 90 percent level. Robert Basmann (1960) proposed an F test of overidentifying restrictions on a structural equation, equivalent to the Anderson-Rubin chi square test in infinite samples but more accurate in small samples.

Friedman in his discussion of Christ's model endorsed the testing of such models against post-sample data, but ventured the

> hunch . . . that attempts to proceed now to the construction of additional models along the same general lines will, in due time, be judged failures. (1951, p. 112)

Instead, he wrote,

> I believe our chief hope is to study the sections covered by individual structural equations separately and independently of the rest of the economy. These remarks obviously have a rather direct bearing on the desultory skirmishing between what have been loosely designated as the National Bureau and the Cowles Commission techniques of investigating business cycles. . . . As the National Bureau succeeds in finding some order, some system, in the separate parts it has isolated for study its investigations will increasingly have to be concerned with combining the parts—putting together the structural equations. As the Cowles Commission finds that its general models for the economy as a whole are unsuccessful, its investigators will increasingly become concerned with studying the individual structural equations, with trying to find some order and system in component parts of the economy. Thus, I predict the actual work of the two groups of investigators will become more and more alike. (p. 114)

This prediction has been confirmed only partly. On the one hand, complete macroeconometric models have proliferated, and many now make useful forecasts of the U.S. economy several quarters ahead (Stephen McNees 1988). On the other hand, it is true that macroeconometric models have not revealed an invariant fundamental structure of the economy, and in recent years the emphasis in mainstream econometric work has shifted toward individual equations or incomplete models. [19]

The last of the Cowles applied econometric studies at Chicago was *A Statistical Study of Livestock Production and Marketing* (Hildreth and Jarrett 1955). [20] It is based on a model of seven equations, describing the livestock production function, the farm demands for feed grain and for protein feed, the farm supply of livestock, the demand for livestock, and supply equations for feed grains and protein feeds. The first five equations were estimated by LIML using annual U.S. data for 1920–1949. Estimated standard deviations were given. For the produc-

---

[19] "The recurrent theme [of Epstein's book] is the persistent gap between the theoretical and empirical achievements of structural estimation" (Epstein 1987, p. 3). Friedman remains skeptical of mainstream econometricians' treatment of single equations such as the demand for money (Friedman and Anna Schwartz 1982, the attack by David Hendry and Neil Ericsson 1991, and the Friedman and Schwartz reply 1991).

[20] Among other applied pieces by Cowles staff in Chicago were the following. Marschak and William H. Andrews, Jr. (1944) estimated the relation between inputs and outputs in the productive process. George Borts (1952) estimated the railroad production function. His study differed perforce from most production function studies because the common carrier law implies that output is a predetermined variable for the railroads, not a decision variable. Allen (1954) estimated a six-equation model of the market for linseed and flaxseed oil. All equations were identified (some were overidentified). They were estimated by LIML using quarterly data for 1926–1939. Estimated standard deviations were given. Forecasts were made for the four quarters of 1940. For most variables in most quarters, naive forecasts assuming no change from 1939 were better than the model's forecasts.

tion function the Anderson-Rubin test rejected the hypothesis that the overidentifying restrictions are correct, but for four other equations it accepted the overidentifying restrictions.

Particularly praiseworthy is Hildreth and Jarrett's procedure for testing whether the estimated equations predict future data well or not: the tests were done with 1950 data, which were not only outside of the sample used for estimation, they were not even available when the model was specified. This means that when the authors chose their model, they could not have been influenced by knowledge of the data that they were going to try to predict. Hence their test is even more stringent than one based on a model's ability to predict data that were already known to the model-builders when they built the model.[21] Most of the model's equations described 1950 as well as they did the sample data, and most of them had smaller errors in 1950 than did the naive models mentioned above.

Many of the Cowles applied studies presented their data, so that other researchers could verify their computations.

6. The Cowles Assumptions

The assumptions under which the Cowles workers derived the asymptotic distributions and properties of their estimators were quite strong. There has been much discussion and criticism of these assumptions in the subsequent literature, especially with regard to their realism, and many modifications have been proposed. (Friedman's criticisms of the Cowles approach were not based on its assumptions, for in his well-known piece on the methodology of economics (1953) he argued that a theory should be judged by its results, rather than by

whether its assumptions are realistic or not.) In most of the Cowles theoretical work, the assumptions included the following:

(a) Economic behavior is governed by simultaneous equations. This assumption has been questioned by Herman Wold (1953). He contends that economic relations cannot be simultaneous, but must be recursive, on the ground that every economic action is a response to some previous action (however short the response time may be). Robert Strotz and Wold (1960) present an interesting explanation of how simultaneous equations can be appropriate tools even if Wold is correct in principle: Suppose that economic interactions are always sequential, not simultaneous, but that there is always a very short delay, say one day, between any agent's action and the next agent's subsequent response; suppose also that all our data correspond to aggregates or averages over a time-interval that is much longer than the one-day response delay, say one calendar year. Then it is not possible to fit a model to the sequence of decisions that occur at one-day intervals: the required daily data are missing. However, if we fit a simultaneous equations model to annual data, we will be approximately correct. For example, if demand decisions follow price-setting decisions by one day, then our demand equation should say that total demand during a calendar year (January 1 through December 31) depends on the average price during the 365-day period starting and ending one day earlier (from December 31 of the preceding year through December 30 of the current year), but we do not make a large error by saying that it depends on the average price during the calendar year. Wold's plea for recursive systems did not convince many economists, and the simultaneous equations framework is widely accepted. Of course, lagged variables can

[21] A defense of this more stringent test is given by Christ (1966, pp. 546–48, and 1993).

be (and often are) included in simultaneous equations to reflect dynamic effects.

(b) The equations of the model are linear in systematic variables and disturbances. This assumption is strong, but may be approximately correct for short periods of time. As noted above, Anderson and Rubin weakened it to require only linearity in unknown parameters, without destroying most of the theoretical econometric results. This weakening permits the handling of the types of nonlinearity that can be removed by a suitable transformation, such as in Cobb-Douglas equations where the appropriate transformation is to take logarithms. In both its forms it is testable, but the Cowles group did not devise tests of it. A procedure for deciding whether a relationship is linear or logarithmic is provided by George E. P. Box and D. R. Cox (1964). Empirical studies have increasingly used nonlinear models in recent years. This represents an advance in technique (not in principle) that has been made possible by the advent of electronic computers and by the derivation of nonlinear estimators (Stephen Goldfeld and Richard Quandt 1972; Takeshi Amemiya 1983).

(c) The systematic variables are observable, without error. The first part of this assumption is strong. Because agents' expectations about the future are not directly observable, they are ruled out of consideration unless one can represent them by observable variables. More about this later. Errors of measurement of variables are real, but most Cowles workers ignored them in favor of disturbances to equations. Exceptions were Koopmans (1937), as noted above, and Chernoff and Rubin (1953).

(d) Variables change at discrete time intervals, such as yearly, or quarterly, or monthly, rather than continuously. This assumption is made essentially for convenience, to allow the use of difference equations to explain dynamic relations among annual, quarterly, or monthly data. It has been adopted in most econometric work.[22]

(e) It is known which variables are exogenous, and which are predetermined at time t. This assumption is strong. If variables are erroneously specified to be predetermined or exogenous, estimators become biased, just as least squares estimators are biased in simultaneous equations systems. More about this later.

(f) The determinant of the coefficients of the jointly dependent variables is not zero, so that the reduced form exists. This assumption has to be made: if it were not true, the model would be useless, because it could not determine the values of the jointly dependent variables.

(g) The predetermined variables are linearly independent, so that their moment matrix can be inverted. This assumption requires that the sample size be greater than or equal to the number of predetermined variables in the model. If that is so, it is easy to satisfy, for if it were false, one could make it true without loss simply by omitting one of the linearly dependent predetermined variables (or more than one, if necessary).

(h) The structural equations are identified by a priori restrictions on their parameters (possibly including restrictions on the parameters of the distribution of disturbances), and these restrictions are correct. This assumption has been severely criticized long ago by Ta-Chung Liu (1960), and more recently by Christopher Sims (1980; see below). As noted earlier, overidentifying restrictions have often been rejected.

(i) The disturbances are normally dis-

---

[22] Clifford Wymer (1972) and Giancarlo Gandolfo (1981) have begun to use continuous-time models and differential equations instead.

tributed random variables with zero means and finite and constant variances and covariances, and their covariance matrix is nonsingular. This assumption is strong. However, the Cowles group showed that normality is not necessary for most of their results. The assumption of zero means has been discussed above, in Section 3a. The assumption of a non-singular covariance matrix is plausible unless the system includes definitional equations that have no disturbances, but this can be handled by eliminating those equations by substitution (this step should be taken prior to estimation of the complete system as a whole).

(j) The disturbances are serially independent. This assumption is testable, but the Cowles group did not devise tests for it. Instead, they used available tests. At first they used the test of B. I. Hart and John Von Neumann (1942). Hildreth and Jarrett (1955) used the more appropriate test of James Durbin and Geoffrey S. Watson (1950, 1951). Serial correlation of disturbances constituted a serious difficulty for the Cowles workers, because most of their theorems assumed it away. (Serial correlation of observed variables is very common, and is no problem.) They did not devote much effort to finding estimators that were appropriate in its presence. Subsequent work has provided solutions to this problem for many cases (John Denis Sargan 1959; Ray C. Fair 1972).

(k) The equation system is dynamically stable. This is assured by assuming that the exogenous variables are considered fixed in repeated samples, and their moments have finite limits as the sample size goes to infinity, and all characteristic roots of the final equations of the system are less than one in absolute value. Some such condition is needed to prove that estimators are consistent and to derive their asymptotic variances and covariances.

The Cowles derivations of the properties of their estimators were almost entirely asymptotic, that is, for infinitely large samples, which we never have in practice. Of course, there is some comfort in knowing that one's estimators are consistent, and asymptotically unbiased and efficient, but this tells nothing about how large the bias or variance may be in samples of size 20 or 30 years, or 60 quarters, which were the sample sizes used in their applied work. Small sample properties are difficult to derive, and the Cowles group made little progress with this problem. The first successes were for very special cases of two or three equations (Basmann 1961, 1963) but progress has now been made with more general cases (Anderson 1982; Peter C. B. Phillips 1983).

Most of the Cowles group dealt with time-series data, because of their interest in the amelioration of business cycles. Their methods are applicable to pure cross section data, where $t = 1,2,3, \ldots$ stands not for the first, second, and third time periods, etc., but for the first, second, and third members of the cross section sample, etc. Note, however, that the concept of serial correlation makes little sense when the data are for cities or counties or families or firms, unless they are arranged in some meaningful order, such as size.

Panel data, consisting of a time series of cross section data, were rare in the 1940s, and the Cowles group did essentially nothing with the problems of estimation from such data.

7. An Evaluation of the Cowles Econometric Contributions

a. A Recapitulation

Let us begin this section with a reminder of what econometrics is about, and a look back at the main features of the Cowles program. Econometrics has been aptly defined by a committee of the Econometric Society as

> the quantitative analysis of actual economic phonomena based on the concurrent development of theory and observation, related by appropriate methods of inference. (Paul Samuelson, Koopmans, and Stone 1954, p. 142)

We have seen that the two mainstays of the Cowles revolution in econometric methods were the probability approach and the concept of a simultaneous equations model.

The probability approach is well established in econometrics, and is no longer in question. Experience has shown that (except for definitional identities) no quantitative theoretical economic relationship fits observed data exactly. Hence each econometric equation is formulated so as to include not only observed variables, but also an unobservable catch-all variable representing the discrepancy between the computed and observed values of the equation. This catch-all variable is treated as stochastic. If plausible assumptions (sometimes testable) are made about the probability distributions of such stochastic variables, then plausible conclusions follow about the distributions of estimators of parameters of the equations, and plausible statistical inferences can be drawn. With the increased attention given to behavior under uncertainty, stochastic elements are also becoming important in economic theory. This is especially evident in the theory of rational expectations. Estimation methods have been developed to take account of rational expectations (Kenneth F. Wallis 1980; Frederic Mishkin 1983). Hence I believe that the obituary in the last sentence of Morgan's otherwise excellent book (1990, p. 264) is premature: "By the 1950s the founding ideal of econometrics, the union of mathematical and statistical economics into a

truly synthetic economics, had collapsed."

Likewise, simultaneous equations models are well established in econometrics—and in economics in general. Economic phenomena are the result of interactions among many agents. Any single economic relationship in which we may be interested interacts with other relationships. Hence we are led from single equations to systems of several equations. The most general case is that of simultaneous equations. Some economists believe that in principle all economic equation systems are recursive, but even if this is correct, as noted earlier, a simultaneous system can be regarded as approximately correct. Hence most economists think in terms of simultaneous equations systems, even when investigating a single equation at a time.

We have seen that the main Cowles contributions in theoretical econometrics were the solution of the identification problem and the development of methods of estimation that have desirable properties for simultaneous equations. These were impressive intellectual achievements, and they have profoundly affected econometrics. But there is controversy even today about their value for applied work. The controversy relates not so much to the probability approach (which is almost universally accepted in econometrics), but rather to the nature and implications of the concept of simultaneous equations. In what follows we shall first consider in several subsections the process of proposing and provisionally adopting the specifications of an econometric model, then consider the present position of the Cowles simultaneous equations estimation methods, and finally sum up.

b. *Why Is Identification Interesting?*

Consider first the identification problem. Remember that structural equations cannot be estimated unless they can be identified. Why is it important to be able to identify and estimate structural equations? After all, the reduced form of the model is what one needs in order to make predictions about the effects of policy changes upon endogenous variables. So why do we care about the structural equations that underlie the reduced form? There are three reasons.

One is that if a structural model is correctly specified and is overidentified, then more efficient estimates of the reduced form can be obtained by solving the estimated structure than by estimating the reduced form by least squares directly. This is implied by the discussion of overidentified equations at the end of Section 4e.

A second is that if the results of using a model are unsatisfactory, it is important to find out what part or parts of the model are at fault. One can test each estimated structural equation separately in order to see which, if any, are performing well, and which one or ones are not. Then one knows which parts of the model to revise.

A third reason is that the economy's structure may undergo a change after it has been estimated, but before the period that one wants to predict. The possibility of a change in the economy's structure was of deep concern to the Cowles group. Marschak (1947, 1953) correctly pointed out that if there is a change in the structure of the economy, that is, if the value of a structural parameter changes (or worse, if the form of a structural equation changes), then in general every reduced form equation changes, and therefore the old reduced form is no longer relevant for forecasting. If one has not estimated the old structure, one has no way of knowing how the reduced form will change. But if one has estimated the old structure, and if one knows the time and the nature of the structural change, one can then find the new struc-

ture, and can solve it to get the new reduced form, and hence can use it to make forecasts for the period after the change. This argument foreshadows the critique of Robert Lucas (1976; see below). Marschak would have agreed with Lucas that it is important to know whether the structure of the economy has changed, and if so, when and how, if one is to make good forecasts from parameter estimates that are based on past data.

c. *The Attacks of Liu and Sims*

The information that would enable one to identify a model comes from the theoretical restrictions that are imposed on the model. There is no controversy over the correctness of the theorems that tell whether a model can be identified. The controversy is over whether information sufficient to identify econometric models can be obtained in practice.

The main attacks have come from Liu (1960) and Sims (1980). Both are based on the view that the simultaneous interactions of economic variables are so pervasive that most structural relationships contain all or nearly all of the variables in the economy, and are therefore not in fact identified. If so, it is pointless to try to estimate them. Liu concluded that in such cases we are forced to retreat to the estimation of reduced form equations, each of which expresses an endogenous variable as a function of exogenous variables and possibly of lagged endogenous variables. Of course this would mean that we are unable to use the Marschak strategy to deduce the new values of reduced form parameters that will prevail if a structural change occurs after we have estimated the old reduced form.

Sims also regards the restrictions that would be needed to identify structural equations as "incredible." But his recommendation is different from Liu's. He proposes the use of vector autoregression (VAR). With this method, one chooses a set of variables thought to be relevant to the problem at hand, and estimates the regression of each one on lagged values of itself and all the others. No exogenous variables are involved (but some could be included, thus making Sims' recommendation more like Liu's). No economic theory is needed to specify a priori restrictions on structural relationships. The only role for economic theory is to assist in the choice of variables and the length of lags (though the latter is usually decided empirically—it cannot be so large that the number of parameters in any single VAR equation exceeds the size of the available sample). Of course a VAR can be regarded as the reduced form of some structural model, one that contains the same variables as the VAR. Epstein (1987, pp. 219–20) properly faults VAR for providing no way to distinguish between competing theories of the way the economy responds to policy changes.

In my view we have sufficient information to identify many structural equations. The usefulness of supply and demand analysis lies in the fact that many of the factors that affect the demand curve of a good have little or no effect on the supply curve, and vice versa. The same is true of saving and investment analysis, and many other types of economic analysis. And we have the Bassmann (1960) test for overidentifying restrictions. It may be the case that some of the restrictions used for identification purposes are only approximately correct. In an important paper Franklin Fisher (1961) explains why it makes sense to use such restrictions.

Related to VAR is another approach which also downplays economic theory, autoregressive integrated moving average (ARIMA) time series analysis (Box and Gwilym M. Jenkins 1970). Here a function of current and lagged values of an observable variable is set equal to a function of current and lagged values of a white noise disturbance (random, serially independent, with zero mean). The autoregressive (AR) part gives the variable's current value in terms of its own past values; the integrated (I) part is needed to undo the difference operator if differences (of first or higher order) rather than levels of the variable are involved; and the moving average (MA) part describes the way the current and lagged white noise disturbances are combined. An ARIMA model implies that the current value of a variable can be explained as a combination of current and (perhaps infinitely many) past values of a white noise disturbance. ARIMA models can be univariate or multivariate. VAR is a special case of a multivariate ARIMA.

Zellner and Franz Palm (1974) propose an ingenious combination of Cowles-type structural modeling and ARIMA modeling: they suggest using a structural model to explain the behavior of endogenous variables in terms of exogenous variables, and an ARIMA model to explain the the behavior of exogenous variables. They show that if this is done, then the behavior of all variables, endogenous as well as exogenous, is modeled by ARIMA processes. But it strikes me as most unsatisfactory to explain everything as the outcome of combinations of white noise disturbances.

d. *The Lucas Critique*

Lucas (1976) issued a serious warning regarding the use of estimated econometric models to predict the effects of future changes in economic policy. He pointed out that if some of the parameters of a model reflect the adaptation of private behavior to a previously maintained policy reaction function, then, if the policy reaction function is changed, private behavior will re-adapt to the new function, and as a result the previously estimated parameters will no longer describe the response of the economy. He and others have given likely examples, based on the hypothesis of rational expectations. This argument is a more sophisticated treatment of structural change than Marschak's. Marschak did not display an explicit understanding of the Lucas critique, though in my view he came close to it.

The Lucas critique implies that if a change in a policy reaction function occurs which changes private behavior parameters, then the reduced form of the system will change, as will any VAR or ARIMA that previously described the system. Hence, in my view, the Lucas critique is just as damaging to Liu's and Sims' procedure, and to ARIMA, as it is to the Cowles procedure. The proper response to the Lucas critique is to specify econometric models in such a way that their parameters are invariant to changes in public policy response functions. Admittedly this is easier said than done.

Thomas Sargent (1976) expressed Lucas's point in a different way. He noted that if the monetary policy regime is to be changed from a constant-money-growth rule to a feedback rule, it is possible to write the reduced form of the system in two versions that are observationally equivalent during a sample period under the constant-money-growth rule, in the sense that both versions describe the sample data with identical residuals, but one of the reduced forms suffers a parameter change when the regime changes, and the other does not. The difference between the two reduced forms lies in the manner in which expectations are formed, and the manner in which they affect behavior. Old-regime estimates of the reduced form, in either version, or in both versions, will not reveal which version will change when the regime changes, and which will remain invariant. Hence reduced-form estimation

alone will not settle the question of whether a feedback rule is better than a constant-money-growth rule.

e. *Model Specifications: Where Do They Come From?*

The Cowles Commisssion approach to econometrics was built on the premise that correct a priori specifications were already available for the models that were to be estimated by its methods. The Cowles theoretical econometric work did not have much to say about the process of specifying models, rather taking it for granted that economic theory would do that, or had already done it.

Ideas for econometric model-building can certainly come from economic theory, by way of the postulate that consumers and producers seek to optimize subject to the constraints they face. But ideas can also come from examining data and searching for patterns. Economic theory is not powerful enough today, and may never be, to tell us everything we want to know about the specification of our models, that is, the variables to be included in each equation, the classification of variables as endogenous or exogenous, the mathematical form of equations (linear, logarithmic, quadratic, or the like), the nature of the random disturbances, and so on. And although economic theory is rather good at deriving equilibrium relationships, it is not very good at deriving the adjustment behavior of a system that is out of equilibrium. Thus there is much room for empirical investigation in the process of model building, even before one arrives at the problem of parameter estimation.[23]

Both VAR and ARIMA can be characterized, with some exaggeration, as mindless data-mining, because both

[23] Heckman in his review (1992) of Morgan (1990) takes a similar view, and objects to Morgan's narrow implicit definition of econometrics.

share the attribute that no use is made of economic knowledge except to choose the variable(s) to be studied and the length of the lags to be used. One can apply these techniques to economic data without knowing much about economics, or to biological data without knowing much about biology. However, data mining can certainly be justified as a method of searching for regularities in the data. And when regularities are found that persist from decade to decade, or from place to place, then there is something for economic theory to try to understand.

In the celebrated exchange between Koopmans and Rutledge Vining concerning Burns and Mitchell's *Measuring Business Cycles* (1946), the magnum opus of the National Bureau of Economic Research as of that time, Koopmans (1947) began by attacking Burns and Mitchell for having no theory about business cycles, and hence having no clear idea about what to measure or what hypotheses to test. Rutledge Vining (1949) replied that Koopmans appeared to reject any style of research that differed from his own, and defended the attempt to increase our understanding of business cycles by careful observation and recording of many economic variables that behave cyclically. In his rejoinder Koopmans (1949) conceded that he and Vining were not so far apart after all, but he reiterated his defense of the Cowles approach. Perhaps as a result of this exchange, the Cowles Commission's original motto, adopted in 1932 and emblazoned on the covers and title pages of early monographs, "Science is Measurement," was changed in 1952, at the suggestion of Hildreth, to "Theory and Measurement" (Christ 1952, p. 62).

f. *Model Specifications: Are They Correct?*

Econometric model specifications must be tested before they can be accepted as correct, or as approximately correct. The Cowles econometric theory workers did not have much to say about how to decide whether a model had been correctly specified or not.

In any applied econometric study, the distinction between variables whose behavior is to be explained and variables whose behavior is to be taken as given is fundamental. This corresponds to the distinction between endogenous and exogenous variables. Although as noted earlier Koopmans (1950b) had given a rigorous statistical definition of exogeneity, the Cowles group had no method of testing whether the designation of variables as exogenous had been done correctly or not. Several such tests are now available (Sims 1972; De-Min Wu 1973; John Geweke 1978, 1984; J. A. Hausman 1978, Robert F. Engle, David Hendry, and Jean-Francois Richard 1983; and Engle 1984).

When post-sample data demand the rejection of the hypothesis that an estimated equation has not changed, there are several possibilities: (1) The form of the equation was correctly specified, and did not change, but its parameters changed after the sample period. (2) The form of the equation was correct during the sample period, but changed after the sample period. (3) Both the form and parameters of the true equation are unchanged, but the form specified by the model builder was incorrect in the first place, so that the estimated equation is only an approximation to the true one, and the approximation no longer held in the post-sample period. For example, suppose that the true relation between two variables is a curve that rises until 1993 and falls thereafter, but a linear equation is fitted to the data before 1993. The fitted equation does not turn down after 1993, but the true relation does, so that post-1993 forecast errors will be large, and will reject the hypothesis that the fitted straight line describes the new data.

The appropriate research strategy differs among these cases: if the form of the equation is correctly specified and only its parameters have changed, one should re-estimate it with post-change data, but if the form of the equation is incorrect, one should try a new form. The Cowles group threw little light on how to distinguish these situations. Subsequent work has made progress with this important problem; among the pioneers are Hausman (1978) and Edward Leamer (1978).

g. The Cowles Simultaneous Equations Estimation Methods

For simultaneous equations models the Cowles theorems about least squares bias and about the consistency of limited and full information maximum likelihood estimators are correct, but these methods are not the most commonly used methods today.

The limited information maximum likelihood method (LIML) has become a curiosum, displaced by the two-stage least squares (2SLS) method of Henri Theil (1953, 1958) and Basmann (1957). The reasons are that 2SLS is much simpler to compute, not requiring iterative computations as does LIML; LIML occasionally gives highly implausible estimates in small samples, which 2SLS does not,[24] and the two methods are asymptotically equivalent. For just identified equations, 2SLS gives the same results as LIML, indirect least squares, and instrumental variables. For overidentified equations, it has a better method than LIML for coming as close as possible

to satisfying the overidentifying restrictions.[25]

The full information maximum likelihood method (FIML) has been largely displaced by three-stage least squares (3SLS), because the two are asymptotically equivalent, and 3SLS is simpler to compute, not requiring iterative computations as does FIML. For a system in which every equation is just identified, 3SLS gives the same result as 2SLS (Zellner and Theil 1962).

Experience suggests that the problem of least squares bias is not very serious. Indeed, it is unusual for least squares estimates to differ much from 2SLS. Hence the least squares method is still quite commonly used even for equations that are part of a simultaneous equations sytem. When a method free of least squares bias is desired, the instrumental variables method is often used because it is so simple to work with, but many popular econometrics programs for personal computers now include 2SLS, and some even include 3SLS and FIML.

8. A Summing Up

Although the Cowles Commission had an indelible effect on the field of econometrics, its lasting contributions are less than what its econometric pioneers hoped for. Those lasting contributions are principally in theoretical rather than applied econometrics: the probability approach, simultaneous equations models, the distinction between structural and reduced-form equations, the distinction between endogenous and exogenous variables, the identification problem and its theoretical solution, and the initiation of research on the construction and statis-

---

[24] Theil (1958, 1961) shows a series of graphs that explain why LIML occasionally yields weird estimates while 2SLS does not. Klein and Mitsugu Nakamura (1962) also throw light on this question.

[25] 2SLS makes the variance difference as close to zero as possible. The variance difference is the difference between the two variances that are described in footnote 15.

tical properties of estimators. It has been left to others to fill the lacunae in the Cowles theoretical econometric effort, such as model specification, specification tests, endogenizing of policy variables, time-varying parameters, serial correlation and heteroskedasticity of disturbances, errors of measurement, and the development of more useful estimators such as two-stage and three-stage least squares and estimators for nonlinear models.

As for applied results, macroeconometric models have established a short-term forecasting record good enough to keep them in business. But Alfred Cowles' dream of predicting the stock market, and Marschak's dream of predicting the effects of economic policy variables so as to control business cycles, are not yet realized.

REFERENCES

ALLEN, STEPHEN G. "Inventory Fluctuations in Flax-seed and Linseed Oil, 1926–1939," *Econometrica*, July 1954, 22(3), pp. 310–27.

AMEMIYA, TAKESHI. "Non-Linear Regression Models," in GRILICHES AND INTRILIGATOR 1983, pp. 333–89.

ANDERSON, THEODORE W. "Small-Sample Distribution Theory," in *Advances in econometrics*. Econometric Society Monographs in Quantitative Economics, Econometric Society Publication No. 2. Ed.: WERNER HILDENBRAND. Cambridge, Eng.: Cambridge U. Press, 1982, pp. 109–22.

———. "Trygve Haavelmo and Simultaneous Equation Models," *Scand. J. Statist.*, Jan. 1991, 18(1), pp. 1–19

ANDERSON, THEODORE W. AND RUBIN, HERMAN. "Estimation of the Parameters of a Single Equation in a Complete System of Stochastic Equations," *Ann. Math. Statist.*, Mar. 1949, 20(1), pp. 46–63.

———. "The Asymptotic Properties of Estimates of the Parameters of a Single Equation in a Complete System of Stochastic Equations," *Ann. Math. Statist.*, Dec. 1950, 21(4), pp. 570–82.

BASMANN, ROBERT L. "A Generalized Classical Method of Linear Estimation of Coefficients in a Structural Equation," *Econometrica*, Jan. 1957, 25(1), pp. 77–83

———. "On Finite Sample Distributions of Generalized Classical Linear Identifiability Test Statistics," *J. Amer. Statist. Assoc.*, Dec. 1960, 55(292), pp. 650–59.

———. "A Note on the Exact Finite Sample Frequency Functions of Generalized Classical Linear

Estimators in Two Leading Overidentified Cases," *J. Amer. Statist. Assoc.*, Sept. 1961, 56(295), pp. 619–36.

———. "A Note on the Exact Finite Sample Frequency Functions of Generalized Classical Linear Estimators in a Leading Three Equation Case," *J. Amer. Statist. Assoc.*, Mar. 1963, 58(301), pp. 161–71.

BORTS, GEORGE H. "Production Relations in the Railway Industry," *Econometrica*, Jan. 1952, 20(1), pp. 71–79.

BOX, GEORGE E. P. AND COX, D. R. "An Analysis of Transformations," *J. Roy. Statist. Soc., Series B*, 1964, 26(2), pp. 211–52.

BOX, GEORGE E. P. AND JENKINS, GWILYM M. *Time series analysis: Forecasting and control.* San Francisco: Holden-Day, 1970.

BRONFENBRENNER, JEAN. "Sources and Size of Least-Squares Bias in a Two-Equation Model," Chapter IX in HOOD AND KOOPMANS 1953, pp. 221–35.

BRUMBERG, RICHARD E. "An Approximation to the Aggregate Saving Function," *Econ. J.*, Mar. 1956, 66(2), pp. 66–72.

BURNS, ARTHUR F. AND MITCHELL, WESLEY C. *Measuring business cycles.* New York: National Bureau of Economic Research, 1946.

CHERNOFF, HERMAN AND DIVINSKY, NATHAN. "The Computation of Maximum-Likelihood Estimates of Linear Structural Equations," Chapter X in HOOD AND KOOPMANS 1953, pp. 236–302.

CHERNOFF, HERMAN AND RUBIN, HERMAN. "Asymptotic Properties of Limited-Information Estimates Under Generalized Conditions," Chapter VII in HOOD AND KOOPMANS 1953, pp. 200–12.

CHRIST, CARL F. "A Test of an Econometric Model for the United States, 1921–1947," in *Conference on business cycles*. Universities-National Bureau Committee for Economic Research, New York: National Bureau of Economic Research, 1951, pp. 35–107.

———. "History of the Cowles Commission, 1932–1952," in *Economic theory and measurement: A twenty year research report 1932–1952*, Chicago: Cowles Commission for Research in Economics, 1952, pp. 3–65.

———. *Econometric models and methods.* New York: Wiley, 1966.

———. "Early Progress in Estimating Quantitative Economic Relationships in America," *Amer. Econ. Rev.*, Dec. 1985, 75(6), pp. 39–52.

———. "Assessing Applied Econometric Results," *Fed. Res. Bank St. Louis Rev.*, Mar./Apr. 1993, 75(2), pp. 71–94.

COBB, CHARLES W. AND DOUGLAS, PAUL H. "A Theory of Production," *Amer. Econ. Rev.*, Mar. 1928, 18(1), pp. 139–65.

COWLES, ALFRED. "Can Stock Market Forecasters Forecast?" *Econometrica*, July 1933, 1(3), pp. 309–24.

DURBIN, JAMES AND WATSON, GEOFFREY S. "Testing for Serial Correlation in Least Squares Regression. I and II," *Biometrika*, Dec. 1950, 37(4), pp. 409–28; June 1951, 38(2), pp. 159–78.

ENGLE, ROBERT F. "Wald, Likelihood Ratio, and Lagrange Multiplier Tests in Econometrics," Chapter 13 in GRILICHES AND INTRILIGATOR, Vol. II, 1984, pp. 776–826.

ENGLE, ROBERT F.; HENDRY, DAVID F. AND RICHARD, JEAN-FRANCOIS. "Exogeneity," *Econometrica*, Mar. 1983, *51*(2), pp. 277–304.

EPSTEIN, ROY J. *A history of econometrics*. Contributions to Economic Analysis No. 165. Amsterdam: North-Holland, 1987.

EZEKIEL, MORDECAI. "Statistical Analyses and the 'Laws' of Price," *Quart. J. Econ.*, Feb. 1928, *42*(1), pp. 199–227.

FAIR, RAY C. "Efficient Estimation of Simultaneous Equations with Auto-Regressive Errors by Instrumental Variables," *Rev. Econ. Statist.*, Nov. 1972, *54*(4), pp. 444–49.

FISHER, FRANKLIN M. "On the Cost of Approximate Specification in Simultaneous Equation Estimation," *Econometrica*, Apr. 1961, *29*(2), pp. 139–70.

_____. *The identification problem in econometrics*. New York: McGraw-Hill, 1966.

FRIEDMAN, MILTON. Review of Tinbergen (1939), *Amer. Econ.Rev.*, Sept. 1940, *30*(3), pp. 657–61.

_____. "Comment" (on Christ 1951), in *Conference on business cycles*. Universities-National Bureau Committee for Economic Research. New York: National Bureau of Economic Research, 1951, pp. 107–14.

_____. "The Methodology of Positive Economics," in *Essays in positive economics*. Chicago: U. of Chicago Press, 1953, pp. pp. 3–43.

_____. *A theory of the consumption function*. Princeton, NJ: Princeton U. Press for the National Bureau of Economic Research, 1957.

FRIEDMAN, MILTON AND BECKER, GARY. "A Statistical Illusion in Judging Keynesian Models," *J. Polit. Econ.*, Feb. 1957, *65*(1), pp. 64–75.

_____."Reply" to Klein (1958), *J. Polit. Econ.*, Dec. 1958, *66*(6), pp. 545–49

FRIEDMAN, MILTON AND SCHWARTZ, ANNA J. *Monetary trends in the United States and the United Kingdom, Their relation to income, prices, and interest rates, 1867–1975*. Chicago: U. of Chicago Press for the National Bureau of Economic Research, 1982.

_____. "Alternative Approaches to Analyzing Economic Data," *Amer. Econ. Rev.*, Mar. 1991, *81*(1), pp. 39–49.

FRISCH, RAGNAR. "Pitfalls in the Statistical Construction of Demand and Supply Curves," *Veröffentlichungen der Frankfurter Gesellschaft für Konjunkturforschung*, Neue Folge, Heft 5. Leipzig: Hans Buske, 1933.

_____. "Statistical Versus Theoretical Relations in Economic Macrodynamics." A memorandum prepared for the Business Cycle Conference at Cambridge, England, July 18th-20th, 1938, to discuss Professor J. Tinbergen's publications of 1938 for the League of Nations. Mimeographed, 19 pp.

GANDOLFO, GIANCARLO. *Qualitative analysis and econometric estimation of continuous time dynamic models*. Amsterdam: North-Holland, 1981.

GEARY, ROBERT C. "Determination of Linear Relations Between Systematic Parts of Variables with Errors of Observation the Variances of Which Are Unknown," *Econometrica*, Jan. 1949, *17*(1), pp. 30–58.

GEWEKE, JOHN. "Testing the Exogeneity Specification in the Complete Dynamic Simultaneous Equation Model," *J. Econometrics*, Apr. 1978, *7*(2), pp. 163–85.

_____. "Inference and Causality in Economic Time Series Models," in GRILICHES AND INTRILIGATOR, Vol. II, 1984, pp. 1102–44.

GIRSHICK, MEYER A. AND HAAVELMO, TRYGVE. "Statistical Analysis of the Demand for Food: Examples of Simultaneous Estimation of Structural Equations," *Econometrica*, Apr. 1947, *15*(2), pp. 79–110; Abridged as Chapter V in HOOD AND KOOPMANS 1953, pp. 92–111.

GOLDFELD, STEPHEN M. AND QUANDT, RICHARD E. *Nonlinear methods in econometrics*. Amsterdam: North-Holland, 1972.

GRANGER, CLIVE W. J. "Investigating Causal Relations by Econometric Models and Cross-Spectral Methods," *Econometrica*, July 1969, *37*(3), pp. 424–38.

GRILICHES, ZVI AND INTRILIGATOR, MICHAEL D., eds. *Handbook of econometrics*, Vols. I, II, and III. Amsterdam: North-Holland, 1983, 1984, 1986.

HAAVELMO, TRYGVE. "The Statistical Implications of a System of Simultaneous Equations," *Econometrica*, Jan. 1943, *11*(1), pp. 1–12.

_____. "The Probability Approach in Econometrics," *Econometrica*, July 1944, *12*(Supplement), pp. 1–115; a preliminary mimeographed version entitled "On the Theory and Measurement of Economic Relations" was issued in Cambridge, MA in 1941.

_____. "Methods of Measuring the Marginal Propensity to Consume," *J. Amer. Statist. Assoc.*, Mar. 1947, *42*(237), pp. 105–22; reprinted as Chapter IV in HOOD AND KOOPMANS 1953, pp. 75–91.

HART, B. I. AND VON NEUMANN, JOHN. "Tabulation of the Probabilites for the Ratio of the Mean Square Successive Difference to the Variance," *Ann. Math. Statist.*, June 1942, *13*, pp. 207–14.

HAUSMAN, J. A. "Specification Tests in Econometrics," *Econometrica*, Nov. 1978, *46*(6), pp. 1251–71.

HECKMAN, JAMES. "Haavelmo and the Birth of Modern Econometrics: A Review of *The History of Econometric Ideas* by Mary Morgan," *J. Econ. Lit.*, June 1992, *30*(2), pp. 876–86.

HENDRY, DAVID F. AND ERICSSON, NEIL R. "An Econometric Analysis of U. K. Money Demand in *Monetary Trends in the United States and the United Kingdom* by Milton Friedman and Anna J. Schwartz," *Amer. Econ. Rev.*, Mar. 1991, *81*(1), pp. 8–38.

HILDRETH, CLIFFORD. *The Cowles Commission in Chicago, 1939–1955. Lecture notes in economics and mathematical systems*. Vol. 271. Berlin: Springer, 1986.

HILDRETH, CLIFFORD AND JARRETT, FRANCIS G. *A statistical study of livestock production and market-*

ing. Cowles Commission Monograph 15. New York: Wiley, 1955.

HOOD, WILLIAM C. AND KOOPMANS, TJALLING C., eds. *Studies in econometric method.* Cowles Commission Monograph 14. New York: Wiley, 1953.

HOTELLING, HAROLD. "Problems of Prediction," *Amer. J. Sociol.*, July 1942, *48*(1), pp. 61–76.

HURWICZ, LEONID. Five papers in KOOPMANS 1950a.

KLEIN, LAWRENCE R. *Economic fluctuations in the United States, 1921–1941.* Cowles Commission Monograph 11. New York: Wiley, 1950.

————. "The Friedman-Becker Illusion," *J. Polit. Econ.*, Dec. 1958, *66*(6), pp. 539–45.

KLEIN, LAWRENCE R. AND NAKAMURA, MITSUGU. "Singularity in the Equation Systems of Econometrics: Some Aspects of the Problem of Multicollinearity," *Int. Econ. Rev.*, Sept. 1962, *3*(3), pp. 274–99.

KOOPMANS, TJALLING C. *Linear regression analysis of economic time series.* Haarlem: de Erven F. Bohn, 1937.

————. "Measurement without Theory," *Rev. Econ. Statist.*, Aug. 1947, *29*(3), pp. 161–72.

————. "Identification Problems in Economic Model Construction," *Econometrica*, Apr. 1949a, *17*(2), pp. 125–44; reprinted with minor revisions as Chapter II in HOOD AND KOOPMANS 1953, pp. 27–48.

————. "A Reply" (to Vining 1949), *Rev. Econ. Statist.*, May 1949b, *31*(2), pp. 86–91.

————, ed. *Statistical inference in dynamic economic models.* Cowles Commission Monograph 10. New York: Wiley, 1950a.

————. "When Is an Equation System Complete for Statistical Purposes?" 1950b; Chapter XVII in KOOPMANS 1950a, pp. 393–409.

KOOPMANS, TJALLING C. AND HOOD, WILLIAM C. "The Estimation of Simultaneous Linear Economic Relationships," Chapter VI in HOOD AND KOOPMANS 1953, pp. 112–99.

KOOPMANS, TJALLING C.; RUBIN, HERMAN AND LEIPNIK, ROY B. "Measuring the Equation Systems of Dynamic Economics," Chapter II in KOOPMANS 1950a, pp. 53–237.

LEAMER, EDWARD E. *Specification searches.* New York: Wiley, 1978.

LENOIR, MARCEL. *Etudes sur la formation et le mouvement des prix.* Paris: Giard et Briere, 1913.

LIU, TA-CHUNG. "Underidentification, Structural Estimation, and Forecasting," *Econometrica*, Oct. 1960, *28*(4), pp. 855–65.

LUCAS, ROBERT E., JR. "Econometric Policy Evaluation: A Critique," *Carnegie-Rochester Conf. Ser. Public Policy*, 1976, *1*, pp. 19–46.

MANN, HENRY B. AND WALD, ABRAHAM. "On the Statistical Treatment of Linear Stochastic Difference Equations," *Econometrica*, July-Oct. 1943, *11*(3&4), pp. 173–220.

MARSCHAK, JACOB. "Economic Structure, Path, Policy, and Prediction," *Amer. Econ. Rev.*, May 1947, *37*(2), pp. 81–84.

————. "Statistical Inference in Economics: An In-

troduction," Chapter I in KOOPMANS 1950a, pp. 1–50.

————. "Economic Measurements for Policy and Prediction," Chapter I in HOOD AND KOOPMANS 1953, pp. 1–26.

MARSCHAK, JACOB AND ANDREWS, WILLIAM H., JR. "Random Simultaneous Equations and the Theory of Production," *Econometrica*, July-Oct. 1944, *12*(3&4), pp. 143–205.

MARSHALL, ANDREW W. "A Test of Klein's Model III for Changes of Structure." Unpub. M.A. thesis, U. of Chicago, 1949; a summary appears in CHRIST 1951.

McNEES, STEPHEN K. "How Accurate Are Macroeconomic Forecasts?" *New Eng. Econ. Rev.*, July-Aug. 1988, pp. 15–36.

MISHKIN, FREDERIC S. *A rational expectations approach to macroeconometrics.* Chicago: U. of Chicago Press for the National Bureau of Economic Research, 1983.

MITCHELL, WESLEY C. *Business cycles.* Berkeley: U. of California Press, 1913.

————. *Business cycles: The problem and its setting.* New York: National Bureau of Economic Research, 1927.

MORGAN, MARY S. *The history of econometric ideas.* Cambridge, Eng.: Cambridge U. Press, 1990.

PHILLIPS, PETER C. B. "Exact Small Sample Theory in the Simultaneous Equations Model," in GRILICHES AND INTRILIGATOR 1983, pp. 449–516.

REDER, MELVIN W. "Chicago Economics: Permanence and Change," *J. Econ. Lit.*, Mar. 1982, *20*(1), pp. 1–38.

REIERSØL, OLAV. "Confluence Analysis by Means of Lag Moments and Other Methods of Confluence Analysis," *Econometrica*, Jan. 1941, *9*(1), pp. 1–24.

————. "Confluence Analysis by Means of Instrumental Sets of Variables," *Arkiv for Mathematik, Astronomi och Fysik*, Aug. 1945, *32*(1), 4, 119 pp.

RUBIN, HERMAN. "The Approximate Distribution of Calculated Disturbances." Cowles Commission Discussion Paper, Statistics, No. 318, duplicated, 1948.

SAMUELSON, PAUL A.; KOOPMANS, TJALLING C. AND STONE, J. RICHARD N. "Report of the Evaluative Committee for Econometrica," *Econometrica*, Apr. 1954, *22*(2), pp. 141–46.

SARGAN, JOHN DENIS. "The Estimation of Relationships with Autocorrelated Residuals by the Use of Instrumental Variables," *J. Roy. Statist. Soc.*, Series B, 1959, *21*(1), pp. 91–105.

SARGENT, THOMAS J. "The Observational Equivalence of Natural and Unnatural Rate Theories of Macroeconomics," *J. Polit. Econ.*, June 1976, *84*(3), pp. 631–40.

SCHULTZ, HENRY. *The theory and measurement of demand.* Chicago: U. of Chicago Press, 1938.

SIMS, CHRISTOPHER A. "Money, Income, and Causality," *Amer. Econ. Rev.*, Sept. 1972, *62*(4), 540–52.

————. "Macroeconomics and Reality," *Econometrica*, Jan. 1980, *48*(1), pp. 1–48.

STROTZ, ROBERT H. AND WOLD, HERMAN O. A. "A

Triptych on Causal Chain Systems," *Econometrica*, Apr. 1960, 28(2), pp. 417–63.

THEIL, HENRI. "Estimation and Simultaneous Correlation in Complete Equation Systems." The Hague: Central Planning Bureau, 1953; reprinted *Henri Theil's Contributions to economics and econometrics*. Eds.: BALDEV RAJ AND J. KOERTS. Dordrecht: Kluwer Academic, 1991, ch. 6.

_____. *Economic forecasts and policy*. Contributions to Economic Analysis No. 15. Amsterdam: North-Holland, first and second editions, 1958 and 1961.

TINBERGEN, JAN. "Bestimmung und Deutung von Angebotskurven: Ein Beispiel," *Z. Nationalokon.*, 1929–30, 1, pp. 669–79.

_____. *An econometric approach to business cycle problems*. Paris: Hermann et Cie., 1937

_____. *Statistical testing of business-cycle theories, Vol. II: Business cycles in the U.S.A. 1919–1932*. Geneva: League of Nations, 1939.

_____. *Selected papers*. Eds.: L. H. KLAASSEN, L. M. KOYCK, AND H. J. WITTEVEEN. Amsterdam: North-Holland, 1959.

VINING, RUTLEDGE. "Koopmans on the Choice of Variables to Be Studied and of Methods of Measurement," *Rev. Econ. Statist.*, May 1949, 31(2), pp. 77–86 (including a "A Rejoinder" to KOOPMANS 1949b, pp. 91–94).

WALLIS, KENNETH F. "Econometric Implications of the Rational Expectations Hypothesis," *Econometrica*, Jan. 1980, 48(1), pp. 49–73.

WEGGE, LEON L. "Identifiability Criteria for a System of Equations as a Whole," *Australian J. Statist.*, Nov. 1965, 7(3), pp. 67–77.

WOLD, HERMAN O. A. in association with LARS JU-

REEN. *Demand analysis: A study in econometrics*. New York: Wiley, 1953.

WORKING, ELMER J. "What Do Statistical 'Demand Curves' Show?" *Quart. J. Econ.*, Feb. 1927, 41(1), pp. 212–35.

WORKING, HOLBROOK AND HOTELLING, HAROLD. "Applications of the Theory of Error to the Interpretation of Trends," *Amer. Statist. Assoc. J.*, Mar. 1929, 24(165A), pp. 73–85.

WRIGHT, PHILIP G. "Review of *Economic Cycles* by Henry Moore," *Quart. J. Econ.*, May 1915, 29(2), pp. 631–41.

_____. *The tariff on animal and vegetable oils*. New York: Macmillan for the Insitutute of Economics, 1928.

WRIGHT, SEWALL. *Corn and hog correlations*. U.S. Department of Agriculture Bulletin No. 1300. Washington, DC: U.S. GPO, 1925.

WRIGHT, SEWALL. with the collaboration of PHILIP G. WRIGHT. "The Method of Path Coefficients," *Ann. Math. Statist.*, 1934, 5, pp. 161–215.

WU, DE-MIN. "Alternative Tests of Independence Between Stochastic Regressors and Disturbances," *Econometrica*, July 1973, 41(4), pp. 733–50.

WYMER, CLIFFORD R. "Econometric Estimation of Stochastic Differential Equation Systems," *Econometrica*, May 1972, 40(3), pp. 565–77.

ZELLNER, ARNOLD AND PALM, FRANZ. "Time Series Analysis and Simultaneous Equation Econometric Models," *J. Econometrics*, May 1974, 2(1), pp. 17–54.

ZELLNER, ARNOLD AND THEIL, HENRI. "Three-stage Least Squares: Simultaneous Estimation of Simultaneous Equations," *Econometrica*, Jan. 1962, 30(1), pp. 54–78.

PART II

ECONOMETRICS AND ITS ASSESSMENT

[4]

A TEST OF AN ECONOMETRIC MODEL FOR THE UNITED STATES, 1921-1947*

CARL CHRIST, *Cowles Commission for Research in Economics; Fellow of the Social Science Research Council*

This paper presents a revision of Lawrence Klein's sixteen-equation Model III for the United States.[1] The starting point of the revision is a test of Klein's model for 1946 and 1947 carried out by Andrew W. Marshall (17), which rejected several of Klein's equations. The equations of the revised model are estimated from a sample consisting of Klein's sample plus the two years 1946 and 1947. The estimates of the equations of the revised model are tested against the 1948 data.

In Sections 1-4 I have drawn freely and without specific acknowledgment on definitions and theorems from the published and unpublished literature, particularly on Anderson and Rubin (1), Haavelmo (5, 6, 7), and Koopmans (14, 15, 16).

I wish to acknowledge the helpful suggestions and criticism given by J. Bronfenbrenner, H. Chernoff, N. Divinsky, M. Friedman, J. Gurland, L. Hurwicz, L. Klein, T. Koopmans, H. Markowitz, J. Marschak, L. Metzler, S. Reiter, and other members of the Cowles Commission staff. I wish also to express my appreciation to the Social Science Research Council, whose fellowship aid made this study possible; to the Cowles Commission for Research in Economics, whose clerical and computing services were put at my disposal; and to the National Bureau of Economic Research, which sponsored the Conference on Business Cycles.

1 ECONOMETRIC MODELS: GENERAL CONCEPTS AND DEFINITIONS

When one thinks of science, one usually thinks also of experiments. In a typical experiment, there is *one* variable whose behavior is studied under various conditions. The experimenter fixes at will the values of all the other variables he thinks are important, and observes the one in which he is interested. He then repeats the process, fixing different values of the other variables each time. Some of these "other variables" may not be

---

* This paper will be reprinted as Cowles Commission Paper, New Series, No. 49.

[1] Klein (11, 13). Numbers in parentheses in contexts like this indicate references listed in Appendix G.

under his control; the important thing is that they are fixed in advance of the experiment.[2] The variables that are fixed in advance are called independent; the one that the experimenter merely observes is called dependent. The experimenter hopes to find a single equation that describes closely the relationship he has observed.

In more complicated situations there may be more than just *one* relationship among the variables studied. This is the case when there is a determinate result *and,* at the same time, there are two or more important variables that are not fixed in advance; there may even be no experimenter. Economics abounds with such situations. The simplest is of course a competitive market, in which neither price nor quantity is fixed in advance. The economist assumes that *two* relations between these variables, a supply equation and a demand equation, must be simultaneously satisfied.

The econometric work discussed here is based on the belief that we will do well to make our theory conform to this state of affairs. Accordingly we deal with systems of simultaneous equations, called structural equations.[3] Each structural equation is assumed to describe an economic relation exactly except for random shocks; hence each contains a non-observable random disturbance (with mean assumed to be zero).[4,5] Effects of errors in measuring variables are here assumed to be small relative to the disturbances (this kind of model is called a shock model, as distinct from an error model).

Time must enter into the equations if they are to describe a dynamic process. The work discussed here treats time as if it came in discrete chunks of equal size, called periods. The raw materials are time series for the variables considered. A given equation is supposed to represent a relation that holds, for any time period t, among a given set of variables evaluated as of the time period t, where t runs over a sequence of periods from 1 to T.

Note that so far we have used the term 'variable' to denote something

---

[2] They may be constants fixed in advance or random variables with probability distributions fixed in advance (such as weather).

[3] Structural equations are divided by Koopmans (14) into four classes: equations of economic behavior such as the consumption function, technical constraints such as the production function, institutional constraints such as tax schedules or reserve requirements, and definitional identities such as income equals consumption plus investment. Another possible type is made up of market adjustment equations, of which equilibrium conditions are a special case.

[4] This means we believe that either (1) there are systematic discoverable causes for *all* the observed variation of the variables but we are satisfied for the time being if we can explain enough of the variation so that the residual appears random, or (2) there really *are* random elements in economic affairs. For present purposes we do not care which of these two is the case.

[5] Identities are meant to be perfectly exact and hence contain no disturbances.

like national income Y or price level p, which can have different values from one period to the next. We shall continue to use 'variable' in this way, but at times we shall use it instead to denote something like national income *in period t*, denoted by Y_t, or price level *in period t*, denoted by p_t. In the first sense, Y_t and Y_{t-1} are different values of the same variable Y in different periods; in the second sense, Y_t and Y_{t-1} are different variables. It will usually be easy to tell from the context the sense in which the term is being used.

We might have G structural equations containing $G + K$ variables (second sense) at time t. Suppose that of the variables at time t, K are fixed in advance of time t, not by an experimenter to be sure, but by society, or by nature, or even by the past operation of the system of equations; they are called predetermined variables at time t. The G variables, which are not fixed in advance but are determined by the economic process we seek to describe (analogous to the dependent variable in the simple experimental case at the beginning), are called jointly dependent variables at time t (sometimes they are called current endogenous). More precisely, the definitions are as follows. (1) Variables (in the first sense) that are stochastically independent of the random disturbances in the equations are called exogenous; they may be arbitrarily fixed by some agency or process, or they may themselves be random. All other variables (in the first sense) are called endogenous. (2) Variables (in the second sense) which for time t are *either* values of exogenous variables at times $t, t - 1, t - 2, \cdots$, *or* lagged values of endogenous variables, i.e., values at times prior to t, are called predetermined variables at time t. Variables (in the second sense) which for time t are current values of endogenous variables, i.e., values at time t, are called jointly dependent variables at time t. Sometimes the phrase "at time t" is omitted, but whenever we speak of jointly dependent or predetermined variables, it is always understood.

Such a system of structural equations is called a *structure*, provided (1) that each equation is completely specified as to form and as to numerical values of parameters, and (2) that it is accompanied by a similarly completely specified joint probability distribution function of the disturbances.[6]

One objective will be to find a structure or structures that will enable us to rationalize past observations of economic variables and to predict future ones.[7] This will be difficult because we cannot observe structures or disturbances directly. However, we can observe samples from the joint

[6] Or, more generally, a structural relation or a distribution may be completely specified by a graph, if it is not expressible in terms of simple functional forms. But such relations are very difficult to work with.

[7] Here the "future" includes the part of the past that was not consulted in the process of finding the structure in question.

conditional probability distribution function $\phi(y \mid z)$ of the jointly dependent variables $y = (y_1, y_2, \cdots)$, given the predetermined variables $z = (z_1,$
$z_2, \cdots)$. It is clear that any given structure generates exactly one such
distribution function, i.e., to any given structure there corresponds exactly
one distribution function $\phi(y \mid z)$ which is consistent with it. It is natural
to ask whether this correspondence is one to one in *both* directions; in
other words whether, if we knew only the conditional distribution $\phi(y \mid z)$
of the jointly dependent variables given the predetermined variables, we
could proceed backwards and find a unique structure that generates it.
In general the answer is no, because in general there are several (or an
infinite number of) structures consistent with a given $\phi(y \mid z)$. Thus even
apart from the sampling problem of estimating $\phi(y \mid z)$ from a finite
sample, it is in general not possible to find a unique structure by studying
observations alone. This would not be serious were it not for the fact that
in general the structures generating a given $\phi(y \mid z)$ are not identical in
their implications about the effects of economic policy decisions (see Sec. 2
for a more detailed discussion).

Sometimes it is possible, on theoretical grounds, i.e., on the basis of
knowledge derived ultimately from other observations not used to estimate
$\phi(y \mid z)$, to find a set of restrictions that we believe must be satisfied by
any structure that can make good predictions. Such a set of restrictions
defines a *model,* i.e., the set of exactly those structures that satisfy the
given restrictions.

A model is said to be structure-identifying, or simply identifying, if each
possible distribution function $\phi(y \mid z)$ is generated by exactly one structure belonging to the model. A structure is said to be identified (or identifiable) within a given model if the model contains no *other* structures
generating the distribution $\phi(y \mid z)$ that is generated by the given structure.
It is important to note that the problem of the identification of structures
is completely separate from the problem of estimating probability distributions from finite samples, and would exist (in the context of simultaneous
equations) even if there were no random elements. It is of course to be
hoped that enough theoretical restrictions are available to permit the construction of identifying models.

It is desirable that the models be more general rather than less. But at
this early stage of the development of econometrics it is convenient to
impose further restrictions in addition to (or even at the expense of some
of) those derived from theory, in order to keep the models fairly simple.
For instance, it is customary for simplicity's sake (though not conceptually
necessary) to choose a model that is a parametric family of structures,
i.e., a set of G simultaneous equations in G jointly dependent variables
and a joint distribution function of disturbances, both having a specified

form but unspecified parameters.[8] Such a model is preferable because of its relative ease of handling: first, the equations and probability distribution function of the model can be set up on the basis of previous knowledge; then observations of appropriate variables can be obtained; then the parameters can be estimated by straightforward statistical procedures (see Secs. 3 and 4).[9]

Revisions of a model in the light of its performance in forecasting are of course permitted and expected; to this subject we shall return in Section 7.

To simplify computational procedures, further restrictions are placed on the model: it is assumed to be linear in the unknown parameters (though not necessarily in the variables); it deals with macro-variables (aggregates) as distinct from micro-; its disturbances are usually assumed to be normally distributed and serially uncorrelated. Obviously some of these restrictions make the model a poor approximation to the actual world. It can be expected that they will be made more realistic as statistical and economic theory, computational facilities, and data permit.

[8] Consider the model represented by the following system of equations and restrictions:

(1) $D = \alpha_1 p + \alpha_2 Y + \alpha_0 + u$
(2) $S = \beta_1 p + \beta_2 w + \beta_0 + v$
(3) u and v are normally distributed, with distribution function $\phi(u,v)$ and means zero.
(4)   successive drawings from $\phi(u,v)$ are independent.
(5) $E(u \mid Y,w) = E(v \mid Y,w) = 0$.

This model will be changed if we restrict any of its parameters to specific values or to specific ranges, or add new terms, or change the assumptions about the distribution $\phi(u,v)$, etc. Two hypothetical structures belonging to it are:

(6) $D = -2p + .10Y + 1.5 + u$
(7) $S = 3p - 2.6w - 0.8 + v$
(8) $\sigma_u^2 = 1,$ $\sigma_v^2 = 4,$ $\sigma_{uv} = -1.5$
(9)   restrictions (3) to (5) above

and

(10) $D = .16Y + 1.2 + u$
(11) $S = 2.8p - 3w - 1.3 + v$
(12) $\sigma_u^2 = 2,$ $\sigma_v^2 = 3,$ $\sigma_{uv} = 0$
(13)   restrictions (3) to (5) above.

[9] In practice, the tendency is to select a model *after* looking at the data to be used to estimate its parameters. This is useful and legitimate, even necessary, as a means of *suggesting* hypotheses. However, the effect is to make spuriously small the estimated standard errors we obtain from the usual formula, i.e., to give us excessive confidence in our estimates, because this formula assumes that all the restrictions implied in our model were derived from some *a priori* source of knowledge *before* we examined the data, whereas in fact some were derived from an examination of the data.

With these restrictions, a model consists of G simultaneous equations in G endogenous variables and a distribution function of disturbances, thus:

(A)
$$\begin{cases} \sum_{j=1}^{J} \alpha_{gj} f^j \ (y_1', \cdots, y_G'; z_1', \cdots, z_M') = u_g, \, g = 1, \cdots, G, G \leqq J. \\[2mm] \phi(u_1, \cdots, u_G) = \text{joint normal distribution with mean zero:} \end{cases}$$

where: $y_h' =$ jointly dependent variables at time t, $h = 1, \cdots, G$.

$z_m' =$ predetermined variables at time t, $m = 1, \cdots, M$.

$f^j =$ functions of the y_h' and the z_m', which are of a given form and contain *no* unknown parameters, $j = 1, \cdots, J$ (for example, X or $(pX - \mathcal{E})/q$ in Klein's model; see Sec. 5). As a special case, f^j might equal y_j' for $j = 1, \cdots, G$ and equal z_{j-G}' for $j = G + 1, \cdots, J$; if so, $J = G + M$ and we have linear equations; we do not restrict the model to this extent.

$\alpha_{gj} =$ known or unknown parameters (some of which may be zero).

successive drawings from $\phi(u_1, \cdots, u_G)$ are independent of one another and of current and previous values of z_m', $m = 1, \cdots, M$.

each variable and disturbance is understood to carry the subscript t to indicate that it is evaluated as of period t, $t = 1, \cdots, T$.

To illustrate (A) concretely, consider the following simple income-consumption model, where C, V, and Y are respectively consumption, investment, and income:

(A')
$$\begin{array}{llll} \alpha_{11} \, C/Y + \alpha_{12} \, Y & + \alpha_{15} & = u_1 \\ Y - C - V & & = 0 \\ \phi(u_1) & & = N \, (0, \sigma^2) \end{array}$$

Here Y and C are the endogenous variables y_1' and y_2', and V is exogenous. $G = 2$ and $J = 5$; $f^j \, (C, Y; V)$ is equal to C/Y when $j = 1$, to Y when $j = 2$, to $-C$ when $j = 3$, to $-V$ when $j = 4$, and to 1 when $j = 5$. $\alpha_{13} = \alpha_{14} = \alpha_{21} = \alpha_{25} = 0$; $\alpha_{22} = \alpha_{23} = \alpha_{24} = 1$; $u_2 = 0$. $N \, (0, \sigma^2)$ is the normal distribution with mean zero and variance σ^2. By checking these statements, the reader can verify that (A') is a special case of (A). Similarly, any system of equations that is linear in the unknown parameters can be expressed in the form (A).

We can rewrite (A) in a more convenient form by separating all the f^j into two classes: (1) those which involve some jointly dependent variables, i.e., some subset of the y_h' (whether or not they also involve any of the z_m'), and (2) those which are completely predetermined, i.e., involve only the z_m'. We call the first group y_i, $i = 1, \cdots, I$, and the second group z_k, $k = 1, \cdots, K$. Then the model becomes

(B) $\begin{cases} \displaystyle\sum_{i=1}^{I} \beta_{gi} y_i + \sum_{k=1}^{K} \gamma_{gk} z_k = u_g, \ g = 1, \cdots, G. \\[2mm] \phi(u_1, \cdots, u_G) = \text{joint normal distribution with mean zero.} \end{cases}$

where: y_i = jointly dependent variables at time t (including functions f^j which depend on any of the y_h' and have no unknown parameters), $i = 1, \cdots, I$.

          z_k = predetermined variables at time t (including functions f^j which depend on no y_h' and have no unknown parameters), $k = 1, \cdots, K$.

          $\beta_{gi} = \alpha_{gj}$ for all i, j such that $f^j = y_i$, $g = 1, \cdots, G$, $i = 1, \cdots, I$, $j = 1, \cdots, J$.

          $\gamma_{gk} = \alpha_{gj}$ for all j, k such that $f^j = z_k$, $g = 1, \cdots, G$, $j = 1, \cdots, J$, $k = 1, \cdots, K$.

      successive drawings from $\phi(u_1, \cdots, u_G)$ are independent of one another, and of current and previous values of z_k, $k = 1, \cdots, K$.

      each variable and disturbance is again understood to carry the subscript t.

This is the form in which we shall use the model. In general $I \geqq G$, so that there appear to be more jointly dependent variables than equations. To complete the model, it is necessary and sufficient to include the identities that define the y_i in terms of the y_h' — thus in the case of Klein's model mentioned above, there would be an equation defining, say, y_2, thus: $y_2 = (pX - \mathcal{E})/q$. There are I such identities.

To illustrate (B) concretely, rewrite (A') as follows, together with the identities defining the y_i:

(B')
$$\begin{aligned} \beta_{11} y_1 + \beta_{12} y_2 &\qquad + \gamma_{12} z_2 = u_1 \\ y_2 + y_3 + z_1 &\qquad = 0 \\ y_1 &\qquad = C/Y \\ y_2 &\qquad = Y \\ y_3 &\qquad = -C \\ \phi(u_1) &\qquad = N(0, \sigma^2) \end{aligned}$$

Here $G = 2$ again of course, $I = 3$, and $K = 2$; $z_1 = -V$, and $z_2 = 1$. $\beta_{11} = \alpha_{11}$, $\beta_{12} = \alpha_{12}$, $\beta_{13} = \alpha_{13} = 0$, $\beta_{21} = \alpha_{21} = 0$, $\beta_{22} = \alpha_{22} = 1$, $\beta_{23} = \alpha_{23} = 1$, $\gamma_{11} = \alpha_{14} = 0$, $\gamma_{12} = \alpha_{15}$, $\gamma_{21} = \alpha_{24} = 1$, $\gamma_{22} = \alpha_{25} = 0$. The reader can verify that (B') is a special case of (B), and that any set of equations of the form (A) can be rewritten in the form (B).

Simple procedures are available for determining whether a model like

(B) is structure-identifying, i.e., whether the structures belonging to (B) are identified. A structure is said to be identified within the model (B) if and only if all its equations are. A necessary condition for the identification of an equation of (B) (if the covariance matrix of the disturbances at time t is completely unknown) is the order condition: K^{**}, the number of predetermined variables z_k in the other equations of the model but *not* in that equation, must be greater than or equal to $H - 1$, where H is the number of jointly dependent variables y_i in that equation. (If K^{**} is greater than $H - 1$, the equation is sometimes said to be overidentified, and to have $K^{**} - H + 1$ overidentifying restrictions.) There is a necessary and *sufficient* condition as well (the rank condition); it is more difficult to apply to an equation in a system where there are unknown parameters, but if it is not satisfied we expect to be notified of the fact when we reach the estimation stage by the presence of large estimated sampling variances of our estimates of the parameters (Koopmans, 15, 16).

There remains one more general remark, concerning the generation of cyclical patterns by an econometric model of the type defined here. Such a model contains lagged values of many of its variables, and therefore is a set of simultaneous difference equations. Whereas the solution of a set of ordinary simultaneous equations (given the values of the exogenous variables) is simply a set of numbers, each giving a single value for one endogenous variable, the solution of a set of difference equations (given the values of the exogenous variables) is a set of functions of time, each giving a path in time for one endogenous variable. Such a time-path gives the future history that an endogenous variable of the model would have, as a function of future values of exogenous variables, if future disturbances were zero. This history may behave in one of several ways as t increases indefinitely:

1) approach a finite limit monotonically.
2) approach a finite limit with oscillations of diminishing amplitude.
3) oscillate indefinitely with constant finite amplitude.
4) approach infinity (positive or negative) monotonically.
5) approach infinity (positive and/or negative) with oscillations.[10]

The oscillations, if any, will have a constant period and a constant 'damping ratio' (which may be less than, equal to, or greater than one according as 2, 3, or 5 above is the case) *if* future disturbances are zero and future exogenous variables are constant. Their limits as t increases indefinitely can be computed. Derivatives of period, damping ratio, and

---

[10] Except during periods of hyperinflation, etc., we expect the solutions of the equations we construct for our economy to be of the first, second, or third kind, i.e., not to 'explode'. This expectation is not included among the restrictions used in the estimation procedures of this paper, however.

amplitude with respect to exogenous variables and parameters can also be computed.[11]

Since econometric models can thus generate cyclical fluctuations that respond to changes in exogenous variables, they recommend themselves as promising analytical tools for business cycle research.[12]

2 PREDICTION: THE REDUCED FORM OF A SYSTEM OF STRUCTURAL EQUATIONS

The ultimate test of an econometric model, as of any theory, comes with checking its predictions. A model of the form of equations (B) in Section 1 is not ready to make predictions of the jointly dependent variables, even if its parameters are known. It must first be solved algebraically, so that each jointly dependent variable is expressed in terms of things that can be at least approximately known when the predictions are being made, i.e., parameters and predetermined variables. If (A) is linear in the y_h', then $y_h' = y_i$ for $h = i$, and (A) and (B) are just alike. Then the solution of (B) or (A) for the jointly dependent variables is simply the solution of a set of G linear equations for G unknowns y_i. It is called the *reduced form* of the model, and looks like this:

$$
\text{(C)} \quad
\begin{cases}
y_i = \sum_{k=1}^{K} \pi_{ik} z_k + v_i, \, i = 1, \cdots, I. \\
\phi(v_1, \cdots, v_I) = \text{joint distribution function of } v_1, \cdots, v_I.
\end{cases}
$$

where: π_{ik} = parameters dependent upon the structural parameters β_{gi} and γ_{gk}, $g = 1, \cdots, G, i = 1, \cdots, I, k = 1, \cdots, K$.

v_i = a random disturbance, equal to a function of the β_{gi} and u_g, $g = 1, \cdots, G, i = 1, \cdots, I$.

all other symbols have the meaning given in Section 1; in particular the y_i are jointly dependent variables at time t (including functions thereof with no unknown parameters), and the z_k are predetermined variables at time t (including functions thereof with no unknown parameters), as defined in Section 1.

We still call (C) the reduced form of (B), even if (A) is not linear in the y_h', though in that case (C) is not actually the solution of (B), but is only a kind of linear approximation of it. The exact solution of (B) for either the y_h' or the y_i is nonlinear in the z_k if (A) is not linear in the y_h'. (C) is a solution of (B) in the sense that each equation of (B) is a linear combination of the equations of (C), as the reader may verify. Since the linear form (C) is more convenient for later purposes than the exact solu-

---

[11] This applies to nonoscillatory solutions too, except for the period.

[12] See, for example, Frisch (4), Kalecki (10), and Tinbergen (23).

tion of (B), we shall use it, and unless otherwise specified, the term reduced form hereafter will refer to it.

We have encountered the reduced form in Section 1, but not under its present name: it specifies the conditional probability distribution $\phi(y \mid z)$ of the jointly dependent variables y given the predetermined variables z.

If the parameters of the reduced form (C) are known or estimated, predictions of any desired jointly dependent y_i for time t may be made simply by substituting the values of the predetermined z_k for time t into the reduced-form equation for the desired y_i.[13] (It is also possible to predict from the structural equations, by the following process: first substitute into the structural equations the known or assumed values of the predetermined variables, and the estimated values of the structural parameters; then solve the system simultaneously to get the predicted values of the jointly dependent variables. This method in effect uses the exact reduced form rather than the linear approximation for predicting; it gives predictions identical with those of the linearized reduced form if and only if the model is linear and just-identifying; in other cases it presumably gives better predictions because it ignores fewer of the available *a priori* restrictions, but in nonlinear models it is more difficult to apply.) As we shall find in Sections 3 and 4, it is easier to obtain suitable estimates for the parameters of the reduced form (C) than for the parameters of the structural equations (B). Thus it appears that in order to predict the jointly dependent variables y_i, we need only know the values of the parameters of the reduced form, not bothering with the structural equations at all. This is true if, between the period for which the reduced form equations are estimated and the period for which predictions are to be made, no change occurs in the distribution $\phi(y \mid z)$, which means no change occurs in the structure that generates the distribution $\phi(y \mid z)$. But if the structure does change, $\phi(y \mid z)$ and hence the reduced-form parameters π_{ik} will change also, and this will invalidate any predictions based upon knowledge of the old π_{ik}. To be valid, predictions must be based upon knowledge of the new π_{ik}. To obtain this we must have (besides knowledge of the old π_{ik}) knowledge of the structural parameters β_{gi} and γ_{gk} before the structural change, and knowledge of the effect upon them of the structural change. Thus, for prediction under known structural change, the reduced form is not enough; we must know the structural parameters as well.[14]

[13] Strictly, a prediction of this kind specifies a probability distribution, not a number. Loosely, we shall use the terms 'predicted value' or 'prediction' to mean 'expected value of predicted distribution'.

[14] Even if the change in a structural parameter is known in *direction* only, not in magnitude, it is still true except in special cases that to find the *direction* of the resulting change in some variable (such as national income) it is necessary to know the *magnitudes* of other parameters of the system. See Samuelson (22), pp. 12-14.

One of the most interesting uses of econometric models will, I hope, be to predict the consequences of alternative public policy measures in order that enlightened decisions can be made. Institution of a new policy can often be interpreted as a change of structure. Information about the effect of such a structural change is likely to be available. Thus prediction under structural change can be expected to assume a very important role.

3 STATISTICAL ESTIMATION PROCEDURES: THE STRUCTURAL PARAMETERS

As we have said, we hope to be able to construct a structure-identifying model, i.e., a model containing exactly one structure able to generate each distribution function $\phi(y \mid z)$ of the jointly dependent variables given the predetermined variables. It is the job of a statistical estimation procedure, given the observations, to find estimates of that structure. We mention three such procedures: the full information maximum likelihood method (which we shall call full information for short), the limited information single-equation maximum likelihood method (which we shall call limited information for short),[15] and the least squares method.

Before describing these three estimation procedures, we shall briefly discuss maximum likelihood estimates in general. Given a sample of observations, the maximum likelihood estimate $\hat{\theta}$ of a parameter θ of the distribution of the observations is the value of θ among all possible values of θ, that yields the highest probability density for the given sample of observations. It is obtained by two steps: (a) forming the *likelihood function* of the unknown parameters given the sample of observations (this is the probability density function of the observable variables, with the actual observed values of the variables substituted into it, so that it is a function only of parameters); (b) maximizing this likelihood function with respect to the unknown parameters, treating them as variables for the moment. For a wide class of distribution functions (including asymptotically normal distributions), maximum likelihood estimates are asymptotically normally distributed. Furthermore, under certain assumptions, they are consistent,[16] and efficient[16] compared with any other estimates that are both consistent and asymptotically normally distributed.[17]

---

[15] The limited information method is treated in Anderson and Rubin (1).

[16] An estimate t of a parameter θ is said to be consistent if $Lim\ Pb(\mid t - \theta \mid > \mathcal{E}) = 0$
$N \to \infty$
for any $\mathcal{E} > 0$, where N is the sample size and $Pb\ (x)$ means the probability of x occurring. A consistent estimate t is said to be efficient compared with another consistent estimate t' if $Lim\ N{\cdot}E(t - \theta)^2 \leqq Lim\ N{\cdot}E(t' - \theta)^2$.
$N \to \infty \qquad\qquad N \to \infty$

[17] The proof that maximum likelihood estimates have these optimal properties is based on the assumption that there is a true structure, which belongs to the model used. Hence the optimal properties of maximum likelihood estimates may not exist if an unrealistic model is used. This is mentioned here as a caution, even though it is

1) The full information maximum likelihood method (full information for short) treats all the jointly dependent variables alike, considering them all dependent as a group on the predetermined variables. It consists of two steps: (a) forming the joint likelihood function of all the parameters, given the observations of all the jointly dependent and predetermined variables in the model; (b) maximizing this likelihood function with respect to all the parameters simultaneously, subject to all the restrictions implied in the model. Its application therefore requires complete specification of the model, plus observed values for all the variables included in the model. Estimates so derived are consistent, and efficient compared to any other estimates which are both consistent and asymptotically normally distributed.

2) The limited information single-equation maximum likelihood method (limited information for short) treats each equation of the model separately, not the whole model at once, but nevertheless recognizes the simultaneous-equations character of the model. For any given equation, it consists of two steps: (a) forming the joint likelihood function of the parameters in the equation, given the observations of the jointly dependent variables in the equation and all the predetermined variables in the model; (b) maximizing this likelihood function with respect to the parameters in the given equation, subject to the restrictions implied in the probability distribution function of the disturbances and in the given equation (including in particular the restrictions stating which predetermined variables do not enter the given equation).[18] Its application to a particular equation therefore uses complete specification of that equation, plus observed values for the jointly dependent variables appearing in that equation, plus observed values for all the predetermined variables appearing in the model. Estimates so derived are consistent, and efficient compared with any other

---

a commonplace that the results of any statistical analysis may fall down if the original assumptions are not fulfilled.

The proof is based also on the assumption of normally distributed disturbances. If this assumption is not true, estimates computed *as if* it were true still retain the property of consistency; such estimates are called quasi-maximum likelihood estimates.

Proofs of consistency in estimation employ also the assumption that the matrix of moments of predetermined variables is bounded in the limit as the sample size increases.

[18] In the process of maximizing this likelihood function, what is done essentially is first to compute the least squares estimates of the parameters of the reduced form (see Sec. 4), and second to transform those estimates into estimates of the structural parameters by means of the inverse of the transformation used to obtain the reduced form (C) from the structural equations (B). This is a complex process only in the case of *overidentified* structural equations.

estimates that (a) are consistent, (b) are asymptotically normally distributed, *and* (c) use the same information, i.e., the same *a priori* restrictions
and the same observations. The limited information estimates are not efficient compared with the full information estimates (in cases where there
is any difference), because the latter use more restrictions and more
observations.

In another variant of the limited information method the likelihood
function that is maximized is an abbreviated version of the one assumed
to be the true one: it is conditional not upon all the predetermined variables
appearing in the model, but only on a subset of them. The subset must
include all the predetermined variables appearing in the equation to be
estimated, and at least $H - 1$ others (where H is the number of jointly
dependent variables in the equation to be estimated), but otherwise it is
arbitrary. In other words, this subset must be large enough to ensure that
the given equation satisfies the necessary condition for identification stated
in Section 1. This abbreviated variant of the limited information method
uses observations on only the jointly dependent and predetermined variables in the given equation plus the $H - 1$ (or more) other predetermined
variables included in the likelihood function. Thus for overidentified equations it yields estimates that (for finite samples) are not unique because
the choice of the $H - 1$ or more other predetermined variables is arbitrary.
Estimates of structural parameters obtained by the abbreviated variant of
the limited information method are consistent. They are less efficient than
ordinary limited information estimates (because the latter use more observations and correct instead of incorrect restrictions), but they are efficient
compared with any other consistent and asymptotically normal estimates
that use the *same* observations and restrictions.[19]

3) The least squares method treats each equation of the model completely
separately, as if there were no other equations. It is not a maximum likelihood method except in special cases. For any given equation, it consists of
three steps: (a) choosing arbitrarily one variable to be regarded as dependent upon the others; (b) forming the likelihood function of the parameters in the equation, given the observed values of the dependent variable
and the other (independent) variables in the equation; (c) maximizing
this likelihood function with respect to the parameters in the equation. Its
application to a particular equation requires complete specification of the
equation, plus observed values for only those variables appearing in the
equation. In the general case of a model with more than one equation,

---

[19] There are still other variants, not discussed here, called limited information subsystem maximum likelihood methods, in which a proper subset of two or more equations of the structure is estimated simultaneously; see Rubin (20).

least squares estimates of the parameters are biased and inconsistent, as Haavelmo (7) has proved. They are also arbitrary within certain limits because of the arbitrary choice of a dependent variable.

In certain cases, depending upon the restrictions implied in the model, the full information method is equivalent to the least squares method, and all three methods lead to identical computation procedures and estimates.[20]

The full information method is most expensive, and therefore has never (to my knowledge) been used for a system of more than three equations, except where for simplicity all disturbances at time *t* were assumed to be independent of one another. The limited information method, though less efficient, is considerably less expensive and has been more extensively used. The least squares method, though known to give biased estimates except in special cases, is computationally much the simplest, and has been traditionally used.

The justifications advanced for the continued use of the least squares method in cases where it yields biased estimates are of two kinds. First, assuming that estimates having the asymptotic properties of consistency and efficiency *are* in fact superior (in terms of the expected value of the square of the error) for small samples as well as for large (although this superiority is proved only for large), the cost of superior estimation may be too high. Second, in the interesting cases the least squares method's bias may be small and the convergence of its estimates as the sample size increases may be rapid, so that its expected errors may be smaller for small samples than those of the full or limited information maximum likelihood methods.[21]

---

[20] An example is the following model, due to Hurwicz:

$$y_1 + \beta y_2 \qquad = u_1$$
$$y_2 + \gamma z = u_2$$

u_1 and u_2 are normally distributed, and serially independent
$$Eu_1 = Eu_1 u_2 = Eu_2 = 0$$
$$E(u_1 \mid z) = E(u_2 \mid z) = 0.$$

The full information estimate of β from a sample of T is

$$\hat{\beta} = -\frac{\sum\limits_{t=1}^{T} y_1 y_2}{T \cdot \sum\limits_{t=1}^{T} y_2^2}$$

which is also the limited information estimate and the least squares estimate. Note that y_2 is exogenous to the first equation of the model because its distribution depends only on z and u_2, so that it is independent of u_1.

[21] Hurwicz has pointed out informally that when estimates of some parameters are obtained using *incorrect* assumptions about the values of others, there is in general both a gain and a loss in accuracy of estimation (measured by the expected value of the squared difference between the estimate and the parameter), as compared with

The least-squares method and the abbreviated variant of the limited information method will be used in this paper. Of these two, the latter appears preferable because it preserves the simultaneous-equations character of economic theory, rather than distorting it by forcing it into a framework designed for only one dependent variable. But until we can recognize in advance the cases in which least-squares error, i.e., bias plus sampling error, in small samples is in fact so large as to make the least-squares method poorer for small samples than the limited information method, it may be just as well to use both methods and compare their results.

4 STATISTICAL ESTIMATION PROCEDURES: THE PARAMETERS OF THE REDUCED FORM

Since the equations of the reduced form contain only one dependent variable each, they are automatically identified. We mention two procedures for estimating the parameters of the reduced form. One is the ordinary least-squares method, and the other is a modification of it which for the purposes of this paper we shall call the restricted least squares method.

1) The ordinary least-squares method is equivalent to forming for each reduced-form equation the likelihood function of its parameters, given the observed values of its dependent variable and its predetermined variables, and then maximizing this likelihood function with respect to the parameters of the equation. Ordinary least-squares estimates of the parameters of any reduced-form equation are unbiased and consistent, provided either that none of the predetermined variables in the model is excluded from the reduced-form equation or that no excluded predetermined variable is correlated with any of the other predetermined variables. But the resulting estimate of the expected value of the jointly dependent variable will remain unbiased and consistent even if some of the predetermined variables are excluded and are correlated with other included ones.[22]

2) The restricted least squares method is the same as the ordinary least-squares method except that for a given reduced-form equation the maxi-

---

the results obtained if the incorrect assumptions are simply dropped. The gain comes from the faster convergence of the estimates to their expected values, and becomes smaller as the sample grows. The loss comes from the fact that the expected values to which the estimates converge are not the true values of the parameters, and is not affected by the sample size. In small samples, therefore, the gain may exceed the loss. Thus least-squares estimates, even if based on incorrect assumptions about the covariances of the disturbances, may be superior in some small sample cases to consistent methods.

[22] Furthermore, the limited information estimates of structural parameters, obtained from least-squares estimates of the parameters of the reduced form as indicated in note 18, will remain consistent as well.

mization is performed subject to a restriction or restrictions implied in the form of a (proper or improper) subset of the set of all those structural equations that contain the jointly dependent variable appearing in the given reduced-form equation.[23] The procedure yields estimates that (for finite samples) are not unique because of the arbitrary choice of the subset of structural equations. If limited information single-equation estimates of the structure have already been computed, it is much the simplest to choose a one-element subset of structural equations because most of the computations have already been made (this is the procedure followed in this paper). The restricted least-squares estimates of the parameters of the reduced form are unbiased and consistent, with the same qualifications as apply to the ordinary least-squares estimates (see the preceding paragraph). They can be expected to be more efficient than the ordinary least-squares estimates because they use more restrictions.

5 KLEIN'S MODEL III

Klein's model III has 15 equations, of which 3 are definitional identities containing no disturbances and no unknown parameters. Thus there are 12 stochastic equations to be estimated.

There are 15 endogenous variables (in the sense of the y_g' in equations (A) in Sec. 1):

C = consumer expenditures, in billions of 1934 dollars.

D_1 = gross construction expenditure for owner-occupied one-family nonfarm housing, in billions of 1934 dollars.

D_2 = gross construction expenditure for rented nonfarm housing, in billions of 1934 dollars.

H = inventories at year end, in billions of 1934 dollars.

I = net private producers' investment in plant and equipment, in billions of 1934 dollars.

i = average corporate bond yield, in per cent.

K = stock of private producers' fixed capital at year end, in billions of 1934 dollars.

$M_1{}^D$ = active cash balances = demand deposits + currency outside banks, in billions of current dollars.

$M_2{}^D$ = idle cash balances = time deposits, in billions of current dollars.

p = general price level, 1934:1.0.

r = nonfarm rent index, 1934:1.0.

v = fraction of nonfarm housing units occupied at year end, in per cent.

W_1 = private wages and salaries, in billions of current dollars.

X = private output (except housing services), in billions of 1934 dollars.

Y = disposable income, in billions of 1934 dollars.

[23] Appendix E gives a fuller description of the nature of these restrictions and how they are applied.

Fourteen variables are assumed to be exogenous (in the sense of the exogenous z_k' in equation (A) in Sec. 1):

D_3 = gross construction expenditures for farm housing, in billions of 1934 dollars.

D'' = depreciation on all housing, in billions of 1934 dollars.

$\mathcal{E}$ = excise taxes, in billions of current dollars.

$\mathcal{E}_R$ = excess bank reserves, in millions of current dollars.

ΔF = increase in number of nonfarm families, in thousands.

G = government expenditures (except transfers and net government interest) + net exports + net investment of nonprofit institutions, in billions of 1934 dollars.

N^S = nonfarm housing units at year end, in millions.

q = price index of capital goods, 1934:1.0.

q_1 = construction cost index, 1934:1.0.

R_1 = nonfarm housing rents, paid or imputed, in billions of current dollars.

R_2 = farm housing rents, paid or imputed, in billions of current dollars.

T = government revenues — net government interest — transfers + corporate saving,
= net national product — disposal income, in billions of 1934 dollars.

t = time, in years; $t = 0$ in 1931.

W_2 = government wages and salaries, in billions of current dollars.

Data for these variables for 1921-41 are presented in Klein (11, 13) and in Appendix A of this paper.

The 12 equations and 3 identities are as follows (they are here grouped as they were by Klein for his limited information estimation, and renumbered by me):

(1) demand for investment

$$I = \beta_0 + \beta_1 \frac{pX - \mathcal{E}}{q}$$
$$+ \beta_2 \left(\frac{pX - \mathcal{E}}{q}\right)_{-1}$$
$$+ \beta_3 K_{-1} + u_2$$

(2) demand for inventory

$$H = \gamma_0 + \gamma_1 (X - \Delta H) + \gamma_2 p$$
$$+ \gamma_3 H_{-1} + u_3$$

(3) output adjustment

$$\Delta X = \mu_0 + \mu_1 (u_3)_{-1} + \mu_2 \Delta p$$
$$+ u_{12}$$

(4) demand for labor

$$W_1 = a_0 + a_1 (pX - \mathcal{E})$$
$$+ a_2 (pX - \mathcal{E})_{-1}$$
$$+ a_3 t + u_1$$

52   PART ONE

(6) demand for consumer goods $C = \delta_0 + \delta_1 Y + \delta_2 t + u_4$

(7) demand for owned housing $D_1 = \varepsilon_0 + \varepsilon_1 \dfrac{r}{q_1} + \varepsilon_2(Y + Y_{-1}$
$+ Y_{-2}) + \varepsilon_3 \Delta F$
$+ u_5$

(8) demand for dwelling space $v = \eta_0 + \eta_1 r + \eta_2 Y + \eta_3 t$
$+ \eta_4 N^S + u_7$

(9) rent adjustment $\Delta r = \theta_0 + \theta_1 v_{-1} + \theta_2 Y$
$+ \theta_3 \dfrac{1}{r_{-1}} + u_8$

(10) demand for rental housing $D_2 = \zeta_0 + \zeta_1 r_{-1} + \zeta_2 (q_1)_{-1}$
$+ \zeta_3 (q_1)_{-2} + \zeta_4 i$
$+ \zeta_5 \Delta F_{-1} + u_6$

(15) demand for active dollars $M_1^D = \iota_0 + \iota_1 p(Y + T) + \iota_2 t$
$+ \iota_3 p(Y + T)t$
$+ u_9$

(16) demand for idle dollars $M_2^D = \kappa_0 + \kappa_1 i + \kappa_2 i_{-1}$
$+ \kappa_3 (M_2^D)_{-1} + \kappa_4 t$
$+ u_{10}$

(11) interest adjustment $\Delta i = \lambda_0 + \lambda_1 \mathcal{E}_R + \lambda_2 i_{-1} + \lambda_3 t$
$+ u_{11}$

(12) definition of net national product $Y + T = C + I + \Delta H + D_1 + D_2$
$+ D_3 - D'' + G$

(13) definition of X $X = Y + T - \dfrac{1}{p}(W_2 + R_1$
$+ R_2)$

(14) definition of K $\Delta K = I$

Observe in Klein's model the following nonlinear functions involving no unknown parameters: $(pX - \mathcal{E})/q$, $pX - \mathcal{E}$, r/q_1, $1/r_{-1}$, $p(Y + T)$, $p(Y + T)t$, and $(1/p)(W_2 + R_1 + R_2)$.

Equations 1, 2, 3, and 6 are related to the market for goods and services, excluding labor and the construction of housing (these two markets will be treated separately immediately below). Demand for consumer goods (6) is a linear function of income and trend.

Demand for net investment in plant and equipment (1) is a linear function of (a) present and lagged values of deflated (by capital goods prices) privately produced national income at factor cost excluding housing, which is similar to profits, and of (b) the stock of plant and equipment at the beginning of the year. This function is meant to show the dependence of demand for investment upon (a) anticipated profits and (b) existing capital.

Demand for inventory stocks to hold (2) is a linear function of sales, of expected price change (assumed to be given by a linear combination of current and lagged prices), and of the stock of inventories at the end of the year (an inertia factor). Lagged prices do not appear because Klein found them to be unimportant statistically.

Equation 3 expresses the change in private nonhousing output as a linear function of unintended inventory accumulation (assumed to be measured by $(u_3)_{-1}$, the lagged disturbance in the demand-for-inventory-stocks equation 4), and of the rate of change in general prices. It is essentially a supply equation.

Equation 4 gives the demand for labor, measured by the total wage bill, as a linear function of trend, and of current and lagged values of privately produced national income at factor cost excluding housing (which is supposed to reflect anticipated receipts from sales, net of excises). Observe that this equation could be omitted without impairing the completeness of the model, because the variable W_1 (wage-bill) does not appear in any other equation; in other words, if this equation were omitted, a system of 14 equations in 14 variables would remain.

Equations 7-11 pertain to the housing market. Demand for owner-occupied one-family nonfarm housing construction (7), which is purchased by consumers, is a linear function of the real value of rents (where the deflator is construction costs), of accumulated cash balances (assumed to be proportional to the sum of incomes during the 3 most recent years), and of the increase in the number of nonfarm families.

Demand for rented nonfarm housing construction (10), which is purchased by entrepreneurs, is a linear function of lagged rents, of anticipated prices of housing (assumed to be given by a linear combination of construction costs lagged one and two years), of corporate bond yield, and of lagged increase in the number of nonfarm families.

Equation 9 describes the determination of the nonfarm rent level, which occurs in the housing-construction equations 7 and 10, by a linear function of lagged rents, lagged occupancy rate, and income.

Equation 11 describes the change in corporate bond yield, which occurs in the rental housing construction equation 10 and in the idle balances equation 16, as a linear function of excess reserves, of lagged interest rate, and of trend. Note that it has only one dependent variable.

Nonfarm occupancy rate, v (8), which occurs lagged in the rent adjustment equation 9, is a linear function of rents, of income, of trend, and of the supply of nonfarm dwelling units. It could, like W_1, be dropped together with its equation 8, since v occurs nowhere else in the model except in lagged form.

Equations 12-14 are definitions containing no disturbances. Equation 12 is an identity defining net national product as a sum of demand for consumer goods, net investment, increase in inventories, housing construction (net), and goods for government use. This sum might be regarded as an aggregate demand; the fact that it is called the definition of net national product indicates that implicit in the model is an assumption that quantity supplied always equates itself to quantity demanded, except for unintended inventory; see equation 3.

Equation 13 defines privately produced real output excluding housing services, which appears in equations 1-4.

Equation 14 defines stock of capital, which appears lagged in the demand for investment equation.

Klein included in his model an equation defining R_1, nonfarm rent, which he classified as endogenous. R_1 is actually exogenous, however, according to the way he treats it,[24] and we shall so regard it.

Equations 15 and 16 could, like 4 and 8, be omitted without impairing the completeness of the model, since the variables M_1^D and M_2^D (active and idle balances, respectively) occur in no other equations. Demand for active balances (15) is a nonlinear function of disposable money income and trend. Demand for idle balances (16) is a linear function of current and lagged corporate bond yield, of lagged idle balances, and of trend.

Equations 1, 2, 4, 6, 7, 8, 10, 15, and 16 are demand equations, describing the behavior of various economic groups in the population. Equations 3, 9, and 11 are market adjustment equations describing responses of certain market variables to disequilibria. Equations 12-14 are identities describing definitional relationships.

Klein's estimates of the parameters of his model, for both least squares and limited information methods, appear in Section 10 below.

The results I am interested in presenting are those flowing from my revision of Klein's model. This revision is based upon a test of Klein's model carried out by Andrew W. Marshall. The next section discusses Marshall's test and its findings.

---

[24] Its time series is obtained as shown in Appendix B and in Klein (13); its defining equation is not used at all except to obtain estimates of its value for 1919-20, for which data are lacking.

6 MARSHALL'S TEST OF KLEIN'S MODEL III

Marshall (17) tested Klein's model III, together with Klein's limited information estimates of its structural parameters, in two ways. Both ways use the *calculated* disturbances to Klein's structural equations for 1946 and 1947. For any time period t, these calculated disturbances (called u_t^*) are obtained from the structural equations by substituting into them the limited information estimates of the structural parameters, together with the values of all the jointly dependent and predetermined variables at time t.

1) Marshall's first test examines each u^* for 1946 and for 1947 to see whether it is larger than would be expected under the hypothesis that Klein's model and estimates describe 1946 and 1947 as well as they describe the sample period. This is done for each structural equation separately by means of a tolerance interval[25] for the calculated disturbances u^*: the hypothesis is accepted for a given equation and a given post-sample year if the value of u^* for that equation and that year falls inside its tolerance interval. Marshall chooses $\gamma = 0.99$ and $P = 0.99$, which means that under the hypothesis the probability is 0.99 that the tolerance interval for a given equation will include at least 0.99 of the population of calculated disturbances u^*.

A tolerance interval is of the form $\bar{x} \pm ks$, where $\bar{x}$ and s are the mean and standard deviation computed from a sample of N, and k is a number depending upon γ, P, and N.[26] In this case, $\bar{x}$ is $\bar{u}^*$, which is zero by the construction of the estimates of the structural parameters. For each structural equation, Marshall uses in place of s an estimated approximation to the standard deviation of the calculated disturbance u^*, analogous to the Hotelling (9) formula for the standard error of forecast from a regression. This approximation, which we call σ^*, is given by Rubin (21). For the gth structural equation and the year t, it looks like this:

$$(17) \quad \sigma^{*2}(g, t) = E(u^{*2})$$
$$= \sigma^2 + \frac{\sigma^2}{T} + tr\Lambda\Omega + \frac{\sigma^2}{T}z_t^* \, M^{-1}_{z^*z^*} \, z_t^{*\prime} + z_t^\circ\Pi^{*\prime\prime}\Lambda\Pi^{**}z_t^{\circ\prime}$$

[25] A tolerance interval is a random variable; it is an interval that encloses, with a certain probability γ, at least a certain proportion P of the individuals in a given probability distribution. This, and not a confidence interval, is what we want here: we are interested in predicting a *future drawing* from our population of years, not in the true mean. Tolerance limits for the normal distribution have been developed by Wald and Wolfowitz (24), and tables have been prepared for constructing them; see Eisenhart, Hastay, and Wallis (3). The size of the tolerance interval depends upon an estimate of the variance of the *calculated* disturbances in the sample period, i.e., it depends partly upon the estimates of the parameters of the equation.

[26] See table in Eisenhart, Hastay, and Wallis (3), pp. 102-7.

where: $\sigma^2 = E(u^2)$

T = number of years in sample.

Λ = covariance matrix of the estimates of parameters of those endogenous variables y_i appearing in the gth structural equation.

Ω = covariance matrix of disturbances v_i of reduced-form equations containing those endogenous variables y_i appearing in the gth structural equation.

$z_t^{\bullet}$ = vector of values in year t of all those predetermined variables z_k appearing in the gth structural equation, measured from their sample means.

$M_{z^{\bullet}z^{\bullet}}$ = moment matrix of $z^{\bullet}$ with $z^{\bullet}$; $m_{ij} = \dfrac{1}{T}\Sigma(z_i - \bar{z}_i)(z_j - \bar{z}_j)$

z_t^{o} = vector of residuals at time t of the regressions of the $z^{\bullet\bullet}$ (i.e., predetermined variables z_k appearing in the system as a whole but not in the gth structural equation, measured from the sample mean) on the $z^{\bullet}$; i.e., $z_t^{o} = z_t^{\bullet\bullet} - M_{z^{\bullet\bullet}z^{\bullet}}\cdot M^{-1}_{z^{\bullet}z^{\bullet}}\, z_t^{\bullet}$.

$\Pi^{\bullet\bullet}$ = matrix of reduced-form parameters of the $z^{\bullet\bullet}$ in those reduced-form equations containing those endogenous variables y_i appearing in the gth structural equation.

For each structural equation the values of T, $z_t^{\bullet}$, and $z_t^{\bullet\bullet}$ are known, and estimates are available for σ^2, Λ, Ω, $M_{z^{\bullet}z^{\bullet}}, M_{z^{\bullet\bullet}z^{\bullet}}$, and $\Pi^{\bullet\bullet}$.[27] Thus an estimate of $\sigma^{\bullet}$ is available for each structural equation. We call this estimate $s^{\bullet}$.

The test for year t then takes the form of constructing a tolerance interval, $\pm\, ks^{\bullet}$, for each structural equation, and rejecting the equation if its calculated disturbance $u^{\bullet}$ falls outside the interval. I shall call it the structural equation tolerance interval test, provisionally, or the SETI test for short.[28]

In applying the SETI test, Marshall computed $ks^{\bullet}$ in five steps, $ks_1^{\bullet}$, $ks_2^{\bullet}$, $ks_3^{\bullet}$, $ks_4^{\bullet}$, and $ks_5^{\bullet} = ks^{\bullet}$, corresponding to the first term of the estimate of 17, the first two terms, $\cdots$, and all five terms. For each equation he compared each of these successively with $u^{\bullet}$, and stopped as soon as he got a region $\pm\, ks_i^{\bullet}$ which enclosed $u^{\bullet}$. In this way he saved some computational effort, because he did not have to compute all the terms of $s^{\bullet}$ for every equation.

2) Marshall's second test examines each calculated disturbance $u^{\bullet}$ for 1946 and 1947 to see whether it is larger than the error one would expect to make by using what he calls "naive models". Naive model I says that next year's value of any variable will equal this year's value plus a random normal disturbance; naive model II says it will equal this year's value plus

[27] See Anderson and Rubin (1).

[28] The name was suggested by John Gurland.

the change from last year to this year plus a random normal disturbance.[29]

For each naive model and each Klein structural equation, Marshall compares the calculated disturbances u^* of 1946 and 1947 with a *tolerance interval* for the calculated disturbance of the one naive-model equation that contains the variable appearing on the left side of the given Klein equation. If both u^*'s for a given Klein equation are outside the interval, Marshall rejects the Klein equation; if one is outside, he puts the Klein equation on probation; if neither is outside, he accepts the Klein equation.

From the viewpoint of this paper, the naive model tests should be applied to the calculated disturbances of the *reduced form,* not to those of the structural equations: the naive model tests are best suited to compare different methods of predicting (because their disturbances are their errors of prediction), and the predictions made by an econometric model are obtained from its reduced form (see Sec. 2), not directly from its structural equations.[30] But if a naive model test *is* applied to the calculated disturbances of the reduced form, and if it is to be a fair comparison between methods of prediction, then the treatment of the errors of the naive model should be symmetrical with the treatment of the errors, i.e., the calculated disturbances, of the reduced form of the econometric model. This means that a direct comparison of errors should be used, instead of a tolerance interval procedure such as Marshall's which will not reject an equation of the reduced form of the econometric model unless the latter's errors are about three times as large as the naive model's errors (because Marshall's value of k in his naive model tests is about 3).

The results of Marshall's SETI test are shown in Table 1. Marshall did not apply the SETI test to equations 3, 6, or 16, because he had already rejected them on the basis of his naive model tests. The SETI test obviously would have rejected them, however. In 1946 and 1947 they have by far the largest calculated disturbances in the model. Also, for each of these equations in 1946 and 1947 the disturbance is between 5 and 6 times as large as its *maximum* value in the sample period, and between 6 and 18 times as large as its estimated standard error.

Therefore, we conclude that by the SETI test equations 3, 6, and 16 are

---

[29] Milton Friedman too has suggested these naive models, though not under this name.

[30] Furthermore, the size of a structural equation's disturbance is not an invariant for this purpose because a structural equation can be normalized arbitrarily on any endogenous variable, but the size of a reduced-form equation's disturbance is a definite quantity because there is only one dependent variable on which to normalize a given reduced-form equation. Marshall comes close to realizing this when he comments that the verdict of a naive model test of a structural equation depends on which variable is selected from the equation as a basis for the test. He always chooses the one Klein has placed on the left side, and he does realize that this is an arbitrary choice. See Marshall (17).

Table 1

RESULTS OF MARSHALL'S SETI TEST OF KLEIN'S MODEL III

Eq.	Var. at left	Yr.	Calc. dist. u^*	ks_1^*	ks_4^*	ks_5^*	Verdict[a]
1	I	46	−5.6		3.4	8.0	
		47	−2.3	2.0	2.9	3.6	
2	H	46	−.7				
		47	−1.9	2.6			
3	ΔX	46	−61.0				
		47	−37.9				[b]
4	W_1	46	7.2		9.2	15.9	
		47	14.7	4.4	8.7	8.9	R
6	C	46	12.7				
		47	14.0				[b]
7	D_1	46	.3		.9		
		47	−1.3	.9	1.3		
8	v	46	1.5		4.5		
		47	4.6	3.6	4.4	8.1	
9	Δr	46	−.1				
		47	−.0ᶜ	.1			
10	D_2	46	.6				
		47	.5	1.2			
11	Δi	46	−.8				
		47	−.6	2.1			
16	M_1	46	1.9		6.4		
		47	−9.0	5.3	6.5	6.9	R
17	M_2	46	12.2				
		47	12.0				[b]

Source: Marshall (17).   [a] R means reject; a blank space means accept.
[b] Marshall did not apply the SETI test to this equation because he rejected it on the basis of his naive model test.
[c] Less than .05 in absolute value, and negative.

rejected; equations 4 and 15 are on probation for having been rejected for either 1946 or 1947; and equations 1, 2, and 7-11 have a clear record so far.

Since neither Klein or Marshall made any explicit computations of the reduced form, results of naive model tests of the reduced form of Klein's model III are not presented here.

7 REVISIONS OF KLEIN'S EQUATIONS

This section presents several equations designed to replace those of Klein's which fared badly in Marshall's SETI test.

The SETI test, as indicated in Section 6, would have rejected three equations: (3) output adjustment, (6) demand for consumption, and (16) demand for idle cash balances. It cast doubt upon two others: (4) demand for labor and (15) demand for active cash balances. These five equations are the ones to be revised or changed here. If theoretically justified, it is permissible to change the number of variables and equations in the model, but the number of equations must not exceed the number of endogenous variables, and the two must be the same if the system is to be complete.

Consider first the demand for money equations (15 and 16). Their function is to determine two variables, M_1^D and M_2^D (active and idle money balances, respectively), which are purely symptomatic in Klein's model. Since they do not enter into any other equations, M_1^D and M_2^D cannot mathematically affect the other variables of the model but can only be affected by them. We are not interested in the quantity of money per se unless it has some effect. Therefore, we drop equations 15 and 16, together with the variables M_1^D and M_2^D.[31] This cuts the number of equations by two but still leaves a complete model.

The demand for dwelling space, equation 8, is in the same position as the demand for money equations. It determines the nonfarm housing occupancy rate, v, whose current value does not appear elsewhere in the model. Therefore it can be dropped, along with variable v. We have now removed three equations and three variables jointly dependent at time t, without affecting the completeness of the model.

Consider the consumption function next. Klein's equation 6 underestimated consumption in 1946 and 1947 by some 13 and 14 billions of *1934* dollars, or about 15 and 16 per cent.[32] The real value of the stock of money at the beginning of each of these years was $110 and $105 billion, respectively, approximately twice the largest value attained during 1921-39. (The real value of the stock of money is here defined as the sum of currency outside banks plus demand deposits adjusted plus time deposits, but not

[31] I believe that a good economic theory will not say that the quantity of money is merely a symptom having no effect upon economic affairs. Accordingly, Klein's theory is amended below, at least with respect to the consumption function. Only lack of time prevented further changes involving the quantity of money in other parts of the model and dictated the dropping of 15 and 16 rather than their revision.

[32] See Marshall (17).

including government deposits, deflated by the 1934-base price index of output as a whole.) For the interwar years Klein (12) was unable to reject the hypothesis that consumption is not dependent upon real cash balances, but this was to be expected because real balances were almost constant during that period except for a smooth trend, so their effect, if any, could not be discovered. The postwar data suggest that real balances may have been important in the consumption function all along. The skewness of the distribution of ownership of real balances among consumers may also be important; we might expect to find that an increase in the holdings of richer people would stimulate consumption less than an equal aggregate increase in the holdings of poorer people (of course the same might be true of income). Time series are not available for this ownership distribution, however.

The proper definition of cash balances for this purpose is total consumer holdings of currency, demand deposits, time deposits, and probably also U. S. Savings Bonds (Series E) as long as they are guaranteed to be immediately redeemable in cash at no loss and yield negligible interest. Holdings by individuals and unincorporated businesses might be a good approximation, but suitable figures do not exist as far as I know, especially if Series E bonds are included. Therefore the definition used in the preceding paragraph seems best.

Lagged disposable income has often been mentioned as a candidate for membership in the consumption function. It is recommended by the fact that people do not adjust themselves immediately to changes in income. Lagged consumption has also been suggested, for a similar reason.[33] As lagged income and lagged consumption are highly correlated (through the consumption function) it is best not to use both.

Accordingly we experiment with fitting the following consumption functions:

$$(6.0) \quad C = \delta_0 + \delta_1 Y + \delta_2 Y_{-1} + \delta_3 \left(\frac{M}{p} \right)_{-1} + \delta_4 t + u_6$$

$$(6.1) \quad C = \delta_0' + \delta_1' Y + \delta_2' Y_{-1} + \delta_3' t + u_6'$$

$$(6.2) \quad C = \delta_0'' + \delta_1'' Y + \delta_2'' \left(\frac{M}{p} \right)_{-1} + \delta_3'' t + u_6''$$

$$(6.3) \quad C = \delta_0''' + \delta_1''' Y + \delta_2''' t + u_6'''$$

$$(6.4) \quad C = \delta_0^{IV} + \delta_1^{IV} Y + \delta_2^{IV} C_{-1} + \delta_3^{IV} \left(\frac{M}{p} \right)_{-1} + \delta_4^{IV} t + u_6^{IV}$$

$$(6.5) \quad C = \delta_0^{V} + \delta_1^{V} Y + \delta_2^{V} C_{-1} + \delta_3^{V} t + u_6^{V}$$

[33] The suggestion was made informally by Klein and by Franco Modigliani.

where M = currency outside banks + demand deposits adjusted + time deposits, at the end of the year; and other symbols are defined in Section 5. Observe that $(M/p)_{-1}$ is a predetermined variable since it is lagged (the same is of course true of Y_{-1} and C_{-1}). Thus we have not added any new current endogenous variables to the system by these modifications of the consumption function.

There remain two equations, (3) output adjustment (which is really a supply function, as mentioned before) and (4) demand for labor. They are closely related theoretically, because under the assumption of profit maximizing, the firm's demand-for-factor equations are deducible from the profit function and the production function; the supply function is then deducible from these demand-for-factor equations and the production function.[34] Equivalently, if the demand-for-factor equations and the supply equation are given, the production function is determined. Thus if we are concerned only with the logical completeness of the model, it does not matter whether it is the production function or the supply function that we include, provided the demand-for-factor equations are present.[35] We

[34] Suppose we are given competitive conditions, a production function

(1) $x = \phi(y_1, \cdots, y_n)$,

and a profit function

(2) $\pi = px - \sum_1^n q_i y_i$,

where x is output and p is its price, y_i is the input of a factor of production and q_i its price, $i = 1, \cdots, n$, and π is profit. Then the firm maximizes (2) with respect to the y_i, subject to the restraint (1), to get

(3) $p\dfrac{\partial \phi}{\partial y_i} - q_i = 0$, $i = 1, \cdots, n$.

If the set of simultaneous equations (1) is solved for the y_i, $i = 1, \cdots, n$, the result is the demand-for-factor equations

(4) $y_i = f_i\left(\dfrac{q_1}{p}, \cdots, \dfrac{q_n}{p}\right)$, $i = 1, \cdots, n$.

The supply equation is obtained by substituting y_i from (4) into (1), $i = 1, \cdots, n$. Results are similar in the noncompetitive case, but elasticities of product demand and factor supply enter in then.

[35] Under the assumption of profit-maximizing, with a profit function such as (2) in the preceding note, and with a set of demand-for-factor equations for the firm that can be uniquely solved for the factor prices, the production function for the firm can be derived from given demand-for-factor equations, uniquely except for a boundary condition such as $\phi(0, \cdots, 0) = 0$, even with no knowledge of the supply function, as follows: By hypothesis it is possible to pass uniquely from (4) to (3) of the preceding note, which can then be divided through by p and integrated to obtain ϕ uniquely except for a constant term (subject to certain integrability conditions which in our case are satisfied), Q.E.D. This proof is due to Koopmans.

This system is not likely to be made overdetermined by including a production function (or alternatively a supply function), however, since an additional variable x is brought along at the same time.

choose here to use a production function, because Klein's output adjustment equation is so far off (overestimating output by 61 and 38 billions of 1934 dollars in 1946 and 1947, respectively) and because the production function is less likely to be affected by possible structural changes.

Variables must be chosen to represent capital input and labor input in the production function. Capital input can be measured by depreciation charges, which would be ideal if depreciation really reflected the services of capital accurately. But since depreciation is a very arbitrary thing, subject to various legal and accounting pressures, it is not a satisfactory measure of capital use. Another possible measure is the stock of producers' capital at the beginning of the year, defined as the sum over time of net investment. This is not free from the effects of the arbitrariness of depreciation charges but it is less sensitive to them because stock of capital is so large in relation to depreciation charges for any one year. It measures capital *existing,* not capital in *use,* which is unfortunate, but we shall try it anyway, perhaps together with some device for indicating the extent to which available capacity is being used.

Labor input, which might appear also in the demand for labor equation, should ideally be measured in man-hours.[36] But data difficulties deter us here; the BLS series for average weekly working hours before 1932 is for manufacturing and railroads only, and does not cover all industries even now. The concept of full time equivalent persons engaged in production, used by Simon Kuznets and the Department of Commerce, is the next best thing. However, it does not regard overtime work as an increase of labor input: it measures roughly the number of persons engaged full time or more (where full time for any person means simply the current customary work week in his job, whether it is 35 hours or 55), plus an appropriate fraction of the number of persons engaged part time (to convert them to full time equivalents). A time trend term will then approximately take care of the secular decrease in weekly working hours that has occurred.[37]

We might choose any one of several forms for the production function. The Cobb-Douglas function, linear in logarithms, is one possibility; a simple linear or quadratic function is another. Investment during the current year might be included on the theory that new capital, because of

[36] It is private labor input that concerns us here, by the way, not total, because only in the private sector is production assumed to be guided by the desire for profit.

[37] Cyclical fluctuations in weekly working hours will be an important source of error here unless their effect is largely explainable by cyclical changes in full time equivalent persons engaged plus a time trend, i.e., if data on weekly working hours (which we do not have), full time equivalent persons engaged, and time trend are not approximately linearly related.

improvements in the design of equipment, is more productive than old capital even after depreciation has been deducted.

In attempting to make the production function reflect the fact that output can be increased if existing capital is used more intensively, we might break our sample into two samples — one containing boom years in which capital was being used at approximately full capacity, and the other containing slack years in which it was not — and then fit two production functions, one to each. The sign of net investment could be used as a crude indicator for classifying the years: in boom years one would expect demand for capital services to exceed existing supply, thereby stimulating an increase in the stock of capital, so that net investment would be positive, and in slack years the opposite. This scheme is undesirable because it sets up a dichotomy where there should be a continuum, and because it reduces the already too small sample. An alternative, suggested during discussions with Jacob Marschak, is to make each parameter of the production function a linear function of net investment, thus: [38]

$$(3.0) \qquad X = (\mu_0 + \mu_1 I) + (\mu_2 + \mu_3 I)N + (\mu_4 + \mu_5 I)K_{-1} + \mu_6 t + u_3$$

where N = private labor input, in millions of full time equivalent man-years (endogenous), and other variables are defined in Section 5. We would expect μ_5 to be positive: a large positive net investment I can be presumed to indicate that capital is being used at a high percentage of capacity, and existing capital K_{-1} can be expected to contribute more to output than otherwise, so that its coefficient $(\mu_4 + \mu_5 I)$ should be high. We might expect μ_3 to be negative because the marginal product of labor is probably less in boom times than otherwise. Of course we expect μ_2, μ_4, and μ_6 to be positive (though μ_6 would be negative if the above mentioned secular drop in working hours were enough to overbalance the increase in per man-hour productivity). We have no presumptions about μ_0 and μ_1, except that μ_1 should probably be positive and not very important.

Another way of trying to solve the problem of unused capacity is to set up a production function in which output depends upon both labor input and existing capital in boom years, but only upon labor input in slack years. This again unfortunately requires a dichotomous classification of all years as either boom or slack. Mainly because of lack of time, estimates of this kind of production function are not presented in this paper; it would be interesting to return to this idea in the future.

[38] Such a production function is dependent upon the assumption that net investment occurs in response to near-capacity use of existing capital. If something happens so that this is no longer true, the production function changes. But nothing of this sort is likely to happen unless the profit maximizing assumption becomes invalid, in which case several other equations will go by the board too.

Besides 3.0, we try the following production functions:

(3.1) $X = \mu_0' + \mu_1'I + \mu_2'N + \mu_3'K_{-1} + \mu_4't + u_3'$

(3.2) $X = \mu_0'' + \mu_1''N + \mu_2''K_{-1} + \mu_3''t + u_3''$

(3.3) $\log X = \mu_0''' + \mu_1'''\log N + \mu_2'''\log K_{-1} + \mu_3'''t + u_3'''$

(3.4) $X = \mu_0^{IV} + \mu_1^{IV}N + \mu_2^{IV}t + u_3^{IV}$

(3.5) $X = \mu_0^{V} + \mu_1^{V}N + \mu_2^{V}NK_{-1} + \mu_3^{V}K_{-1} + \mu_4^{V}t + u_3^{V}$

(3.6) $X = \mu_0^{VI} + \mu_1^{VI}N + \mu_2^{VI}N^2 + \mu_3^{VI}NK_{-1} + \mu_4^{VI}K_{-1}^2$
$$+ \mu_5^{VI}K_{-1} + \mu_6^{VI}t + u_3^{VI}$$

In 3.1 to 3.4 we would expect all parameters (except possibly the μ_0's) to be positive. In 3.5 and 3.6 we would expect μ_2^{V}, μ_4^{V}, μ_3^{VI}, and μ_6^{VI} to be positive, and μ_1^{V}, μ_3^{V}, μ_2^{VI}, and μ_4^{VI} to be negative (this can be seen more easily by examining the expressions for marginal productivity of labor and capital implicit in the two equations).

Equation 3.3 is a Cobb-Douglas function with a time trend to take approximate account of technological improvements. 3.2 is a linear approximation. 3.1 is like 3.2 except that it treats new and old capital differently. 3.4 is a linear approximation which attempts to account for the existence of unused productive capacity by (1) disregarding the quantity of *existing* capital and (2) assuming (more or less plausibly) that capital input (not measurable) is proportional to labor input, so that output can be expressed as a function of labor input alone. 3.5 and 3.6 are attempts at more accurate approximation than a linear function provides: they have marginal productivity functions that vary with inputs instead of being constant.

Observe that by replacing Klein's output adjustment equation with any of the production functions 3.0 to 3.6, we have added a new endogenous variable, N. Before we finish our revisions, we must therefore find a corresponding additional equation, if we are to end with a complete system.

Now that the wage-salary bill and labor input are both in the model, it is natural to include the wage rate too:

(18) $w = \dfrac{W_1}{N}$

where w = private wage-salary rate, in thousands of current dollars per full time equivalent man-year (endogenous), and W_1 and N are defined in Section 5 and in this section, respectively.

Adding 18 will not affect the completeness of the system. We have here one new equation and another new endogenous variable, w, so we still need to find an additional equation.

If the wage rate is to mean merely total labor earnings per unit of labor input, the definition is satisfactory in the simple form (18). However, if it is to mean the hourly wage, the thing over which workers and employers bargain, overtime payments, premiums for night-shift work, etc., must be allowed for; furthermore, labor input must be measured in man-hours. The advantage of using the hourly wage is that it enables us to introduce an equation describing the bargaining process and its dependence upon price movements, level of employment, and any other relevant variables. This wage adjustment equation could serve also as the additional one required by the introduction of the two new endogenous variables, w and N, with only the one equation 18. But existing data do not permit us to incorporate overtime payments and premiums for shift-work into the wage rate or, as we have seen, to define labor input in man-hours.

Accordingly we retain 18 as it stands. We assume that our w is closely representative of hourly wage,[39] and use a wage adjustment equation such as:

$$(5.0) \qquad w = \kappa_0 + \kappa_1 \Delta p + \kappa_2 (N_L - N) + \kappa_3 w_{-1}$$
$$+ \kappa_4 (N_L - N)_{-1} + \kappa_5 t + u_5$$

or

$$(5.1) \qquad w = \kappa_0' + \kappa_1' \Delta p + \kappa_2' (N_L - N) + \kappa_3' w_{-1} + \kappa_4' t + u_5'$$

where N_L = labor force, including work relief employees but excluding other government employees,[40] in full time equivalent man-years (exogenous),[41] and other variables are as defined above. These wage adjustment

[39] A study in the *Monthly Labor Review* for November 1942, pp. 1053-56, shows the estimated average number of overtime hours per worker per week in manufacturing in 1942 as a function of average total hours per worker per week. Using this study and the BLS series for average weekly hours in manufacturing, and assuming that the 1942 study is valid for all years and that all time over forty hours is paid at time and a half, one concludes that if overtime pay had been the sole cause of the difference between our w and the straight-time hourly wage, this difference would have been less than 2 per cent in all interwar years and less than 3 per cent in 1946 and 1947. Thus we are not risking more than about 3 per cent from this cause. Shift premiums probably do not contribute a larger error than this. And we are more comfortable if we remember that the manufacturing industries probably had more extensive shift premiums and more complete observance of the time and a half for overtime rule than did the economy as a whole.

[40] $N_L - N$ is meant to measure unemployment including relief workers, and N excludes government workers. Therefore if $N_L - N$ is to be a correct measure, N_L must exclude government nonrelief workers.

[41] Labor force is the only measure we have for labor supply, and it is expressible in man-years, but not in man-hours except by some trick assumption. Hence unemployment and employment, which add up to labor force, must also be in man-years instead of man-hours. Hence, there is another advantage in defining labor input N in man-years as we have done.

equations tell us that the wage level depends upon the past wage level (reflecting the downward rigidity of wages), upon price changes (reflecting wage increases following increases in the cost of living and in the prices received by employers), upon unemployment (reflecting the state of the labor market), and upon trend (reflecting the growth in productivity and/or in the strength of unions).

By adding a wage adjustment equation, we have completed our system again.

The demand for labor equation (4) is still to be considered. It was put on probation, not completely rejected. Therefore we try it again, but we also try two alternatives which express the demand for labor in real terms as a function of the real wage rate, of real output, and possibly of trend. The real wage rate enters as a result of the profit maximizing assumption. Output is relevant on the theory that if producers receive more orders they will demand more labor even if the real wage does not fall.[42] Trend may be necessary to reflect the long-term rise in per man-hour productivity. Our alternative equations are:

$$(4.0) \qquad W_1 = a_0 + a_1(pX - \mathcal{E}) + a_2(pX - \mathcal{E})_{-1} + a_3 t + u_4$$

$$(4.1) \qquad N = a_0' + a_1'\frac{w}{p} + a_2'X + a_3't + u_4'$$

$$(4.2) \qquad N = a_0'' + a_1''\frac{w}{p} + a_2''X + u_4''$$

Klein's equation 4.0 is not as different from the others as it looks at first: if we divide 4.0 through by w we get

$$(19) \qquad \frac{W_1}{w} = N = \frac{a_0}{w} + \frac{a_1 X}{w/p} - a_1\frac{\mathcal{E}}{w} + \cdots$$

which also depends on real wage w/p and on real output X, though there is only one parameter, a_1, to take care of both, and there are other terms involving w and $\mathcal{E}$ and lagged quantities meant to account for expectations.

Whether we finally choose 4.0 or 4.1 or 4.2, we still have a complete system of fourteen equations (including four definitional identities) in fourteen jointly dependent variables: $I, H, X, W_1, w, C, D_1, r, D_2, i, Y, p, K,$ and N.[43] It should be understood that there are additional identities which define as additional variables the following nonlinear functions in

---

[42] The dependence of the demand for labor upon output cannot be found from the profit maximizing assumption and the usual production function, which may indicate a weakness in one of these two.

[43] Klein (13) at least hints at most of the changes made in this section, and even includes exploratory computations on some.

the system: $(pX - \mathcal{E})/q$, $pX - \mathcal{E}$, w/p, M/p, r/q_1, $1/r_{-1}$, and $(1/p)(W_2 + R_1 + R_2)$.

8 DESCRIPTION OF TESTS USED

Several tests are available for application to a model or structure obtained by the methods described in this paper. They may be divided into two groups according to the information required for their use. The first group comprises tests dependent only on observations and restrictions available for use in the estimation process; these are essentially tests of internal consistency. The second group comprises tests that use observations concerning events outside (usually subsequent to) the sample period; these are tests of success in extrapolation and prediction, and therefore are of higher authority. We describe here the tests applied in this paper.

a) Tests of internal consistency

First, there are certain qualitative procedures that perhaps should not be called tests at all: the estimates of the structural parameters can be examined to see whether they have the approximate magnitudes and particularly the algebraic signs to be expected on the basis of theoretical and other information about elasticities, marginal propensities, etc. The estimated sampling variance of each estimate can be examined to see how much confidence can be placed in its sign or in its approximate size. The calculated disturbances can be examined to see whether they are very large according to some intuitive standard of how large they are expected to be. This last procedure is of doubtful usefulness because it is not always possible to tell whether disturbances are due to the existence of several systematic factors that have been neglected, or to a real randomness in the phenomenon studied, especially if the disturbances appear to be random.

Second, for any equation of the model there is a test of all the restrictions used in the limited information estimation of that equation. The test is applied to the largest characteristic root λ_1 of the equation

(20) $det[W(W^* - W)^{-1} - \lambda I] = 0$

which is used in the estimation process. Here W is the covariance matrix of disturbances to the regressions *of* the H jointly dependent variables in the equation to be estimated *on* the predetermined variables assumed to be known to appear in the entire model; W^* is the covariance matrix of disturbances to the regressions *of* the same H jointly dependent variables in the equation to be estimated *on* the predetermined variables in the equation to be estimated; the roots $\lambda_1 \geq \lambda_2 \geq \cdots \geq \lambda_H$ are scalars; and I is the identity matrix. Anderson and Rubin (1) have shown that under the assumptions of the limited information method, the quantity $T \ log \ (1 + 1/\lambda_1)$ has the χ^2 distribution asymptotically as the sample size T increases, with the number of degrees of freedom equal to the number of overidentifying restrictions, i.e., to the excess of K^{**}, the number of pre-determined variables assumed to be known to enter the model but not the given equation, over $H-1$, where H is the number of jointly dependent variables in the given equation. $1 + 1/\lambda_1$ can never be less than 1, and if it is close to 1 in an overidentified model it means that the effect of exclud-ing the excluded predetermined variables is only slightly detrimental to the variances, i.e., increases them only slightly, which is what we want. This χ^2 test of the largest root λ_1 is a sort of over-all test of the totality of restrictions and assumptions applied in estimating an equation; if in a particular equation, λ_1 takes a value that is very improbable under the hypothesis that all these assumptions are true, then for that equation we have only a very generalized alarm signal which cannot point to a specific remedy. (Of course, if we have a high degree of a priori confidence in some *specific* set of identifying restrictions, this test can be regarded as a test of the remaining, overidentifying, restrictions.) The test is of questionable usefulness for this paper because it is derived on the assumptions of the ordinary limited information method, and this paper uses the abbreviated variant of the limited information method.

Third, for any equation of the model there is a test of the assumption that the disturbances are serially uncorrelated, based on the distribution of the statistic δ^2/S^2. For a given equation and sample period, δ^2 is the mean square successive difference of the disturbances u, given by

$$(21) \qquad \delta^2 = \frac{1}{T-F-1} \sum_{t=2}^{T} (u_t - u_{t-1})^2$$

and S^2 is the variance of the disturbances u over the sample, given by

$$(22) \qquad S^2 = \frac{1}{T-F} \sum_{t=1}^{T} u_t^2$$

where T is the sample size and F is the number of parameters to be esti-mated in the equation. The question of the proper number of degrees of freedom is not solved, so we follow Marshall in using $T-F$ arbitrarily, as if we were dealing with least squares. The distribution of δ^2/S^2 has been tabulated by Hart and von Neumann (8).[44]

b) Tests of success in extrapolation and prediction

First, there is the SETI test, described in Section 6. As stated there, the SETI test tells whether each structural equation describes events in future

[44] Since we never *observe* the disturbances, being forced to calculate their values on the basis of estimates of the structural parameters, there may be some bias in using the tables given by Hart and von Neumann. In fact, Orcutt and Cochrane (18) have found in sampling experiments that there is a high probability of bias against finding serial correlation, especially when the number of parameters to be estimated is large.

periods as well as it does those in the past sample period. A similar test could be applied to the estimates of the equations of the reduced form; it might be called the reduced form tolerance interval test, or the RFTI test for short. The RFTI test is a test of *predictions,* but in case of poor prediction it cannot tell us which structural equations should be changed.[45] The SETI test examines each structural equation separately, and is therefore more useful in this respect.[46]

Second, there are the naive model tests of the predicting ability of the reduced form of the econometric model, mentioned in Section 6. We want the errors of prediction made by the reduced form, i.e., the calculated disturbances to the reduced form equation in the years for which predictions are made, to be at least as small in absolute value as the errors made by the noneconomic naive models.[47] If this condition is not met, we cannot have much confidence in the predicting ability of the econometric model. But observe that even if such a naive model does predict about as well as our econometric model, our model may still be preferable because it may be able to predict consequences of alternative policy measures and of other exogenous changes, while the naive model cannot.

Third, a comparison can be made to see whether the limited information method or the least squares method yields smaller calculated disturbances to the structural equations in the years for which predictions are made.

[45] 'Autonomy' of an equation is the name given to a concept that is useful here. It is not numerically defined, but corresponds to the degree to which the equation is invariant under possible or probable changes in structure. Structural equations are the most autonomous, since each depends on the structural parameters of only one equation, namely itself. Reduced form equations are the least autonomous. The advantage of autonomous equations is obvious for prediction under changes of structure. See Haavelmo (6).

[46] If a structural equation with limited information estimates of its parameters fails to pass the SETI test, we can be reasonably confident that the trouble (apart from sampling variation) lies with the form of *that* equation and not with the other equations of the model, because in estimating that equation no information from the rest of the model was used, except for observations on a list of predetermined variables. This statement could fail to be true only if the rest of the model contained a seriously wrong set of predetermined variables. But observe this caution: even if all the calculated disturbances fell inside their tolerance intervals, we still might not have a good structure; we might instead have a poor structure which, however, is not worse in the prediction period than it was in the sample period (this remark arose in discussions with Harry Markowitz).

[47] To test this, we can make point predictions (as opposed to tolerance interval predictions) with both methods for a number of years, and apply a simple t-test to the hypothesis that the means of the absolute values of their errors are the same, using as an alternative the hypothesis that the mean of the absolute values of the econometric model's errors is larger. As we are likely to have very small samples for this test as well as for the SETI test (Marshall would have had a sample of two, for instance) its results will not be conclusive.

9 PLAN OF COMPUTATIONS

Klein has estimated the equations of his model (Sec. 5) by the least squares and limited information methods; the estimates are given in Klein (13).[48] Certain of these equations have been rejected by Marshall's SETI test on the basis of Klein's limited information estimates and the data for 1946 and 1947; the results are given in Section 6 above. The rejected equations have been revised, replaced, or eliminated (see Sec. 7).

The estimates presented here are for the unrejected Klein equations, and for the new or revised equations of Section 7. They are based in each case on a sample consisting of the years used by Klein for his limited information estimates plus 1946 and 1947,[49] which were added in order to bring the estimates up to date and give the model a fairer chance to do a good job of describing 1948. The war years 1942-45 were omitted because some of the ordinary economic relationships were set aside in favor of direct government controls during that period. Some controls, e.g., rent controls, continued after 1945, however, and some period of readjustment may be required before the postwar economy finds its stride. After a few years, when the sample of postwar years has grown, it may be wise to drop 1946 as well as 1942-45.

All the unrejected and new equations are estimated by least squares, and the estimated standard errors of the disturbances and of the estimates are computed. Then *one* form is chosen from the theoretically acceptable alternative forms of each equation, e.g., one production function from equations 3.0 to 3.6, etc., and estimated by the limited information method.[50]

---

[48] The estimates appearing in Klein (11) have been revised because of the discovery of an error in the time series for X. The revised series is used in Klein (13) and in this paper.

[49] This means that my sample is 1922-41 plus 1946-47 for all equations except 10.0 and 11.0, for which it is 1921-41 plus 1946-47.

See Appendix C for a discussion of certain peculiarities in the time series obtained for 1946 and 1947.

[50] The choice is based partly on theoretical grounds (but not wholly, or else it could be made before any empirical work is done), and partly on the least squares estimates. There is a presumption that if an equation fits well by least squares, i.e., if its residuals and the estimated standard errors of the estimates of parameters are small, there is likely to be a relation among its variables that can be consistently estimated by the limited information method. This is particularly true if the variance of the disturbance to the equation is small; see Jean Bronfenbrenner (2). I realize that this procedure is not satisfactory to the uncompromising advocate of consistency in estimation. Ideally all the alternative forms of each equation should be estimated by the limited information method, but as this is an expensive process the least squares estimates are used as a kind of screening device. How misleading they can be is shown in the cases of equations 1.0 and 4.0, discussed below.

For each equation estimated by the limited information method, estimates are prepared for: the standard error of the disturbance; the covariances of the estimates of the parameters; the successive values of ks_i^* required for the SETI test, where $P = .95$ and $\gamma = .99$; the value of the ratio δ^2/S^2; and the quantities needed for the characteristic root test. The calculated disturbances for 1948 are computed for Klein's limited information estimates, for my least-squares estimates, and for my limited information estimates. The SETI test is applied to the last.

The parameters of the reduced form are estimated by the ordinary least-squares method and by the restricted least-squares method.[51] The naive model tests are applied to both sets of estimates, with the single year 1948 as a sample.

The results of all these computations appear in the next section.

10 RESULTS OF COMPUTATIONS

Table 2 shows the computational results that are applicable directly to structural equations (as opposed to equations of the reduced form): the estimates of parameters and variances, the calculated 1948 disturbances, and the quantities needed for the SETI test, the serial correlation test, and the characteristic root test.

Table 3 presents results pertaining to the equations of the reduced form of the revised model. For each of the endogenous variables,[52] it shows: (1) the observed 1948 value; (2) the change in the observed value from 1947 to 1948; (3) the average absolute value of the annual change in the observed value, over the 24 periods 1920-21 to 1940-41 and 1945-46 to 1947-48; (4) and (5) the two 1948 predictions made by the reduced form of the revised model, as estimated by the ordinary least squares method and by the restricted least squares method, respectively; (6) and (7) the 1948 predictions made by naive models I and II; (8) and (9) the errors of the two reduced form predictions, i.e., the observed values minus the predicted values; (10) and (11) the errors of the naive models; (12) to (15) a comparison of each reduced form error with each naive model error, to see in each case which is smaller in absolute value; (16) the percentage error of the least squares prediction, using the 1948 observed

[51] In this paper each reduced form equation includes only the predetermined variables that appear in the corresponding group of structural equations. See Appendix D for the grouping and Section 4 for remarks about the properties of the estimates.

[52] Endogenous in the sense of the y_i' in section 2. The equations of the reduced form are *linear* regressions on certain predetermined variables. Therefore, the predicted value of a nonlinear function such as w/p cannot be expected to be the same when obtained from the quotient of the predictions of w and p as when obtained directly from a regression. Predictions of such nonlinear functions are not presented here.

Table 2: Results of Computations on Structural Equations of Revised Model[a]

Eq. (1)		Estimates of Parameters and Standard Errors[b]					S (8)	δ^2/S^2 (9)	Obs. value 1948 (10)[e]	Calc. value 1948 (11)[e]	Calc. dist. 1948 (12)[e]	$ks_1^* = kS$ (13)[d]	1948 SETI test result (14)[*]	Pb of getting a smaller λ_t (15)[t]
		$\dfrac{pX-\varepsilon}{q}$ (2)	$\left(\dfrac{pX-\varepsilon}{q}\right)_{-1}$ (3)	K_{-1} (4)	1 (5)	(6)	(7)								
1.0 Investment	I														
KLS	1	.08 (.02)	.07 (.02)	−.12 (.02)	5.24			.42	1.81	1.89	4.82	−2.93			
KLI	1	.12 (.023)	.043 (.023)	−.098 (.023)	2.59 (2.7)			.47	1.59	1.89	5.39	−3.50			
CLS	1	.130 (.04)	−.041 (.03)	−.040 (.05)	.18			1.01		1.89	3.15	−1.26			
CLI	1	1.271 (2.0)	−.846 (1.4)	.52 (.32)	−78.38 (400)			6.62	1.50	1.89	10.26	−8.37	21.72	A	.45
2.0 Inventory	H	$X-\Delta H$	p	H_{-1}	1										
KLS	1	.13 (.02)	4.66 (1.2)	.48 (.08)	1.06			.57	2.17	34.34	36.86	−2.52			
KLI	1	.12 (.02)	4.59 (1.1)	.50 (.07)	1.17 (1.6)			.58	2.26	34.34	36.58	−2.24			
CLS	1	.110 (.02)	1.42 (1.3)	.467 (.11)	6.08			.82		34.34	33.16	1.18			
CLI	1	.082 (.02)	1.93 (1.4)	.539 (.12)	5.22 (1.9)			.87	1.64	34.34	33.15	1.19	2.86	A	.30
3.0[g] Production	X	I	IN	N	IK_{-1}	K_{-1}	t								
CLS	1	19.8 (2.0)	−.40 (.19)	3.966 (.84)	−.06 (.15)	−.146 (.24)	.29 (.31)	3.05		90.26	98.49	−8.23			
3.1 Production	X	I	N	K_{-1}	1	1	t								
CLS	1	.37 (1.38)	2.657 (.66)	−.303 (.17)	.62 (.29)	−19.75		3.33		90.26	98.54	−8.28			

3.2 Production

	X	N	K_{-1}	t	1				
CLS	1	2.820 (.25)	−.296 (.16)	.55 (.14)	−26.50	3.23	90.26	99.02	−8.76
CLS*	1	2.812 (.22)	−.426 (.16)	.63 (.17)	−12.18	2.99	90.26	96.74	−6.48
CLS**	1	2.956 (.19)	−.482 (.16)	.70 (.14)	−11.77	2.90	90.26	95.43	−5.17

3.3 Production − log X

	X	$\log N$	$\log K_{-1}$	t	1				
CLS	1	2.119 (.17)	−.313 (.28)	.003 (.001)	−1.030	.006	1.956	2.025	−.070

3.4 Production X

	X	N	t	K_{-1}	1							
CLS	1	3.074 (.22)	.43 (.13)	−68.13		3.42		90.26	99.16	−8.90		
CLI	1	2.917 (.24)	.48 (.13)	−61.93 (9.4)		3.47	1.52	90.26	98.08	−7.82	11.18	A .08

3.5 Production X

	X	N	NK_{-1}	K_{-1}	t	1				
CLS	1	−.928 (3.7)	.034923 (.035)	−1.706 (1.4)	.63 (.16)	124.83	3.23	90.26	98.84	−8.57

3.6[1] Production X

	X	N	N^2	NK_{-1}	K^2_{-1}	K_{-1}	t				
CLS	1	12.234 (8.5)	−.095663 (.050)	−.015062 (.049)	.042003 (.031)	−8.708 (7.0)	.77 (.17)	3.04	90.26	91.83	−1.57

4.0 Labor

	W_1	$pX - \varepsilon$	$(pX - \varepsilon)_{-1}$	t	1							
KLS	1	.47 (.03)	.12 (.03)	.19 (.04)	4.70	.96	1.27	114.65	107.31	7.34		
KLI	1	.41 (.03)	.17 (.03)	.17 (.04)	5.04 (1.0)	1.00	1.89	114.65	104.67	9.98		
CLS	1	.480 (.04)	.158 (.03)	.20 (.05)	2.08	1.47		114.65	112.63	2.02		
CLI	1	−8.286 (127)	8.949 (128)	3.49 (48)	15.17 (195,000)	76.2	1.36	114.65	24.09	90.56	249.9	A .10

Continued overleaf

Table 2 (cont.)

4.1 Labor

Eq. (1)	N	w/p (2)	X (3)	t (4)	1 (5)	(6)	(7)	S (8)	δ²/S² (9)	Obs. value 1948 (10)	Calc. value 1948 (11)	Calc. dist. 1948 (12)	$ks_1^* = kS$ (13)	1948 SETI test result (14)	Pb of getting a smaller λ_1 (15)
CLS	1	-8.46 (8.5)	.344 (.05)	-.06 (.06)	28.52			1.06		52.07	49.42	2.65			

4.2 Labor

Eq. (1)	N	w/p (2)	X (3)	1 (4)	(5)	(6)	(7)	S (8)	δ²/S² (9)	Obs. value 1948 (10)	Calc. value 1948 (11)	Calc. dist. 1948 (12)	$ks_1^* = kS$ (13)	1948 SETI test result (14)	Pb (15)
CLS	1	-13.81 (6.3)	.364 (.05)	32.09				1.06		52.07	49.93	2.14			
CLI	1	-23.08 (7.9)	.456 (.06)	35.20 (3.9)				1.19	1.09	52.07	51.30	.77	3.83	A	.04

5.0 Wage

Eq. (1)	w	Δp (2)	$N_L - N$ (3)	w_{-1} (4)	$(N_L - N)_{-1}$ (5)	t (6)	1 (7)	S (8)	δ²/S² (9)	Obs. value 1948 (10)	Calc. value 1948 (11)	Calc. dist. 1948 (12)	(13)	(14)	(15)
CLS	1	.54 (.11)	-.022 (.004)	.75 (.08)	.008 (.006)	.007 (.002)	.37	.019		2.20	2.06	.14			

5.1 Wage

Eq. (1)	w	Δp (2)	$N_L - N$ (3)	w_{-1} (4)	t (5)	1 (6)	(7)	S (8)	δ²/S² (9)	Obs. value 1948 (10)	Calc. value 1948 (11)	Calc. dist. 1948 (12)	$ks_1^* = kS$ (13)	1948 SETI test result (14)	Pb (15)
CLS	1	.64 (.08)	-.018 (.002)	.67 (.03)	.01 (.002)	.48		.020		2.20	2.03	.17			
CLI	1	.81 (.13)	-.011 (.004)	.73 (.05)	.005 (.002)	.37 (.07)		.026	1.57	2.20	2.03	.17	.085	A'	.05

6.0 Consumption

Eq. (1)	C	Y (2)	Y_{-1} (3)	$(M/p)_{-1}$ (4)	t (5)	1 (6)	(7)	S (8)	δ²/S² (9)	Obs. value 1948 (10)	Calc. value 1948 (11)	Calc. dist. 1948 (12)	(13)	(14)	(15)
CLS	1	.558 (.08)	.053 (.10)	.270 (.07)	-.24 (.11)	6.70		1.60		82.84	75.76	7.08			

6.1 Consumption

Eq. (1)	C	Y (2)	Y_{-1} (3)	t (4)	1 (5)	(6)	(7)	S (8)	δ²/S² (9)	Obs. value 1948 (10)	Calc. value 1948 (11)	Calc. dist. 1948 (12)	(13)	(14)	(15)
CLS	1	.502 (.10)	.361 (.09)	.08 (.10)	4.67			2.24		82.84	74.46	8.39			

Estimates of Parameters and Standard Errors[b]

6.2 Consumption — dep. var. C

	C	Y	$(M/p)_{-1}$	t	1						R^x
CLS	1	.583 (.06)	.297 (.04)	−.27 (.10)	7.07	1.57		82.84	75.97	6.87	5.22 / .08
CLI	1	.543 (.06)	.315 (.05)	−.27 (.10)	8.56 (2.9)	1.59	.91	82.84	75.96	6.88	

6.3 Consumption — dep. var. C

	C	Y	t	1	Y_t					
KLS	1	.77 (.04)	.76 (.06)	9.70	−.01 (.004)	1.17	1.46	82.84	70.58	12.26
KLI	1	.73 (.04)	.04 (.06)	11.87 (2.5)	.....	1.36	1.20	82.84	70.83	12.01
CLS	1	.811 (.08)	.21 (.13)	7.31	.....	2.88		82.84	75.66	7.18

6.4 Consumption — dep. var. C

	C	Y	C_{-1}	$(M/p)_{-1}$	t	1				
CLS	1	.512 (.06)	.214 (.09)	.208 (.06)	−.21 (.10)	3.80	1.42	82.84	77.52	5.32

6.5 Consumption — dep. var. C

	C	Y	C_{-1}	t	1					
CLS	1	.512 (.07)	.462 (.08)	.03 (.09)	.08	1.39		82.84	79.21	3.63

7.0 Owned housing — dep. var. D_1

	D_1	r/q_1	$\Sigma_{-1}\,^\circ Y$	ΔF	C	t	1							A
KLS	1	3.14 (.52)	.02 (.003)	.0039 (.001)	−7.49			.21	1.80	1.86	4.93	−3.07		
KLI	1	3.74 (.50)	.024 (.003)	.0043 (.001)	−9.03 (1.2)			.21	2.26	1.86	5.07	−3.21		
CLS	1	1.80 (.8)	.0061 (.004)	.0015 (.0005)			−2.65	.36	.80	1.86	1.87	−.02		
CLI	1	1.79 (.9)	.0072 (.004)	.0014 (.0005)			−2.77	.36		1.86	1.83	.03	1.17	.01

Continued overleaf

Table 2 (cont.)

Eq. (1)	Estimates of Parameters and Standard Errors[b] (2)	(3)	(4)	(5)	(6)	(7)	S (8)	δ^2/S^2 (9)	Obs. value 1948 (10)[e]	Calc. value 1948 (11)[e]	Calc. dist. 1948 (12)[e]	$kS_1^* = kS$ (13)[d]	1948 SETI test result (14)[e]	Pb of getting a smaller λ_1 (15)[f]
9.0 Rent Δr	Y	v_{-1}	$1/r_{-1}$	**1**										
KLS	.0013 (.0007)	.020 (.002)	.16 (.04)	-2.13			.03	1.09	.066	.110	-.044			
KLI	.00071 (.0007)	.020 (.002)	.17 (.04)	-2.15 (.20)			.03	1.04	.066	.051	.015			
CLS	-.0003 (.0008)	.018 (.003)	.16 (.06)	-1.81			.033		.066	.059	.007			
CLI	-.0006 (.0008)	.018 (.003)	.17 (.06)	-1.85 (.27)			.033	.96	.066	.055	.011	.109	A	.04
10.0 Rental housing D_2	i	r_{-1}	$(q_1)_{-1}$	$(q_1)_{-2}$	ΔF_{-1}	**1**								
KLS	-.25 (.07)	2.93 (.39)	.16 (.5)	-.44 (.5)	.0013 (.0006)	-1.99	.25	2.16	1.44	2.03	-.59			
KLI	-.18 (.07)	2.81 (.34)	.02 (.5)	-.44 (.5)	.0016 (.0005)	-2.14 (.40)	.26	2.07	1.44	2.01	-.56			
CLS	-.25 (.06)	3.05 (.36)	.04 (.5)	-.53 (.5)	.0011 (.0005)	-1.79	.25		1.44	1.59	-.14			
CLI	-.20 (.07)	2.89 (.38)	.0007 (.5)	-.47 (.5)	.0012 (.0005)	-1.92 (.43)	.25	1.86	1.44	1.63	-.19	.85	A	.40
11.0' Interest Δi	ε_R	i_{-1}	t	**1**										
K	-.17 (.10)	-.37 (.17)	-.005 (.035)	2.00			.47	1.77	.22	.70	-.48			
C	-.092 (.07)	-.34 (.16)	-.03 (.03)	1.69			.46	1.73	.22	.15	.07	1.49	A	'

Notes to Table 2

ᵃ The equations are numbered here just as they are in the text except that equations 1, 2, 4, 7, 9, 10, and 11 in the text appear here as 1.0, 2.0, $\cdots$, 11.0.

The variables in each equation are listed in the same row with the equation number, jointly dependent variables first and predetermined variables next. Each equation has a short title.

The units in which each variable is measured are given in Section 5 except that $\mathcal{E}_R$ is here converted to billions of current dollars, so that all quantities whose dimensions are current or 1934 dollars are measured in billions.

KLS and *KLI* refer to Klein's estimates by the least squares and limited information methods, respectively, based on a sample period ending in 1941, and found in Klein (13). (The sample was 1921-41 for all *KLS* equations except 1.0 and 9.0, and for *KLI* equations 10.0 and 11.0; the sample was 1922-41 for all other *KLI* and *KLS* equations.)

CLS and *CLI* refer to my estimates by the least squares and limited information methods, respectively, based on the *KLI* sample plus 1946 and 1947. (Thus the sample was 1921-41 and 1946-47 for *CLS* and *CLI* equations 10.0 and 11.0, and 1922-41 and 1946-47 for all other *CLS* and *CLI* equations.)

In the interest of not wasting effort in accurate computation of small quantities which will be added to larger and less accurate ones, relatively few significant figures are given for estimates of parameters attached to variables having small numerical values.

ᵇ The numbers in parentheses in columns 1-7 are estimates of the standard errors of the estimates of the parameters. The numbers not in parentheses are the estimates of the parameters. They are arranged in such a way that any equation may be read off directly in the form in which it is given in the text. For example, the *CLI* estimate of the consumption equation 6.2 is seen to be

$$C = .543Y + .315 \ (M/p)_{-1} - .27t + 8.56.$$

ᶜ Column 10 gives the observed 1948 value of the variable appearing on the left side of each equation, i.e., the variable in column 1 of the table. Column 11 gives the value of the linear combination on the right side of each equation. Column 12 is column 10 minus column 11, the calculated disturbance. If this is positive, the equation has underestimated the variable on its left side. Column 10 minus 11 may not equal column 12 exactly because of rounding.

ᵈ The values of k for $\gamma = 0.99$ and $P = 0.95$, from Eisenhart, Hastay, and Wallis (3), p. 102, are as follows:

d.f.	k	d.f.	k	d.f.	k
15	3.507	18	3.279	21	3.121
16	3.421	19	3.221	22	3.078
17	3.345	20	3.168	23	3.040

ᵉ A = accept; R = reject (*CLI* equations only).

ᶠ Column 15 gives the approximate probability of obtaining a value of λ_1 smaller than was in fact obtained. A low probability indicates that our confidence in the *a priori* restrictions imposed must be low. See Table 4 for more details.

ᵍ The constant term in the *CLS* estimate of equation 3.0 is -84.76.

ʰ *CLS** and *CLS*** under equation 3.2 refer to some special exploratory computations based on different series for K_{-1}. They are discussed in the text below.

^{i} The constant term in the *CLS* estimate of equation 3.6 is 233.45.

^{j} The value of ks^* for equation 5.1 is .181, which is larger than .17, the calculated disturbance. Hence the verdict is acceptance.

^{k} The value of ks^* for equation 6.2 is 6.39, which is smaller than 6.88, the calculated disturbance. Hence the verdict is rejection.

^{l} The *LS* and *LI* estimates of equation 11.0 are identical since it has only one dependent variable. No value of λ_1 is available for this equation.

value as a base; (17) the least-squares predicted change from 1947 to 1948; (18) a notation as to whether this predicted change was in the right direction.

11 DISCUSSION OF RESULTS OF COMPUTATIONS[53]

We shall look first at the results of (a) the SETI test and (b) the naive model tests. Also we shall (c) compare the 1948 calculated disturbances obtained from different estimates of each structural equation. Then we shall go back and look at the results of the tests of internal consistency described in the first part of Section 8: (d) the serial correlation test; (e) the characteristic root test; and (f) the qualitative examination of the estimates, in particular those for equations 1.0 and 4.0, where anomalous results appear.

a) There are ten stochastic equations in our revised econometric model, namely those estimated by the limited information method with a sample including 1946-47: the CLI equations 1.0, 2.0, 3.4, 4.0 or 4.2, 5.1, 6.2, 7.0, 9.0, 10.0, and 11.0. All are accepted for 1948 by the SETI test with $P = 0.95$ and $\gamma = 0.99$, except for the consumption function 6.2. If P and γ are both relaxed to 0.95, only one additional equation, the wage adjustment equation 5.1, is rejected by the SETI test. Even if P and γ are both relaxed to 0.75, all equations except 3.4, 5.1, and 6.2 are accepted by the SETI test with room to spare.[54] This means that nearly every equation fits 1948 as well as could be expected on the basis of its performance during the sample period.

b) For 1948, each of the two naive models predicts 7 out of 13 endogenous variables better, i.e., has smaller errors, than do the equations of the reduced form as estimated by the ordinary least squares method. Naive model I predicts better in 15 cases out of 21 than the reduced form as estimated by the restricted least-squares method, and naive model II pre-

[53] The results of all the computations in this paper of course depend upon the time series used for the variables for 1946 and 1947. See Appendix C for a discussion of certain peculiarities in those time series.

[54] To verify this, compare Table 2, columns 8 and 12, and Eisenhart, Hastay, and Wallis (3), p. 102.

Table 3

Results of Naive Model Tests

Variable[a]	Eq.	Obs. Value 1948 (1)	Change in Obs. Value 1947-48 (2)	Average Absolute Change in Obs. Value[b] (3)	Predictions 1948 — Reduced Form[c] LS (4)	RLS (5)	Naive Models I (6)	II (7)	Errors 1948[d] — Reduced Form[c] LS (8)	RLS (9)	Naive Models I (10)	II (11)	Verdicts[e] LS I (12)	LS II (13)	RLS[c] I (14)	RLS II (15)	Pre-diction Error as % of (1) (16)	Pre-dicted Change 1947-48 (17)	Pre-diction of Direction of Change (18)
Investment I	1.0	1.89	-.38	1.02	1.00	.98	2.27	3.22	.89	.91	-.38	-1.33	N	RF	N	RF	47	-1.27	right
Inventories H	2.0	34.3	3.04	1.25	27.4	34.4	31.3	31.6	6.9	-.1	3.0	2.7	N	N	RF	RF	20	-3.9	wrong
Price level p	2.0 / 5.1	2.03	.15	.07	2.17	2.24 / 2.17	1.88	2.19	-.14	-.21 / -.14	.15	-.16	RF	RF	N / N	N / RF	-7	.29	right
Private output X	3.4 / 4.2	90.3	2.96	5.03	72.5	96.7 / 79.5	87.3	79.3	17.8	-6.4 / 10.8	3.0	11.0	N	N	N / RF	RF / RF	20	-14.8	wrong
Private employment N	3.4 / 4.2 / 5.1	52.1	1.05	1.81	48.7	51.6 / 49.4 / 45.9	51.0	53.5	3.4	.5 / 2.7 / 6.2	1.1	-1.4	N	N	RF / N / N	RF / N / N	7	-2.3	wrong
Private wage bill W_1	4.0	114.7	9.93	4.93	107.6	110.1	104.7	117.9	7.1	4.6	10.0	-3.2	RF	RF	RF	N	6	2.9	right
Private wage rate w	5.1	2.20	.15	.07	2.10	2.08	2.05	2.22	.10	.12	.15	-.02	RF	RF	RF	N	5	.05	right
Consumption C	6.2	82.8	1.13	2.86	80.2	67.8	81.7	76.9	2.6	15.0	1.1	5.9	N	N	N	N	3	-1.5	wrong
Disposable income Y	6.2 / 7.0 / 9.0	79.9	1.74	4.15	70.9	65.0 / 78.4 / 70.9	78.2	66.4	9.0	14.9 / 1.5 / 9.0	1.7	13.5	N	RF	N / RF / RF	N / RF / RF	11	-7.3	wrong
Owned housing D_1	7.0	1.86	.23	.23	2.04	1.62	1.63	1.92	-.18	.24	.23	-.06	RF	RF	N	N	-10	.41	right
Rent level r	7.0 / 9.0	1.24	.07	.05	1.25	.81 / .84	1.18	1.21	-.01	.43 / .40	.06	.03	RF	RF	N / N	N / N	-1	.07	right
Rental housing D_2	10.0	1.44	.28	.22	1.49	1.73	1.16	1.38	-.05	-.29	.28	.06	RF	RF	RF	N	-3	.33	right
Interest rate i	10.0 / 11.0	3.08	.22	.38	2.73	2.59 / 2.73	2.86	2.98	.35	.49 / .35	.22	.10	N	N	N / N	N / N	11	-.13	wrong
													7/13	7/13	15/21	13/21			

Fraction of cases in which naive model error is less than reduced form error

[a] Only the endogenous variables in the sense of the y_t' in Section 1 appear in this table. Each reduced form prediction is obtained from a reduced form equation containing all the predetermined variables in the group to which the predicted variable belongs. See Appendix D for the grouping.

[b] Average of the 24 periods 1920-21 to 1940-41 and 1945-46 to 1947-48.

[c] *LS* means least-squares estimates; *RLS* means restricted least-squares estimates.

[d] Error equals observed value minus predicted value. A positive error means underestimation.

[e] *RF* means that the reduced form's error is smaller than the naive model's error; *N* means the reverse.

dicts better in 13 cases out of 21 than the reduced form as estimated by the restricted least-squares method.[55]

These results do not permit us to say that there is any significant difference between the predicting abilities of the ordinary least squares estimates of the equations of the reduced form on the one hand and the naive models on the other. They suggest that, at least in the absence of structural change, predictions by the restricted least-squares estimates of the reduced form are inferior, both to predictions by the ordinary least-squares estimates of the reduced form and to those made by the naive models. The econometric model used here has failed, at least in our sample consisting of the one year 1948, to be a better predicting device than the incomparably cheaper naive models, even though almost every structural equation performs as well, i.e., has just as small an error, in extrapolation to 1948 as it does in the sample period.

It might be noted that the variables that are predicted better for 1948 by naive model *I* than by the reduced form (as estimated by either of the two ways) are almost exactly the same as those for which the change from 1947 to 1948 was less than the average (absolute value) of the annual changes over the sample period (see Table 3, col. 2, 3, 12, and 14). In other words, roughly speaking, naive model I predicted better the variables that changed *less* than usual, and the econometric model through its reduced form predicted better the variables that changed *more* than usual. This is not surprising, because naive model *I* assumes no change, and so of course will do well when there are only small changes, and poorly when there are large changes. On the other hand, the variables that are predicted better for 1948 by naive model *II* than by the reduced form include some for which the 1947-48 change was greater than average and some for which it was less (see Table 3, col. 2, 3, 13, and 15). But the variables whose *predicted* 1947-48 changes (based on the reduced form) were greater than average are not uniformly better predicted by the reduced form than by either naive model (see Table 3, col. 2, 12, 13, and 17). We conclude that it is not possible to tell in advance which variables are likely to be predicted better by the reduced form and which by a naive model.

However, an econometric model may be preferable, even though a naive model predicts equally well, because an econometric model may be able to predict the effects of alternative policy measures or other exogenous changes (including changes in structure if they are known about beforehand), while the naive model can only say that there will be no effect. Unfortunately we do not know how to tell rigorously in advance whether

[55] Incidentally, neither naive model is shown to be superior to the other; naive model II predicts better than naive model I in 7 out of 13 cases.

this will be true in a particular case, but it appears likely to be true when large or irregular changes occur in the exogenous variables, because it is then that the naive models are at their greatest disadvantage.

c) Table 2 shows that for every structural equation whose *KLI* and *CLS* estimates were both computed, the *CLS* estimates yield the smaller calculated disturbance. This suggests that for small samples a short extrapolation of least-squares estimates (i.e., from 1947 to 1948) may be more reliable than a prolonged extrapolation of limited information estimates (i.e., from 1941 to 1948). Table 2 shows also that for the eleven equations whose *CLI* and *CLS* estimates were both computed, the *CLS* estimates yield appreciably smaller calculated disturbances in four cases, the *CLI* yield smaller ones in two cases, and there is approximately a tie in five cases.[56] This suggests that short extrapolations based on least-squares estimates may be more reliable for samples as small as 22 than those based on limited information estimates.

We have here two comparisons of ordinary least-squares estimates with others known to be asymptotically superior (three if we recall that the ordinary least-squares estimates of the reduced form equations yield better predictions for 1948 than do the restricted least-squares estimates). In these comparisons the results suggest that in our problem the least-squares estimates lead to smaller errors in extrapolation. Now this is not surprising if there is no change in the underlying mechanism generating the observations, i.e., no change in structure. The argument is as follows: The least-squares method yields an estimate of the expected value of the conditional probability distribution of one variable, the one chosen to be "dependent", given the others. This distribution remains fixed as long as there is no change in structure. Therefore the least-squares estimates, which by construction produce the smallest possible calculated root-mean-square residual over the sample period, will continue to produce small residuals in extrapolation to subsequent periods as long as there is no change in structure.[57] But if the structure changes after the sample period and before the prediction period, the conditional probability distribution of the chosen dependent variable, given the others, will change in a complicated way, depending on the old and new structures. Then the least-squares estimates will no longer yield small errors in extrapolation, because they are estimates of the expected value of a distribution that is no longer relevant.

[56] The cases are, respectively: 1.0, 4.0, 9.0, 10.0; 3.4, 4.2; 2.0, 5.1, 6.2, 7.0, 11.0. Equation 11.0 *must* produce a tie because the *CLS* and *CLI* estimates are identical.

[57] The size of the error in extrapolation by any method will increase with the length of the extrapolation. For the case of least squares this is described by the Hotelling (9) formula for the standard error of forecast.

This is why it is desirable to estimate structural relations as well as simple regressions.

d) The limited information estimates presented here, as indicated in Section 1, are computed on the assumption that disturbances to the structural equations are not serially correlated.[58] For a sample of 22, if there is no serial correlation, the probability is 0.95 that the value of δ^2/S^2 will lie between approximately 1.26 and 2.93.[59] For the *CLI* estimates of equations 4.2, 6.2, 7.0, and 9.0, δ^2/S^2 is less than 1.26, indicating positive serial correlation of their disturbances.[60] Klein's limited information estimates give evidence of positive serial correlation of the disturbances to equations 6.3 and 9.0. There is no obvious relation between the performance of an equation in the SETI test and the serial correlation of its disturbances; no attempt has been made here to assess the error incurred by assuming zero serial correlation of disturbances.

Table 4

CHARACTERISTIC ROOT TEST RESULTS

Eq.	K^{**}[a]	$H-1$[a]	λ_1	T	$T\log$ $(1+1/\lambda_1)$	$K^{**}-H+1$ $=d.f.$[a]	Pb of getting a smaller λ_1
	(1)	(2)	(3)	(4)	(5)	(6)	(7)
1.0	6	1	1.662	22	4.50	5	.45
2.0	7	2	1.160	22	5.94	5	.30
3.4	7	1	.450	22	11.18	6	.08
4.0	6	1	.605	22	9.32	5	.10
4.2	8	2	.345	22	13.00	6	.04
5.1	6	2	.587	22	9.50	4	.05
6.2	4	1	1.012	22	6.57	3	.08
7.0	5	2	.109	22	22.14	3	.01
9.0	4	1	.686	22	8.60	3	.04
10.0	2	1	12.96	23	.71	1	.40

[a] K^{**} is the number of predetermined variables that are assumed to be known to be in the model but not in the equation to be estimated; H is the number of jointly dependent variables in the equation to be estimated; and $K^{**}-H+1$ is the number of overidentifying restrictions, i.e., the number of degrees of freedom of $T\log(1+1/\lambda_1)$; see Section 8.

e) Table 4, an expanded version of column 15 in Table 2, gives the results of the characteristic root test as applied to each equation of the revised model. At the 95 per cent significance level four equations are

[58] Chernoff and Rubin have developed a consistent method of estimation, as yet unpublished, that does not require this assumption, but no computations have as yet been made with it.

[59] δ^2/S^2 is defined in Section 8, and its distribution is tabulated in Hart and von Neumann (8), p. 213. See also note 44 above.

[60] At the 90 per cent significance level the interval containing δ^2/S^2 is smaller, but no additional equations show serial correlation.

rejected by the characteristic root test: 4.2, 5.1, 7.0, and 9.0. Furthermore, at the 90 per cent significance level three other equations are rejected as well: 3.4, 4.0, and 6.2. Again, there is no obvious relation between the performance of an equation on this test and its performance on the SETI test, but this test rejects all equations rejected by the test of δ^2/S^2.

f) In the following discussion of the estimates presented in Table 2 we use abbreviated designations, such as "KLS 1.0" for "the Klein least squares estimates of equation 1.0."

In the demand for investment equation, CLS 1.0, the estimate of the coefficient of $\left(\dfrac{pX - \mathcal{E}}{q}\right)_{-1}$, which is closely related to lagged profits, has become negative, though not significantly. This may be due to sampling variation, or it may mean that entrepreneurs invest partly in response to *increases* in profits rather than only in response to high present and past profits. Thus, by means of the identity $\Delta x = x - x_{-1}$, CLS (1.0) can be equivalently written as

$$(1.0') \qquad I = .089 \left(\frac{pX - \mathcal{E}}{q}\right) + .041\Delta \left(\frac{pX - \mathcal{E}}{q}\right) - .040K_{-1} + .18.$$

In CLS 3.0, 3.1, 3.2, and 3.3, i.e., in all the CLS production functions containing K_{-1} but no cross-product term in NK_{-1}, the marginal product of capital emerges as negative, though not significantly. At first this seemed to be due to the *fall* in K_{-1} from 110.1 in 1941 to 98.8 in 1946, coupled with the tremendous rise in X; it did not seem reasonable that the stock of productive capital in private hands had decreased 10 per cent during the war. But CLS* 3.2 and CLS** 3.2, each based on an upward-revised postwar series for K_{-1},[61] yield even more strongly negative estimates of the marginal product of capital than CLS 3.2.[62] An examination of the

[61] The values of K_{-1} used in CLS, CLS* and CLS** 3.2 are, respectively,

	K_{-1}	$K_{-1}{}^*$	$K_{-1}{}^{**}$
1946	98.787	102.600	111.400
1947	101.098	108.168	116.968

$K_{-1}{}^*$ is like K_{-1} except that additions are made to correct understatements during the war years due to the amortization of war plants in five years or less, allowed under the wartime revenue acts; the transfer of surplus producer goods from government to private hands; and (less defensible) the fact that the joint SEC-Department of Commerce series for plant and equipment expenditures, used in defining K, is smaller beginning in 1941 than the Department of Commerce series that appears in the national income accounts (the two series are almost identical before 1941). $K_{-1}{}^{**}$ is like $K_{-1}{}^*$ except that it assumes that the 1946 value is 111.4, as assumed in Klein (11), p. 135.

[62] CLS* 3.2 and CLS** 3.2 have smaller calculated disturbances in 1948 than CLS 3.2 or CLS 3.4 or CLI 3.4, despite their negative marginal products of capital, because all the production functions have negative disturbances which are made smaller in magnitude by the presence of a larger negative term in stock of capital.

time series for X and K_{-1} shows that for about half of the sample period
the two variables move in opposite directions; consequently, given the
time series the result is not unreasonable. The conclusion to be drawn is
either that the K_{-1} series does not measure stock of capital, as it is meant
to, or that the stock of capital sometimes does not limit output. A less
aggregative theory might be helpful in solving the problem. Equation 3.4
is the immediate solution chosen here.[63]

In *CLS* 3.0 the estimated coefficient of IK_{-1} is nearly zero when it is
expected to be positive. But this is not a new cause for alarm, given the
fact that the coefficient of K_{-1} is negative.

CLS 3.0 has one additional independent variable besides those in *CLS*
3.2, yet its disturbance has a larger estimated standard error, S. The same
is true of *CLS* 6.0 and *CLS* 6.2, respectively, and of *CLS* 6.4 and *CLS* 6.5,
respectively. This seems odd because when a new independent variable
is added to a regression, it cannot increase the sum of squares of residuals.
The answer lies in the fact that the reduction in the number of degrees of
freedom caused by the introduction of the new variable more than uses up
the reduction in the sum of squares brought about by the same cause. In
such a case the additional variable is not worth its extra cost in degrees
of freedom, except in larger samples where the cost is negligible.

The time trend term in the demand for labor equation *CLS* 4.1 has a
very small coefficient not significantly different from zero, and therefore
might reasonably be omitted. But the coefficient of w/p in *CLS* 4.1 and
CLS 4.2 is very sensitive to the presence or absence of the trend term. As
it too has a coefficient not significantly different from zero, however, its
sensitivity might be attributed to sampling variation. It is apparent that in
both 4.1 and 4.2 the chief relationship being estimated is that between X
and N, namely the backbone of the production function. Indeed 3.4 is
almost identical with either 4.1 or 4.2, numerical estimates and all — the
term in w/p contributes relatively little to 4.1 or 4.2. It may be noted that
4.1 is not identified if 3.4 is in the model at the same time. Since 3.4 is the
most satisfactory of our production functions, except for 3.5 and 3.6,
which were tried later, we want to keep it, and so we replace 4.1 by 4.0 or
4.2.[64] Since all other equations meet the necessary condition (order con-

---

[63] The nonlinear equations 3.5 and 3.6, theoretically preferable to 3.2 and 3.4 because of having non-constant marginal productivities, were not estimated by the
limited information method because of lack of time. Their least-squares estimates,
particularly for 3.6, yield smaller calculated residuals for 1948 than any of the
other production equations, however.

[64] This decision to drop 4.1 from the model is open to criticism because it is made
in order to satisfy the necessary conditions for the identification of all equations, and
not on theoretical or empirical grounds.

dition) for identifiability with room to spare, the probability is high that they meet the necessary and sufficient (rank) condition as well (see Sec. 1).

The consumption functions *CLS* 6.0, *CLS* 6.2, *CLI* 6.2, and *CLS* 6.4 show significantly positive coefficients for real cash balances $(M/p)_{-1}$. The addition of this term alone is enough to reduce the calculated disturbance in 1948 almost half — see *CLI* 6.2 — as compared with that of equation 6.3 which does not contain $(M/p)_{-1}$. But apparently the introduction of $(M/p)_{-1}$ is not sufficient to correct the consumption function, for *CLI* 6.2 is rejected by the SETI test. Another indication that $(M/p)_{-1}$ is not sufficient is that consumption has not fallen relative to disposable income since 1944, but $(M/p)_{-1}$ has been falling since 1946. Thus a term in $(M/p)_{-1}$ can explain the high postwar *average* level of consumption relative to income as compared with prewar, but it cannot explain the fact that consumption has remained high in 1947 and 1948, even exceeding disposable income, while $(M/p)_{-1}$ has been declining. It is evident that some other variable in addition to or in place of $(M/p)_{-1}$ is needed.

As can be seen from an examination of *CLS* 6.4 and *CLS* 6.5, lagged consumption expenditure C_{-1} appears to help matters, and more so when used *instead of* $(M/p)_{-1}$ than when used *in addition to* it.[65] *CLS* 6.5 has a smaller estimated standard error *S* and a smaller calculated 1948 disturbance than any of the other consumption equations estimated from the sample that includes 1946 and 1947.[66]

The estimated coefficients of disposable income *Y* in the rent adjustment equation *CLS* 9.0 and *CLI* 9.0 are negative. The explanation may lie in sampling variation, since the standard errors are of the same order of magnitude as the estimates. However, the controlled rise in postwar rents and the fall of *Y* from 1946 to 1947 may be responsible (see App. C).

The estimated coefficients of twice lagged construction costs $(q_1)_{-2}$ are negative in all four estimates of the demand for the construction of rental housing, equation 10.0. As their standard errors are about as large as the estimates, this need not be taken seriously. However, some response to expected costs, based on the past behavior of costs, may be indicated.

The *CLI* estimates of equations 1.0 and 4.0, as we have seen, are far out of line with our expectations. Unlike the *CLI* estimates of the other equations, they do not remotely resemble the *CLS, KLS,* and *KLI* estimates. Their calculated disturbances are often of the same order of magnitude as

---

[65] This is because the addition of $(M/p)_{-1}$ to 6.5 costs more in degrees of freedom than it is worth in reducing the sum of squares of residuals, as discussed in the third paragraph above.

[66] Limited information estimates were not computed for equations 6.4 and 6.5 because of lack of time; these equations were not considered until all the other computations were finished and the inadequacy of 6.2 became obvious.

the variables they contain, but they do not show clear signs of serial correlation.

One obvious possibility must be rejected immediately, namely that for each of these two equations the 1946 and 1947 observations may be nowhere near the line fitted to the 1922-41 sample, so that the line is radically changed by the addition of the 1946 and 1947 points. If this were true, the least squares estimates would be radically changed and the estimated standard error of disturbances greatly increased; but neither happens. Equations 1.0 and 4.0 are clearly cases where there is an approximately linear *empirical* relation among the variables (as evidenced by the least squares fits) but where the limited information method yields a straight line very different in slopes and intercepts from this empirical relation.

Sampling variation cannot be excluded as a possible explanation, especially since the estimated standard errors are so large that the *CLI* estimates do not differ *significantly,* i.e., by more than two or three times their respective standard errors, from the other estimates. Furthermore, nothing in the derivation of the limited information method requires it to yield small residuals and estimates close to the least-squares estimates, even though it has usually done so in the past.

There are two differences between the two procedures used in obtaining the *KLI* and the *CLI* estimates of equations 1.0 and 4.0. One is, obviously, that 1946 and 1947 are in the *CLI* sample but not in the *KLI* sample. The other is that the list of predetermined variables z^{**} (explained in App. D) for the *CLI* estimates differs from the list for the *KLI* estimates in that the variables X_{-1} and H_{-2} are omitted and the variables w_{-1} and $(N_L - N)_{-1}$ added. In other words, certain of the reduced form equations in the *CLI* case are regressions on a set of predetermined variables which differs from the corresponding set in the *KLI* case by containing w_{-1} and $(N_L - N)_{-1}$ instead of X_{-1} and H_{-2}, and accordingly the estimates of the parameters of equations 1.0 and 4.0 depend upon observations of a slightly different set of predetermined variables.

To separate the effects of these two changes, equation 4.0 was estimated four times: (1) (*KLI*) with the *Klein* z^{***}'s and *without* 1946-47; (2) with *my* z^{***}'s and *without* 1946-47; (3) with the *Klein* z^{***}'s and *with* 1946-47; (4) (*CLI*) with *my* z^{***}'s and *with* 1946-47. The results indicate that the anomalous *CLI* estimates of equation 4.0 are not due to the change in the list of predetermined variables z^{**}, but are somehow due instead to the addition of 1946 and 1947 to the sample.[67]

[67] (1)   (*KLI*) $W_1 =$ .41 $(pX - \mathcal{E})$ + .17 $(pX - \mathcal{E})_{-1}$ + .17t + 5.04
  (2) $W_1 =$ .413 $(pX - \mathcal{E})$ + .175 $(pX - \mathcal{E})_{-1}$ + .17t + 5.05
  (3) $W_1 =$ 8.17 $(pX - \mathcal{E})$ − 7.56 $(pX - \mathcal{E})_{-1}$ − 2.68t − 9.42

12 SUMMARY AND CONCLUSION

The revised version of Klein's model, consisting of equations 1.0, 2.0, 3.4, 4.0 or 4.2, 5.1, 6.2, 7.0, 9.0, 10.0, 11.0, and the identities 12, 13, 14, and 18, has been subjected to several tests.[68] Table 5 summarizes the results of tests pertaining to the structural equations. Table 3 presents the results of the naive model tests, which pertain to the equations of the reduced form.

Table 5

SUMMARY OF RESULTS OF STRUCTURAL EQUATION TESTS

Equation	SETI Test[a] $P=.95$ $\gamma=.99$	$P=.75$ $\gamma=.75$	Smaller Calc. Dist. in 1948	Serial Correlation Test[a] 95% level	90% level	Characteristic Root Test[a] 95% level	90% level
1.0 Investment			CLS				
2.0 Inventory			neither				
3.4 Production		R	CLI				R
4.0 Labor			CLS				R
4.2 Labor			CLI	R	R	R	R
5.1 Wage		R	neither			R	R
6.2 Consumption	R	R	neither	R	R		R
7.0 Owned housing			neither	R	R	R	R
9.0 Rent			CLS	R	R	R	R
10.0 Rental housing			CLS				
11.0 Interest			neither				

Source: Tables 2 and 4, and Section 11, parts (a) and (d).
[a] R means reject; a blank space means accept.

With the exception of the consumption function 6.2,[69] all the equations estimated by the limited information method fit the post-sample year 1948 just as well as they fit the data of the sample period. This is shown by the SETI test.

The predictions for 1948 made by the equations of the reduced form are, on the average over all equations, no better (measured by whether their errors are smaller in absolute value) than predictions made by naive models which simply extrapolate either the value of each variable from the preceding year or the trend between the two preceding years (Table 3).[70]

Note 67 concluded:
(4) (CLI) $W_1 = -8.29$ $(pX - \mathcal{E}) + 8.95$ $(pX - \mathcal{E})_{-1} + 3.49t + 15.17$
Note the similarity between 1 and 2 and (except for sign) between 3 and 4. (This sign difference is not an error in computation; it is due to a change in sign of a determinant entering the estimate of the parameter on which the estimates are normalized.)

[68] The equations are given in Sections 5 and 7, and more compactly in Table 2.

[69] And, if P and γ are both relaxed to 0.75, the production function 3.4 and the wage adjustment equation 5.1.

[70] In fact they are worse if the restricted least squares method is used instead of the ordinary least squares method.

However, the reduced form predictions are quite consistently better than the predictions of naive model I for variables that changed more than usual in 1948. Further, the equations of the reduced form may be preferable to naive models for predicting effects of exogenous changes even when both methods make equally large errors in the ordinary prediction of the magnitudes of economic variables, especially when the exogenous changes are unusually large.

The least squares method yields on the average smaller calculated disturbances for 1948 than do our asymptotically superior methods, for both structural and reduced form equations.[71] This is seen by a simple pairwise comparison of calculated disturbances in Tables 2 and 3.

Four equations, as estimated by the limited information method, are rejected by the two-sided test for serial correlation of disturbances, at either the 95 or the 90 per cent level of significance.

Four equations are rejected at the 95 per cent significance level by the characteristic root test of the totality of *a priori* restrictions imposed on a given equation, and seven at the 90 per cent significance level.

Several avenues of future work suggest themselves on the basis of the experience of this paper.

1) Better use could be made of existing economic theory. That is, equations to be estimated should be consistent with the known properties of the equations of micro-economics. Also, a better theory of economic expectations and of behavior under uncertainty would be useful.

2) Studies of narrower sectors of the economy would probably be fruitful, because it is desirable whenever possible to refine our approximations by using variables and equations that apply to more homogeneous groups of firms or individuals. Furthermore, there are several industries and economic sectors for which data, as well as facts pertaining to the technical and institutional environment, are much more plentiful than for the economy as a whole.

3) Cross-section data, i.e., data pertaining to different parts of the economy as of a given point in time such as are obtained in surveys, are becoming increasingly available. It will be possible to combine time series and cross section studies to advantage.

4) One misfortune of the econometrician is that exogenous variables do not vary enough to give him a good idea of their respective influences. The war years are very valuable in this regard, because exogenous changes are ordinarily much larger than in peacetime. Therefore they might be included

---

[71] This is something to be expected if there are no important changes of structure, and is not contrary to the claims made for limited information estimation; see Section 11, part (c).

in the sample, of course together with appropriate changes in certain parts of the model to allow it to accommodate the wartime government policies.

5) The use of quarterly data would multiply the effective sample size by approximately four,[72] thus producing more accurate estimates, provided the problem of serial correlation can be solved (see next item).

6) The development of practical methods of estimation that do not require the assumption of zero serial correlation of disturbances would be useful. As already mentioned, Chernoff and Rubin have worked on this problem but as yet no attempt has been made to use their results.

7) Mathematical (or experimental)[73] studies to determine the size of the small-sample bias in the estimation of structural parameters by the least-squares method and by the various maximum likelihood methods would be very helpful in deciding which procedure to use.

8) Studies might be made of the effect of estimating the parameters of a model by using data generated by a structure not belonging to the given model, i.e., the effect of estimating from the wrong model. This is a general problem which includes the case of estimating by the least squares method when to do so is not theoretically justified. If a "slightly incorrect" model always or often leads to absurd results, the type of econometrics presented in this paper will suffer a severe setback, because we know from the start that our models are at least slightly incorrect.

9) It would be interesting, though expensive, to estimate the parameters of a fairly large system of equations by the full information maximum likelihood method and analyze the results. But this would not be likely to be immediately useful in getting better estimates unless the sample size were much larger than 22.

Appendix A

TIME SERIES

Until 1942 all time series are as given in Klein (11), pp. 141-3, except that those marked with an asterisk below have been revised as indicated

---

[72] The effective sample size would be multiplied by *exactly* 4, except for several small points: the fact that one degree of freedom goes into the estimation of each parameter; the possibility of adding four new parameters in order to allow for seasonal changes (this is done by introducing four new exogenous variables x_1, x_2, x_3, x_4, such that in the ith quarter all are 0 except x_i which is 1, and estimating the parameter of each); etc.

[73] Orcutt and Cochrane (18, 19) have used sampling experiments of a type that might be widely applied in getting information of any desired degree of statistical reliability about certain problems that seem to be secure against direct mathematical attack.

in Appendix B, and the X series presented here reflects the correction of a computational error, which has been corrected in Klein (13) also.

	C	I	q	ΔH	D_1	q_1	D_2	D_3	D''
1941						1.348*			
1942		−1.748	1.303	−.379	.870	1.497	.831	.174	1.977
1943		−3.648	1.331	−.436	.514	1.565	.611	.183	1.965
1944	76.833	−3.950	1.351	−1.224	.473	1.621	.539	.143	1.947
1945	80.451	−3.267	1.398	−.425	.462	1.683	.429	.118	1.926
1946	86.517	1.311	1.619	4.020	1.334	2.000	.941	.182	1.926
1947	81.708	2.266	1.964	.345	1.629	2.671	1.162	.172	1.943
1948	82.840	1.889	2.160	3.041	1.858	3.039	1.443	.173	1.969

	G	$Y+T$	Y	p	W_2	W_1	R_1	R_2	r
1939					8.116*	39.959*			
1940					8.348*	43.940*			
1941					9.436*	55.053*			
1942					14.458				
1943					23.224				1.144
1944	70.902	141.769	99.705	1.333	28.211	87.834	10.613	.820	1.146
1945	59.604	135.446	96.286	1.369	29.595	84.908	11.002	.889	1.147
1946	22.835	115.214	89.930	1.561	18.257	91.550	11.790	.978	1.150
1947	17.946	103.285	78.186	1.876	16.008	104.718	12.868	1.105	1.178
1948	17.273	106.548	79.928	2.025	17.529	114.650	14.287	1.162	1.244

	ΔF	v	N'	i	ε_R	K	ε	X	H
1943				3.16					
1944				3.05				112.299	27.361
1945	571	100.0	31.3	2.87		98.787	7.9	105.142	26.936
1946	1088	100.0	31.8	2.74	976	101.098	9.4	95.339	30.956
1947	1381	100.0	32.7	2.86	853	103.364	10.0	87.304	31.301
1948	1582	100.0	33.6	3.08	888	105.253	10.6	90.263	34.342

	M	N	N_L	w	X
1920	38.464	38.335	38.609	1.080	40.3
1921	38.1005	34.737	39.259	.921	38.8
1922	40.6235	36.335	39.950	.938	42.8
1923	43.249	39.035	40.815	1.040	49.3
1924	46.826	38.744	41.592	1.035	48.5
1925	49.981	39.379	42.044	1.056	52.5
1926	50.876	40.748	43.072	1.087	55.6
1927	53.802	40.792	44.103	1.086	55.8
1928	55.355	40.969	45.128	1.118	56.0
1929	54.555	42.489	46.247	1.132	58.1
1930	53.248	40.397	46.757	1.067	52.3
1931	47.861	37.214	47.313	.951	44.1
1932	44.854	33.816	47.967	.787	35.1
1933	41.532	33.770	48.627	.728	36.7
1934	46.270	36.177	49.127	.788	42.2
1935	51.273	37.162	49.583	.840	47.1
1936	56.360	39.142	49.961	.902	55.3
1937	55.815	41.026	50.433	.999	57.5
1938	58.066	38.657	50.908	.957	52.6
1939	63.253	40.014	51.437	.999	61.0
1940	70.008	41.851	51.722	1.050	66.9
1941	76.336	45.369	51.653	1.213	79.8
1942		47.678	51.427		
1943		48.149	49.821		
1944	130.225	47.111	48.900	1.864	112.299
1945	150.793	45.662	48.181	1.859	105.142
1946	164.004	48.533	52.145	1.886	95.339
1947	170.010	51.019	54.937	2.053	87.304
1948	168.700	52.066	56.021	2.202	90.263

Appendix B

SOURCES OF DATA AND CONSTRUCTION OF TIME SERIES

Construction of time series for 1942 and later, and for the few of Klein's figures for years before 1942 that were revised, is indicated below. My time series are intended to be as consistent as possible with Klein's, since they are extensions of Klein's. The variables denoted by numbers in parentheses correspond to those in the appendices to Klein (11, 13), with the exception of my numbers (13), (14), (15), and (38). The following abbreviations are used:

BAE: Bureau of Agricultural Economics
BLS: Bureau of Labor Statistics
C.C.M.: Construction and Construction Materials
F.R.B.: Federal Reserve Bulletin
H.L.S.: Handbook of Labor Statistics
Klein: L. R. Klein, The Use of Econometric Models as a Guide to Economic Policy, *Econometrica,* 15 (1947), pp. 111-51.
M.L.R.: Monthly Labor Review
S.A.U.S.: Statistical Abstract of the United States
S.C.B.: Survey of Current Business
C: consumption, in billions of 1934 dollars.

$$C = \frac{(1) + (2)}{(3)}$$

(1) = consumer expenditures, Department of Commerce old series, *S.A.U.S.,* 1947, p. 273, for years through 1946. 1947-48 values were obtained from a regression (1939-46) of the old series on the new series (*S.C.B.,* July 1948, p. 16, Table 2; and July 1949, p. 10, Table 2).

(2) = imputed rents on owner-occupied residences, *S.C.B.,* July 1948, p. 24, Table 30; and July 1949, p. 23, Table 30.

(3) = price index of consumption goods, 1934: 1.00, weighted average of the BLS consumers' price index for moderate-income families in large cities (*M.L.R.,* Table D-1) and the BAE index of prices paid by farmers for living (*S.A.U.S.,* 1948, p. 642, and *S.C.B.,* Feb. 1949, p. S-4). The weights are proportional to the urban and rural populations, respectively[1] (*S.A.U.S.,* 1946, p. 14; 1947, p. 15; and 1948, p. 15; and U. S. Bureau of Census, *Current Population Reports,* Series P-20, No. 22, p. 6).

[1] Weights used were, respectively: 1944, .596 and .404; 1945, .586 and .414; 1946, .600 and .400; 1947, .590 and .410; 1948, .584 and .416.

I: net investment in private producers' plant and equipment, in billions of 1934 dollars.

$$I = \frac{(4)}{(5)} + \frac{(6)}{(7)} - \frac{(8)}{(9)} - \frac{(10)}{(7)}$$

(4) = gross expenditures on private producers' nonagricultural plant and equipment, *S.C.B.,* March 1948, p. 24; and February 1949, back cover.

(5) = price index of business capital goods, 1934: 1.00, regression on Solomon Fabricant's index (*Capital Consumption and Adjustment,* pp. 178-9, and private correspondence) of a weighted average of the Aberthaw index (*S.A.U.S.,* 1948, p. 792, and *S.C.B.,* Feb. 1949, p. S-6), the American Appraisal Co. index (*S.A.U.S.,* 1948, p. 792, and *C.C.M.,* May 1949, p. 54), and the BLS index for metals and metal products (*S.A.U.S.,* 1948, p. 296, *M.L.R.,* March 1949, p. 381); weights a, β, and γ, respectively, are such that the weighted average is the same as Fabricant's index in 1934, in 1941, and on the average for 1934-41.

(6) = gross expenditures on farm service buildings and machinery; equal to expenditures on farm buildings excluding operators' dwellings, farm machinery excluding motor vehicles, farm trucks, and farm autos used in production (assumed to be 50 per cent of expenditures on autos in 1942-45 and 40 per cent thereafter), BAE, private correspondence.

(7) = price index of farm capital goods, 1934: 1.00, weighted average of price indexes for building materials for other than housing (*Agricultural Statistics,* 1947, p. 524, and BAE, private correspondence), farm machinery (same), and motor vehicles (BLS metals and metal products index;[2] see (5) above). The weights are proportional to expenditures on each of the three categories of capital goods, respectively. (Because of an error, current dollar expenditures were used as weights instead of constant dollar expenditures, but as the resulting error in *I* is less than 1 per cent in all cases, and less than 0.1 per cent in most cases, no recomputation was made.)

(8) = depreciation charges on private producers' nonagricultural plant and equipment, regression (1929-43) of Mosak's nonagricultural depreciation (*Econometrica,* 13, 1945, p. 46) on the Department of Commerce depreciation series (*S.C.B.,* July 1947 Supplement, p. 20, Table 4; July 1948, p. 17, Table 4; and July 1949, p. 11, Table 4).

---

[2] The *BAE* index of motor vehicle prices was discontinued at the start of the war.

(9) = price index underlying depreciation charges, 1934: 1.00, regression (1934-41) of Fabricant's depreciation price index (Fabricant, *Capital Consumption and Adjustment,* p. 183, and private correspondence) on (5).

(10)= depreciation charges on farm service buildings and machinery, BAE, private correspondence.

q: price index of private investment goods, 1934: 1.00.

$$q = \frac{(5) \times (4) + (7) \times (6)}{(4) + (6)}$$

ΔH: value of the change in inventories, in billions of 1934 dollars.

$$\Delta H = \frac{(11)}{(12)}$$

(11) = value of change in inventories, Department of Commerce old series, *S.A.U.S.,* 1947, p. 273, and *S.C.B.,* May 1942, p. 12, for years through 1946. 1947-48 values were obtained from a regression (1939-46) of the old series on the new series (*S.C.B.,* July 1948, p. 16, Table 2, and July 1949, p. 10, Table 2).

(12) = BLS wholesale price index of all commodities, 1934:1.00, *F.R.B.,* March 1949, p. 297.

D_1: gross construction expenditures on permanent, owner-occupied, single family, nonfarm residences, in billions of 1934 dollars.[3]

$$D_1 = \frac{1.076 \times 1.126 \, [0.63 \times (13) \times (14) + .32 \times (15)]}{(16)}$$

(13) = ratio of *1-family* permanent nonfarm residences started to *total* permanent nonfarm units started, *H.L.S.,* 1947, p. 193; and *M.L.R.,* February 1949, p. 179 (graph), and May 1949, p. 620.

(14) = gross private construction expenditures for new permanent nonfarm residences, *H.L.S.,* 1947, pp. 170-1, and *C.C.M.,* May 1949, p. 6.

(15) = private repairs and maintenance expenditures on nonfarm residences, *C.C.M.,* May 1948, p. 15. (This figure is not available after 1944; hence total residential repairs and maintenance was multiplied by the ratio of *nonfarm* to *total* new residential construction to get an approximation; *C.C.M.,* May 1949, pp. 6, 15.)

1.076= ratio of average permit valuation of *single-family* urban units to *all* urban units in 1942, *BLS Bulletin 786,* The Construction Industry in the U. S., p. 21, Table 11.

---

[3] 0.63 = fraction of single-family, nonfarm dwelling units constructed 1935-40 that were owner-occupied in 1940, *Census of Housing, 1940,* III, Part I, Table A-4 (quoted by Klein, p. 144).

1.126 = ratio of average rental value of *owner-occupied* single-family non-farm residences (constructed 1935-40) to that of *all* single-family nonfarm residences (constructed 1935-40), *Census of Housing, 1940,* III, Part I, Table A-4 (Klein, p. 144).

.32 = ratio of *owner-occupied single-family* nonfarm units to *total* nonfarm units in 1940 (Klein, p. 144).

(16) = American Appraisal Co. index of construction costs (national average), 1934: 1.00, *S.A.U.S.,* 1948, p. 792, and *C.C.M.,* May 1949, p. 54.

q_1: construction cost index, 1934: 1.00.

$$q_1 = (16)$$

D_2: gross construction expenditures on rented nonfarm residences, in billions of 1934 dollars.

$$D_2 = \frac{(17)}{(16)} - D_1$$

(17) = (14) + (15).

D_3: gross construction expenditures on farm residences, in billions of 1934 dollars.

$$D_3 = \frac{(18)}{(19)}$$

(18) = gross construction expenditures on farm residences, *C.C.M.,* May 1948, pp. 8, 15; and May 1949, pp. 8, 15.

(19) = BAE index of farm dwelling construction costs, 1934: 1.00, *C.C.M.,* May 1948, p. 56, and May 1949, p. 58.

D'': depreciation of all residences (farm and nonfarm), in billions of 1934 dollars (on the basis of 3 per cent per year).

$$D'' = (67.6)(.97)^{t-1934}(.03) + \sum_{i=1934}^{t-1} (D_1 + D_2 + D_3)_i$$

$$(.985)(.97)^{t-1-1934}(.03) + (D_1 + D_2 + D_3)_t (.015) \qquad \text{for } t > 1934$$

67.6 = estimated value, January 1, 1934, of the stock of residential dwellings in the U. S. (Klein, p. 145).

G: government expenditures for goods and services (not excluding government interest payments) plus net exports plus net investment of non-profit institutions, in billions of 1934 dollars.

$$G = \frac{(20) - (21) - (22)}{(23)} + \frac{(22)}{(16)} + \frac{(24)}{(12)} + \frac{(25) - 0.1}{(16)}$$

(20) = government expenditures for goods and services, Department of Commerce old series, *S.A.U.S.,* 1947, p. 273, for years through 1946. 1947-48 values were obtained from a regression (1939-46)

of the old series on the new series (*S.C.B.,* July 1948, p. 16, Table 2; and July 1949, p. 10, Table 2).

(21) = government interest payments, *S.C.B.,* July 1948, p. 17, Table 4; and July 1949, p. 11, Table 4.

(22) = public construction expenditures (including work-relief construction), *S.C.B.,* July 1948, p. 25, Table 31; and July 1949, p. 24, Table 31.

(23) = BLS wholesale price index of nonfarm products, 1934: 1.00, *H.L.S.,* 1947, p. 126, and *M.L.R.,* March 1949, p. 381.

(24) = net exports of goods and services and gold, equal to net foreign investment, *S.C.B.,* July 1948, p. 16, Table 1; and July 1949, p. 10, Table 1.

(25)= gross construction expenditures by nonprofit institutions, *S.C.B.,* July 1947 Supplement, p. 44, Table 31; July 1948, p. 25, Table 31; and July 1949, p. 24, Table 31.

0.1 = estimate of depreciation of nonprofit institutions' plant, based on a rate of approximately 3 per cent (Klein, p. 146).

$Y + T$: net national product, in billions of 1934 dollars.

$$Y + T = C + I + \Delta H + D_1 + D_2 + D_3 - D'' + G$$

Y: disposable income, in billions of 1934 dollars.

$$Y = \frac{1}{(3)} \left[(1) + (2) + (4) + (6) - \frac{(8)}{(9)} (5) - (10) + (11) + (17) \right.$$
$$+ (18) - (16)D'' + (20) + (24) + (25) - 0.1$$
$$\left. - (26) - (27) - (28) + (29) \right]$$

(26) = federal government receipts, *S.C.B.,* July 1948, p. 17, Table 8; and July 1949, p. 12, Table 8.

(27) = state and local government receipts, same sources as for (26).

(28) = net corporate savings (undistributed corporate profits after taxes plus corporate inventory valuation adjustment, plus excess of wage accruals over disbursements, *S.C.B.,* July 1948, p. 17, Table 4; and July 1949, p. 11, Table 4).

(29) = government transfer payments, same sources as for (28).

p: price index of output as a whole, 1934: 1.00.

$$p = \frac{1}{Y + T} \left[(1) + (2) + (4) + (6) - \frac{(8)}{(9)} (5) - (10) + (11) + (17) \right.$$
$$\left. + (18) - (16)D'' + (20) + (24) + (25) - 0.1 - (21) \right]$$

W_2: government wage-salary bill, in billions of current dollars.

$$W_2 = (31)$$

(31) = government wages and salaries, including work relief, Department of Commerce old series, *S.A.U.S.,* 1947, p. 269, for years through 1946. 1947-48 values were obtained from a regression (1939-46) of the old series on the new series with adjustments for income in kind to armed forces (*S.C.B.,* July 1948, p. 16, Table 1; and July 1949, p. 10, Table 1).

W_1: private wage-salary bill, in billions of current dollars.

$$W_1 = (30) - (31)$$

(30) = total employee compensation, including work relief, Department of Commerce old series, *S.A.U.S.,* 1947, p. 269, for years through 1946. 1947-48 values were obtained from a regression of the old series on the new series (*S.C.B.,* July 1948, p. 16, Table 1; and July 1949, p. 10, Table 1).

R_1: nonfarm rentals, paid and imputed, in billions of current dollars.

$$R_1 = (32)$$

(32) = sum of owner-occupied and tenant-occupied nonfarm rents, *S.C.B.,* July 1948, p. 24, Table 30; and July 1949, p. 23, Table 30.

R_2: farm rentals, paid and imputed, in billions of constant dollars.

$$R_2 = (33)$$

(33) = farmhouse rentals, same sources as for (32).

r: index of rents, 1934: 1.00.

$$r = (34)$$

(34) = rent component, 1934: 1.00, of *BLS* consumers' price index for moderate-income families in large cities, *S.A.U.S.,* 1948, p. 302, and *M.L.R.,* March 1949, p. 375.

ΔF: thousands of new nonfarm families.

$$\Delta F = (35)$$

(35) = increase in nonfarm families, thousands, *S.A.U.S.,* 1948, p. 46, and Bureau of Census, *Current Population Reports,* Series P-20, No. 21, p. 9. As the number of families is not given as of the same date each year, adjustments were based on linear interpolation between dates given.

v: percentage of nonfarm housing units occupied at the end of the year, assumed equal to 100.

N^s: millions of available nonfarm housing units at the end of the year.

$$N^s = 31.3 + \sum_{i=1946}^{t} (38)_i$$

(38) = millions of nonfarm housing units finished during the year, *M.L.R.,* March 1948, p. 368, for 1946 and 1947. This series has

been discontinued; for 1948 the number of nonfarm units started was used as an approximation (*M.L.R.,* May 1949, p. 620).

31.3 = millions of available nonfarm dwelling units in November 1945, assuming $v = 100$, *S.A.U.S.,* 1947, p. 799.

i: average corporate bond yield.

$$i = (40)$$

(40) = Moody's corporate bond yield, *F.R.B.,* 1947, p. 1519; and 1949, p. 275.

$\mathcal{E}_R$: excess reserves, in millions of current dollars.

$$\mathcal{E}_R = (43)$$

(43) = annual average of monthly figures for excess reserves, *F.R.B.,* 1947, pp. 551, 987, 1377; 1948, pp. 187, 523, 965, 1373; 1949, p. 137.

K: end of year stock of private producers' plant and equipment, in billions of 1934 dollars.

$$K = 107.8 + \sum_{i=1935}^{t} I_i \qquad t \leqq 1945$$

$$K = 1.0 + 107.8 + \sum_{i=1935}^{t} I_i \qquad t \geqq 1946$$

107.8 = end of 1934 stock of private producers' plant and equipment (Klein, p. 148).

1.0 = estimate of surplus property transferred to the private sector at the close of the war (Klein, p. 150).

H: end of year stock of inventories, in billions of 1934 dollars.

$$H = 21.8 + \sum_{i=1935}^{t} (\Delta H)_i$$

21.8 = end of 1934 stock of inventories (Klein, p. 149).

$\mathcal{E}$: excise taxes, in billions of current dollars.

$$\mathcal{E} = (45)$$

(45) = excise taxes, regression (1931-41) of Klein's excise series (p. 149) on the sum of federal excises plus state and local sales and social insurance taxes (*S.C.B.,* July 1947 Supplement, p. 21, Table 8; July 1948, p. 17, Table 8; and July 1949, p. 12, Table 8).

X: private output excluding housing services, in billions of 1934 dollars.

$$X = Y + T - \frac{1}{p}(W_2 + R_1 + R_2)$$

M: end of year money supply, in billions of current dollars.

$$M = (46) \qquad t \leqq 1922$$
$$M = (47) \qquad t \geqq 1923$$

(46) = demand and time deposits adjusted plus currency outside banks, average of June 30 figures before and after, Federal Reserve Board, *Banking and Monetary Statistics,* p. 34.

(47) = demand and time deposits adjusted plus currency outside banks, Dec. 31 figures, *Banking and Monetary Statistics,* pp. 34-5, and *F.R.B.,* 1949, p. 265.

N: labor input, in millions of full time equivalent man-years.

$$N = (48) \qquad t \leqq 1928$$
$$N = (49) \qquad t \geqq 1929$$

(49) = number of full time equivalent persons engaged in production in all private industries, excluding work relief, *S.C.B.,* July 1947 Supplement, p. 40, Table 28; July 1948, p. 23, Table 28; and July 1949, p. 22, Table 28.

(48) = regression (1929-38) of (49) on Kuznets' estimates of total persons engaged in private production (*National Income and Its Composition,* pp. 314-5, 346-7).

N_L: labor force, including work-relief employees but excluding other government employees, in millions of man-years.

$$N_L = (50) - (51)$$

(50) = civilian labor force, Census definition, *H.L.S.,* 1947, p. 36, and *S.C.B.,* February 1949, back cover, for years after 1928. 1920-28 values were obtained from a regression (1929-39) of the Census series on the National Industrial Conference Board series (*Economic Almanac,* 1944-45, p. 43).

(51) = government full time equivalent civilian employees excluding work-relief employees, *S.C.B.,* July 1947 Supplement, p. 36, Table 24; July 1948, p. 22, Table 24; and July 1949, p. 20, Table 24, for years after 1929. 1920-28 values were obtained from a regression (1929-38) of the above series on Kuznets' estimates of the same quantity (*National Income and Its Composition, 1919-1938,* pp. 314-5).

w: private money wage rate, in thousands of current dollars per man-year.

$$w = \frac{W_1}{N}$$

Appendix C

TIME SERIES FOR 1946-1947

During the discussion at the Conference on Business Cycles Research in November 1949, Lawrence Klein pointed out a discrepancy in the time series for 1946 and 1947 which were used in this paper: the series for real net national product $Y + T$ and for real private output X show decreases of about 10 per cent from 1946 to 1947, while during the same two years the series for private employment N rose about 5 per cent and the Federal Reserve Board index of industrial production rose 10 per cent. Since these four series are meant to measure magnitudes that have to move closely together (except that the agricultural sector is not represented in the Federal Reserve index), it is clear that something is wrong. It is difficult to see how the series for employment and industrial production could be seriously in error for this period, but the series for $Y + T$ and X might be thrown off by either or both of two causes.

First, the series for $Y + T$ and X are constructed by adding component series, each of which is first expressed in current prices, then deflated by an appropriate price index. It is very likely that the published price indexes (which were used in the paper) are too low for the years toward the end of the reign of price controls, including 1946, because of failure to take account of reductions in quality and service, black market activities, and the practice on the part of manufacturers of concentrating their output in their more expensive lines. This understatement has been estimated by the Technical Committee on the consumers' price index (also known as the Mitchell Committee) not to exceed about 4 per cent in any year (see the *Economic Report of the President,* January 1950, pp. 156 and 169), and by various others to be considerably larger. It can be expected to have disappeared by some time in 1947, because virtually all controls were lifted in November 1946, and many had been lifted or relaxed before then. Therefore it is a good surmise that while the published price indexes are too low in 1946, they again measure approximately what we want them to measure in 1947. If this is true, the deflated series for $Y + T$ and X are too high in 1946, and therefore their apparent drop from 1946 to 1947 is partly or wholly illusory — there may even have been a rise, camouflaged by the understated 1946 price indexes. My guess would be that the entire discrepancy is not to be explained in this manner, however.

Second, as indicated in Appendix B, the time series used were extensions of Klein's own time series, based like his on the series released by the Department of Commerce before the publication in 1947 of its revised national income series. Some of the 1947-48 figures were obtained from regressions of the unrevised series on the corresponding revised series. It would have been sounder to adjust all the time series, including Klein's, to conform to the revised Department of Commerce series, or failing that, to obtain the 1947-48 extrapolations of the unrevised series by adjusting the revised series for changes in definition instead of using regressions.

Similar discrepancies, of comparable magnitude, are obtained for

1946-47 for the whole economy and for separate industries if the national income originating in the economy and in each of several industries, deflated by the corresponding wholesale price index, is compared industry-wise with the number of full time equivalent persons engaged in production or with the Federal Reserve index of industrial production. (They are clearly visible, even though the industrial classifications are not quite the same in the Federal Reserve index and national income accounts as in the wholesale price index.) Because these discrepancies are comparable in magnitude to the one pointed out by Klein, it seems likely that it is unnecessary to look to my regression technique for an explanation of the error in the relationship of the 1946 to the 1947 figures; it even seems likely that the regression technique made no significant contribution to that error (though no doubt it introduced others).

It remains to determine the effect of the discrepancies on the results of the paper. Of course the most reliable way would be to revise all the data and re-estimate all the equations. Here it is possible only to try to obtain a rough idea of the effect, by means of some approximation 'corrections' consisting of making changes in some of the 1946-47 time series so that they become consistent with the Federal Reserve index of industrial production, then re-estimating certain of the structural and reduced form equations by the ordinary least squares method. The detailed steps and results of this exploratory 'correction' procedure are explained below.

The time series for real private output X, disposable income Y, and consumption C are accepted as correct for 1947, and are 'corrected' for 1946. Let unprimed symbols stand for the values underlying the original computations of the paper, and primed symbols for the 'corrected' values. Then,

$$X'_{1946} = \frac{170}{187} X_{1947}$$

where $\frac{170}{187}$ is the ratio of the 1946 to 1947 values of the Federal Reserve index of industrial production. (If employment were used as the correction standard instead, a less drastic reduction factor than $\frac{170}{187}$ would result; however, we use $\frac{170}{187}$ so as to be sure not to *under*estimate the effect of the discrepancy we are analyzing.) Also,

$$Y'_{1946} = \frac{X'_{1946}}{X_{1946}} Y_{1946}$$

$$C'_{1946} = \frac{X'_{1946}}{X_{1946}} C_{1946}$$

$$\left[\left(\frac{M}{p}\right)_{-1}\right]'_t = \frac{X'_{1946}}{X_{1946}}\left[\left(\frac{M}{p}\right)_{-1}\right]_t \qquad t = 1946, 1947$$

The purpose of these changes is to gear output X for 1946 to the Federal Reserve index (while accepting X for 1947), and then to make the same percentage change in the 1946 values of C, Y, and $\left(\frac{M}{p}\right)_{-1}$ as was made in the 1946 value of X. The 'corrected' values are shown in Table C1.

Table C1

CORRECTED TIME SERIES

	X	C	Y	$(M/p)_{-1}$
1946	79.367	72.023	74.864	91.695
1947	....	....	....	87.462

Then the production functions (3.2) and (3.4), the consumption function (6.2), and the reduced form equations for C and Y are re-estimated by the ordinary least squares method, incorporating the above changes into the time series. The results of the structural re-estimation are shown as the CLS' estimates in Table C2, which reproduces the relevant CLS estimates from Table 2 for convenience in comparison.

Table C2

RE-ESTIMATION OF CERTAIN STRUCTURAL EQUATIONS

Eq.		Estimates of Parameters (and of Standard Errors)				S (8)	Obs. Value 1948 (10)	Calc. Value 1948 (11)	Calc. Dist. 1948 (12)
	(1)	(2)	(3)	(4)	(5)				
3.2 Production	X	N	K_{-1}	t	1				
CLS	1	2.820 (.25)	−.296 (.16)	.55 (.14)		−26.50	3.23	90.26	99.02	−8.76
CLS'	1	2.771 (.23)	−.044 (.15)	.34 (.13)		−51.8	2.94	90.26	93.73	−3.47
3.4 Production	X	N	t	1					
CLS	1	3.074 (.22)	.43 (.13)	−68.13			3.42	90.26	99.16	−8.90
CLS'	1	2.809 (.18)	.32 (.11)	−58.01			2.87	90.26	93.65	−3.39
6.2 Consumption	C	Y	$(M/p)_{-1}$	t	1				
CLS	1	.583 (.06)	.297 (.04)	−.27 (.10)		7.07	1.57	82.84	75.97	6.87
CLS'	1	.614 (.08)	.329 (.10)	−.30 (.18)		3.88	2.20	82.84	77.65	5.19

The results of the re-estimation of the reduced form equations are shown opposite the primed variables in Table C3, which reproduces certain parts of Table 3 for convenience in comparison.

Table C3

RE-ESTIMATION OF CERTAIN REDUCED FORM EQUATIONS

	Obs. Value	Predictions 1948			Errors 1948			Naive Model Test Verdicts	
		RF	Naive Models		RF	Naive Models			
Var.	1948	LS	I	II	LS	I	II	I	II
	(1)	(4)	(6)	(7)	(8)	(10)	(11)	(12)	(13)
C	82.8	80.2	81.7	76.9	2.6	1.1	5.9	N	RF
C′	82.8	90.3	81.7	91.4	−7.5	1.1	−8.6	N	RF
Y	79.9	70.9	78.2	66.4	9.0	1.7	13.5	N	RF
Y′	79.9	86.1	78.2	81.5	−6.2	1.7	−1.6	N	N

From Table C2 it appears that the differences between the estimates obtained in this paper and the estimates that would be obtained if the time series discrepancies were corrected are not likely to be negligible, and that some of the structural equations would be likely to fit better in 1948 as a result of the corrections. From Table C3 it appears that the correction process would be likely to produce non-negligible changes in the predictions made by the reduced form. But Table C3 does not indicate that *better* predictions of the important variables C and Y would be obtained if the time series discrepancies were corrected.

The variables whose time series are most likely to be changed by a revision of the data, in a way important enough to influence the results, are $C, I, q, \Delta H, G, Y, T, p,$ and X. Those likely to be affected in an unimportant way (because they are small or stable) are $D_1, q_1, D_2, D_3, D'', r, K,$ and H. Those not likely to be affected at all (because they are independent of price indexes) are $(pX - \mathcal{E}), W_1, W_2, R_1, R_2, \Delta F, v, N^s, i, \mathcal{E}_R, \mathcal{E}, M, N, N_L,$ and w. Accordingly, equations 1.0, 2.0, 3.4, 4.2, and 6.2 are likely to be affected in a significant way because they are dominated by variables from the first of the aforementioned groups. Similarly, equations 4.0, 5.1, 7.0, 9.0, 10.0, and 11.0 are not likely to be affected significantly because they are not dominated by variables from the first group.

Naive model I as applied to 1948 is unaffected by the changes made here because it does not reach as far into the past as 1946. Naive model II is affected, however, and will be led by the changes to make uniformly higher predictions of deflated quantities (usually an improvement in performance) and a lower prediction of the general price index (also an improvement).

The upshot of the calculations based on these approximate 'corrections' is something like this: if the data were revised and the equations re-estimated, the estimates of the parameters would be changed, and the 1948 fit of some structural equations would probably be improved, but there is no evidence that the predictions of important variables by the reduced form would be improved.

Appendix D

CHOICE OF PREDETERMINED VARIABLES FOR ESTIMATION BY THE
ABBREVIATED VARIANT OF THE LIMITED INFORMATION METHOD

The limited information estimates of any structural equation depend upon observations of a subset of the predetermined variables that are not in the equation being estimated but are in the system. The elements of this subset are called z''''s and there must be at least as many as $H - 1$ of them if H is the number of jointly dependent variables in the equation being estimated (see text, Sec. 1). Of course, there may be more than $H - 1$; if so, the estimates will be better. In our model the largest value of $H - 1$ for any equation is 4, for equation 3.0; if this is excepted, the largest value is 2, for each of several equations. Therefore the number of z''''s *required* for any equation is 2 except in the case of equation 3.0, which requires 4.

Now there are 25 predetermined variables in the complete model, and no equation contains more than 4. Thus, for each equation there are at least 21 variables available for use as z''''s, and so there is an arbitrary choice of z''''s to be made for each equation. If there were no costs in money and in degrees of freedom, one would always use all the available variables as z''''s. Because of these costs, a proper subset of the available variables has been used in each case, i.e., the abbreviated variant of the limited information method has been used.

The stochastic equations have been divided into four groups in such a way as to minimize the intersection of the set of jointly dependent variables in any group with the corresponding set for any other group; in fact every such intersection is empty. Then for any equation the set of z''''s is the set of *all* predetermined variables in the group to which the equation belongs, minus the set of predetermined variables appearing in the equation (see the accompanying table).

		VARIABLES	
GROUP	EQUATIONS	Jointly Dependent	Predetermined
I	(1.0), (2.0), (3.4), (4.0), (4.2), (5.1)	$pX - \mathcal{E}$, $I, \dfrac{}{q}$, H, p, $(X - \Delta H)$, X, N, W_1, $(pX - \mathcal{E})$, w/p, w, Δp, $(N_L - N)$	$\left(\dfrac{pX - \mathcal{E}}{q}\right)_{-1}$, K_{-1}, H_{-1}, t, $(pX - \mathcal{E})_{-1}$, w_{-1}, $(N_L - N)_{-1}$, p_{-1}
II	(6.2), (7.0), (9.0)	C, Y, D_1, r/q_1, $(Y + Y_{-1} + Y_{-2})$, Δr	$(M/p)_{-1}$, t ΔF, v_{-1}, $1/r_{-1}$
III	(10.0)	D_2, i	r_{-1}, $(q_1)_{-1}$, $(q_1)_{-2}$ ΔF_{-1}, i_{-1}, t
IV	(11.0)	Δi	i_{-1}, $\mathcal{E}_R$, t

Klein's grouping of equations was quite similar. In particular for group I he used exactly the same predetermined variables as I did, except that in place of w_{-1} and $(N_L - N)_{-1}$ he used H_{-2} and X_{-1}. This is mentioned here because of its possible bearing on certain anomalies in the *CLI* estimates of equations 1.0 and 4.0 of group I. The matter is discussed in the text in Section 11, part (f).

Appendix E

ESTIMATION OF THE PARAMETERS OF THE REDUCED FORM

This appendix is a note on the restricted least-squares method of estimating reduced form parameters, referred to in Section 4. We first describe the method assuming that a one-element subset of structural equations is chosen to provide the restrictions.

Suppose there is a model consisting of G equations in G jointly dependent variables y and K predetermined variables z. Suppose that one of its equations is

$$(1) \qquad \beta_1 y_1 + \cdots + \beta_H y_H + 0 + \cdots + 0 + \gamma_1 z_1 + \cdots$$
$$+ \gamma_{K^*} z_{K^*} + 0 + \cdots + 0 = u$$

where $H < G$ and $K^* < K$. Consider H equations of the reduced form,

$$(2) \qquad y_i = \sum_1^{K^*} \pi_{ik} z_k + \sum_{K^*+1}^{K^*+K^{**}} \pi_{ik} z_k + v_i \qquad i = 1, \cdots, H$$

where K^{**} is the number of predetermined variables assumed to be known to be in the model but not in 1. Then $K^{**} \leq K - K^*$. The parameters π_{ik} can be estimated by least-squares. The least-squares estimates can be made more efficient by altering them to take account of the restrictions implied by the zeros in 1, as follows. It must be possible to get equation 1 from a linear combination of equations 2, in fact, from that combination obtained by taking β_i times the ith equation of 2, $i = 1, \cdots, H$, and summing the results. This means that there are K^{**} equations, one for each z_k excluded from 1, thus:

$$(3) \qquad \sum_{i=1}^{H} \beta_i \pi_{ik} = 0 \qquad k = K^* + 1, \cdots, K^* + K^{**}$$

Now if $K^{**} > H - 1$, i.e., if 1 is overidentified, 3 is overdetermined. Hence if 3 is to hold, and it must, a restriction is implied on the matrix of the $\pi_{ik}, i = 1, \cdots, H, k = K^* + 1, \cdots, K^* + K^{**}$, keeping its rank down to $H - 1$. This restriction may be applied to the matrix of least-squares estimates of the π_{ik}, to make them conform to the restrictions implied by the zeros in 1. The computation is not difficult, once the limited information estimates for 1 are obtained.

Similarly, if there are other structural equations besides 1 which also contain some one of the jointly dependent variables $y_1, \cdots, y_H$, say y_1, the estimates of the parameters of the reduced-form equation for y_1 can be made to conform simultaneously to the restrictions implied in the form of two, three, ···, or all these other structural equations as well. This further increases the efficiency of the estimates, but makes them more difficult to compute.

Appendix F

CALCULATED DISTURBANCES FOR CLI LIMITED INFORMATION
ESTIMATES OF EQUATIONS

	1.0	2.0	3.4	4.0	4.2	5.1	6.2	7.0	9.0	10.0	11.0
1921										.03	.37
1922	2.11	−.26	3.04	37.07	−1.08	.033	−.61	.15	−.010	−.01	−.66
1923	3.93	1.05	1.19	97.88	.09	.019	−.89	.18	−.014	.06	.18
1924	6.38	−.38	.76	−6.20	.28	−.017	.37	.38	.016	.10	−.09
1925	−2.56	.12	2.43	59.97	−.93	−.033	.05	.44	−.004	.18	−.24
1926	−2.60	.73	1.06	34.73	−.41	−.003	.83	.20	−.002	.19	−.25
1927	.56	.25	.65	−18.03	.03	.005	1.54	.19	.010	.06	−.29
1928	−3.41	−.23	−.14	−.51	.59	.009	2.18	.28	.018	.02	−.13
1929	−3.55	1.21	−2.96	10.87	1.54	.003	1.33	−.16	.034	.34	.19
1930	2.45	.64	−3.13	−98.53	1.68	−.016	−.11	−.25	.041	−.75	−.08
1931	7.87	−.53	−2.52	−149.14	2.07	.012	−2.25	−.36	.013	−.28	.76
1932	12.19	−1.18	−2.09	−141.32	1.41	−.028	−3.27	−.47	−.050	−.21	1.38
1933	2.35	−.43	−.83	−20.27	−.12	−.036	−1.24	−.58	−.079	−.01	−.25
1934	−1.11	−.63	−2.83	44.62	−.09	−.043	−.48	−.41	−.019	.004	−.40
1935	−2.36	−.83	−1.29	28.41	−.88	−.022	−.09	−.13	.009	.13	−.17
1936	−5.34	.53	.66	42.52	−1.40	.006	.47	−.04	.019	−.004	−.40
1937	1.63	.09	−3.11	9.26	.64	.003	.80	−.07	.039	.02	−.03
1938	8.27	−1.33	−1.58	−108.97	.56	−.004	2.08	.12	.029	−.06	.32
1939	−6.04	−.28	2.38	27.75	−.73	.025	1.01	.21	.006	.30	−.06
1940	−4.85	.49	2.45	12.84	−.76	.002	.34	.38	.010	.17	.20
1941	−17.27	1.49	4.61	115.82	−1.25	.036	−2.22	.58	.019	.04	.08
1946	1.48	.71	8.53	−38.12	−2.26	−.033	−1.55	−.46	−.050	.15	−.33
1947	1.70	−1.36	−7.24	60.24	1.25	.013	1.88	−.16	−.032	−.22	−.10
1948	−8.37	1.19	−7.82	90.56	.77	.17	6.88	.03	.011	−.19	.07

Appendix G

REFERENCES

1) Anderson, T. W., and H. Rubin, Estimation of the Parameters of a Single Equation in a Complete System of Stochastic Equations, *Annals of Mathematical Statistics,* 20 (1949), pp. 46-63, and The Asymptotic Properties of Estimates of the Parameters of a Single Equation in a Complete System of Stochastic Equations, *Annals of Mathematical Statistics,* 21 (1950), pp. 570-82.

2) Bronfenbrenner, J., 'Extent of Least Squares Bias in Estimating a Single Stochastic Equation in a Complete System', Cowles Commission Discussion Paper (unpublished), 1949.

3) Eisenhart, C., M. Hastay and W. A. Wallis (editors), *Techniques of Statistical Analysis* (McGraw-Hill, 1947), Ch. 2.

4) Frisch, Ragnar, Propagation Problems and Impulse Problems in Dynamic Economics, *Economic Essays in Honour of Gustav Cassel* (London, Allen & Unwin, 1933).

5) Haavelmo, T., The Statistical Implications of a System of Simultaneous Equations, *Econometrica,* 11 (1943), pp. 1-13.

6) Haavelmo, T., The Probability Approach in Econometrics, *Econometrica,* 12 (1944), Supplement.

7) Haavelmo, T., Methods of Measuring the Marginal Propensity to Consume, *Journal of the American Statistical Association,* 42 (1947), pp. 105-22.

8) Hart, B. I., and John von Neumann, Tabulation of the Probabilities for the Ratio of the Mean Square Successive Difference to the Variance, *Annals of Mathematical Statistics,* 13 (1942), pp. 207-14.

9) Hotelling, Harold, Problems of Prediction ('The Prediction of Personal Adjustment': A Symposium), *American Journal of Sociology,* 48 (1942-43), pp. 61-76.

10) Kalecki, M., *Essays in the Theory of Economic Fluctuations* (London, Allen & Unwin, 1939).

11) Klein, L. R., The Use of Econometric Models as a Guide to Economic Policy, *Econometrica,* 15 (1947), pp. 111-51.

12) Klein, L. R., Theories of Effective Demand and Employment, *Journal of Political Economy,* 50 (1947), pp. 108-31.

13) Klein, L. R., *Economic Fluctuations in the United States, 1921-1941,* Cowles Commission Monograph 11 (Wiley, 1950).

14) Koopmans, T., Identification Problems in Economic Model Construction, *Econometrica,* 17 (1949), pp. 125-44.

15) Koopmans, T., Statistical Methods of Measuring Economic Relations, Cowles Commission Discussion Paper (unpublished), 1948.

16) Koopmans, T. (editor), *Statistical Inference in Dynamic Economic Models,* Cowles Commission Monograph 10 (Wiley, 1950).

17) Marshall, A., A Test of Klein's Model III for Changes of Structure, to be published.

18) Orcutt, G., and D. Cochrane, Application of Least Squares Regression to Relationships Containing Auto-Correlated Error Terms, *Journal of the American Statistical Association,* 44 (1949), pp. 32-61.

19) Orcutt, G., and D. Cochrane, A Sampling Study of the Merits of Auto-regressive and Reduced Form Transformations in Regression Analysis, *Journal of the American Statistical Association,* 44 (1949), pp. 356-72.

20) Rubin, H., 'Systems of Linear Stochastic Equations', Cowles Commission Discussion Paper (unpublished), 1947.

21) Rubin, H., 'The Approximate Distribution of Calculated Disturbances', Cowles Commission Discussion Paper (unpublished), 1948.

22) Samuelson, P. A., *Foundations of Economic Analysis* (Harvard University Press, 1947).

23) Tinbergen, Jan, *Statistical Testing of Business Cycle Theories, II: Business Cycles in the United States of America, 1919-1932* (League of Nations, Economic Intelligence Service, Geneva, 1939).

24) Wald, A., and J. Wolfowitz, Tolerance Limits for a Normal Distribution, *Annals of Mathematical Statistics,* 17 (1946), pp. 208-15.

INTERNATIONAL ECONOMIC REVIEW
Vol. 16, No. 1, February, 1975

JUDGING THE PERFORMANCE OF ECONOMETRIC MODELS OF THE U. S. ECONOMY

BY CARL F. CHRIST[1]

INTRODUCTION

ECONOMETRIC MODELS OF THE U.S. economy have been developed to the point where forecasters who use them can forecast real and nominal GNP two or three quarters ahead with root mean square errors of less than one percent, and six quarters ahead with RMS errors of one to two percent. The best of them now usually do better than forecasters who do not use such models. Are the models then so reliable that we can believe what they say about the effects that particular fiscal or monetary policy actions will have, immediately and in the long run? And how can we learn the answer to such questions, either for today's models, or tomorrow's? That is what this paper is about. It draws heavily on the extensive and intensive work of the authors of the other papers in this symposium, and could not have been written without them.

My main contentions will be as follows. First, it is important to test econometric models as abstract representations of reality, as well as to test the forecasting performance of the people who use them. Second, testing of a model requires that the model be tried against data that occurred after the model was built, i.e., after the specifications were decided upon concerning which variables appear in each equation, which variables are endogenous and which exogenous, what is the functional form of each equation, what is the lag structure of each, what restrictions the parameters are to obey, etc. A common way to do this is to make forecasts for a period that is subsequent to the building of the model, and then examine the errors of those forecasts. Third, though the models forecast well over horizons of four to six quarters, they disagree so strongly about the effects of important monetary and fiscal policies that they cannot be considered reliable guides to such policy effects, until it can be determined which of them are wrong in this respect and which (if any) are right.

1. TESTING ECOMOMETRIC MODELS AND FORECASTERS

Every econometric model in this symposium is a system of equations intended to determine a vector of endogenous variables y_t at time t, in terms of a vector of exogenous variables x_t, vectors of lagged endogenous variables $y_{t-1}, \cdots, y_{t-L}$, a matrix of parameters A, and a vector of stochastic disturbances u_t. The system of equations can be symbolized by the following, where F is a (possibly non-linear) vector function:

[1] This work was supported by a grant from the National Science Foundation to The Johns ♦ Hopkins University. Helpful comments were made by L. R. Klein and G. Fromm.

54

$$(1) \qquad F(y_t, y_{t-1}, \cdots, y_{t-L}, x_t, A) = u_t.$$

The reduced form of the system, obtained by solving (1) for y_t, can be expressed as

$$(2) \qquad y_t = G(y_{t-1}, \cdots, y_{t-L}, x_t, A) + v_t$$

where v_t is a stochastic disturbance vector depending on u_t and A. If (1) is nonlinear, so will (2) be; then (2) may have to be obtained by numerical methods rather than by explicit solution, and if (2) is not unique, spurious solutions must be rejected.

A model—once it has been specified by listing its endogenous variables, its exogenous variables, the functional form of each of its equations (including the lag structure), and any other restrictions upon its parameters—is an impersonal theoretical construct, that can and should be tested like any scientific theory, by comparing its implications against observed data. We use a sample of data $(t = 1, \cdots, T)$ to obtain an estimate $\hat{A}$ of the parameters, and then see how closely the estimated equations (1) and (2) describe the values of the variables in the model during a chosen test period, which may be either the same sample period that was used for estimation, or a different (usually subsequent) period. In practice, this means substituting the estimate $\hat{A}$ into (1) and (2), and finding the values $\hat{u}_t$ and $\hat{v}_t$ that must be taken by the disturbance terms in the test period to maintain the equalities in the estimated equations (1) and (2). The more accurately the equations describe the data, i.e., the smaller are $\hat{u}_t$ and $\hat{v}_t$, in the test period, the more confidence we have in the model, *ceteris paribus*. More about this below.

It is worthwhile to distinguish between testing an econometric model, and testing a practical human forecaster who forecasts by means of an econometric model. The forecaster obtains, from some source extraneous to the model, ex ante forecasts of the exogenous variables x_t, and substitutes them into his estimate of the reduced form (2), and then calculates his forecasts of the future values of the endogenous variables y_t. Of necessity, his forecast period comes *after* the time when his model was specified, and *after* the sample period used to estimate its parameters. Sometimes, just before he is to announce a forecast, he may believe (based on recent events not explicitly included in the model) that the model is going to make (or has made) an incorrect forecast; in some cases he then may adjust one or more of the model's constant terms or slopes in a way that (in his judgment) is likely to improve the forecast. Therefore the correctness of such practical econometric forecasts is dependent in a complex way on the forecaster's ability to forecast the exogenous variables and to adjust the model in a subjective manner, as well as on the adequacy of the model itself.

In order to test an econometric model, as distinct from a forecaster who uses a model, it is of course necessary to make *no* subjective adjustments to the constant terms or slopes (adjustments made according to a pre-announced mechanical rule are acceptable, for the rule can be regarded as part of the model;

see the "PSS" forecasts in Hirsch *et. al.* [12]). It is also necessary to use *actual* values of exogenous variables, rather than ex ante forecasts thereof.

To test an econometric model of the U. S. economy, it is crucial to use a test period that occurs *after* the model has been specified. A test period that occurred before the model was specified does not provide a meaningful test. This is because, although economic theory plays an important part in building these models, it is not able to do the whole job alone; hence alternative functional forms and alternative lag structures are quite properly tried out against the data that are available at the time, and (again quite properly) any specification that does not describe those data with rather high R^2's is rejected right then. Therefore, any U. S. econometric model that is released by its builders will already have been shown to fit rather well the data that occurred before the model was specified.[2] Experience teaches that it is uncommon for such models to fit subsequent data as closely, and that the fit typically deteriorates as one moves to data occurring later and later after the time when the model was specified. This is a common finding, even after allowing for the deterioration in fit that would be expected as one extrapolates a correctly specified and properly estimated equation to data outside the sample period.[3] Testing a model by means of a test period that occurs after the model was built is the only way to discriminate between the (inferior) models that have been chosen to fit primarily the random and non-enduring features of the pre-model-building data, and the (superior) models that have been chosen to fit primarily the systematic and enduring features of the economy.

These crucial tests, using a test period that occurs after the building of the model, are most commonly made by first estimating the model (1) using the pre-model-building data, and then using the reduced form (2) to make conditional forecasts for the post-model-building test period, given actual values of the exogenous variables for the test period and actual initial values of the lagged endogenous variables at the beginning of the test period. This is the type of forecast to which most emphasis will be given in this paper. Such forecasts (whether they use actual or ex ante exogenous values) are often called post-sample forecasts, which indeed they are, but it is more important that they are forecasts of data from the post-model-building period, for reasons noted above. (In particular, it is not sufficient to divide the pre-model building period into two parts, and estimate the model from the earlier part, and then use the latter part as a post-sample test period: this yields a pre-model-building test period, and hence does not provide the crucial test that is needed.) Root mean square errors (RMSE's) for post-model-building forecasts are presented and discussed below.

---

[2] This conclusion applies even if the explicit screening procedure described in the text is not used in building the model, because the model builder knows a great deal about recent economic events in his country, and designs the model with them in mind.

[3] One makes the required allowance by means of the standard error of forecast, proposed by Hotelling [13] and extended to econometric model forecasts by Brown [4] and by Goldberger, Nagar, and Odeh [10].

2. POLICY SIMULATION

If and when an econometric model of the economy has been shown to be a reliable predictor of post-model-building data, it can be relied upon to tell us the time-paths of the multiplier effects of alternative government policies that appear in the model. The usual vehicle for obtaining such multipliers is the *policy simulation*. It is constructed by comparing two dynamic simulations computed from the model over the same time period, one of which uses actual values of all the exogenous variables, and the other of which uses the same set of exogenous values *except* that, at some chosen instant, the time-path of one of the policy variables is given a step-wise increase or decrease and thereafter follows a path that is a fixed distance above or below the actual path. The resulting paths of the endogenous variables in the two simulations differ by amounts that are attributed to the policy change. Multipliers are then computed, showing the effect on an endogenous variable divided by the step-change in the policy variable, after the lapse of one quarter, two quarters, etc.

Even if an econometric model is not yet shown to be a reliable predictor, dynamic simulations based on it are of great interest, for they show what the model implies about the time-paths of the multiplier effects of policy changes. Such multipliers will be discussed below.

3. ROOT MEAN SQUARE ERRORS OF THE MODELS' FORECASTS

Table 1 lists the models in this symposium,[4] and shows for each the number of equations, stochastic equations, and exogenous variables; the sample period used to estimate it; the types of forecasts for which root mean square errors are presented by the authors; and the types of policy simulations that are presented.

Table 2 shows the root mean square errors of post-sample forecasts of nominal and real GNP, and of the GNP deflator, that are presented in the symposium, for forecasts one quarter ahead, two quarters ahead, and so on up to eight quarters ahead. Almost all the forecasts deteriorate as the horizon lengthens. The semi-naive forecasts made by the "ARIMA" (auto-regressive integrated moving average) method, based only on past values of the variable that is being forecast, are uniformly the poorest. Apart from them, the largest RMSE for any variable and length of horizon is about twice the smallest. The forecasts in the American Statistical Association-NBER survey of regular forecasters are about as good as the median of the econometric forecasters for nominal GNP and for short-horizon price level forecasts, and better than most of the econometric forecasts for real GNP and for 4- and 5-quarters-ahead price level forecasts. The Wharton III forecasts, which are *subjectively adjusted* and based on *ex ante* exogenous variable values, are the best of the econometric forecasts for nominal GNP, and

---

[4] Tables 1-4 and the ensuing discussion omit RMSE's and policy simulations for the Brookings, MPS, and Wharton annual models because papers presenting them did not reach me before press time.

TABLE 1

MODEL SIZES, SAMPLE PERIODS, TYPES OF FORECASTS FOR WHICH ROOT MEAN SQUARE ERRORS ARE PRESENTED, AND TYPES OF POLICY SIMULATIONS PRESENTED

Line	Model (Quarterly unless otherwise stated)	Number of: Stoch Eqs.	Number of: Eqs.	Number of: Exog. Variables	Sample Period	RMSE's of forecasts: Within sample — Exog variable values used	RMSE's of forecasts: Post sample — Exog variable values used	Policy Simulations: Fiscal — Gov. Purchases	Policy Simulations: Fiscal — Taxes	Policy Simulations: Fiscal — Balanced Budget	Policy Simulations: Monetary — Unborrowed Reserved	Policy Simulations: Monetary — Treas bill rate
a	b	c	d	e	f	g	h	j	k	l	m	n
1	BEA	67	117		54.1–71.4	—	actual and ex ante	×	×			
2	Fair[1]	14	19	20	56.1–73.2	actual	actual and ex ante					
3	DRI[2]	477	698	184	61.1–72.4	actual	ex ante	×	×	×	×	
4	MQEM	35	59	63	54.1–70.4	actual	—	×				×
5	St. Louis[1,3]	5	9	3	53.1–68.4	—	actual					
6	Wharton III[2]	68	191	92	53.3–70.1	actual	ex ante	×	×	×	×	
7	Wharton III[2] anticipations	79	202		53.3–70.1	actual	—	×	×		×	
8	Liu-Hwa[3] monthly	51	131	27	54Ja–71Dc	actual	actual	×	×		×	
9	Hickman-Coen annual	50	70		24–40, 49–66	actual	actual	×	×		×	

[1] The Fair and St. Louis models are re-estimated before each forecast.

[2] For some equations the sample period was different from the typical period shown in column f.

[3] The papers on the St. Louis and Liu-Hwa models do not give RMSE's, but the authors kindly supplied them to me.

nearly the best for real GNP and the price level. The BEA EAF3 forecasts, which are also *subjectively adjusted* and based on *ex ante* exogenous values, are very good for short-horizon forecasts, but deteriorate rather rapidly as the horizon lengthens. The (*unadjusted*) Fair model that uses *actual* exogenous values is about third best, especially for nominal GNP and the price level. On the other hand, two other *unadjusted* or *mechanically adjusted* models using *actual* exogenous values (St. Louis and BEA PSS) are in many cases the poorest. The Fair model does better when using *actual* exogenous values than when using *ex ante* ones. On the other hand, the *subjectively adjusted* BEA model does worse when using *actual* than when using *ex ante* exogenous values (compare the EPF and EAF3 forecasts). We return to this below. The DRI model, which uses *ex ante* exogenous values, does quite well with real and nominal GNP one quarter ahead, but gets worse rapidly for longer horizons. The Liu-Hwa forecasts (*unadjusted*, and based on *actual* exogenous values) are good, but their horizon is too short (eight months, or about three quarters) to be very revealing. The Hickman-Coen forecast errors were not shown separately for different horizons.

In general, it appears that *subjectively adjusted* forecasts using *ex ante* exogenous values are better than the others. It is no surprise that subjective adjustment helps. It may surprise some that the use of actual exogenous values does not help, and sometimes hinders. But there is likely to be some interaction, in the sense that if a forecaster feels that the preliminary forecast turned out by his model is unreasonable, he may both adjust the model and change his ex ante forecast of the exogenous variables, in order to obtain a final forecast that he thinks is more reasonable. This suggests that when unadjusted models are used, *actual* exogenous values should yield better forecasts than ex ante values. The two sets of forecasts from the Fair model bear this out. It also suggests that if *subjectively adjusted* models are used, *ex ante* exogenous values should yield better forecasts than actual values. A comparison of the EAF3 and EPF forecasts from the BEA model beares this out.

To test econometric models, free from the subjective judgment of the human forecasters who use them, we want to see the RMSE's of forecasts made without subjective adjustment, and with actual exogenous values. Such RMSE's are present in some but not all of the papers in this symposium. Fortunately, they have been computed for all the models that are represented in the NBER/NSF Model Comparison Seminar. The first report presenting them is Fromm and Klein [8], and the second one is Fromm and Klein [9], to appear in the *Annals of Economic and Social Measurement*. The authors have kindly given me permission to make use of these forthcoming results. They are graphed in Figures 1, 2, and 3, respectively, for nominal GNP, real GNP, and the GNP deflator. For reference, the ASA/NBER forecasts are included also. The forecast periods are not identical, but all begin no earlier than 1965.4 and end no later than 1972.4. A comparison of Table 2 with the graphs indicates once again that econometric model forecasts can be improved by the use of subjective judgment.

The forecasts deteriorate rapidly as the forecast horizon is lengthened, with

TABLE 2

RMSE's (ROOT MEAN SQUARE ERRORS) OF POST-SAMPLE FORECASTS OF NOMINAL GNP, REAL GNP, AND THE GNP DEFLATOR

Line	Forecaster	Forecast Period	Forecast Type[1]	Exog. Variable Values	Adjustments to Model[2]	RMSE's (Root Mean Square Errors)[9] of Post-Sample Forecasts — Number of Quarters Ahead							
						1	2	3	4	5	6	7	8
a	b	c	d	e	f	g	h	j	k	l	m	n	p
Part I: GNP in Billions of Current Dollars													
1	ASA-NBER[3,5]	70.3-73.2	—	—	—	4.9	7.9	11	13	16			
2	ARIMA[4]	"	—	—	—	11	19	27	27	46	58		
3	BEA (EAF3)	"	A	ex ante	subj	3.2	7.0	8.4	13	16	15		
4	BEA (EPF)	"	C	actual	subj	6.4	8.9	14	16	14	14		
5	BEA (PSS)	"	D	actual	mech	8.7	13	13	12	17	20		
6	Fair[5]	"	B	ex ante	none	5.3	11	16	18	22			
7	Fair[5]	"	D	actual	none	5.1	7.2	8.5	11	12			
8	DRI	69.4-73.4	A	ex ante	subj	4.3	7.9	12	15	18	18	21	26
9	St. Louis[6]	69.1-73.3	D	actual	none	8.2	12	16	18	22	26	28	27
10	Wharton III	71.2-74.1	A	ex ante	subj	4.8	6.2	6.7	7.5	9.5	10	12	9.5
11	Liu-Hwa[6,7]	72Ja-Dc	D	actual	none	5.4	6.5	4.2					
12	Hickman-Coen	67-72										27[8]	
Part II: GNP in Billions of 1958 Dollars													
13	ASA-NBER[3,5]	70.3-73.2	—	—	—	3.5	3.7	6.1	7.9	8.8			
14	ARIMA[4]	"	—	—	—	8.7	13	17	23	29	36		
15	BEA (EAF3)	"	A	ex ante	subj	2.5	4.7	5.2	8.2	9.3	7.2		

No.	Model	Sample	Type	e	f								
16	BEA (EPF)	"	C	actual	subj	5.4	8.3	12	15	13	9.2	9.1	1.3
17	BEA (PSS)	"	D	actual	mech	7.9	11	11	11	15	17		
18	Fair[5]	"	B	ex ante	none	6.1	9.5	10	13	7.5			
19	Fair[5]	"	D	actual	none	4.4	6.6	7.8	11	10			
20	DRI	69.4–73.4	A	ex ante	subj	3.1	5.6	7.8	7.7	10	9.1	9.1	1.3
21	St. Louis[6]	69.1–73.3	D	actual	none	6.4	11	11	15	17	20	23	25
22	Wharton III	71.2–74.1	A	ex ante	subj	3.2	4.9	5.7	6.9	8.8	9.7	10	8.9
23	Liu-Hwa[6,7]	72Ja–Dc	D	actual	none	6.2	7.8	7.4					
24	Hickman-Coen	67–72									18[8]		

Part III: GNP Deflator (1958 : 100)

No.	Model	Sample	Type	e	f								
25	ASA-NBER[3,5]	70.3–73.2	—	—	—	.6	1.1	1.3	1.1	1.0	3.8		
26	ARIMA[4]	"	—	—	—	.8	1.3	2.1	2.8	3.0	1.1		
27	BEA (EAF3)	"	A	ex ante	subj	.5	.8	1.4	1.9	1.7	1.1		
28	BEA (EPF)	"	C	actual	subj	.5	1.0	1.3	1.5	1.7	2.0		
29	BEA (PSS)	"	D	actual	mech	.6	.6	.6	.7	1.0	1.4		
30	Fair[5]	"	B	ex ante	none	.8	1.1	1.3	1.5	1.4			
31	Fair[5]	"	D	actual	none	.7	1.0	1.2	1.2	1.1			
32	St. Louis[6]	69.1–73.3	D	actual	none	.6	1.1	1.4	1.7	2.0	2.3	2.6	2.6
33	Wharton III	71.2–74.1	A	ex ante	subj	.5	.8	1.2	1.3	1.4	1.5	1.5	1.5
34	Liu-Hwa[6,7]	72Ja–Dc	D	actual	none	.7	.8	.8					
35	Hickman-Coen	67–72											

[1] Forecasts of types A and B use ex ante exogenous variable values.
Forecasts of types C and D use actual exogenous variable values.
Forecasts of types A and C use subjective adjustments to the model.
Forecasts of types B and D use either no adjustments to the model, or adjustments made by a mechanical rule stated in advance.
See columns e and f.

[2] Abbreviations are as follows :
"subj" = subjective

Continued overleaf

TABLE 2 (cont.)

"mech" = by a mechanical rule stated in advance.

[3] Forecast errors from the ASA/NBER Survey of Regular Forecasters, as reported by Fair [7].

[4] ARIMA stands for auto-regressive integrates moving average forecasts, using only the lagged values of the variable being forecast, according to a Box-Jenkins technique described in Hirsch *et al.* [12]. It is a semi-naive method.

[5] Fair gives mean absolute errors. I have multiplied them by 1.22, 1.26, and 1.26 respectively for Parts I, II, and III to transform them approximately to RMSE's.

[6] Anderson and Carlson [2] and Liu and Hwa [15] do not present RMSE's but the authors kindly supplied to me the RMSE's shown here.

[7] Liu and Hwa [15] use a monthly model. The RMSE's shown for 1, 2, and 3 quarters ahead are their RMSE's for the middle month of each quarter, i.e., 2, 5, and 8 months ahead.

[8] Hickman and Coen [11] present only one post-sample RMSE for each variable; it is for forecasts of annual data during 1967–72, based on a dynamic simulation beginning with initial conditions for 1967.

[9] Fair [7A] and McNees [16] examine the errors of post-sample forecasts made with ex ante values of exogenous variables, by several model builders, for periods different from the ones reported in this Table. Tee average errors reported by those authors differ, sometimes rather substantially, from the RMSE's shown here for DRI and Wharton forecasts. Those authors show the DRI, Michigan, and Wharton forecasts about equal when ex ante exogenous values are used.

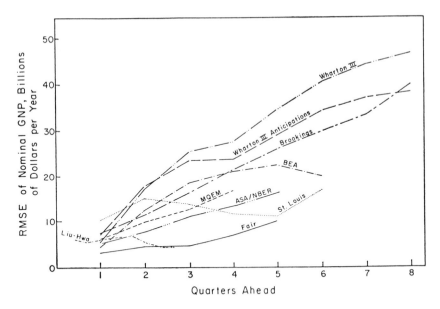

FIGURE 1

ROOT MEAN SQUARE ERRORS OF POST-SAMPLE FORECASTS OF NOMINAL GNP
USING ACTUAL EXOGENOUS VARIABLE VALUES AND NO SUBJECTIVE
ADJUSTMENTS. SOURCE: FROMM AND KLEIN [9], TABLE 1.

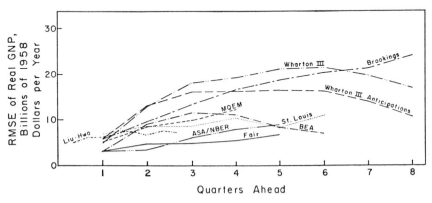

FIGURE 2

ROOT MEAN SQUARE ERRORS OF POST-SAMPLE FORECASTS OF REAL GNP USING
ACTUAL EXOGENOUS VARIABLE VALUES AND NO SUBJECTIVE
ADJUSTMENTS. SOURCE: FROMM AND KLEIN [9], TABLE 1.

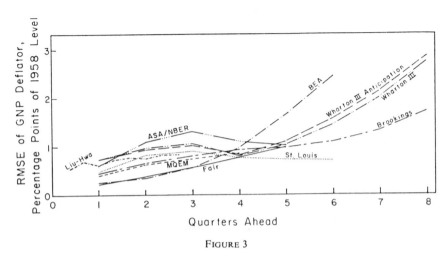

FIGURE 3

ROOT MEAN SQUARE ERRORS OF POST-SAMPLE FORECASTS OF THE GNP DEFLATOR
USING ACTUAL EXOGENOUS VARIABLE VALUES AND NO SUBJECTIVE
ADJUSTMENTS. SOURCE: FROMM AND KLEIN [9], TABLE 3.

few exceptions. Typically the RMSE doubles or trebles as we go from one quarter ahead to 5 quarters ahead. This makes it clear, if indeed it was not clear already, that these econometric models are at best only approximations to the economy as it existed when they were built and estimated; they do not state fundamental immutable laws of human behavior.

There are substantial differences in the forecasting abilities of the models unassisted by judgment, as shown in the graphs. All have RMSE's for real and nominal GNP that are 1% or less for one quarter ahead, and 3% or less for five or six quarters ahead. The Fair model looks relatively good here, and so does the St. Louis model after one or two quarters, but remember that each treats as exogenous certain variables that convey a lot of information about income and employment, and are difficult to forecast ex ante. For the Fair model the chief such variables are consumer and business anticipations, financial variables related to the housing market, and potential output. For the St. Louis model they are high-employment Federal expenditures, and potential output. This helps explain both their good performance and the fact that their errors do not grow very much as the horizon grows. The Michigan model sometimes takes the Treasury bill rate as exogenous, which gives it some advantage.

To make a comparison of models without giving an advantage to a model that treats a hard-to-forecast variable as exogenous, one can compare models via unadjusted forecasts that use ex ante values of the exogenous variables. Unfortunately, the only model for which such forecasts are presented in this symposium is Fair's, so no such comparisons can be made here.

4. POLICY SIMULATIONS YIELDED BY THE MODELS

Government-purchases multipliers (without accommodating monetary policy) are presented for the models in this symposium in Table 3, and monetary policy multipliers in Table 4. Similar multipliers for real and nominal GNP are presented in Fromm and Klein [9]. For real GNP they are shown in Figures 4 and 5.[5]

All the quarterly models in Table 3 agree fairly closely on fiscal multipliers for GNP, both real and nominal, for about the first two years after the fiscal policy change: the two-year government purchases multiplier is put between 1.9 and 2.8 for nominal GNP, and between 1.4 and 2.4 for real GNP. All the quarterly models in Fromm and Klein [9] agree approximately with these results, except for the St. Louis model which puts the five-quarter (and later) fiscal multipliers close to zero. But after two years, the agreement begins to evaporate.

Consider nominal GNP first. The MPS model shows a substantial decline in the fiscal multiplier from 3.1 at seven quarters to 1.8 at 20 quarters, when the policy simulation was stopped. The other models show fiscal multipliers still increasing at 40 quarters, some with small cycles and some without, except possibly the Fair and Liu-Hwa models, whose policy simulations do not go that far.

Consider real GNP next. Here the disagreement is even more spectacular. Three models show substantial negative government-purchases multipliers after a time: -0.5 at 20 quarters for MPS, -3 at 40 quarters for Wharton III, and -23 at 40 quarters for BEA! Four models show declines in the government-purchases multiplier from its peak, amounting to ten percent in one case and about 66 percent in the others, by the end of the policy simulation: Wharton III anticipations model and Wharton annual model at 20 quarters, and the Brookings and DRI models at 40 quarters. The Michigan model's multiplier falls to zero at 40 quarters. The Hickman-Coen multiplier is still rising after 40 quarters. The Hickman-Coen multiplier is still rising after 40 quarters, but turns down at 56 quarters and is still falling at 64 quarters.

This is a strikingly varied set of results concerning the long-run effect of an increase in government purchases.

Consider now the effects of a \$1 billion increase in annual government purchases on prices, shown in Table 3. All the models find the effect to be less than one percent, but they do not agree very well. The Hickman-Coen model shows the effect peaking after 16 quarters, but the others show it still increasing at the end of the policy simulation, 16 to 40 quarters after the policy change.

Consider now the response over time to an easing of monetary policy, as shown in Table 4. There is very serious disagreement here, and it begins immediately after the policy change. Most models do agree that both real and nominal GNP will be increased, but the DRI model shows a negative effect on both from about 20 to 40 quarters after the change, and the Hickman-Coen model shows a small negative effect on both at 52 to 56 quarters and a small

---

[5] For the MPS model the results graphed in Figure 4 were computed by Albert Ando, while those in Figures 1–3 and 5 were computed by the Model Comparison Seminar.

TABLE 3

FISCAL MULTIPLIER EFFECTS OF A $1 BILLION INCREASE IN NOMINAL[1] GOVERNMENT PURCHASES UPON NOMINAL GNP, REAL GNP, AND THE GNP DEFLATOR, WITHOUT ACCOMMODATING MONETARY POLICY

Part I: Nominal GNP in Billions of Dollars

Fiscal Multiplies[2] as a Function of Time Elapsed — Number of Quarters Elapsed

Line (a)	Model (b)	Simulation Period (c)	1 (d)	4 (e)	8 (f)	12 (g)	14 (h)	16 (j)	20 (k)	28 (l)	40 (m)	56 (n)	64 (p)	q	r
1	BEA[3]	66.1-70.4	.9	2.2	2.8	3.1		2.9	2.9*						
2	DRI[1]	63.1-72.4	1.5	2.3	2.5	2.3	2.3	2.4	2.6	3.3	3.7*				
3	MQEM	58.1-67.4	.7	1.9	2.3	1.8		1.3	1.5	2.3	2.5*				
4	MQEM	64.1-73.4	.8	2.1	2.7	2.8		2.8	3.3	4.7	5.7*				
5	Wharton III[4]	62.1-65.4	1.3	1.8	2.2	2.5	2.5	2.5*							
6	Liu-Hwa	61Ja-67Dc	.6	1.5	1.9	2.4	2.6*								
7	Liu-Hwa	68Ja-71Dc	.6	1.3	1.8	2.3	2.4*								
8	Hickman-Coen	51-66		2.7	2.5	2.9		3.5	3.7	3.6	3.9	4.4	4.3		

Part II: Real GNP in Billions of 1958 Dollars

Number of Quarters Elapsed

Line	Model	Simulation Period	1	4	6	8	12	14	16	20	24	28	40	56	64
9	BEA[3]	66.1-70.4	.8	1.7	1.5	1.4	.7		.2	-.3					
10	DRI[1]	63.1-72.4	1.5	2.2	2.2	2.2	1.8	1.7	1.7	1.8	2.1	2.3	1.8		
11	MQEM	58.1-67.4	.8	1.9	2.2	2.1	1.4		.7	.8	1.2	1.2	.5		

#	Model	Period	1	4	8	12	16	20	28	40	56	64		
12	MQEM	64.1–73.4	.8	2.0	$\overline{2.2}$	2.1	1.2		.2	$\overline{.1}$	$\overline{.5}$	.2	−1.0	
13	Wharton III[4]	62.1–65.4	1.3	2.0	2.2	2.4	$\overline{2.5}$	2.3	2.2	1.6		2.1		
14	Wharton III anticipations	62.1–66.4	1.1	1.7	1.8	$\overline{1.8}$			1.7	1.6				
15	Liu-Hwa	61Ja–67Dc	.6	1.5	$\overline{1.7}$	$\overline{1.7}$	1.6	1.6						
16	Liu-Hwa	68Ja–71Dc	.5	1.1	$\overline{1.1}$	1.1	1.1	1.0				2.1		
17	Hickman-Coen	51–66		$\overline{1.6}$		$\overline{.9}$	1.1		1.6	$\overline{1.6}$	$\overline{1.6}$	1.7	$\overline{2.4}$	1.9

Part III: GNP Deflator (1958 : 100)

#	Model	Period	Number of Quarters Elapsed									
			1	4	8	12	16	20	28	40	56	64
18	BEA[3]	66.1–70.4	0	.04	.20	.34	.41	.45*	.15	.27*		
19	MQEM	58.1–67.4	−.02	−.01	.02	.07	.11	.12	.59	.89*		
20	MQEM	64.1–73.4	0	−.01	.06	.20	.37	.43				
21	Wharton III[4]	62.1–65.4	−.02	−.14	−.10	.05	$\overline{.30}$*		.43	.36	.33	.31
22	Hickman-Coen	51–66		.34	.44	.47	$\overline{.50}$	.50				

[1] For the DRI model's fiscal simulation, the increase in government purchases was in real terms.

[2] An asterisk * means the multiplier was still growing at the end of the simulation. An overline ‾ or an underline _ denotes a peak or a trough, respectively.

[3] This is the BEA simulation that kept the unemployment rate at 4%.

[4] This is the Wharton III simulation that increased nondefense purchases.

TABLE 4

MONETARY POLICY: EFFECTS OF A $1 BILLION INCREASE IN UNBORROWED RESERVES, OR A CUT OF 50 BASIS POINT IN THE TREASURY BILL RATE, ON NOMINAL GNP, REAL GNP, AND THE GNP DEFLATOR

Part I: Nominal GNP in Billions of Dollars

| Line | Model | Simulation Period | Policy Variable[1] | Monetary Policy Effects[2] as a Function of Time Elapsed — Number of Quarters Elapsed | | | | | | | | | | | |
(a)	(b)	(c)	(d)	1 (e)	4 (f)	8 (g)	10 (h)	12 (j)	14 (k)	16 (l)	20 (m)	32 (n)	36 (p)	56 (q)	64 (r)
1	DRI	63.1-72.4	RU	0	7	11	9	7	5	3	-1	-2	-3		
2	MQEM	58.1-67.4	TBR	0	1.6	8.4	9.1	8.8		7.4	6.3	7.5	7.4		
3	MQEM	64.1-73.4	TBR	0	2.8	8.4	10	12		13	11	11	10		
4	Wharton III	62.1-65.4	RU	1.3	4.2	6.8	7.6	8.1	7.9	7.5					
5	Wharton III	65.1-68.4	RU	1.0	3.2	5.3	6.2	6.7	7.0	7.2*					
6	Liu-Hwa	61Ja-67Dc	RU	0	2.2	14	21	27	31*						
7	Liu-Hwa	68Ja-71Dc	RU	0	2.2	13	20	24	28*						
8	Hickman-Coen	51-66	RU	0	2.9	4.0		2.5		.4	.4	.3	1.1	-.2	.2*

Part II: Real GNP in Billions of 1958 Dollars

| Line | Model | Simulation Period | Policy Variable[1] | Number of Quarters Elapsed | | | | | | | | | | | |
(a)	(b)	(c)	(d)	1 (e)	4 (f)	8 (g)	10 (h)	12 (j)	14 (k)	16 (l)	24 (m)	28 (n)	36 (p)	56 (q)	64 (r)
9	DRI	63.1-72.4	RU	0	7	9	8	6	2	0	-4	-3	-2*		
10	MQEM	58.1-67.4	TBR	0	1.6	8.0	8.4	7.8		5.3	2.9	3.2	2.7		
11	MQEM	64.1-73.4	TBR	0	2.7	7.5	8.6	8.4		5.8	1.6	1.3	.6		

			1	3	4	8	16	20	28	32	36	40	56	64
12	Wharton III	62.1-65.4	RU	1.4	4.5	7.2	8.0	$\overline{8.4}$	8.0	7.8					
13	Wharton III	65.1-68.4	RU	1.1	3.4	5.2	5.7	$\overline{6.0}$	5.8	5.6					
14	Wharton III anticipations	62.1-66.4	RU	.7	1.7	2.6		$\overline{2.9}$		2.7					
15	Liu-Hwa	61Ja-67Dc	RU	0	2.2	13	17	20	22*						
16	Liu-Hwa	68Ja-71Dc	RU	0	$\underline{1.8}$	10	14	15	16*						
17	Hickman-Coen	51-66	RU		$\underline{1.7}$	1.7	.6		-.3		.4	.4	$\overline{.7}$	$\underline{-.1}$	.1*

Part III: GNP Deflator (1958 : 100)

				Number of Quarters Elapsed										
				1	3	4	8	16	20	28	32	36	40	56	64
18	MQEM	58.1-67.4	TBR	0	.01	0	.05	.35	.50	$\overline{.58}$	.61	.65	.66*		
19	MQEM	64.1-73.4	TBR	0	0	-.02	0	.79	1.10	$\overline{1.26}$	1.22	1.14	.95		
20	Wharton III	62.1-65.4	RU	-.04	-.20	-.12	-.18	-.09							
21	Wharton III	65.1-68.4	RU	0	-.01	-.01	-.01	0							
22	Hickman-Coen	51-66	RU			.36	$\underline{.62}$	.17	$\underline{.07}$	$\underline{.10}$	$\underline{.04}$	$\overline{.09}$	.04	$\underline{-.02}$	0*

[1] RU = unborrowed reserves

TBR = Treasury bill rate

[2] An asterisk * means the effect was still increasing at the end of the simulation. An overline ⌐ or underline _ denotes a peak or a trough in the effect, respectively.

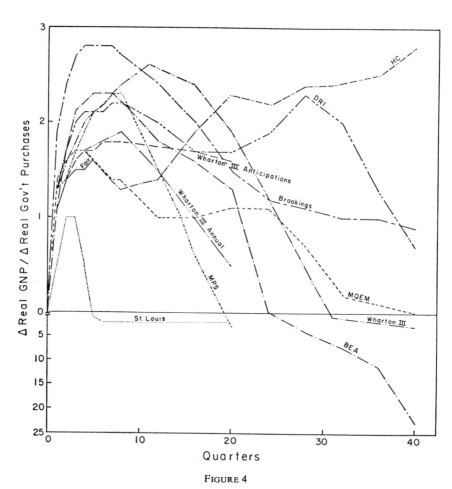

FIGURE 4

DYNAMIC MULTIPLIER EFFECTS OF A MAINTAINED $1 BILLION INCREASE IN REAL
GOVERNMENT PURCHASES UPON REAL GNP WITHOUT ACCOMODATING
MONETALY POLICY AS A FUNCTION OF TIME ELAPSED.
SOURCE: FROMM AND KLEIN [9], TABLE 5.

negative effect on real GNP at 16 quarters. The amounts of increase obtained
by the other models differ by factors of three and four after eight to 12 quarters,
and more after that. Some models show a monotonically increasing effect over
time, and some show cycles. The four models whose monetary policy effects
are reported in Fromm and Klein [9] but not in Table 4 are equally at variance
with each other and with the rest. The MPS model shows very large effects
of a $1 billion step increase in unborrowed reserves, rising to $36 billion for
nominal GNP and to $16 billion for real GNP at the end of 20 quarters. The
Wharton annual model shows similar effects, except that its effect on real GNP

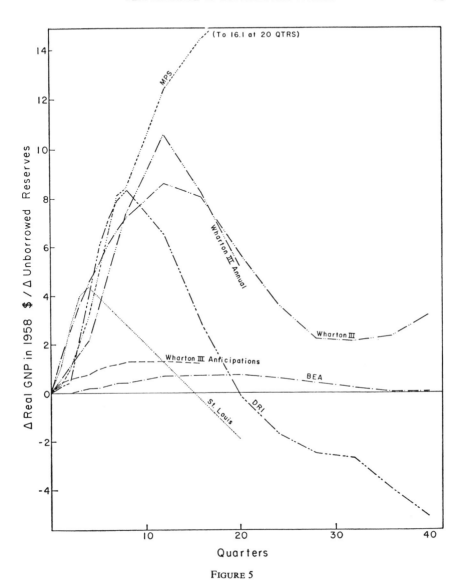

FIGURE 5

DYNAMIC MULTIPLIER EFFECTS OF A MAINTAINED $1.0 BILLION INCREASE IN UNBOR-
ROWED RESERVES UPON REAL GNP AS A FUNCTION OF TIME ELAPSED (EXCEPT
FOR ST. LOUIS MODEL, WHERE THERE IS A $1 BILLION INCREASE IN M_1).
SOURCE: FROMM AND KLEIN [9], TABLE 8.

turns down at about 12 quarters. According to the St. Louis model, the effect
on nominal GNP rises to about $5 billion after four quarters and stabilizes there,
while the effect on real GNP follows the nominal effect for about four quarters

and then turns down, becoming slightly negative at 16 and 20 quarters. The BEA model shows the effect on nominal GNP rising throughout 40 quarters, and the effect on real GNP being near zero for five quarters, rising to $0.7 billion at 16 quarters, and returning to zero at 36 to 40 quarters.

The models differ almost as much on the effect of an easing of monetary policy on the price level, as shown in Table 4. The Wharton III model shows virtually no effect (at least for 16 quarters), the Hickman-Coen model shows an interim increase but no effect remaining at 64 quarters, and the Michigan model shows a positive effect, still increasing at the end of the 1958–67 policy simulation period, but decreasing at the end of the 1964–73 period.

The models disagree very strongly about the effects that follow from important fiscal and monetary policy actions. This is probably due in part to the use of different simulation periods. We face great uncertainty about this vital matter, until we can determine which of the models are wrong about it, and which (if any) are right. It would be valuable to have post-model-building RMSE statistics over much longer horizons than the eight quarters shown in Table 2 and the graphs, and policy simulations over periods having identical starting dates. Failing this, it will be difficult to make the important choice among models that have similar multiplier paths over short periods but extremely different paths over long periods.

An important aspect of the evaluation of an econometric model is the analysis of the economic theory contained in its equations. It is desirable to relate the theoretical structure of each model to the results it yields, including the character of the time-paths predicted by the model for the effects of important policy changes. That is too large an undertaking to be carried out in this paper. It will certainly be the subject of much future research. Each of the papers in this symposium has made a valuable contribution toward this end.[6]

5. SUGGESTIONS FOR TESTING MODELS AND FORECASTERS

For the future, the following types of computations would be helpful in testing and comparing the performance of econometric models, and the forecasting prowess of those who use them. Some of these computations are already being published by some model builders.

Errors of forecasts for periods that occur after the building of the model.

Errors of forecasts over longer horizons that have typically been used so far: at least eight quarters, and preferably much longer. Of course, a model cannot be evaluated in this way until several years after it is built.

Residuals of structural equations in post-model-building periods, to determine which structural equations stand up over time and which do not.

RMSE's (root mean square errors) of forecasts and residuals that are based on
   (a) true exogenous values, and again ex ante exogenous values.

---

[6] Since I have criticized some macro-econometric models for not taking account of the government budget restraint, it is a pleasure to agree with Ando [3] that the simplified version of the MPS model presented there contains the government budget restraint implicitly.

(b) subjective adjustments to the model, and again no adjustments.
(c) a model that has been re-estimated using all data right up to the beginning of the forecast period, and again a model that has not been re-estimated.
(d) preliminary data as available at the beginning of the forecast peried, and again final revised data.

Policy simulations for periods of 20 years in order to find which policies have cyclical effects and which have monotonic effects, and whether the policy multipliers appear to converge eventually, and if so, to what values.

Comparisons of policy multipliers over time and between models, and the attempt to find which models yield the most reliable multipliers over long periods. For this purpose, the abovementioned RMSE's over longer forecasting horizons will help.

Stochastic as well as exact policy simulations, to determine whether exact simulations are a reliable guide in a world where nonstochastic equations do not perfectly describe events. Starting dates for simulations should be identical.

Performance in predicting turning points for the period after the model was built.[7] This includes an assessment of whether actual turing points are correctly predicted, and also of whether the model predicts the occurrence of turning points that do not actually occur.

The Johns Hopkins University, U.S.A.

REFERENCES

[1] ADAMS, F. GERARD AND VIJAYA G. DUGGAL, "Anticipations Variables in an Econometric Model: The Anticipations Version of Wharton Mark III," *International Economic Review*, XV (June, 1974), 267-284.
[2] ANDERSEN LEONALL C. AND KEITH CARLSON, "St. Louis Model Revisited," *International Economic Review*, XV (June, 1974), 305-327.
[3] ANDO, ALBERT, "Some Aspects of Stabilization Policies, the Monetarist Controversy, and the MPS Model," *International Economic Review*, XV (October, 1974), 541-571.
[4] BROWN, T. M., "Standard Error of Forecast of a Complete Econometric Model," *Econometrica*, XXII (April, 1954), 178-192.
[5] DUGGAL, VIJAYA G., LAWRENCE R. KLEIN, AND MICHAEL D. McCARTHY, "The Wharton Model Mark III: A Modern IS-LM Construct," *International Economic Review*, XV (October, 1974), 572-594.
[6] ECKSTEIN, OTTO, EDWARD W. GREEN, AND ALLEN SINAI, "The Data Resources Model: Uses, Structure and Analysis of the U. S. Economy," *International Economic Review*, XV (October, 1974), 595-615.
[7] FAIR, RAY, "An Evaluation of a Short-Run Forecasting Model," *International Economic Review*, XV (June, 1974), 285-304.
[7A] McNEES, STEPHEN K., "The Predictive Accuracy of Econometric Forecasts," *New England Economic Review* (September/October, 1973), 3-27.
[8] FROMM, GARY AND LAWRENCE R. KLEIN, "A Comparison of Eleven Econometric Models of the United States," *American Economic Review*, LXIII (May, 1973), 385-393.

[7] Adams and Duggal [1] discuss the performance of the Wharton III anticipations model at turning points, but only within the sample, where the performance can be expected to be better than for post-sample and post-model-building periods.

74   CARL F. CHRIST

[9] _____, AND _____, "The NBER/NSF Model Comparison Seminar: An Analysis of Results," forthcoming in *Annals of Economic and Social Measurement*.

[10] GOLDBERGER, ARTHUR S., A. L. NAGAR, AND H. S. ODEH, "The Covariance Matrices of Reduced-Form Coefficients and of Forecasts for a Structural Econometric Model," *Econometrica*, XXIX (October, 1961), 556-573.

[11] HICKMAN, BERT G., MICHAEL D. HURD, AND ROBERT M. COEN, "The Hickman-Coen Annual Growth Model: Structural Characteristics and Policy Responses," *International Economic Review*, XVI (February, 1975).

[12] HIRSCH, ALBERT A., BRUCE T. GRIMM, AND GORTI V. L. NARASIMHAM, "Some Multiplier and Error Characteristics of the BEA Quarterly Model," *International Economic Review*, XV (October, 1974), 616-631.

[13] HOTELLING, HAROLD, "Problems of Prediction," *American Journal of Sociology*, XLVIII (1942-43), 61-76.

[14] HYMANS, SAUL H. AND HAROLD T. SHAPIRO, "The Structure and Properties of the Michigan Quarterly Econometric Model of the U. S. Economy," *International Economic Review*, XV (October, 1974), 632-653.

[15] LIU, TA-CHUNG AND ERH-CHENG HWA, "Structure and Applications of a Monthly Econometric Model of the U. S. Economy," *International Economic Review*, XV (June, 1974), 328-365.

[16] FAIR, RAY C., "Forecasts from the Fair Model and a Comparison of the Recent Forecasting Records of Seven Forecasters," Princeton University Econometric Research Program, July, 1973 (duplicated).

[6]

Indian Economic Review, Special Number, 1992, pp. 325–328

Decomposition of the Expected Squared Error of Forecast from a Linear Forecasting Equation

CARL F. CHRIST

The Johns Hopkins University, Baltimore

1. THE PROBLEM

Multivariate linear equations are often used to forecast future values of dependent variables, based on sample-period estimates of the parameters of the equations, and on forecasts somehow obtained for the future values of the independent variables. Error in such a dependent variable forecast can arise from three causes, even assuming (as we shall) that the true equation is linear. First, there is typically a disturbance associated with the equation, with in general has a nonzero value for the forecast period. Second, the forecasts of the independent variables may be incorrect. Third, the estimated values of the parameters may be incorrect for three reasons: because of sampling error in the estimation process, because of a structural change in the parameters occurring between the sample period and the forecast period, and because of error in specifying the forecasting equation.

For example, if an independent variable is *erroneously excluded* from the forecasting equation, then of course the estimate of its parameter will be zero, which is itself incorrect, and bias may be introduced in the estimation of other parameters as well. On the other hand, if an independent variable is *erroneously included* in the forecasting equation, and if the estimator used has desirable properties (e.g., efficiency), we may expect to obtain good estimates of all the parameters, including an estimate of the wrongly included variable's parameter that is near the true value of zero, though of course it will have a positive variance, and the variances of the estimators of other parameters may be increased by the incorrect inclusion.

This note decomposes the expected squared error of such a forecast of a dependent variable into 9 components arising from (1) the variance of the equation's disturbance, (2) bias in the estimation of the parameters for any of the three reasons mentioned above, (3) the covariance matrix of the estimated parameters, (4) bias in the forecasting of the independent variables, (5) the covariance matrix of the forecasts of the independent variables, and (6) to (9) four types of interactions among the foregoing.

2. THE MODEL

Let the observations in the sample period, upon which estimation is based, be indexed $t = 1, \ldots, T$. Let the subsequent period for which the forecast is to be made be indexed by $t = T + \tau$. Let the true equation at time $T + \tau$ be denoted by

$$y_{T+\tau} = \beta' z_{T+\tau} + u_{T+\tau}$$

207

and let the equation specified and estimated for forecasting be

$$y_{F, T+\tau} = \hat{\beta}' z_{F, T+\tau}$$

Here $y_{T+\tau}$ and $y_{F, T+\tau}$ denote respectively the actual and the forecast values of the dependent variable for time $T + \tau$; β' and $\hat{\beta}'$ denote respectively the true value as of time $T + \tau$ and the estimated value of the row vector of the equation's parameters; $z_{T+\tau}$ and $z_{F, T+\tau}$ denote respectively the column vectors of true and forecast values of the independent variables for time $T + \tau$; and $u_{T+\tau}$ denotes the true disturbance at time $T + \tau$. For simplicity we shall omit the subscripts $T + \tau$ henceforth unless clarity demands them.

We regard both the vectors z and z_F as containing all of the variables that have nonzero parameters in the true equation, and also all the variables that the erroneorsly included in the specification of the forecasting equation. Then the vectors z, z_F, β' and $\hat{\beta}'$ all have the same order. The values of β_i are zero for those z_i that are erroneously included in the forecasting equation, and the values of $\hat{\beta}_i$ are zero for those z_i that are erroneously excluded from the forecasting equation.

We adopt the following additional notation. E_c and cov_c will deonote respectively conditional expectations and conditional covariances, given the valus of z for appropriate times. $\hat{\beta}$ is conditional upon $z_1, \ldots, z_T$. z_F is conditional on $z_1, \ldots, z_T$ and, if the forecaster cares to use them, also on $z_{T+1}, \ldots, z_{T+\tau-1}$. y is condiitonal on z at time $T + \tau$. θ will deonte $Ez_F - z$, the bias in forecasting z. δ will denote $E\hat{\beta} - \beta$, the bias in estimating β.

We use the following assumptions. $Eu_{T+\tau} = 0$, $Eu_{T+\tau}^2 = \sigma^2$, and $Eu_s u_{T+\tau} = 0$ for all $s \leq T$. The forecast-period disturbance u is independent of the estimator $\hat{\beta}$ and of the forecast-period values z and z_F. The forecasting error $z_F - z$ is independent of z and of $\hat{\beta}$. Therefore z is predetermined at time $T + \tau$, but is not necessarily exogenous. The following symmetrical table summarizes the assumed independences and the permitted dependences (only the below-diagonal elements are entered):

	u	z	z_F	$z_F - z$
z	ind	—		
z_F	ind	dep	—	
$z_F - z$	ind	ind	dep	—
$\hat{\beta}$	ind	dep	dep	ind

3.   DECOMPOSITION OF THE EXPECTED SQUARED ERROR

The expected squared error of the *ex ante* forecast of y for period $T + \tau$, made prior to that time but after time T, on the basis of the estimated parameter vector $\hat{\beta}$ and the forecast z_F of the independent variables, is

$$E_c(y_F - y)^2 = E_c(\hat{\beta}' z_F - \beta' z - u)^2$$
$$= E_c[-u + \hat{\beta}'(z_F - z) + (\hat{\beta}' - \beta')z]^2$$

Squarring, taking the expectation of the resulting sum, and using the facts that u in independent of $\hat{\beta}$, z, and z_F, and has mean zero, we obtain

$$= \sigma^2 + E_c[\hat{\beta}'(z_F - z)]^2 + E_c[(\hat{\beta}' - \beta')z]^2 + 2E_c[\hat{\beta}'(z_F - z)(\hat{\beta}' - \beta')z]$$

Expressing each vector product in terms of the individual elements of the vectors, and evaluating the indicated squares and cross products of the resulting sums, we obtain

$$= \sigma^2 + E_c \Sigma\Sigma\hat{\beta}_i\hat{\beta}_j(z_{Fi} - z_i)(z_{Fj} - z_j) + E_c\Sigma\Sigma(\hat{\beta}_i - \beta_i)(\hat{\beta}_j - \beta_j)z_iz_j + 2E_c\Sigma\Sigma\hat{\beta}_i(\hat{\beta}_j - \beta_j)(z_{Fi} - z_i)z_j$$

where each double sum runs over i and j from 1 to K, K being the order of the vectors $\hat{\beta}$, β, z_F, and z. Taking advantage of the independence assumptions and the conditional expectations, we obtain

$$= \sigma^2 + \Sigma\Sigma(E_c\hat{\beta}_i\hat{\beta}_j)E(z_{Fi} - z_i)(z_{Fj} - z_j) + \Sigma\Sigma[E_c(\hat{\beta}_i - \beta_i)(\hat{\beta}_j - \beta_j)]z_iz_j + 2\Sigma\Sigma[E_c\hat{\beta}_i(\hat{\beta}_j - \beta_j)][E(z_{Fi} - z_i)]z_j$$

Nothing that the expectation of the product of two random variables is their covariance minus the product of their expectations, and using the definitions of θ and δ, and keeping the 4 main terms in the same order as above, we obtain

$$= \delta^2 + \Sigma\Sigma[\mathrm{cov}_c(\hat{\beta}_i, \hat{\beta}_j) + \beta_i\beta_j + \delta_i\delta_j + \beta_i\delta_j + \delta_i\beta_j][\mathrm{cov}(z_{Fi} - z_{Fj}) + \theta_i\theta_j] + \Sigma\Sigma[\mathrm{cov}_c(\hat{\beta}_i, \hat{\beta}_j) + \delta_i\delta_j]z_iz_j$$
$$+ 2\Sigma\Sigma[\mathrm{cov}_c(\hat{\beta}_i, \hat{\beta}_j) + \delta_i\delta_j + \beta_i\delta_j]\theta_iz_j$$

Performing the indicated multiplications and collecting similar terms, we obtain the final expression for the decomposition of the expected squared error of an *ex ante* forecast, as follows, where the terms are numbered from 1 to 9 and labeled for easy reference:

	$E_c(y_F - y)^2$	
1	$= \sigma^2$	var (u)
2	$+ \Sigma\Sigma\delta_jz_iz_j$	bias of $\hat{\beta}$
3	$+ \Sigma\Sigma \, \mathrm{cov}_c(\hat{\beta}_i, \hat{\beta}_j)z_iz_j$	cov of $\hat{\beta}$
4	$+ \Sigma\Sigma\theta_i\theta_j\beta_i\beta_j$	bias of z_F
5	$+ \Sigma\Sigma \, \mathrm{cov}(z_{Fi}, z_{Fj})\beta_i\beta_j$	cov of z_F
6	$+ \Sigma\Sigma \, \mathrm{cov}_c(\hat{\beta}_i\hat{\beta}_j) \, \mathrm{cov}(z_{sub}Fi, z_{Fj})$	covs of $\hat{\beta}$ and z_F
7	$+ 2\Sigma\Sigma \, \mathrm{cov}_c(\hat{\beta}_i, \hat{\beta}_j)\theta_i(z_j + \frac{1}{2}\theta_j)$	cov of $\hat{\beta}$ and bias of z_F
8	$+ 2\Sigma\Sigma \, \mathrm{cov}(z_{Fi}, z_{Fj})\delta_i(\beta_j + \frac{1}{2}\delta_j)$	cov of z_F and bias of $\hat{\beta}$
9	$+ 2\Sigma\Sigma[\delta_i\delta_j\theta_i(z_j + \frac{1}{2}\theta_j) + \beta_i\delta_j\theta_i(z_j + \theta_j)]$	bias of $\hat{\beta}$ and z_F

4.   INTERPRETING THE DECOMPOSITION

This is a generalization of the familiar expression for the variance of forecast from a regression equation given by Hotelling (1942), which includes only terms 1 and 3 above. Observe that if the true parameter β that prevails during the forecast period is estimated without bias by $\hat{\beta}$, then $\delta = E\hat{\beta} - \beta = 0$, and terms 2, 8, and 9 drop out. If there were no sampling variation in the estimation of the parameters, then $\mathrm{cov}_c(\hat{\beta}_i, \hat{\beta}_j)$ would be zero, and terms 3, 6, and 7 would drop out. If the forecasts of the independent variables are unbiased, then $\theta = Ez_F - z = 0$, and terms 4, 7, and 9 drop out. If the forecasts of the independent variables for time $T + \tau$ were nonstochastic so that $\mathrm{cov}(z_{Fi}, z_{Fj}) = 0$, then terms 5, 6, and 8 would drop out. If the expected squared error is desired for *ex post* forecasts that are based on correct values of the independent variables, it can be obtained by dropping terms 4 through 9.

Note what happens if a variable, say z_K, is erroneously omitted from the equation. Its estimated parameter $\hat{\beta}_K$ is assigned the value zero. Hence the bias in estimating that parameter is $\delta_K = E\hat{\beta}_K - \beta_K = -\beta_K$. Bias may enter into the estimation of other parameters as a result of the exclusion of z_K, particularly if z_K is correlated with the correctly included variables. Because $\hat{\beta}_K$ is nonstochastic, its variance will be zero, as will its covariance with every other parameter. The forecast z_{FK} of z_K becomes irrelevant, and can be replaced by an arbitrary constant, because whatever value is chosen for it, it will be multiplied by the zero value of $\hat{\beta}_K$; hence the variance of z_{FK} becomes zero, as does the covariance of z_{FK} with every other forecast z_{Fi}. Because of these simplifications, term 2 is affected, certain expressions in terms 3, 5, 6, 7, and 8 drop out (those involving $i = K$ and $j = K$), and certain expressions cancel out in terms 4 and 9 (again those involving $i = K$ and $j = K$).

If a varaible is incorrectly included in the equation, then as noted earlier the corresponding component of β will be zero, so that the corresponding expressions in terms 4, 5, and 9 drop out. Notice that nothing has been said about the estimation method used to obtain $\hat{\beta}$. The assumptions made are not strong enough to insure that least squares estimation of β will be unbiased, consistent, or efficient. The result applies to any estimation method for β, unbiased or not.

REFERENCE

Hotelling, Harold (1942), Problems of prediction, *American Journal of Sociology*, Vol. 48 (1942–43), 61–76.

Carl F. Christ

Carl F. Christ is a professor of economics at The Johns Hopkins University. Helpful comments on an earlier draft were made by Jonathan Ahlbrecht, Stephen Blough, Pedro de Lima and William Zame. Any remaining shortcomings are my responsibility.

Assessing Applied Econometric Results

*I*T IS A GREAT HONOR to be asked to participate in this conference to celebrate the work of Ted Balbach, who has long upheld the standard of relevant, independent, intelligible economic studies at the Federal Reserve Bank of St. Louis.

My invitation to this conference asked for a philosophical paper about good econometric practice. I have organized my views as follows. Part I of the paper defines the concept of an ideal econometric model and argues that to tell whether a model is ideal, we must test it against new data—data that were not available when the model was formulated. Such testing suggests that econometric models are not ideal, but are approximations to a changing reality. Part I closes with a list of desirable properties that we can realistically seek in econometric models. Part II is a loosely connected set of comments and criticisms about several econometric techniques. Part III discusses methods of evaluating econometric models by means of their forecasts and summarizes some results of such evaluations, as proposed in part I. Part IV resurrects an old, plain-vanilla equation relating monetary velocity to an interest rate and tests it with more recent data. The rather remarkable result is that it still does about as well today as it did nearly 40 years ago. Part V is a brief conclusion.

HOW TO RECOGNIZE AN IDEAL MODEL IF YOU MEET ONE

The Goal of Research and the Concept of an Ideal Model

The goal of economic research is to improve knowledge and understanding of the economy, either for their own sake, or for practical use. We want to know how to control what is controllable, how to adapt to what is uncontrollable, and how to tell which is which. The goal of economic research is analogous to the prayer of Alcoholics Anonymous (I do not suggest that economics is exactly like alcoholism)—"God grant me the serenity to accept the things I cannot change; the courage to change the things I can; and the wisdom to know the difference."

The goal of applied econometrics is *quantitative* knowledge expressed in the form of mathematical equations.

I invite you to think of an ideal econometric model, by which I mean a set of equations, complete or incomplete, with numerically estimated parameters, that describes some interesting set of past data, closely but not perfectly, and that

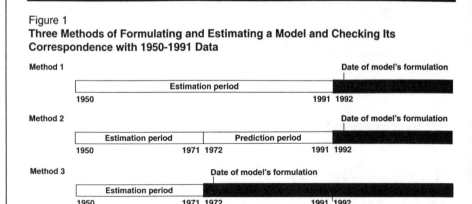

Figure 1

Three Methods of Formulating and Estimating a Model and Checking Its Correspondence with 1950-1991 Data

will continue to describe all future data of that type.

The Need for Testing Against New Data

How can we tell whether we have found an ideal econometric model? We can certainly tell how well a model describes a given set of *past* data. (We will discuss what is meant by a good description later). Suppose we have a model in 1992, with estimated parameters, that closely describes past data for 1950–91. To tell whether it is the ideal model we seek, we must try it with future data. Suppose that after three years we try the model with data for 1992–94, and it describes them closely. Still, in 1995 all we will be sure of is that it describes data closely for a past period, this time from 1950 through 1994. In principle we can never be sure we have found an ideal model because there will always be more future data to come, so we will never be able to say that a model is ideal. The longer the string of future data that a model describes closely, however, the more confidence we have in it.

Is this only a matter of the *amount* of data that the model describes, or is there something else involved? I argue that something else is involved.

Suppose again that in 1992 we have a model that closely describes an interesting data set for the past period 1950–91. Consider the following three methods, shown in figure 1, by which this model might have been obtained and by which its ability to describe data for 1950 through 1991 might have been assessed:

1. It was formulated in *1992*, and fitted to data for the *entire* period 1950–91.

2. It was formulated in *1992*, fitted to data for the *sub-period* 1950–71, and used to predict data from 1972 through 1991.

3. It was formulated in *1972*, fitted to data for the *sub-period* 1950–71, and used to predict data from 1972 through 1991.

Methods 1 and 2 differ in that method 1 fits the model to *all* the available data, whereas method 2 fits it to the first part only and uses the result to predict the second part, from 1972 onward. 1972 is not a randomly chosen date. It was the year before the first oil crisis. Method 3 differs in that the model builder did not yet know about the oil crisis when formulating the model.

Now consider the following question: Given the goodness of fit of this model to data for the whole period 1950–91, does your confidence in the model depend on which of these three methods was used to obtain it? I argue that it should. In particular, I argue that an equation obtained by a method similar to method 3, which involves testing against data that were not available to the model builder when the model was formulated, deserves more confidence than the same equation obtained by either of the other two methods.

The argument has to do with the goal of an econometric model—to describe not only past data, but also future data. It is easy to formulate a model that can describe a given set of past data perfectly but cannot describe future observations at all. Of course, such a research strategy should be avoided.

Here is a simple example. Imagine a pair of variables whose relationship we want to describe. Suppose we have two observations on the pair of variables. Then a line, whose equation is linear, will fit the data perfectly. Now suppose we obtain a third observation. It will almost certainly not lie on the line determined by the first two observations. But a parabola, whose equation is quadratic (of degree 2), will fit the three observations perfectly. Now suppose a fourth observation becomes available. It will almost certainly not lie on the parabola. But a sort of S-curve, whose equation is cubic (of degree 3), will fit the four observations perfectly. And so on. In general, a polynomial equation of degree n will fit a set of $n + 1$ observations on two variables perfectly, but a polynomial of higher degree will be required if the number of observations is increased. Methods of this type can describe any set of past data perfectly but almost certainly cannot describe any future data.

If a model is to describe future data, it needs to capture the enduring systematic features of the phenomena that are being modeled and it should avoid conforming to accidental features that will not endure. The trouble with the exact-fitting polynomial approach just discussed is that it does not try to distinguish between the enduring systematic and the temporary accidental features of reality. In the process of fitting past data perfectly, this approach neglects to fit enduring systematic features even approximately.

This relates to the choice among methods 1, 2 and 3 for finding a model that describes a body of data. When formulating a model, researchers typically pay attention to the behavior of available data, which perforce are past data. One tries

different equation forms and different variables to see which formulation best describes the data. This process has been called data mining. As a method of formulating tentative hypotheses, data mining is fine. But it involves the risk of being too clever, of fitting the available data too well and hence of choosing a hypothesis that conforms too much to the temporary accidental and too little to the enduring systematic features of the observed data. In this respect it is similar to the exact-fitting polynomial approach described earlier, though not as bad.

The best protection against having done too good a job of making a model describe past data is to test the model against new data that were not available when the model was formulated. This is what method 3 does, and that is why a model obtained by method 3 merits more confidence, other things equal.

Trygve Haavelmo once said to me, not entirely in jest, that what we economists should do is formulate our models, then go fishing for 50 years and let new data accumulate, and finally come back and confront our models with the new data.

Wesley Mitchell put the matter very well when he wrote the following:[1]

> The proposition may be ventured that a competent statistician, with sufficient clerical assistance and time at his command, can take almost any pair of time series for a given period and work them into forms which will yield coefficients of correlation exceeding ±.9. It has long been known that a mathematician can fit a curve to any time series which will pass through every point of the data. Performances of the latter sort have no significance, however, unless the mathematically computed curve continues to agree with the data when projected beyond the period for which it is fitted. So work of the sort which Mr. Karsten and Professor Fisher have shown how to do must be judged, not by the coefficients of correlation obtained within the periods for which they have manipulated the data, but by the coefficients which they get in earlier or later periods to which their formulas may be applied.

Milton Friedman, in his review of Jan Tinbergen's pioneering model of the U.S. economy, referred to Mitchell's comment and expressed a similar idea somewhat differently:[2]

> Tinbergen's results cannot be judged by ordinary tests of statistical significance. The reason is that

---

[1]See Mitchell (1927).

[2]See Friedman (1940) and Tinbergen (1939).

the variables with which he winds up, the particular series measuring these variables, the leads and lags, and various other aspects of the equations besides the particular values of the parameters (which alone can be tested by the usual statistical technique) have been selected after an extensive process of trial and error *because* they yield high coefficients of correlation. Tinbergen is seldom satisfied with a correlation coefficient less than .98. But these attractive correlation coefficients create no presumption that the relationships they describe will hold in the future. The multiple regression equations which yield them are simply tautological reformulations of *selected* economic data. Taken at face value, Tinbergen's work "explains" the errors in his data no less than their real movements.

That last statement can be strengthened. Tinbergen's method, which has been the method of most model builders ever since, explains whatever temporary accidental components there may be in the data (regardless of whether they are measurement errors), as well as the enduring components.

Most macroeconometric models formulated before the 1973 oil crisis had no variables representing the prices and quantities of oil and energy. Most of these models were surprised by the oil crisis and its aftermath, and most of them made substantial forecast errors thereafter. Many models formulated after 1973 pay special attention to oil and energy. Of course many of those models provide better explanations of the post-oil-crisis data than do models that ignore oil and energy. But my point is different. A model that was formulated after the oil crisis was specifically designed to conform to data during and after the crisis, and if there are temporary accidental variations, the model will conform to them just as much as to the systematic variations. Hence the task of explaining data between the onset of the 1972 oil crisis and 1992 is easier for a model that was formulated in 1992 than for a model that was formulated before the crisis. Therefore if both models do equally well at describing data from 1950 to 1991, the one formulated before the crisis has passed a stricter test and merits more confidence.

What about the relative merits of methods 1 and 2? Sometimes method 2 is recommended; that is, it is recommended that researchers estimate a model using only the earlier part of the available data and use the later part as a test of the model's forecasting ability. When thinking about this proposal, consider a model that has

been formulated with access to all of the data. It does not make much difference whether part of the data is excluded from the estimation process and used as a test of that model, as in method 2, or whether it is included, as in method 1. Either way, we draw the same conclusions. If the model with a set of constant coefficients describes both parts of the data well, method 1 will yield a good fit for the whole period and method 2 will yield a good fit for the estimation period and small errors for the forecast period. If the model with a set of constant coefficients does not describe both parts of the data well, in method 1 the residuals, if examined carefully, will reveal the flaws, and in method 2 the residuals, the forecast errors or both will reveal the flaws. And with both methods 1 and 2 we have a risk that the model was formulated to conform too much to the temporary accidental features of the available data.

One noteworthy difference between methods 1 and 2 is that if the model's specification is correct, method 1 will yield more accurate estimates of the parameters because it uses a larger sample and thus has a smaller sampling error.

Econometric Models Are Approximations

When I began work in econometrics, I believed a premise that underlies much econometric work—namely, that a true model that governs the behavior of the economy actually exists, with both systematic and random components and with true parameter values. And I believed that ultimately it would be possible to discover that true model and estimate its parameter values. My hope was first to find several models that could tentatively be accepted as ideal and eventually to find more general models that would include particular ideal models as special cases. (One way to top your colleagues is to show that their models are special cases of yours. Nowadays this is called "encompassing.")

Experience suggests that we cannot expect to find ideal models of the sort just described. When an estimated econometric model that describes past data is extrapolated into the future for more than a year or two, it typically does not hold up well. To try to understand how this might happen, let us temporarily adopt the premise that there is a true model. Of course, we do not know the form or parameters of this true model. They may or may not be changing, but if they are changing according to some rule, then in principle it is possible to incorporate that rule into a more general unchanging true model.

Suppose that an economist has specified a model, which may or may not be the same as the true model. If the form and parameters of the economist's model are changing according to some rule (not necessarily the same as the rule governing the true model), again in principle it is possible to incorporate that rule into a more general unchanging model.

Now consider the following possible ways in which the economist's model might describe past data quite well but fail to describe future data:

1. The form and parameter values of the economist's model may be correct for both the past period and the future period, but as the forecast horizon is lengthened, the forecasts get worse because the variance of the forecast is an increasing function of the length of the horizon. This will be discussed later.

2. The form of the economist's model may be correct for both the past period and the future period, but some or all of the true parameters may change during the future period.

3. The form of the economist's model may be correct for the past period but not for the future period because of a change in the form of the true model that is not matched in the economist's model.

4. The form of the economist's model may be incorrect for both periods but more nearly correct for the past period.

The last possibility is the most likely of the four in view of the fact that the economy has millions of different goods and services produced and consumed by millions of individuals, each with distinct character traits, desires, knowledge and beliefs.

These considerations lead to the conjecture that the aforementioned premise underlying econometrics is wrong—that there is no unchanging true model with true parameter values that governs the behavior of the economy now and in the future. Instead, every estimated econometric model is at best an approximation of a changing economy—an approximation that becomes worse as it is applied to events that occur further into the future from the period in which the model was formulated. In this case we should not be surprised at our failure to find an ideal general model as defined earlier. Instead, we should be

content with models that have at best only a temporary and approximate validity that deteriorates with time. We should sometimes also be content with models that describe only a restricted range of events—for example, events in a particular country, industry or population group.

Desiderata for an Econometric Model

If no ideal model exists, what characteristics can we realistically strive for in econometric models regarded as scientific hypotheses? The following set of desiderata are within reach:

1. The estimated model should provide a good description of some interesting set of past data. This means it should have small residuals relative to the variation of its variables—that is, high correlation coefficients. The standard errors of its parameter estimates should be small relative to those estimates, that is, its t-ratios should be large. If it is estimated for separate subsets of the available data, all those estimates should agree with each other. Finally, its residuals should appear random. (If the residuals appear to behave systematically, it is desirable to try to find variables to explain them.)

2. The model should be testable against data that were not used to estimate it and against data that were not available when it was specified.

3. The estimated model should be able to describe events occurring after it was formulated and estimated, at least for a few quarters or years.

4. The model should make sense in the light of our knowledge of the economy. This means in part that it should not generate negative values for variables that must be non-negative (such as interest rates) and that it should be consistent with theoretical propositions about the economy that we think are correct.

5. Other things equal, a simple model is preferable to a complex one.

6. Other things equal, a model that explains a wide variety of data is preferable to one that explains only a narrow range of data.

7. Other things equal, a model that incorporates other useful models as special cases is preferable to one that does not. (This is almost the same point as the previous one.)

In offering these desiderata, I assume that the purpose of a model is to state a hypothesis that describes an interesting set of available data and that may possibly describe new data as well. Of course, if the purpose is to test a theory that we are not sure about, the model should be constructed in such a way that estimates of its parameters will tell us something about the validity of that theory. The failure of such a model to satisfy these desiderata may tell us that the theory it embodies is false. This too is useful knowledge.

COMMENTS AND CRITICISMS ABOUT ECONOMETRIC TECHNIQUES

Theory vs. Empiricism

Two general approaches to formulating a model exist. One is to consult economic theory. The other is to look for regularities in the data. Either can be used as a starting point, but a combination of both is best. A model derived from elegant economic theory may be appealing, but unless at least some of its components or implications are consistent with real data, it is not a reliable hypothesis. A model obtained by pure data mining may be consistent with the body of data that was mined to get it, but it is not a reliable hypothesis if it is not consistent with at least some other data (recall what was said about this earlier), and it will not be understood if no theory to explain it exists.

The VAR Approach

Vector autoregression (VAR) is one way of looking for regularities in data. In VAR, a set of observable variables is chosen, a maximum lag length is chosen, and the current value of each variable is regressed on the lagged values of that variable and all other variables. No exogenous variables exist; all observable variables are treated as endogenous. Except for that, a VAR model is similar to the unrestricted reduced form of a conventional econometric model. Each equation contains only one current endogenous variable, each equation is just identified, and no use is made of any possible theoretical information about possible simultaneous structural equations that might contain more than one current endogenous variable. In fact, no use is made of any theoretical information at all, except in the choice of the list of variables to be included and the length of the lags. In macroeconomics it is not practical to use many variables and lags in a VAR because the number of coefficients to be estimated in each equation is the product of the number of variables times the number of lags and because one cannot estimate an equation that has more coefficients than there are observations in the sample.

The ARIMA Approach

The Box-Jenkins type of time-series analysis is another way to seek regularities in data. Here each observable variable is expressed in terms of purely random disturbances. This can be done with one variable at a time or in a multivariate fashion. In the univariate case an expression involving current and lagged values of an observable variable is equated to an expression involving current and lagged values of an unobservable white-noise disturbance; that is, a serially independent random disturbance that has a mean of zero and constant variance. Such a formulation is called an autoregressive integrated moving average (ARIMA) process. The *autoregressive* part expresses the current value of the variable as a function of its lagged values. The *integrated* part refers to the possibility that the first (or higher-order) differences of the variable, rather than its levels, may be governed by the equation. Then the variable's levels can be obtained from its differences by undoing the differencing operation—that is, by integrating first differences once, integrating second differences twice, and so on. (If no integration is involved, the process is called ARMA instead of ARIMA.) The *moving average* part expresses the equation's disturbance as a moving average of current and lagged values of a white-noise disturbance. To express a variable in ARIMA form, it is necessary to choose three integers to characterize the process. One gives the order of the autoregression (that is, the number of lags to be included for the observable variable); one gives the order of the moving average (that is, the number of lags included for the white-noise disturbance); and one gives the order of integration (that is, the number of times the highest-order differences of the observable variable must be integrated to obtain its levels). The choice of the three integers (some of which may be zero) is made by examining the time series of data for the observable variable to see what choice best conforms to the data. After that choice has been made, the coefficients in the autoregression and moving average are estimated. The multivariate form of ARIMA modeling is a generalization of the univariate form. And, of course, VAR modeling is a special case of multivariate ARIMA modeling.

VAR and ARIMA models can be useful if they lead to the discovery of regularities in the data. If enduring regularities in the data are discovered, we have something interesting to try to understand and explain. In my view, however, one disadvantage of both approaches is that they make almost no use of any knowledge of the subject matter being dealt with. To use univariate ARIMA on an economic variable, one need know nothing about economics. I think of univariate ARIMA as mindless data mining. To use multivariate ARIMA, one need only make a list of variables to be included and choose the required three integers. To use VAR, one need only make a list of the variables to be included and choose a maximum lag length. Knowledge of the subject the equations deal with can enter into the choice of variables to be included.

It may seem that the ARIMA approach and the conventional econometric model approach are antithetical and inconsistent with each other. Zellner and Palm (1974), however, have pointed out that if a conventional model's exogenous variables are generated by an ARIMA process, the model's endogenous variables are generated the same way.

General-to-Specific Modeling

General-to-specific modeling starts with an estimated equation that contains many variables and many lagged values of each. Its approach is to pare this general form down to a more specific form by omitting lags and variables that do not contribute to the explanatory power of the equation. Much can be said for this technique, but of course it will not lead to a correct result if the general form one starts with does not contain the variables and the lags that belong in an equation that is approximately correct.

The Error Correction Mechanism

The error correction mechanism (ECM) provides a way of expressing the rate at which a variable moves toward its desired or equilibrium value when it is away from that value. Economic theory is at its best when deriving desired or equilibrium values of variables, either static positions or dynamic paths. ECM has so far not been good at deriving the path followed by an economy that is out of equilibrium. Error correction models are appealing because they permit the nature of the equilibrium to be specified with the aid of the-

ory but permit the adjustment path to be determined largely by data.

Testing Residuals for Randomness

I have already discussed testing residuals for randomness. If an equation's residuals appear to follow any regular or systematic pattern, this is a signal that there may be some regular or systematic factor that has not been captured by the form and variables chosen for the equation. In such a case it is desirable to try to modify the equation's specification, either by including additional variables, by changing the form of the equation, or both, until the residuals lose their regular or systematic character and appear to be random.

Stationarity

It is often said that the residual of a properly specified equation should be stationary, that is, that its mean, variance and autocovariances should be constant through time. However, for an equation whose variables are growing over time, such as an aggregate consumption or money-demand equation, it would be unreasonable to expect the variance of the residual to be constant. That would mean that the correlation coefficients for the equation in successive decades (or other time intervals) would approach one. It would be more reasonable to expect the standard deviation of the residual to grow roughly in proportion to the dependent variable, to one of the independent variables, or to some combination of them.

The Lucas Critique

Robert Lucas (1976) warned that when an estimated econometric model is used to predict the effects of changes in government policy variables, the estimated coefficients may turn out wrong and hence the predictions may also turn out wrong. Under what conditions can this be expected to occur? Lucas says that this occurs when policymakers follow one policy rule during the estimation period and begin to follow a different policy rule during the prediction period. The reason for this, he argues, is that in many cases the parameters that were estimated are not constants that represent invariant economic relationships, but instead are variables that change in response to changes in policy rules. This is because they depend both on constant parameters and on varying expectations that private agents formulate by observing policymakers and trying to discover what policy rule is being followed. Jacob Marschak (1953) foreshadowed this idea when he cautioned that predictions made from an estimated econometric model will not be valid if the structure of the model (that is, its mathematical form and its parameter values) changes between the estimation period and the prediction period. Therefore, to make successful predictions after a structural change, one must discover the nature of the structural change and allow for it.

I take this warning seriously. It need not concern us when policy variations whose effects we want to predict are similar to variations that occurred during the estimation period. But when a change in the policy rule occurs, private agents will eventually discover that their previous expectation formation process is no longer valid and will adopt a new one as quickly as they can. As they do so, some of the estimated parameters will change and make the previously obtained estimates unreliable.

Goodhart's Law

Lucas' warning is related to Goodhart's Law, which states that as soon as policymakers begin to act as if some previously observed relationship is reliable, it will no longer be reliable and will change.[3] A striking example is the short-run, downward-sloping Phillips curve.

Are Policy Variables Exogenous?

Most econometric models treat at least some policy variables as exogenous. But public policy responds to events. Policy variables are not exogenous. The field of public choice studies the actions of policymakers, treating them as maximizers of their own utility subject to the constraints they face. Econometric model builders have so far not made much use of public choice economics.

BY THEIR FORECASTS YE SHALL KNOW THEM (MODELS, THAT IS)

Methods of Evaluating Models' Forecasts

A conventional econometric model contains disturbances and endogenous and exogenous variables. Typically some of the endogenous variables appear with a lag. Consider an annual model with data for all variables up to and including 1992.

Suppose that at the end of 1992 we wish to forecast the endogenous variables for 1993, one

year ahead. This is an *ex ante* forecast. For this we need estimates of the model's parameters, which can be computed from our available data. In addition, we need 1993 values for the lagged endogenous variables. These we already have because we have values for the years 1992 and earlier. Further, we need predicted 1993 values for the disturbances. We usually use zeros here because disturbances are assumed to be serially independent with zero means. (Some modelers, however, would use values related to the residuals for 1992 and possibly earlier years if the disturbances were thought to be serially correlated.) Finally, we need predicted 1993 values for the exogenous variables. These predictions must be obtained from some source outside the model.

Our predictions of the endogenous variables for 1993 will be conditional on our estimated model and on our predictions of the disturbances and exogenous variables. If we make errors in forecasting the endogenous variables, it may be because our estimated model is wrong, because our predictions of the disturbances or exogenous variables are wrong, or because of some combination of these.

It is possible—and desirable—to test the forecasting ability of an estimated model independently of the model user's ability to forecast exogenous variables. This is done with an *ex post* forecast. An *ex post* forecast for one period ahead, say for 1993, is made as follows: Wait until actual 1993 data for the exogenous variables are available, use them instead of predicted values of the exogenous variables to compute forecasts of the 1993 endogenous variables, and examine the errors of those forecasts.

When comparing forecasts from different models, bear in mind that the models may differ in their lists of exogenous variables and that this may affect the comparison. For example, a model that has hard-to-forecast exogenous variables is not going to be helpful for practical *ex ante* forecasting, even if it makes excellent *ex post* forecasts.

Errors of *ex ante* and *ex post* forecasts tell us different things. *Ex ante* forecasting errors tell us about the quality of true forecasts but do not allow us to separate the effects of incorrect estimated models from the effects of bad predictions of exogenous variables and disturbances. *Ex post* forecasting errors tell us how good an estimated model has been as a scientific hypothesis, which is

---

[3]See Goodhart (1981).

Table 1

Root Mean Square Percentage Errors of *Ex Post* Forecasts with No Subjective Adjustments of the Forecasts, from about 1965 to 1973, Averaged over Eight Models

Variable	Horizon		
	1 quarter	4 quarters	8 quarters
Nominal GNP	0.7	2.0	4.5
Real GNP	0.7	1.9	2.5
GNP Deflator	0.4	0.6	1.9

distinct from anyone's ability to forecast exogenous variables and disturbances. If you are interested in the quality of practical forecasting, you should evaluate *ex ante* forecasts. If you are interested in the quality of a model as a scientific theory, you should evaluate *ex post* forecasts. *Ex post* forecasts are usually more accurate than *ex ante* forecasts because the predictions of the exogenous variables that go into *ex ante* forecasts are usually at least somewhat wrong.

What if we want to make forecasts *two* years ahead, for 1994, based on data up to and including 1992? We need 1993 values for the endogenous variables to use as lagged endogenous values for our 1994 forecast; however, we do not have actual 1993 data. Hence we must make a one-year-ahead forecast for 1993 as before. Then we can make our 1994 forecast using our 1993 forecasts as the lagged values of the endogenous variables for 1994. Thus the errors of our 1994 forecast will depend partly on the errors of our 1993 forecast and partly on the values we use for the 1994 exogenous variables and disturbances. If we want to make forecasts for n years ahead instead of two years ahead, the situation is similar except that n steps are required instead of two. We can still consider either *ex ante* or *ex post* forecasts. As before, *ex post* forecasts use actual values of the exogenous variables.

When making *ex ante* forecasts, the typical econometric forecaster does not automatically adopt the forecasts generated by a model. Instead the forecaster compares these forecasts with his subjective judgment about the future of the economy, and if there are substantial discrepancies, he makes subjective adjustments to his model's forecasts. This is usually done with subjective adjustments to the predicted disturbances. Thus the accuracy of *ex ante* forecasts

typically depends not only on the adequacy of the estimated model, but also on the model builder's ability to forecast exogenous variables and to make subjective adjustments to the model's forecasts. Paul Samuelson once caricatured this situation at a meeting some years ago by likening the process that produces *ex ante* econometric forecasts to a black box inside which we find only Lawrence R. Klein!

Errors of Forecasts from Several Econometric Models

Most presentations of forecasting accuracy are based on *ex ante* rather than *ex post* forecasts, often with subjective adjustments, perhaps because of the interest in practical forecasting. I like to look at *ex post* forecast errors without adjustments because I am interested in econometric models as scientific hypotheses.

Fromm and Klein (1976) and Christ (1975) discuss root mean square errors (RMSEs) of *ex post* quarterly forecasts of real GNP, nominal GNP and the GNP deflator one quarter to eight quarters ahead by eight models with *no subjective adjustment* by the forecaster. The models were formulated by Brookings, the U.S. Bureau of Economic Analysis, Ray Fair, Leonall Andersen of the Federal Reserve Bank of St. Louis, T. C. Liu and others, the University of Michigan and the Wharton School (two versions). For GNP they show RMSEs rising from 0.7 percent to 2.5 or 4.5 percent of the actual value as the horizon increases from one quarter to eight quarters. For the GNP deflator they show RMSEs rising from 0.4 percent to 1.9 percent, as shown in table 1.

In a series of papers over the past several years, Stephen McNees (1986, 1988 and 1990) has reported on the accuracy of *subjectively* adjusted *ex ante* quarterly forecasts of several macroeconometric models, for horizons of one to eight quarters ahead, and has compared them with two simple mechanical forecasting methods. One is the univariate ARIMA method of Charles Nelson (1984), which is called BMARK (for benchmark). The other is the Bayesian vector autoregression method of Robert Litterman (1986), which is called BVAR. The models discussed in McNees (1988) are those formulated by the U.S. Bureau of Economic Analysis, Chase Econometrics, Data Resources Inc., Georgia State University, Kent Institute, the University of Michigan, UCLA and Wharton.

McNees' results for *quarterly* forecasts may be summarized in the following five statements:

1. The models' forecast errors were usually smaller than those of BMARK.[4]

2. The models' forecast errors were usually slightly smaller than those of BVAR for nominal GNP and most other variables and slightly larger than those of BVAR for real GNP. Thus BVAR was usually better than BMARK for real GNP.[5]

3. Forecast errors for the *levels* of variables became worse as the forecast horizon lengthened from one quarter to eight quarters, roughly quadrupling for most variables and increasing tenfold for prices. However, forecast errors for the *growth rates* of many variables (but not for price variables) improved as the horizon lengthened. In other words, for many variables, the forecasts for growth rates averaged over several quarters were better than the forecasts for short-term fluctuations.[6]

4. Mean absolute errors (MAEs) of the models' forecasts of the level of nominal GNP were usually about 0.8 percent of the true level for forecasts one quarter ahead and increased gradually to about 2.2 percent for forecasts one year ahead and about 4 percent for forecasts two years ahead. Real GNP forecast errors were somewhat smaller. Errors for other variables were comparable. Price-level forecast errors were smaller for the one-quarter horizon but grew faster and were larger for the two-year horizon.[7]

5. When subjectively adjusted forecasts were compared with unadjusted forecasts, the adjustments were helpful in most cases, though sometimes they made the forecast worse. Usually the adjustments were larger than optimal.[8]

One-year-ahead *annual* forecasts of real GNP by the University of Michigan's Research Center in Quantitative Economics, by the Council of Economic Advisers and by private forecasters covered by the ASA/NBER survey all had MAEs of about 0.9 percent to 1.1 percent of the true level, and RMSEs of about 1.2 percent to 1.5 percent of the true level.[9] (The relative sizes of the MAEs and RMSEs are roughly consistent with the fact that for a normal distribution, the RMSE is about 1.25 times the MAE.)

Implications of Worsening Ex Post Forecast Errors

Because the root mean square error of an econometric model's *ex post* forecasts roughly quadruples when the horizon increases from one quarter to eight quarters as in table 1, can we conclude that the model is no longer correct for the forecast period? The answer is possibly, but not certainly.

For a static model we could conclude this because the error of each forecast would involve disturbances only for the period being forecast, not for periods in the earlier part of the horizon. Hence there is no reason to expect great changes in the size of the forecasting error for a static model as the horizon increases. Small increases will occur because of errors in the estimates of the model's parameters if the values of the model's independent variables move further away from their estimation-period means as the horizon lengthens. This is because any errors in the estimates of equations' slopes will generate larger effects as the distance over which the slopes are projected increases.

But most econometric forecasting models contain lagged endogenous variables. Therefore, as noted previously, to forecast n periods ahead, we must first forecast the lagged endogenous-variable values that are needed for the n-periods-

---

[4]See McNees (1988 and 1990).
[5]See McNees (1990).
[6]See McNees (1988).

[7]See McNees (1988).
[8]See McNees (1990).
[9]See McNees (1988).

ahead forecast. This involves a chain of n steps. The first step is a forecast one period ahead, whose error involves disturbances only from the first period in the n-period horizon. The second step is a forecast two periods ahead, whose error involves disturbances from the second period in the horizon and also disturbances from the first period because they affect the one-period-ahead forecast, which in turn affects the two-periods-ahead forecast. And so on, until the nth step, whose forecast error involves disturbances from all periods in the horizon from one through n. Thus, for a dynamic model, the variance of a forecast n periods ahead will depend on the variances and covariances of disturbances in all n periods of the horizon, and except in very special circumstances, it will increase as the horizon increases.

To decide whether the evidence in table 1 shows that the estimated models it describes are incorrect for the forecast horizon of eight quarters, we need to know whether the RMSEs of a *correct* model would quadruple as the forecast horizon increases from one quarter to eight quarters. If they would, then the quadrupling observed in the table is not evidence of incorrectness of the estimated models. If they would not, then evidence of incorrectness exists. We do not have enough information about the models underlying the table to settle this issue definitively, but some simple examples will illustrate the principle involved.

Suppose the model is linear and perfectly correct, and suppose it contains lags of one quarter or more (as most models do). Then the variance of the error of an n-periods-ahead forecast will be a linear combination of the variances and covariances of the disturbances in all periods of the horizon. In the simple case of a single-equation model, if the disturbances are serially independent and if the coefficients in the linear combination of disturbances are all equal to one, the variance of the linear combination of disturbances for a horizon of eight quarters will be eight times that of one quarter. So the RMSE of *ex post* forecast errors from a correct model will increase by a factor of the square root of eight (about 2.8) as the horizon goes from one quarter to eight quarters. If the coefficients in the linear combination are less than one, as in the case of a stable model with only one-period lags, the variance of the linear combination for

eight quarters will be less than eight times that for one quarter. Hence the RMSE of *ex post* forecast errors from a correct model will increase by less than a factor of the square root of eight as the horizon goes from one quarter to eight quarters. In such a case, if the observed RMSEs approximately quadrupled, it would cast some doubt on the validity of the model.

Consider a single-equation model with a single lag, and no exogenous variables as follows:

$$y_t = \alpha + \beta y_{t-1} + \varepsilon_t$$

where ε is a serially independent disturbance with zero mean and constant variance σ^2. Suppose that the values of α and β are known and thus no forecast error is attributable to incorrect estimates of these coefficients. Then the variance of the error of a one-period-ahead forecast is σ^2, that of a two-periods-ahead forecast is $(1 + \beta^2) \sigma^2$, that of a three-periods-ahead forecast is $(1 + \beta^2 + \beta^4)\sigma^2$, and so on. The variance of an n-periods-ahead forecast is $\sum_0^{N-1} \beta^{2i} \sigma^2$, which is equal to $(1 - \beta^{2N}) \sigma^2/(1 - \beta^2)$.

Table 2 shows how the standard deviation of such a forecast error increases as the horizon increases from one quarter to eight quarters for several values of the parameter β. Table 2 suggests that if the RMSE of a model's forecasts quadruples as the horizon increases from one quarter to eight quarters, either β (the rate of approach of the model to equilibrium) must be large or close to one, or the model is inadequate as a description of the forecast period.

Corresponding expressions can be derived for multi-equation models with many lags and serially correlated disturbances, but they are rather cumbersome.

AN OLD, PLAIN-VANILLA EQUATION THAT STILL WORKS, ROUGHLY

Nearly 40 years ago Henry Allen Latané published a short paper in which he reported that for 1919–52 the inverse of the GNP velocity of M1 is described by a simple least squares regression on the inverse of a long-term, high-grade bond rate RL as follows:[10]

(1) M1/GNP = .100 + .795/RL, $\bar{r}^2$ = .75
   (t-ratio)   (10)

---

[10]See Latané (1954).

82

Table 2

Standard Deviation of Error of N-Periods-Ahead Forecast from the Equation $y_t = \alpha + \beta y_{t-1} + \varepsilon_t$
Relative to the Standard Deviation of ε, as a Function of N and β, when α and β Are Known

β	β^2	Horizon, N				
		1	2	4	8	∞
0.7070	0.50	1.00	1.22	1.37	1.41	1.41
0.8944	0.80	1.00	1.34	1.72	2.04	2.24
0.9486	0.90	1.00	1.38	1.85	2.39	3.16
1.0000	1.00	1.00	1.41	2.00	2.83	∞

Here and in what follows, I have expressed interest rates in units of percent per year, so a 5 percent rate is entered as 5, not as 0.05, and its inverse 0.20, not 20. The Appendix gives the definitions and data sources for variables in this and subsequent equations. Latané showed the unadjusted correlation coefficient r, but showed neither the standard deviation nor the t-ratio of the slope. I calculated the adjusted $\bar{r}^2$ and the t-ratio. The latter is the square root of r^2 (df)$/(1 - r^2)$, where df, the number of degrees of freedom, equals 32.

This specification has some of the properties of a theoretical money demand equation—namely, a positive income elasticity (restricted to be constant and equal to one by construction) and a negative interest elasticity (restricted to have an absolute value less than one and not constant). But its least-squares estimate would almost certainly be biased or inconsistent, even if the form of the equation were correct, because the bond rate is almost certainly not exogenous and hence not independent of the equation's disturbances.

Nevertheless, this specification has continued to work fairly well for other periods. Nearly 30 years ago M1/GNP was described for 1892–1959 by a similar regression on the inverse of Moody's Aaa bond rate with almost the same coefficients, as follows:[11]

(2) M1/GNP $= .131 + .716/$RAaa, $\bar{r}^2 = .76$
(t-ratio)   (14)

[11]See Christ (1963).

For 1959–91 the same specification describes the ratio of M1 to GNP with almost the same coefficients, as follows:

(3) M1/GNP $= .085 + .774/$RAaa, $\bar{r}^2 = .90$
(t-ratio)   (13)   (17)

If GNP in equation (3) is replaced by the new output variable GDP for 1959–91, the result is almost identical, as follows:

(4) M1/GDP $= .086 + .771/$RAaa, $\bar{r}^2 = .91$
(t-ratio)   (13)   (18)

David Dickey's discussion is based on the 1959–91 data that underlie equation (3).

For 1892–1991 a similar result is again obtained, as follows:

(5) M1/GNP $= .083 + .874/$RAaa, $\bar{r}^2 = .89$
(t-ratio)   (11)   (28)

Table 3 shows the estimated equations (1)–(5) and several other estimated equations that will be described soon. Equations (1′) and (2′) are attempts to duplicate the results in equations (1) and (2) using the same data base that is used in equations (3), (5) and later equations. The Appendix gives data sources.

Figure 2 shows the graphs of M1/GNP and 1/RAaa over time. Figures 3 and 4 show the scatter diagrams for equations (3) and (5), respectively. (I should add that, of the four

Table 3

Regressions of M1/GNP or M1/GDP on 1/RAaa and Other Variables* (t-ratios are in parentheses)

				Estimated Coefficient (and t-ratio)			
Eq	Sample	Constant	1/RAaa	$(M1/GNP)_{-1}$	$(1/RAaa)_{-1}$	$\bar{R}^2$	DW
PLAIN-VANILLA EQUATIONS							
1	1919–1952	.100	.795(10)			.75	
1'	1919–1952	.136(7)	.713(10)			.75	.56
2	1892–1959	.131	.716(14)			.76	
2'	1892–1959	.132(9)	.712(14)			.73	.62
3	1959–1991	.085(13)	.774(17)			.90	.38
4	1959–1991	.086(13)	.771(18)			.91	.36
5	1892–1991	.083(11)	.874(28)			.89	.48
AR(1) EQUATIONS**							
15	1960–1991	.013	.267(2.8)	.896(26)	−.239	.98	1.82
17	1893–1991	.020	.711(7)	.831(12)	−.591	.95	1.60
ECM EQUATIONS**							
18	1960–1991	.016(2.2)	.275(2.8)	.857(11)	−.212(−2.2)	.98	1.78
19	1893–1991	.016(2.1)	.593(5)	.807(12)	−.428(−3.6)	.95	1.59

*The dependent variable is M1/GNP in all equations except equation (4), where it is M1/GDP. Definitions and data sources for the variables M1, GNP, GDP and RAaa are given in the Appendix. As explained in the Appendix, a uniform set of data for M1, GNP and RAaa was used for equations (1'), (2'), (3), (5) and later equations; slightly different data were used for equations (1), (2) and (4). David Dickey's discussion is based on equation (3) and the data underlying it. Equations (1') and (2') are attempts to reproduce equations (1) and (2), respectively, using the same data that were used for equations (3), (5) and later equations.
**AR(1) means "first-order autoregressive." ECM means "error correction mechanism."

equations that can be obtained by regressing either the velocity of M1 or its inverse on either RAaa or its inverse, the form that is presented here fits the best.)

It is rather remarkable that this plain-vanilla specification continues to describe the relation between M1's velocity and the long-term Aaa bond rate with such similar regression and correlation coefficients for the four periods, especially in view of the changes in interest-rate regulation and in the definition of M1 that have occurred over the last century. However, the differences among the four estimated versions are not negligible, as seen in a comparison of the computed values of M1/GNP that they yield. For 1959–91 these computed values are shown in figure 5 together with the actual values of M1/GNP. Note that those computed from equations (1) and (2) using 1919–52 and 1892–1959 data are *ex post* forecasts, whereas those from equations (3) and (5) using 1959–91 and 1892–1991 data are within-sample calculated values. Figure 6 shows the values of M1/GNP obtained when equation (3) based on 1959–91 data is used to backcast M1/GNP for 1892–1958, and it also

shows the actual values and the calculated values from equation (5) using 1892–1991 data. The forecasting and backcasting errors are by no means negligible, but the general pattern of behavior of M1/GNP is reproduced.

The estimates of the plain-vanilla equation are rather stable across time, as indicated by figures 7 and 8 which show the behavior of the slope as the sample period is gradually lengthened by adding one year at a time. In figure 7 the sample period starts with 1959–63 and is extended a year at a time to 1959–91. In figure 8 the sample period starts with 1892–97 and is gradually extended to 1892–1991. In each figure the slope settles down quickly after jumping around at first and varies little as the sample is extended thereafter.

However, this simple specification does not by any means satisfy all of the desiderata listed previously. In particular, the 1959–91 Durbin-Watson statistic is a minuscule 0.38, and the 1892–1991 Durbin-Watson statistic of 0.48, is not much better, which suggests that the residuals have a strong positive serial correlation. This by itself would not create bias in the estimates if

84

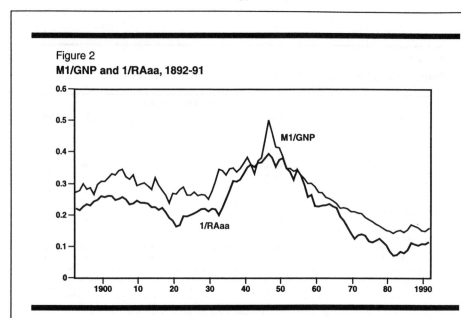

Figure 2
M1/GNP and 1/RAaa, 1892-91

Figure 3
Regression of M1/GNP on 1/RAaa, 1959-91

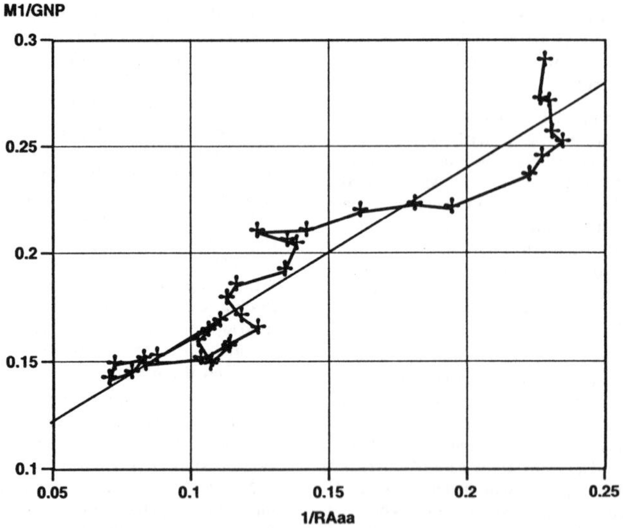

Figure 4
Regression of M1/GNP on 1/RAaa, 1892-91

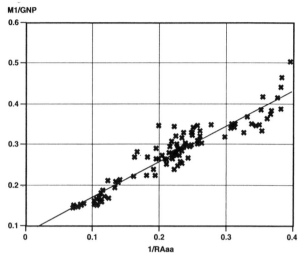

Figure 5
**Actual, Computed and Forecast Values of M1/GNP from Regressions on
1/RAaa for Four Periods**

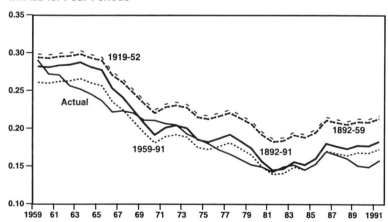

86

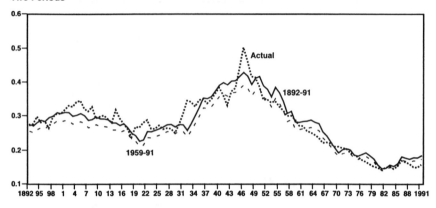

Figure 6
Actual, Computed and Backcast Values of M1/GNP from Regressions on 1/RAaa for Two Periods

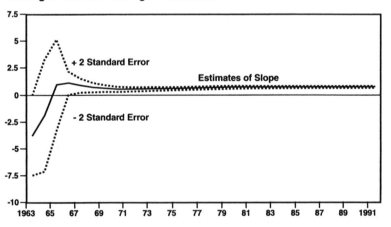

Figure 7
Estimates of Slope in Regression of M1/GNP on 1/RAaa for Samples Starting in 1959 and Ending in 1963...1991

Figure 8
Estimates of Slope in Regression of M1/GNP on 1/RAaa for Samples Starting in 1892 and Ending in 1897...1991

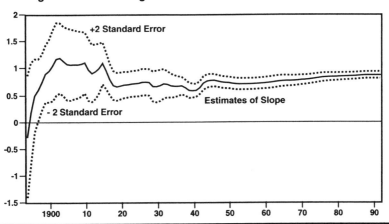

the equation form were correct and if the disturbance were independent of the interest rate and had zero mean and constant variance. But it certainly suggests strongly that the equation has not captured all its relevant systematic factors. The graph of the residuals of the 1959–91 equation (3) against time is illuminating. It shows an almost perfect 12-year cycle of diminishing amplitude with peaks (positive residuals) in 1959 (or possibly earlier), 1970 and 1982 and troughs (negative residuals) in 1965, 1977 and 1990. It also suggests a negative time trend. The residuals of the 1892–1991 equation (5) show a roughly similar pattern. (See figures 9 and 10.)

The very low Durbin-Watson statistics suggest that the equation should be estimated either using the first differences of its variables, or better, using the levels of its variables with a first-order autoregressive [AR(1)] correction applied to its residuals. Estimation in levels with an AR(1) correction would be appropriate if the disturbance u in the original equation were equal to its own lagged value times a constant, ρ, plus a serially independent disturbance, ε, with constant variance, as follows:

(6) $u_t = \rho u_{t-1} + \varepsilon_t$

In this case, if the original equation is

(7) $y_t = \alpha + \beta x_t + u_t = \alpha + \beta x_t + \rho u_{t-1} + \varepsilon_t$,

the AR(1) correction subtracts ρ times the lagged version of equation (7) from equation (7) itself and produces the following equation:

(8) $y_t = \rho y_{t-1} + (1 - \rho) \alpha + \beta x_t - \beta \rho x_{t-1} + \varepsilon_t$

This equation is nonlinear in the parameters because the coefficient of lagged x, $-\beta\rho$, is the negative of the product of the coefficients of x and lagged y. If that restriction is ignored and the coefficient of lagged x is denoted by γ, the equation becomes as follows:

(9) $y_t = \rho y_{t-1} + (1 - \rho) \alpha + \beta x_t + \gamma x_{t-1} + \varepsilon_t$

This equation can be given the following error correction interpretation. Suppose that the equilibrium value y* of a dependent variable y is linear in an independent variable x, as follows:

(10) $y_t^* = \alpha + \beta x_t$

and that the change in y depends on both the change in the equilibrium value and an error

88

Figure 9
Residuals from Regression of M1/GNP on 1/RAaa, 1959-91

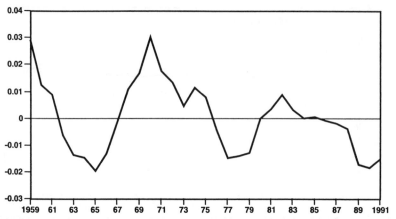

Figure 10
Residuals from Regression of M1/GNP on 1/RAaa, 1892-1991

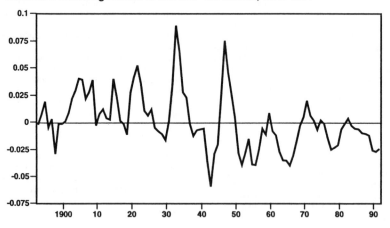

correction term proportional to the gap between the lagged equilibrium and the lagged actual values, as follows:

(11) $\Delta y_t = \theta \Delta y_t^* + (1 - \rho)(y_{t-1}^* - y_{t-1}) + \varepsilon_t$

Substitution from equation (10) into equation (11) implies an equation with the same variables as the AR(1) equation (8) but with some different parameters, as follows:

(12) $y_t = \rho y_{t-1} + (1 - \rho)\alpha + \theta \beta x_t + (1 - \rho - \theta)\beta x_{t-1} + \varepsilon_t$

If the adjustment parameter θ in equation (12) were equal to one, then equation (12) would become the same equation as (8).

Estimates in first differences would be appropriate if the value of ρ in equation (6), (7) and (8) were one. In this case, equation (8) becomes a first-difference equation, as follows:

(13) $\Delta y_t = \beta \Delta x_t + \varepsilon_t$.

The least-squares estimate of equation (8) in levels with the AR(1) correction for 1960–91 is as follows:

(14) M1/GNP – .896(M1/GNP)$_{-1}$

$= (1 - .896).126 + .267(1/\text{RAaa} - .896/\text{RAaa}_{-1})$
(t-ratio)   (8)   (2.8)   (26)

with an adjusted R squared of .98 and DW equal to 1.82. This is equivalent to the following equation:

(15) M1/GNP = .896(M1/GNP)$_{-1}$

+ .013 + .267/RAaa – .239/RAaa$_{-1}$

There is no evidence of a trend.

The least-squares estimate in levels with the AR(1) correction for 1893–1991 is as follows:

(16) M1/GNP – .831(M1/GNP)$_{-1}$
$= (1 - .831).117 + .711(1/\text{RAaa} - .831/\text{RAaa}_{-1})$
(t-ratio)   (5)   (7)   (12)

with an adjusted R squared of .95 and DW equal to 1.60. This is equivalent to the following equation:

(17) M1/GNP = .831(M1/GNP)$_{-1}$
+ .020 + .711/RAaa – .591/RAaa$_{-1}$

There is again no evidence of a trend.

Least-squares estimation of the ECM equation (12) for 1960–91 (without restricting θ to be one) yields the following equation:

(18) M1/GNP = .857(M1/GNP)$_{-1}$
(t-ratio)   (11)
+ .016 + .275/RAaa – .212/RAaa$_{-1}$
(2.2)   (2.8)   (–2.2)

with an adjusted R squared of .98 and DW equal to 1.78. This is quite close to the AR(1) result in equation (15), which suggests that the adjustment coefficient θ in equation (12) is not very different from one. The hypothesis that in equation (18) the coefficient of lagged 1/RAaa is equal to the negative of the product of the coefficients of 1/RAaa and lagged M1/GNP, as required by equation (8) and as satisfied by equation (15), is strongly accepted by a Wald test (the p-value is .59).

Least-squares estimation of equation (12) for 1893–1991 (again without restricting θ to be one) yields the following equation:

(19) M1/GNP = .807(M1/GNP)$_{-1}$
(t-ratio)   (12)
+ .016 + .593/RAaa – .428/RAaa$_{-1}$
(2.1)   (5)   (–3.6)

with an adjusted R squared of .95 and DW equal to 1.59. This is quite close to the AR(1) result in equation (17), which again suggests that the adjustment coefficient θ in equation (12) is not very different from one. The hypothesis that in equation (19) the coefficient of lagged 1/RAaa is equal to the negative of the product of the coefficients of 1/RAaa and lagged M1/GNP, as required by equation (8) and as satisfied by equation (17), is accepted by a Wald test (the p-value is .11).

Equations (15), (17), (18) and (19) are better than the plain-vanilla equations (3) and (5) in some respects, and worse in others. They have substantially higher adjusted R-squared values, much less serial correlation in their residuals, no evidence of a time trend, and significant coefficients. The ECM equations (18) and (19), however, are very unstable over time. In equation (18) the coefficient of 1/RAaa varies from about .6 for 1960–70, to .05 for 1960–78 and 1960–81, to .3 for 1960–86 and 1960–91. In equation (19) the coefficient of 1/RAaa varies almost as much but remains at about .7 or .6 for samples that include at least the years 1893–1950.

90

Table 4

Regressions of Δ(M1/GNP) on Δ(1/RAaa) without a Constant* (t-ratios are in parentheses)

Eq	Sample	Coef of Δ(1/RAaa)	$\bar{R}^2$	DW
24	1960–1991	.380(3.6)	.05	1.23
25	1893–1991	.494(4.1)	.15	1.76

*Definitions and data sources for the variables M1, GNP and RAaa are given in the appendix.

I conjecture that in the AR(1) equations (15) and (17) the coefficient of 1/RAaa is also unstable across time because the AR(1) and ECM equation estimates are quite similar.

By comparing equations (12) and (18), one can solve for the 1960–91 estimates of the four parameters ρ, α, β and θ, in that order, to obtain:

(20) $\hat{\rho}$ = .857, $\hat{\alpha}$ = .112, $\hat{\beta}$ = .441 and $\hat{\theta}$ = .624

This implies that the equilibrium relation in equation (10) embedded in the ECM is as follows:

(21) (M1/GNP)* = .112 + .441/RAaa

Similarly, by comparing equations (12) and (19) one can solve for the 1893–1991 estimates of the four parameters as follows:

(22) $\hat{\rho}$ = .807, $\hat{\alpha}$ = .083, $\hat{\beta}$ = .855 and $\hat{\theta}$ = .694

This implies that the equilibrium relation in equation (10) embedded in the ECM is as follows:

(23) (M1/GNP)* = .083 + .855/RAaa

The two equilibrium relations in equations (21) and (23) for the two periods 1960–91 and 1893–1991 are quite different, which is consistent with the instability of the ECM specification across time.

Now let us return to the first-difference equation (13). The least-squares estimate for 1960–91 is as follows:

(24) Δ(M1/GNP) = .380Δ(1/RAaa), $\bar{r}^2$ = .05
      (t-ratio)   (3.6)

with DW = 1.23. For 1893–1991 it is as follows:

(25) Δ(M1/GNP) = .494Δ(1/RAaa), $\bar{r}^2$ = .15
      (t-ratio)   (4.1)

with DW = 1.76. Table 4 shows the estimated equations (24) and (25). The estimates of this first-difference specification are not quite as stable across time as those of the specification in levels of the variables. This can be seen by comparing equations (24) and (25) and also from figures 11 and 12, which show the values of the estimates as the sample is increased one year at a time, starting respectively with 1960 and 1893. In each figure the estimates stabilize after an initial period of instability, but the values at which they settle differ by a factor of about .75.

If a constant term is included in equation (24), which implies a trend term in equation (3), the constant is small but significantly negative, the slope falls to about .3, and the adjusted R-squared and DW values improve slightly. The estimated slope, however, becomes wildly unstable across time. If a trend variable is included in equation (3), its coefficient is small but significantly negative, the interest-rate coefficient falls to .49 and remains highly significant, the adjusted R-squared and the DW values rise slightly, and again the estimated slope is wildly unstable across time.

If a constant term is included in equation (25), it is small and insignificantly negative, the rest of the equation is almost unchanged, and the slope becomes quite unstable through time, varying from .6 to zero and back to .6 again. If a trend is included in equation (5), its coefficient is small but significantly negative, the interest-rate coefficient is almost unchanged at .81, the adjusted R-squared value rises a bit, the DW value rises a bit, and the coefficient is again wildly unstable across time.

Figure 11
Estimates of Slope in Regression of Δ(M1/GNP) on Δ(1/RAaa) for Samples Starting in 1960 and Ending in 1962...1991

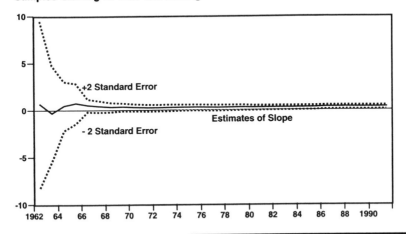

Figure 12
Estimates of Slope in Regression of Δ(M1/GNP) on Δ(1/RAaa) for Samples Starting in 1893 and Ending in 1896...1991

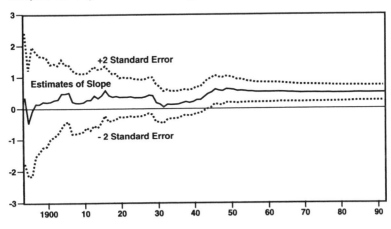

92

On the whole, the first-difference specification does not stand up well.

Where do matters stand? On the one hand, we have the plain-vanilla equation such as equation (3), which fits only moderately well and has severe serial correlation in its residuals but has an estimated slope that is rather stable across time. On the other hand, we have more complicated dynamic equations such as the ECM equation (18), which fit much better and have nice Durbin-Watson statistics but have estimated coefficients that vary greatly across time. Neither is quite satisfactory, but if the aim is to find an estimated equation that will describe the future as well as it does the past, I think I would now bet on the plain-vanilla specification, even though the relation of its estimated coefficients to structural parameters is unclear.

CONCLUSION

Econometrics has given us some results that appear to stand up well over time. The price and income elasticities of demand for farm products are less than one. The income elasticity of household demand for food is less than one. Houthakker (1957), in a paper commemorating the 100th anniversary of Engel's law, reports that for 17 countries and several different periods these income elasticities range between .43 and .73. Rapid inflation is associated with a high growth rate of the money stock. Some short-term macroeconometric forecasts, especially those of the Michigan model, are quite good.

But there have also been some nasty surprises about which econometrics gave us little or no warning in advance. The short-run downward-sloping Phillips curve met its demise in the 1970s. (Milton Friedman [1968] and Edmund Phelps [1968] predicted that it would.) The oil embargo of 1973 and its aftermath threw most models off. The slowdown of productivity growth beginning in the 1970s was unforeseen. The money demand equation, which appeared to fit well and be quite stable until the 1970s, has not fit so well since then.

How then should we approach econometrics, for science and for policy, in the future? As for science, we should formulate and estimate models as we usually do, relying both on economic theory and on ideas suggested by regularities observed in past data. But we should not fail to test those estimated models against new data

that were not available to influence the process of formulating them. As for policy, we should be cautious about using research findings to predict the effects of any large policy change of a type that has not been tried before.

REFERENCES

Christ, Carl F. "Interest Rates and 'Portfolio Selection' among Liquid Assets in the U.S.," in Christ et al., *Measurement in Economics: Studies in Mathematical Economics and Econometrics in Memory of Yehuda Grunfeld* (Stanford University Press, 1963).

_____. "Judging the Performance of Econometric Models of the U.S. Economy," *International Economic Review* (February 1975), pp. 54–74.

Friedman, Milton. Review of "Business Cycles in the United States of America, 1919–1932" by Jan Tinbergen, *American Economic Review* (September 1940), pp. 657–60.

_____. "The Role of Monetary Policy," *American Economic Review* (March 1968), pp. 1–17.

Fromm, Gary, and Lawrence R. Klein. "The NBER/NSF Model Comparison Seminar: An Analysis of Results," *Annals of Economic and Social Measurement* (Winter 1976), pp. 1–28.

Goodhart, Charles. "Problems of Monetary Management: The U.K. Experience," in A. S. Courakis, ed., *Inflation, Depression, and Economic Policy in the West* (Barnes and Noble Books, 1981).

Houthakker, Hendrik. "An International Comparison of Household Expenditure Patterns, Commemorating the Centenary of Engel's Law," *Econometrica* (October 1957), pp. 532–51.

Kendrick, John. *Productivity Trends in the United States* (Princeton University Press, 1961).

Latané, Henry Allen. "Cash Balances and the Interest Rate—A Pragmatic Approach," *Review of Economics and Statistics* (November 1954), pp. 456–60.

Litterman, Robert B. "Forecasting with Bayesian Vector Autoregressions—Five Years of Experience," *Journal of Business and Economic Statistics* (January 1986), pp. 25–38.

Lucas, Robert E. Jr. "Econometric Policy Evaluation: A Critique," *The Phillips Curve and Labor Markets*, Carnegie-Rochester Conference Series on Public Policy, vol. 1, (North-Holland, 1976), pp. 19–46.

Marschak, Jacob. "Economic Measurements for Policy and Prediction," in William C. Hood and Tjalling C. Koopmans, eds., *Studies in Econometric Method, Cowles Commission Monograph No. 14* (Wiley, 1953), pp. 1–26.

McNees, Stephen K. "The Accuracy of Two Forecasting Techniques: Some Evidence and an Interpretation," *New England Economic Review* (March/April 1986), pp. 20–31.

_____. "How Accurate Are Macroeconomic Forecasts?" *New England Economic Review* (July/August 1988), pp. 15–36.

_____. "Man vs. Model? The Role of Judgment in Forecasting," *New England Economic Review* (July/August 1990), pp. 41–52.

Mitchell, Wesley C. *Business Cycles: The Problem and Its Setting* (National Bureau of Economic Research, 1927).

Nelson, Charles R. "A Benchmark for the Accuracy of Econometric Forecasts of GNP," *Business Economics* (April 1984), pp. 52–58.

Phelps, Edmund. "Money-Wage Dynamics and Labor-Market Equilibrium," *Journal of Political Economy* (Part II, July/August 1968), pp. 678–711.

Tinbergen, Jan. *Business Cycles in the United States of America, 1919–1932, Statistical Testing of Business Cycle*

Theories, vol. 2, (League of Nations, 1939).

Zellner, Arnold, and Franz Palm. "Time Series Analysis and Simultaneous Equation Econometric Models," *Journal of Econometrics* (May 1974), pp. 17–54.

Appendix
On Data For Tables 3 and 4

A. Data for equations (1′), (2′), (3), (5), (14–19), and (24–25):

M1 = currency plus checkable deposits, billions of dollars

    1892–1956, June 30 data: U.S. Bureau of the Census. *Historical Statistics of the U.S. from Colonial Times to 1957* (Government Printing Office, 1960), p. 646, series X-267.

    1957–58, June 30 data: *Economic Report of the President*, 1959, p. 186.

    1959–91, averages of daily data for December, seasonally adjusted: *Economic Report of the President*, 1992, p. 373.

    Note: December data, seasonally adjusted, are close to June 30 data.

GNP = gross national product, billions of dollars per year

    1892–1928: Kendrick (1961), pp. 296–7.

    1929–59: *Economic Report of the President*, 1961, p. 127.

    1960–88: *Economic Report of the President*, 1992, p. 320.

    1989–91: *Survey of Current Business*, July 1992, p. 52.

RAaa = long-term high-grade bond rate, percent per year

    1892–1918: Macaulay's unadjusted railroad bond rate, U.S. Bureau of the Census. *Historical Statistics of the United States from Colonial Times to 1957* (Government Printing Office, 1960), p. 656, series X-332.

    1919–91: Moody's Aaa corporate bond rate:

    1919–38: U.S. Bureau of the Census. *Historical Statistics of the United States from Colonial Times to*

1957 (Government Printing Office, 1960), p. 656, series X-333.

    1939–91: *Economic Report of the President*, 1992, p. 378.

Note: For pre-1959 data I used sources that were available in 1960, in an attempt to make equation 2′ reproduce the 1892–1959 equation 2, which originally appeared in Christ (1963). These same sources also yield equation 1′, which is an approximate reproduction of the 1919–52 equation 1, from Latané (1954).

B. Data for 1959–91 for equation (4):

M1 = currency plus checkable deposits, billions of dollars: same as above.

GDP = gross domestic product, billions of dollars per year: *Economic Report of the President*, 1992, pp. 298 or 320.

RAaa = Moody's Aaa corporate bond rate, percent per year: same as above.

C. Data for 1919–52 for equation (1), as described in Latané (1954), p. 457:[1]

M1: "demand deposits adjusted plus currency in circulation on the mid-year call date, (Federal Reserve Board Data)."

    U.S. Bureau of the Census. *Historical Statistics of the United States from Colonial Times to 1957* (Government Printing Office, 1960). Series X-267

GNP: "Department of Commerce series from 1929 to date; 1919–28 Federal Reserve Board estimates on the same basis (National Industrial Conference Board, *Economic Almanac*, 1952, p. 201)."

---

[1] Though Latané's work was published in 1954, research analysts at the Federal Reserve Bank of St. Louis used more recent data to replicate his work.

94

RAaa: "interest rate on high-grade long-term corporate obligations. The U.S. Treasury series giving the yields on corporate high-grade bonds as reported in the *Federal Reserve Bulletin* is used from 1936 to date. Before 1936 we use annual averages of Macaulay's high-grade railroad bond yields given in column 5, Table 10, of his *Bond Yields, Interest Rates, Stock Prices,"* pp. A157–A161. Macaulay, Frederick R. *Bond Yields, Interest Rates, Stock Prices* (National Bureau of Economic Research, 1938).

D. Data for 1892–1959 for equation (2), as described in Christ (1963), pp. 217–18:[2]

M1: "currency outside banks" plus "demand deposits adjusted", "billions of dollars as of June 30."

U.S. Bureau of the Census. *Historical Statistics of the United States from Colonial Times to 1957* (Government Printing Office, 1960). Series X-267

U.S. Bureau of the Census. *Historical Statistics of the United States from Colonial Times to 1957; Continuation to 1962 and Revisions* (Government Printing Office, 1965). Series X-267

RAaa: "long-term interest rate (Moody's Aaa corporate bond rate, extrapolated before 1919 via Macaulay's railroad bond yield index)", "percent per year."

GNP: "gross national product, billions of dollars per year."

---

[2]Though Christ's work was published in 1963, research analysts at the Federal Reserve Bank of St. Louis used more recent data to replicate his work.

PART III

THE GOVERNMENT BUDGET RESTRAINT AND ITS IMPLICATIONS

[8]

A SHORT-RUN AGGREGATE-DEMAND MODEL OF THE INTERDEPENDENCE AND EFFECTS OF MONETARY AND FISCAL POLICIES WITH KEYNESIAN AND CLASSICAL INTEREST ELASTICITIES*

By CARL F. CHRIST
*Johns Hopkins University
and University of Essex*

The purposes of this paper are (1) to emphasize that major domestic monetary and fiscal policies are interdependent because of the existence of the government budget restraint, which allows the authorities only N-1 degrees of freedom in the setting of N monetary and fiscal policy variables; (2) to present a theoretical economic model of aggregate demand that incorporates important features of U.S. domestic monetary and fiscal policy, including the government budget restraint but excluding foreign trade; and (3) to analyze the effects of the four main domestic monetary and fiscal policy variables upon the short-run equilibrium of the economy represented by the model when there is short-run rigidity of the price level.

Results for two of the policy variables—government purchases and the high powered money stock—are as follows. Remember that they are only very approximate, and that they refer to short-run equilibria of real aggregate demand, with rigid prices.

1. The multiplier effect of increased government purchases upon real aggregate demand can be as low as 1.1 (under pure tax finance), or as high as 6.2 (under financing purely by printing high-powered money), or anywhere in between. For example, it is 3.7 when the financing is purely by borrowing from private lenders.

2. The multiplier effect of an increased stock of high-powered money upon real aggregate demand can be as low as 1.7 (where the new money and the resulting induced taxes are spent in buying government bonds from private holders), or as high as 7.9 (where the new money and the resulting induced taxes are spent for increased government purchases of goods and services), or anywhere in between. For example, it is 5.1 if the new money is used purely to replace tax finance, or 2.5 if the new money is used purely to buy government bonds from private holders.

* The research underlying this paper was supported in part by a grant from the National Science Foundation to the Johns Hopkins University. I am indebted for helpful comments to Don Patinkin, Kelvin Lancaster, William Poole, William Oakland, Karl Brunner, G. C. Archibald, O. H. Brownlee, Harry G. Johnson, Robert A. Mundell, Helen F. Popkin, and James J. Sullivan.

434

This confirms what all good economists know (but most commonly used macro models fail to reflect properly); namely, the effects of fiscal policy depend heavily on how deficit financing is divided between printing money and borrowing from the private sector, and the effects of a change in the high-powered money stock depend heavily on how that change occurs.

The next few paragraphs describe the method of analysis. A ten-equation model of aggregate demand is used. There are two sectors: government (including the treasury and the central bank) and private (including commercial banks and local government).[1] Three assets are explicitly considered: physical capital, government bonds, and high-powered money. Intrasector claims may exist, such as bank deposits and corporate securities, but they cancel out in the consolidated sectors used here.[2]

The ten endogenous variables are c=real consumption, i=real net investment, k=real physical capital, r=yield on perpetual government bonds, r'=yield on physical capital, t=real tax receipts less transfers, w=real private wealth, x=real net national product (NNP), y=real disposable income, and z=real capital gains on government bonds and high-powered money. The four policy variables considered are g=real government purchases, H=high-powered money stock, t_0=autonomous flow of real taxes less transfers, and B=number of government bonds in private hands (each bond being a perpetuity paying \$1.00 per year). The price level P is predetermined and held fixed. So is the marginal tax transfer rate t_1.[3] Stocks are as of the end of the period.

The ten equations are:

(1)	$x = c + i + g$	real NNP definition
(2)	$k = k_{-1} + i$	real physical capital identity
(3)	$w = k + H/P + B/rP$	real private wealth definition
(4)	$t = t_0 + t_1 x$	tax transfer equation
(5)	$y = x - t$	real disposable income definition (excluding capital gain on bonds and high-powered money)

[1] Note that this renders the model incapable of dealing with changes in required reserve ratios, or changes in interest ceilings on bank deposits, unless certain parameters of the model are permitted to vary, because such policies affect the distribution of claims within the private sector and also affect the private sector's aggregate behavior.

[2] The model does exclude any assets (except high-powered money and government bonds) that will arise from claims between the private and government sectors and hence do not cancel out when each sector is consolidated; e.g., Federal Reserve claims against commercial banks as a result of discounting and Treasury deposits in commercial banks. These exclusions are quantitatively minor.

[3] This results in no loss of generality in the analysis, because a change in the marginal tax-transfer rate t_1 can always be linearly approximated by that change in the autonomous tax-transfer rate t_0 which yields the same change in the flow of total taxes less transfers.

(6) $z = H\Delta(1/P) + B\Delta(1/rP)$ real capital gain on bonds and high-powered money

(7) $c = \phi(y, z, w_{-1}, r, r')$ real consumption

(8) $i = \theta(x, k_{-1}, r, r')$ real net investment

(9) $H/P = \psi(x, w, r, r')$ real high-powered money demanded

(10) $B/rP = \beta(x, w, r, r')$ real government bonds demanded

Now government purchases must be financed by some combination of (1) taxes less transfers, (2) printing high-powered money, and (3) borrowing from the private sector, including commercial banks. This requirement is the government budget restraint (11).

(11) $g = t_0 + t_1 x + (1/P)\Delta H + (1/rP)\Delta B$

The four policy variables g, t_0, H, and B must be chosen subject to this restraint. Hence only three of them can be exogenous—any three. The fourth one becomes endogenous in a model that incorporates the government budget restraint as its eleventh equation. Thus the model determines short-run equilibrium values of any one policy variable and the other ten endogenous variables, given the values of the other three policy variables, and given also P, t_1, and all the lagged variables. (The equilibrium will not be stationary if the budget is unbalanced, or if net investment is not zero, for the stocks of assets will not then be constant.)

The method of analysis is comparative statics. The first difference of the model is taken, setting $\Delta P = \Delta t_1 = 0$. For simplicity the lagged first differences of all variables are set equal to zero (this does not affect the results very much, for the annual changes in variables rarely exceed 10 percent).

Numerical values are assigned to the initial equilibrium levels of all variables, roughly approximating recent U.S. data, and numerical values are assigned to the partial derivatives of the four behavior functions, based on econometric studies of the U.S. where possible, and otherwise on plausible guesses subject to relevant theoretical restrictions. The first set of values so assigned is labeled Case 1.[4]

[4] They are as follows. Flows in billions of dollars per year: $c = 430$, $i = 50$, $g = t = 120$, $t_0 = 0$, $x = 600$, $y = 480$, $z = 0$. (Note that the budget is assumed to be initially balanced). Stocks in billions of dollars: $H = 60$, $B/r = 240$, $k = 2100$, $w = 2400$. Yields: $r = .0333$ ($3\frac{1}{3}$ percent), $r' = .0667$ ($6\frac{2}{3}$ percent). $P = 1.0$ (index number) and $t_1 = 0.2$ (pure number). Slopes and elasticities:

$$\phi_y = 0.7, \quad \phi_z = 0.07, \quad \eta_{\phi r} = \eta_{\phi r'} = -0.05, \quad \theta_x = 0.1,$$

$$\eta_{\theta r} = -\eta_{\theta r'} = -0.1, \quad \eta_{\psi x} = \eta_{\psi w} = -\eta_{\psi r} = 1, \quad \eta_{\psi r'} = -0.4,$$

$$\eta_{\beta x} = 0.1, \quad \eta_{\beta w} = 1, \quad \eta_{\beta r} = 0.55, \quad \eta_{\beta r'} = -0.25.$$

Sources for these slopes and elasticities are included in the list at the end of the paper. The theoretical restrictions take account of the fact that the demand function for physical capital must be identically equal to total wealth minus the demand functions for real bonds and real high-powered money.

The resulting system of equations for the differences in variables (denoted by Δ's) as between the initial equilibrium and the new one, in Case 1, is as follows:[5]

(1') $$\Delta x = \Delta c + \Delta i + \Delta g$$

(2') $$\Delta k = \Delta i$$

(3') $$\Delta w = \Delta k + (1/P)\Delta H + (1/rP)\Delta B - (B/r^2 P)\Delta r$$
$$= \Delta k + \Delta H + 30\Delta B - 7200\Delta r$$

(4') $$\Delta t = \Delta t_0 + t_1 \Delta x = \Delta t_0 + 0.2\Delta x$$

(5') $$\Delta y = \Delta x - \Delta t$$

(6') $$\Delta z = -(B/r^2 P)\Delta r = -7200\Delta r$$

(7') $$\Delta c = \phi_y \Delta y + \phi_z \Delta z + \phi_r \Delta r + \phi_{r'} \Delta r'$$
$$= 0.7\Delta y + 0.07\Delta z - 645\Delta r - 322.5\Delta r'$$

(8') $$\Delta i = \theta_x \Delta x + \theta_r \Delta r + \theta_{r'} \Delta r'$$
$$= 0.1\Delta x - 150\Delta r + 75\Delta r'$$

(9') $$(1/P)\Delta H = \psi_x \Delta x + \psi_w \Delta w + \psi_r \Delta r + \psi_{r'} \Delta r'$$
$$= \Delta H = 0.1\Delta x + 0.025\Delta w - 1800\Delta r - 360\Delta r'$$

(10') $$(1/rP)\Delta B = \beta_x \Delta x + \beta_w \Delta w + (\beta_r + B/r^2 P)\Delta r + \beta_{r'}\Delta r'$$
$$= 30\Delta B = 0.04x + 0.1\Delta w + 11160\Delta r - 900\Delta r'$$

(11') $$\Delta g = \Delta t_0 + t_1 \Delta x + (1/P)\Delta H + (1/rP)\Delta B$$
$$= \Delta t_0 + 0.2\Delta x + \Delta H + 30\Delta B$$

By a policy we shall mean a set of arbitrary values for the changes in any three of the four policy variables, Δg, ΔH, Δt_0, and $30\Delta B$ ($30\Delta B$ is the value of the change in government bonds privately held, since $1/rP = 30$). For any such policy, the foregoing eleven equations will determine the changes in the other eleven variables required to reach the resulting new short-run equilibrium.

Twelve different stimulating policies were chosen for analysis. They are described in the first column of Table 1. For simplicity, the three exogenous changes in policy variables are always chosen to be either 0 or $1 billion, as shown in three of the columns 2 through 5. The endogenous response of the economy to each of the twelve policies, under the conditions of Case 1, is shown in the other columns, including the endogenous response of the remaining policy variable.

For example, consider policy c. It consists of a $1 billion open market purchase of government bonds ($30\Delta B = -1$ in column 4), with no

---

[5] If real output were regarded as fixed by the full employment of given resources, and the price level were regarded as endogenous, then one would set $\Delta x = 0$ rather than $\Delta P = 0$, and these equations would contain ΔP rather than Δx.

TABLE 1

EFFECTS OF TWELVE SELECTED MONETARY AND FISCAL POLICIES UPON THE SHORT-RUN EQUILIBRIUM
VALUES OF THE ELEVEN DEPENDENT VARIABLES IN CASE 1

Policy	Changes in Policy Variables Δt_0	Δg	$30\Delta B$	ΔH
(1)	(2)	(3)	(4)	(5)
(a) a switch from autonomous tax finance to a combination of induced tax finance and printing high-powered money.................................	−1	0	0	.50
(b) an increase in government purchases, financed by printing high-powered money except to the extent that induced taxes less transfers contribute to the financing.	0	1	0	.39
(c) an open market purchase of government bonds, financed by printing high-powered money except to the extent that induced taxes less transfers contribute to the financing..	0	0	−1	.75
(d) a switch from autonomous tax finance to a combination of induced tax finance and borrowing from the private sector.....................................	−1	0	.66	0
(e) an increase in government purchases, financed by borrowing from the private sector except to the extent that induced taxes less transfers contribute to the financing...	0	1	.52	0
(f) printing high-powered money, and using it and the induced taxes less transfers to buy government bonds from the private sector; it is the same as policy (c) except for a scale factor..	0	0	−1.33	1
(g) an increase in government purchases, financed entirely by autonomous and induced taxes less transfers (the balanced budget multiplier case).............	.78	1	0	0
(h) a switch from tax finance to borrowing from the private sector; it is the same as policy d except for a scale factor.......................................	−1.51	0	1	0
(i) a switch from tax finance to printing high-powered money; it is the same as policy a except for a scale factor..	−2.01	0	0	1
(j) a switch from debt finance to printing high-powered money, with no change in total taxes less transfers (any induced increase being offset by an equal autonomous cut)...	−.50	0	−1	1
(k) an increase in government purchases, financed entirely by printing high-powered money, with no change in total taxes less transfers (an induced increase being offset by an equal autonomous cut)......................................	−1.23	1	0	1
(l) an increase in government purchases, financed entirely by borrowing from the private sector, with no change in total taxes less transfers (any induced increase being offset by an equal autonomous cut)...............................	−.73	1	1	0

NOTES: Numerical results were obtained by solving equations (1')–(11') for each policy selected. The tax-transfer function (4') requires that column 6 equal column 2+0.2 times column 7. The budget restraint (11') requires that column 3 equal the sum of columns 4, 5, and 6. In each row, 3 policy variables have arbitrarily been chosen as exogenous, and the remaining one (having entries other than 0 or 1 in its column) is dependent.

Continued overleaf

change in tax rates or government purchases ($\Delta t_0 = \Delta g = 0$ in columns 2 and 3). The high-powered money stock is left to adjust endogenously. In the new equilibrium, NNP is higher by $1.24 billion ($\Delta x = 1.24$ in column 7). At a 20 percent marginal rate this yields induced taxes less transfers of $0.25 billion ($\Delta t = .25$ in column 6). Hence the amount of high-powered money that must be issued in order to complete the financing of the open market purchase, and satisfy the budget restraint, is only $0.75 billion ($\Delta H = .75$ in column 5). Changes in the short-run equilibrium values of the other variables are shown in columns 8–14. Any of the other policies' effects can be read from Table 1 in the same way.

We now compute "multipliers" to express the effects of each monetary and fiscal policy variable upon the short-run equilibrium value of real NNP, for each of the twelve policies. Each multiplier is defined as the quotient of the change in the short-run equilibrium level of real NNP divided by the change in the policy variable in question, thus: $\Delta x/\Delta g$,

TABLE 1—Continued

Effect of the Policy Shown in Columns 2–5 Upon the Ten Dependent Variables (Other than the Dependent Policy Variable)									Linear Combination of 3 Basic Policies $(a), (b), (c)$
Δt	Δx	Δy	Δz	Δc	$\Delta i = \Delta k$	Δw	Δr	$\Delta r'$	
(6)	(7)	(8)	(9)	(10)	(11)	(12)	(13)	(14)	(15)
$-.50$	2.51	3.01	.35	2.28	.23	1.08	$-.00005$	$-.0037$	$a = .50i$
.61	3.06	2.45	.16	1.76	.31	.86	$-.00002$	$-.00005$	$b = -.61i + k$
.25	1.24	1.00	1.22	1.16	.09	1.06	$-.00017$	$-.00082$	$c = -.25i + j$
$-.66$	1.69	2.35	$-.46$	1.51	.17	.37	.00006	.00017	$a - .66c = .66(i-j)$
.48	2.42	1.94	$-.47$	1.16	.26	.31	.00006	.00037	$b - .52c = -.4 - .52j + k$
.33	1.66	1.33	1.63	1.54	.12	141.	$-.00023$	$-.00109$	$1.33c = -.33i + 1.33j$
1	1.11	.11	$-.11$	$-.01$	.13	.02	.00001	.00024	$-.78a + b = -i + k$
-1	2.55	3.55	$-.70$	2.29	.26	.56	.00010	.00026	$1.51a - c = 1.51d = i - j$
-1	5.05	6.05	.70	4.58	.46	2.16	$-.00010$	$-.00074$	$2.01a$
0	2.50	2.50	1.40	2.30	.20	1.60	$-.00019$	$-.00100$	$.50a + c = i - h$
0	6.16	6.16	.59	4.57	.59	2.18	$-.00008$	$-.00050$	$1.23a + b = g + i$
0	3.66	3.66	$-.80$	2.27	.39	.58	.00011	.00050	$.73a + b - c = g + h = -j + k$

$\Delta x/\Delta t_0$, $\Delta x/\Delta H$, and $\Delta x/30\Delta B$. They are shown in Table 2. (Note that the different multipliers shown for each policy are different ways of expressing the total effect of that policy; to add them together would be double counting, and hence improper.)

For example, in policies a, b, and c the multipliers $\Delta x/\Delta H$ for the high-powered money stock are respectively 5.05, 7.90, and 1.66. The highest and lowest values of each multiplier obtainable among the twelve policies are shown at the foot of each column in Table 2.

We can now summarize the multiplier effects of monetary and fiscal policy variables upon the short-run equilibrium level of real NNP demanded using the foregoing eleven equations in Case 1:

The government purchases multiplier of real NNP may be as great as 6.16 (for policy k which finances the purchases purely by printing high-powered money), and as low as 1.11 (for the balanced-budget multiplier policy g). See column 3.

The high-powered money stock multiplier of real NNP may be as high as 7.90 (for policy *b* which uses the additional high-powered money to help finance government purchases, the remaining financing being via induced taxes less transfers), and as low as 1.66 (for policy *c* which is an open market purchase of government bonds, financed by the additional high-powered money except to the extent that induced taxes less transfers contribute to the financing). See column 5.

The autonomous tax-transfer multiplier of real NNP may be as great as $+1.43$ (for the balanced-budget multiplier policy *g*), and as low as

TABLE 2

REAL NNP MULTIPLIER, Δ (REAL NNP) $\div \Delta$ (POLICY VARIABLE), IN CASE 1
FOR THE TWELVE SELECTED MONETARY AND FISCAL POLICIES IN TABLE 1

POLICY	REAL NNP MULTIPLIER, $\Delta x/\Delta$ (POLICY VARIABLE), FOR CHANGES IN THESE POLICY VARIABLES:			
(1)	t_0 (2)	g (3)	$30B$ (4)	H (5)
a, i	−2.51	—	—	5.05
b	—	3.06	—	7.90
c, f	—	—	−1.24	1.66
d, h	−1.69	—	2.55	—
e	—	2.42	4.70	—
f, c	—	—	−1.24	1.66
g	1.43	1.11	—	—
h, d	−1.69	—	2.55	—
i, a	−2.51	—	—	5.05
j	—	—	−2.50	2.50
k	—	6.16	—	6.16
l	—	3.66	3.66	—
Max	1.43	6.16	4.70	7.90
Min	−2.51	1.11	−2.50	1.66

SOURCE: Column 7 of Table 1÷column (*n*) of Table 1 (*n*=2, · · · , 5).

−2.51 (for policy *a* which is a switch from tax finance to printing high-powered money). See column 2.

The private bondholdings multiplier of real NNP may be as great as $+4.70$ (for policy *e* which issues the bonds in order to help finance government purchases, the remaining financing being via induced taxes less transfers), and as low as -2.50 (for policy *j*, which is a pure switch between debt finance and printing high-powered money). See column 4.

Next we study the sensitivity of the real NNP multipliers to changes in some of the parameters of the system. We concentrate on interest elasticities of expenditure and asset demand, for it is here that "Keynesian" and "classical" advocates differ most.

For simplicity we consider only three policies, *a*, *b*, and *c*, though others can be examined in the same way.

In Figure 1, the absolute interest elasticity of investment, $|\eta_{\partial r}|$, varies from the Keynesian extreme of 0 at the left to the strongly classical value of 1 at the right. In computing the NNP multipliers shown in Figure 1, all four interest elasticities of expenditure have been

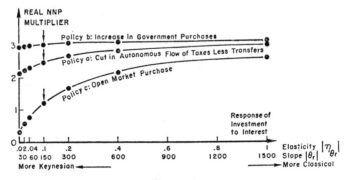

FIGURE 1

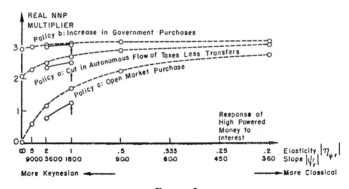

FIGURE 2

varied in proportion to each other, and other parameters have been kept at their Case 1 values.

In Figure 2, the absolute interest elasticity of high-powered money demand, $|\eta_{\psi r}|$, varies from the Keynesian extreme of infinity at the left to the strongly classical value of 0.2 at the right. In computing the NNP multipliers shown by the solid curves in Figure 2, all four interest elasticities of asset demand have been varied in proportion to each other, and other parameters have been kept at their Case 1 values. The dotted curves are the same except that the four interest elasticities of expenditure have been kept at double their Case 1 values.

The two figures show that the real NNP multiplier effects of government purchases in policy a and taxes less transfers in policy b are not very sensitive to variations in interest elasticities, and the real NNP multiplier effect of open market operations in policy c is sensitive only toward the Keynesian extremes where expenditure elasticities are low and asset demand elasticities are high. A similar analysis of policies j, k, and l (not shown here) yields the same qualitative result. Hence if we can find a set of parameter values representing the most Keynesian character that the system might realistically have, we can then find a lower bound for the multiplier effect of open market operations. Let us try.

Consider the points in Figure 1 marked by arrows. Here $|\eta_{\theta r}| = 0.1$, as assumed in Case 1, and the absolute investment slope $|\theta_r| = 150$. This would imply that a substantial change of 0.01 in the bond yield r (from $3\frac{1}{3}$ percent to $4\frac{1}{3}$ percent) would cut investment demand by only $1.5 billion, from $50 billion to $48.5 billion. I submit that this is so small as to be a reasonable lower limit, although admittedly we do not have firm econometric evidence on this point.

Consider now the points in Figure 2 marked by arrows. Here $|\eta_{\psi r}| = 1$, as assumed in Case 1, and the absolute high-powered money slope $|\psi_r| = 1800$. This would imply that a change of 0.01 in r (from $3\frac{1}{3}$ to $4\frac{1}{3}$ percent) would cut high-powered money demand by a whopping $18 billion, from $60 billion to $42 billion. I submit that this is so large as to be conservative upper limit, and there is some supporting econometric evidence here; see the references to Christ, Latané, and Meltzer.

If it is accepted that the interest elasticity of investment is no less than 0.1, and that the interest elasticity of high-powered money demand is no more than 1, and that the other assumptions of Case 1 are near the truth, then Figures 1 and 2 show that we can expect a real NNP multiplier of at least $1\frac{1}{4}$ from policy c; that is, from open market purchases financed partly by printing high-powered money and partly by the induced taxes less transfers that arise at existing tax-transfer rates. If open market operations are financed entirely by printing money as in policy j, the multiplier is of course higher, about $2\frac{1}{2}$. These multipliers are too high to justify the neglect of monetary policy.

To summarize: (1) Government policy variables are subject to a budget restraint. Therefore (2) the effect of a change in any single policy variable depends on how other policy variables are varied in order to satisfy the budget restraint.

Therefore (3) the proper object of analysis is not a single policy variable, but a policy (defined as as set of arbitrary values of all but one of the policy variables, the remaining one being determined endogenously by the system). (4) Our rough quantitative results suggest forcefully that both the extreme fiscal advocates and the extreme monetary advocates are wrong: Fiscal variables strongly influence the effect of a given change in the high-powered money stock, and open market operations strongly influence the effects of given changes in government expenditures and taxation.

REFERENCES AND RELATED WORKS

1. *Phillip D. Cagan, "The Demand for Currency Relative to the Total Money Supply," *J.P.E.*, Aug., 1958, pp. 303–28.
2. *Carl F. Christ, "Interest Rates and 'Portfolio Selection' Among Liquid Assets in the U.S.," in Carl F. Christ and (eleven) others, *Measurement in Economics: Studies in Mathematical Economics and Econometrics in Memory of Yehuda Grunfeld* (Stanford Univ. Press, 1961), pp. 201–18.
3. Morris A. Copeland, "Tracing Money Flows Through the United States Economy," *A.E.R.*, May 1947, pp. 31–49.
4. *Robert Eisner and Robert Strotz, "Determinants of Business Investment," in Commission on Money and Credit, *Impacts of Monetary Policy* (Prentice-Hall, 1963), pp. 59–337, esp. pp. 151–79.
5. Alain C. Enthoven, "A Neo-classical Model of Money, Debt, and Economic Growth," Mathematical Appendix to *Money in a Theory of Finance*, by John G. Gurley and Edward S. Shaw (Brookings Institution, 1960), pp. 303–59, esp. pp. 315 ff.
6. *Milton Friedman, "The Demand for Money: Some Theoretical and Empirical Results," *J.P.E.*, Aug., 1959, pp. 327–51.
7. Bent Hansen, *The Economic Theory of Fiscal Policy*, translated by P. E. Burke (London, Allen and Unwin, and Cambridge, Harvard Univ. Press, 1958), Chap. 3.
8. *Henry Allen Latané, "Cash Balances and the Interest Rate—A Pragmatic Approach," *Rev. of Econ. and Statis.*, Nov., 1954, pp. 456–60.
9. Assar Lindbeck, *A Study in Monetary Analysis*, Stockholm Economic Studies, New Series III (Stockholm, Almqvist and Wicksell, 1963), pp. 144, 146–47.
10. *Allan H. Meltzer, "The Demand for Money: The Evidence from the Time Series," *J.P.E.*, June, 1963, pp. 219–46.
11. Lloyd Metzler, "Wealth, Saving, and the Rate of Interest," *J.P.E.*, Apr., 1951, pp. 93–116.
12. Richard A. Musgrave, *The Theory of Public Finance: A Study in Public Economy* (McGraw-Hill, 1959), Chap. 22.
13. Don Patinkin, *Money, Interest and Prices* (Row Peterson, 1956), pp. 361–65.
14. *Richard T. Selden, "Monetary Velocity in the United States," in Milton Friedman, ed., *Studies in the Quantity Theory of Money* (Univ. of Chicago Press, 1956), pp. 179–257.

* Note: Starred items contain econometric evidence about elasticities. The other items contain conceptual antecedents to this paper.

9

Reprinted from THE JOURNAL OF POLITICAL ECONOMY
Vol., 76, No. 1, January/February 1968
Copyright 1968 by The University of Chicago
Printed in U.S.A.

A Simple Macroeconomic Model with a Government Budget Restraint

Carl F. Christ*

Johns Hopkins University

In choosing a mix of monetary and fiscal policies, government authorities (including the central bank) are bound by a government budget restraint. This restraint is less severe than a private individual's or firm's restraint because government authorities can issue fiat money. Nevertheless, the government budget restraint is important. It requires that in each period total government expenditure (transfer payments plus purchases of goods and services) must be equal to the total flow of financing from *all sources* (including printing money). This means there is a constraint upon the government's freedom to choose arbitrary values of such policy variables as expenditures, taxes, net amount of borrowing from the private sector, and net amount of new money issued. For example, if a government has already decided upon its expenditures, taxes, borrowing, and all other means of finance besides printing money, then it has no further choice about how much money to issue: The net amount issued must be just enough so that the total of flows of financing is equal to expenditure.

It is the purpose of this paper to introduce the government budget restraint into a very simple theoretical static macroeconomic model of aggregate demand with a rigid price level, and to show how the analysis of macroeconomic policies is affected by the budget restraint.[1]

To summarize: the results indicate that the multiplier effect of a change in government purchases cannot be defined until it is decided how to finance the purchases, and the value of the multiplier given by the generally

* The work underlying this paper was done partly at the University of Essex and partly supported by a National Science Foundation grant to the John Hopkins University. I am indebted for helpful comments to G. C. Archibald, H. G. Johnson, J. Johnston, D. E. W. Laidler, R. A. Mundell, and F. G. Pyatt.

[1] The government budget restraint has also been recognized by Patinkin (1956, pp. 361–65), Hansen (1958, chap. iii), Musgrave (1959, chap. xxii), and Enthoven (1960, pp. 303–59, esp. pp. 315 ff.), among others. After this paper was accepted for publication, two related pieces of work came to my attention: Ritter (1955–56) and Ott and Ott (1965). Both employ the idea of a government budget restraint, but neither carries the analysis as far as is done here.

53

accepted analysis (which ignores the government budget restraint) is in general incorrect. The *one-year impact* multiplier effect of government purchases may be greater or less than the value obtained by ignoring the budget restraint, depending on whether the method of financing is mainly by printing money or mainly by taxation. The same applies to the *long-run* multiplier effect of government purchases. A striking result is that the long-run multiplier effect of an increase in government purchases, with no change in tax rates, is equal to the inverse of the marginal tax rate.[2]

Our point of departure is a simple static model of aggregate demand with rigid prices, stemming from the Keynesian model in Hicks (1937). We incorporate into it a governmental budget restraint in the simplest possible manner. The variables used are as follows: e, t, x, y, g, and v are flows:

e = Real private expenditure (consumption + investment);
r = Interest rate;
t = Real taxes less government transfer payments, hereafter referred to as "taxes" (thus transfers are regarded as negative taxes);
x = Real national income;
y = Real disposable income;
g = Real government purchases;
H = High-powered money stock, end of period;
u = Marginal tax rate;
v = Autonomous real tax flow;
P = Price level, assumed rigid.

The six equations of the model appear below. For simplicity the two behavior equations have been linearized. The first five equations are fairly standard features of the generally accepted static demand model that underlies the well-known IS and LM curves, with some exceptions noted later. Equation (6) is the government budget restraint, stating that in each period real government purchases must equal the total flow of real financing available from all sources; in this very simple model the only two sources are taxes, t, and the real value of the net increase in the high-powered money stock, $\Delta H/P$.

$x = e + g$	real income definition	(1)
$t = ux + v$	tax equation	(2)
$y = x - t$	real disposable income definition	(3)
$e = \epsilon_y y + \epsilon_r r + \epsilon_0$	real private expenditure equation	(4)
$H/P = \lambda_x x + \lambda_r r + \lambda_0$	real high-powered money demand equation	(5)
$g = t + \Delta H/P$	government budget restraint	(6)

[2] By the marginal tax rate is meant the derivative of aggregate tax receipts with respect to aggregate income.

A few points of interpretation should be noted. First, as the budget restraint shows, there are no government bonds in this model; budget deficits or surpluses must be offset by changes in the outstanding high-powered money stock. Government bonds could be introduced, and with them the possibility of financing expenditures by borrowing from the private sector, but for simplicity that has not been done here.[3]

Second, the money stock as usually defined (currency outside banks plus bank deposits) does not appear explicitly in the model. This is because the banks and the non-banking private sector are regarded as consolidated into a single private sector; then, banks' deposit liabilities ca..cel out against private holdings of deposits, leaving the *net* money holdings of the consolidated private sector equal to the high-powered money stock as in equation (5).[4] This is an appropriate simplification because the high-powered money stock is a policy variable, whereas the ordinary money stock is endogenously determined by the behavior of bankers and their customers within the private sector; to study that behavior it would be necessary to complicate the model greatly.

Third, the treasury and central bank are consolidated in a single government sector; it is their net combined outstanding monetary liabilities (currency and central-bank deposits) that constitute the stock of high-powered money held by the private sector including banks.

Fourth, and most important, the government budget restraint places a restriction on the four policy variables—g, H, u, and v—so that the authorities are free to assign arbitrary values to only three of them. When that has been done, the model determines the value of the fourth policy variable and of the other five dependent variables: e, r, t, x, and y. Therefore, the six dependent variables of the system consist of e, r, t, x, y, and any *one* of the four policy variables, while the predetermined variables consist of the other three policy variables and P and H_{-1} (which appears in ΔH, defined as $H - H_{-1}$).

Fifth, note that the model is static if the government budget restraint (equation [6]) is ignored but becomes dynamic when it is included. This dynamic system is in long-run equilibrium only when none of its variables

---

[3] I have expanded the impact multiplier analysis of this paper to include government bonds and their interest rate, but the algebraic solutions obtained for policy multipliers then become so complicated that a simulation approach is easier to handle (see Christ, 1967).

[4] This result depends on the simplifying assumption that the Treasury holds no deposits in private banks. It is also assumed here that the central bank does not make loans to financial institutions at their request, that is, there is no discount window. (The falsification introduced by these two assumptions is quantitatively minor.) Thus the model includes no claims between the consolidated private sector on the one hand and the Treasury and central bank on the other except high-powered money. Of course there may be claims of one part of the private sector against another, such as bank deposits, bank loans, corporate securities, and so on, but they cancel out in the consolidation adopted here.

are changing, including the high-powered money stock, H. Hence for long-run equilibrium the government budget must be balanced, that is, $g = t$ in equation (6).

Even before embarking on the formal analysis of the model, one can now see why the long-run multiplier effect of an increase in government purchases, with no change in either of the tax-rate variables u or v, is equal to $1/u$. Suppose that the budget is initially balanced and that then the annual rate of government purchases is raised to a new level \$1 billion higher than before. The first-period effect will be to raise real income; this will lead to an induced increase in taxes of less than \$1 billion, so there will be a budget deficit met by an increase in the high-powered money stock, H. In the second period there is no further change in government purchases, but the budget deficit requires the issue of more money, which raises real income further. And so on in later periods. The rise in real income will come to an end only when the issue of money stops; that will occur only when the budget is again balanced; that will occur only when the annual level of tax receipts has risen by \$1 billion to match government purchases, and *that* will occur only when annual real income has risen by \$$1/u$ billion. Hence the long-run multiplier is $1/u$ for government purchases at given tax rates.

Now let us turn to the formal analysis of the model. The effect of any policy change upon the system can be found by a technique akin to comparative statics: Take the first difference of equations (1)–(6), assign arbitrary values to the changes in the predetermined variables, and solve for the changes in the six dependent variables. This method will be followed below. The first difference of the system is as follows:

$$\Delta x = \Delta e + \Delta g \tag{1'}$$
$$\Delta t = u\Delta x + x\Delta u + \Delta v \tag{2'}$$
$$\Delta y = \Delta x - \Delta t \tag{3'}$$
$$\Delta e = \epsilon_y \Delta y + \epsilon_r \Delta r \tag{4'}$$
$$\Delta H/P - H\Delta P/P^2 = \lambda_x \Delta x + \lambda_r \Delta r \tag{5'}$$
$$\Delta g = \Delta t + \Delta H/P - \Delta H_{-1}/P - \Delta H\Delta P/P^2 \tag{6'}$$

Since prices are taken to be rigid, ΔP will be set equal to 0 henceforth.

Notice that Δu and Δv occur only in the additive expression $x\Delta u + \Delta v$, in equation (2'). This means that to a linear approximation a change Δv in the autonomous tax flow has the same effect as that change Δu in the marginal tax rate which produces a change equal to Δv in tax revenue at the original level of income. Therefore we shall consider that there are only three policy variables: $x\Delta u + \Delta v$, Δg, and ΔH. Then the government budget restraint implies that the authorities are free to fix *any two* of these, the remaining one being endogenously determined.

The simplest kind of policy to analyze is one having only two non-zero changes of policy variables, any other policy variables being held constant.

We have just seen that in this model there are only three policy variables. Hence there are only three families of such simple policies: $\Delta g = 0$ with ΔH and $x\Delta u + \Delta v$ non-zero, $x\Delta u + \Delta v = 0$ with Δg and ΔH non-zero, and $\Delta H = 0$ with Δg and $x\Delta u + \Delta v$ non-zero. These families can be represented by the following three simple policies, where in each case the predetermined non-zero change has been given a *sign* so that the effect is to increase national income, and a *magnitude* so that the initial change in the flow of government purchases or financing is one unit:

Policy A: $\Delta g = 0$, $x\Delta u + \Delta v = -1$, and ΔH is dependent. This is a tax-rate cut, offset by printing money (ΔH) except to the extent that induced taxes ($u\Delta x$) reduce the initial loss of revenue.

Policy B: $x\Delta u + \Delta v = 0$, $\Delta g = 1$, and ΔH is dependent. This is an increase in government purchases, financed by printing money (ΔH) except to the extent that induced taxes ($u\Delta x$) contribute to the financing.

Policy C: $\Delta H = 0$, $\Delta g = 1$, and $x\Delta u + \Delta v$ is dependent. This is an increase in government purchases financed entirely by taxes (partly induced [$u\Delta x$], and the rest [$x\Delta u + \Delta v$] arising from an increase in tax rates), that is, the balanced-budget-multiplier policy.

A fourth policy that is interesting to analyze is:

Policy D: $\Delta g = 1$, $\Delta H/P = 1$, and $x\Delta u + \Delta v$ is dependent. This is an increase in government purchases, financed in the first period entirely by printing money: Tax rates are cut so that in the first period there is no change in total tax revenue.[5]

Note that policies A and B can be regarded as a set of basic policies, in the sense that any monetary-fiscal policy that is possible in this model can be expressed as a linear combination of policies A and B. For example, policy C is equivalent to a combination of a unit positive dose of policy B (which will make $\Delta g = 1$) and a negative dose of policy A just large enough to undo the change in H caused by policy B (thus making $\Delta H = 0$).[6]

---

[5] Each of these four policies has a twin, obtained by interchanging the independent and dependent non-zero changes. For example, for policy A, the twin would be $\Delta g = 0$, $\Delta H/P = 1$, and $x\Delta u + \Delta v$ is dependent; this would clearly have the same effect as an appropriate-size dose of policy A, and so it need not be analyzed separately.

[6] If government borrowing is introduced into the model, then there are four policy variables, not three, and hence the number of basic policies becomes three, not two (see Christ, 1967).

Let us now analyze the *first-period* effects of policies A to D, starting from a position of long-run equilibrium in which the budget is balanced and the high-powered money stock is constant. Then, for the first period during which the new policy is in force, we have $\Delta H_{-1} = 0$. The first-period effects of any policy are found by solving equations (1′)–(6′), using the predetermined variables as given by the policy, and using $\Delta H_{-1} = 0$ and $\Delta P = 0$ as already explained. These short-period effects of policies A to D are set forth algebraically in Table 1. For policy A we can see the tax-rate cut costing one unit of revenue at the initial equilibrium level of income in column (1), no change in government purchases in column (2), the resulting real increase in the high-powered money stock in column (3), the resulting increase in real income in column (5), and the resulting net decrease in real tax revenue in column (4). The effects of policies B, C, and D can be read from Table 1 similarly. Observe that for any policy the change in government purchases in column (2) equals the sum of the changes in financing in columns (3) and (4), as required by equation (6′).

For each dependent variable change shown in Table 1, the range of possible variation is given in parentheses. These ranges are derived from the usual assumptions about the values of the derivatives of the expenditure, liquidity, and tax functions:[7]

$$1 > \epsilon_y > 0, \quad \epsilon_r < 0, \quad \lambda_x > 0, \quad -\infty < \lambda_r < 0, \quad \text{and} \quad 1 > u > 0. \tag{7}$$

In square brackets in Table 1 are given illustrative numerical magnitudes of the first-period changes in the dependent variables. They have been obtained by the use of a set of numerical values thought to be plausible for the parameters appearing in the algebraic formulas in the table.[8]

The effects of the four simple policies on the first-period level of real income can be compared more readily if multipliers are computed for each policy, showing the change in the value of real income per unit change in each policy variable. These multipliers are shown in the first four rows of Table 2. For each of the four simple policies, multipliers are shown for the two policy variables that change, but of course not for the policy variable that is held fixed.

For comparison, Table 2 also shows in row I the real income multipliers that are obtained by the commonly used but incorrect method of ignoring

---

[7] For example, consider $x\Delta u + \Delta v$ under policy C in column (1) of Table 1. These assumptions imply that $(1 - \epsilon_y)(1 - u)$ and $\epsilon_r \lambda_x / \lambda_r$ are positive, so the numerator is positive. Similarly, $1 - \epsilon_y$ is positive also, so the denominator is positive. Hence the fraction is positive. Furthermore, $1 - u$ is less than 1, so the fraction is less than 1. Hence $0 < x\Delta u + \Delta u < 1$, as stated in row C and column (1) of Table 1.

[8] The values are: $u = 0.2$, $\epsilon_y = 0.8$, $\lambda_x = 0.1$, $\epsilon_r = -645$, and $\lambda_r = -2160$. The latter two slopes have been obtained by assuming that $r = 0.06$, $H/P = \$60$ billion, $e = \$480$ billion a year, and interest elasticities $\eta_{er} \cong -0.08$ and $\eta_{\lambda r} \cong -2$. There is some econometric evidence to support very approximately these values for the United States, except for η_{er}, for which I simply chose a small negative number.

TABLE 1

FIRST-PERIOD EFFECTS OF FOUR SELECTED MONETARY-FISCAL POLICIES UPON REAL TAXES, t, AND REAL AGGREGATE DEMAND, x

POLICY	CHANGES IN POLICY VARIABLES			CHANGES IN SELECTED DEPENDENT VARIABLES	
	$x\Delta u + \Delta v$ (1)	Δg (2)	$\Delta H/P = \Delta g - \Delta t$ (3)	$\Delta t = u\Delta x + x\Delta u + \Delta v$ (4)	Δx (5)
A: Cut in tax rates, offset by induced taxes and printing money. . .	-1	0	$\dfrac{1 - \epsilon_y + (\epsilon_r/\lambda_r)\lambda_x}{1 - \epsilon_y(1 - u) + (\epsilon_r/\lambda_r)(\lambda_x + u)}$ (0 to 1) [0.511]	$\dfrac{-(1 - \epsilon_y + (\epsilon_r/\lambda_r)\lambda_x)}{1 - \epsilon_y(1 - u) + (\epsilon_r/\lambda_r)(\lambda_x + u)}$ (-1 to 0) [-0.511]	$\dfrac{\epsilon_y + (\epsilon_r/\lambda_r)}{1 - \epsilon_y(1 - u) + (\epsilon_r/\lambda_r)(\lambda_x + u)}$ (1 to $1/u$) [2.444]
B: Rise in purchases, financed by induced taxes and printing money. . .	0	1	$\dfrac{(1 - \epsilon_y)(1 - u) + (\epsilon_r/\lambda_r)\lambda_x}{1 - \epsilon_y(1 - u) + (\epsilon_r/\lambda_r)(\lambda_x + u)}$ (0 to 1) [0.422]	$\dfrac{u(1 + \epsilon_r/\lambda_r)}{1 - \epsilon_y(1 - u) + (\epsilon_r/\lambda_r)(\lambda_x + u)}$ (0 to 1) [0.578]	$\dfrac{1 + \epsilon_r/\lambda_r}{1 - \epsilon_y(1 - u) + (\epsilon_r/\lambda_r)(\lambda_x + u)}$ (1 to $1/u$) [2.889]
C: Rise in purchases, financed entirely by taxes	$\dfrac{(1 - \epsilon_y)(1 - u) + (\epsilon_r/\lambda_r)\lambda_x}{1 - \epsilon_y + (\epsilon_r/\lambda_r)\lambda_x}$ (0 to 1) [0.826]	1	0	1	$\dfrac{1 - \epsilon_y}{1 - \epsilon_y + (\epsilon_r/\lambda_r)\lambda_x}$ (0 to 1) [0.870]
D: Rise in purchases, financed entirely by printing money. . .	$\dfrac{-u(1 + \epsilon_r/\lambda_r)}{1 - \epsilon_y + (\epsilon_r/\lambda_r)\lambda_x}$ (negative) [-1.130]	1	1	0	$\dfrac{1 + \epsilon_r/\lambda_r}{1 - \epsilon_y + (\epsilon_r/\lambda_r)\lambda_x}$ (positive) [5.652]

SOURCE: Solution of equations (1')–(6') for each policy, after setting $\Delta P = \Delta H_{-1} = 0$ (see text).

TABLE 2

FIRST-PERIOD IMPACT MULTIPLIERS, $\frac{\Delta x}{\Delta \text{(policy variable)}}$, FOR REAL AGGREGATE DEMAND, x, FOR THE FOUR SELECTED POLICIES IN TABLE 1, AND FOR THE MODEL IGNORING THE GOVERNMENT BUDGET RESTRAINT

POLICY	FIRST-PERIOD MULTIPLIERS, $\frac{\Delta x}{\Delta \text{(policy variable)}}$		
	$\dfrac{\Delta x}{x\Delta u + \Delta v}$ (Tax Rate) (1)	$\dfrac{\Delta x}{\Delta g}$ (Government Purchases) (2)	$\dfrac{\Delta x}{\Delta H/P}$ (High-powered money) (3)
A	$\dfrac{-(\epsilon_y + \epsilon_r/\lambda_r)}{1 - \epsilon_y(1 - u) + (\epsilon_r/\lambda_r)(\lambda_x + u)}$ [−2.44]		$\dfrac{\epsilon_y + \epsilon_r/\lambda_r}{1 - \epsilon_y + (\epsilon_r/\lambda_r)\lambda_x}$ [4.78]
B		$\dfrac{1 + \epsilon_r/\lambda_r}{1 - \epsilon_y(1 - u) + (\epsilon_r/\lambda_r)(\lambda_x + u)}$ [2.89]	$\dfrac{1 + \epsilon_r/\lambda_r}{(1 - \epsilon_y)(1 - u) + (\epsilon_r/\lambda_r)\lambda_x}$ [6.84]
C	$\dfrac{1 - \epsilon_y}{(1 - \epsilon_y)(1 - u) + (\epsilon_r/\lambda_r)\lambda_x}$ [1.05]	$\dfrac{1 - \epsilon_y}{1 - \epsilon_y + (\epsilon_r/\lambda_r)\lambda_x}$ [0.87]	$\dfrac{1 + \epsilon_r/\lambda_r}{1 - \epsilon_y + (\epsilon_r/\lambda_r)\lambda_x}$ [5.65]
D	$-\dfrac{1}{u}$ [−5.00]	$\dfrac{1 + \epsilon_r/\lambda_r}{1 - \epsilon_y + (\epsilon_r/\lambda_r)\lambda_x}$ [5.65]	
I: Ignore government budget restraint	$\dfrac{-\epsilon_y}{1 - \epsilon_y(1 - u) + (\epsilon_r/\lambda_r)\lambda_x}$ [−2.05]	$\dfrac{1}{1 - \epsilon_y(1 - u) + (\epsilon_r/\lambda_r)\lambda_x}$ [2.56]	$\dfrac{\epsilon_r/\lambda_r}{1 - \epsilon_y(1 - u) + (\epsilon_r/\lambda_r)\lambda_x}$ [0.77]
Rank in column	$C > 0 > I > A > D$	$D > B > I > C > 0$	$B > D > A > I > 0$

SOURCES: Rows A–D: Table 1, col. (5) ÷ col. (n), $n = 2, 3, 4$. Row I: Solve equations (1')–(5'), ignoring (6').

the budget restraint, that is, solving equations (1')–(5') alone. Note that these multipliers differ from those associated with the simple policies analyzed here: In no case is the multiplier in row I the same as any others in its column.[9]

The multipliers of real income with respect to any given policy variable, shown in a column of Table 2, can now be compared to see which policy gives the largest multiplier, which the next largest, and so on.

Consider first the government-purchases multipliers, $\Delta x/\Delta g$, shown in column (2) of Table 2. All are positive. The largest is for policy D, where purchases are financed entirely by printing money. The next largest is for policy B, where purchases are financed by induced taxes and printing money. The smallest is for the balanced-budget multiplier, policy C, where financing is entirely by taxes. The multiplier obtained by ignoring the budget restraint understates the effect of policy D or B by ignoring the effect of issuing money and (as is well known) overstates the effect of the balanced policy C by ignoring the effect of the increased tax rate. These inequalities are summarized at the foot of column (2); analogous inequalities are reported for the multipliers in column (1) and in column (3); all may be derived from the assumptions (7) mentioned earlier about the derivatives of the functions in the model. In square brackets in Table 2 are shown illustrative numerical values of these first-period multipliers, based on the set of assumptions given in footnote 8.

Consider next the tax multipliers, $\Delta x/(x\Delta u + \Delta v)$, shown in column (1) of Table 2. The largest one is for policy C, the balanced budget multiplier policy: It is positive since an increase in taxes, offset by increased purchases, increases income. The smallest (algebraically) is for policy D, and the next smallest (algebraically) is for policy A: They are both negative since a tax-rate increase, offset in part by a decline in the money stock, reduces income. The multiplier obtained by ignoring the budget restraint is also negative, but of course it understates the absolute magnitude of the effect of policy A or D because it ignores the monetary tightening required by those policies.

Consider finally the high-powered money-stock multipliers, $P\Delta x/\Delta H$, shown in column (3) of Table 2. They are all positive. The largest occurs when the newly issued money is used together with induced taxes to buy goods and services (policy B), the next largest when it is used alone to buy goods and services (policy D), and the third largest when it is used to offset a tax cut (policy A). The multiplier obtained by ignoring the budget restraint of course understates the effects of all three policies A, B, and D, because it neglects both the tax-rate cut and the increased expenditures, one or a combination of which must offset the issue of money.

[9] It is of course possible to find the linear combination of policies A and B that yields the same multiplier as is shown in row I of Table 2 for the policy variable in question, if one wishes to do so.

First-period multiplier effects for any permissible monetary-fiscal policy mix can be obtained in an analogous manner.

Now let us examine the *long-run* effects of policies A to D, starting from a position of long-run equilibrium. For each policy, they can be found as follows: First, solve the system in (1)–(6) for its reduced form.[10] Second, manipulate the reduced form equations to obtain for each dependent variable a difference equation that contains no lagged values of any other dependent variables. Third, solve each of the resulting difference equations for the time path of its dependent variable. Fourth, check the stability of the solution. Fifth, if it is stable, find the new long-run equilibrium level of the variable, and see how much the long-run equilibrium level has changed as a result of the policy. Inequalities (7) given above insure that the solutions for all policies are stable.

The long-run results of the four policies are shown in Table 3, and the corresponding long-run multipliers are shown in Table 4. In each case, if a bar appears above the symbol for the change in a variable, it denotes the change in the long-run equilibrium value of the variable. Thus $\overline{\Delta x}$ refers to the difference between the new and the old long-run equilibrium levels of real income, after and before the policy change. As before, every possible policy is a linear combination of policies A and B.[11] And as before, numbers in square brackets in the tables are illustrative values based on the assumptions in footnote 8.

The derivation of some of Table 3's results for policies A and B will now be illustrated. The reduced form equations for policies A and B are the same, since the sets of predetermined variables in the two policies are the same.

Consider first the effects on *income*. The reduced form equation for real income, x, under either policy A or policy B is:[12]

$$x = \frac{(1 + \epsilon_r/\lambda_r)g - (\epsilon_y + \epsilon_r/\lambda_r)v + (\epsilon_r/\lambda_r)H_{-1}/P + [\epsilon_0 - (\epsilon_r/\lambda_r)\lambda_0]}{1 - \epsilon_y(1 - u) + (\epsilon_r/\lambda_r)(\lambda_x + u)}. \tag{8}$$

The difference equation for real income, x, under policy A or B is obtained by eliminating H_{-1} from (8), by means of a relationship between H_{-1} and x_{-1} that is derived from the lagged version of (1)–(5); the result is:

$$x = \frac{(\epsilon_r/\lambda_r)(g - v) + \Delta g - \epsilon_y \Delta v + [1 - \epsilon_y(1 - u_{-1}) + (\epsilon_r/\lambda_r)\lambda_x]x_{-1}}{1 - \epsilon_y(1 - u) + (\epsilon_r/\lambda_r)(\lambda_x + u)}. \tag{9}$$

[10] $\Delta P = 0$ as before because of the rigid price level, but now ΔH_{-1} is not zero in all periods, because H may change during the long-run adjustment process.

[11] Notice that in Tables 1 and 3, policy C is a combination of a unit positive dose of policy B and $-k_{C1}$ units of policy A, where k_{C1} is the entry in row C, column 1 of Table 1. Also, policy D is a combination of a unit positive dose of policy B and k_{D1} units of policy A, where k_{D1} is the entry in row D, column 1 of Table 1. In the numerical examples shown in square brackets in the tables, $k_{C1} = 0.8261$ and $k_{D1} = -1.1304$.

[12] The first-period multipliers shown in Table 2 for $\Delta x/\Delta g$ under policy B and $\Delta x/\Delta v$ under policy A can be read from equation (8).

TABLE 3

LONG-RUN EFFECTS OF FOUR SELECTED MONETARY-FISCAL POLICIES UPON THE REAL HIGH-POWERED MONEY STOCK, H/P; REAL TAXES, t; AND REAL AGGREGATE DEMAND, x

POLICY	CHANGE IN LONG-RUN EQUILIBRIUM VALUE		
	$\dfrac{\Delta \overline{H}}{P}$ (1)	$\Delta \bar{t}$ (2)	$\Delta \bar{x}$ (3)
A	$\dfrac{1 - \epsilon_y + (\epsilon_r/\lambda_r)\lambda_x}{u\epsilon_r/\lambda_r}$ [3.833]	0	$\dfrac{1}{u}$ [5.00]
B	$\dfrac{(1 - \epsilon_y)(1 - u) + (\epsilon_r/\lambda_r)\lambda_x}{u\epsilon_r/\lambda_r}$ [3.167]	1	$\dfrac{1}{u}$ [5.00]
C	0	1	$\dfrac{1 - \epsilon_y}{1 - \epsilon_y + (\epsilon_r/\lambda_r)\lambda_x}$ [0.870]
D	$\dfrac{1 - \epsilon_y(1 - u) + (\epsilon_r/\lambda_r)(\lambda_x + u)}{u\epsilon_r/\lambda_r}$ [7.500]	1	$\dfrac{1}{u} + \dfrac{1 + \epsilon_r/\lambda_r}{1 - \epsilon_y + (\epsilon_r/\lambda_r)\lambda_x}$ [10.652]

SOURCE: Long-run solution of equations (1)–(6) after setting $\Delta P = 0$ (see text).

TABLE 4

LONG-RUN MULTIPLIERS FOR REAL AGGREGATE DEMAND, x, FOR THE FOUR SELECTED POLICIES IN TABLE 1, AND FOR THE MODEL IGNORING THE GOVERNMENT BUDGET RESTRAINT

	LONG-RUN MULTIPLIERS		
POLICY	$\dfrac{\Delta x}{x\Delta u + \Delta v}$ (1)	$\dfrac{\Delta x}{\Delta g}$ (2)	$\dfrac{\Delta x}{\Delta H/P}$ (3)
A	$-\dfrac{1}{u}$ [−5.00]	. . . .	$\dfrac{\epsilon_r/\lambda_r}{1 - \epsilon_y + (\epsilon_r/\lambda_r)\lambda_x}$ [1.30]
B	. . . .	$\dfrac{1}{u}$ [5.00]	$\dfrac{\epsilon_r/\lambda_r}{(1 - \epsilon_y)(1 - u) + (\epsilon_r/\lambda_r)\lambda_x}$ [1.58]
C	$\dfrac{1 - \epsilon_y}{(1 - \epsilon_y)(1 - u) + (\epsilon_r/\lambda_r)\lambda_x}$ [1.05]	$\dfrac{1 - \epsilon_y}{1 - \epsilon_y + (\epsilon_r/\lambda_r)\lambda_x}$ [0.87]	. . . .
D	$-\dfrac{1 - \epsilon_y + u + (\epsilon_r/\lambda_r)(\lambda_x + u)}{u^2(1 + \epsilon_r/\lambda_r)}$ [−9.42]	$\dfrac{1}{u} + \dfrac{1 + \epsilon_r/\lambda_r}{1 - \epsilon_y + (\epsilon_r/\lambda_r)\lambda_x}$ [10.65]	$\dfrac{[1 - \epsilon_y + u + (\epsilon_r/\lambda_r)(\lambda_x + u)]\epsilon_r/\lambda_r}{[1 - \epsilon_y + (\epsilon_r/\lambda_r)\lambda_x] \times [1 - \epsilon_y(1 - u) + (\epsilon_r/\lambda_r)(\lambda_x + u)]}$ [1.42]
I:	$\dfrac{-\epsilon_y}{1 - \epsilon_y(1 - u) + (\epsilon_r/\lambda_r)\lambda_x}$ [−2.05]	$\dfrac{1}{1 - \epsilon_y(1 - u) + (\epsilon_r/\lambda_r)\lambda_x}$ [2.56]	$\dfrac{\epsilon_r/\lambda_r}{1 - \epsilon_y(1 - u) + (\epsilon_r/\lambda_r)\lambda_x}$ [0.77]
Rank	$C > 0 > I > A > D$	$D > B > I > C > 0$	$B > D > A > I > 0$

SOURCE: ROWS A–D: Col. (1): Table 3 col. 3 + Table 1 col. 1; col. (2): Table 3 col. 3 + Table 1 col. 2; col. (3): Table 3 col. 3 ÷ Table 3 col. 1. Row I: Same as Table 2 row I.

Note that lagged values of the predetermined policy variables appear in this equation, namely, in u_{-1}, Δg, and Δv. In the second period after a policy change, however, Δg and Δv become 0, and u_{-1} becomes equal to u, so thenceforth the equation has constant coefficients. Its characteristic root, which is the coefficient of x_{-1} with u_{-1} set equal to u, is between 0 and 1 because of inequalities (7), so that the time path of real income, x, is stable. The long-run equilibrium level of x under policy A or B is obtained from (9) by setting $\Delta g = \Delta v = 0$, $u_{-1} = u$, and $x_{-1} = x$, and then solving for x; the result is:

$$\text{Long-run equilibrium of } x = \frac{g - v}{u}. \tag{10}$$

The derivatives of this equation show that the same long-run effects on real income, x, are obtained from a unit increase in government purchases, g, under policy B as from a unit cut in autonomous taxes v under policy A, namely, either one will raise the long-run equilibrium level of real income, x, by $1/u$.[13]

Now consider the derivation of Table 3's results for the *real high-powered money stock*, H/P, under policies A and B. The relevant reduced form equation is

$$\frac{H}{P} = \frac{\begin{aligned}&\{[(1 - \epsilon_y)(1 - u) + (\epsilon_r/\lambda_r)\lambda_x]g - [1 - \epsilon_y + (\epsilon_r/\lambda_r)\lambda_x]v \\ &\quad + [1 - \epsilon_y(1 - u) + (\epsilon_r/\lambda_r)\lambda_x]H_{-1}/P - u[\epsilon_0 - (\epsilon_r/\lambda_r)\lambda_0]\}\end{aligned}}{[1 - \epsilon_y(1 - u) + (\epsilon_r/\lambda_r)(\lambda_x + u)]}. \tag{11}$$

This happens also to be the difference equation for H/P. Its characteristic root is of course the same as that of equation (9), so it too is stable. The long-run equilibrium level of H/P under policy A or B is obtained by putting $H_{-1} = H$, and solving for H.

Long-run equilibrium of H/P

$$= \frac{\begin{aligned}&[(1 - \epsilon_y)(1 - u) + (\epsilon_r/\lambda_r)\lambda_x]g \\ &\quad - [1 - \epsilon_y + (\epsilon_r/\lambda_r)\lambda_x]v - u[\epsilon_0 - (\epsilon_r/\lambda_r)\lambda_0]\end{aligned}}{u(\epsilon_r/\lambda_r)}. \tag{12}$$

This equation's partial derivatives give the long-run effects on the real high-powered money stock, H/P, of a unit increase, Δg, under policy B, or a unit decrease, Δv or $x\Delta u$, under policy A, as shown in Table 3. Other results in Table 3 have been derived in a similar way.

---

[13] Note that from equation (10) $\partial x/x\partial u = -(g - v)/u^2 x = -1/u$, so that we have $\overline{\Delta x}/x\Delta u = \overline{\Delta x}/\Delta v = -1/u$. Thus we see again that $x\Delta u$ and Δv have the same effects, to a linear approximation. If the marginal tax rate is changed by more than an infinitesimal amount, then the correct value for the multiplier effect $\overline{\Delta x}/x\Delta u$ is minus the inverse of the new marginal tax rate, that is, $-1/(u + \Delta u)$. Note that the stability of the equilibrium in equation (10) depends upon the assumption, made above, that $\epsilon_r/\lambda_r > 0$. If this ratio is zero or negative, then an increase in real balances has no effect or an inhibiting effect on real expenditure, and the system is unstable.

Several aspects of these results deserve comment:

1. Long-run static equilibrium requires a balanced budget. It is this feature of the analysis that yields a long-run government-purchases multiplier of $1/u$ when tax rates are fixed, and a long-run tax-receipts multiplier of $-1/u$ when government purchases are fixed, as in policies A and B in Table 4. Because changes in private holdings of high-powered money influence private behavior through the equations for money demand and expenditure, real income cannot reach a long-run equilibrium level until the budget deficit has been erased.[14]

2. The amount of money that must be issued to re-balance the budget and re-establish long-run equilibrium is less for a unit increase of government purchases at given tax rates (policy B) than for a unit cut in initial tax revenue at a given level of government purchases (policy A), although both have the same effect on real income in the long run: Compare rows A and B in Table 4. The difference between the two new long-run equilibria arises because, under the increased-purchases policy B, private expenditure is lower and the interest rate is higher than under the decreased-tax-rate policy A.

3. The balanced-budget-multiplier policy C has the same effects in the long run as it does in the first period; this is because there is no deficit and hence no change in the money stock. It is shown by the fact that rows C in Tables 1 and 2 are the same respectively as in Tables 3 and 4. Observe also that if one ignores the government budget restraint, then the first-period and long-run results are the same (and are inappropriate for both cases); this is because the model used here is static apart from the budget restraint. Compare rows I in Tables 2 and 4.

4. The simple elementary-textbook version of the government-purchases multiplier is the inverse of the private marginal propensity not to spend out of national income. In the presence of a marginal tax rate, and in the notation of our model, this can be expressed as:

$$\frac{\Delta x}{\Delta g} = \frac{1}{1 - \epsilon_y(1 - u)}. \tag{13}$$

This result is incorrect in general. But it emerges as a special case of the first-period result given here for policy B in which tax rates are unchanged, provided we assume that changes in the high-powered money stock have no effect on private expenditure. This assumption means that $\epsilon_r/\lambda_r = 0$, which may be because either the demand for money is infinitely elastic ($\lambda_r = -\infty$), or private expenditure has zero interest elasticity ($\epsilon_r = 0$), or both. In this case, the existence of a budget deficit will lead to the issue of

---

[14] Observe that if $u = 0$, so that increases in income do not result in increased tax receipts, then the long-run multipliers discussed in this paragraph are infinite (under the linear approximations used for behavior equations in this paper).

money, and possibly (that is, if $\lambda_r > -\infty$) to a fall in the interest rate, but will have no effect on real income or tax receipts. Then the effect on real income of increased government purchases with given tax rates becomes the same in the long run as in the first period. It may be obtained by setting $\epsilon_r/\lambda_r = 0$ in Table 1, row B, column (5). The corresponding multiplier is obtained by setting $\epsilon_r/\lambda_r = 0$ in Table 2, row B, column (2); it is the same as equation (13).

5. The version of the government-purchases multiplier obtained by including a money equation in the model, but ignoring the government budget restraint, is also incorrect in general; it appears in Table 2 or 4, row I, column (2). If $\epsilon_r/\lambda_r = 0$, it reduces to equation (13) and becomes correct. But if a money equation is to be included in the system, and if changes in the real high-powered money stock can influence private expenditure, then correct results require that the government budget restraint be taken into account, as in Tables 1–4.

References

Christ, Carl F. "A Short-Run Aggregate-Demand Model of the Interdependence and Effects of Monetary and Fiscal Policies with Keynesian and Classical Interest Elasticities," *A.E.R.*, LVII (May, 1967), 434–43.

Enthoven, Alain C. "A Neo-classical Model of Money, Debt, and Economic Growth," in John G. Gurley and Edward S. Shaw, Mathematical Appendix to *Money in a Theory of Finance*. Washington: Brookings Institution.

Hansen, Bent. *The Economic Theory of Fiscal Policy*. Translated by P. E. Burke. London: Allen & Unwin; Cambridge, Mass.: Harvard Univ. Press, 1958.

Hicks, J. R. "Mr. Keynes and the 'Classics,'" *Econometrica*, V (April, 1937), 147–59. Reprinted in *Readings in the Theory of Income Distribution*. Philadelphia: Blakiston Co., 1949.

Musgrave, Richard A. *The Theory of Public Finance: A Study in Public Economy*. New York: McGraw-Hill Book Co., 1959.

Ott, David J., and Ott, Attiat. "Budget Balance and Equilibrium Income," *J. Finance*, XX (March, 1965), 71–77.

Patinkin, Don. *Money, Interest and Prices*. Evanston, Ill.: Row, Peterson & Co., 1956.

Ritter, L. S. "Some Monetary Aspects of Multiplier Theory and Fiscal Policy," *Rev. Econ. Studies*, XXIII (2), No. 61 (1955–56), 126–31.

10

CARL F. CHRIST

Monetary and Fiscal Influences on U.S. Money Income, 1891–1970

I. INTRODUCTION AND SUMMARY*

This paper presents some estimates of the effects of monetary and fiscal policy variables upon money income in the United States since 1891. These results bear on the recent monetarist controversy. They can be thought of as pertaining to aggregate demand in money terms, which is one important factor underlying inflation. The decomposition of the level of aggregate spending in money terms into its two components, real output and the price level, is also important, but is not dealt with here.

The conceptual core of this study is an equation describing money income as a function of policy variables that appear in the government budget restraint and certain other variables that are taken here to be exogenous. This equation is a reduced-form equation of a suitably specified macroeconomic model describing aggregate demand and its components in money terms, and including the government budget restraint as one of its equations. Several forms of such an equation for money income are discussed, and estimates are computed for several subsets of the sample period 1891-1970, using annual data.

A macroeconomic model is not specified here, but the discussion will indicate some of the properties that such a model must have in order to give rise to reduced-form equations like those estimated.

The main results of the paper may be summarized as follows.

*The work underlying this paper was supported in part by a grant from the National Science Foundation to The Johns Hopkins University, for which the author expresses his thanks. He is indebted to Joan Schneider and Paul De Grauwe for assistance in the preparation of data and in the computations, to John W. Kendrick and Maude Pech for assistance in obtaining data from Kendrick's work sheets, to Anna J. Schwartz for help with data for gold before 1916, and to Jürg Niehans, Edward Kane, Harold Shapiro, Milton Friedman, Louis Maccini, Charles Hulten, Susan Vroman, Akinbolaji Iwayemi, and Richard Friedman for valuable suggestions.

Carl F. Christ is professor of political economy at Johns Hopkins University.

In the United States since 1891, both federal government purchases and the high powered money stock have had substantial stimulating effects upon money income. The magnitudes of the effects do not appear to have been constant over time.

Government purchases appear to exert their effect rather promptly, inasmuch as the current value of government purchases almost always has a significant positive coefficient while values lagged one, two, three, and four years typically have insignificant coefficients.

The speed of response of money income to high powered money is not clearly established by this study, inasmuch as the inclusion of values lagged two years or more leads to substantial changes in the estimated speed (but not the total magnitude) of response. Indeed, it often leads to a negative coefficient for the current value of high powered money.

The effect of federal debt upon money income appears to have been positive since 1948, but not in most sample periods beginning in 1929 or earlier.

The speed of adjustment of money income to changes in the explanatory variables appears to have decreased markedly over the 80-year period.

II. THE UNDERLYING MODEL OF MACROECONOMIC POLICY

Since the purpose here is to understand policy effects upon money income, the macroeconomic model underlying our reduced form equations will be conceived in money terms.

Notation is as follows. All stocks are at year-end in billions of current dollars, and flows are in billions of current dollars per year. Sources and data are shown in appendices.

B = federal debt privately held (i.e., held outside the U.S. government and Federal Reserve), net of U.S. government holdings of private debts.

D = U.S. Treasury deposits at commercial banks.

Δ = first difference operator (e.g., $\Delta B_t = B_t - B_{t-1}$).

$E = \Delta D + \Delta F$ = change in U.S. government holdings of deposits at commercial banks and of gold and foreign exchange.

F = gold and foreign exchange holdings of the U.S. government including the Federal Reserve.

G = federal government purchases of goods and services.

H = unborrowed high powered money stock (high powered money less member bank borrowings from the Federal Reserve).

P = GNP deflator, 1958 : 1.00.

r_f = interest rate on federal debt, percent per year.

T = federal government tax receipts, less transfer expenditures other than interest.

X = net exports (exports less imports).

Y = GNP.

Z = other net liabilities of the consolidated Treasury and Federal Reserve balance sheet, besides those mentioned above.

One of the equations of a macroeconomic policy model is the federal government budget restraint.[1] It is a reflection of the year-to-year change in the consolidated balance sheet of the Treasury and Federal Reserve. It states that the total of all federal expenditures must be equal to the total of all federal financing. That is, for each year, the sum of federal purchases of goods and services G, plus federal interest payments $r_f B$ to the private sector, plus federal transfer payments other than interest, equals the sum of federal tax receipts, plus the increase in unborrowed high powered money ΔH, plus the increase in privately held federal debt ΔB, less the increase in federal government deposits at commercial banks ΔD, less the increase in federal government and Federal Reserve holdings of gold and foreign exchange ΔF, plus the net increase in other liabilities of the consolidated federal government and Federal Reserve ΔZ. In equation form,

$$G + r_f B = T + \Delta H + \Delta B - \Delta D - \Delta F + \Delta Z.$$

The term ΔZ is included for conceptual completeness. In the empirical work it is included with the disturbance terms since it is relatively small.

Behavior equations in a macroeconomic policy model of aggregate demand in money terms should explain expenditure for consumption, investment, and—in a detailed model—imports and exports. Behavior equations should also explain the private sector's demand for money and federal debt. In a detailed financial model, there will be separate sectors for the private banking system and for the private nonbank sector, with supply and demand equations for the claims of each against the other as well as vis-à-vis the consolidated Treasury and Federal Reserve sector. Appropriate identities complete the model.

Under fixed exchange rates, the exchange rate is an exogenous variable, and changes in government gold and foreign exchange reserves ΔF are not a policy variable, but are determined by the balance of payments, which is equal to net exports plus net capital inflow. Rather than treat the foreign sector as endogenous and include in the reduced-form equations and predetermined variables that affect exports, imports, and capital flow, this study takes ΔF and net exports X to be exogenous non-policy variables. Net capital inflow can be obtained as $\Delta F - X$, if desired, but it plays no role in this study.

Banks and the nonbank private sector are here consolidated, as in Christ [4]. Therefore the stock of money as usually defined (currency outside banks plus demand deposits adjusted) does not appear as a variable. Rather, the high-powered money stock appears, since it is the net holdings of money by the private sector (including banks).

Borrowings by member banks from the Federal Reserve can be represented by a separate structural equation, since they are determined largely by member banks' decisions in the light of the exogenously set discount rate and other money-market conditions. The high-powered money stock is then in part endogenous because of

[1] For a discussion of its role in the analysis of macroeconomic policy, see Christ [4,5] and Steindl [11].

member bank borrowing. Hence in this study the stock of high-powered money less borrowings is taken as the exogenous monetary total.

The variable *B*, federal debt in private hands, is defined net of U.S. government holdings of private debt, because government loans to the private sector can be expected to offset private holdings of federal debt in their macroeconomic effects. The amounts of government loans to the private sector were very small until 1933 when many such programs were introduced or broadened in an attempt to ease the effects of the Great Depression. By 1970, the total had grown to $57 billion. Two alternative debt variables are discussed later.

A complete structural model of aggregate demand in money terms is not specified here. If such a model were specified, however, in accordance with the foregoing discussion, its reduced-form equation for money income (and of course its other reduced-form equations, if one wanted them) would include the following exogenous variables: net exports *X*, the change in government and Federal Reserve holdings of gold and foreign exchange reserves ΔF, and four of the following five macroeconomic policy variables: federal government purchases *G*, federal taxes less transfers other than interest *T*, the unborrowed high-powered money stock *H*, private holdings of federal debt *B*, and federal government deposits at commercial banks *D*. Lagged values of at least some of these would also appear, for as the government budget restraint points out, it is the increase in stocks of federal liabilities, and the decrease in federal assets, that contributes to the financing of federal expenditures, not simply the stocks themselves.

The reason why only four of the above-mentioned macropolicy variables are exogenous, of course, is that the government budget restraint operates together with the behavior equations of the private sector to determine the fifth one whenever any four of them have been chosen by the authorities.[2] In principle, the authorities could set the values of any of the four, leaving the remaining one to be determined by the operation of the system including the budget restraint.

In practice, the Congress typically sets tax and transfer schedules, which together with income and its distribution determine tax receipts less transfers *T*. Also, Congress and the executive branch typically set government purchases *G*, although their exact timing is affected somewhat by endogenous factors such as the speed of completion of work by government contractors. This sets the deficit (or surplus). The Treasury typically sets the level (and hence by implication the change) in government deposits in commercial banks. What remains of the deficit (or surplus) is the portion to be financed by the sum of borrowing from the private sector plus issuing unborrowed high-powered money. The Treasury must issue (or for a surplus retire) federal debt in this amount. The Federal Reserve, by deciding continuously what quantity of Treasury debt to hold in its own portfolio, determines whether the private sector's holdings of federal debt increase by just this amount (if the Fed keeps its portfolio constant) or by more or by less (if the Fed sells or buys).

In this study, the four policy variables taken to be exogenous are *G*, *H*, *B*, and *D*,

---

[2] For a more detailed discussion, see Christ [5, pp. 55-57] including footnote 5.

266 Econometrics, Macroeconomics and Economic Policy

CARL F. CHRIST : 283

with taxes less transfers (other than interest) T taken to be endogenous. This treatment has the advantage of avoiding the necessity for specifying the form of the tax-transfer equation and for obtaining time series data for the rates at which taxes are levied and transfers are paid, which would be rather difficult to do. Instead of determining the amount of taxes less transfers in that way, the model envisioned here does so by the operation of the government budget restraint in conjunction with the rest of the model. It is not difficult to show that once the equations of a macroeconomic model have been specified, including the government budget restraint, then the model yields the same effects for a given set of values of policy variables no matter whether it is taxes less transfers (as here), or one of the other four policy variables that is taken to be the endogenous one.

III. THE REDUCED-FORM EQUATION FOR MACROECONOMIC POLICY EFFECTS ON MONEY INCOME

Macroeconomic theory leads us to expect that the algebraic signs of the parameters in the reduced-form equation for money income will be as follows: positive for government purchases G, high-powered money H, and net exports X, uncertain for federal debt B, and negative for increases in government holdings of commercial bank deposits ΔD and of gold and foreign exchange reserves ΔF.

Reasons for these expected signs may be briefly suggested in simple economic terms, although in each case analysis of a complete structural model would be needed to establish theoretical presumptions as to sign. Recall that taxes less transfers T are endogenous here, so that when we examine the sign of the effect of an exogenous policy variable on money income, all other macroeconomic policy variables except T are being held constant. Net exports add to final demand, both directly and (through the multiplier) indirectly. So do government purchases, but they require extra taxes (or else cuts in government transfers) to pay for them, so that we are considering a balanced budget multiplier here, and should expect a coefficient for government purchases that is smaller than that of net exports, but that need not be equal to unity. High-powered money creation adds to private wealth and depresses interest rates, and also must be accompanied by tax cuts (or increased transfers), which can be expected to stimulate aggregate demand. An increase in privately held federal debt adds to private wealth (except to the extent that taxpayers make a downward adjustment in their perceptions of their net worth on account of the present value of the stream of future taxes that is needed to cover the interest on the debt—presumably this adjustment amounts to something between zero and 100 percent of the value of federal debt in private hands), and also must be accompanied by tax cuts (or increased transfers); on the other hand it presumably raises interest rates; thus its gross effects operate in both inflationary and deflationary directions. It is not clear whether the inflationary wealth and income effects outweigh the deflationary interest effects. Increases in government holdings of commercial bank deposits and gold and foreign exchange reserves have no direct effect in themselves, but must be accompanied by either increases in taxes or cuts in transfers, thus inhibiting aggregate demand. Analysis of a complete model would not only provide a more rigorous derivation of the direction of policy effects than the simple discussion given above, but would probably lead to the inclusion of additional predetermined variables in the reduced form.

The functional form of a reduced-form equation naturally depends upon the form of the structural equations underlying it. Since the latter have not been specified, the reduced-form equations for money income dealt with here can best be thought of as approximations to equations of unknown form. If the true reduced-form equation were nonlinear (or nonlogarithmic) then the parameters in a linear (or logarithmic) approximation to it would be expected to be different for different time-periods, because the values of the variables change from time to time, and hence the shape of the non-linear function at the point of linearization will change accordingly.

IV. ESTIMATION OF REDUCED-FORM EQUATIONS FOR MONEY INCOME

The reduced-form equations reported here are linear in levels of the variables. Some preliminary estimates were made using equations linear in first differences, linear in logarithms of levels, and linear in first differences of logarithms of levels. (Logarithms of first differences do not make sense because first differences are often negative numbers which have no logarithms.) These alternative forms gave broadly similar results, equations in levels being somewhat more uniform and usually fitting better than those in first differences, and linear equations fitting somewhat better than logarithmic equations.

Some equations linear in levels of the variables were estimated after including lagged money income Y_{t-1} as an explanatory variable. Its coefficient can be thought of as related to either a distributed lag expectations-formation process or a delayed adjustment process. Its value is expected to lie in the interval from 0 to 1 inclusive. It measures 1 minus the rate of adjustment.

The general form of the linear equations used to explain money income is then as follows:

$$Y_t = a + \Sigma\, b_i G_{t-i} + \Sigma\, c_i H_{t-i} + \Sigma\, d_i B_{t-i} + \Sigma\, e_i \Delta D_{t-i}$$
$$+ \Sigma\, f_i \Delta F_{t-i} + \Sigma\, g_i X_{t-i} + h Y_{t-1} \tag{1}$$

where the lower case letters a through h are coefficients to be estimated, and each sum runs from $i = 0$ to the number of lags that are included in the equation for the variable in question. The number of lags need not be the same for all variables. Indeed it may be zero for some variables, in which case the sum for that variable contains only one term, namely that for the current value of the variable.

The structure of the model from which the reduced-form equation for money income is derived may imply some restrictions on the parameters of equation (1). For example, in one very simple model of 8 equations from which such a reduced form equation was derived, the change in Treasury deposits at commercial banks

ΔD and the change in gold and foreign exchange reserves ΔF appear in the same way and hence have the same coefficient. This implies that e_0 and f_0 are equal. A crude test did not reject this.[3] If their lagged values also enter in the same way, then $e_i = f_i$ for all of the current and lagged coefficients of these two variables. Accordingly, many of the equations were estimated subject to this restriction. The easiest way to do this is to remove the variables ΔD and ΔF from equation (1) and use their sum instead, namely $E = \Delta D + \Delta F$. Then the terms in current and lagged ΔD and ΔF in (1) are replaced by $\Sigma e_i E_{t-i}$.

The same very simple model implies that the coefficient of government purchases G is the sum of the coefficients of E and net exports X. However, the results contradict this restriction, so it was not imposed in this paper.

Annual data were used, in order that the early period could be studied on the same basis as more recent periods. The original aim was to begin in 1869 in order to study the substantial price deflation that occurred from the end of the Civil War to about 1896, but suitable data before 1889 for some of the variables have not been found and prepared. Hence the data used run from 1889 through 1970. The sample starts with 1891 because two-year lags are used.

Since the equations estimated are of the reduced-form type, the estimation method used was least squares, which under suitable assumptions leads to consistent estimators of the parameters of reduced-form equations.[4]

Several different versions of equation (1) were estimated, using the entire sample period as well as several different subperiods, and using different numbers of lags for the explanatory variables. The results varied considerably among different time periods, but not very much among different lengths of lag. Accordingly, estimates for two forms of equation (1) that are fairly typical are presented below, and then some summary statistics are given regarding the other forms that were estimated. The estimated equations chosen for presentation are as follows, except that some omit the term in Y_{t-1} :

$$Y_t = a_0 + b_0 G_t + c_0 H_t + c_1 H_{t-1} + d_0 B_t + d_1 B_{t-1} + e_0 E_t$$
$$+ e_1 E_{t-1} + g_0 X_t + h Y_{t-1} . \tag{2}$$

Reasons for this choice are given below.

V. NUMERICAL RESULTS

Estimates for equation (2) are shown in Table 1 for the periods 1948-70, 1929-47, 1913-47, 1913-28, 1913-70, 1891-1912, and 1891-1970. In Table 1, column 5,

---

[3] The crude test was to compare R^2s in two equations, identical except for the fact that in one equation the variables ΔD and ΔF are free to have different coefficients, while in the other they are required to have the same coefficient. The imposition of this restriction reduced R^2 only from .976 to .972, thus raising the unexplained variation only from 2.4 percent of the total to 2.8 percent.
[4] See for example Christ [3], pp. 369-70, 374-78, and 468.

Estimates of Equation (2) Explaining Money Income (Y)*

Estimated Coefficients and t-Ratios†

Sample Period‡ (1)	$\bar{Y}$ (2)	DW (3)	s (4)	R^2 (5)	a_1 (6)	b_0/G (7)	c_0/H (8)	c_1/H_{-1} (9)	c_0+c_1 (10)	d_0/B (11)	d_1/B_{-1} (12)	d_0+d_1 (13)	e_0/E (14)	e_1/E_{-1} (15)	e_0+e_1 (16)	g_0/X (17)	h/Y_{-1} (18)
1948-70	530	.91	33	.985	-1290	3.6	5.6	9.2	14.8	.6	3.7	4.3	-13.2	-9.3	-22.5	10.6	.9845
					-2.9	3.8	1.1	1.7	5.5	.3	1.8	1.8	-2.6	-1.6	-2.7	2.9	9.8
		2.59	12	.9982	-250	.19	4.4	-3.6	.8	-.54	1.82	1.28	-1.36	.64	-.72	-.75	
					-1.3	.4	2.5	-1.6	.4	-.7	2.4	1.4	-.6	.3	-.2	-.4	
1929-47	121	.89	12	.977	63	2.7	-3.2	3.8	.6	-1.21	1.08	-.13	.93	.96	1.9	12.4	.612
					7.7	1.9	-.9	1.0	.4	-.7	.7	-.4	.5	.5	.6	1.8	3.1
		1.24	9.0	.989	17	1.4	-1.8	3.1	1.3	-.51	.19	-.32	.52	.46	1.0	7.0	
					1.1	1.2	-.7	1.0	1.1	-.4	.2	-1.4	.4	.3	.4	1.3	
1913-28	73	2.14	3.9	.985	-18	4.6	-5.2	20.0	14.9	-4.0	4.8	.3	9.0	5.8	14.8	2.9	.193
					-2.2	2.3	-1.3	5.0	9.2	-2.2	2.7	.8	1.7	1.2	1.6	2.7	.84
		2.39	3.9	.987	-16	3.4	-4.8	17.3	12.5	-3.5	3.7	.2	6.0	6.8	12.8	2.9	
					-1.9	1.4	-1.2	3.3	3.8	-1.4	1.6	.5	.9	1.3	1.3	2.7	
1913-47	99	.34	16	.928	58	1.3	-4.7	7.2	2.5	-.50	.63	.12	.1	-1.5	-1.4	-.62	.846
					10	.9	-1.1	1.5	2.7	-.3	.4	.4	.05	-1.1	-.5	-.2	8.5
		1.31	8.2	.982	4.9	.71	-2.4	4.0	1.5	-.15	-.17	-.31	.14	-.31	-.18	2.3	
					.7	.9	-1.1	1.6	3.3	-.1	-.2	-1.6	.1	-.4	-.1	1.6	
1913-70	270	1.32	40	.979	37	7.5	-8.7	14.9	6.2	-8.1	6.5	-1.6	3.5	.2	3.7	9.5	.9712
					3.3	12.6	-2.2	3.8	4.3	-9.6	6.5	-5.7	1.5	.1	1.0	2.8	23
		1.85	12	.9983	-1.3	.55	1.53	-.64	.89	-.51	.30	-.21	.41	-.34	.07	1.22	
					-.4	1.6	1.3	-.5	1.9	-1.2	.7	-2.1	.6	-.6	.1	1.2	
1891-1912	22	2.29	.79	.9939	-11	2.2	4.7	6.7	11.4	-11.7	8.2	-3.4	24.0	5.3	29.3	-4.0	-.11
					-.03	.3	1.5	2.1	8.6	-2.8	2.7	-.9	5.0	1.1	3.9	-2.5	-.5
		2.11	.82	.9940	.2	1.9	5.0	7.8	12.7	-11.9	7.7	-4.2	24.8	6.6	31.3	-4.0	
					.1	.2	1.5	1.9	4.0	-2.8	2.3	-1.0	4.8	1.2	3.5	-2.4	
1891-1970	202	1.14	35	.981	18	7.1	-7.5	14.5	7.0	-7.7	6.0	-1.7	3.8	1.0	4.8	11.2	.9683
					2.8	14	-2.3	4.2	5.7	-11	7.0	-7.4	1.9	.6	1.5	3.9	30
		1.85	9.6	.9986	-.7	.58	1.47	-.59	.89	-.54	.33	-.21	.41	-.36	.05	1.2	
					-.4	2.2	1.5	-.5	2.2	-1.7	1.1	-2.1	.7	-.7	.1	1.4	
Presumed range						>0			>0						<0	>0	0 to 1

*$\bar{Y}$ is the mean of national income during the sample period, in billions of current dollars per year. DW is the Durbin Watson statistic for serial correlation of disturbances. s is the standard error of the residuals. R^2 is the squared multiple correlation coefficient, not adjusted for degrees of freedom.

†For symbols, refer to the description of notation in the text.

‡The first line of numbers for each period gives the estimated coefficients, and the second line gives the t-ratios.

all squared correlation coefficients are high (.928 or higher). For government purchases in column 7, all coefficients are positive, as expected.

Consider first the equations in Table 1 that *exclude lagged income* Y_{t-1}. The coefficients for government purchases in column 7 range from 1.3 to a surprisingly large 7.5. Their t-ratios are all 1.9 or more except for 0.9 in 1913-47 and 0.3 in 1891-1912. (In no year of that early period did government purchases exceed 2.2 percent of money income, so it is not surprising that the coefficient is not significant.)

For high-powered money the sum of the current and lagged coefficients in column 10 is always positive, as expected. The sums range from 0.6 in 1929-47 to 14.9 in 1913-28, and the t-ratio for the sum is always 1.8 or more, except for 1929-47. However, the coefficient for current high-powered money is negative for every period except 1948-70 and 1891-1912, twice significantly so. The coefficient for lagged high-powered money is always positive, and larger both algebraically and absolutely than that for current high-powered money. More about this later.

For privately-held federal debt (referred to henceforth simply as "debt" unless otherwise noted), 1948-70 has positive values in columns 11 and 12 for both current and lagged coefficients, but all other periods have positive values only for the lagged coefficient, with negative values for the current coefficient and often for the sum of the two. Four of the six negative debt coefficients are significant, and some are highly so. More about this later also.

For E (the sum of the increases in government demand deposits at commercial banks and in gold and foreign exchange reserves), the coefficients in columns 14-16 and 1948-70 are negative, as expected, but for other periods most are positive. Few are significant; all the significant ones have the expected negative sign except for periods beginning in 1891.

Net exports has a positive coefficient in column 17 as expected in every period, except 1913-47 and 1891-1912. One of the two negative coefficients is not significant, and all of the positive ones have $t \geq 1.8$.

Now consider the equations in Table 1 that *include lagged income* Y_{t-1}. The estimated coefficients of the other variables are short-run coefficients. Long-run coefficients are obtained by dividing the short-run coefficients by the speed of adjustment, that is, by 1 minus the coefficient of Y_{t-1} in column 18. These long-run coefficients are generally similar to the coefficients obtained when Y_{t-1} is excluded, if one takes account of the sampling variation in the estimates of the speed of adjustment. It is interesting that there appears to be a strong downward trend in the speed of adjustment during the 80-year sample period. Column 18 of Table 1 shows that for the 1891-1912 subperiod it is 1.11, which is outside the expected range of 0 to 1, but it is not significantly different from 1 or even from 0.9. Then it declines to 0.81 for 1913-28, to 0.39 for 1929-47, and to 0.0155 (not significantly different from zero) for 1948-70. Note that R^2 is substantially increased by the inclusion of Y_{t-1} (except for 1891-1912 when Y_{t-1} has an insignificant coefficient).

The Durbin-Watson statistic in column 3 indicates positive serial correlation among the residuals except when lagged money income was included as an explanatory variable; this was typical of all the estimated equations.

Table 1 also shows for reference in columns 2 and 4 the mean value of money income in billions of current dollars for each period, and the root mean square residual. These statistics, together with the estimated coefficients, emphasize that if equation (2) is used to explain the behavior of money income since 1891, even though it does so for that whole period with $R^2 \geq .98$, the coefficients that fit best are substantially different among the subperiods (for some variables even as regards sign). Hence at best equation (2) is an approximation, and either it does not have the correct form, or its parameters have been changing. Note further that for many of the variables both the 1913-70 and 1891-1970 estimates of the slope lie outside of the extremes of the estimates for the four short subperiods, in the equations excluding Y_{t-1}.

Table 2 shows, for the equations of Table 1 that exclude lagged income, a measure of the importance of each explanatory variable, together with the t-ratio from Table 1. The measure is the regression coefficient times the ratio of the standard error of the explanatory variable to the standard error of the dependent variable, money income Y. When this measure is 0.40, as in the case of government purchase G in 1948-70, it means that a change in G equal to one standard deviation of G will be associated with a change in Y equal to 0.40 standard deviations of Y, other explanatory variables being held fixed. Of course only those measures associated with statistically significant coefficients should be taken seriously. Table 2 shows that

TABLE 2

Importance of the Explanatory Variables in Equation (2)
Excluding Lagged Income Y_{t-1}, as Measured by the
Regression Coefficient Times the Ratio of the
Standard Error of the Explanatory Variable
to the Standard Error of Money Income (Y)*

Measure of Importance, and t-Ratio

Sample Period	b_0 G	c_0 H	c_1 H_{-1}	d_0 B	d_1 B_{-1}	e_0 E	e_1 E_{-1}	g_0 X
(1)	(2)	(3)	(4)	(5)	(6)	(7)	(8)	(9)
1948-70	.40	.25	.40	.01	.07	-.10	-.07	.11
	3.8	1.1	1.7	.3	1.8	-2.6	-1.6	2.9
1929-47	1.33	-.74	.88	-1.50	1.34	.09	.09	.65
	1.9	-.9	1.0	-.7	.7	.5	.5	1.8
1913-28	.72	-.26	1.02	-1.9	2.0	.18	.11	.16
	2.3	-1.3	5.0	-2.2	2.7	1.7	1.2	2.7
1913-47	.58	-1.16	1.78	-.59	.74	.01	-.12	-.03
	.9	-1.1	1.5	-.3	.4	.05	-1.1	-.2
1913-70	.96	-.78	1.33	-2.7	2.1	.05	.002	.10
	12.6	-2.2	3.8	-9.6	6.5	1.5	.1	2.8
1891-1912	.03	.41	.59	-.16	.11	.17	.04	-.08
	.3	1.5	2.1	-2.8	2.7	5.0	1.1	-2.5
1891-1970	.90	-.71	1.37	-2.6	2.1	.05	.01	.11
	14	-2.3	4.2	-11	7.0	1.9	.6	3.9

*Computed for those equations in Table 1 that exclude lagged money income Y_{t-1}.

TABLE 3

Ranges of Significant Coefficients (i.e., those with $t > 1.6$) in Variants
of Equation (1) Explaining Money Income (Y) without
Lagged Income (Y_{t-1})*

Sample Period	Independent Variables†				
	G	H	B	E	X
(1)	(2)	(3)	(4)	(5)	(6)
1948–70‡	2.9 to 5.9	9.6 to 19.1	3.8 to 20.8	−25.0 to −11.6	10.6 to 17.3
1929–47	2.6 to 4.1	1.9 to 4.0	−.08 to .4	1.7 to 2.4	10.0 to 12.6
1917–47§	2.9 to 4.7	1.0 to 2.5	−.2 to −.2	−1.9 to 2.1	none signif.
1917–28	5.1 to 6.1	6.9 to 24.0	−1.3 to −.6	−6.2 to −6.2	none signif.
1917–70§	1.9 to 8.1	3.2 to 16.2	−2.4 to −1.1	.3 to 3.9	8.0 to 12.1
All of the above	1.9 to 8.1	1.0 to 24.0	−2.4 to 20.8	−25.0 to 3.9	8.0 to 17.3
Presumed sign	+	+		−	+

*Ranges in this table refer to the sum of coefficients of the current and all included lagged values of each variable, that is, to the steady-state effect of the variable without regard to the distribution of the effect over time.
†For symbols, refer to the description of notation in the text.
‡When lags of three or four years were included, the sample period was shortened to 1950–70 in order not to introduce any wartime data (1945 or earlier) among the lagged values used.
§When lags of two years were included, the sample was shortened to begin in 1918 since the time series used begin in 1916.

government purchases G are important in every period except 1891-1912 (the reason for the exception was noted above). The high-powered money stock H is always important, and often the privately-held government debt B is also. Net exports X and changes in government holdings of bank deposits and gold and foreign exchange E are usually not very important contributors to the explanation of money income.

A number of other variants of equation (1) for money income were estimated for several subperiods, usually without lagged income. Table 3 shows, for each period, the lower and upper limits of the statistically significant estimates obtained for the sum of current and lagged coefficients for each variable when lagged income is excluded. The criterion of significance used here was an absolute value of the t-ratio greater than 1.6. Had a larger value of the t-ratio been used as the criterion, of course, the ranges shown in Table 3 would have been narrower. Within each of the four short sub-periods, the range of estimates is at most 2.5 to 1 (that is, the largest estimate is at most 2.5 times the smallest, and of the same sign) for the variables G, H, and X, with the single exception of H in 1917-28. If equations that don't include E or X are set aside, the largest estimate in that case becomes 9.4 rather than 24.0, so that the range then is well under 2.5 to 1. For the period 1917-70, the range of estimated coefficients for G and the range for H are both much larger than 2.5 to 1, again underscoring the nonhomogeneity of the longer sample period at least as far as equations like (1) are concerned. The ranges for the debt variable B and for E sometimes encompass both negative and positive values.

An idea of the goodness of fit of these variants of equation (1) is given by Table 4, which shows their squared multiple correlation coefficients, and also the ratio of the root mean square error to the mean level of income, a kind of average

TABLE 4

Squared Multiple Correlation Coefficients (R^2) and Ratio of Mean Square Residual
to Mean Income ($s/\overline{Y}$) for Variants of Equation (1), Explaining Money
Income (Y), without Lagged Income (Y_{t-1})

Independent Variables (with Number of Lagged Values of Each, if any)*	Sample Period									
	1948-70†		1929-47		1917-47‡		1917-28		1917-70‡	
	R^2	$s/\overline{Y}$	R^2	$s/\overline{Y}$	R^2	$s/\overline{Y}$	R^2	$s/\overline{Y}$	R^2	$s/\overline{Y}$
(1)	(2)	(3)	(4)	(5)	(6)	(7)	(8)	(9)	(10)	(11)
G, H, B	.954	.09	.939	.13	–	–	.48	.12	.923	.26
$G, H(1), B(1)$	.969	..08	–	–	–	–	–	–	–	–
$G, H(1), B(1), E(1)$	.976	.07	–	–	–	–	–	–	–	–
$G, H(1), B(1), E(1), X$	.985	.06	.977	.10	.960	.11	.989	.03	.979	.14
$G, H(1), B(1), E(1), X(1)$	.986	.06	.978	.11	.961	.11	–	–	.982	.13
$G, H(2), B(2), E(1), X$	.988	.06	.979	.11	.970	.10	–	–	.985	.12
$G(3), H(3), B(3)$	.9906	.06	–	–	–	–	–	–	–	–
$G(4), H(4), B(4)§$	.9919	.05	–	–	–	–	–	–	–	–

*For symbols, refer to the description of notation in the text.
†When lags of three or four years were included, the sample period was shortened to 1950-70 in order not to introduce any wartime data (1945 or earlier) among the lagged values used.
‡When lags of two years were included, the sample was shortened to begin in 1918 since the time series used begin in 1916.
§This equation was estimated using a second-degree polynomial distributed lag following Shirley Almon [1], with unconstrained weights.

percentage error. Notice that with the exception of the short period 1917-28, the current values of the three variables G, H, and B alone explain over 90 percent of the variation in money income. Two of the values of R^2 from Table 1 appear in the fourth row of numbers in Table 4, for comparison. Note also that the average percentage error $s/\overline{Y}$ does not exceed 14 percent except for the 1917-70 equation (described in the first line of Table 4) that includes as explanatory variables only the current values of government purchases G, high powered money H, and government debt B. The average percentage error is smaller for short sample periods, especially 1948-70, than for the long period 1917-70. The ratio $s/\overline{Y}$ in Table 1 (column 4 divided by column 2) behaves in a similar way.

Several variants of equation (1) containing lagged income are not reported in the tables. In most of them, the lagged income coefficient is significantly different from zero, but in some cases it is not significantly different from 1 and in a few cases it is negative or greater than 1. Small or even negative values are especially common for short periods that begin in 1891 or 1913 or 1917, and large values occur for later periods, as noted above.

Longer lags than in equation (2) were used in several equations not reported in the tables. Lags up to four years were tried in equation (1) for G, H, and B. Lags up to three years were tried for E, and up to two years for X. Lagged income was excluded in most of these cases. Three and four year lags were tried only for 1948-1970.

The steady-state effect of G, H, and X is not much affected by the number of lags used. That is, for any of these variables the sum of the current and all lagged coefficients is not very sensitive to the number of lags used. For government purchases G

and net exports X, the current value is usually significant, and usually none of the lagged values are. Hence in equation (2) only the current values of G and X are used. For high-powered money H, whenever values of two years ago or longer were included in the equation, the current value had a negative coefficient, and as Table 1 shows, sometimes this occurred also when only the current and one-year-lagged values were included.[5] Hence in equation (2) only the current and one-year-lagged values of H are used.

For E, when lags of one and two years are included, the two-year lagged coefficient is typically not significant, but when lags of one year or one and two years are included, the one-year lagged coefficient is often significant, and the sum of the current and one-year lagged coefficients is often larger than the current coefficient obtained when no lags are included. Hence in equation (2) the current and one-year lagged values are included.

For debt B, the current coefficient is often negative, whether or not any lagged values are included. The one-year lagged coefficient is almost always positive and significant. The two-year lagged coefficient is of irregular sign. The coefficients of B with three- and four-year lags are positive but most of them are not significant. Hence in equation (2) only the current and one-year lagged values are included.

To investigate whether the definition chosen for the debt variable B might be responsible for its negative coefficients, some preliminary estimates were computed for 1916-1970 using two alternative concepts of the federal debt, namely:

$B1$ = federal debt privately held (i.e., held outside the U.S. government and the Federal Reserve). $B1$ exceeds B by the amount of U.S. government holdings of private debt.

$B2$ = marketable interest-bearing federal debt privately held (i.e., held outside the U.S. government and the Federal Reserve). $B1$ exceeds $B2$ by the amount of privately-held federal debt that is not both marketable and interest-bearing.

The rationale for using B, which is privately-held federal debt net of federal holdings of private debt, is (as noted above) that federal loans to the private sector can be expected to cancel out the effects of a like amount of private loans to the federal government. However, these loans are not all homogeneous: some are marketable and hence have yields that vary with market conditions, and some are not marketable and have yields fixed under various legislative or administrative programs of the federal government. Most of the federally-held private debt is not marketable and has yields that respond only slightly and sluggishly to market conditions. Thus it might happen that when market interest rates rise, the relatively fixed rates for federal loans to the private sector may appear more attractive so that the private sector actually borrows more from the federal government when market rates are high, and less when they are low. Hence the debt variable $B1$, which is not net of

---

[5] Negative coefficients for current unborrowed high powered money were also found by deLeeuw and Kalchbrenner [9] in their quarterly study of changes in current-dollar GNP.

federally-held private debt, was tried to see whether it would behave differently than does B. Since U.S. savings bonds and a few other federal issues also have relatively fixed yields and are not marketable, the variable $B2$, which consists only of private holdings of marketable interest-bearing federal debt, was tried for the same reason. However, in the simple equations in which $B1$ and $B2$ were tried in place of B, there was practically no difference among the results.

For 1948-70 a few equations were fitted using the polynomial distributed lag technique of Shirley Almon [1] with a second-degree polynomial, i.e., a parabola, for each of the three variables G, H, and B, when lagged income and other explanatory variables were omitted. Correlation coefficients were high when none of the weights of the lagged values were constrained to be zero, $R^2 = .99$ or higher. See Table 4.

Some logarithmic and/or first difference equations were estimated for money income, as noted earlier. Also, a few equations explaining the price level and real income were estimated, using the same group of explanatory variables except that in the real income equation the explanatory variables are deflated by the price level. In general, money income was explained better than either of its two components, real income or the price level. Table 5 shows R^2 from several such equations, confirming the foregoing comparison.

First-difference equations, as usual, have lower R^2 than equations in levels. Note that the linear equations fit somewhat better than the logarithmic ones, in general. The pattern of individual coefficients in logarithmic and first-difference equations for money income does not appear very different from that described above for linear equations in the level of money income.

Wartime years have not been excluded from the sample period for this study. In many time series studies they are excluded on the ground that wartime controls interfere with the operation of behavior equations. However, the largest changes in

TABLE 5

Multiple Correlation Coefficients (R^2) for Alternative Equations Explaining
Money Income (Y), Price Level (P), and Real Income (Y/P)
Without Lagged Income

Dependent Variable*		Y		Y		P		P		Y/P†	
Form of Equation		Linear		Log		Linear		Log		Linear	Log
Sample Period		1948 to 1970	1917 to 1970	1948 to 1970	1917 to 1970	1948 to 1970	1917 to 1970	1948 to 1970	1917 to 1970	1948 to 1970	
Type of Data (1)	Independent Variables (2)	(3)	(4)	(5)	(6)	(7)	(8)	(9)	(10)	(11)	(12)
Levels	G, H, B	.954	.923	.932	.86	.921	–	.912	–	.939	.85
Levels	$G, H, B,$ H_{-1}, B_{-1}	.969	–	.954	–	–	–	–	–	–	–
First Differences	G, H, B	.59	.42	.59	.23	.54	.06	.57	.36	–	–

*For symbols, refer to the description of notation in the text.

†Explanatory variables for these equations were in real terms.

monetary variables and in the federal budget occur during wartime, and hence for the study of the effects of these variables it is desirable to include the wartime years. Money income was probably somewhat lower during the price control period of 1942 to 1945 than it would have been without the controls, but the controls did not completely prevent prices from rising, and money income rose rapidly during the period. Table 6 shows residuals for money income for the years 1939-48 computed from estimates of equation (2) for four different sample periods, excluding lagged income. Notice that for seven of the eight equations, the average absolute residual during World War II (1942-45) is less than the root mean square error over the corresponding sample period, and that in the remaining one it is only slightly larger. Indeed, twenty-seven of the thirty-two wartime residuals are less than the corresponding sample period root mean square error, and only five are greater, as Table 6 shows. The residuals for 1939 to 1948 certainly do not suggest that the years of World War II are outlying observations in equation (2). Note that equation (2) as fitted to all four sample periods underestimates money income in 1942, and overestimates it in 1946.

The implications of these results for macroeconomic policy are that both government purchases and the high-powered money stock have substantial stimulating effects upon aggregate demand as measured by money income, but that the amount of federal debt in private hands does not have a well-established effect. Thus the findings of this paper are more in accord with those of deLeeuw and Kalchbrenner [9] than with the monetarist findings of Andersen and Jordan [2] and Friedman.

Mention was made earlier of the negative coefficient that appears for the current value of the high-powered money stock whenever lags of two years or more for that variable were included in the equation. Coupled with the fact that the total of all the coefficients of high-powered money, current and lagged, is not very sensitive to the number of lags included, this suggests that the speed of response of money income to changes in high-powered money is not well established, but that it may be quite slow. Three other recent studies obtained rather similar results. One was de Leeuw and Gramlich [7], in which the quarterly time path of the response of GNP to policy changes was simulated with the FRB-MIT model. On page 27 they show that a step increase in unborrowed reserves increases GNP with a multiplier of about 11 after 3 years, but that less than 20 percent of the effect is felt in the first 4 quarters. (On page 29 they show that a step increase in government defense purchases increases GNP with a multiplier of about 3 in the 4th quarter, with the multiplier rising to about 3.6 and then declining to 3 again after 12 quarters; this is similar to the rapid response of money income to government purchases noted above.)

The other studies use more recent versions of the FRB-MIT model to simulate the effect of a step increase in reserves upon GNP. One is de Leeuw and Gramlich [8] and one is Kaufman and Laurent [10]. Both show GNP rising gradually to a peak after about 12 quarters, and then declining at about the same rate for another 4 to 8 quarters, suggesting that a cycle in GNP may be generated. The time paths for these three studies are graphed in Christ [6, p. 445].

TABLE 6

Residuals during and near World War II from Equation (2) for Money Income (Y) as Estimated from 4 Sample Periods (Billions of Current Dollars per Year)

Year	Observed Money Income	Residuals from Equation (2)							
		Excluding Y_{t-1}				Including Y_{t-1}			
		1929-47	1913-47	1913-70	1891-1970	1929-47	1913-47	1913-1970	1891-1970
(1)	(2)	(3)	(4)	(5)	(6)	(7)	(8)	(9)	(10)
1939	90.5	4.9	5.5	-4.0	-3.7	1.8	2.2	-7.5	-7.5
1940	99.7	.2	6.6	-30.0	-34.7	-3.0	-.1	-8.2	-8.1
1941	124.5	.1	-1.2	-52.0	-55.0	-.8	-.8	10.0	9.9
1942	157.9	2.3	10.6	8.8	4.4	1.1	3.3	10.9	11.0
1943	191.6	-4.6	5.7	-36.8	-35.2	1.3	4.8	10.0	9.9
1944	210.1	.01	-4.3	-19.8	-17.6	-1.0	-2.4	-8.6	-8.7
1945	211.9	3.9	-7.4	5.8	1.4	-1.1	-4.7	-13.2	-13.0
1946	208.5	-2.0	-3.1	-59.6	-59.0	-1.1	-.3	-10.6	-10.7
1947	231.3	-.2	-1.8	-43.4	-44.8	1.0	1.5	-2.9	-3.0
1948	257.6	—	—	8.3	-5.9	—	—	8.4	8.8
Average Absolute Residual, 1942-45		2.7	7.0	17.8	14.7	1.1	3.8	10.7	10.7
Root Mean Square Residual, Sample Period		12.3	15.9	40.0	35.0	9.0	8.2	11.5	9.6

VI. LIMITATIONS

The work reported in this paper has many limitations of which the author is painfully aware. Among the more important ones are the following. The private sector is not broken down into a banking and a nonbanking sector, and therefore the quantity of money as usually defined is not analyzed. This may contribute to some of the large residuals that occurred during the Great Depression, for the money stock declined much more drastically than did the high-powered money stock during that period. The equations estimated are not explicitly derived from a fully specified macroeconomic model, but rather are arrived at by considering only some of the main features of such a model. There is no explicit treatment of policy changes with regard to tax rates and transfer payment schedules. Net exports X and government holdings of gold and foreign exchange F are taken to be exogenous. Changes in exchange rates are ignored, as is the effect of discount rate changes. The high-powered money stock is not adjusted for changes in reserve requirements. The period studied does not go back to 1869 as had originally been intended. The data used are annual, not quarterly (though as noted above, the reason for this is to permit treatment of the early years on the same basis as recent years). And perhaps most important, the results do not give clear evidence concerning the speed of response of money income to changes in monetary and debt variables, and the question of how changes in money income are allocated as between price changes and changes in real output has not been dealt with here.

LITERATURE CITED
(See also Appendix I)

1. Almon, Shirley. "The Distributed Lag Between Capital Appropriations and Expenditures," *Econometrica,* 33 (January, 1965), 178-96.

2. Andersen, Leonall C., and Jerry L. Jordan. "Monetary and Fiscal Actions: A Test of Their Relative Importance in Economic Stabilization," *Review of the Federal Reserve Bank of St. Louis* (November, 1968), 11-24.

3. Christ, Carl F. *Econometric Models and Methods.* New York: John Wiley and Sons, 1966.

4. _____ . "A Short-Run Aggregate-Demand Model of the Interdependence and Effects of Monetary and Fiscal Policies with Keynesian and Classical Interest Elasticities," *American Economic Review,* 57 (May, 1967), 434-43.

5. _____ . "A Simple Macroeconomic Model with a Government Budget Restraint," *Journal of Political Economy,* 76 (January/February 1968), 53-67.

6. _____ . "Econometric Models of the Financial Sector," *Journal of Money Credit and Banking,* 3 (May, 1971, Part II), 419-49.

7. deLeeuw, Frank and Edward Gramlich. "The Federal Reserve-MIT Econometric Model," *Federal Reserve Bulletin,* 54 (January, 1968), 11-40.

8. _____ . "The Channels of Monetary Policy: A Further Report on the Federal Reserve–MIT Model," *Journal of Finance,* 24 (May, 1969), 265-90, and *Federal Reserve Bulletin* (June, 1969), 472-91. (The duplicated version made available at the December, 1968 meetings of the economics association provides more detail.)

9. deLeeuw, Frank and John Kalchbrenner. "Monetary and Fiscal Actions: A Test of Their Relative Importance in Economic Stabilization–Comment," *Review of the Federal Reserve Bank of St. Louis* (April, 1969), 6-11, followed by a reply by Andersen and Jordan.

10. Kaufman, George G., and Robert D. Laurent. "Three Experiments with Simulating a Modified FRB-MIT Model," duplicated, Federal Reserve Bank of Chicago, 1969.

11. Steindl, Frank J. (1971), "A Simple Macroeconomic Model with a Government Budget Restraint: A Comment," *Journal of Political Economy* (May/June 1971), 675-79.

APPENDIX A: SOURCES OF DATA

In this appendix the following abbreviations are used:

ARST: *Annual Report of the Secretary of the Treasury,* various issues.

BMS: *Banking and Monetary Statistics,* Washington, Federal Reserve System, 1943.

ERP: *Economic Report of the President,* February, 1971.

F of F: *Flow of Funds Accounts 1945-1968,* Washington, Federal Reserve System, 1970.

FRB: *Federal Reserve Bulletin.*

HSUS: *Historical Statistics of the U.S. from Colonial Times to 1957,* Washington, USGPO, 1960.

Kendrick: John W. Kendrick, *Productivity Trends in the United States,* Princeton for NBER, 1961.

Kendrick worksheets: worksheets giving unpublished detail in support of data in Kendrick's book, above.

MonHist: *A Monetary History of the United States 1867-1960* by Milton Friedman and Anna J. Schwartz, Princeton for NBER, 1963.

MonHist worksheets: worksheets underlying Mon Hist.

MonStat: *Monetary Statistics of the United States* by Milton Friedman and Anna J. Schwartz, New York, NBER, 1970.

Nat Income: *The National Income and Product Accounts of the United States, 1929-1965,* Washington, USGPO, no date.

SCB: *Survey of Current Business.*

For the meanings of the alphabetical symbols, see the description of notation in the text of the paper. Numbers in parentheses below, from (1) through (14), denote series that were constructed in the process of obtaining the data for the variables used in the paper. The time series data are given in Appendix B.

$B = (2) - (1)$.

(1) = U.S. Government holdings of private credit market debt, December 31
1969-70: FRB March, 1971, p. A71.12
1945-68: F of F pp. 50-51
1942-44 and 1934: FRB 1953, p. 1355, 1944 p. 1222, 1935 p. 88

  1935-41: BMS, p. 517

  1917-33: HSUS, pp. 663 and 286, series X389 and K163

  1889-1916: zero

(2) for 1945-70 = U.S. public debt and budget agency securities held privately (outside U.S. Government accounts and the Federal Reserve), obtained as holdings outside U.S. Government accounts less holdings of the Federal Reserve, December 31

  1969-70 from FRB March 1971 pp. A71.12-13

  1945-68 from F of F pp. 50-51 and 58-9

(2) for 1889-1944 = U.S. Government debt, direct and agency issues, guaranteed and non-guaranteed, held privately, December 31

 = (3) + (4)

(3) = U.S. Government agencies' nonguaranteed debt, December 31

  1934-44: same sources as (1)

  1917-33: approximated by HSUS, p. 286, series K163

  1889-1916: zero

(4) = U.S. Government debt, direct and guaranteed, privately held, December 31

  1940-44: FRB 1953, p. 1362

  1889-1939: (5) + (6)

(5) = U.S. Government debt, direct and guaranteed, non-interest-bearing, December 31

  1916-44: BMS, pp. 509-10 and 512

  1889-1915: sum of matured non-interest-bearing U.S. Government debt from ARST plus June 30 data interpolated to December 31 for U.S. Government debt bearing no interest less gold reserve fund for U.S. notes, from ARST

(6) = U.S. Government debt, direct and guaranteed, interest-bearing, privately held, December 31

  1936-39: BMS, p. 512

  1916-35: June 30 data from BMS, p. 512, interpolated to December 31 via data for U.S. Government debt, direct and guaranteed, interest bearing, BMS, pp. 509-10 and 511

  1889-1915: interest-bearing U.S. government debt from ARST, less Federal Reserve holdings from BMS, p. 330 for 1914 and 1915 (prior values are zero)

$B1 = (2)$

$B2 =$ for 1916-41 $= (6) - (7)$

$B2 =$ for 1942-70 $= (8) - (9) - (10)$

 (7) = nonmarketable public issues, December 31, BMS, pp. 509-10

 (8) = total marketable public issues, direct and guaranteed, December 31, FRB various issues from May, 1943 to February, 1971

 (9) = same as (8), except (9) is holdings of U.S. agencies and trust accounts

 (10) = same as (8), except (10) is holdings of the Federal Reserve

D for 1889-46: MonHist pp. 749-761, December 31 (1889-1906 data are interpolated from June 30 data)

D for 1947-69: FRB 1970 pp. 895-98, December 31

D for 1970: FRB February 1971 p. A17, December 31

F for 1916-70 = (11) - (12) - (13) - (14)

       (11) for 1946-70 = U.S. reserve assets, total, December 31, ERP p. 304

       (11) for 1941-45 = total gold stock, December 31, from Supplement No. 14 to BMS, p. 5

       (11) for 1916-40 = gold stock, December 31, BMS p. 536

       (12) = IMF gold deposits at the Federal Reserve, December 31; 1965-70 data from FRB February issues 1966-71; 1916-64 values are zero

       (13) for 1916-33 = gold certificates in circulation (outside the Treasury and Federal Reserve), December 31, BMS, pp. 410-12

       (13) for 1934-70 = zero

       (14) for 1916-33 = gold coin in circulation (outside the Treasury and Federal Reserve), December 31, BMS p. 410-12

       (14) for 1934-70 = zero

F for 1889-1920: MonHist worksheets giving unpublished December 31 data for gold in the Treasury (and, beginning in November, 1914, in Federal Reserve Banks) to match June data in MonHist, pp. 130 and 179. They agree with (11) - (12) - (13) - (14) for 1916-20.

G for 1929-70: Nat Income, pp. 2-3 and SCB recent issues

G for 1889-28: Kendrick worksheets (his book publishes total government purchases, but does not give federal purchases separately)

H for 1889-1960: MonHist, pp. 799-808, December 31 (1889-1906 data are interpolated from June 30 data), less member bank borrowings obtained as follows:

  1914-41: BMS, pp. 330-32

  1941-60: BMS Supplement No. 9, pp. 5-7

H for 1961-70 = currency in circulation + member bank reserves on deposit at the Federal Reserve - float - member bank borrowings, December 31, FRB February and March issues, 1966 and 1971

P for 1929-70: ERP p. 200 and SCB May, 1971 p. 14

P for 1889-28: ratio of Kendrick's money income to real income, Kendrick, pp. 293-94 and 296-97, adjusted to 1958 = 1.00

X for 1929-70: Nat Income, pp. 2-3 and SCB recent issues

X for 1889-28: Kendrick, pp. 296-97

Y for 1929-70: Nat Income, pp. 2-3 and SCB recent issues

Y for 1889-28: Kendrick, pp. 296-97

APPENDIX B: DATA

Time series data used in computing the estimates reported in this paper are as follows (see the description of notation in the text of the paper):

Year	B	B1	B2	D	F	G	H	P	X	Y
1889	1.07			.039	.191	.12	1.34	.260	−.09	12.4
1890	.92			.028	.149	.14	1.40	.254	−.11	13.1
1891	.88			.020	.131	.15	1.48	.251	−.02	13.5
1892	.86			.014	.121	.16	1.52	.241	−.05	14.2
1893	.86			.014	.081	.17	1.54	.246	−.04	13.8
1894	.96			.014	.086	.16	1.54	.231	.00	12.6
1895	1.03			.016	.063	.15	1.45	.227	−.12	13.9
1896	1.12			.016	.137	.16	1.46	.222	.08	13.2
1897	1.13			.032	.161	.18	1.62	.222	.13	14.6
1898	1.33			.062	.247	.33	1.76	.229	.40	15.3
1899	1.22			.087	.237	.32	1.88	.237	.26	17.3
1900	1.09			.099	.247	.28	2.01	.248	.41	18.6
1901	1.03			.111	.263	.27	2.11	.246	.33	20.6
1902	1.01			.135	.271	.28	2.20	.254	.15	21.5
1903	.99			.128	.266	.30	2.33	.257	.22	22.8
1904	.98			.090	.230	.33	2.44	.260	.15	22.8
1905	.99			.081	.285	.34	2.55	.266	.16	25.1
1906	1.02			.135	.314	.35	2.72	.273	.14	28.7
1907	1.02			.237	.249	.37	3.07	.284	.11	30.4
1908	1.02			.120	.232	.44	3.10	.282	.23	27.6
1909	1.00			.047	.242	.45	3.14	.292	−.16	32.1
1910	1.00			.045	.254	.45	3.22	.299	−.15	33.3
1911	1.05			.051	.276	.46	3.30	.298	.05	34.2
1912	1.04			.048	.300	.46	3.38	.310	.04	37.3
1913	1.04			.082	.263	.48	3.48	.312	.16	39.0
1914	1.04			.062	.504	.49	3.46	.315	−.11	36.4
1915	1.04			.031	.757	.50	3.85	.325	1.5	38.7
1916	1.16	1.1	.9	.031	.982	.62	4.4	0.366	2.9	49.7
1917	7.17	7.1	6.9	.63	1.83	3.04	4.8	0.451	3.2	59.9
1918	20.7	20.9	19.4	.41	2.25	13.75	4.7	0.526	2.1	76.1
1919	25.3	25.6	24.2	.59	2.23	6.59	4.6	0.539	3.8	78.9
1920	23.3	23.6	22.3	.26	2.23	2.40	4.4	0.614	2.8	88.8
1921	22.6	23.0	21.7	.26	3.04	1.94	5.1	0.523	1.6	73.9
1922	22.1	22.7	20.8	.34	3.20	.99	5.8	0.494	.6	73.9
1923	21.3	22.1	20.6	.21	3.25	1.06	6.0	0.508	.4	86.1
1924	20.1	21.0	19.3	.22	3.12	.98	6.7	0.502	.9	87.5
1925	19.3	20.3	18.6	.28	2.87	1.10	6.5	0.510	.6	91.3
1926	17.5	19.0	17.2	.21	2.99	1.09	6.4	0.513	.4	97.6
1927	16.5	18.0	16.3	.26	2.90	1.14	6.6	0.501	.7	96.2
1928	16.0	17.4	15.8	.23	2.75	1.25	6.0	0.504	1.0	98.1
1929	14.5	16.0	14.5	.1	3.0	1.2	6.3	0.506	1.1	103.1
1930	13.9	15.7	14.2	.2	3.1	1.3	6.8	0.492	1.0	90.4
1931	15.4	17.4	15.9	.3	3.1	1.4	7.1	0.447	.5	75.8
1932	16.1	19.4	17.9	.5	3.4	1.4	7.7	0.402	.4	58.0
1933	18.3	22.6	20.9	.8	3.7	2.0	8.2	0.392	.4	55.6
1934	20.6	29.5	26.6	1.5	8.2	2.9	9.4	0.421	.6	65.1

300 : MONEY, CREDIT, AND BANKING

Appendix B: Data–*Continued*

Time series data used in computing the estimates reported in this paper are as follows (see the description of notation in the text of the paper):

Year	B	B1	B2	D	F	G	H	P	X	Y
1935	22.4	31.8	29.3	.8	10.1	2.9	11.5	0.426	.1	72.2
1936	26.5	35.6	32.5	.8	11.2	4.9	13.2	0.427	.1	82.5
1937	27.8	36.5	33.1	.7	12.7	4.6	13.6	0.445	.3	90.4
1938	29.0	37.8	34.2	.7	14.5	5.4	15.5	0.438	1.3	84.7
1939	31.4	40.0	35.6	.7	17.6	5.1	19.2	0.432	1.1	90.5
1940	33.8	42.5	37.1	.6	21.9	6.0	23.1	0.438	1.7	99.7
1941	44.7	53.9	43.0	1.4	22.7	16.8	23.7	0.472	1.3	124.5
1942	86.6	95.4	71.2	8.4	22.7	51.8	27.6	0.530	0.0	157.9
1943	134.9	142.9	103.4	10.4	21.9	81.1	32.3	0.568	-2.0	191.6
1944	186.2	193.0	138.6	20.8	20.6	89.0	38.5	0.581	-1.8	210.1
1945	222.0	227.2	167.5	24.6	20.0	74.1	43.0	0.596	- .6	211.9
1946	197.1	204.6	147.0	3.1	20.7	17.2	43.9	0.667	7.5	208.5
1947	186.4	198.2	137.9	1.0	24.0	12.5	44.8	0.746	11.5	231.3
1948	178.7	191.8	128.6	1.8	25.7	16.5	47.2	0.795	6.4	257.6
1949	184.3	198.8	130.9	2.8	26.0	20.1	42.9	0.791	6.1	256.5
1950	180.5	195.7	126.3	2.4	24.2	18.4	43.5	0.801	1.8	284.8
1951	175.8	192.3	116.7	2.7	24.2	37.6	47.5	0.856	3.7	328.4
1952	178.2	196.2	120.7	4.9	24.7	51.7	49.5	0.874	2.2	345.5
1953	182.2	202.1	125.1	3.8	23.4	57.0	49.1	0.883	.4	364.6
1954	185.9	205.5	129.4	5.0	22.9	47.3	48.2	0.896	1.8	364.8
1955	184.5	204.8	134.2	3.4	22.7	44.0	48.1	0.908	2.0	398.0
1956	178.0	198.9	130.4	3.4	23.6	45.5	48.8	0.939	4.0	419.2
1957	175.8	197.4	133.6	3.5	24.8	49.5	49.0	0.974	5.7	441.1
1958	181.5	204.6	142.6	3.9	22.5	53.5	48.8	0.999	2.2	447.3
1959	186.5	211.4	154.2	4.9	21.5	53.6	48.9	1.016	.1	483.7
1960	182.6	208.5	153.5	4.7	19.3	53.5	47.1	1.032	4.0	503.7
1961	186.7	214.2	158.6	4.9	18.7	57.4	49.1	1.046	5.6	520.1
1962	189.4	219.4	162.5	5.6	17.2	63.3	49.8	1.057	5.1	560.3
1963	189.1	220.5	162.0	5.1	16.8	64.2	52.4	1.071	5.9	590.5
1964	189.5	223.6	163.2	5.5	16.6	65.1	55.0	1.088	8.5	632.4
1965	184.6	221.5	160.4	4.6	15.4	66.8	58.1	1.108	6.9	684.9
1966	180.3	221.5	159.1	3.4	14.6	77.7	60.8	1.139	5.3	749.9
1967	184.0	229.8	160.7	5.0	14.5	90.7	65.5	1.175	5.2	793.9
1968	188.3	239.3	168.4	5.0	15.4	99.5	69.6	1.223	2.5	865.0
1969	177.7	231.4	159.7	5.6	16.7	101.3	73.2	1.281	1.9	931.4
1970	182.2	239.2	165.8	7.1	14.3	99.7	77.1	1.348	3.6	976.5

[11]

Journal of Monetary Economics 4 (1978) 45–70. North-Holland Publishing Company

SOME DYNAMIC THEORY OF MACROECONOMIC POLICY EFFECTS ON INCOME AND PRICES UNDER THE GOVERNMENT BUDGET RESTRAINT

Carl F. CHRIST*

The Johns Hopkins University, Baltimore, MD 21218, U.S.A.

Consider a macroeconomic model with constant capacity, an inflation adjustment process depending on excess demand, a government budget restraint, and plausible assumptions. Steady-state equilibrium paths have constant (possibly zero) inflation rates. Stability is assured if the endogenous policy variable is money, government purchases, or the tax rate; if it is government debt instability is assured (contrary to Blinder–Solow). Exogenous increases in money or government purchases raise prices in the short and long run. An open market purchase raises prices in the short run, but if money is endogenous it reduces money and prices in the long run.

1. Introduction

This paper studies the dynamic theory of real output and the price level (including the inflation rate) as a result of the interaction of monetary and fiscal policy.

The analysis is based on a simple macroeconomic model that incorporates the following points. The government budget restraint limits the freedom of the authorities in choosing the monetary-fiscal policy mix. The productive capacity of the economy imposes an upper limit on real output. The expected rate of inflation (not necessarily zero) influences the private sector's behaviour. There is an inflation-adjustment mechanism, whereby the price level rises at the expected inflation rate, or faster or slower, depending on whether real aggregate demand matches or exceeds or falls short of the economy's capacity.

Previous work has dealt with macroeconomic policy effects under the government budget restraint, combining some of the features analyzed here. Previously accepted macroeconomic conclusions were altered when the conventional *IS–LM* curve analysis was modified in the light of the government budget restraint.[1]

*Research underlying this paper was supported in part by a National Science Foundation grant to The Johns Hopkins University. The Foundation does not necessarily subscribe to the statements made herein. Helpful comments were made by Karl Brunner, Rudiger Dornbusch, Louis Maccini, Eshragh Motahar, Jürg Niehans, and a referee.

[1]This modification was begun by Ritter (1955–56), Patinkin (1956), Hansen (1958), Musgrave (1959), Enthoven (1960), Lindbeck (1963), Modigliani (1963), and Ott and Ott (1965). Explicit dynamic analysis by Christ (1968, 1969) and by Blinder and Solow (1973) derived

D

2. Summary of results

The economy analyzed here has a steady-state equilibrium path. Along this path real variables (including real output and real asset holdings) are constant, and nominal variables (including the price level and nominal income and asset values) are growing at the constant rate at which policymakers choose to expand the nominal stocks of money and government bonds. If they expand these stocks at a zero rate, the equilibrium path will have a balanced budget and a stable price level. If they expand these stocks at a constant positive rate, the equilibrium path will have a constant real budget deficit and steady inflation.

Policymakers are free to choose exogenously the values or growth rates of all the policy variables except one. The behaviour of the remaining one, whichever it is, will be determined endogenously by the government budget restraint interacting with the private sector. The economy's adjustment path, starting from a disequilibrium, will depend upon the choice as to which policy variable is to adjust endogenously.

When just two policy variables change, the steady-state multiplier does not depend on which of the two policy variables is endogenous, but the stability conditions do. Of course the adjustment path does not converge to the steady-state path in unstable cases.

If the endogenous policy variable is chosen to be either the high powered money stock or a tax-transfer variable, then plausible inequality assumptions concerning the parameters of the model are sufficient to guarantee that the steady-state equilibrium path is locally stable. But if the endogenous policy variable is either government purchases of goods and services or the outstanding stock of privately held government bonds, stability cannot be so guaranteed.[2]

However, further light is thrown on stability in those cases by the sign of the long-run multiplier effect of the high powered money stock upon the price

the result that the long-run multiplier effect upon real income of an increase in government purchases financed by printing money is the inverse of the marginal tax rate. Of course, this result is of limited relevance because it applies only to situations where aggregate demand does not become large enough to press against the economy's productive capacity. Christ (1969) dealt with two cases, in which either the price level is fixed and real output varies, or the other way around. Brunner and Meltzer (1972) presented a model incorporating both price changes and output changes, and also capital stock growth, price expectations, and considerable detail about the private banking system, but did not present explicit dynamic analysis of equilibrium paths and their stability conditions. Scarth (1975a) and Shinkai (1975) included the government budget restraint in a model of an open economy. Scarth (1975b) considered inflation and expectations concerning it, but only in a context where equilibrium requires zero inflation.

[2] Blinder and Solow (1973) studied the stability of the static equilibrium in a related model with a government budget restraint. They assumed a constant price level, and put no capacity constraint upon real output. They too found that plausible inequality assumptions on the parameters do assure the stability of equilibrium when the money stock is endogenous (p. 329), and do not when bonds are endogenous (p. 330).

level. Consider first the case where the endogenous policy variable is government purchases. If an exogenous increase in high powered money then has a positive long-run effect on the equilibrium path of the price level, the equilibrium path is stable, and conversely. Consider second the case where the endogenous policy variable is privately held government bonds. If an endogenous increase in high powered money then has a positive long-run effect on the equilibrium path of the price level the equilibrium path is unstable. These considerations suggest that the equilibrium path is stable if government purchases are endogenous, and unstable if the privately held stock of government bonds is endogenous.[3] Jürg Niehans has devised an independent way of inquiring whether the stability conditions are met, which concurs, as noted below. Of course stability is an empirical matter.

The stability characteristics of the real economy may not be like those of the model analyzed here. But if they are, there may be danger of instability in a policy that chooses a constant rate of growth for the high powered money stock, and fixes tax-transfer rates and real government purchases of goods and services so that the real deficit is of the right size on the average to be financed by increasing both bonds and high powered money at the rate chosen for the latter, and then allows the government budget restraint to be satisfied during disequilibria by endogenous variation in the outstanding stock of government bonds. For that policy is just the one that this paper suggests is unstable. If it is stable, then in this paper an exogenous increase in the high powered money stock when bonds are endogenous must reduce prices in the long run.

Some of the policy multiplier effects are as follows (only the stable cases are recorded here, for long-run multipliers are of no practical interest in unstable cases; it is here presumed that equilibrium is stable when government purchases are endogenous).

Exogenous increases in high powered money increase prices in the short and long run run, whether the endogenous variable is government purchases or taxes less transfers.

Exogenous increases in government purchases increase prices in the short and long run, whether high powered money or taxes less transfers are endogenous,

An open market purchase increases prices in the short run, but if high powered money adjusts endogenously the long-run effect is to reduce the price level[4] and the high powered money stock.

All policy multiplier effects on output are zero in the long run in this model since equilibrium requires that output be at the capacity level.

---

[3]Blinder and Solow (1973) properly find that it is an empirical question whether the system is stable when bonds are endogenous (pp. 328, 330). But they accept unequivocally the statement that the steady-state equilibrium of income, after an increase in government purchases, is higher if bonds are endogenous than if money is endogenous (p. 327), a statement that can be shown to be equivalent in their model to the statement that the system is stable when bonds are endogenous.

[4]Brunner *et al.* (1973) also obtained this result.

Other impact and long-run multipliers are shown in table 1 below. The results reported here for stability and for long-run multipliers pertain to the case where the inflation rate is at or near zero; the method of analysis is equally suitable for inflation rates far from zero.

3. The economy to be analyzed

The economy studied here is divided into two sectors: a consolidated government sector consisting of the Treasury and the Central Bank, and the private sector including the private banking system. State and local governments are included in the private sector, since they cannot finance their deficits by printing money as the Federal government can. Foreign transactions are assumed away.

The consolidated government sector is assumed to hold no deposits in private banks, and to make no loans to the private sector (thus there is no Central Bank discount window).[5] Then private bank deposits cancel out in the consolidated balance sheet of the private sector. Hence the conventional money stock (currency outside banks plus deposits in private banks) does not appear. The Central Bank's holdings of Treasury debt cancel out in the balance sheet of the consolidated government sector; hence only the private holdings of government debt appear. The Treasury's debt consists only of perpetuities. It is assumed that private securities (which net out in the consolidated private balance sheet) are a perfect substitute for government debt, so that the same interest rate rules for both.

Government transfer payments are treated as negative taxes. Taxes less transfers are assumed to have an autonomous nominal component unaffected by income, and an induced component proportional to income. Government interest is included in transfers, and is taxable. The tax-transfer system is progressive in terms of money income, so that taxes less transfers rise in real terms if the price level rises with no change in real income; this provides a built-in stabilizing effect.

Under these conditions, government authorities have 5 monetary and fiscal policy variables: the high powered money stock, the amount of government debt outstanding in private hands, government purchases of goods and services, the marginal tax-transfer rate, and the level of autonomous nominal taxes less transfers. The government budget restraint includes all 5 policy variables; it requires that the government deficit (purchases plus transfers less taxes) be financed by some combination of issuing high powered money and borrowing from the private sector.

Because of the government budget restraint, the authorities may choose levels or constant growth rates for only 4 of these policy variables exogenously

---

[5]These restrictions do not deprive the monetary authority of its most potent policy weapon, namely buying and selling government securities for high powered money.

(any 4, to be sure), the path of the remaining one being determined endogenously by the interaction of government budget restraint and the private economy.

For simplicity it has been assumed that productive capacity is exogenous, unaffected by monetary and fiscal policy. Output can exceed capacity, if aggregate demand warrants it. Then the inflation rate is greater than expected, and this results in a reduction in demand and output as will be seen below. Output can also fall short of capacity. In that case the inflation rate is less than expected, and this results in an increase in demand and output as will be seen below.

The expected inflation rate is taken to be exogenous for simplicity. It could be made endogenous by the addition of a third differential equation. This has not been done because the formation of expectations about inflation is not well understood, and because a third differential equation would complicate the analysis.

4. Notation and some inequality assumptions

The five policy variables are as follows (four are to have levels or growth rates fixed exogenously, and the path of one is endogenously determined dynamically by the system):

B = number of privately held government bonds, each being a perpetuity yielding \$1 a year in nominal terms. Thus B equals the annual interest expenditure for privately held government bonds.

g = real government purchases of goods and services.

H = nominal high powered money stock.

u = marginal rate of taxes less government transfers, $0 < u < 1$.

V = autonomous taxes less government transfers in nominal terms ($V < 0$, that is, the tax-transfer system is progressive).

The six endogenous variables in the model are as follows:

x = real private expenditure net of depreciation.

P = price level.

r = nominal interest rate. The unmodified term 'interest rate' refers to it.

t = real tax receipts less government transfers (government interest is included in transfers).

y = real net national product and income.

One of the 5 policy variables listed above.

The seven exogenous variables in the model are as follows:

f = full-employment capacity level of real net national product.

π = expected rate of inflation expressed as an annual rate.

τ = time.

Four of the 5 policy variables listed above.

The parameters of the system are all positive except perharps the intercepts α_0 and λ_0, as follows:

α_i = parameters of the private expenditure function;
    $0 < \alpha_2 < \alpha_1 \leq 1$ (see below).
λ_j = parameters of the asset equilibrium function.
ρ = speed of inflation adjustment to excess supply or demand.

Other notation is as follows:

β = ratio of change in B to change in H, assumed constant when both are endogenous.
$\Delta, \Delta_B, \Delta_g, \Delta_H, \Delta_V$ = determinants defined in Appendix A1.
e = 2.71828 ..., the base of natural logarithms.
r' = expected real interest rate. This does not appear explicitly in the model, since it is expressed by definition in terms of the nominal interest rate r and the expected inflation rate π, thus: $1 + r' = (1 + r)/(1 + \pi)$.
θ = rate of growth chosen by the authorities for the exogenous nominal policy variables.
ϕ = functional symbol for aggregate demand.

For the nominal variables P, B, H, and V an asterisk (e.g. P^*) denotes the steady-inflation equilibrium path value as a function of time; a subscript zero denotes the value at time $\tau = 0$ (e.g. $P^* = P_0^* e^{\theta\tau}$); and a prime denotes the actual value at any time, deflated by $e^{\theta\tau}$ (e.g. $P' = P/e^{\theta\tau}$). These notations will be used to simplify the analysis of the case where the long-run equilibrium path has nonzero rates of change of the nominal variables. A dot denotes a time derivative, e.g. $\dot{P} = dP/d\tau$.

5. The Model

The six equations of the model are given here and interpreted below.

(1) $y = x + g$,   real income = expenditure,
(2) $t = V/P - B/P + uB/P + uy$,   real taxes less transfers,
(3) $x = \alpha_0 + \alpha_1 y - \alpha_2 t + \alpha_3/r$
    $\quad + \alpha_4 H/P + \alpha_5 B/P + \alpha_6 \pi$,   real private expenditure
(4) $1/r = \lambda_0 - \lambda_1 y + \lambda_2 H/P - \lambda_3 B/P$,   asset equilibrium,
(5) $g = t + \dot{H}/P + \dot{B}/rP$,   government budget restraint,
(6) $\dot{P}/P = (y/f - 1)\rho + \pi$,   price adjustment.

Equation (1) states that total real private expenditure x (for consumption and net investment) plus government purchases g equals real income y.

Equation (2) says that real tax collections less government transfers t are equal to deflated autonomous nominal taxes less transfers V/P, less deflated nominal public debt interest B/P, plus induced taxes less induced transfers

$uB/P+uy$. This means that government interest is included in transfers, and affects induced taxes less transfers at the same marginal rate u as does other income.[6]

Equation (3) says that total real private expenditure x is a linear function of real income y, real taxes less transfers t, the inverse of the interest rate $1/r$, real high powered money H/P, real government bond interest B/P, and the expected inflation rate π. This equation has been obtained by starting with a function of real income y, real taxes less transfers t, the expected real interest rate r' (expressed as noted above in terms of the nominal interest rate r and the expected inflation rate π), and real holdings of high powered money H/P and government bonds B/rP; and then linearizing in y, t, $1/r$, H/P, B/P, and π. The parameters α_1 and α_2 may be different, because while real income and taxes less transfers presumably affect consumption by equal but opposite amounts, they may have different effects on the investment component of private expenditure. We assume that $0 < \alpha_2 \leq \alpha_1 < 1$.

Equation (4) says that when asset markets are in equilibrium, the inverse of the interest rate $1/r$ is a linear function of real income y, real high powered money H/P, and real government bond interest B/P. This has been derived from a portfolio balancing process in which the desired proportion between private holdings of high powered money H/P and government bonds B/rP depends on income and the rate of interest, and then linearizing the result in $1/r$, y, H/P, and B/P.

The decision to linearize equations (3) and (4) in the variables $1/r$ and B/P (rather than in r and B/rP) is particularly convenient, because it means that when the aggregate demand equation is obtained from the *IS* and *LM* equations as in equation (7) below, its denominator is free of all policy variables except for the marginal tax-transfer rate u. It may seem restrictive to express private behaviour by linear functions, but the dynamic stability analysis below is an approximation based on the linearization of the system about its equilibrium, and hence equations (3) and (4) are to be regarded as so linearized.

Equation (5) is the government budget restraint, requiring that government purchases plus transfers be equal to the total amount of financing available from all sources: taxes, issuing high powered money $\dot{H}/P$, and borrowing from the private sector $\dot{B}/rP$. Open market operations are covered by this restraint. They involve equal but opposite changes in high powered money H and private holdings of government debt B/r. Observe that transfer payments appear as a negative component of t. Observe also that since $P > 0$, $B > 0$, $V < 0$, and $u < 1$, we must have $uy > g$ when the budget is balanced.

Equation (6) says that the rate of inflation $\dot{P}/P$ is equal to the expected rate of inflation π, plus an amount proportional to excess demand (which may be negative) deflated by full-employment capacity output $[(y-f)/f$, or what is

---

[6]This equation corrects oversights regarding government bond interest in Christ (1967° 1969).

the same thing, $y/f-1$]. If real income and output y exceed the full-employment level, prices will rise faster than expected. The price adjustment process is symmetrical: excess supply leads to a rate of inflation less than expected and possibly to a decline in prices.[7]

6. Relation to the familiar static aggregate-demand model

Notice that if inflation expectations are ignored, the first four equations correspond to the familiar simple static Keynesian aggregate-demand *IS–LM* model. It would determine real income, real private expenditure, real taxes less transfers and the interest rate, if one assumed a rigid price level, for given levels of fiscal and monetary policy variables (namely, government purchases, tax and transfer rates, the high powered money stock, and the amount of privately held government debt), ignoring the government budget restraint, the productive capacity constraint, and the price-level adjustment mechanism. Such a model is inadequate because it permits real income to remain forever above or forever below the capacity level, and it permits a perpetual constant deficit or a perpetual constant surplus with no effect on private asset holdings.

The same first four equations (ignoring inflation expectations) correspond equally well to the familiar simple static classical model. It would determine the price level, real private expenditure, real taxes less transfers, and the interest rate, if one assumed that real income is fixed by full employment of given resources, for given levels of the fiscal and monetary policy variables, again ignoring the government budget restraint and the productive capacity constraint, and assuming that prices adjust with no delay. Such a model is inadequate because it provides no possibility of real income ever deviating from capacity, and it too permits a perpetual constant deficit or a perpetual surplus with no effect on private asset holdings.

By including capacity, the inflation adjustment mechanism, and the government budget restraint, we allow both output and inflation to respond to excess demand, and we recognize the effects of deficits or surpluses on the future levels of high powered money and the government debt.

Equations (5) and (6), namely the government budget restraint and the inflation adjustment equation, make the system dynamic, for they introduce the rates of change of the price level $\dot{P}$, high powered money $\dot{H}$, and privately held bonds $\dot{B}$. The inflation adjustment equation (6) is always dynamic, prescribing that inflation proceeds faster or slower than expected depending on the existence of excess demand or excess capacity, and remains as expected ($\dot{P}/P = \pi$) only when demand and capacity are just balanced. The government

[7]Note that the capacity level of output f can correspond to 4 % or 5 % or any other level of unemployment. What is required for the purposes of this paper is that f be the level of output at which inflation proceeds at the expected rate.

budget restraint (5) is either dynamic or static, depending upon which policy variable is chosen to be endogenous: it is dynamic if either high powered money H or privately held government bonds B is chosen to be endogenous, because then either $\dot{H}$ or $\dot{B}$ appears in the model via (5); it is static if both H and B are fixed exogenously, for then neither $\dot{H}$ nor $\dot{B}$ appears.

7. Reduction of the model to three equations

We are chiefly interested in the relations among real income, the price level, and the policy variables. Accordingly, we shall simplify our analytical task by eliminating the variables t, x, and r by substituting from equations (2), (3) and (4), respectively, into the other equations. The result is the following system of three equations, interpreted below:

$$\dot{P}/P = (y/f-1)\,\rho+\pi, \tag{6}$$

$$y = \frac{\alpha_0+\alpha_3\lambda_0+\alpha_6\pi-\alpha_2 V/P+(\alpha_2(1-u)-\alpha_3\lambda_3+\alpha_5)B/P+(\alpha_4+\alpha_3\lambda_2)H/P+g}{1-\alpha_1+\alpha_2 u+\alpha_3\lambda_1}$$

$$= \phi(P, \pi, B, g, H, u, V), \tag{7}$$

$$g = V/P-(1-u)B/P+uy+H/P+(\lambda_0-\lambda_1 y+\lambda_2 H/P-\lambda_3 B/P)/\dot{B}P. \tag{8}$$

Equation (6) is the inflation adjustment equation as before. Equation (7) is the aggregate demand function obtained by substituting equations (2)–(4) into (1), and solving the result for y. It expresses real income y in terms of the price level P, the expected inflation rate π, and the policy variables.[8] The functional symbol ϕ is used simply to express the aggregate demand function concisely. Equation (8) expresses the government budget restraint in terms of real income y, the price level P, and the policy variables. It is obtained by substitution of (2) and (4) into (5).

The remainder of the paper will be concerned with the analysis of the behaviour of three-equation system (6)–(8). Its exogenous variables are the same as those of the original system. Its three endogenous variables are real income y, the price level P, and one endogenous policy variable. Its behaviour with respect to these three variables is the same as that of the original system. Once this behavior has been understood, then it is easy to study the behavior of x, t, and r by returning to equations (1), (2), and (4) respectively, if desired.

8. Properties of the aggregate demand equation

Equation (7) is the reduced form equation for real income in the static aggregate-demand *IS–LM* sub-model (1)–(4), when the price level and the

---

[8]If desired equation (7) can be solved for P to show the price level at which a fixed level of output y would be demanded for given values of the policy variables.

expected inflation rate are exogenous and the government budget restraint is ignored. We shall need to know the directions of response of aggregate demand in equation (7) to changes in the price level, in the expected inflation rate, and in the policy variables. Some of these directions of response can be deduced from the foregoing assumptions as follows: (a) The *IS* curve slopes downward. (b) The *LM* curve slopes upward. (c) The denominator of (7) is positive. For a given price level, and given values of all policy variables but one, the level of real aggregate demand generated by this equation is (d) *increased* by an increase in government purchases g, that is, $\partial\phi/\partial g > 0$; (e) *increased* by an increase in the high powered money stock H, that is, $\partial\phi/\partial H > 0$; (f) *decreased* by an increase in the marginal tax-transfer rate u, that is $\partial\phi/\partial u < 0$; (g) *decreased* by an increase in the autonomous nominal tax-less-transfer payment V, that is, $\partial\phi/\partial V < 0$; and (h) *increased* by an increase in the expected inflation rate, that is, $\partial\phi/\partial\pi > 0$.

We shall make the plausible assumption that (i) an increase in the price level shifts the *LM* curve (4) to the left, given the nominal asset stocks H and B, i.e. $\lambda_2 H > \lambda_3 B$. This implies that (j) the level of aggregate demand given by (7) is *decreased* by an increase in the price level, i.e. $\partial\phi/\partial P < 0$. We shall also make the plausible assumption that (k) an open market purchase *increases* the level of aggregate demand given by (7) for a fixed price level, i.e. $\partial\phi/\partial H > r\partial\phi/\partial B$. This requires that $\partial\phi/\partial B$ be either negative or smaller than $\partial\phi/r\partial H$.

9. The steady-state equilibrium path

We consider steady-state equilibrium paths along which all real quantities are constant, and all nominal quantities are growing at a common constant rate (which may be positive, negative, or zero), as noted earlier. On such an equilibrium path, $\dot{P}/P$ must be constant because y is constant in equation (6). And H, B, and V must all be growing at the same rate $\dot{P}/P$, to insure that the real quantities H/P, B/P, and V/P are constant. Denote by θ the common constant rate of growth of the nominal exogenous policy variables. Then in equilibrium, $P/\dot{P} = \theta$, since the inflation rate must equal the growth rate of all nominal variables.[9]

[9]Sections 9 and 10 would be greatly simplified if attention were restricted to the case where the equilibrium is static, with a constant price level, instead of permitting dynamic equilibrium paths having steady inflation. Readers who wish to concentrate on this simple case may do so, as follows. First, skip the remainder of this section except for equations (9)–(11) and the paragraph following them, and skip section 10 except for its last paragraph. Second, from here onward, set both θ and π equal to zero, and ignore the primes that appear on symbols for nominal variables. Third, note that in this simple case the static equilibrium position for the system (6)–(8) is given by setting equal to zero the time-derivatives $\dot{P}$, $\dot{H}$, and $\dot{B}$, thus obtaining static equilibrium conditions as expressed by equations (9)–(11) with $\theta = 0$. (Equations (19)–(21) with $\theta = 0$ describe the same equilibrium in this special case.) Fourth, note that static equilibrium requires that the budget be balanced (as shown by equation (11) or (21) when $\theta = 0$).

Note that if the expected inflation rate is equal to the equilibrium inflation rate, $\pi = \theta$, then from (6) we have equilibrium output equal to the capacity level, $y = f$. If the expected and equilibrium inflation rates differ (which the model would permit because both π and θ are exogenous), then equilibrium output will differ from the capacity level: from (6) we will have $y = (1 + (\theta - \pi)/\rho)f$. If policymakers inflate faster than expected, so that $\theta > \pi$, the model implies that equilibrium output will exceed capacity, $y > f$; and if policymakers inflate less rapidly than expected, the model implies $y < f$. These two situations are unrealistic for the long run for in reality the expected inflation rate will not long remain different from the actual rate if inflation continues at a constant rate. Hence we shall restrict our attention to the realistic equilibria where the two exogenous variables π and θ are equal.

The equilibrium solution of the system (6)–(8), and also of the original system (1)–(6), can now be obtained by setting $\dot{P} = \theta P$, $\dot{B} = \theta B$, and $\dot{H} = \theta H$ in (6)–(8), This results in the following three equilibrium equations, respectively. Here y^* and P^* denote values on the equilibrium path, y^* being constant and P^* growing at the constant rate θ. (The endogenous policy variable's equilibrium value could bear an asterisk also, but it has been omitted in order to allow the equilibrium equations to apply to an arbitrary choice as to which policy variable is endogenous.)

$$y^* = f \quad \text{(since in equilibrium } \dot{P}/P = \theta = \pi\text{)}, \tag{9}$$

$$f = \phi(P^*, \pi, B, g, H, u, V), \tag{10}$$

$$g = V/P^* - (1-u)B/P^* + uy^* + \theta H/P^* + (\lambda_0 - \lambda_1 y^* + \lambda_2 H/P^* - \lambda_3 B/P^*)\theta B/P^*. \tag{11}$$

These equations say that in equilibrium, (9) output will be equal to the capacity level; (10) output will be equal to aggregate demand; and (11) the real deficit will be exactly financed by the issue of bonds and high powered money at the constant rate θ.

Note that on this equilibrium path, all nominal variables are growing at the rate θ, namely P, B, H, and V. And all real quantities are constant, namely y, g, u, B/P, H/P, and V/P. The interest rate is constant in equilibrium also, its inverse being given from (4) by the expression in parentheses in the last term of (11). The equilibrium paths of the nominal variables are as follows, where a subscript zero indicates the value at time $\tau = 0$:

$$P^* = P_0^* e^{\theta\tau}, \quad B^* = B_0^* e^{\theta\tau}, \quad H^* = H_0^* e^{\theta\tau}, \quad V^* = V_0^* e^{\theta\tau}. \tag{12}$$

When the system is in disequilibrium, the real endogenous variables may be above or below their equilibrium levels, and the nominal endogenous variables may be above or below their equilibrium paths which grow exponentially at the rate θ.

10. Transformation of nominal variables to remove the exponential trend

Dynamic analysis will be simplified by a transformation that removes the exponential trend from the nominal variables, in order to obtain a transformed system whose equilibrium is static. This is done by dividing each nominal variable by $e^{\theta\tau}$. The transformed nominal variables are denoted by primes, thus:

$$P' = P/e^{\theta\tau}, \quad B' = B/e^{\theta\tau}, \quad H' = H/e^{\theta\tau}, \quad V' = V/e^{\theta\tau}. \tag{13}$$

The equilibrium values of the transformed nominal variables will be constant levels (dependent of course on the paths chosen for the exogenous variables), equal via (12) to the levels at $\tau = 0$ of the untransformed equilibrium paths, as follows:

$$P'^* = P^*/e^{\theta\tau} = P_0^*, \qquad B'^* = B^*/e^{\theta\tau} = B^*,$$

$$H'^* = H^*/e^{\theta\tau} = H_0^*, \qquad V'^* = V^*/e^{\theta\tau} = V_0^*. \tag{14}$$

Fig. 1 shows the relationship between the time paths of the untransformed price level P (top panel) and the transformed price level P' (bottom panel) for an illustrative case of stable oscillations about a steady-inflation path. In the top panel, the dashed line shows the equilibrium *path* of the price level, growing exponentially at the rate θ. The solid wavy line shows the actual time path of the price level, satisfying initial conditions at $\tau = 0$, oscillating about the equilibrium path and approaching it. In the bottom panel, the dashed line shows the static equilibrium *value* of the transformed price level. The solid wavy line shows the actual path of the transformed price level, satisfying corresponding initial conditions at $\tau = 0$, oscillating about the static equilibrium value and approaching it. Of course if the exogenous conditions are changed at some later time (i.e. the levels of real exogenous variables and the constant-growth rate paths of the nominal exogenous variables), then at that time the old equilibrium path becomes irrelevant, a new equilibrium path must be determined on the basis of the new exogenous conditions, and the system will then start to adjust in relation to that new equilibrium path.

In order to express the three fundamental equations (6)–(8) in terms of the transformed nominal variables, we need to evaluate the dynamic expressions $\dot{P}/P$, $\dot{B}/P$, and $\dot{H}/P$ (which appear in (6)-(8)) in terms of the transformed variables and their time derivatives:

$$\dot{P}/P = \dot{P}'/P'+\theta, \quad \dot{B}/P = \dot{B}'P'+\theta B'/P', \quad \dot{H}/P = \dot{H}'/P'+\theta H'/P'. \tag{15}$$

Now the fundamental equations (6)–(8) can be rewritten, using (12)–(15), in terms of the transformed nominal variables as follows:

$$\dot{P}'/P' = (y/f - 1)\rho + \pi - \theta \quad \text{(but recall that } \pi = \theta\text{)}, \tag{16}$$

$$y = \phi(P', \pi, B', g, H', u, V'), \tag{17}$$

$$g = V'/P' - (1-u)B'/P' + uy + \dot{H}'/P' + \theta H'/P'$$

$$+ (\lambda_0 - \lambda_1 y + \lambda_2 H'/P' - \lambda_3 B'/P')(\dot{B}'/P' + \theta B'/P'). \tag{18}$$

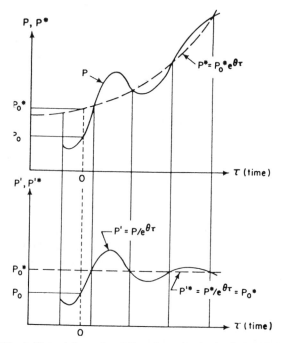

Fig. 1. Untransformed and Transformed price levels P and P'.

The transformed aggregate demand equation (17) employs the same function ϕ as did the original one (7), and it is homogeneous of degree zero in nominal variables, so that all the derivations and assumptions about ϕ and its derivatives in section 8 above apply here, after the nominal variables have been transformed. The inflation adjustment equation (16) is similar to (6) except that π is cancelled by $-\theta$ in (16). The government budget restraint (18) is of the same form as (8) except for the appearance in (18) of the terms $\theta H'/P'$ and $\theta B'/P'$, (Note that if $\theta = 0$, i.e. if nominal exogenous policy variables are assigned constant values, then the transformed nominal variables become the same as the untransformed ones, and equations (16)–(18) reduce to (6)–(8) as they should.)

The *dynamic* equilibrium *path* of the original system (6)–(8), with nominal variables growing at the rate ϕ, can now be conveniently expressed as the *static* equilibrium *level* of the transformed system (16)–(18). It is obtained by setting $\dot{P}'$, $\dot{B}'$, and $\dot{H}'$ equal to zero in (16)–(18), thus:

$$y^* = f, \tag{19}$$

$$f = \phi(P'^*, \pi, B', g, H', u, V'), \tag{20}$$

$$g = V'/P'^* - (1-u)B'/P'^* + uy^* + \theta H'/P'^*$$

$$+ (\lambda_0 - \lambda_1 y^* + \lambda_2 H'/P'^* - \lambda_3 B'/P'^*)\theta B'/P'^*. \tag{21}$$

The behaviour of the original system (6)–(8) can now be determined by studying the simpler behaviour of the static system (16)–(18). This is the purpose of the transformation that removes the exponential trend.

11. Graphical description of the equilibrium in the transformed system

The top panel of fig. 2 shows the three equilibrium conditions (19)–(21) on a graph[10] of the transformed price level P' versus output y. (There is implicitly a third dimension, not shown, representing the endogenous policy variable, whatever it may be. Only when this variable is at its own equilibrium will the 3 lines intersect in a single point as shown.)

The vertical dotted line shows the requirement that output be at the capacity level, as in equation (19).

The solid negatively sloping line shows the requirement that output be equal to aggregate demand, as in equation (20). Its negative slope was discussed in section 8.

The dashed negatively sloping line shows the requirement that the real budget deficit is constant and is financed by issuing bonds and high powered money at the constant rate θ, as in equation (21). Its slope must be negative if $\theta = 0$, that is if nominal exogenous policy variables are constant so that in equilibrium the budget is balanced and there is no inflation or deflation; this can be seen by differentiating (21) to obtain $\partial y^*/\partial P'^*$ and then putting $\theta = 0$ to obtain $\partial y^*/\partial P'^* = [V' - (1-u)B']/uP'^{*2} < 0$. The slope of (21) remains negative unless θ is given a value too far from zero.

In fig. 2 the solid line representing the equilibrium of output and aggregate demand has been drawn less steep than the dashed line representing the equilibrium of the government budget restraint, but the assumptions made above about the parameters do not require this.

[10]This graph was suggested to me by Rudiger Dornbusch.

The disequilibrium adjustment of the system is based on the following responses. First, for all points to the right of the vertical dotted line, output exceeds capacity, so that inflation is accelerating relative to the expected rate; the reverse holds for points to the left. Second, for all points to the right of the dashed government budget restraint equilibrium line, the real deficit is below its equilibrium level, so that nominal bonds or high powered money must increase slower than the rate θ, so that private nominal wealth is either rising slower than its equilibrium rate or falling; the reverse holds for points to the left. Both of these responses influence output through their influence on aggregate demand in equation (20).

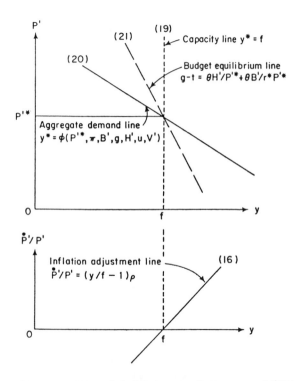

Fig. 2. Three equilibrium conditions (19)–(21) (top panel). Response of $\dot{P}'/P'$ to real income (bottom panel).

The bottom panel of fig. 2 shows the inflation adjustment line from equation (16), $\dot{P}'/P'$ being plotted against output y. The line shows that when output equals capacity the inflation rate is equal to the expected rate π which equals the issue-rate of bonds and high powered money.

12. Results concerning stability

In this section the results dealing with dynamic stability conditions are presented. We deal with 4 cases, corresponding to 4 possible choices as to which of the policy variables is to be determined endogenously: the number of privately held bonds B', real government purchases g, high powered money H', or the intercept V' of the nominal tax-transfer function.[11] We also discuss a 5th case, in which bonds and high powered money are both endogenous subject to the restriction that a fixed proportion β is mantained between their changes. The marginal tax-transfer rate u is not discussed, because in the small the effects of $y\mathrm{d}u$ and $(\mathrm{d}V)/P$ are the same. The derivation of these results is left to the appendix.

The stability of the system depends in part on θ, the rate of increase chosen for exogenous nominal policy variables. We consider the case where θ is at or near zero. The results are as follows. The necessary and sufficient conditions for local stability are unambiguously satisfied, given the assumptions we have made in sections 4 and 8, if the endogenous policy variable is either the tax-transfer variable V' or the high powered money stock H'. Our assumptions above do not determine whether the stability conditions are satisfied if the endogenous policy variable is either government purchases g or bonds B'.

However, if g is endogenous, then stability is equivalent to a positive long-run value of $\partial P'/\partial H'$, that is, the system is stable if and only if the new equilibrium price path after an exogenous increase in the high powered money stock is higher than the old equilibrium price path. And if B' is endogenous, then stability implies a negative long-run value of $\partial P'/\partial H'$, that is, if the system is stable then the new equilibrium price path after an exogenous increase in high powered money is lower than the old equilibrium price path.[12] Historical and empirical evidence strongly suggests that when high powered money is increased, the equilibrium price level does not fall, but rises. Hence it appears likely that the system will be stable when government purchases g are endogenous, and unstable when privately held bonds B' are endogenous. This is supported by a result of Niehans.[13] The stability results are in column 3 of table 1.

[11]Each once-for-all exogenous change in a policy variable must be accompanied by an initial endogenous change in some other policy variable so as to satisfy the government budget restraint at the instant when the exogenous policy change is made. During the subsequent adjustment period, the policy variable that is permitted to change endogenously (with all other policy variables held fixed) need not be one of the two policy variables involved in the initial change. For convenience, however, we analyze only those cases in which this is so.

[12] Note that there are three different long-run multipliers depending upon whether the endogenous policy variable is B',g, or V'. See table 2 in the appendix, column 5.

[13]Jürg Niehans (1976) has proposed an independent procedure for examining the stability of the Blinder–Solow model when bonds are endogenous. I have applied this procedure to the model of this paper, and it supports the view that the system is stable when government purchases g are endogenous, and unstable when bonds B' are endogenous. Niehans' pro-

Table 1

Summary of effects on real output y, the price level P', and the endogenous policy variable resulting from exogenous increases in privately held bonds B', real government purchases g, high powered money H', and autonomous taxes less transfers V' in a simple dynamic macroeconomic model containing a government budget restraint.[a]

Choice of endogenous policy variable	No. of differential equations	Locally stable?	Type of effect	Effect on real output y of an exogenous increase in				Effect on price level P' of an exogenous increase in				Effect on endogenous policy variable of an exogenous increase in			
(1)	(2)	(3)	(4)	B' (5)	g (6)	H' (7)	V' (8)	B' (9)	g (10)	H' (11)	V' (12)	B'[d] (13)	g[e] (14)	H' (15)	V' (16)
(1) B' = bonds[b]	2	no[b]	impact	na	+	+	−	na	+	+	−	na	+	−	−
			long-run[b]	na	0	0	0	na	+?	+	−?	na	−	+	+
(2) g = government purchases[c]	1	yes[c]	impact	+	na	+	−	+	na	+	+	+	na	+	+
			long-run	+	na	+	−	−?	na	+	+	−	na	+	+
(3) H' = high powered money	2	yes	impact	−	+	na	−	+	+	na	+	+	+	na	−
			long-run	0	0	na	0	+	+	na	+	+	−	na	−
(4) V' = autonomous taxes less transfers	1	yes	impact	+	+	+	na	+	+	+	na	+	+	+	na
			long-run	0	0	0	na	−?	+	+	na	+	−	−	na

[a] The entries $+$, $-$, 0, na mean respectively an increase, a decrease, no change, and not applicable. A question mark after a $+$ (or a $-$) means that the long-run multiplier in question is a positive (or negative) expression, plus a term of unknown sign that is proportional to $\partial\phi/\partial B$ (this derivative is discussed in section 8).

[b] Results in row 1 are those that obtain if, when B' is endogenous, the long-run multiplier $\partial P'/\partial H' > 0$ and hence the system is unstable.

[c] Results in row 2 are those that obtain if, when g is endogenous, $\partial P'/\partial H' > 0$ and hence therefore never be attained. The long-run multipliers in row 1 would therefore never be attained.

[d] The signs of the long-run multipliers in column 13 are ambiguous if one uses only the assumptions in sections 4 and 8, but the signs of $\partial H'/\partial B'$ and $\partial V'/\partial B'$ are the same. However under the presumptions of notes b and c, the signs of the long-run multipliers in column 13 become correct.

[e] The signs of the long-run multipliers in column 14 are ambiguous if one uses only the assumptions in sections 4 and 8, but the signs of $\partial H'/\partial g$ and $\partial V'/\partial g$ are the same. However, under the presumptions of notes b and c, the signs of the long-run multipliers in column 14 become correct.

E

62   *C.F. Christ, Macroeconomic policy effects*

Consider the 5th case, in which both bonds and high powered money are endogenous, and the change in B' is kept equal to β times the change in H', i.e. $\dot{B}' = \beta\dot{H}'$, where β is a constant chosen by the monetary authorities. If β is chosen to be zero, this reduces to the above case where H' is endogenous, and the system is stable. If β is chosen to be plus infinity, this reduces to the above case where B' is endogenous; suppose that in this case the long-run value of $\partial P'/\partial H' > 0$, and hence the system is unstable. Then as β is gradually increased from zero without limit, the system will at first be stable, but will reach a critical value of β beyond which the system is unstable.

13. Results concerning impact and long-run multipliers

Table 1 also shows the algebraic signs of impact and long-run multiplier effects of exogenous policy changes upon three endogenous variables: real output y, the price level P', and the endogenous policy variable, for cases in which the value of θ (the growth rate of the exogenous nominal policy variables) is at or near zero. The derivations and the explicit long-run multipliers are left to the appendix.

All long-run policy multipliers for real output are zero in this model, because output equals productive capacity when the system is on an equilibrium path. Columns 5–8 show this.

Observe that the impact effects of any policy change upon output and the price level are always in the same direction. Compare impact effects in Columns 6 and 10, or 7 and 11, or 8 and 12. This occurs because inflation accelerates when output exceeds capacity, and decelerates when output falls short of capacity.

We shall discuss two pairs of cases in table 1, and then leave the reader to interpret the rest.

(i) We begin with a pair of cases involving increases in *government purchases* and *high powered money*. First consider the case of an exogenous increase in government purchases g, with the high powered money stock H' adjusting endogenously so as to satisfy the government budget restraint. Look at Columns 3, 6, 10 and 14 in row 3 of table 1. The system is stable. The impact effect is to increase H', which raises aggregate demand and output; this accelerates inflation. When the new equilibrium path is reached, real income has returned to its capacity level, and the price level is on a higher path than before. The rise in the price level's equilibrium path can be seen from the equilibrium budget equation (21), where $\partial P'^*/\partial g > 0$ when θ is at or near zero.

cedure is to postulate that the goverment budget restraint returns to equilibrium instantly but there is lagged adjustment of output to aggregate demand, and postulate that this system is stable; the result is that the stability condition for the Blinder–Solow case where bonds are endogenous cannot be satisfied.

In economic terms, the higher price path is required to reduce the real value of fixed nominal transfers (including interest) less taxes, i.e. the real value of $(1-u)B' - V'$ so as to restore budget equilibrium at the new higher level of real government purchases g with the same real induced tax revenue uy. The cumulative effect on H' here is positive if and only if the system is stable when g is endogenous (see appendix).

Second, consider the related case of an exogenous step-increase in high powered money H' ,with goverment purchases g adjusting so as to satisfy the government budget restraint. Look at columns 3, 7, 11, and 15 in row 2 of table 1. The system is presumed stable. The impact effects are of course the same as those of the previous case, for both involve initial increases in g and H' so as to satisfy the government budget restraint. The dynamic adjustment paths in the two cases are not the same, however, since in the previous case it is the high powered money stock H' that adjusts over time as the economy approaches its new equilibrium, and in the present case it is government purchases g. However, presuming stability in this case, the long-run effect is the same no matter whether g or H' is endogenous.

The symmetry of impact effects just illustrated (and of long-run effects too, given stability), as between two cases involving the same two policy variables, one of which is endogenous in the one case and the other of which is endogenous in the other case, runs right through table 1.

(ii) Consider next a pair of cases where the initial disturbance is a once-for-all open market purchase of government bonds by the Central Bank i.e. an increase in *high powered money H'* accompanied by a decrease in private holdings of *government bonds B'*. If B' is endogenous in the subsequent adjustment process, we are in row 1, columns 7, 11 and 15. If H' is endogenous, we are in row 3, columns 5, 9 and 13, but we must reverse the signs shown in columns 5 and 9 because the signs there correspond to an open market *sale* (i.e. an increase in B' balanced by a decrease in H'). In both cases, the impact effect of an open market purchase is an increase in aggregate demand and hence in output, and inflation is accelerated. The dynamic adjustment paths for the two cases differ, however.

If high powered money H' is endogenous, then the system is stable and the new equilibrium price path following an open market purchase is *below* the old equilibrium path (see the + sign that shows the long-run price-increasing effect of an open market *sale* in row 3, column 9). This is the only case in table 1 where the initial and final price effects are unambiguously in opposite directions. The lower equilibrium price path is required in this case because an open market purchase leads to a decline in nominal interest payments B' to the private sector; the only way for the budget to regain its equilibrium at full capacity is for the price level to decline slightly, enough so that the real value of fixed nominal transfer payments (including interest) less taxes, i.e. the real value of $(1-u)B' - V'$, can be raised back up to its old level.[14] See the budget equilibrium equation (21), where $\partial P'^*/\partial B' > 0$ for θ at or near zero. In the preceding section we presumed that when bonds are endogenous, an exogenous increase in high powered money raises the equilibrium path of the price level. This is equivalent (see appendix) to the statement that in the present case (an open market purchase with high powered money adjusting endogenously thereafter), the equilibrium path of high powered money is lowered (row 3, column 13). Then all three equilibrium paths for bonds, the price level, and high powered money are lowered.

If bonds B' are endogenous instead of H' following the open market purchase, then the presumption noted in the preceding paragragh implies that the system is unstable, and is equivalent to the statement that the equilibrium paths of the price levels and bonds (which will not be attained because of their instability) are raised; see the $+$ signs in row 1, columns 11 and 15, in table 1.

The reader may use table 1 to find the effects of other policies. For example, a step-increase in exogenous taxes less transfers V', accommodated by endogenous adjustments in high powered money H', will be found in row 3, columns 8, 12, and 16.

14. Limitations

The analysis in this paper has a number of limitations, each significant for some purposes but not for others. The real equilibrium of the presently analyzed system is a static one, rather than a dynamic path. This is related to the fact that capacity is taken as exogenous, rather than being affected by technological change or endogenously determined by available quantities of labor and capital that grow in response to economic conditions. The inflation adjustment mechanism used here is a very simple one responding only to the current inflationary or deflationary gap and people's exogenous anticipations about future rates of inflation. There is assumed to be no delay in the adjustment of output to changes in the level of aggregate demand. Discretionary countercyclical policies have not been examined. The analysis uses only two sectors, the Federal government and private sectors. This means that foreign trade and payments are ignored. It also means that the private banking sector is not dealt with separately, so that monetary policy is confined to Central Bank open market operations and participations in Treasury financing. Although these are the most important monetary policy tools, it is important for many purposes to separate the bank and non-bank parts of the private sector and thus deal explicitly with the conventional stock of money (currency outside banks plus deposits), bank loans, bank capital, and bank reserve requirements.

---

[14]As noted earlier, Brunner *et al.* (1973) also obtained this result.

Appendix: Derivation of the results

A1. Long-run multipliers

The long-run multiplier effects of macroeconomic policy variables are obtained from the three equilibrium conditions (19)–(21) by choosing one policy variable to be endogenous, and then finding partial derivatives of that endogenous policy variable and of real income y and the price level P' with respect to the remaining policy variables (which are exogenous). As noted earlier, long-run policy multipliers for real income are zero in this model. For the case where $\theta = 0$, i.e. where all the nominal exogenous variables are constant, other results are summarized in table 2 below. The top half of table 2 corresponds to columns 9–12 of table 1, and the bottom half to columns 13–16. In table 2, partial derivatives of the aggregate demand function ϕ in equation (7) are denoted by ϕ with a subscript, e.g. $\phi_H = \partial\phi/\partial H'$; Δ denotes the denominator of equation (7); Δ_B denotes the denominator of the long-run multipliers when B' is endogenous; Δ_g, Δ_H and Δ_V denote respectively the denominators of the long-run multipliers when g, H', and V' are endogenous.

The reasoning underlying the signs indicated in table 2 is as follows. First, recall that under the assumptions of sections 4 and 8 about the model's parameters, the following inequalities were established:

Positive: $\alpha_1 \ldots \alpha_6$, $1-\alpha_1$, $1-\alpha_2$, $\lambda_1 \ldots \lambda_3$,

$$u, 1-u, B', g, H', P', \Delta, \phi_H, \phi_g, \lambda_2 H' - \lambda_3 B', \text{ and } \phi_H - r\phi_B. \qquad (22)$$

Negative : V', ϕ_p, ϕ_u, ϕ_V, and perhaps ϕ_B.
Second, under those same assumptions, the denominators of the long-run multipliers turn out as follows:

$$\Delta_H = ((1-u)B' - V')\phi_H/P'^2 > 0, \qquad (23)$$

$$\Delta_V = ((1-u)B' - V')\phi_V/P'^2 - \phi_P/P' > 0, \qquad (24$$

$$\Delta_g = ((1-u)B' - V')\phi_g/P'^2 + \phi_P \gtreqless 0, \qquad (25)$$

$$\Delta_B = ((1-u)B' - V')\phi_B/P'^2 + (1-u)\phi_P/P' \gtreqless 0. \qquad (26)$$

The positive sign of Δ_V becomes apparent if one obtains the derivatives ϕ_V and ϕ_P from (7) and substitutes them into (24). Third, note that, when g is endogenous, if the long-run multiplier $\partial P'/\partial H'$ in row 4, column 5 of table 2 is to be positive, then Δ_g must be negative, and conversely. From this, we find that Δ_g is likely to be negative. (Below it is shown that a negative Δ_g is necessary and sufficient for stability when g is endogenous.) Fourth, note that when B' is endogenous, if the long-run multiplier $\partial P'/\partial H'$ in row 3, column

Table 2

Long-run multipliers from equations (19)–(21) when $\theta = 0$.

Long-run multiplier effects of exogenous policy variables, with signs of numerator and denominator

(1)	Endogenous policy variable (2)	(3) $\partial P'/\partial B'$	(4) $\partial P'/\partial g$	(5) $\partial P'/\partial H'$	(6) $\partial P'/\partial V''$
Effects on the price level P'	(3) B' bonds	na	$\dfrac{\phi_B-\dfrac{1-u}{P'\Delta}}{\Delta_B}$ $-\;?$	$\dfrac{-\phi_H\dfrac{1-u}{P'}}{\Delta_B}$ $-\;?$	$\dfrac{-\phi_V\dfrac{1-u}{}-\dfrac{\phi_B}{}}{\Delta_B}$ $+\;?$
	(4) g gov. purch.	$\dfrac{-\phi_B+\dfrac{1-u}{P'\Delta}}{\Delta_g}$ $+\;?$	na	$\dfrac{-\phi_H}{\Delta_g}$ $-\;-$	$\dfrac{-\phi_V-\dfrac{1}{P'\Delta}}{\Delta_g}$ $-\;-$
	(5) H' money	$\dfrac{\phi_H\dfrac{1-u}{P'}}{\Delta_H}$ $+\;+$	$\dfrac{\phi_H}{\Delta_H}$ $+\;+$	na	$\dfrac{\dfrac{\phi_H}{P'}}{\Delta_H}$ $-\;+$
	(6) V' tax-transfer	$\dfrac{\phi_V\dfrac{1-u}{P'}+\dfrac{\phi_B}{P'}}{\Delta_V}$ $-\;?$	$\dfrac{\phi_V+\dfrac{1}{P'\Delta}}{\Delta_V}$ $+\;+$	$\dfrac{\dfrac{\phi_H}{P'}}{\Delta_V}$ $+\;+$	na

(1)	(7)	$\partial/\partial B'$	$\partial/\partial g$	$\partial/\partial H'$	$\partial/\partial V'$
Effects on the endogenous policy variable	(8) B' bonds	na	$\dfrac{-\Delta_g}{\Delta_B}$ $+$	$\dfrac{-\Delta_H}{\Delta_B}$ $-$	$\dfrac{-\Delta_V}{\Delta_B}$ $-$
	(9) g gov. purch.	$\dfrac{-\Delta_B}{\Delta_g}$ $+$	na	$\dfrac{-\Delta_H}{\Delta_g}$ $-$	$\dfrac{-\Delta_V}{\Delta_g}$ $-$
	(10) H' money	$\dfrac{-\Delta_B}{\Delta_H}$ $+$	$\dfrac{-\Delta_g}{\Delta_H}$ $+$	na	$\dfrac{-\Delta_V}{\Delta_H}$ $-$
	(11) V' tax-transfer	$\dfrac{-\Delta_B}{\Delta_V}$ $+$	$\dfrac{-\Delta_g}{\Delta_V}$ $+$	$\dfrac{-\Delta_H}{\Delta_V}$ $+$	na

5 of table 2 is to be positive, then Δ_B must be negative, and conversely. From this we find that Δ_B is likely to be negative. (Below it is shown that $\Delta_B < 0$ implies instability when B' is endogenous.) This determines the signs of all denominators in table 2, and the signs of numerators in the bottom half of the table. The signs of numerators in the top half of the table can be determined from (22); the question marks arise because the sign of ϕ_B is indeterminate. The results in table 2 hold when θ is zero; the algebraic signs hold when θ is not too far from zero; when θ is far from zero, the procedure is the same, but terms in θ (neglected in table 2) then have to be taken into account.

Note that the numerators in the top half of table 2 form a skew-symmetric matrix, i.e. the *ij*th element is equal to the negative of the *ji*th element. Note also that all denominators in any row of table 2 are identical, all numerators in any column of the bottom half of table 2 are identical, and the *ij*th element of the bottom half is equal to the inverse of the *ji*th element.

A2. Stability when high powered money H' is endogenous

When high powered money H' is the endogenous policy variable, we suppose that the other 4 policy variables B', g, u, and V' are all exogenously fixed and held constant. We study the dynamic behavior of the three endogenous variables, real income y, price level P', and high powered money H'. Observe that $\dot{B}' = 0$ because B' is fixed. The three-equation system (16)–(18) in y, P', and H' then becomes:

$$\dot{P}'/P' = (y/f - 1)\rho, \tag{16}$$

$$y = \phi(P', \pi, B', g, H', u, V',), \tag{17}$$

$$g = V'/P' - (1-u)B'/P' + uy + \dot{H}'/P' + 0H'/P'$$
$$+ (\lambda_0 - \lambda_1 y + \lambda_2 H'/P' - \lambda_3 B'/P')\theta B'/P'. \tag{18'}$$

The static equilibrium position of this system, when $\dot{P}' = \dot{H}' = 0$, is of course the same as the general form given by (19)–)21).

We now examine the stability of the system in the small, when H' is the endogenous policy variable. For simplicity we present the case where $\theta = 0$. First, eliminate y from (16)–(17)–(18') to obtain a pair of differential equations in $\dot{P}', P', \dot{H}'$, and H'. Then solve them algebraically for $\dot{H}'$ and $\dot{P}'$, thus:

$$\dot{H} = P'g - P'u\phi + (1-u)B' - V',$$

$$\dot{P} = (\phi/f - 1)\rho P'.$$

Then linearize these two equations by means of Taylor series expansions of their right hand sides about the equilibrium values H'^* and P'^*, remembering that the constant terms in such an expansion must be zero because both $\dot{H}'$ and $\dot{P}'$ are zero at equilibrium, and that $\phi/f - 1 = 0$ at equilibrium, thus:

$$\dot{H}' = 0 - P'^*u\phi_H(H' - H'^*) + (g - u\phi - P'^*u\phi_P)(P' - P'^*), \tag{27}$$

$$\dot{P}' = 0 + (\rho P'^*/f)\phi_H(H' - H'^*) + (0 + (\rho P'^*/f)\phi_P)(P' - P'^*). \tag{28}$$

The characteristic equation of this linear system, obtained by setting equal to zero the determinant formed from the matrix of its coefficients by subtracting λI, where I is a 2×2 identity matrix, is as follows:

$$\begin{vmatrix} -P'^*u\phi_H - \lambda & g - u\phi - P'^*u\phi_P \\ (\rho P'^*/f)\phi_H & (\rho P'^*/f)\phi_P - \lambda \end{vmatrix} = 0, \tag{29}$$

After evaluating the determinant and cancelling two terms, this reduces to

$$\lambda^2 + [P'^*u\phi_H - (\rho P'^*/f)\phi_P]\lambda - (\rho P'^*/f)(g - u\phi)\phi_H = 0. \tag{30}$$

Upon evaluating ϕ and its derivatives at the equilibrium point, and making use of our assumptions about the values of variables and signs of parameters, we find that the determinant is positive and its trace is negative, so that the real parts of both roots of this characteristic equation are negative. This is necessary and sufficient for stability in the neighborhood of equilibrium. This result is entered in table 1, column 3, row 3. The discriminant of the characteristic equation is positive, so the roots must be real; hence the approach to equilibrium is monotonic.

A3. Stability when government debt B' is endogenous

We now suppose that the 4 policy variables g, H', u, and V' are exogenously fixed and held constant, and that the government debt B' is the endogenous policy variable. We study the behaviour of B', y, and P'. The three-equation system in B', y, and P' now is the same as (16)–(18) except that the term $\dot{H}'/P'$ is absent from (18) because H' is constant. The static equilibrium solution is given by (19)–(21).

To examine the stability of the system in the small, again when $\theta = 0$, first eliminate y from (16)–(18) to obtain a pair of differential equations in $\dot{B}'$, B', $\dot{P}'$, and P'. Then solve algebraically for $\dot{B}'$ and $\dot{P}'$. Then use a Taylor series to linearize about the equilibrium point. Then from the characteristic equation of the linear system, which will be of the form $\lambda^2 + m\lambda + n = 0$, and examine its roots. The system is stable if and only if both roots have negative real parts, which occurs if and only if two inequalities are satisfied. One is that the trace be negative, i.e. $m > 0$, which is equivalent to

$$\phi_B > [1-u+\phi_P\rho P'^*/r^*f]/P'^*u, \quad \text{which is} \gtreqless 0. \tag{31}$$

The other is that the determinant be positive, i.e. $n > 0$, which is equivalent to

$$\phi_B > \phi_P(1-u)/(g-u\phi), \quad \text{which is} > 0. \tag{32}$$

Hence if ϕ_B is positive, and not too small, i.e. if it exceeds the expressions in (31) and (32), the system will be stable in the neighborhood of equilibrium when B' is the endogenous policy variable. However, stability condition (32) cannot be satisfied if, as we found likely in section A1, Δ_B is negative: this can be seen by comparing (26) and (32), remembering that in equilibrium when $\theta = 0$, $P'(u\phi - g) = (1-u)B' - V'$. Hence we find that the system is unlikely to be stable when B' is endogenous. As noted earlier, Niehans' procedure supports this view. This result is entered in table 1, Column 3, row 1. The discriminant is positive, so there are no cycles.

A4. Stability when government purchases g are endogenous

We now suppose that the 4 policy variables B', H', u, and V' are held constant, and that government purchases g adjust endogenously. We study the behaviour of g, y, and P'. The three-equation system in g, y, and P' is now the same as (16)–(18) except that the terms invoving $\dot{H}'/P'$ and $\dot{B}'/P'$ in (18) are now absent because both B' and H' are constant. The static equilibrium solution is again given by (19)–(21).

To examine the stability of the system in the small, again when $\theta = 0$, first eliminate both y and g from (16)–(18) to obtain a single differential equation in $\dot{P}'$ and P'. (This can be done because, with both B' and H' fixed, the only dynamic element in the system is provided by the price adjustment equation that governs $\dot{P}'/P'$). Next, solve this differential equation algebraically for $\dot{P}'$. Next, differentiate the right hand side with respect to P' to obtain $d\dot{P}'/dP'$, and and examine its sign. A negative sign is necessary and sufficient for stability. This derivative turns out to be simply Δg. Hence a negative Δg is necessary and sufficient for stability. We found in section A1 that Δ_g is likely to be negative. Hence the system is likely to be stable when g is endogenous. As noted earlier, Niehans' procedure supports this view. This result is entered in table 1, Column 3, row 2.

A5. Stability when autonomous nominal taxes less transfer V' are endogenous

The procedure in this case is analogous to that in the preceding section.

Under our assumptions when $\theta \geqq 0$, the system is unambiguously stable in the neighborhood of equilibrium. When $\theta = 0$ the proof of stability uses the fact that the derivative $d\dot{V}'/dV'$ has the same sign as $-\Delta_V$, which is negative as shown in section A1. This is recorded in table 1, column 3, row 4.

When θ is near zero, the stability results obtained in this appendix continue to apply. When θ is far from zero, the procedure is the same, but terms in θ which have been neglected here must be taken into account. For plausible numerical values of the parameters, and for all four choices as to which policy variable is endogenous, the degree to which the stability conditions are met is an increasing function of θ, and the system becomes unstable if θ decreases to become sufficiently far below zero.

References

Blinder, Alan S. and Robert M. Solow, 1973, Does fiscal policy matter?, Journal of Public Economics 2, 319–337.

Brunner, Karl and Allan H. Meltzer, 1972, Money, debt and economic activity, Journal of Political Economy 80, Sept.–Oct., 951–977.

Brunner, Karl et al., 1973, Fiscal and monetary policies in moderate inflation, Journal of Money, Credit and Banking 5, February, Part II, 313–353.

Christ, Carl F., 1968, A simple macroeconomic model with a government budget restraint, Journal of Political Economy 76, January/February, 53–67.

Christ, Carl F., 1969, A model of monetary and fiscal policy effects on the money stock, price level, and real output, Journal of Money, Credit, and Banking 1, November, 683–705.

Enthoven, Alain C., 1960, A neo-classical model of money, debt, and economic growth, mathematical appendix to: Money in a theory of finance by John G. Gurley and Edward S. Shaw (Brookings Institution, Washington) 303–359, esp. 315 ff.

Hansen, Bent, 1958, The economic theory of fiscal policy. Translated by P.E. Burke (Allen and Unwin, London, and Harvard University Press, Cambridge) Chapter 3.

Hansen, Bent, 1973, On the effects of fiscal and monetary policy: A taxonomic discussion, American Economic Review 63, September, 546–571.

Lindbeck, Assar, 1963, A study of monetary analysis, Stockholm Economic Studies, New Series III (Almqvist and Wicksell, Stockholm) 144, 146–147.

Modigliani, Franco, 1963, The monetary mechanism and its interaction with real phenomena, Review of Economics and Statistics 45, February, Part 2, 79–107.

Monissen, Hans G., 1972, Including a government budget restraint in standard macroeconomic analysis: Some fiscal and monetary policy implications, Finanzarchiv 31, no. 2, 193–223.

Musgrave, Richard A., 1959, The theory of public finance: A study in public economy (McGraw Hill, New York) chapter 22.

Niehans, Jürg, 1976, A comment on stabilization paradoxes, Manuscript, 12 pp.

Ott, David J. and Attiat F. Ott, 1965, Budget balance and equilibrium income, Journal of Finance 20, March, 71–77.

Patinkin, Don, 1956, Money interest and prices (Row Peterson, Evanston, Illinois) 361–365.

Ritter, L.S., 1955–56, Some monetary aspects of multiplier theory and fiscal policy, Review of Economic Studies 23, 126–131.

Scarth, William M., 1975a, Fiscal policy and the government budget constraint under alternative exchange-rate systems, Oxford Economic Papers 27, March, 10–20.

Scarth, William M., 1975b, The effects on economic stability of indexing the tax system and government bond yields for inflation, Canadian Journal of Economics 8, August, 383–398.

Shinkai, Yoichi, 1975, Stabilization policies in an open economy: A taxonomic discussion, International Economic Review 16, October, 662–681.

Reprinted from

THE AMERICAN ECONOMIC REVIEW

© The American Economic Association

On Fiscal and Monetary Policies and the Government Budget Restraint

By CARL F. CHRIST*

Recognition of the government budget restraint has altered the way economists think about macroeconomics. This is especially true concerning what policy options are available, stability conditions, long-run multipliers, and the nature of equilibrium. One purpose of this paper is to describe and illustrate the way the government budget restraint affects macroeconomic analysis.

Several writers have found that a particular monetarist type of policy is or may be unstable, to wit: fix government expenditures and tax-transfer schedules, make the money stock grow at a constant moderate rate, and issue or retire government bonds to match any budget deficit or surplus. A second purpose of this paper is to show how the stability of such a policy can at least be made possible for some parameter values, by including government interest (gross of income tax) in the government expenditure variable that is fixed.

I. The Role of the Government Budget Restraint

In this section, before embarking upon mathematical seas, I describe the distinguishing features of macro-economic analysis in the presence of the government budget restraint (*GBR*). The *GBR* is the requirement that the total of government expenditure for all purposes must equal the total of financing from all sources, including printing money,

thus:

$$
\left.\begin{array}{l}
\text{government purchases of} \\
\quad \text{goods and services} \\
+ \text{ debt interest} \\
+ \text{ transfer payments} \\
\quad \text{other than interest}
\end{array}\right\}
=
\left\{\begin{array}{l}
\text{taxes on debt interest} \\
+ \text{ other taxes} \\
+ \text{ borrowing from} \\
\quad \text{private sector} \\
+ \text{ high-powered} \\
\quad \text{money issued} \\
+ \text{ gold and foreign} \\
\quad \text{exchange reserves} \\
\quad \text{spent}
\end{array}\right.
$$

We consider the *GBR* of the federal government, excluding state and local governments because they cannot print money (they are accordingly included in the private sector). We consolidate the Federal Reserve with the federal government because the effects of their separate and joint policies depend on the actions of their consolidated sector vis-à-vis the rest of the economy, independent of any additional transactions that they may undertake between themselves alone. We consider only a closed economy, ignoring gold and foreign exchange reserves, because of space limitations. We consolidate the banking and the private nonbank sectors for simplicity.

The most fundamental implication of the *GBR* is that the authorities cannot fix arbitrary paths for all of the macro-economic policy variables at once. At least one policy variable must have its path endogenously determined by the joint action of the *GBR* and the economy's structure. For instance, if the authorities fix constant-level paths for purchases of goods and services, tax rates, transfer rates, and privately held government debt, then the path of the high-powered money stock will be determined by the *GBR* and the economy: Whenever income and the price level are such that the budget is in deficit, high-powered money must be issued to finance it; similarly, when the budget is in surplus or is balanced, the high-powered money stock must decline or be constant.

*Johns Hopkins University. I am glad to acknowledge helpful discussions on the subject of this paper with Willem H. Buiter, Frank De Leeuw, Chi-Hung Leung, Louis Maccini, Bennett McCallum, Jürg Niehans, William Poole, Jerome Stein, and Naoyuki Yoshino. The research underlying the paper was supported in part by an *NSF* grant to the Johns Hopkins University. The views expressed here are not necessarily those of *NSF*. Any errors of course are my own.

The authorities can decide which one of the N policy variables is to be endogenous, and can then fix paths for the other $N-1$. Or they can permit two policy variables to vary endogenously by fixing the ratio between them (for example, the ratio of high-powered money to privately held government debt), and fix paths for the other $N-2$.

It is not possible to change just one policy variable from its previous path, leaving all others on their previous paths. If one is changed, at least one other must be changed to satisfy the *GBR*. For example, if currency is dropped from airplanes during a short interval, not only does the high-powered money stock increase, but transfers become temporarily large during that interval.

The path of the economy after a policy change depends not only on which two (or more) policy variables are changed initially, but also on the choice of which policy variable is to be endogenous afterwards. For example, the effect of an open market purchase of bonds, if private bondholdings are held fixed afterward and high-powered money adjusts endogenously to cover any budget imbalance, will not be the same as if high-powered money is held fixed afterward and bonds adjust endogenously. The effect will be different again, if *both* bonds and high powered money are held fixed afterwards, and some other policy variable (a government expenditure or tax variable) is endogenous in the subsequent adjustment period.

For simplicity, I will usually confine attention to those policy changes where only two policy variables are changed initially, and where just one of those two is allowed to be endogenous afterward. Such a policy change can be described by specifying one policy variable whose path is to be changed exogenously, and one other policy variable that is to adjust endogenously both initially and afterward.

The questions that can be answered by theoretical macro-economic analysis using the *GBR* are familiar, though the answers are sometimes different when the *GBR* is brought into the picture. Does a particular policy permit the existence of long-run equilibrium, either a static equilibrium position or a dynamic equilibrium path? If so, is it stable? And what are the long-run equilibrium multiplier effects of exogenous changes in each policy variable? The stability conditions and the long-run equilibrium multipliers turn out to depend upon the choice of which policy variable is to be endogenous.

We do not have generally accepted definitions of pure monetary policy and pure fiscal policy. In my view, the quest for such definitions is futile because a change in the money stock or in government purchases or tax transfer rates alone does not describe a policy change adequately: at least two policy variables must be changed initially if policy is to be changed, and then at least one policy variable must be allowed to adjust endogenously afterward. Discussions of macro-economic policy would be much clearer if each policy change were completely described by specifying which two (or more) policy variables are changed initially, and which one (or more) is chosen to adjust endogenously afterward.

II. A Simple *GBR* Model

To analyze theoretically the implications of the *GBR*, one must specify a complete macro-economic model. For illustrative purposes, consider the model that is analyzed in my 1978 paper. It is simple enough to understand easily, yet complex enough to permit the study of constant-inflation dynamic equilibrium paths as well as constant-price-level static equilibrium positions. It consists of the following six equations. The meaning of each is described briefly below. A list of notation is provided for reference.

$$(1) \qquad y = x + g$$

$$(2) \qquad t = V/P - B/P + uB/P + uy$$

$$(3) \qquad x = \alpha_0 + \alpha_1 y - \alpha_2 t + \alpha_3/r$$
$$\qquad\qquad + \alpha_4 H/P + \alpha_5 B/P + \alpha_6 \pi$$

$$(4) \qquad 1/r = \lambda_0 - \lambda_1 y + \lambda_2 H/P - \lambda_3 B/P$$

$$(5) \qquad g - t = DH/P + DB/rP$$

$$(6) \qquad DP/P = (y/f - 1)\rho + \pi$$

List of Notation

A_i = characteristic matrix of dynamic system when i is the endogenous policy variable

B = nominal bond interest, \$/yr, > 0

D = d/dt, the time-derivative operator

f = real capacity output, \$/yr, > 0

g = real government purchases, \$/yr, > 0

$g' = g + (1 - u)B/P$, \$/yr, > 0

$g'' = g + B/P$, \$/yr, > 0

H = nominal high-powered money, \$, > 0

P = price level, > 0

r = nominal interest rate, $(yr)^{-1}$, > 0

t = real taxes less all transfers, \$/yr

u = marginal tax rate, dimensionless, $0 \leq u < 1$

V = nominal tax-transfer intercept, \$/yr, < 0

x = real private expenditure, \$/yr, > 0

y = real income, \$/yr, > 0

α_i = private expenditure parameters, > 0 (except possibly α_0)

Δ = denominator of ϕ in equation (7), > 0

Δ_i = determinant of equilibrium system when i is the endogenous policy variable

θ = equilibrium growth rate of B, H, V, P

λ_i = money demand parameters, > 0 (except possibly λ_0)

π = expected inflation rate, $(yr)^{-1}$, $= \theta$

ρ = speed of adjustment of inflation rate, > 0

ϕ = aggregate demand function in equation (7)

ϕ_i = partial derivative of ϕ

Equation (1) is the national income identity. It says that real national income y is the sum of private expenditure x (for consumption and investment) plus government purchases of goods and services g.

Equation (2) is the tax-transfer equation. Assume that the macro-economic effects of transfer payments are the same as those of taxes except for sign. Thus we use one equation for real tax receipts less real transfers, all denoted by t. Consider the four terms on the right-hand side in turn: V is nominal autono-

mous taxes, less autonomous transfers other than government interest. Its real value is V/P. The term B/P is the real value of interest income received by private holders of government bonds. Assume that all bonds are perpetuities paying \$1 a year each in nominal terms; then B stands for both the number of government bonds in private hands, and the nominal interest income thereon. The term uB/P is the induced real tax on government debt interest, at the constant marginal rate u. The term uy is the real induced tax less induced transfers based on real national income, at the marginal rate u. Let us assume that $0 \leq u < 1$ and that V is negative so that the tax transfer system is progressive.

Equation (3) is the real private expenditure equation. All the slope coefficients α_i are positive. Real private expenditure depends positively on real income y, negatively on real taxes less transfers t, negatively on the nominal interest rate r, positively on the real high-powered money stock H/P, positively on real private holdings of government debt B/rP (but note that the equation has been linearized in $1/r$ and B/P for convenience—this is consistent with the linearization that will be performed later for stability analysis), and positively on the expected inflation rate π. Assume that $\alpha_2 \leq \alpha_1 < 1$; the first of these inequalities permits a zero or positive marginal propensity to invest, $\alpha_1 - \alpha_2$.

Equation (4) is the demand equation for real high-powered money H/P. It is obtained thus: First express H/P in the usual way as depending positively on real income y and real private holdings of government debt B/rP, and negatively on the nominal interest rate r; then linearize in $1/r$ and B/P; and then solve for $1/r$. This simplifies the form of equation (7) below. All the slope coefficients λ_i are positive.

Equation (5) is the government budget restraint, stating that the real government deficit $g - t$ must be financed by some combination of printing high-powered money DH/P and borrowing from the private sector DB/rP.

Equation (6) is the inflation adjustment equation. It says that the actual inflation rate DP/P will be equal to the exogenous expected rate π, unless real income is above or below the full-employment level f, in which case actual inflation will, respectively, accelerate or slow down ($\rho > 0$) as compared with the expected rate π.

This model has six endogenous variables: y, t, x, r, P, and *one* of the five policy variables (B, g, H, u, V). The exogenous variables are f, π, and *four* of the five policy variables. The capital stock is assumed to change so little that it and f can be taken as fixed.

The model generates a static long-run equilibrium position at the full-employment real income level $y = f$, if all exogenous variables are assigned constant values and if zero inflation is expected. It generates a static *real* equilibrium position at $y = f$ and a steady-growth dynamic *nominal* equilibrium path, if all *real* exogenous variables are assigned constant values and all *nominal* exogenous variables (which must be chosen from the set of B, H, and V) are assigned steady-growth paths all with the same growth rate, and if furthermore the expected inflation rate is equal to this common growth rate of the nominal exogenous policy variables. This latter assumption makes long-run sense because in reality expectations about inflation will not long remain different from the actual inflation rate if the latter remains constant. The short-run meaning of the assumption amounts to a rational expectations postulate, for it says that inflationary expectations promptly mirror the decision of the authorities regarding the growth rate of the nominal exogenous policy variables.

Note that the equations are of two types: (5) and (6) are dynamic, each describing how some variable changes through time, either the price level or a stock of assets; (1)–(4) are static, describing short-run equilibrium conditions for given values of the price level and the asset stock whose evolution is prescribed by the dynamic equations.

III. Steps in Analyzing a *GBR* Model

A useful method of analysis consists of the following steps (a)–(g). It is a standard dynamic analysis method, adapted for use with the *GBR*.

(a) Solve the static equations for the short-run equilibrium values of all endoge-nous variables except those whose time derivatives appear in the dynamic equations, taking the latter and the exogenous variables as given. In a simple *IS–LM* model, this amounts to finding the intersection of the *IS* and *LM* curves. In the foregoing model, (4) is the *LM* curve, and the *IS* curve is obtained from (1)–(3). If the interest rate is eliminated between the *IS* and *LM* curves, the result is the usual aggregate demand curve relating real output negatively to the price level, thus:

$$(7) \quad y = \phi(P, \pi, B, g, H, u, V)$$
$$= [\alpha_0 + \alpha_3\lambda_0 + \alpha_6\pi - \alpha_2 V/P$$
$$+ [\alpha_2(1 - u) - \alpha_3\lambda_3 + \alpha_5] B/P$$
$$+ (\alpha_4 + \alpha_3\lambda_2) H/P + g]$$
$$\div [1 - \alpha_1 + \alpha_2 u + \alpha_3\lambda_1]$$

Assume that $V < 0$, $f > 0$, and the slope coefficients α_i, λ_i, and ρ are > 0, with $0 < \alpha_2 \leq \alpha_1 < 1$. We deduce that the denominator of ϕ in (7) is > 0, and that the partial derivatives ϕ_g, ϕ_H, and ϕ_π are > 0 while ϕ_u and ϕ_V are < 0. Assume $\lambda_2 H > \lambda_3 B$, i.e., that a price rise shifts the *LM* curve to the left via (4). This implies that $\phi_p < 0$. Also assume $\phi_H > r\phi_B$, i.e., that an open market purchase raises income in the short run via (7).

(b) Find the long-run equilibrium conditions for the system by setting all growth rates equal to their long-run equilibrium values. If a static equilibrium position is to be studied, then all growth rates are set to zero. If a dynamic steady-state growth path equilibrium is to be studied, then each growth rate is set equal to the value it is to have along that path.

For a static equilibrium in the above model, expected inflation π must be zero, and the static equilibrium conditions are like (1)–(6) except that (5) (after substituting for t from (2)) and (6) reduce, respectively, to

$$(5') \quad g - uy - V/P$$
$$+ (1 - u)B/P = 0 \quad \text{(balanced budget)}$$
$$(6') \quad\quad\quad\quad y = f \quad \text{(output = capacity)}$$

For a dynamic equilibrium with steady inflation at the rate $DP/P = \theta$ per year, but constant real variables such as y, g, H/P, etc., expected inflation π must be equal to θ, so that equation (6') remains but (5') becomes

$$(5'') \quad g - uy - V/P + (1 - u)B/P =$$
$$\theta \ (H/P + B/rP)$$

Note that in the inflationary equilibrium, condition (5'') provides not for a balanced budget, but for a constant real deficit, financed by the continual issue of bonds and high-powered money at the constant growth rate θ.

(c) Decide which policy variable is going to adjust endogenously. Notice that there is no need to make this decision until now, because it does not affect either the short-run solution of the static equations in step (a), or the set of long-run equilibrium conditions in step (b).

(d) Solve the long-run equilibrium conditions obtained in step (b) for the long-run equilibrium values of the endogenous variables, assuming given values of the exogenous variables. Long-run equilibrium multipliers can then be obtained by differentiating these solutions partially with respect to each exogenous variable. They will depend on the partial derivatives of ϕ found in step (a). Notice that the long-run equilibrium solutions, and the multipliers obtained by differentiating them, depend upon the decision as to which policy variable is to adjust endogenously.

The long-run equilibrium form of the foregoing model is block recursive. Equation (6') alone shows that real income must equal the exogenous capacity level f in long-run equilibrium. The existence of any further recursiveness among the long-run equilibrium conditions depends on the choice of endogenous policy variable. For simplicity, consider static long-run equilibria and look at equations (7) and (5').

Suppose first that high-powered money H is the endogenous policy variable. Then (5') alone determines the long-run equilibrium price level:

$$(8) \qquad P = \frac{(1 - u)B - V}{uf - g}$$

This equilibrium value is positive if and only if $uf - g$ is positive, that is, if and only if the

constant marginal tax rate applied to capacity income yields more than enough revenue to cover government purchases g. When considering static equilibria we shall assume that this is the case. (For inflationary equilibrium paths, $uf - g$ need not be positive; of course the negative static equilibrium price level that results from (8) in such a case is of no practical interest. I shall return to this point later, in Section XI.) Once the equilibrium price level has been obtained from (8), the equilibrium high-powered money stock H can be obtained from (7). Suppose second that any other policy variable is endogenous instead of H. Then (5') and (7) determine its long-run equilibrium value and that of P simultaneously, not recursively.

In an inflationary equilibrium, the equilibrium inflation rate θ must satisfy the GBR (5'').

Note that for any choice of endogenous policy variable, the long-run equilibrium solution and the associated multipliers are of no practical interest unless the long-run equilibrium is stable, because the path of the economy will not converge to an unstable equilibrium. If the static equilibrium price level is negative, it cannot be stable in a plausible model.

(e) Substitute the short-run equilibrium solutions found in step (a) into the dynamic equations of the model, thus obtaining a dynamic set of equations containing only those endogenous variables whose time derivatives appeared in the original model. This system will be different for different choices of endogenous policy variable.

(f) Linearize the dynamic system obtained in step (e) about its equilibrium. Then write the Routh-Hurwitz necessary and sufficient conditions for the stability of this system, and try to determine whether they are satisfied. In this model they involve the partial derivatives of ϕ found in step (a). Note that different stability conditions apply, depending on the choice of endogenous policy variable. Since there are as many of these conditions as there are dynamic equations in the model, it is sometimes not possible to determine whether all are satisfied, without empirical estimation. In such cases it is sometimes possible to discover theoretically that one of the conditions is definitely not satisfied, which proves instability.

(g) In unstable cases, examine the behavior of the system through time to see whether the unstable variables approach a constant-growth-rate path, such that certain ratios of the unstable variables (for example, real balances H/P) approach a constant value and thus are stable. This sometimes reveals that a system with an unstable price level has a stable rate of inflation and stable real variables.

I have noted that the choice of which policy variable is to adjust endogenously is important, because it affects the block recursiveness of the system, the long-run equilibrium multipliers, and the stability of the system. However, different choices of endogenous policy variable can lead the system to the same long-run equilibrium path, in the following sense: Any given long-run equilibrium path can be attained, from any initial position near that path, by any choice of endogenous policy variable for which the system is stable, provided that the paths chosen for the exogenous policy variables coincide with the given equilibrium path.

IV. Brief Comments on Selected *GBR* Models

Early work on the *GBR* (see my 1968 paper; Alan Blinder and Robert Solow; James Tobin and Willem Buiter, Sec. 3–5) used simple models in which the price level was assumed constant. This is unrealistic, for clearly one of the important effects of changes in the high-powered money stock, at least in some cases, is to change the price level. Later models treat prices as endogenous, and determine a long-run equilibrium price level. Some of these (see William Scarth; Tobin-Buiter, Sec. 6; my 1978 paper) treat productive capacity as fixed. This too is unrealistic, for capacity can be increased by growth in the capital stock. Several others allow for capacity growth as a result of capital accumulation (see Jürg Niehans, 1974, 1978, ch. 11; Tobin-Buiter, Sec. 6; Buiter, 1976, 1977; Karl Brunner and Allan Meltzer; Stephen Turnovsky, 1977, ch. 8; 1978). A few recent models analyze steady-inflation equilibria (see David Pyle and Turnovsky; David Currie, 1976; Turnovsky, 1977, ch. 8; my 1978 paper). A few deal with steady-state real growth based on population growth (see Buiter, 1977; Turnovsky, 1978).

V. Five Types of Equilibrium

Five types of long-run equilibrium can usefully be distinguished:

(i) A static equilibrium position for all real and nominal variables. Here equilibrium requires a balanced budget. (See my 1968 paper; Blinder-Solow; Tobin-Buiter.)

(ii) A dynamic steady-state growth equilibrium path for all aggregate real variables, but a static equilibrium position for all aggregate nominal stock and flow variables. Here too equilibrium requires a balanced budget; it also requires a steadily declining price level so that real balances can grow in proportion to population while nominal balances are constant. (See Buiter, 1977.)

(iii) A dynamic steady-state growth equilibrium path for aggregate real variables, and a constant price level. This requires steady-state growth of nominal stocks and flows, and a constant real budget deficit.

(iv) A static equilibrium position for aggregate real variables, but a steady inflation. This requires steady-state growth in nominal stocks and flows, and a constant real budget deficit. (See Turnovsky, 1977, ch. 8; my 1978 paper.)

(v) A dynamic steady-state growth equilibrium path for aggregate real variables, and a steady inflation. This requires steady-state growth of nominal stocks and flows at a rate approximately the sum of the growth rates of real variables and prices. (See Turnovsky, 1978.)

Note that in equilibria of types (iii)–(v) where nominal stocks and flows grow steadily without limit, the system must fail to satisfy stability conditions pertaining to a static equilibrium of nominal aggregate levels. However, the dynamic equilibrium path may be stable. If so, it will satisfy stability conditions regarding real per capita stocks and flows.

TABLE 1—STABILITY CONDITIONS IN THE MODEL OF EQUATIONS (1)–(6)
FOR VARIOUS CHOICES OF ENDOGENOUS POLICY VARIABLE

	Endogenous Policy Variable			
	V	g	H	B
Determinant appearing in long-run equilibrium multipliers and in stability conditions with sign if known	$\Delta_V = \dfrac{[(1-u)B - V]\phi_V}{P^2} - \dfrac{\phi_P}{P} > 0$	$\Delta_g = \dfrac{[(1-u)B - V]\phi_g}{P^2} + \phi_P$	$\Delta_H = \dfrac{[(1-u)B - V]\phi_H}{P^2} > 0$	$\Delta_B = \dfrac{[(1-u)B - V]\phi_B}{P^2} + \dfrac{(1-u)\phi_P}{P}$
Long-run equilibrium multiplier $\partial P/\partial H$	$(\phi_H/P)/\Delta_V$	$-\phi_H/\Delta_g$		$-[(1-u)\phi_H/P]/\Delta_B$
Necessary and sufficient conditions for local stability of static equilibrium[b]	$\dfrac{dDP}{dP} = \dfrac{-P^2\rho\Delta}{(1-\alpha_1+\alpha_3\lambda_1)f}\Delta_V < 0$	$\dfrac{dDP}{dP} = \dfrac{P\rho\Delta/f}{1-\alpha_1-(1-\alpha_2)u+\alpha_3\lambda_1}\Delta_g < 0$	$tr\ A_H = P(-u\phi_H + \rho\phi_P/f) < 0$ $det\ A_H = \dfrac{P^2\rho}{f}\Delta_H > 0$	$tr\ A_B = r(1 - u - Pu\phi_B) + P\rho\phi_P/f < 0$ $det\ A_B = \dfrac{P^2\rho r}{f}\Delta_B > 0$
Determinantal stability condition restated in terms of Δ_i	$\Delta_V > 0$	$P\Delta_g < 0^a$	$\Delta_H > 0$	$\Delta_B > 0$
Determinantal stability condition restated in terms of $\partial P/\partial H$	$P\dfrac{\partial P}{\partial H} > 0$	$P\dfrac{\partial P}{\partial H} > 0$		$P\dfrac{\partial P}{\partial H} > 0$
Is stability condition satisfied if the static equilibrium price level P is positive?	yes	yes iff $\partial P/\partial H > 0$	*tr* yes *det* yes	*tr* uncertain *det* no iff $\partial P/\partial H > 0$

[a] Assuming that $[1 - \alpha_1 - (1 - \alpha_2)u + \alpha_3\lambda_1] > 0$.
[b] *tr* denotes the trace and *det* the determinant value.

VI. Stability and Multipliers in the Model of Section II

I now review the stability conditions and long-run price multipliers derived in my 1978 paper for the foregoing model, equations (1)–(6). This will illustrate some of the ideas mentioned above, and also prepare the way for a partial solution of the instability problem that appears in some cases when bonds are endogenous.

Table 1 presents the results. Each column of the table corresponds to a different choice of endogenous policy variable. The first row presents important determinants, which (according to Samuelson's correspondence principle) appear both in the stability conditions and in the long-run equilibrium multipliers. The second row presents the equilibrium multipliers for the effect of the high-powered money stock on the price level, $\partial P/\partial H$. The denominator of each is the determinant in the first row. The numerator of each depends on the positive partial derivative ϕ_H from equation (7). (The second row has no entry when H is endogenous, of course.) The third row presents the necessary and sufficient conditions for stability of a static equilibrium. If V or g is endogenous, there is just one dynamic equation, based on (6), and hence one necessary and sufficient stability condition; see the columns labeled V and g. When H or B is endogenous, there are two dynamic equations, based on (5) and (6), and hence two necessary and sufficient conditions: the characteristic matrix of the dynamic system must have a negative trace and a positive determinant; see columns H and B. The fourth and fifth rows restate the determinantal stability conditions from the third row in terms of the sign of the determinant shown in the first row, and in terms of the sign of the equilibrium multiplier $\partial P/\partial H$, respectively. The last row indicates whether each stability condition is satisfied under the assumptions made in Section III, step (a) above, and the assumption that the static equilibrium price level is positive, i.e., that $uf > g$, recall equation (8). Then we see in the last row that the system is unambiguously stable when either V or H is chosen to be the endogenous policy variable, but stability is related to the sign of the equilibrium multiplier $\partial P/\partial H$ when either g or B is made endogenous. In particular, when g is endogenous a positive sign for $\partial P/\partial H$ is necessary and sufficient for stability, but when B is endogenous a positive sign for $\partial P/\partial H$ implies instability. Ettore Infante and Jerome Stein, p. 492, found the same result when B is endogenous.

In the cases where g or B is endogenous, can we find plausible conjectures about stability and about the signs of the long-run equilibrium multipliers $\partial P/\partial H$? Or must these questions be left for empirical estimation of parameters? Historical evidence suggests that the effect of the money stock on prices is positive, not negative, and that the economy does not run away to plus or minus infinity when the money stock and tax transfer rates are held fixed. This suggests that $\partial P/\partial H$ is positive and the economy is stable. We have seen that in this model when g is endogenous these two statements are compatible (indeed, they are equivalent) so we might conjecture they are correct, but when B is endogenous they are incompatible.

Three conjectures are then open for the case of endogenous bonds: 1) $\partial P/\partial H$ is positive and the system is unstable; 2) $\partial P/\partial H$ is negative and the system is stable; or 3) any model that requires a choice between 1) and 2) is incorrect. History has not performed the crucial experiment that would decide among these three, namely, starting from an equilibrium, increase the money stock by an open market operation and forever afterward hold constant the money stock and all other policy variables except B. If the model be accepted, I am inclined to believe in instability when B is endogenous, partly because of doubt that $\partial P/\partial H$ is negative in a stable system, and partly because of a different stability argument proposed by Niehans (1977), to which I now turn.

Niehans' argument is this. Assume that the government budget restraint is always kept in equilibrium, but that output responds to aggregate demand with a lag. Postulate that this dynamic system is stable (this postulate is widely accepted). Note the resulting restrictions on the parameters of the IS and LM curves. Then note the implications of those restrictions for the stability of the original system. Niehans applied this argument to the first (i.e., the fixed-price) model in Blinder and Solow; he found that it restricts their IS and LM curves so that their system is unstable when bonds are endogenous. I have applied it to the model consisting of equations (1)–(6), assuming that the price level adjusts to equilibrium instantly. It implies restrictions on the IS and LM parameters, which in turn require that $\Delta_B < 0$ in Table 1, that is, that when bonds are endogenous in (1)–(6) the system is unstable and $\partial P/\partial H$ is positive. (The same argument establishes stability when g is endogenous, confirming the conjecture above.)

Note that when H is endogenous, the discriminant $tr^2 A_H - 4\ det\ A_H$ can be either negative or positive, so cycles may or may not occur. When B is endogenous, if Δ_B is negative, the discriminant is positive, so there are no cycles.

VII. Instability when Bonds are Endogenous

Several other writers in the GBR literature have found a similar theoretical result, namely that stability is impossible (or un-likely) when bonds are endogenous, but certain (or likely) when money is endogenous. This result occurs in studies that use government purchases g as the government expenditure variable, including Blinder-Solow, Infante-Stein, and my 1978 paper as noted above, and Scarth and Pyle-Turnovsky. It also occurs in Tobin-Buiter (Sec. 6) and Buiter (1976, 1977) which use, as the government expenditure variable, government purchases plus government interest net of tax, denoted by g':

$$(9) \qquad g' = g + (1 - u)B/P$$

The policy that is unstable (or likely to be so) in these studies resembles a policy that has been advocated by some of the monetarists, that is, fix government purchases and tax-transfer schedules, make the money stock grow at a constant moderate rate, and allow any variation in deficits or surpluses to be covered by issuing or retiring government debt. For example, Milton Friedman says,

> The right policy—not alone for this episode but as a general rule—is to *let the quantity of money increase at a rate that can be maintained indefinitely without inflation* (about 5 per cent per year) and to keep taxes and spending at levels that will *balance the budget at high employment.* [p. 92]

It is not known whether the *U.S.* economy has stability properties like the models in these studies, but if it does, a policy of constant moderate growth of the money stock with fixed g or g', fixed tax-transfer rates, and endogenous bonds would appear to have stability problems.

The difficulty appears to be associated with the fact that when bonds are issued to finance a deficit, the deficit is not thereby reduced. First, if g is the expenditure variable held constant during the disequilibrium, the *GBR* equation (5) with taxes given by (2) shows that when the debt rises to cover a deficit, the deficit *increases* because of the increase in the term $(1 - u)B/P$ which represents interest payments net of tax. Thus the system is moved further from equilibrium, rather than

toward it. Second, if g' is the expenditure variable held constant, the term in B/P disappears from the *GBR*, which becomes

$$(10) \quad g' - uy - V/P = DH/P + DB/rP$$

Hence the deficit *does not change* as more bonds are issued, and so the system is not moved toward equilibrium.

VIII. Some Hope for Stability when Bonds are Endogenous

This suggests that a solution to the instability problem when bonds are endogenous might be to use a different government expenditure variable, namely, government purchases plus debt interest *gross* of tax, denoted by g'':

$$(11) \qquad g'' = g + B/P$$

(This suggestion was made independently by Frank De Leeuw in correspondence.) The *GBR* (5) then becomes the following:

$$(12) \quad g'' - uy - V/P - uB/P = \\ DH/P + DB/rP$$

In this case, when bonds are issued to finance a deficit with g'' constant, the term $(-uB/P)$ decreases algebraically, which *decreases* the deficit and moves the system toward equilibrium, *ceteris paribus*. What causes the difference, of course, is that any increase in debt interest must be counteracted by an equal decrease in government purchases, g.

Let us proceed to analyze the stability of the model when g'' is used as the expenditure variable rather than g. It is first necessary to replace g by $g'' - B/P$ not only in the original *GBR* (5) to obtain (12), but also in (1), (5'), and (5''). We shall make the same assumptions as in Section III, step (a) above, after replacing g by $g'' - B/P$ in the numerator of ϕ in (7). We shall again assume the equilibrium price level is positive; this is equivalent to $uf > g$ or g' or g'' in the three models, respectively. And we shall assume that $-uB - V > 0$, i.e., a price rise moves the budget toward surplus; see equation (12).

Table 2 summarizes the results for the model using g'' in the third row. For comparison, it also shows in the first and second rows

TABLE 2—STABILITY OF THE MODELS FOR THREE DIFFERENT GOVERNMENT EXPENDITURE VARIABLES AND VARIOUS CHOICES OF ENDOGENOUS POLICY VARIABLE

Government Expenditure Variable	Endogenous Policy Variable			
	V	g or g' or g''	H	B
g = Purchases of Goods and Services	Stable	Stable iff $\partial P/\partial H > 0$	Stable	Unstable if $\partial P/\partial H > 0$, because the condition that $\det A_B > 0$ is equivalent to $\partial P/\partial H < 0$
$g' = g$ + Interest Net of Tax $= g + (1 - u)B/P$	Stable iff $\partial P/\partial H > 0$	Stable iff $\partial P/\partial H > 0$	Stable	Unstable if $\partial P/\partial H > 0$, because the condition that $\det A_B$ be > 0 implies that $\partial P/\partial H = 0$[a]
$g'' = g$ + Interest Gross of Tax $= g + B/P$	Stable iff $\partial P/\partial H > 0$	Stable iff $\partial P/\partial H > 0$	Stable	Possibly stable: the condition that $\det A_B$ be > 0 is satisfied iff $\partial P/\partial H > 0$, but the condition that $tr\, A_B$ be < 0 is uncertain

Notes: See Table 1. The stability conditions above are obtained under the assumption that the equilibrium price level is positive. When g' or g'' is used instead of g, the expression $1 - u$ that appears in Table 1, in the four determinants in the first row above, and in the expressions for $\partial P/\partial H$ and $tr\, A_B$ in column B, is replaced respectively by zero or by $- u$.

[a]Here $\partial P/\partial H \neq 0$ iff $\det A_B = 0$. In cases like this where the linearized system is unstable because a zero value appears where stability would require a positive one, it sometimes happens that the original non-linear system is stable.

the results for the original model using g (taken from Table 1, last row), and for the model that uses g'. The third column shows that when H is endogenous, all three models are stable. The second column shows that when government expenditure is endogenous, stability in all three models is equivalent to a positive sign for $\partial P/\partial H$. The first column shows that when V is endogenous, the shift from g to either g' or g'' makes stability equivalent to a positive sign for $\partial P/\partial H$. And the fourth column shows that when B is endogenous, the shift from either g or g' to g'' reverses the previous relation between the sign of $\partial P/\partial H$ and the sign of the stability determinant: a positive sign for $\partial P/\partial H$ is now equivalent to a *positive* sign of that determinant, so that the system may now be stable, depending upon the trace condition (whose satisfaction is uncertain under our assumptions).

Suppose the first model in Blinder-Solow is modified to use g'', government purchases plus gross interest, as the expenditure variable. Then a similar argument shows that the model remains stable when money is endoge-

nous, and that when bonds are endogenous a positive sign for the equilibrium multiplier $\partial Y/\partial H$ is equivalent to stability, where Y is their income variable. Further, the Niehans (1977) argument applied to the Blinder-Solow model thus modified also indicates that it is definitely stable when either bonds or money is endogenous.

Tobin-Buiter (Sec. 6) found that their model with static expectations is definitely unstable when bonds are endogenous because the determinant of the characteristic equation is unambiguously negative. When that model is modified to use government purchases plus gross interest (rather than net interest, which they use), the sign of the determinant of the characteristic equation becomes uncertain so that stability is now possible.

We have found that in three models (see my 1978 paper; Blinder-Solow, first model; Tobin-Buiter, Sec. 6, static-expectations model), the use of g'', government purchases plus gross interest, as the expenditure variable weakens the conclusion that the stability determinants are negative and that the models are therefore unstable when bonds are endogenous, though it does not definitely establish stability except in the first Blinder-Solow model. Thus the above mentioned monetarist policy of fixing a moderate constant growth rate of the money stock with bonds as the endogenous policy variable is not yet completely rescued from the demon of instability, but it is given some hope.

IX. When is the Multiplier Equal to the Inverse of the Tax Rate?

A rather common result in the *GBR* literature is that the equilibrium multiplier effect of government expenditure on income is simply the inverse of marginal tax rate, $1/u$. This is a striking result, for the behavior parameters of the economy have no effect on it. However, it is unrealistically special. My 1968 paper and Blinder-Solow obtain it when the endogenous policy variable is high-powered money (but not when it is bonds) in a simple model where the price level is rigid, there is excess capacity, and the government expenditure variable is government purchases. Of course, such a result makes no practical sense except temporarily in a deep depression, for in reality prices are not rigid and capacity limits output.

Tobin-Buiter (Sec. 6) and Buiter (1976, 1977) obtain the same multiplier, $1/u$, when the endogenous policy variable is bonds in a full-employment model where prices and capacity are endogenous, bonds are short term, the tax-transfer system is proportional ($V = 0$, in my notation), and the government expenditure variable is government purchases plus interest net of tax (g' in my notation). Buiter (1976) shows that the same multiplier arises in his model when the endogenous variable is high-powered money. In fact the same is true of the Tobin-Buiter model, as is easily shown.

In general, when prices are endogenous and capacity limits output, the equilibrium multiplier effect of government expenditure on income is not equal to the inverse of the marginal tax rate. Two special features of the Tobin-Buiter and Buiter models combine to produce this special result. One is the assumption of a proportional tax system ($V = 0$). The other is the use of g', government purchases

plus net interest, as the expenditure variable. With these two modifications, the static-equilibrium balanced-budget version of the *GBR* in (5') becomes

$$(13) \qquad g' - uy = 0$$

From this it is clear that the multiplier $\partial y/\partial g'$ equals $1/u$ regardless of whether the endogenous policy variable is bonds or high-powered money. If a nonzero intercept V is introduced into their tax-transfer function, the multipliers $\partial Y/\partial g'$ for endogenous bonds and for endogenous high-powered money are no longer equal to each other or to $1/u$. The same occurs if the government expenditure variable g' is replaced by g or by g''.

X. When are Money-Financed Expenditures More Powerful than Bond-Financed Expenditures?

Blinder-Solow and Pyle-Turnovsky have inquired whether bond-financed expenditure is more expansionary than money-financed expenditure, and have concluded, respectively, that the answer is yes or maybe. They did so by comparing the long-run equilibrium multipliers for the two cases when the endogenous policy variable is bonds or high-powered money. Blinder-Solow compared multiplier effects on income (recall they assumed prices fixed), while Pyle-Turnovsky compared multiplier effects on the inflation rate. This method is appropriate only if the system is stable under both endogenous bonds and endogenous money so that when disturbed, it does converge to the state that is described by the multipliers. However, we have seen reason to believe that the Blinder-Solow first model is unstable when bonds are endogenous. If so, the equilibrium multiplier for bond finance (though inappropriate because of instability) is less than $1/u$, the equilibrium multiplier for money finance. The Pyle-Turnovsky equilibrium multipliers may also be inappropriate because they find that their system may be unstable under either bond finance or money finance, more likely so under bond finance.

When the Blinder-Solow first model is modified to use g'', government purchases plus gross interest, as the expenditure variable, and when the multiplier $\partial Y/\partial H$ is positive, the model is stable and the multiplier for bond finance (now appropriate because of stability) becomes less than $1/u$, the multiplier for the money finance. Thus in this case money finance is unambiguously more powerful than bond finance. When the model in my 1978 paper is modified in the same way, the price multiplier $\partial P/\partial g''$ for bond finance (now appropriate if bond finance is stable, which it may be) also becomes less than the price multiplier $\partial P/\partial g''$ for money finance. Thus also in this case money finance is more powerful than bond finance if the latter is stable.

XI. Instability in Nominal Terms is Compatible with Stability in Real Terms

Consider the original model of equations (1)–(6) again, but now assume (as promised earlier) that government purchases exceed the revenue brought in by the marginal tax transfer rate applied to capacity income, so that $g > uf$. Then, as noted earlier, the equilibrium price level in (8) becomes negative, and is irrelevant for the economy's actual behavior.

Consider the case where high-powered money H is endogenous, with bonds B and nominal taxes less transfers V fixed. Then the determinant condition for stability is satisfied, but the trace condition is violated at the negative equilibrium price, which is therefore unstable (recall Table 1, column H). There is a continual deficit which is financed by issuing money. The price level rises without limit as does the money stock. The real values of bond interest B/P and autonomous taxes less transfers V/P go to zero as P goes to infinity. Thus the system approaches one in which taxes less transfers are strictly proportional to income and there is no government debt.

There may be a stable inflationary equilibrium path along which real balances H/P and the inflation rate θ are constant and the constant real deficit $g - uy$ is financed by the so-called inflation tax yielding a real "revenue" of $\theta H/P$. In that case the inflationary-equilibrium GBR in (5") becomes

$$(14) \qquad g - uy = \theta H/P$$

This situation can occur with the expected

inflation rate π equal to the actual rate θ, provided that the deficit is small enough so that there exists a pair of noncomplex values of the inflation rate and real balances demanded such that their product $\theta H/P$ can equal the deficit. If the deficit is too large, it cannot be financed by issuing money at a steady rate because the attempt to do so will create such a rapid inflation that real balances, which are the taxable base of the inflation tax, are driven down too low. Mathematically, we are seeking a simultaneous solution to equations (14) and (7) for the two variables θ and H/P, after modifying (7) by dropping out the terms in V/P and B/P (which go to zero), replacing income y by capacity f and replacing the expected inflation rate π by the actual rate θ. There are two solutions because (14) is a hyperbola while (7) is linear. Suppose (7) traverses the first quadrant of the $(\theta, H/P)$ space. It slopes negatively. The lines intersect twice in the first quadrant, or have a single tangency point there, or else don't intersect at all. If they don't intersect, the solutions are complex numbers and there is no equilibrium for θ and H/P in the domain of real numbers. If they do intersect, both solutions are real and positive. Given the expected inflation rate, only one solution can be attained. It is the one whose inflation rate is expected. The stability analysis is simplified because the two dynamic variables DH and DP can be combined into one, $D(H/P)$, so that there is only a single dynamic equation in the system. Under our assumptions it is easy to show that this equilibrium is stable.

A similar situation arises if the deficit is financed not by money alone, but by money and bonds in a fixed proportion, except that then the real debt approaches a positive equilibrium value rather than zero. In each case there is no stable static equilibrium for the price level and nominal income and asset holdings, but there may be one for the inflation rate and real income and asset holdings.

A parallel situation also arises in the presence of steady-state real aggregate growth, where there is no stable equilibrium for aggregate real income, but there may be one for per capita real income.

XII. GBR Models Provide an Impartial View of the Monetarist-Fiscalist Controversy

The theory of *GBR* models does not require the extreme monetarist conclusion that the effect of a macro-economic policy change depends solely upon what happens to the stock of money. Nor does it require the extreme fiscalist conclusion that the effect of a macro-economic policy change is independent of what happens to the stock of money. It suggests that changes in the money stock, the debt, government purchases, transfers, and taxes all have effects, depending on which variables are fixed and which are allowed to vary endogenously.

XIII. Limitations

This paper is subject to many limitations. There is no foreign sector. There is no banking sector and no conventional quantity of money. Dynamic systems of at most two differential equations are considered. Endogenous short-run expectations about prices and inflation are not considered. Steady-state real growth paths are barely mentioned. There are no lags in the adjustment of output to aggregate demand. The Phillips curve is assumed vertical in the long run. Empirical problems and results are not considered. There is no discussion of discretionary stabilization policy or of policy optimization.

REFERENCES

A. S. Blinder and R. M. Solow, "Does Fiscal Policy Matter?," *J. Publ. Econ.*, Nov. 1973, *2*, 319–37; "Does Fiscal Policy Matter? A Correction," *J. Publ. Econ.*, Jan./Feb. 1976, *5*, 183–84.

K. Brunner and A. H. Meltzer, "An Aggregate Theory for a Closed Economy," in Jerome L. Stein, ed., *Monetarism*, Amsterdam 1976, 69–103.

W. H. Buiter, "Capacity Constraints, Government Financing and the Short Run and Long Run Effects of Fiscal Policy," mimeo., Princeton Univ. 1976.

———, "An Integration of Short Run Neo-Keynesian Analysis and Growth Theory," *De Economist*, No. 3, 1977, *125*, 340–59.

C. F. Christ, "A Simple Macroeconomic Model with a Government Budget Restraint," *J. Polit. Econ.*, Jan./Feb. 1968, *76*, 53–67.

———, "Some Dynamic Theory of Macroeconomic Policy Effects on Income and Prices under the Government Budget Restraint," *J. Monet. Econ.*, Jan. 1978, *4*, 45–70.

D. A. Currie, "The Government Budget Constraint and Inflation: Some Dynamic Implications," disc. paper, Queen Mary College, London 1976.

———, "Macroeconomic Policy and Government Financing," Association of University Teachers of Economics *Proceedings*, 1977.

Milton Friedman, *An Economist's Protest*, Glen Ridge 1972, 41; reprinted from *Newsweek*, October 17, 1966, p. 92.

E. F. Infante and J. L. Stein, "Does Fiscal Policy Matter?," *J. Monet. Econ.*, Nov. 1976, *2*, 473–500.

Jürg Niehans, "Monetary Policy with Full Stock Adjustment," *Z. Wirtsch. Sozialwiss.*, No.1, 1974, 17–43.

———, "A Comment on Stabilization Paradoxes," in Horst Albach, Ernst Helmstadter and Rudolf Henn, eds., *Quantitative Wirtschaftsforschung, Wilhelm Krelle zum 60. Geburtstag*, Tubingen 1977, 513–21.

———, *The Theory of Money*, Baltimore 1978.

D. H. Pyle and S. J. Turnovsky, "The Dynamics of Government Policy in an Inflationary Economy," *J. Money, Credit, Banking*, Nov. 1976, *8*, 411–37.

W. M. Scarth, "The Effects on Economic Stability of Indexing the Tax System and Government Bond Yields for Inflation," *Can. J. Econ.*, Aug. 1975, *8*, 383–98.

J. Tobin and W. H. Buiter, "Long-Run Effects of Fiscal and Monetary Policy on Aggregate Demand," in Jerome L. Stein, ed., *Monetarism*, Amsterdam 1976, 273–309.

Stephen J. Turnovsky, *Macroeconomic Analysis and Stabilization Policy*, Cambridge 1977.

———, "Macroeconomic Dynamics and Growth in a Monetary Economy," *J. Money, Credit, Banking*, Feb. 1978, *10*, 1–26.

[13]

CHANGES IN THE FINANCING OF THE FEDERAL DEBT AND THEIR IMPACT ON THE U.S. ECONOMY, 1948-90

By Carl F. Christ*

CONTENTS

TABLES

*The Johns Hopkins University.

(93)

94

ACKNOWLEDGMENTS

I am especially indebted to Elizabeth Fogler of the Flow of Funds Section of the Federal Reserve staff for patient and detailed help in understanding the flow of funds accounts, including the definitions of the sectors and of the myriad stock, flow, and discrepancy items that appear, and for preparing the computer-printed tables and charts below according to my instructions. Stephen Taylor and Judith Ziobro of the Flow of Funds Section and Stanley Sigel, formerly of that section and now Assistant to the Board, were also very helpful. Any conceptual errors are my responsibility.

George Krumbhaar, Louis Maccini, Hyman Minsky, William Poole, Timothy Roth, Stephen Taylor, and James Tobin read an early draft of this paper and made valuable suggestions.

I. SUMMARY, INTRODUCTION, AND MAIN RECOMMENDATIONS

A. Summary

The current U.S. inflation could not have happened without an important and substantial change in the financing of the Federal debt. This change was begun in 1961, and was accelerated after 1965. It produced a temporary boom and a short-run improvement in unemployment in 1966–69, but that improvement has long since worn off.

95

In the 1970's we were left with considerably more inflation than in 1960, and no better unemployment.

What was this important change in U.S. Government debt financing? It was a substantial increase in the Federal Reserve's rate of purchases of Treasury securities. Such purchases are paid for chiefly with newly created additions to the monetary base (high powered money), created by the Federal Reserve for that purpose. Thus the growth rate of the monetary base was substantially increased, especially after 1965. That is a sure recipe for inflation, whatever its other effects.

Federal budget deficits have become more common since 1965. And their size in proportion to gross national product (GNP) has grown. Indeed, in 1975 the deficit was 4.6 percent of GNP, a higher percentage even than during the Great Depression of the thirties. Deficits are not very inflationary as long as they are financed by sales of securities to private and foreign investors rather than to the Federal Reserve. However, deficits do increase the amount of debt that has to be financed. This may lead the Federal Reserve to buy more of it than price stability would dictate. Also, large persistent deficits are likely to result in the crowding out of some private capital investment, thus reducing future growth.

The period since World War II falls into three parts, concerning macro-economic policy. First, from 1948 to 1960 the growth rate of the monetary base was kept under 1 percent a year on the average, and the average inflation rate measured by the consumer price index (CPI) was under 2 percent a year. Second, in 1961–65 there was a transition to more rapid growth of the monetary base. Third, from 1966 to October 1979, the growth rate of the monetary base was further increased, exceeding 8 percent a year in the late seventies, and the inflation rate rose to the same range.

It is perfectly possible to stop inflation and achieve an approximately constant price level. What is required is to reduce the use of monetary expansion as a means of financing the Federal debt. We should return to very slow and fairly steady growth rates for the monetary base and other stocks of money. They should average about 1 to 3 percent a year after a transition phase. A gradual policy carried out over a period of 5 to 10 years will be best. It will begin to be successful after we pass through one recession and recovery without abandoning it, so that the public will believe that it will be adhered to.

At this writing the Federal Reserve appears to have embarked on such a policy beginning in October 1979. At first it is likely to cause a temporary reduction in output and employment (the reverse of the 1966–69 boom). Such adverse cyclical effects can be ameliorated by a temporary slowdown in the reduction of monetary growth (provided the long-run goal is met) and by a temporary budget deficit.

A reduction in the average level of Federal budget deficits would be desirable, to at most about 0.5 percent of GNP on the average over the business cycle. The budget should not be balanced at all times. To ameliorate the business cycle, it should be in deficit during recessions and in balance or in surplus during prosperity.

This paper supports these statements with a description of the relationships between Federal debt financing and such important variables as output, employment, the several stocks of money, inflation, interest rates, the exchange rate, and the balance of payments;

with annual data on the Federal deficit and its financing from 1946 through 1979, in nominal and real terms and as a ratio to GNP; and with an analysis of our present difficult macroeconomic situation, how we got into it, and how we can get out of it. Conditional predictions are offered for the period from 1980 to 1990.

B. Introduction

The financing of the Federal debt is of high importance to the economy. This is because of its close direct relations with (a) the amount of Federal debt securities in domestic private and foreign hands, (b) the monetary base (sometimes called the high powered money stock), (c) several other stocks of money, and (d) the country's stock of gold, SDR's and foreign exchange, Through these asset stocks and in other ways, the Federal debt is related to such important variables as employment, output, the rate of inflation, interest rates, and the international value of the dollar.

In sections II and III we describe in a simplified way the essential nature of the relationships between Federal debt financing and these important asset stocks. In section II we emphasize the domestic relationships, temporarily assuming for simplicity that the U.S. is involved in no international claims or transactions. In section III we bring economic relations with the rest of the world into the picture. In each of these sections we make use of a table of intersectoral claims that embodies the balance sheets of each of the four sectors into which we divide the economy. From the year-to-year change in the balance sheet of the U.S. Government sector (including the Federal Reserve System) is derived an important relationship called the *Government budget restraint*. It says that the Government's decisions about spending, taxing, printing money, borrowing, spending reserves of gold and foreign exchange, etc., cannot all be made independently. This is because the total of government spending must be equal to the total of government financing from all sources. Such restraint plays a leading role in explaining the relations between the financing of the Federal debt and the behavior of the economy.

In section IV we present annual data for the variables in the U.S. Government budget restraint for 1946 through 1979. They are based on the flow of funds accounts that are published by the Federal Reserve System.

In section V we discuss the macroeconomic effects of Federal debt financing upon the stocks of money, inflation, employment, interest rates, exchange rates, and the balance of payments.

In section VI we venture some conditional projections for the U.S. economy to 1990, indicating what kinds of policies will lead to the perpetuation or acceleration of inflation, and what kinds will lead to price stability.

The appendix describes the manner in which we obtained the consolidated U.S. Government and Federal Reserve sector by combining the U.S. Government sector and the monetary authorities sector as they are defined in the flow of funds accounts.

A supplementary note discusses some aspects of Federal debt management that are related, but not central, to the subject of this paper.

97

C. Main Recommendations

A number of recommendations are made in the course of this paper. For convenience the main ones are given here, together with a reference to the subsection where each may be found:

1. For the long run, the Federal Reserve should provide noninflationary and fairly steady growth of the stocks of money. To reach this long-run state, the growth rates of the money stocks must be reduced from their recent range of 6 to 10 percent a year to their 1948–60 range of around 1 to 3 percent a year. (The noninflationary growth rates will not be the same for the several stocks of money.) This transition should be accomplished gradually, over a period of 5 to 10 years, by small reductions averaging 0.5 to 1 percent each year. The transition should not be reversed in the event of a recession, but it could be temporarily slowed, provided the long-run goal is met. (See section I.A, V.D, V.E, and VI.)

2. For the short run, the money stocks should not be permitted to rise very fast in booms, nor to decline during recessions. (During the transition mentioned just above, they should not be permitted to decline more rapidly in recession than at other times.) (See section I.A. and V.D.)

3. For the long run, the Congress should reduce the frequency and average size of Federal budget deficits, so that on the average over the business cycle they amount to at most about 0.5 percent of gross national product (GNP). (See section I.A., V.D, V.E, and VI.)

4. For the short run, the size of the deficit should not be made the same every year. In particular, a Constitutional amendment to require a balanced budget every year would be pernicious. There should be deficits during recessions, and surpluses or roughly balanced budgets during business cycle peaks. (See section I.A, V.E, and VI.)

5. The Federal Reserve should not attempt to control interest rates directly, but rather should secure their decline by following recommendation 1 above. (See section V.F.)

6. The Congress should provide for the gradual increase and final abolition of statutory ceilings on interest rates (See section V.G. and supplementary note.)

7. The minimum wage law should be abolished, or at least amended to exclude teenagers and young adults. (See section VI.)

8. Unemployment compensation should be made to start after a few weeks of unemployment rather than immediately, and to continue longer than at present. (See section VI.)

II. The Essential Relation Between the Federal Deficit and Asset Stocks in a Closed Economy

A. Introduction

In sections II and III we describe in a simplified way the important relationship between Federal debt financing and the asset stocks that influence inflation, output, employment, interest rates, and

98

international economic events. The essence of this relationship is most clearly seen in an economy that is closed to all foreign transactions. This is the subject of section II. Foreign transactions are introduced in section III.

There are three main points in section II concerning a closed economy. First, the Congress and the executive branch, together with the private sector, determine the Federal budget deficit (or surplus). Second, the deficit (or surplus) is matched by an equal net increase (or decrease) in the sum of private holdings of Federal debt plus the monetary base. Third, the Federal Reserve cannot control this sum, but does control its composition as between private holdings of Federal debt and the monetary base.

We will argue later that over any long period, by its control of the monetary base, the Federal Reserve controls the rates of growth of the other money stocks and the rate of inflation.

B. Balance Sheets for a Simple Closed Economy

In section II we will consider only the bare essentials of monetary and fiscal policy action in a closed economy. The Federal Government makes expenditures and sets tax rates. It issues debt if it has a deficit, and retires debt if it has a surplus. That is all we permit it to do in this section. In particular, it holds no assets.

The Federal Reserve holds a portfolio of Federal Government securities, balanced by a liabliity in the form of the monetary base. The base is held partly by banks in the form of reserves and partly by nonbank private agents in the form of currency. The Federal Reserve buys and sells Federal securities, issuing new additions to the monetary base when it buys, and retiring part of the monetary base when it sells. That is all we permit it to do in this section.

The rest of the domestic economy will be called the private sector. It holds all of the monetary base, and some of the outstanding Federal securities (those not held by the Federal Reserve). It goes about its business of producing, consuming, saving, and investing. Our consolidation of the private banks and all other private agents in a single private sector serves well to bring out the main points of sections II and III, but of course it suppresses detail that is useful for other purposes.

The balance sheets of all three sectors are displayed in table 2.1. There is a row for each sector, containing its liabilities, and a column for each sector, containing its assets. There are a row and a column for a fictitious sector called the capital account which by construction holds the net worths of all other sectors as its assets and carries all physical assets as its liabilities. Every balance-sheet item is a claim of some sector against another. All claims of A against B are in A's column and B's row, while all claims of B against A are in B's column and A's row. Thus the balance sheet of any sector can be read from its column (assets) and row (liabilities). For example, the private sector's balance sheet can be read as follows:

Private sector assets:
    Treasury securities_____
    Monetary base_____
    Physical assets_____

Private sector liabilities:
    Net worth.

Total assets.

Total liabilities.

99

TABLE 2.1.—INTERSECTORAL CLAIMS IN A SIMPLIFIED CLOSED ECONOMY

	Assets of—				
	Private sector	Federal Government (excluding Federal Reserve)	Federal Reserve	Capital account	Total
Liabilities of—					
Private sector		0	0	Net worth of private sector.	Net worth.
Federal Government (excluding Federal.	Federal securities held by private sector.		Federal securities held by Federal Reserve.	Net worth of Federal Government (negative).	Total Federal securities plus net worth of Federal Government equals 0.
Federal Reserve	Monetary base	0		0	Monetary base.
Capital account	Physical assets	0	0		Physical assets.
Total	Federal securities held by private sector plus monetary base plus physical assets.	0	Federal securities held by Federal Reserve.	Net worth of private sector plus net worth of Federal Government.	Grand total.

Note: Each sector's balance sheet can be read from this table, assets from the sector's column, and liabilities from its row.

C. The Government Budget Restraint for a Simple Closed Economy

We are now ready to develop the relation of the Federal budget deficit or surplus to private holdings of Federal debt and the monetary base.

First, note that the Federal debt came into existence because of Federal deficits in the past. Further deficits increase the debt, and surpluses decrease it. The debt is held partly by the private sector and partly by the Federal Reserve (as shown by the Government sector's row in table 2.1). Therefore we have this simple equation:

Federal deficit=net increase in combined holdings of Federal debt by the private sector and the Federal Reserve   (2.1)

This equation can equally well be expressed in terms of the Federal surplus, rather than the deficit, thus:

Federal surplu=net decrease in combined holdings of Federal debt by the private sector and the Federal Reserve   (2.2)

Since a negative surplus is the same as a positive deficit, and vice versa, it is clear that equations (2.1) and (2.2) say the same thing: either one can be obtained by multiplying both sides of the other by −1. When the budget is in deficit, both sides of (2.1) are positive numbers, and both sides of (2.2) are negative. When the budget is in surplus, the reverse is true. In what follows, we will usually use (2.1) and speak of the deficit, even when it is negative. But sometimes, especially when discussing the national income accounts and the flow of funds accounts, we will follow their practice and use (2.2), and speak of the surplus, even when it is negative.

The deficit is determined by the Congress and the Executive Branch, interacting with the private sector. Therefore, because of equation (2.1), the same process determines the net increase of the combined Federal debt holdings by the private sector and the Federal Reserve.

The essential function of the Federal Reserve is to decide how much of this combined total of Federal debt is to be held by the private sector, and (by subtraction) how much is to be held by the Federal Reserve itself. It does this by buying or selling Federal securities in return for high powered money. When it buys, it creates additional new high powered money, and when it sells, it retires high powered money, in amounts equal to the value of the purchase or sale. Therefore we have another simple equation:

increase in Federal Reserve holdings of Federal debt equals increase in the monetary base   (2. 3)

Now replace the increase in the Federal Reserve's holdings of Federal debt in (2.1) by the equal increase in the monetary base from (2.3), and obtain the following equation:

Federal deficit equals increase in Federal debt holdings by the private sector plus increase in the monetary base   (2. 4)

This important relation is called the *Government budget restraint*. It says (in this simplified world) that the budget deficit must be equal to the increase in the total of two types of asset held by the private sector: Federal securities and the monetary base.

Another useful interpretation of the Government budget restraint follows. Consolidate the U.S. Government and the Federal Reserve into a single sector, netting out the only claim between them (Federal debt). Next, take the first difference (that is, the year-to-year change) of the balance sheet of this consolidated government sector. Finally, replace the net increase in the sector's net worth by the negative of the Federal budget deficit. The result is the Government budget restraint (2.4).

To summarize, the role of the Congress and the Executive is to control the size of the deficit, and therefore to control the change in the private sector's total holdings of Federal debt and monetary base, without controlling the composition of the total. The role of the Federal Reserve is to control the mix of this total as between privately held government debt and the monetary base, without controlling the total itself. This kind of division of responsibility requires cooperation to achieve success.

The budget deficit and the monetary base are among the most important variables that economic policy deals with. Their effects on employment, output, inflation, interest rates, and international economic events will be dealt with in later sections. But first, in section III, we must take international transactions and claims into account.

III. The Essential Relation Between the Federal Deficit and Asset Stocks in an Open Economy

A. Introduction

In this section we extend the discussion to an economy that is open to foreign transactions. The results are similar to those obtained in section II for a closed economy, except that there is now an additional market, the foreign exchange market. The authorities can either fix the exchange rate and let the balance of payments fluctuate, or fix the balance of payments at zero and let the exchange rate float freely, or follow a middle course: A managed (or "dirty") float.

B. Balance Sheets for a Simple Open Economy

In section III we consider the bare essentials of monetary and fiscal policy action in an economy that is open to foreign transactions, but is otherwise as simple as the one in section II. The foreign sector (consolidated public and private) is assumed to hold some of our country's government debt and monetary base, as well as some physical assets; its liabilities consist of its net worth and some of its money which is held by our government as a foreign exchange reserve. Table 3.1 shows the assets (in columns) and liabilities (in rows) of each sector, on the same plan as table 2.1. Of course, table 3.1 has a new row and column representing the foreign sector.

TABLE 3.1.—INTERSECTORAL CLAIMS IN A SIMPLIFIED OPEN ECONOMY

| Liabilities of— | Assets of— | | | | |
	Private sector	Federal Government (including Federal Reserve)	Foreign sector	Capital account	Total
Private sector		0	0	Net worth of private sector.	Net worth.
Federal Government (including Federal Reserve).	Private holdings of monetary base and Federal securities.		Foreign holdings of monetary base and Federal securities.	Net worth of Government sector.	Total monetary base plus Federal securities. plus net worth of Government sector.
Foreign sector	0	Foreign exchange reserves.		Net worth of foreign sector.	Foreign exchange reserves plus foreign net worth.
Capital account	Private physical assets.	0	Foreign physical assets.		Total physical assets.
Total	Private holdings of monetary base, Federal securities, plus physical assets.	Foreign exchange reserves.	Foreign holdings of monetary base, Federal securities, plus physical assets.	Total net worth.	Grand total.

Note: Each sector's balance sheet can be read from this table, assets from the sector's column and liabilities from its row.

For convenience we have consolidated the Federal Government and Federal Reserve sectors into a single sector. This consolidation causes no difficulty, for the claims and transactions that are thus netted out are of no great interest for our purpose. Recall that the important relationship in section II, the Government budget restraint (2.4), deals with the consolidated Government sector.

The balance sheet of each sector can be read from Table 3.1. For example, the balance sheet of the consolidated Government sector can be read as follows:

Government assets:
   foreign exchange reserves_____

Government liabilities:
   monetary base (held by private and foreign sectors).
   Federal Government debt (held by private and foreign sectors).
   Government net worth (negative).

Total assets.   Total liabilities.

C. *The Government Budget Restraint for a Simple Open Economy*

We are now ready to present the relation of the Federal deficit to the amounts of private and foreign holdings of Federal debt, the monetary base, and the stock of foreign exchange reserves. As before, this

102

relation is the first difference (i.e., the year-to-year change) of the balance sheet of the consolidated Government sector, thus:

Federal deficit = increase in private and foreign holdings of Federal debt + increase in the monetary base — increase in foreign exchange reserves   (3.1)

As before, it is called the Government budget restraint. This time it says (in this still simplified world) that the Federal deficit must be equal to the increase in the net total of Federal debt and monetary base held by the private and foreign sectors minus the increase in U.S. foreign exchange reserves.

As before, the Congress and the Executive (interacting with the private sector and now with the foreign sector too) determine the size of the budget deficit and therefore determine the net flow given by the right side of the Government budget restrait (3.1)without determining its composition. As before, the Federal Reserve's role is to control the composition of the net asset total whose net increase appears as the right side of (3.1), without controlling the total itself. Again there is a division of responsibility.

But now the Federal Reserve has three types of assets to deal with and two degrees of freedom in its actions, rather than (as in the closed economy of section II) two types of asset and one degree of freedom. It can still buy and sell Federal securities in return for high powered money, as before, but now it can also buy and sell foreign exchange as well.

Under a fixed exchange rate, one degree of freedom is used up in choosing the rate and in buying and selling whatever amounts of foreign exchange will maintain that rate; the other degree of freedom allows the Federal Reserve to buy or sell Federal securities in return for high powered money as in a closed economy.

Under a freely (cleanly) floating exchange rate, one degree of freedom is used up in holding foreign exchange reserves constant (possibly zero) so that the rate will be determined freely by market forces. The other degree of freedom is available as before for trading Federal securities for high powered money.

Under the more general situation of a managed (or "dirty") float, the Federal Reserve can determine the levels of any two of the three assets in the Government budget restraint (3.1); namely, Federal securities in private and foreign hands, the monetary base, and U.S. foreign exchange reserves. The third asset level will be determined by the operation of the Government budget restraint and past levels of the three assets.[1]

D. A Net Surplus Identity for an Open Economy

For any open economy, national accounting conventions require that the surpluses and deficits of the three sectors (private, government, and foreign) be related as follows:

excess of private investment over private saving plus government budget deficit plus excess of exports over imports equals 0 (3.2)

---

[1] The five preceding paragraphs of this subsection are written for the case where the Federal Reserve, not the Treasury, holds the foreign exchange reserves and deals on the foreign exchange market. If the Treasury does this, instead of the Federal Reserve, the balance sheets in table 3.1 and the Government budget restraint (3.1) are not affected, because we have consolidated the Federal Reserve with the Government; the only difference would be that the Federal Reserve would lose the degree of freedom representing foreign exchange transactions, and the Treasury would gain it.

103

This is because GNP can be expressed either as the sum of consumption plus private gross investment plus government purchases of goods and services plus net exports, or as the sum of consumption plus private gross saving plus taxes less transfers. Subtracting one of these sums from the other and rearranging terms results in equation (3.2). Of course private saving and private investment must both be defined in the same way with respect to depreciation: either both gross or both net. If the deficit in (3.2) applies to the Federal Government only, then State and local governments must be included in the private sector (as is done in this paper).

Equation (3.2) is a useful reminder that policy actions influencing the Government budget deficit must also influence the deficit and/or surplus of one or both of the other two sectors. In the closed economy of section II equation (3.2) would always hold, but the excess of exports over imports would always be zero.

IV. Financing the U.S. Government Deficit, 1946–79

A. Introduction

In sections II and III we considered the bare essentials of fiscal and monetary policy action. We found that fiscal actions, interacting with other actions, determine the budget deficit. The deficit then determines (is equal to) the increase in the net liabilities of the consolidated government sector that are held by the private sector and the rest of the world. The three important assets and liabilities that we considered in section III were the Federal debt in private and foreign hands, the monetary base, and U.S. foreign exchange reserves. In section IV we develop the corresponding relation for the actual U.S. economy.

The relationship that will emerge from section IV gives the Federal budget deficit (NIA basis) as the sum of the items shown (with appropriate algerbraic signs) in table 4.1. Lines 5, 6, and 7 correspond to the three terms on the right side of equation (3.1). The remaining items in table 4.1 were assumed away for simplicity in the discussion of sections II and III. They will be explained below.

TABLE 4.1.—U.S. GOVERNMENT BUDGET RESTRAINT, SHOWING THE FINANCING OF THE U.S. GOVERNMENT DEFICIT, WITH DATA FOR 1979

[In billions of dollars per year]

Line	Add or subtract	Item	1979 flow
1		Total: U.S. Government deficit, national income accounting (NIA) basis	11.450
2	Subtract	Increase in Treasury deposits at commercial banks	.490
3	Subtract	Increase in Federal Reserve loans to member banks	.282
4	Subtract	Increase in U.S. Government loans except to member banks	30.400
5	Subtract	Increase in U.S. reserves of gold, SDR's, and foreign exchange	−.578
6	Add	Increase in the monetary base (high powered money)	9.524
7	Add	Increase in U.S. Government debt held in private and foreign hands	30.320
8	Add	Mineral rights sales by U.S. Government	4.745
9	Add	Increase in financial net worth of monetary authorities	.390
10	Subtract	Statistical discrepancy between national income accounts (NIA) and flow of funds accounts (FofF)	2.935

Source: Table 4.3. See text of section IV.B for explanation.

104

We use the national income accounts (NIA) definition of the budget deficit. We use the flow of funds (FofF) accounts for the U.S. Government and the monetary authorities,[2] which we consolidate into a single government sector as in table 3.1. In table 4.3 we present annual data for the period from 1946 through 1979, corresponding to table 4.1, showing in detail how the Federal deficit was financed. In section V we use these data to interpret the change from relatively stable prices in 1948–60 to continuous inflation in 1966–79. In section VI we venture some projections for 1980–90, indicating what types of financing will be consistent with continued inflation and what types will be consistent with a return to price stability. Output, employment, interest rates, and the international value of the dollar will also be considered.

B. Derivation of the Empirical U.S. Government Budget Restraint

The U.S. Government budget restraint, which shows the financing of the budget deficit as in table 4.1, is derived as follows from NIA and FofF data. In the derivation we follow the official statistics and speak of the surplus rather than the deficit. At the end of the derivation we will reverse all the signs to obtain the Government budget restraint in terms of the deficit.

The FofF accounts are used because they provide consistent stock and flow accounts for both the U.S. Government and the monetary authorities, which we want to consolidate into a single sector.[3]

Step one in the derivation is to reconcile the U.S. Government surplus on the NIA basis with the change in the financial net worth of the U.S. Government of the FofF basis. This has already been done in the FofF accounts as follows. (The figures accompanying the next several equations are flows for the year 1979 in billions of dollars, from table A. 2.)[4]

> U.S. Govt surplus (NIA basis) (−11.450) equals increase in life and retirement insurance reserves (8.303) minus mineral rights sales by U.S. Government (4.745) plus FofF discrepancy (2.935) plus increase in financial net worth of U.S. Government (−17.943)   (4.1)

Note that the FofF Accounts ignore nonfinancial assets altogether. That is, the FofF balance sheet lists only financial assets on its asset side, and shows financial net worth rather than total net worth on its liability side; financial net worth is defined as total net worth minus the value of nonfinancial assets. Thus the balance sheet still balances.

---

[2] See Board of Governors [1975] for explanation, and [1976] or [1978] for tables of annual stock and flow data.

[3] In the FofF accounts, the monetary authorities sector is defined as the Federal Reserve plus the monetary accounts of the Treasury; the latter are accordingly not included in the U.S. Government sector in the FofF accounts. This causes us no difficulty, because we are interested in the consolidation of the two accounts, which is not affected by the transfer of the Treasury's monetary accounts.

[4] Several points should be noted about this relationship. First, annual data for it can be found in the FofF table of annual flows for the U.S. Government sector, lines 10, 11, 13, 36, and 15; see Board of Governors [1976], pages 22–24, or [1978], table 46. Updated data for 1946–79 can be found below in table A.2, lines 48–52. Second, the item that is here called "increase in financial net worth of U.S. Government" is called "net financial investment" [of the U.S. Government] in the FofF publications just cited. Third, the item "increase in life and retirement insurance reserves" refers to reserves of the U.S. Government employees' insurance system and the railroad retirement insurance system, but not social security. (See Board of Governors [1975], p. 31.) Fourth, the item "mineral rights sales of U.S. Government" consists mainly of receipts from offshore oil leases. It is not included in government receipts on the NIA basis (presumably because it is not a payment for productive services rendered by factors of production), but it is treated as revenue in the FofF accounts. Fifth, the remaining discrepancy is discussed in Board of Governors [1975], pp. 30–34.

Step two is to consolidate the FofF balance sheet accounts of the U.S. Government sector and the monetary authorities sector by netting out all claims between them so that the only claims vis-a-vis the consolidated sector are claims vis-a-vis the private sector, the foreign sector, and the capital account. Details of the consolidation are given in the appendix. The result is the following balance sheet equation for the consolidated U.S. Government and monetary authorities sector.[5]

> Treasury deposits at commercial banks plus member bank borrowing plus U.S. Government loans except to member banks plus gold, SDR's, and foreign exchange equals monetary base plus U.S. Government debt in private and foreign hands plus life and retirement insurance reserves plus financial net worth of U.S. Government plus financial net worth of monetary authorities (4.2)

The network of intersectoral claims corresponding to this consolidation is given in table 4.2.

TABLE 4.2.—INTERSECTORAL CLAIMS UNDERLYING THE U.S. GOVERNMENT BUDGET RESTRAINT IN TABLE 4.1

Liabilities of—	Financial assets of—			
	Private domestic sector	Government sector including monetary authorities	Foreign sector	Capital account excluding physical assets
Private domestic sector		Treasury deposits at commercial banks; loans to member banks; U.S. Government loans to private domestic sector.	0	Financial net worth (private domestic).
Government sector including monetary authorities.	Monetary base privately held; U.S. Government debt privately held; life and retirement insurance reserves.		Monetary base held by foreign sector; U.S. Government debt held by foreign sector.	Financial net worth of U.S. Government including monetary authorities.
Foreign sector	0	U.S. Government loans to foreign sector; U.S. foreign exchange, gold, and SDR reserves.		Financial net worth of foreign sector.
Capital account excluding physical assets.	0	0	0	

Note: Each sector's financial balance sheet can be read from this table, financial assets from the sector's column and liabilities from its row. In order to save space, the row and column totals are not printed.

Step three is to solve the foregoing balance sheet equation (4.2) for the financial net worth of the consolidated U.S. Government and monetary authorities sector, thus:

> Financial net worth of U.S. government plus financial net worth of monetary authorities equals Treasury deposits at commercial banks plus member bank borrowing plus U.S. government loans except to member banks plus gold, SDR's, and foreign exchange minus monetary base minus U.S. government debt in private and foreign hands minus life and retirement insurance reserves (4.3)

---

[5] The item "gold, SDR's, and foreign exchange" includes the IMF gold tranche of the United States. Data for equations (4.2)–(4.3) are in table A.1, lines 56–61, 49, 52 and 54.

106

Step four is to write down the annual flows version of the preceding consolidated U.S. Government sector balance sheet equation (4.3): [6]
Increase in financial net worth of U.S. government (−17.943) plus increase in financial net worth of monetary authorities (0.390) equals increase in Treasury deposits at commercial banks (0.490) plus member bank borrowing (0.282) plus U.S. government lending except to member banks (30.400) plus increase in gold, SDR's and foreign exchange (−.578) minus increase in the monetary base (9.524) minus increase in U.S. government debt in private and foreign hands (30.320) minus increase in life and retirement insurance reserves (8.303)   (4.4)

Step five is to substitute, for the increase in financial net worth of the U.S. Government in equation (4.1), the equivalent expression obtained from equation (4.4). This yields an expression for the U.S. Government surplus (NIA basis) in terms of the changes in the assets and liabilities in the balance sheet of the consolidated government sector. It is the U.S. Government budget restraint expressed in terms of the Federal surplus. Data for it are shown in table 4.3.

Step six is to multiply the equation obtained in step five by −1, thus obtaining the U.S. Government budget restraint expressed in terms of the Federal deficit, as follows:
U.S. government deficit (NIA basis) (11.450) equals minus increase in Treasury deposits at commercial banks (0.490) minus member bank borrowing (.282) minus increase in U.S. government loans except to member banks (30.400) minus increase in U.S. gold, SDR's, and foreign exchange reserves (−.578) plus increase in the monetary base (9.524) plus increase in U.S. government debt in private and foreign hands (30.320) plus mineral rights sales by U.S. government (4.745) plus increase in financial net worth of monetary authority (0.390) minus NIA–FofF discrepancy (2.935)   (4.5)

This corresponds precisely to table 4.1, and to (−1) times table 4.3.

C. Tables of Data for 1946–79

Tables 4.3 to 4.6 present annual data for the U.S. Government budget restraint for 1946–79, inclusive, including the same components of the Government deficit as are shown in table 4.1. Table 4.3 gives nominal data in billions of dollars. It is the same as lines 55–64 of table A.2. Table 4.4 gives real data in billions of 1972 dollars using the implicit GNP deflator. Table 4.5 expresses the budget deficit and its components as ratios to GNP. Table 4.6 expresses them as ratios to the financial net worth of the U.S. Government and monetary authorities at year-end. (This net worth is negative; hence these ratios are negative in years when there was a deficit, and positive in years when there was a surplus.)

---

[6] The source is the FofF tables of annual flows for the U.S. Government and monetary authorities sectors; see table A.2, lines 52, 54, 56–61, and 49. The consolidation is done on the same principles as that for the preceding equation. The annual flows are not always equal to the first differences of the stocks, for two reasons. First, asset revaluations are not recorded in the flow accounts, though they do affect the stocks and hence the first differences. Important examples of this are the issue of SDR's by the IMF to the U.S. Government, the revaluation of the gold stock, and write-offs of foreign-aid loans as bad debts. In each case it is the flows we want in the government budget restraint, not the first differences of stocks. Second, there are some items that are carried as constants in the FofF stock accounts because stock data are not available for them. For both reasons, we work with the flows rather than with the first differences of stocks.

Figures 4.1 to 4.4 present some of the same information in graphical form, plotted against time. Figure 4.3 summarizes the data that underlie the main thrust of this study. It shows that Federal budget deficits have been made more frequent, and larger as a ratio to GNP, since 1961. And it shows, if taken in connection with the initial level of the monetary base (table A.1, line 26), that growth of the monetary base has been made more rapid since 1961 as well.

There are two respects in which the government deficit in the national income accounts, as shown in tables 4.1 and 4.3–4.6, does not give a complete picture. It overstates the real value of the deficit during inflation in that it does not recognize the capital gain to the government that comes from the erosion of the real value of the government's monetary liabilities (securities and the monetary base); see section V.E below for further discussion. On the other hand, the national income accounts deficit understates the true deficit in that it does not provide for the unfunded future liabilities being built up by the social security system.

Table 4.3—Continued

11 JUNE 1980
ANNUAL FLOWS, 1946-79

U.S. GOVERNMENT SURPLUS, N.I.A. BASIS, AND ITS COMPONENTS

BILLIONS OF DOLLARS PER YEAR

	1975	1976	1977	1978	1979	1948-60	CODE	BILLIONS OF DOLLARS PER YEAR	
1	-70.584	-53.595	-46.331	-27.685	-11.450	8.941	316061105	U.S. GOVT. SURPLUS, N.I.A.	1
2	-1.479	1.062	2.981	7.158	490	4.987	324000005	DEPOSITS AT COML. BANKS	2
3	-70	-204	240	907	282	-9	713068001	F.R. LOANS TO MEMBER BANKS	3
4	16.709	15.416	12.826	29.979	30.400	21.622	324030035	LOANS EXCEPT TO MEMBER BANKS	4
5	593	2.366	271	-1.044	-578	-4.240	323011095	GOLD, SDR'S & OFF.FGN.EXCH.	5
6	7.013	6.276	11.806	15.187	9.524	3.184	324100035	- HIGH-POWERED MONEY	6
7	78.264	65.387	51.689	48.560	30.320	11.150	324130035	- U.S. GOVERNMENT DEBT	7
8	1.323	3.973	2.470	1.973	4.745	-	105030003	- MINERAL RIGHTS SALES	8
9	236	48	223	680	390	273	715000005	- FINANCIAL N.W., MON. AUTH.	9
10	499	3.449	3.539	1.715	2.935	1.188	317005005	N.I.A.-F.O.F. DISCREPANCY	10

ANNUAL FLOWS, 1946-79

Table 4.3—Continued

11 JUNE 1980
ANNUAL FLOWS, 1946-79

U.S. GOVERNMENT SURPLUS, N.I.A. BASIS, AND ITS COMPONENTS

ANNUAL FLOWS, 1946-79

BILLIONS OF DOLLARS PER YEAR					CODE	BILLIONS OF DOLLARS PER YEAR	
1961-65	1966-74	1975-79	1966-79	1948-79			
-10.616	-81.042	-209.645	-290.687	-292.362	316061105	U.S. GOVT. SURPLUS, N.I.A.	1
-830	-894	10.212	9.318	13.475	324000005	DEPOSITS AT COML. BANKS	2
71	203	1.155	1.358	1.420	713058001	F.R. LOANS TO MEMBER BANKS	3
18.331	41.027	105.330	146.357	166.310	324030035	LOANS EXCEPT TO MEMBER BANKS	4
-3.884	-4.734	1.608	-3.126	-11.250	323011095	GOLD, SDR'S & OFF.FGN.EXCH.	5
10.358	45.083	49.806	94.889	108.431	324100035	- HIGH-POWERED MONEY	6
12.876	60.229	276.220	334.449	358.475	324130035	- U.S. GOVERNMENT DEBT	7
-	12.990	14.484	27.474	27.474	105030003	- MINERAL RIGHTS SALES	8
-273	431	1.577	2.008	2.008	715000005	- FINANCIAL N.W. MON. AUTH.	9
-1.343	2.089	12.137	14.226	14.071	317005005	N.I.A.-F.O.F. DISCREPANCY	10

Table 4.5—Continued

11 JUNE 1980
ANNUAL FLOWS, 1946-79

ANNUAL FLOWS, 1946-79

U.S. GOVERNMENT SURPLUS, N.I.A. BASIS, AND ITS COMPONENTS

RATIOS TO GROSS NATIONAL PRODUCT

	1975	1976	1977	1978	1979	AVERAGE 1948-60	CODE		RATIOS TO GROSS NATIONAL PRODUCT	
1	-4.616	-3.148	-2.438	-1.300	-82	297	316061105	U.S. GOVT. SURPLUS, N.I.A.	1
2	-96	61	156	335	20	111	324000005	DEPOSITS AT COML. BANKS	2
3	-4	-11	12	42	11	-	713068001	F.R. LOANS TO MEMBER BANKS	3
4	1.092	905	674	1.408	1.282	510	324030035	LOANS EXCEPT TO MEMBER BANKS	4
5	38	138	13	-48	-23	-62	323011095	- GOLD, SDR'S & OFF.FGN.EXCH.	5
6	458	368	621	713	401	62	324100035	- HIGH-POWERED MONEY	6
7	5.118	3.840	2.720	2.281	1.279	201	324130035	- U.S. GOVERNMENT DEBT	7
8	86	232	129	92	199	-	105030003	- MINERAL RIGHTS SALES	8
9	14	2	11	31	15	6	715000005	- FINANCIAL N.W., MON. AUTH.	9
10	32	202	185	80	123	7	317005005	N.I.A.-F.O.F. DISCREPANCY	10

Table 4.5—Continued

11 JUNE 1980
ANNUAL FLOWS, 1946-79

ANNUAL FLOWS, 1946-79

U.S. GOVERNMENT SURPLUS, N.I.A. BASIS, AND ITS COMPONENTS

AVERAGE RATIOS TO GROSS NATIONAL PRODUCT

	1961-65	1966-74	1975-79	1966-79	1948-79	CODE		
1	-377	-855	-2,397	-1,406	-553	316061105	U.S. GOVT. SURPLUS, N.I.A.	1
2	-20	7	95	38	59	324000005	DEPOSITS AT COML. BANKS	2
3	2	4	10	6	3	713068001	F.R. LOANS TO MEMBER BANKS	3
4	610	422	1,073	654	589	324030035	LOANS EXCEPT TO MEMBER BANKS	4
5	-130	-54	23	-26	-57	323011095	GOLD, SDR'S & OFF.FGN.EXCH.	5
6	338	487	513	496	295	324100035	- HIGH-POWERED MONEY	6
7	470	645	3,048	1,503	813	324130035	- U.S. GOVERNMENT DEBT	7
8		115	148	127	55	105030003	- MINERAL RIGHTS SALES	8
9	-7	3	15	8	5	715000005	- FINANCIAL N.W., MON. AUTH.	9
10	-38	17	125	56	21	317005005	N.I.A.-F.O.F. DISCREPANCY	10

136

Figure 4.1

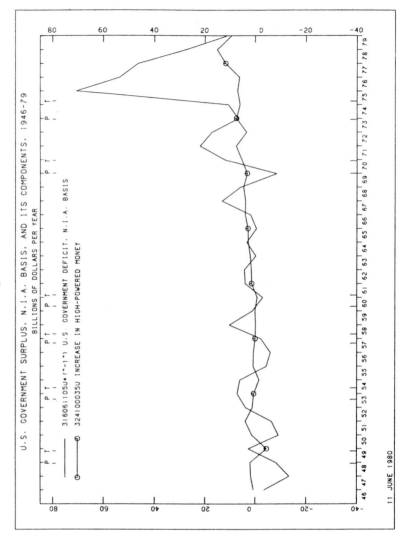

138

Figure 4.3

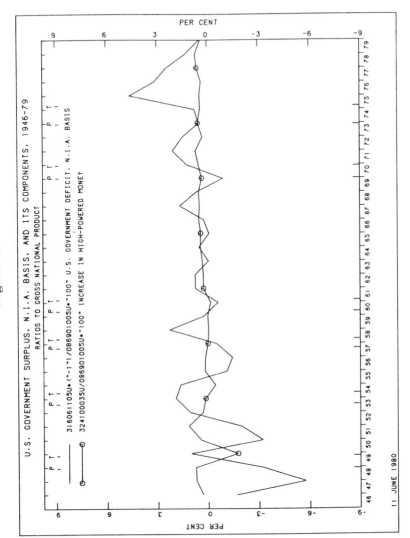

140

V. Macroeconomic Effects of Federal Debt Financing

A. Introduction

In this section we discuss the relations of Federal debt financing to inflation, employment, the money stocks, interest rates, the exchange rate, and the balance of payments, with special reference to experience since World War II. Its main results are summarized in section I above.

B. The Relation Between Inflation and the Several Concepts of the Stock of Money

So far we have emphasized only one of the several concepts of the stock of money; namely, the monetary base (high powered money). Its definition and data as used in this study are found in table A.1, lines 26–29. There are several other concepts that have important uses, and that behave somewhat differently than does the monetary base. Also, so far we have not discussed the variation that exists in the relation between the growth rate of the monetary base and the rate of inflation. In this subsection we address these matters.

We will consider briefly four additional recently adopted concepts of the stock of money, known as M1A, M1B, M2, and M3. (The formerly used concepts were called M_1, M_2, and M_3.) M1A is the sum of currency outside banks plus commercial bank demand deposits adjusted, excluding U.S. Government deposits, interbank deposits, and deposits held by foreign banks and official institutions. M1A is almost the same as old M_1. M1B is M1A plus checkable deposits at all depositary institutions. It includes NOW accounts and automatic funds transfer service accounts at banks and thrift institutions, demand deposits at mutual savings banks, and credit union share draft accounts. M2 is M1B plus savings and small-denomination time deposits at all depositary institutions, overnight repurchase agreements at commercial banks, overnight Eurodollars held by U.S. residents other than banks at Caribbean branches of member banks, and money market mutual fund shares. M3 is M2 plus large-denomination time deposits at all depositary institutions and term repurchase agreements at commercial banks and savings and loan associations.[7]

Obviously, M3 exceeds M2, which exceeds M1B, which exceeds M1A. Less obviously, M1A exceeds the monetary base. Why? The ratio of M1A to the monetary base is the ratio of (currency outside banks + demand deposits) divided by (currency outside banks plus bank reserves). And demand deposits exceed bank reserves (roughly by the amount of interest-earning assets that banks hold). Therefore M1A exceeds the monetary base. One can think of each dollar of reserves as supporting more than a dollar of deposits. (That is why the names "monetary base" and "high powered money" make sense.)

The ratios of these four M's to each other and to the monetary base can and do change through time, in response to demand and supply conditions in the financial markets, and to government regulation of interest rates, of bank reserve ratios, and so on. These changes are

---

[7] Data for these money stocks are published by the Federal Reserve. See the *Federal Reserve Bulletin* for February, 1980 for a description of the new concepts of M1A, M1B, M2, and M3 and their relationships to old M_1, M_2, and M_3. See the *Federal Reserve Bulletin* for April 1980 and Board of Governors [1980] for data for the new concepts since 1959.

usually gradual except when government regulation is involved. For example, if there is a ceiling on the interest rate payable on one kind of deposit, and the market rate rises to that ceiling and would rise further if allowed to, then depositors will rather abruptly switch to other forms of deposit whose interest rates are not regulated, even if financial institutions have to invent such forms of deposit (which they often do: witness the invention of the certificate of deposit and the money market mutual fund). Or if the Federal Reserve abruptly increases the required reserve ratios of banks, other things equal, then banks must reduce the amount of loans outstanding, thus reducing M1A. In a severe recession or depression, M1A can decline substantially more than the monetary base, as bank deposits and loans decline. Indeed, in the 1929–33 depression, old M_1 declined drastically but the base did not decline.

The *adjusted monetary base* is the monetary base plus an adjustment (sometimes negative) to allow for the effects of changes in required reserve ratios against deposits and for changes in the distribution of deposits among accounts that have different required ratios. The advantage of the adjusted monetary base is that it is a single time series that reflects monetary policy actions to increase or decrease M1A regardless of whether these changes come from changes in the (unadjusted) monetary base or from changes in required reserve ratios. Data for the adjusted monetary base are published by the Federal Reserve Bank of St. Louis.

Because the stocks of money, differently defined, can change relative to each other, their growth rates need not be identical (and usually they are not). Of course this raises the question as to which money stock, if any, should be used as a guide for monetary policy. We will return to this question presently.

But first we consider the relation between inflation and the growth rates of the various stocks of money. A useful identity for this purpose is the so-called equation of exchange. It says that nominal GNP can be expressed in two equivalent ways, thus:

nominal GNP equals real GNP times price level equals money
stock times velocity of circulation of money   (5. 1)

This equation defines the velocity of circulation of money, which is not directly observable, in terms of variables that are directly observable. Of course, for every definition of the money stock, there is a corresponding money velocity given by the ratio of nominal GNP to that money stock.

The velocity of money varies through the years, no matter which definition of the money stock one chooses. It varies more for some definitions than others but it is not constant for any of them. However, it does not vary rapidly or unsystematically. It rises when the use of money becomes more expensive, as when interest rates are high and/or when inflation is rapid, because people find it worthwhile to reduce their average real holdings of money, thus increasing its velocity. It falls when incomes rise, because people feel they can afford the convenience that comes from holding larger stocks of money per unit of income, thus decreasing its velocity.

Return to equation (5.1), and consider the growth rate of nominal GNP. The growth rate of a product of two variables is approximately equal to the sum of the growth rates of the two. Therefore we see from (5.1) that, approximately,

142

Growth rate of nominal GNP equals growth rate of real GNP plus inflation rate equals growth rate of money stock plus growth rate of velocity of money   (5. 2)

This too is true for each definition of the money stock that one may choose.

Now let us look at the data for the growth rates that appear in equation (5.2). They are calculated in table 5.1 for the three periods 1960 to 1965 (5 years), 1965 to 1979 (14 years), and 1960 to 1979 (19 years).

TABLE 5.1.—SEVERAL MONEY STOCKS (NOT SEASONALLY ADJUSTED) AND THEIR VELOCITIES OF CIRCULATION WITH GROWTH RATES FOR 1960 THROUGH 1979

Money stock or other variable	Levels			Average annual growth rates, percent			Velocity of money					
							Levels			Average annual growth rates, percent		
	1960	1965	1979	1960 to 1965	1965 to 1979	1960 to 1979	1960	1965	1979	1960 to 1965	1965 to 1979	1960 to 1979
(1)	(2)	(3)	(4)	(5)	(6)	(7)	(8)	(9)	(10)	(11)	(12)	(13)
Nominal GNP	506.0	688.0	2,369.0	6.3	9.2	8.5						
Real GNP	737.0	926.0	1,432.0	4.7	3.2	3.6						
GNP deflator	68.7	74.3	165.5	1.6	5.9	4.7						
Monetary base	50.0	60.5	155.4	3.9	7.0	6.2	10.1	11.4	15.2	2.5	2.1	2.2
Adjusted monetary base	44.4	57.5	154.0	5.3	7.3	6.8	11.4	12.0	15.4	1.0	1.8	1.6
M1A	145.3	173.7	381.1	3.6	5.8	5.2	3.48	3.96	6.22	2.6	3.3	3.1
M1B	145.3	173.7	397.3	3.6	6.1	5.4	3.48	3.96	5.96	2.6	3.0	2.9
M2	314.2	461.5	1,526.0	8.0	8.9	8.7	1.61	1.49	1.55	-1.5	-.3	-.2
M3	316.1	482.1	1,779.0	8.8	9.8	9.5	1.60	1.43	1.33	-2.2	-.5	-1.0

Sources:
Nominal GNP (billion dollars per year), real GNP (billions of 1972 dollars per year), and GNP deflator (1972:100): national income accounts.
Monetary base, year-end (billions of dollars): Table A.2.
Adjusted monetary base, December (billions of dollars): Federal Reserve Bank of St. Louis, "Review" and "Monetary Trends."

M1A, M1B, M2, M3, December (billions of dollars): Board of Governors [1980] and "Federal Reserve Bulletin", April 1980.
Velocities: Calculated as nominal GNP for the year divided by the December money stock.
Growth rates: For nominal and real GNP and the GNP deflator, growth rates are computed from each year's average. For stocks, growth rates are computed from each year's December figure. For velocities, growth rates are computed from each year's velocity ratio.

144

All six money stocks were allowed to grow too fast for price-level stability since the end of 1960, and especially since the end of 1965. From then until the end of 1979 each of their average rates was between 5.8 and 9.8 percent, substantially too high.

None of the six velocities was constant during any of the three periods, though the velocity of M2 was nearly constant. But notice that none of the velocities changed very rapidly over any of the three periods: The largest change was for M1A's velocity, which grew from 1965 to 1979 at an average rate of 3.3 percent a year. This modest growth of M1A's velocity together with the nearly constant velocity of M2 and the slight decline in M3's velocity are attributable to the fact that during these periods nominal interest rates were rising on all the components of M2 and M3 except the M1A component, which has had a legal interest ceiling of zero; people were gradually shifting their holdings out of currency and demand deposits (especially the latter) into interest-paying deposits and savings shares. These changes in velocity are not only gradual and roughly predictable; they also reinforce rather than counteract the effects of changes in the growth rates of the money stocks. Increases in monetary growth rates create more inflation, which increases interest rates and velocities and thus compounds the inflationary effect as shown by equation (5.2). Similarly, decreases in monetary growth rates dampen inflation, which lowers interest rates and velocities, thus compounding the deflationary effect.

We conclude that although the relation between the inflation rate and the growth rates of the money stocks is not immutable, it changes slowly enough so that it is reliable as an approximate guide to the kind of monetary policy that is required to stop inflation. The message is that the growth rates of *all* the money stocks must be brought down. The Federal Reserve exerts direct control over the monetary base, and must reduce its growth rate substantially if inflation is to be brought to a halt. If there are to be substantial changes in required reserve ratios in the future, the *adjusted* monetary base is the better base to stabilize, since it incorporates reserve requirement changes. If interest ceilings and other regulations combine with changes in the inflation rate to produce rapid shifts of the public's asset holdings among different forms of money, as in the late 1970's, the monetary base may temporarily be a better quantity to stabilize than M1A or M1B or M2. In normal times M2 may be the best choice since it has had a more nearly constant velocity than the others. In the remainder of this paper we will conduct the discussion mainly in terms of the monetary base.

Variations in velocity are not likely to be abrupt in the future, but if velocity does change over long periods, gradual adjustments in the growth rate of the monetary base should be made accordingly. This process cannot easily be made precise in advance, but it can be administered in such a way as to stop inflation and maintain approximate price level stability over long periods in the future.

C. Inflation, Unemployment, and Phillips Curves

At one time, in the middle and late sixties, it was thought by some that the Phillips curve diagram gave a reliable picture of a stable trade-off between the inflation rate and the unemployment rate. (How-

145

ever, Phillips himself did not say this. See Lipsey [1978] for a good review.) Subsequent data for many countries combined with further theoretical work have destroyed that view.

It is instructive to look at a Phillips curve diagram for the U.S.; see figure 5.1. For the period from 1959 to 1961, it suggests a stable negative relation between unemployment and inflation, such that by accepting a somewhat higher permanent inflation rate we could attain a permanently lower unemployment rate. If this were true, most people would probably be willing to accept permanent inflation at the moderate rate of say 3 percent in order to achieve a permanent reduction in the unemployment rate to say 4 percent. However, the apparently stable relation fell to pieces as more data became available. Instead of a stable negatively sloping curve, the graph became a series of loops, containing segments with positive, zero, or infinite slopes as well as negative. This happened not only for the U.S. but also for Canada, France, Germany, Italy, Japan, the Netherlands, Sweden, and the United Kingdom: see McCracken *et al.* [1977], pp. 105–6, 314, and 339–41.

A somewhat more complex theory, known as the "natural rate of unemployment" hypothesis, is more nearly (but not completely) consistent with the data. It distinguishes a long-run Phillips curve from a series of short-run curves. It says that the long-run Phillips curve applies to situations where the actual and expected inflation rates are equal, and that this curve is approximately vertical at the so-called natural rate of unemployment which is approximately independent of the inflation rate; though the natural rate can change for other reasons. (See below.) It says further that for each different

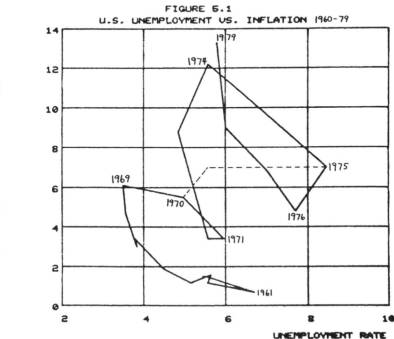

FIGURE 5.1
U.S. UNEMPLOYMENT VS. INFLATION 1960-79

146

expected rate of inflation there is a different negatively sloped short-run Phillips curve which crosses the long-run curve at the expected rate of inflation. It says still further that people change their expectations of inflation slowly, partly in response to recently observed actual rates. Thus it seeks to explain figure 5.1 by supposing that the natural unemployment rate in the U.S. was about 4¾ percent in the 1960's and is about 6¾ percent now, and that inflationary expectations behaved as follows: Were quite steady at a rate of about 1 to 1.5 percent in 1959–67 so that the short-run Phillips curve for those years was quite stable; rose in 1968–70 so that the data for 1968, 1969, and 1970–72 were on new and successively higher short-run Phillips curves; rose again in 1973–74 so that the data for 1974–75 were on a still higher short-run curve; receded somewhat in 1976 so that the data for 1976–78 were on a somewhat lower short-run curve, but not as low as the one for 1970–72; and rose again in 1979. According to this hypothesis, the sections of the diagram where the curve slopes positively or is vertical or horizontal correspond to changes in inflationary expectations, upward for movements up and/or toward the right, and downward for movements down and/or toward the left. (The price data understate the actual inflation rate for 1971–73 because price controls were in effect, and overstate it for 1974 because part of the observed 1974 increase reflects delayed 1971–73 inflation that did not come into the open until controls were lifted in 1974. A point representing the 1971–74 average is shown on the diagram, connected to 1970 and 1975 by dashed lines, as a reminder of this.)

When inflation is expected, the contracts that people make for future payments of money reflect an adjustment for the decline in the purchasing power of the dollar that is expected to occur with the inflation. Nominal interest rates are important cases in point. Long-term interest rates have risen substantially since being set free by the Treasury-Federal Reserve accord of 1951, in a manner broadly consistent with the kind of inflationary expectations that rationalize figure 5.1 via the natural rate hypothesis. See section V.F. below.

D. *Inflation, Unemployment, and Federal Debt Financing*

Next we look at postwar statistics for the Federal budget deficit and its financing, and their relation to unemployment and inflation, for the period since the beginning of 1948. We choose 1948 as a starting point because it was the first normal peacetime year after the readjustments of prices and production following World War II.

Table 5.2 shows the cumulative Federal deficit and its financing by means of additions to the monetary base, borrowing from the private and foreign sectors, and other sources for the entire period 1948–79 inclusive, and several subperiods. This table corresponds to equation (4.5) which states the U.S. Government budget restraint in terms of the deficit. The source is table 4.3 which states the same relation in terms of the surplus. Budgetary data mentioned in the text of this subsection come from table 5.2 unless otherwise stated.

147

TABLE 5.2.—CUMULATIVE U.S. GOVERNMENT DEFICIT AND ITS FINANCING FOR 1948 THROUGH 1979 AND SELECTED SUBPERIODS

[Flows In billions of dollars]

	1948–60	1961–65	1966–74	1975–79	1966–79	1948–79
1. U.S. Government deficit, NIA basis	−8.9	10.6	81.0	209.6	209.7	292.4
2.—Treasury deposits at commercial banks	5.0	−.8	−.9	10.2	9.3	13.5
3.—Federal Reserve loans to member banks	−0	.1	.2	1.2	1.4	1.4
4.—U.S. Government loans except to member banks	21.6	18.3	41.0	105.3	146.4	186.3
5.—U.S. gold, SDR and foreign exchange reserves	−4.2	−3.9	−4.7	1.6	−3.1	−11.2
6. Monetary base (high-powered money)	3.2	10.4	45.1	49.8	94.9	108.4
7. U.S. Government debt in private and foreign hands	11.2	12.9	60.2	274.2	334.4	358.5
8. Mineral rights sales by U.S. Govt.	0	0	13.2	14.5	27.5	27.5
9. Financial net worth of monetary authorities	.3	−.3	.4	1.6	2.0	2.0
10.—NIA–FofF discrepancy	1.2	−1.3	2.1	12.1	14.2	14.1

Source: Table 4.3, last columns

The management of the budget since 1948 falls into three distinct periods. The first is 1948 through 1960. It was characterized by a small cumulative budget surplus of $8.9 billion, offset mainly by $10.4 billion in net leanding by the Federal Government ($10.4 billion is the difference between Federal lending of $21.6 billion and Federal borrowing of $11.2 billion from private and foreign lenders). The surplus averaged 0.3 percent of GNP. (See table 4.5.) It was a period of very stable monetary policy on the average: the cumulative increase in the monetary base was $3.2 billion, from $46.8 billion at the beginning of 1948 to $50.0 billion at the end of 1960 (see table A.1) for an average growth rate of 0.5 percent a year. For the same period old M1 rose at 1.7 percent a year on the average, and old M2 at 2.3 percent a year. The price level was nearly stable: The CPI rose at an average rate of 1.7 percent a year from 1948 to 1960. Concern was expressed about this high rate of inflation at the time! But in comparison with recent experience that period looks very good. There were three mild recessions—in 1949, 1954, and 1958— with annual unemployment rates rising 2 to 2½ percentage points from their previous lows to peaks of 5.9, 5.5, and 6.8 percent, and and with quarterly real GNP declining from its previous peak by 1.4, 3.3, and 3.2 percent, respectively. The budget was in deficit by 1 to 2 percent of GNP in each recession, with surpluses before and after (see table 4.5), thus providing some built-in stabilization. The monetary base and the other money stocks were not managed in a cyclically stabilizing manner; however: table 4.3 shows that the base was allowed to decline somewhat in each of these three recessions. Old M1 and M2 were allowed to grow more slowly as well. A policy of maintaining undiminished growth rates for the base and other money stocks during recessions would be preferable. It would of course allow short-term interest rates to go lower in recessions than did the policy of reducing the base.

The second period is 1961 through 1965. The year 1961 is chosen as its starting point because in 1961–63 there was an abrupt increase in Federal Reserve purchases of Treasury debt, from $0.4 billion a year in 1948–60 on average to $3 billion a year in 1963–65 on average.

148

(See Board of Governors [1976], pp. 25–27.) In 1961 through 1965 the authorities provided a small cumulative deficit amounting to $10.6 billion over the 5 years, averaging 0.4 percent of GNP (see table 4.5). The Federal Reserve financed it by increasing the monetary base somewhat faster than before; by $10.4 billion—from $50.0 billion to $60.5 billion (see table A.1)—for an average annual growth rate of 3.9 percent. The growth rates of M1A and M1B averaged 3.6 percent a year; the growth rate of M2, 8 percent. There was one mild recession, in 1960–61, when the annual unemployment rate rose 1.2 percentage points to 6.7 percent, and quarterly real GNP declined 1.2 percent from its previous peak. The expansionary shift in fiscal and monetary policy during this period helped to reduce the unemployment rate to 4.5 percent in 1965 (it was to go still lower in 1966–69), and there was as yet no sign of the faster inflation that follows more rapid increases of the monetary base. It was a time when the Administration could briefly claim that fine tuning of the economy was now possible in such a way as to maintain high employment with very little inflation (recall the points for 1959–65 in figure 5.1). Even as late as January 1969, President Johnson wrote in "The Economic Report of the President" (p. 4):

Ever since the historic passage of the Employment Act in 1946, economic policies have responded to the fire alarm of recession and boom. In the 1960's, we have adopted a new strategy aimed at fire prevention—sustaining prosperity and heading off recession or serious inflation before they could take hold.

The third period is 1966 through 1979. Much more expansionary policies were followed beginning in 1966. It is sobering now to read the testimony of William McChesney Martin as Chairman of the Federal Reserve Board urging that Congress abolish (as in fact Congress did) the 25 percent gold reserve requirement against Federal Reserve deposits in 1965, and against Federal Reserve notes in 1968. Mr. Martin stated in 1968: "Removal of this requirement would in no way reduce our determination to preserve the soundness of the dollar." See the Federal Reserve Bulletin for February, 1965 and for February, 1968, p. 125.

Because of the unusually large deficits associated with the recession of 1975, let us consider 1966–74 and 1975–79 separately. (It is important to put all of the years 1971–74 into the same subperiod because much of the 12 percent increase in the consumer price index (CPI) during 1974 really belongs to 1971–73 but it could not come into the open until the price controls were lifted in 1974.)

In 1966–74 there was a deficit every year except 1969 when there was a surplus of $8.5 billion, not quite 1 percent of GNP. (See tables 4.3 and 4.5.) For the 9 years the deficit aggregated $81.0 billion, and averaged 0.9 percent of GNP. (See table 4.5.) Even though only about half of it, $45.1 billion, was financed by additions to the monetary base, this brought a large increase in the base, to $105.6 billion at the end of 1974. (See table A.1.) This meant that the average growth rate of the base during 1966 through 1974 was raised again, to 6.4 percent a year, clearly incompatible with price stability. The average growth rates of M1A, M1B and M2 were 5.6, 5.6, and 7.8 percent a year. The average CPI inflation rate from 1965 to 1974 was 5.1 percent a year. There was one mild recession, in 1970–71, with the annual employment rate rising 2.4 points to 5.9 percent and quarterly real GNP

149

declining 1.1 percent from its previous peak. The expansionary policies of 196–168 held the average unemployment rate to 3.7 percent in 1966–69, but this effect began to wear off as the slower-acting price effect began to appear. The annual unemployment rate was 4.9 percent in 1970 and again in 1973 but has not been below 5.6 percent in any other year since 1970.

In 1975–79 there was a deficit every year. For the 5 years it aggregated $209.6 billion and averaged 2.4 percent of GNP. In 1975 the deficit was $70.6 billion, or 4.6 percent of GNP. (See tables 4.3 and 4.5). This was a larger fraction of GNP than in any year of the Great Depression of the thirties (though it did not approach the 1944 wartime peak of 26 percent). Even though only about one-fourth of the cumulative deficit for 1975–79 was financed by additions to the monetary base, the increase was large ($49.8 billion in 5 years) which brought the base to $155.4 billion at the end of 1979 (see table A.1) for a still higher average growth rate of 8.4 percent a year, again clearly incompatible with price stability. The average annual growth rates of M1A, M1B, and M2 were 6.1, 7.0, and 10.9 percent.

The recession of 1975 was more severe than any since World War II, with the annual unemployment rate rising 3.5 percentage points to 8.5 percent, and quarterly real GNP declining 7 percent from its previous peak. The severity was partly due to the increase in imported oil prices which forced some reduction in our standard of living.

This brief sketch of macroeconomic policy in the United States since World War II gives strong support to the view that the authorities raised the growth rate of the monetary base too high, beginning in 1961, after a period of successfully limited monetary growth and nearly stable prices. This resulted in too-rapid growth of the money stocks M1A, M1B, and M2, without which the inflation could not have occurred.

Why was this inflationary policy followed? Arthur Burns, Chairman of the Federal Reserve from 1970 to March, 1978, had this to say [1979, p. 15]: "Viewed in the abstract, the Federal Reserve System had the power to abort the inflation at its incipient stage fifteen years ago or at any later point, and it has the power to end it today. At any time within that period, it could have restricted the money supply and created sufficient strains in financial and industrial markets to terminate the inflation with little delay. It did not do so because the Federal Reserve was itself caught up in the philosophic and political currents that were transforming American life and culture." He then referred to the Full Employment Act of 1946, which proclaims the responsibility of the Federal Government "to promote maximum employment, production, and purchasing power" without mentioning price stability among those goals.

According to the natural unemployment rate hypothesis, a rise in the inflation rate is accompanied by a temporary decrease in unemployment, and a decline in the inflation rate is accompanied by a temporary rise in unemployment. By how many percentage-point years was unemployment reduced between 1960 and 1973 by the stimulative policies that also increased the inflation rate? If we could answer this question, we could get a rough idea of how many percentage-point years of above-normal unemployment might be required to reduce the inflation rate to its 1948–59 level. Suppose that the natural

150

unemployment rate were 4.57 percent (the 1948–59 average) at the end of 1959, 6.77 percent (the 1973–78 average) in mid-1973, and followed a straight-line growth path between these two time points. The accompanying table 5.3 suggests that about 9.8 percentage-point years of unemployment were prevented by the stimulative policies of 1960–73, which also gave us the increase in the inflation rate. (Each period in table 5.3 begins and ends at a cyclically low rate of unemployment.) If the reverse process has an effect of similar size, this suggests we might expect about 10 percentage-point years of extra unemployment as an unpleasant side effect of reducing the inflation to its 1948–1959 level, e.g., 2½ percent for 4 years, or 2 percent for 5 years, or the like. Of course this is not a prediction, it is only an indication of a possible order of magnitude.

TABLE 5.3.—ROUGH ESTIMATE OF PERCENTAGE-POINT YEARS OF UNEMPLOYMENT PREVENTED BY STIMULATIVE POLICIES IN 1960–73

(1) Period (inclusive)	1948–59	1960–68	1969 to mid-1973	Mid-1973 to 1978	Sum for 1960 to mid-1973
(2) Years	12	9	4½	5½	13½
(3) Number of cycles	3	1	1	1	2
(4) Average unemployment rate, percent	4.57	4.92	4.97	6.77	....
(5) Assumed natural unemployment rate, percent, average [1]	4.57	5.30	6.40	6.77	....
(6) Difference, (5)−(4), percent	0	.38	1.43	0	....
(7) Percentage-point years of unemployment prevented, (2)×(6) except for last column	0	3.4	6.4	0	9.8

[1] Defined by linear interpolation between 4.57 percent (the 1948–59 average) at the end of 1959 and 6.77 percent (the 1973–78 average) in mid-1973.

In October 1979, the Federal Reserve announced its intention to reduce the growth of the money stocks gradually until noninflationary growth rates are attained. If this program is carried through, late 1979 will mark the beginning of a fourth postwar period for macroeconomic policy in which inflation is brought under control.

E. The Relation Between the Federal Debt and the Monetary Base

The frequency of government deficits and their magnitude in relation to GNP were increased after 1960, and those deficits were financed to a significant degree by the too-large increases in the monetary base, as we have seen. Perhaps if the deficits had not been so large, the Federal Reserve would not have been led to contribute so heavily to their financing by such large increases in the monetary base. That is the subject of this subsection.

Consider the relationship between the size of the Federal deficit and the rate of growth of the monetary base. When the financial authorities run a large deficit, do the monetary authorities have any choice but to help finance it by large additions to the monetary base? What would happen if the monetary authorities tried to maintain a slow growth rate of the base in the face of a large deficit?

Return again to table 5.2. It shows the sources of deficit finance that are available. Large continuing deficits can be financed only by the sale of securities either to the Federal Reserve (which increases the monetary base) or to private and foreign buyers on the open market

151

(which has other disadvantages as we will see). The other sources of finance, e.g., depletion of foreign exchange reserves, can make important contributions in the short run, but they would be exhausted by large sustained deficits in the long run.

When there is a large deficit, and hence a large issue of securities by the Treasury to finance it, the Federal Reserve is the agency that decides how much of that debt issue will be dumped on the open market (at whatever prices and interest rates will persuade the market to buy them) and how much will be transformed into an increase in the monetary base through purchase by the Federal Reserve.

Suppose the deficit is large and sustained. Then the Federal Reserve is in a box because undesirable consequences will follow no matter what it does.

To understand the nature of this box, it is helpful to make the distinction between nominal and real interest rates. Nominal rates are those typically quoted in the market, on savings accounts, mortgages, bonds, etc. Real rates are nominal rates adjusted for the rate of inflation. The adjustment is made according to this formula:

$$\text{real interest rate} = \frac{1 + \text{nominal interest rate}}{1 + \text{inflation rate}} - 1 \qquad (5.3)$$

For example, if the inflation rate were 20 percent a year and the nominal interest rate were 32 percent a year, then the real rate of interest would be $(1.32/1.20) - 1 = 1.10 - 1 = .10 = 10$ percent. If the nominal interest rate and the inflation rate are both small, say both less than 10 percent, then a quick approximation to the real interest rate can be found by subtracting the inflation rate from the nominal interest rate. This approximation for the preceding example yields (32 percent -20 percent) $= 12$ percent, which is 2 percentage points too high.

The significance of this distinction is that business borrowers and consumer borrowers care more about the real rate of interest than about the nominal rate, for the real rate is what determines the cost of borrowing in terms of real resources such as labor, capital, and materials.

Note that the budget deficit, as stated in the Government budget restraint equation and in the corresponding tables 5.2 and 4.3, does not account for the erosion of the real purchasing power of the outstanding stocks of money and government bonds that occurs during inflation. This erosion is a capital loss to the holders of money and bonds but a gain to the Government. Thus the real value of the Government deficit, taking account of this capital gain, is less than the amounts shown in the tables when inflation is occurring. In early 1980, with privately held Federal Government debt net of Federal loans to the private sector amounting to about $350 billion and inflation in the neighborhood of 10 percent a year, the overstatement of the real value of the deficit amounted to about $35 billion a year.

Now let us return to the question of what difference the Federal Reserve's actions make when there is a large and sustained deficit.

Suppose first that the Federal Reserve buys only a small amount of the Treasury's sustained debt issues; just enough to maintain a small average growth rate of the monetary base, say at 1 or 2 percent a year

152

which would be consistent with a roughly constant price level. The great bulk of the Treasury's securities would be offered on the open market, year after year. The immediate effect, when the process begins, would be a reduction in bond prices and an increase in interest rates (both real and nominal since the price level is nearly constant). The longer term effect as the process continues would be still lower bond prices and still higher interest rates (real and nominal), as the market is asked to hold increasing quantities of government bonds. Some private borrowers would be priced out of the market, and thus private investment in plant and equipment and technology would be reduced. This is called "crowding out" of private investment by the government's borrowing. The average deficit in 1966–79 was 1.4 percent of GNP (table 4.5), which amounts to about one-fifth of net private domestic investment: a significant fraction.

Suppose instead that the Federal Reserve buys a large amount of the Treasury's sustained debt issues, enough to create rapid growth in the monetary base (as it has done since 1966). This produces first a temporary period of high employment and output (as in 1966–69), followed by continuous inflation. The effect on nominal interest rates is to reduce them when the process first starts but to raise them later by building an inflation premium into them as borrowers and lenders come to expect inflation to continue. The effect on real interest rates is to lower them at first, but the long-run effect is small and we are not sure whether it is positive or negative. However, if the sustained deficits are due to increased government purchases (rather than to reduced taxes), there will also be some crowding out of private expenditure.

In the first case, where the Federal Reserve sticks to slow monetary growth for the sake of price stability, we get high nominal interest rates, high real rates, and some crowding out of private investment. In the second case, where the Federal Reserve creates rapid monetary growth to help finance the deficits, we get inflation, high nominal interest rates, and perhaps some crowding out of private investment. Neither outcome is desirable. The fault here is not with the Federal Reserve, but with the fiscal authorities (the Congress and the Executive) for continuing to have large deficits.

Thus the happiest outcome would be obtained with small deficits, averaging at most about 0.5 percent of GNP over the business cycle, and a small average growth rate of the monetary base, about 1 or 2 percent a year for approximate price-level constancy.

Why is 0.5 percent of GNP about the highest acceptable size for the deficit, on the average? Consider that the net total of the monetary base, plus Federal debt in private and foreign hands, and less U.S. Government loans outstanding at the end of 1978, was $510 billion (table A.1, lines 26+30–7) or about 22 percent of GNP. A deficit of 0.5 percent of GNP would be about $12 billion, or about 2 percent of that $510 billion net total. Thus if the ratio of the monetary base to that net total were kept constant, a deficit of 0.5 percent of GNP would require a growth rate of about 2 percent a year in the monetary base, which would be about right for price stability. A smaller deficit than 0.5 percent of GNP, a balanced budget, or a small surplus—on the average over time, after an adjustment period—would also be acceptable. But deficits averaging much over 0.5 percent of GNP would risk either inflation or the crowding out of investment.

The foregoing discussion does not support the proposal to amend the Constitution to require that the Federal budget be balanced every year. In fact, it would be pernicious to balance the budget every year in both high and low stages of the business cycle. The reason is that our fiscal system now has built-in stabilizing forces that increase the deficit (or decrease the surplus) in recession—thus helping to cushion the economy against the decline in expenditure that characterizes recession—and that decrease the deficit (or increase the surplus) at business cycle peaks, thus helping to moderate the high expenditure that characterizes the peak. If the budget were balanced every year, this would deprive us of those stabilizing effects, and business cycles would be rendered more severe.

F. Interest Rates

In this subsection we shall argue that if the average size of the budget deficit and the average growth rate of the monetary base are chosen correctly, the determination of interest rates can be left to the market, and no attempt need (or should) be made to control them.

Interest rates are important prices. They enter into decisions to consume, to save, and to invest. They affect many people. Large unforeseen changes in interest rates create large unforeseen capital gains and losses on long-term assets. Consequently it is not surprising that economic policymakers pay attention to variations in interest rates.

Interest rates are influenced by monetary policy. One rather popular view of monetary policy supposes that changes in interest rates are a reliable indicator of changes in the ease or tightness of monetary policy, and in particular that a rise in interest rates indicates a tightening of monetary policy, and a decline indicates an easing. However, for reasons alluded to earlier, this supposition is not reliable. Sometimes it is correct and sometimes just the reverse is correct. To understand the relation between monetary policy and variations in interest rates, it is necessary to distinguish short-term and long-term reactions to changes in monetary policy and to recognize that the long-term effect can be in the opposite direction from the short-term effect.

Imagine an initial situation in which the money stock is growing slowly and prices are stable. Imagine now a departure from that situation for a period of two months: The money stock is increased 2 percent the first month, returned to its former path the second month, and thereafter made to follow the same slow-growth path it was following before. Then the aforementioned popular view is correct: Interest rates will fall during the first month when the money stock is expanded, because higher asset prices and lower interest rates are required to persuade people to hold the larger money stock. Similarly, for the opposite reason, interest rates will rise to approximately their former path during the second month when the money stock is reduced to its former path.

Start from the same initial situation as before, but now imagine that the money stock is made to embark on a 2-percent-per-month

154

compound-growth path (which amounts to 27 percent a year) and is held to that path for several years. In the first month, interest rates will fall just as in the previous case. However, after several years of monetary growth at 27 percent a year, the economy will develop a rapid inflation, and interest rates will (if free to be determined in the market without regulation) rise to levels above the inflation rate, thus affording a positive real return. Then for the long-run effect the popular view is just backwards: The high interest rates are an indication that monetary policy has been so easy as to create rapid inflation. To make interest rates come back down and *remain down*, it is necessary to slow or stop the inflation. This requires a reduction in the rate of growth of the money stock. Its short-run effect will be to raise interest rates briefly, as money becomes scarcer than expected, but when the inflation rate comes down interest rates will come down too.

The fact that long-run and short-run effects of money-stock growth upon interest rates can be in opposite directions makes it impossible to deduce the degree of ease or tightness of current monetary policy from current changes in interest rates. Rising interest rates today may possibly be due to a tightening of monetary policy today, or they may be due to an easing of monetary policy last year which is now generating inflation and thus driving interest rates up as the continuation of inflation comes to be expected. Attempts to stabilize interest rates by open market operations can easily go wrong if the authorities try to hold the interest rate at a level that is not consistent with the going rate of inflation. For example, if the current inflation rate is 10 percent and the corresponding *equilibrium* short-term interest rate is 12 percent—with the authorities trying to maintain the *actual* short-term rate at 11 percent, the result will be an acceleration of inflation; this because in order to keep the rate below 12 percent the authorities must buy Treasury securities more rapidly than is consistent with 10-percent inflation.

If the average growth rate of the money stock is kept low in order to maintain price stability, and if the average budget deficit is kept small in order to avoid crowding out private borrowers, then interest rates will fluctuate mildly as the economy experiences mild business cycles, but they will not reach the extreme high levels that we have seen accompanying the inflation of the 1970's and early 1980.

It has been the Federal Reserve's practice for many years to conduct a large volume of open market operations in order to remove the seasonal variation that would otherwise occur in interest rates thus transferring the seasonal variation to the money stock (especially the currency stock). In view of the difficulty of interpreting the meaning of changes in interest rates, it would be preferable to cease seasonal variations in the money stock, or perhaps in the monetary base, and allow the seasonal changes in the demand for currency relative to deposits to be accompanied by seasonal variations in interest rates. Private investors and speculators are equal to this task. The Federal Reserve would then be better able to concentrate its attention on the growth rate of the money stock, where it belongs.

Interest-rate ceilings on bank deposits, savings and loan shares, certificates of deposit, and mortgages generally have harmful effects.

They should be gradually increased and then, after they have been raised above prevailing market rates, they should be abolished. Interest ceilings have existed for some years, doing little harm because they were usually above the rates set by the market and hence usually had no effect. With the adoption of inflationary monetary policy, however, market rates rose as the inflationary premium was incorporated into them. When market-clearing rates rose above the ceilings, lenders naturally switched their funds to other channels where interest rates could reflect market equilibrium. This had a particularly unfortunate effect on financial institutions that typically lend at long term and borrow at short term: they were locked into portfolios of long-term loans and investments made in earlier years at low rates, and were competing for borrowed short-term funds in a market where short rates became very high because of inflation. This is one of the many problems that would not have arisen had a noninflationary monetary policy been followed.

G. Uncertainty

When the future rate of inflation is uncertain, as at present, long-term planning by both savers and investors is seriously interferred with. Long-term financial commitments become very risky, for the real value of future payments will be high or low depending upon whether inflation is lower or higher than was expected. This applies to decisions about life insurance, retirement plans (including social security), long-term leases, and long-term financing of housing, plant, equipment, and technology. Part of the recent decline in capital spending and in productivity growth is surely due to uncertainty over future inflation rates.

In principle, once a constant inflation rate has been established and adjusted to, it doesn't matter whether it is plus 10 percent, minus 10 percent, or zero. Of course, during the adjustment period required to switch from one constant inflation rate to another, large unanticipated wealth transfers occur between parties to long-term contracts, and there is much uncertainty until inflation has been constant at the new rate long enough that people come to expect it to continue to be constant at the new rate. This adjustment period can be very long, perhaps 50 years, because there are many long-term pension and insurance and other contracts outstanding.

Although any constant moderate inflation rate will do as well as any other, once it has become established and adjusted to, experience strongly suggests that it is not possible to maintain any inflation rate approximately constant on the average over a long period, unless it is approximately zero. Whenever the inflation rate is much above zero, strong pressures arise to change it in both directions. Those who advocate an activist policy to stimulate aggregate demand will press for faster monetary growth, and those who seek a return to price stability will press for slower. An average inflation rate of zero appears to be easier to maintain than any other rate.

Another aspect of inflationary uncertainty concerns the effective real tax rate that individuals and firms will have to pay under our present tax law. Inflation pushes wages and salary earners into higher tax brackets and thus increases their real tax burden even though

156

wages and salaries before tax may exactly keep up with inflation. Income from interest, dividends, and profits is subject to much worse distortion. Imagine for simplicity a corporation in the 50 percent tax bracket. Suppose it earns 10 percent in real terms before tax. If the inflation rate is zero, there is no distortion: its real tax rate is 50 percent and its after-tax return is 5 percent. But if the inflation rate is 11.1 percent, the nominal rate of return is 22.2 percent (since $1.10 \times 1.111 = 1.222$), the real tax rate is 100 percent, and the after-tax return is zero. And if the inflation rate is 25 percent, the nominal rate of return is 37.5 percent (since $1.1 \times 1.25 = 1.375$), the real tax rate is 150 percent, and the after-tax return is minus 5 percent. In principle it is possible to rewrite the tax code so that the real tax rate on everyone is independent of the inflation rate, but in practice it is very difficult and probably will never be done. This is another reason to opt for price stability.

H. The Exchange Rate, the Balance of Payments, and Foreign Exchange Reserves

In a closed economy, the values of government expenditures, tax receipts, the monetary base, and government debt in private hands are required to satisfy the Government budget restraint, equation (2.4). Therefore the authorities cannot exogenously fix the paths of all four of these policy variables. They can fix paths for at most three of them, any three. The Government budget restraint and the private economy together determine the fourth endogenously.

In an open economy, foreign exchange reserves appear as an additional variable in the Government budget restraint. (See equation (3.1).) The net increase in foreign exchange reserves is related to the exchange rate. We measure the exchange rate in dollars per unit of foreign currency. Then, after an adjustment period, a higher exchange rate (meaning a lower foreign value of the dollar) goes with a larger net increase in foreign exchange reserves. The authorities have two more variables to think about than in a closed economy: Foreign exchange reserves and the exchange rate. They can choose a path for either one of them exogenously and let the market determine the other one endogenously.

(a) Suppose the authorities choose a flexible exchange rate regime, a clean float. To do so, they exogenously fix the change in foreign exchange reserves at zero and let the market demand and supply of dollars determine the exchange rate endogenously. This is compatible with the choice of any one of the closed economy's four policy variables as endogenous (expenditures, taxes, the monetary base, and government debt held outside the Federal Reserve).

(b) Suppose the authorities choose to fix the exchange rate exogenously. They do so as follows. Whenever more dollars are supplied than demanded in the market at the chosen exchange rate, the authorities step in and buy the excess dollars, spending part of their foreign exchange reserves. This prevents the foreign value of the dollar from falling. Whenever more dollars are demanded than supplied at the chosen rate, the authorities sell the excess dollars, receiving foreign exchange in return, which they add to their reserves. This prevents the foreign value of the dollar from rising. Thus the exchange rate is maintained at the chosen level, while the stock of foreign exchange reserves is determined endogenously, falling when dollars are in excess supply and rising when dollars are in excess demand. This too is compatible with the choice of any one of the closed economy's four policy variables as endogenous, with one proviso: that we do not run out of foreign exchange reserves. If we do run out, we no longer have the wherewithal to buy any excess supply of dollars, and so we can no longer prevent a decline in the foreign value of the dollar.

(c) Suppose the authorities choose to fix all four of the closed economy's policy variables exogenously, and leave both the exchange rate and foreign reserves to be determined endogenously. In principle this should be possible, but it might lead to rather wide fluctuations in the exchange rate because foreign exchange reserves must move in such a way as to satisfy the Government budget restraint (3.1); and the variable that must bear the burden of adjusting to make this happen is the exchange rate. This policy too might break down through the exhaustion of the stock of foreign exchange reserves.

(d) What if the authorities try to fix exogenously both the exchange rate and the change in foreign exchange reserves? Can they do so? No, because they cannot foresee disturbances quickly and accurately enough to offset them before they affect either the exchange rate or foreign exchange reserves. The difficulty here is similar to the difficulty of trying to fix the path of real income exogenously. It may be possible to fix an average path, about which the actual values fluctuate, but not the actual values themselves.

(e) The authorities may choose a managed ("dirty") float, by using either explicitly or implicitly a rule determining when to intervene in the foreign exchange market and by how much. Then both the exchange rate and foreign exchange reserves would be endogenous. This regime too would break down if foreign exchange reserves fell to zero, unless the rule prescribed floating rates at that juncture.

We have found that in an open economy, the authorities must consider the following 6 variables: Government expenditures, taxes, the monetary base, government debt outside the Federal Reserve, the exchange rate, and the change in foreign exchange reserves. Four of them can be chosen exogenously; two (at least) must be determined endogenously. Any choice is possible, with the following exceptions: (1) It is not possible to fix exogenously both foreign exchange reserves and the exchange rate; (2) if foreign exchange reserves are made endogenous and subsequently foreign exchange reserves fall to zero, the regime will break down because they cannot be negative.

J. Changes and Continuity Since World War II

The two most important changes in the financing of the Federal debt since World War II, as noted above, have been an increase in the frequency and size of Federal budget deficits (even as compared to GNP) and an increase in the use of additions to the monetary base as a means of financing. Other changes in Federal debt financing have been of minor importance in comparison.

It is important to note that there are some things that have not changed since World War II and on which we still can rely. One is

158

the positive relation between the rate of inflation and the growth rate of the monetary base. It remains true that rapid inflation cannot continue in the absence of, and cannot be stopped in the presence of, sustained rapid growth of the monetary base. As we have seen, this relationship, although not arithmetically precise, is compelling, and policymakers cannot successfully fly in the face of it.

Another is the negative relation between the amount of slack in the economy and the difference between the actual rate of inflation and the expected rate. This relation was incorrectly perceived when a stable Phillips-curve tradeoff was thought to exist between the rate of unemployment and the rate of inflation. A more nearly correct view is that the tradeoff is between the unemployment rate and the difference between the actual and expected rates of inflation. Abnormally low unemployment leads to an inflation rate higher than expected, while abnormally high unemployment leads to an inflation rate lower than expected (though perhaps still at a positive rate, if expected inflation was high). Thus it is possible to understand the simultaneous existence of inflation and unemployment in the 1970's.

VI. PROJECTIONS TO 1990

In this section we offer some conditional projections concerning the financing of the Federal debt and its implications to the year 1990. The reason the projections must be conditional is that no one knows how large the deficits in the Federal budget will be for the next decade nor how rapidly the Federal Reserve will accumulate Federal debt in its portfolio thus increasing the monetary base. We shall make our projections for three different values of each of these two magnitudes; one value that approximates recent policy decisions, one considerably lower (as recommended in this paper), and one considerably higher. The three values assumed for the budget deficit as a percentage of GNP are 0.5 percent which is the upper limit recommended herein, 3 percent which was the approximate average in the years 1975–79, and 6 percent. The three annual growth rates assumed for the monetary base are 1 percent as recommended approximately herein, 8 percent as in the years 1974–79, and 15 percent.

We shall base our projections on two additional assumptions. One is that real GNP will grow at an average rate of 2.5 percent a year (slightly less than 3.5 percent growth rate from 1948–79) as it did in the last complete business cycle peak to peak (1973–79). This of course will depend on the amounts of employment, investment and technical progress in the coming decade, which will be influenced in turn by the tax, expenditure, and monetary policies followed by the Federal Government.

The second additional assumption is that the income velocity of the monetary base will increase at an average rate of 2 percent a year, as it did from 1960 to 1978 with relatively little fluctuation. (See again table 5.1). This is consistent with a roughly constant velocity of M2. Of course, if the inflation rate is brought down, interest rates and the velocity of money will come down too.

The projections below are all based for simplicity on these two uniform assumptions concerning the growth rates of real output and of velocity. If as time passes these assumptions turn out to be incorrect, the projections can and should be adjusted to reflect the changes.

We will apply equation (5.2) to the monetary base, thus:

159

Growth rate of nominal GNP equals growth rate of real GNP
plus inflation rate equals growth rate of monetary base plus
growth rate of income velocity of monetary base   (6.1)
Using our assumptions about the growth rate of real GNP and of the
income velocity of the monetary base and rearranging terms in
equation (6.1), we find the following expression for the rate of inflation:
Inflation rate equals growth rate of monetary base plus growth
rate of income velocity of monetary base minus growth rate
of real GNP equals growth rate of monetary base plus 2 percent minus 2.5 percent equals growth rate of monetary base
minus 0.5 percent   (6.2)
Table 6.1 records the different assumptions made, in columns (1),
(3), and (8). It shows the conditional projections made for the 1990
values of the monetary base in column (2), the price level on a 1979
base in column (4), nominal GNP in columns (5) and (6), the increase
in the monetary base as a percent of GNP in column (7), the nominal
Federal budget deficit in column (9), the amount of deficit financing
required from sources other than additions to the monetary base,
expressed as a percentage of GNP, in column (10), and the net Federal
debt as a percent of GNP in column (11).
Line 1 of table 6.1 shows the policy combination that we ought to
be approximately following on a long-term basis, according to this
paper: A growth rate of the monetary base averaging about 1 percent
a year in column (1), and a Federal deficit averaging about 0.5 percent
of GNP in column (8). If 1979 is taken as a benchmark, and if this
policy had been in effect before 1979 and were continued until 1990,
then prices would be essentially stable, growing at only 0.5 percent a
year in column (3) to reach only 5.6 percent above the 1979 level by
1990 in column (4). The deficit would be $16 billion in 1990 in
column (9), and the amount of deficit financing required from sources
other than additions to the monetary base would be a modest 0.45
percent of GNP on the average in column (10), not enough to crowd
out any significant amount of private investment.
It would be unwise to embark upon such a combination of policies
abruptly, because a much more inflationary mix of monetary and
fiscal policies has been followed in recent years, approximately the mix
shown in line 5 of table 6.1. A gradual approach to the noninflationary
and noncrowding-out policies of line 1 is to be preferred in order to
give the economy time to adjust its expectations toward price stability
and thus reduce the severity of any ensuing recession. A reduction in
growth rate of the monetary base by 0.5 to 1 percentage point a year
would be suitable. Starting from a growth rate of 8 percent a year as
in late 1979, this would require a transition period of about 5 to 10
years. The Federal Reserve may have embarked on such a path in
October 1979.
A continuation of the policies of the 1970's would yield a result
approximately like line 5 of the table. Inflation would continue at
about 7.5 percent a year, resulting in a price level more than twice
as high in 1990 as in 1979. The nominal budget deficit by 1990 would
be $203 billion. The amount of deficit financing required from sources
other than additions to the monetary base would be about 2.6 percent
of GNP, approximately the same as the average for 1975–79. This
represents, in recent years, a third of net investment as a proportion
of GNP and, therefore, gives cause for concern about the risk of
crowding out.

TABLE 6.1.—CONDITIONAL PROJECTIONS TO 1990 FOR INFLATION AND THE U.S. GOVERNMENT DEFICIT AND ITS FINANCING

[Growth rates in percent]

Line	Monetary base		Price level		Nominal GNP		(Increase in monetary base)÷GNP 1990 1×2÷6	Deficit÷GNP	Nominal deficit 1990 6×8	(Deficit to be financed other than by adding to the monetary base)÷GNP 1990 8−7	(Federal debt held privately and abroad net of Federal loans)÷GNP 1990
	Growth rate	1990 level	Growth rate	1990 level	Growth rate	1990 level					
	(1)	(2)	(3)	(4)	(5)	(6)	(7)	(8)	(9)	(10)	(11)
1	1	173	0.5	1.056	3	3,279	0.0005	0.005	16	0.0045	0.15
2								.03	98	.0295	.39
3								.06	197	.0595	.67
4	8	362	7.5	2.216	10	6,759	.004	.005	34	.001	.05
5								.03	203	.026	.23
6								.06	406	.056	.45
7	15	723	14.5	4.435	17	13,323	.008	.005	67	−.003	.01
8								.03	400	.022	.15
9								.06	799	.052	.32

Sources: Cols. 1, 3, and 8: assumption. Col. 5: col. 3+2.5 percent. Cols. 2, 4, and 6: 1979 level projected to 1990 at indicated growth rate. Cols. 7, 9 and 10: as indicated at the head of the column. Col. 11: [cumulation of (deficit—increase in monetary base)]÷col. 6.

Units of measurement: Cols. 1, 3, 5: annual growth rates. Col. 2: billions of dollars. Col. 4: index with 1979 value equal to 1.000. Cols. 6 and 9: billions of dollars per year. Cols. 7, 8, and 10: pure numbers, ratios without any units.
Assumptions: see text.

161

Line 9 of the table portrays a policy of more inflation and more crowding out than we have been following recently. It would more than quadruple the price level by 1990 and would require deficit financing (other than by adding to the monetary base) in an amount that approaches recent total net investment as a proportion of GNP, thus posing a grave threat of crowding out private investment.

Numerical projections of unemployment are not presented in table 6.1, for cycles are difficult to project accurately. At the business cycle peak in 1979, the lowest monthly unemployment rate was 5.7 percent and the average for 1979 was 5.8 percent. At the trough in 1975, the annual average unemployment rate was 8.5 percent. These rates are about 2 percentage points higher than was typical of the 1950's. Several reasons have been suggested for this increase in unemployment rates. Among them are an increase in the labor force participation of women and youths (whose unemployment rates are typically somewhat higher than men's), improved unemployment compensation programs, broadened coverage of the minimum wage law, the 1972 requirement that in order to be eligible for AFDC welfare and for food stamps one must register with the U.S. Employment Service for work, and the deterioration of the quality of education in some schools. None of these factors appears headed for a spectacular reversal in the next decade or so. Hence it seems likely that unemployment rates in normal business cycles will fluctuate between about 6 and 8 percent. If the Federal Reserve adheres to the policy of gradually reducing the growth rates of the money stocks which was announced in October 1979, there will probably be a temporary increase in unemployment rates, just as there was a temporary decrease in 1966–69 following the adoption of a policy of more rapid monetary growth (recall table 5.3). How long would this temporary unemployment last? Until the general public and officials of firms and labor unions begin to believe that the anti-inflationary policy actually will be carried through. They are not likely to believe this until we have passed through one recession and recovery without abandoning the policy. Action, not just talk, is needed. The credibility of government pronouncements about the future effectiveness of anti-inflation programs is now almost nil. A period of 3 to 5 years might be required before unemployment subsides to a long-run normal path.

To ameliorate unemployment during this transition and in future recessions, I propose several measures. One is the abolition of the minimum wage law or at least the exemption of teenagers and young adults. Surely there are potential employers and workers who would like to get together at an annual wage of $6,000 for a year's work of 50 weeks at 40 hours a week, but that is illegal in 1980. And $6,600 will be illegal by January of 1981.

A second is the alteration of the unemployment compensation program—to have benefits begin after several weeks of unemployment rather than immediately but continue for a longer period than at present—in order to give protection against long bouts of unemployment but not against short ones.

A third is the use of countercyclical expenditure and tax programs designed to run a deficit during recessions but not during prosperity and financed only slightly by additions to the monetary base so that the growth of the base is maintained at a low non-inflationary rate on the average over time.

162

A fourth is mild countercyclical monetary policy to prevent the money stocks from declining in recession and from rising rapidly in prosperity as they have usually been allowed to do in the past.

APPENDIX. CONSOLIDATION OF THE FLOW-OF-FUNDS ACCOUNTS FOR THE U.S. GOVERNMENT SECTOR AND THE MONETARY AUTHORITIES SECTOR

The U.S. Government budget restraint given by equation (4.5) and tables 4.1 and 4.3 concerns the funds flows for the sector that is obtained by consolidating the U.S. Government sector and the monetary authorities sector in the flow-of-funds (FofF) accounts, canceling out all claims of either one against the other. This appendix describes how the author carried out the consolidation. (See the acknowledgement at the beginning of the study.)

The FofF statements of year-end outstandings and annual flows for the U.S. Government sector and the monetary authorities sector are given for 1946–75 in Board of Governors [1976], pages 22–27 and 110–115. The nine-digit numerical code numbers that identify each item in the FofF accounts, together with data for 1973–77, are given in Board of Governors [1978]; the two sectors in question are treated in tables 46–47 and 546–547. The data in these two sources are now obsolete, having been somewhat revised since their release. Quarterly updates and revisions are released by the Board of Governors under the title *Flow of Funds Accounts ( )th Quarter 19( )*.

Table A.1 shows the year-end outstandings for the consolidated U.S. Government and monetary authorities (USG + MA) sector for 1945 through 1978. We begin by describing the items in this table with the aid of the first four digits of the nine-digit code numbers that are found in the "CODE" column.

Look first at the third and fourth digits of the codes. Asset items are denoted by "30" or "40". Liability items are denoted by "31" or "41". Financial net worth items are denoted by "50".

Look now at the first two digits of the codes. Items that appear in the FofF statement for the USG sector are denoted by "31". Items that appear in the FofF statement for the MA sector are denoted by "71" [8] or "72" ("72" refers to the commercial banking sector; that is the source of the "vault cash of commercial banks" item in line 28, which is a liability of the MA sector). Items that were created in the consolidation of the USG and MA sectors are denoted by "32". The definition of each "32" item can be read from the indenting of the verbal descriptions of each line of the table, having regard to the minus signs that appear in those verbal descriptions For example, "deposits at commercial banks" in line 2 is defined as line 3 − line 4 + line 5. "Total financial assets" in line 1 is defined as the sum of lines 2, 6, 7, and 21. "U.S. government debt" in line 30 (held outside the Federal Reserve) is defined as the sum of lines 31, 32, 34, 36, 37, and 38 minus the sum of lines 33 and 35. And so on.

The consolidation of the USG and MA sectors was carried out as follows. First, find the FofF statements of year-end outstandings in one of the FofF publications. Board of Governors [1978] is especially convenient for this purpose because it contains the code number of each item. Second, put all the asset items from both the USG sector and the MA sector on the left side of an aggregate balance sheet, and all the liability and net worth items on the right side. Third, obtain the consolidated balance sheet of the USG + MA sector by netting out claims of the USG sector against the MA sector and claims of the MA sector against the USG sector. This is done by canceling out items that are included on both sides of the aggregate balance sheet that was obtained in the second step; these items are discussed individually below.

A fourth step was taken to obtain table A.1. Combine some of the individual items in the consolidated balance sheet into subtotals, shown in lines 2, 6, 7, 21, 26, 30, 39, and 40 in table A.1. The subtotals are the same year-end outstandings that appear in equation (4.3) in the text, namely, Treasury deposits at commercial banks (line 2), member-bank borrowing (line 6), U.S. Government loans except member-bank borrowing (line 7), gold and SDR's and foreign exchange reserves (line 21), the monetary base (high powered money, line 26), U.S. Government debt held outside the Federal Reserve (line 30), U.S. Government life and

---

[8] There is one exception, regarding items whose codes begin with "71"; it is noted in the memorandum to table A.2.

163

retirement insurance reserves (line 39), and financial net worth of the USG + MA sector (line 40).

The items netted out in the consolidation are as follows. Each is indicated explicitly in the stub of table A.1 by a particular line carrying a minus sign.

Line 4 is Treasury holdings of currency and of deposits at the Federal Reserve. It is a liability of the monetary authority (note that its code begins with 7131), and is also included in the U.S. Government's asset item "demand deposits and currency" (whose code begins with 3130, in line 3). Hence it is netted out so that the consolidated asset item "deposits at commercial banks" in line 2 will not include any claims of the U.S. Government against the monetary authority.

Line 14 is a U.S. Government liability. It is the seignorage on currency issued by the Treasury plus the value of SDR certificates held by the Federal Reserve. Line 15 is a monetary authority asset representing the face value of currency issued by the Treasury plus the value of the same SDR certificates. They are netted against each other to cancel out the value of SDR certificates and the seignorage; the difference between them is the value of the silver at cost that is in the currency issued by the Treasury. It is a rather small item and does not seem to belong naturally to any of the eight major balance-sheet items. Hence it was combined with the two miscellaneous asset items, lines 19 and 20, and allocated to the major item "loans except to member banks" (line 7) which is the least homogeneous of the asset items and is large.

Lines 33 and 35 are Federal Reserve holdings of direct and guaranteed U.S. debt and of budget agency issues and loan participations. As such they are netted out against the total of U.S. Government debt in order to obtain the amount held outside the Federal Reserve (line 30).

There is one netting-out operation in table A.1 that is not the result of canceling out claims between the USG and MA sectors: Line 24, foreign deposits at the Federal Reserve excluding those held by the IMF, is an offset to foreign exchange reserves and hence is netted against them to obtain line 21, "gold, SDR's and official foreign exchange."

The original FofF statements of year-end outstandings for the separate USG and MA sectors can be recovered from table A.1, if desired, as follows. Ignore all items in table A.1 whose codes begin with "32". Ignore the minus signs that appear in the stub of the table. Put on the asset aide of the USG sector statement all items whose codes begin with "3130", and on the liability side all items whose codes begin with "3131". Put on the asset side of the MA statement all items whose codes begin with "7130" and the liability side all items whose codes begin with "7131" and also line 28 whose code begins with "7230" (this item was discussed earlier in the appendix).

This completes the description of table A.1, which is the statement of year-end outstandings for the consolidated USG + MA sector.

Table A.2 contains in lines 1–42 the corresponding statement of annual flows for the years 1946–1978. Recall that it is not exactly the same as the year-to-year change in outstandings for reasons explained in footnote 6 in the text.

Lines 43–48 show U.S. Government receipts, expenditures, and surpluses according to the national income accounts (NIA).

Lines 48–54 correspond precisely to equation (4.1) in the text. This is the reconciliation (carried out in the FofF accounts) between the NIA and the FofF accounting system.

Lines 55–64 correspond to equation (4.5) and to tables 4.1 and 4.3 in the text, which express the U.S. government budget restraint.

Tables 4.3 to 4.6 in the text are the same as lines 55–64 of table A.2.

Table A.1—Continued

11 JUNE 1980
YEAR-END OUTSTANDINGS, 1945-79

SECTOR STMT.OF FINANCIAL ASSETS & LIABILITIES, U.S. GOVT. & MONETARY AUTHORITY

YEAR-END OUTSTANDINGS, 1945-79

BILLIONS OF DOLLARS

#	1975	1976	1977	1978	1979		CODE	#
1	142.136	160.819	177.526	214.874	246.214	TOTAL FINANCIAL ASSETS	324090035	1
2	3.957	5.019	8.000	15.158	15.649	DEPOSITS AT COMMERCIAL BANKS	324000005	2
3	11.153	15.141	14.628	18.652	19.211	DEMAND DEPOSITS & CURRENCY	313029101	3
4	7.768	10.853	7.506	4.436	4.569	- TREAS.CASH & F.R. DEPOSITS	313031003	4
5	572	731	878	942	1.007	TIME DEPOSITS	313061003	5
6	229	25	285	1.172	1.494	F.R. LOANS TO MEMBER BANKS	713068001	6
7	122.208	137.675	150.562	184.358	210.958	LOANS EXCEPT TO MEMBER BANKS	324030035	7
8	7.012	10.750	10.095	23.825	32.050	SPONS.AGCY.ISSUES—TREAS.	313061703	8
9	5.623	6.401	7.865	9.254	8.248	SPONS.AGCY.ISSUES—F.R.	713061713	9
10	13.517	10.455	10.225	9.854	8.690	MORTGAGES	313065005	10
11	61.607	75.455	80.222	95.832	109.005	OTHER LOANS	313059005	11
12	5.800	11.337	10.054	13.594	17.290	TAXES RECEIVABLE	313078005	12
13	6.695	6.968	6.186	8.912	10.856	TRADE CREDIT	313070003	13
14	8.670	9.859	10.159	10.693	12.293	- TREAS. CURR. & SDR CTFS.	313112C03	14
15	10.632	12.010	12.581	13.146	14.883	TREAS.CURR. & SDR CTFS.	313012003	15
16	3.688	2.601	3.810	6.516	6.767	F.R. FLOAT	713022000	16
17	1.126	991	954	587	704	ACCEPTANCES	713069603	17
18	—	—	—	—	—	LOANS ON GOLD TO R.O.W.	713068103	18
19	6.114	7.078	7.752	8.519	9.438	MISC. ASSETS OF U.S. GOVT.	313090005	19
20	3.214	3.008	2.424	2.953	3.130	MISC. ASSETS OF F.R.	713093005	20
21	15.742	18.100	18.699	17.976	18.143	GOLD.SDR'S & OFF.FGN.EXCH.	323011095	21
22	4.571	7.004	7.603	5.402	5.330	GOLD.SDR'S & OFF.FGN.EXCH.	313011005	22
23	11.655	11.763	11.714	13.248	13.628	GOLD & FOREIGN EXCHANGE	713022003	23
24	434	647	618	674	785	- FGN. DEPOSITS EXCL. I.M.F.	713122605	24
25	530.854	606.366	677.008	748.922	798.322	TOTAL LIABILITIES	324190035	25
26	112.599	118.875	130.681	145.868	155.392	HIGH-POWERED MONEY	324100035	26
27	26.052	25.158	26.870	31.223	29.792	MEMBER BANK RESERVE DEP.	713113001	27
28	12.252	12.121	13.922	15.470	18.488	VAULT CASH OF COML. BANKS	723025001	28
29	74.295	81.596	89.889	99.175	107.112	CURR. OUTSIDE COML. BANKS	713125001	29
30	368.350	432.847	485.034	534.538	566.111	U.S. GOVERNMENT DEBT	324130035	30
31	67.363	72.018	76.762	80.691	79.876	SAVINGS BONDS	313133000	31
32	369.943	434.427	487.332	538.516	578.092	DIRECT & GUAR.TREAS. SECS.	313161105	32
33	87.934	97.021	102.819	110.562	117.458	- F.R. HOLDINGS DIR. & GUAR.	713061101	33
34	8.967	9.311	8.425	6.993	5.592	BUDG.AGCY.ISS.,MTG.& L.P.	313161755	34
35	567	671	590	516	461	- F.R. HOLDINGS B.A.I.& L.P.	713061705	35
36	5.651	10.012	11.682	14.056	14.458	TRADE DEBT	313170005	36
37	1.150	675	25	25		MISC. U.S.G. LIABILITIES	313190005	37
38	3.797	4.096	4.217	5.235	5.987	MISC. F.R. LIABILITIES	713190C05	38
39	49.995	54.644	61.293	68.516	76.819	LIFE & RETIREMENT RESERVES	313154005	39
40	-388.718	-445.547	-499.482	-533.948	-552.108	FINANCIAL N.W., U.S.G. & M.A.	325060535	40
41	-388.718	-445.547	-499.482	-533.948	-552.108	FINANCIAL N.W. U.S. GOVT.	315000005	41
42	—	—	—	—	—	FINANCIAL N.W., MON. AUTH.	715000005	42

Table A.2—Continued

11 JUNE 1980
ANNUAL FLOWS, 1946-79

BILLIONS OF DOLLARS PER YEAR

SECTOR STATEMENT OF SAVING & INVESTMENT, U.S. GOVERNMENT & MONETARY AUTHORITY

ANNUAL FLOWS, 1946-79

BILLIONS OF DOLLARS PER YEAR

1975	1976	1977	1978	1979	1948-60	CODE		
15,753	18,640	16,318	37,000	30,594	22,360	324090035	TOTAL FINANCIAL ASSETS	1
-1,479	1,062	2,981	7,158	490	4,987	324000605	DEPOSITS AT COMMERCIAL BANKS	2
2,896	3,988	-513	4,024	559	3,492	313022001	DEMAND DEPOSITS & CURRENCY	3
4,470	3,085	-3,347	-3,070	134	-1,344	713123101	- TREAS.CASH & F.R. DEPOSITS	4
95	159	147	64	65	151	313031003	TIME DEPOSITS	5
-70	-204	240	907	282	-9	713068001	F.R. LOANS TO MEMBER BANKS	6
16,709	15,416	12,826	29,979	30,400	21,622	324030035	LOANS EXCEPT TO MEMBER BANKS	7
4,504	3,738	5,345	7,730	8,225	37	313061703	SPONS.AGCY.ISSUES—TREAS.	8
4,955	778	1,454	-352	735	-	713061713	SPONS.AGCY.ISSUES—F.R.	9
3,224	-3,062	-230	-371	1,036	4,823	313065005	MORTGAGES	10
7,357	8,236	6,716	13,048	13,292	7,957	313069005	OTHER LOANS	11
-3,001	5,537	-1,283	3,540	3,696	2,109	313078005	TAXES RECEIVABLE	12
1,190	-162	-162	2,726	1,944	1,790	313070003	TRADE CREDIT	13
937	1,889	300	524	1,610	278	313112003	- TREAS. CURR. & SDR CTFS.	14
959	1,398	571	505	1,257	836	313012002	TREAS. CURR. & SDR CTFS.	15
1,687	-1,087	1,209	2,706	251	1,333	313022000	F.R. FLOAT	16
127	-135	-37	-367	217	74	713069103	ACCEPTANCES	17
-	-	-	-	-	-44	713068103	LOANS ON GOLD TO R.O.W.	18
683	955	717	749	800	2,818	313098005	MISC. ASSETS OF U.S. GOVT.	19
21	-206	-584	529	177	167	713093005	MISC. ASSETS OF F.R.	20
593	2,366	271	-1,044	-578	-4,249	323011095	GOLD-SDR'S & OFF.FGN. EXCH.	21
470	2,441	271	-2,634	-1,195	363	313011005	GOLD-SDR'S & OFF.FGN. EXCH.	22
84	88	-29	1,646	728	-809	713011005	GOLD & FOREIGN EXCHANGE	23
-39	163	-29	56	111	-206	713122605	- FGN. DEPOSITS EXCL. I.M.F.	24
89,073	76,402	70,144	70,970	48,147	25,391	324100035	TOTAL LIABILITIES	25
7,013	6,276	11,806	15,187	9,524	3,184	324100035	HIGH-POWERED MONEY	26
209	-894	-81	-353	-1,431	-818	713113001	MEMBER BANK RESERVE DEP.	27
612	-131	1,801	1,548	3,018	1,130	723025001	VAULT CASH OF COML. BANKS	28
6,192	7,301	8,293	9,286	7,937	2,872	713125001	CURR. OUTSIDE COML. BANKS	29
78,264	65,387	51,689	48,560	30,320	11,650	324130035	U.S. GOVERNMENT DEBT	30
4,025	4,655	4,744	3,929	-815	-594	313133000	SAVINGS BONDS	31
81,823	65,484	52,905	51,184	39,576	14,194	313161105	DIRECT & GUAR.TREAS. SECS.	32
7,433	9,087	5,798	7,743	6,896	4,825	713061101	- F.R. HOLDINGS DIR. & GUAR.	33
-443	-112	-886	-1,432	-1,491	1,872	313161755	BUDG.AGCY.ISS.=MTGS.&L.P.	34
-18	104	-81	-74	-55	-	713061705	- F.R. HOLDINGS B.A.=I.& L.P.	35
1,445	4,361	1,670	2,374	402	3,145	313170005	TRADE DEBT	36
-709	939	-925	-276	-1,130	-3,108	313190005	MISC. U.S.G. LIABILITIES	37
-462	251	-102	450	709	466	713190005	MISC. F.R. LIABILITIES	38
3,796	4,739	6,649	7,223	8,303	11,057	313154005	LIFE & RETIREMENT RESERVES	39
-73,320	-57,762	-53,826	-33,970	-17,553	-3,031	325000535	FINANCIAL N.W. USG & MA	40
-73,556	-57,810	-54,049	-34,650	-17,943	-3,304	315000005	FINANCIAL N.W. U.S. GOVT.	41
236	48	223	680	390	273	715000005	FINANCIAL N.W. MON. AUTH.	42

Table A.2—Continued

11 JUNE 1980
ANNUAL FLOWS, 1946-79

CONTINUED
ANNUAL FLOWS, 1946-79

SECTOR STATEMENT OF SAVING & INVESTMENT, U.S. GOVERNMENT & MONETARY AUTHORITY

BILLIONS OF DOLLARS PER YEAR

	1975	1976	1977	1978	1979	1948-60	CODE		
43	286.241	331.421	375.384	432.066	497.588	894.402	316010005	U.S. GOVT. RECEIPTS, N.I.A.	43
44	356.825	385.016	421.715	459.751	509.038	885.461	316900005	U.S.GOVT. EXPENDITURES, N.I.A.	44
45	123.058	129.707	144.379	152.590	166.649	533.810	316901001	GOODS & SERVICES	45
46	23.199	26.754	28.983	34.816	43.072	64.234	316132001	NET INTEREST	46
47	210.568	228.555	248.353	272.345	299.317	267.617	316400205	TRANSFERS, ETC.	47
48	-70.584	-53.595	-46.331	-27.685	-11.450	8.941	316060105	U.S. GOVT. SURPLUS, N.I.A.	48
49	3.796	4.739	6.649	7.223	8.303	11.057	313154005	LIFE & RETIREMENT RESERVES	49
50	1.323	3.973	2.470	1.973	4.745	—	105030003	- MINERAL RIGHTS SALES	50
51	499	3.449	3.539	1.715	2.935	1.188	317005005	N.I.A.-F.O.F. DISCREPANCY	51
52	-73.556	-57.810	-54.049	-34.650	-17.943	-3.304	315900005	FINANCIAL N.W. U.S. GOVT.	52
53	-73.320	-57.762	-53.826	-33.970	-17.553	-3.031	325000535	- FINANCIAL N.W., USG & MA	53
54	236	48	223	680	390	273	715000005	- FINANCIAL N.W., MON. AUTH.	54
55	-70.584	-53.595	-46.331	-27.685	-11.450	8.941	316061105	U.S. GOVT. SURPLUS, N.I.A.	55
56	-1.479	1.062	2.981	7.158	490	4.987	324000005	DEPOSITS AT COML. BANKS	56
57	-70	-264	240	907	282	-9	713068001	F.R. LOANS TO MEMBER BANKS	57
58	16.709	15.416	12.826	29.979	30.400	21.622	324030035	LOANS EXCEPT TO MEMBER BANKS	58
59	593	2.306	271	-1.044	-578	-4.240	323011095	GOLD, SDR'S & DEF.FOR.EXCH.	59
60	7.013	6.276	11.806	15.187	9.524	3.184	324100035	- HIGH-POWERED MONEY	60
61	78.264	65.387	51.689	48.560	30.320	11.150	324130035	- U.S. GOVERNMENT DEBT	61
62	1.323	3.973	2.470	1.973	4.745	—	105030003	- MINERAL RIGHTS SALES	62
63	236	48	223	680	390	273	715000005	- FINANCIAL N.W., MON. AUTH.	63
64	499	3.449	3.539	1.715	2.935	1.188	317005005	N.I.A.-F.O.F. DISCREPANCY	64

MEMORANDUM:

EACH LINE IN LINES 1-64 ABOVE (OTHER THAN TOTALS HAVING CODE NUMBERS BEGINNING WITH 321) APPEARS IN THE FLOW OF FUNDS TABLE OF FLOWS FOR EITHER THE U.S. GOVERNMENT SECTOR OR THE MONETARY AUTHORITY SECTOR, EXCEPT FOR 713061713 AND 713061705 IN LINES 9 AND 35. THEIR SUM APPEARS IN THE MONETARY AUTHORITY SECTOR TABLE AS THE ASSET ITEM "AGENCY ISSUES" 713061703.

Table A.2—Continued

11 JUNE 1986
ANNUAL FLOWS, 1946-79

SECTOR STATEMENT OF SAVING & INVESTMENT, U.S. GOVERNMENT & MONETARY AUTHORITY

ANNUAL FLOWS, 1946-79

BILLIONS OF DOLLARS PER YEAR — BILLIONS OF DOLLARS PER YEAR

1961-65	1966-74	1975-79	1966-79	1948-79	CODE		
13,688	35,602	118,305	153,907	189,955	324090035	TOTAL FINANCIAL ASSETS	1
-530	-894	10,212	9,318	13,475	324000005	DEPOSITS AT COMMERCIAL BANKS	2
-252	-1,230	10,954	9,724	12,984	313020001	DEMAND DEPOSITS & CURRENCY	3
566	-169	1,272	1,103	385	713123101	- TREAS.,CASH & F.R. DEPOSITS	4
-12	227	530	757	896	313031003	TIME DEPOSITS	5
71	223	1,135	1,358	1,420	713068001	F.R. LOANS TO MEMBER BANKS	6
18,331	41,027	105,330	146,357	186,410	324030035	LOANS EXCEPT TO MEMBER BANKS	7
-	2,463	29,542	32,005	32,050	313061703	SPONS.AGCY.ISSUES—TREAS.	8
-	4,628	3,620	8,248	8,268	313065713	SPONS.AGCY.ISSUES—F.R.	9
53	4,440	597	5,037	9,913	313065005	MORTGAGES	10
10,807	31,257	48,649	79,906	98,670	313066005	OTHER LOANS	11
4,346	-8,120	8,389	269	6,724	313070005	TAXES RECEIVABLE	12
1,332	2,183	5,551	7,734	10,856	313070003	TRADE CREDIT	13
378	4,782	4,560	9,342	9,998	313112003	- TREAS. CURR. & SDR CTFS.	14
177	4,234	5,230	9,464	10,477	713012003	TREAS. CURR. & SDR CTFS.	15
491	-247	4,766	4,519	6,253	713022000	F.R. FLOAT	16
113	812	-295	517	704	713069603	ACCEPTANCES	17
33	-41		-41	-52	713068103	LOANS ON GOLD TO R.O.W.	18
1,306	1,458	3,904	5,362	9,686	313099005	MISC. ASSETS OF U.S. GOVT.	19
133	2,742	-63	2,679	2,979	713093005	MISC. ASSETS OF F.R.	20
-3,842	-4,734	1,608	-3,126	-11,250	323011095	GOLD, SDR'S & OFF.FGN. EXCH.	21
-556	309	-647	-338	-531	313011005	GOLD, SDR'S & OFF.FGN. EXCH.	22
-3,353	-4,721	2,517	-2,204	-10,366	713011005	GOLD & FOREIGN EXCHANGE	23
-25	322	262	584	353	713122605	- FGN. DEPOSITS EXCL. I.M.F.	24
29,455	124,684	354,736	479,420	534,266	324190035	TOTAL LIABILITIES	25
10,358	45,083	49,806	94,889	108,431	324109035	HIGH-POWERED MONEY	26
1,172	7,396	3,949	11,345	11,699	713113001	MEMBER BANK RESERVE DEP.	27
1,505	6,797	6,848	13,645	16,280	723025001	VAULT CASH OF COML. BANKS	28
7,681	30,890	39,009	69,899	80,452	713125001	CURR. OUTSIDE COML. BANKS	29
12,876	60,229	274,220	334,449	358,475	324193035	U.S. GOVERNMENT DEBT	30
4,053	13,643	16,538	30,181	33,640	313133000	SAVINGS BONDS	31
19,532	79,896	289,972	369,868	403,594	313161105	DIRECT & GUAR.,TREAS. SECS.	32
13,384	39,733	36,957	76,690	94,899	713061101	- F.R. HOLDINGS DIR. & GUAR.	33
2,575	4,875	-4,274	601	5,048	313161755	BUDG.AGCY.ISS.,MTGS.& L.P.	34
-	585	-124	461	461	713061705	- F.R. HOLDINGS B.A.I.& L.P.	35
721	-1,162	10,252	9,090	12,956	313170005	TRADE DEBT	36
-954	1,394	-2,281	-1,187	-5,249	313190005	MISC. U.S.G. LIABILITIES	37
333	2,201	846	3,047	3,846	713190005	MISC. F.R. LIABILITIES	38
6,221	19,372	30,710	50,082	67,360	313154005	LIFE & RETIREMENT RESERVES	39
-15,767	-89,082	-236,431	-325,513	-344,311	325000535	FINANCIAL N.W. USG & MA	40
-15,494	-89,513	-238,008	-327,521	-346,319	315000005	FINANCIAL N.W., U.S. GOVT.	41
-273	431	1,577	2,008	2,008	715000005	FINANCIAL N.W., MON. AUTH.	42

Table A.2—Continued

11 JUNE 1980
ANNUAL FLOWS, 1946-79

CONTINUED
ANNUAL FLOWS, 1946-79

SECTOR STATEMENT OF SAVING & INVESTMENT, U.S. GOVERNMENT & MONETARY AUTHORITY

BILLIONS OF DOLLARS PER YEAR

	1961-65	1966-74	1975-79	1966-79	1968-79	CODE	BILLIONS OF DOLLARS PER YEAR	
43	557.910	1829.137	1922.700	3751.837	5204.149	316010005	U.S. GOVT. RECEIPTS, N.I.A.	43
44	568.526	1910.179	2132.345	4042.524	5496.511	316900005	U.S.GOVT. EXPENDITURE, N.I.A.	44
45	318.225	872.534	716.383	1588.917	2460.952	316901001	GOODS & SERVICES	45
46	36.678	125.101	156.824	281.925	382.837	316132001	NET INTEREST	46
47	213.623	912.544	1259.138	2171.682	2652.722	316400205	TRANSFERS, ETC.	47
48	-10.616	-81.042	-209.645	-290.687	-292.362	316061105	U.S. GOVT. SURPLUS, N.I.A.	48
49	6.221	19.372	30.710	50.082	67.360	313154005	LIFE & RETIREMENT RESERVES	49
50	-	12.990	14.484	27.474	27.474	105030003	- MINERAL RIGHTS SALES	50
51	-1.343	2.089	12.137	14.226	14.071	317005005	N.I.A.-F.O.F. DISCREPANCY	51
52	-15.499	-89.513	-238.008	-327.521	-346.319	315000005	FINANCIAL N.A., U.S. GOVT.	52
53	-15.767	-89.082	-236.431	-325.513	-344.311	325000535	FINANCIAL N.W., USG & MA	53
54	-.273	.431	1.577	2.008	2.008	715000005	- FINANCIAL N.A., MON. AUTH.	54
55	-10.616	-81.042	-209.645	-290.687	-292.362	316061105	U.S. GOVT. SURPLUS, N.I.A.	55
56	-.830	-.894	10.212	9.318	13.475	324000005	DEPOSITS AT COML. BANKS	56
57	.71	.203	1.155	1.358	1.420	713068001	F.R. LOANS TO MEMBER BANKS	57
58	18.331	41.027	105.330	146.357	186.310	324030035	LOANS EXCEPT TO MEMBER BANKS	58
59	-3.884	-4.734	1.608	-3.126	-11.250	323011095	GOLD, SDRS & OFF.FGN.EXCH.	59
60	10.358	45.083	49.806	94.889	108.431	324100035	- HIGH-POWERED MONEY	60
61	12.876	60.229	276.220	336.449	358.475	324130635	U.S. GOVERNMENT DEBT	61
62	-	12.990	14.484	27.474	27.474	105030003	- MINERAL RIGHTS SALES	62
63	-.273	.431	1.577	2.008	2.008	715000005	- FINANCIAL N.A., MON. AUTH.	63
64	-1.343	2.089	12.137	14.226	14.071	317005005	N.I.A.-F.O.F. DISCREPANCY	64

MEMORANDUM:

EACH LINE IN LINES 1-44 ABOVE (OTHER THAN TOTALS HAVING CODE NUMBERS
BEGINNING WITH 32) APPEARS IN THE FLOW OF FUNDS TABLE OF FLOWS FOR EITHER
THE U.S. GOVERNMENT SECTOR OR THE MONETARY AUTHORITY SECTOR, EXCEPT FOR
713061713 AND 713061705 IN LINES 9 AND 35. THEIR SUM APPEARS IN THE MONETARY
AUTHORITY SECTOR TABLE AS THE ASSET ITEM "AGENCY ISSUES" 713061703.

184

A SUPPLEMENTARY NOTE ON DEBT MANAGEMENT

In this note we mention some aspects of Federal debt management that would be treated in any thorough account of the subject, though some of them are not central to the subject of this paper.

Debt management is carried out by the Treasury subject to legislation enacted by the Congress. It is concerned with such matters as the following.

What should be the term structure of the Federal debt? That is, how much should be in 13-week bills, how much in long-term bonds, and how much in intermediate maturities? The average term to maturity of the Federal debt is now rather short. Very short-term issues are regarded by the public as relatively close substitutes for money since the value of a short-term instrument fluctuates only insignificantly as market interest rates fluctuate. Long-term bonds are poor substitutes for money because their values do fluctuate (in reverse) as market interest rates change. Open market operations in long-term bonds have a greater impact than those in short-term bills because the securities being exchanged for money are less like money.

What interest rates should be offered by the Treasury? Here the answer is simple, for the Treasury must offer rates comparable to the going market rates for similar private securities or it will find no private takers. (At times like the present, when discriminatory Federal interest ceilings deny to small savers the right to receive yields as high as the market is paying, the Treasury may possibly be able to sell some of its small-denomination U.S. Savings Bonds to small savers, but one hopes that such interest ceilings are not long for this world.)

In what denominations should Federal securities be offered? In recent years the Treasury has increased the minimum size of those securities whose interest rates are market-determined (such as Treasury bills: their minimum denomination was raised a few years ago from $1,000 to $10,000). The only small denominations now offered carry interest rates considerably below going market rates. It is not very important whether the Treasury offers its own securities in small denominations for small savers, so long as private financial institutions are permitted to accept small amounts of savings from individuals. What is important, in fairness, is that small savers not be denied access to market yields because of discriminatory government regulations as at present.

What kind of commitment to pay interest and principal should be offered? Currently, almost all U.S. Government debt carries the promise to pay in dollars, regardless of what the purchasing power of those dollars may be when the payment is due. It would be possible to promise to pay in dollars of constant purchasing power according to some price index, in gold, or in some foreign currency such as German marks. When a country's currency has been stable in purchasing power in the past, and is expected to remain so, promises to pay interest and principal in that currency are quite satisfactory. However, when the future inflation rate is uncertain, a long-term promise to pay in dollars is a very risky thing: it will turn out very valuable if inflation is stopped dead the day after the promise is made, but nearly worthless if the inflation rate rises much further than expected. In inflationary uncertainty, many lenders might prefer a promise in terms of indexed dollars or gold in order to protect themselves from this uncertainty. A difficulty with such promises is that governments have caused them to be broken before and might do so again. The gold clause in certain contracts was abrogated by the courts after the U.S. abandoned the gold standard in the thirties.

A crucial related question has to do with the tax treatment of interest and principal payments. During an inflationary period, the interest rates agreed upon in the marketplace carry an inflation premium to allow for the decline in purchasing power of the dollar that is expected to occur during the life of the loan. For example, if borrower and lender agree that the expected inflation rate for the next year will be 10 percent and that a real interest rate of 3 percent is appropriate, then they will agree on an interest rate of 13.3 percent for a one-year loan to be repaid in dollars $(1.10 \times 1.03 = 1.133$, which requires an interest rate of 0.133 = 13.3 percent). Under present U.S. tax law, written for an era of stable prices, the entire 13.3 percent is regarded as income and is taxed at the lender's marginal tax rate. But this amounts in fact to a confiscation of part of his original capital. If he received 10 percent interest during a 10 percent inflation, he would have no income at all in terms of real purchasing power. If he receives 13.3 percent interest, then only the 3 percent real return should be regarded as income and taxed. Under present tax law, it is virtually impossible for the Treasury to offer interest rates that will protect lenders against future inflation. Inflation plus taxation of nominal interest and dividends and capital gains equal confiscation of capital.

185

The remaining items of debt management to be mentioned are rather minor and technical. Should interest on Federal securities be paid periodically during their life, or should it be accumulated and paid at maturity? Answer: Whatever lenders prefer. There is no harm in offering a variety of securities. Should Federal securities be sold at auction, as Treasury bills are, or through an offering of a stated amount of securities at a fixed interest rate? Answer: The auction method works well where the Treasury wants to be sure in advance how much money it will raise through the sale of the issue. Offerings at fixed interest rates work well where that advance certainty is not important. Should Federal securties be negotiable (as most current issues are), or should they be redeemable only by the original buyer (or his or her heirs)? Answer: Negotiability is important to most lenders, and accordingly the Treasury can borrow at slightly lower rates if it issues negotiable securities. This, it should do.

List of References

Burns, Arthur F. [1979], *The Anguish of Central Banking: The 1979 Per Jacobsson Lecture.* Washington, The Per Jacobsson Foundation, International Monetary Fund.

Federal Reserve Bulletin, various recent issues.

Lipsey, Richard G. [1978], "The Place of the Phillips Curve in Macroeconomic Models." Pp. 49–75 in *Stability and Inflation*, edited by A. R. Bergstorm. Sussex, Wiley.

McCracken, Paul *et al.* [1971], *Towards Full Employment and Price Stability.* Paris, OECD.

U.S. Board of Governors of the Federal Reserve System [1975], *Introduction to Flow of Funds.* Washington.

———— [1976], *Flow of Funds Accounts 1946–1975: Annual Total Flows and Year-End Assets and Liabilities.* Washington.

————, *Flow of Funds Accounts (th) Quarter 19(   ).* Quarterly. Washington.

———— [1978], *Flow of Funds Table Codes.* Washington.

———— [1980], "Redefined Money Stock Measures, Liquid Assets, and Related Components," February 13, 1980, processed. Washington.

U.S. President, *Economic Report of the President,* various annual issues. Washington, U.S.G.P.O.

The Financing of the Government Budget in Japan and Its Relation to Macroeconomic Variables*

Carl F. Christ**

I. Introduction

This paper deals with the relation of government finance in Japan to the rate of inflation and other macroeconomic variables. For the past decade, Japan's anti-inflation record has been one of the best in the world: its annual inflation rate came down very quickly from 25% in 1974, and subsequently declined gradually, reaching 2% in 1985. This has been brought about by the action of the Bank of Japan which limited the growth rates of high powered money (to be denoted by H), M_1, and M_2 + CD. Velocities of circulation and money multipliers did not change rapidly during the past decade. This suggests that it was a fairly simple task conceptually (though perhaps not simple practically, since so few countries succeeded!) to control inflation by keeping the average growth rate of the money supply close to the average growth

* This paper was written while the author was a Visiting Scholar from Abroad at the Institute for Monetary and Economic Studies, Bank of Japan. The author is grateful to helpful assistance, advice, and comments from Sei Kuribayashi, Hiroshi Matsuura, and Naohiro Yashiro of the Economic Planning Agency; Takayoshi Hatayama, Sumihide Jinnouchi, Yoshihiko Noguchi and Teiichi Yasuda of the Research and Statistics Department, the Bank of Japan, and Dr. Michael Dotsey (the former Visiting Scholar from Abroad; now at the Federal Reserve Bank of Richmond), Yasuhiro Horiye, Suzu Ishihara, Takashi Kanzaki, Munehisa Kasuya, Misako Kimura, Masataka Kotani, Yoshiharu Oritani, Takashi Oyama, Hiromichi Shirakawa, Dr. Yoshio Suzuki, and Dr. Philip Turner (the former Visiting Scholar from Abroad; now at OECD) of the Bank's Institute for Monetary and Economic Studies. Helpful comments on an earlier draft were made by members of the seminars at Doshisha, Hitotsubashi, International Christian, Kobe, Kyoto, Osaka, Saitama, and Tokyo Universities, and at the Ministry of Finance. Especially detailed comments were received from Professors: Kazumi Asako, Hidekazu Eguchi, Masaaki Homma, and Hiromitsu Ishi. Any errors or inadequacies are the author's.

** Abram G. Hutzler Professor of Economics, Johns Hopkins University.

1

rate of real output.

Beginning in 1975 the Japanese government budget has gone heavily into deficit, with deficits in the neighborhood of 4 or 5% of GNP. Had these deficits been financed by high powered money creation, the result would have been a poorer anti-inflation record. Instead, they were financed largely by the sale of government bonds to investors outside the Bank of Japan. So far there appear to have been no serious adverse effects of these deficits, financed in this way. However, the experience of many countries shows that there is such a thing as borrowing too much, relative to the capacity of the country's tax system to raise the revenue needed to service the debt. In general, as Table 1 and Figure 1 indicate, countries with severe inflation are countries with government deficits in excess of 3% of GNP, while countries without severe inflation are countries with government deficits below 3% of GNP. This is not an inviolable rule: Japan has been an exception for the past 5 or 6 years. But in many countries, when the deficit becomes large, heavy political pressure falls on the central bank to issue high powered money faster so as to help finance the deficit. And this can only result in inflation.

Table 1   Relationship between Government Deficit and Inflation

(Average of 1980–1984, %)

		General government deficit/nominal GNP(GDP) X 100	Rate of increase of consumer prices
Countries with high government deficit and high inflation	Ireland	△12.4	15.0
	Italy	△11.4	16.2
	Greece	△ 8.3	21.8
	Sweden	△ 4.4	10.3
	Spain	△ 4.2	13.6
	Denmark	△ 6.2	9.5
	United Kingdom	△ 3.2	9.6
	Canada	△ 4.4	8.7
Countries with low government deficit and low inflation	Germany	△ 2.9	4.6
	Austria	△ 2.5	5.5
	United States	△ 2.5	7.5
Exceptions	Japan	△ 3.6	3.9
	Netherlands	△ 5.8	5.1

Source: OECD *Economic Outlook* May 1986

Figure 1   Relationship between Government Deficit and Inflation
(Average of 1980-1984,%)

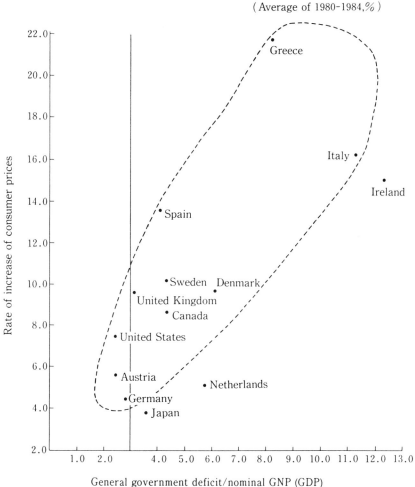

General government deficit/nominal GNP (GDP)

There is considerable discussion in the literature about government debt. At least two strands can be distinguished. One strand deals with how to incorporate government debt into macroeconomic analysis, and centers on the government budget restraint (GBR). The GBR equation says that the total of government expenditures must be equal to the total of financing by all methods, one of those methods being the sale of government debt to private and foreign investors. This is one of the ways government debt enters into the analysis. Other ways include its effect on taxes and transfer payments (since government interest is a transfer and is typically taxed), and its effect on the behavior of its holders.

Another strand deals with the question of whether government debt really has any significance in macroeconomic analysis at all, in spite of the GBR. This strand argues that under appropriate stringent assumptions investors do not regard government debt as net wealth, because the present value of expected future taxation to service the debt is a liability which is exactly equal to the debt's current market value. In such a world tax finance and debt finance of government expenditure are equivalent; when the paths of government expenditure and the high powered money stock have been chosen, the behavior of interest rates, output, and prices is determined, regardless of what mix of taxation and debt sale to investors is used to satisfy the GBR. Then the only role of the GBR is to determine investors' holdings of government debt, but these holdings have no feedback effect on interest rates, prices, or output. This is known as the Ricardian equivalence theorem, recently brought to prominence by Barro (1974, 1976). The assumptions include the following. All taxes are of the lump-type, having no allocative effects. When government debt is issued, it is certain that the interest and principal payments required to service the debt will be covered by future taxes (not by issuing money). And everyone lives forever and maximizes an intertemporal utility function. This last assumption may be relaxed by assuming that everyone has ancestors and descendants, and family members engage in intergenerational wealth transfers so as to maximize the intertemporal utility function of the family.

While the Ricardian equivalence theorem is well established as a theoretical proposition, the issue of its applicability to actual economies is still not decided in the minds of many economists, and is the subject of active research and debate.

This paper is in three parts. The first part II presents data for money multipliers and velocities in Japan since 1965, in support of the claim that they varied little, and that therefore it was relatively easy to control inflation by controlling the growth of monetary aggregates. The second part III-V describes the GBR, assembles data for it, and shows how the government deficits in Japan have been financed. It also shows the theoretical relation of the deficit to the rate of inflation. It then estimates the inflation rate that can be expected in long-run balanced-growth equilibrium, as a function of the ratio of the deficit to GNP. The third part VI-XII introduces a government debt variable and a GBR into a simple macroeconomic model. It then shows how the GBR interacts with the model when the Ricardian equivalence theorem does not hold, and when it does hold. XIII is a brief conclusion.

II.   Recent Short-Run Behavior of Velocity and Money Multipliers

Table 2 shows the high powered money stock H, M_1, and M_2 + CD for Japan, together with their velocities, and the money multipliers for M_1 and M_2 + CD, and

Table 2   Japanese Monetary Aggregates at End of Fiscal Year and Their Velocities and Money Multipliers

F.Y.	H	M_1	M_2+CD	$m(M_1)$	$m(M_2$+CD)	Y	y	p	V(H)	$V(M_1)$	$V(M_2$+CD)
1965	2655.4	10065.1	25687.4	3.79	9.67	33602.3	92027.6	36.5	12.654	3.338	1.308
1966	2979.8	11377.6	29731.0	3.82	9.98	39508.9	102209.9	38.7	13.259	3.473	1.329
1967	3565.7	12945.2	34169.2	3.63	9.58	46239.4	113182.4	40.9	12.968	3.572	1.353
1968	4118.3	14817.0	39435.1	3.60	9.58	54760.4	127709.1	42.9	13.297	3.696	1.389
1969	5039.5	17798.2	46612.7	3.53	9.25	64920.0	142993.8	45.4	12.882	3.648	1.393
1970	5799.2	21167.3	55002.0	3.65	9.48	75152.0	153915.4	48.8	12.959	3.547	1.366
1971	6601.5	27062.5	68224.8	4.10	10.33	82806.3	161688.1	51.2	12.544	3.060	1.214
1972	8840.7	34475.3	85346.2	3.90	9.65	96539.1	176627.9	54.7	10.920	2.800	1.131
1973	11229.6	39778.8	98235.8	3.54	8.75	116679.2	184569.3	63.2	10.390	2.933	1.188
1974	12977.4	43671.2	109374.8	3.37	8.43	138155.8	183797.8	75.2	10.646	3.164	1.263
1975	13503.8	49755.2	126234.7	3.68	9.35	152209.4	190874.7	79.7	11.272	3.059	1.206
1976	15036.1	54854.6	142350.0	3.65	9.47	171152.5	199630.1	85.7	11.383	3.120	1.202
1977	16150.6	58814.5	157331.8	3.64	9.74	190034.8	210234.4	90.4	11.766	3.231	1.208
1978	17853.2	66619.9	177587.5	3.73	9.95	208780.9	221243.0	94.4	11.694	3.134	1.176
1979	20274.7	71005.8	194734.9	3.50	9.60	225452.6	232878.3	96.8	11.120	3.175	1.158
1980	20639.0	68023.3	208097.4	3.30	10.08	245162.7	242130.9	101.3	11.879	3.604	1.178
1981	21272.0	74484.0	230485.7	3.50	10.84	259668.8	250158.8	103.8	12.207	3.486	1.127
1982	23021.0	78675.1	247926.5	3.42	10.77	272382.9	258240.9	105.5	11.832	3.462	1.099
1983	24431.3	80512.1	267172.4	3.30	10.94	284121.0	267782.0	106.1	11.629	3.529	1.063
1984	25543.2	87675.6	291609.6	3.43	11.41	303155.7	281102.2	107.8	11.866	3.458	1.040

Source: See the Appendix

Units: For stocks :   billion yen
       For   Y   :   billion yen per year
       For   y   :   billion 1980 yen per year
       For money multipliers :   none
       For velocities :   per year

real and nominal GNP and the GNP deflator, annually for fiscal years 1965-1984. Sources are given in the Appendix. Figure 2 shows the behavior of the velocities and Figure 3 shows the money multipliers through time. Neither the velocities nor the money multipliers have changed rapidly in the past decade, since the Bank of Japan began its successful anti-inflationary policy. $V(M_1)$ (the velocity of M_1) shows the most variation, but its annual growth rate for 1975-84 averaged only $+1.4\%$, and did

Figure 2   Velocities of M_1, M_2 + CD, and H (High Powered Money)

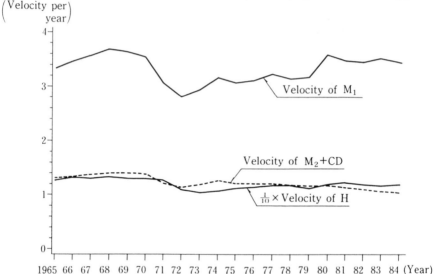

Figure 3   Money Multipliers for M_1 and M_2 + CD

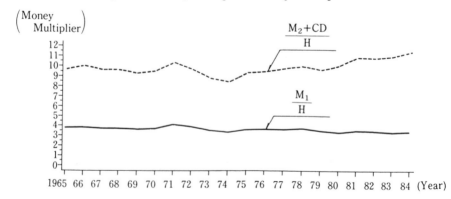

not deviate much from that average. Even for the period 1972-84 its growth rate averaged only 1.8% a year. This evidence about Japan supports the view that rather slow average growth of a monetary aggregate, at approximately the growth rate of the real economy, with occasional adjustments to account for changes in velocity, will control inflation.

III. Bonds and the Government Budget Restraint in a Macaroeconomic Model

Many macroeconomic models contain government purchases of goods and services (henceforth to be called simply government purchases), government transfer payments, tax variables, and the money supply, but not government debt. Sometimes the omission of government debt is defended by stating that the bond equation, being dependent on the other equations of the model by Walras' Law, can be omitted.

In general this is not correct, as the following reasoning shows. Any equation that is dependent upon other equations can be derived from those other equations. Hence, every variable that appears in such a dependent equation must also appear somewhere among the other equations. Therefore, when a dependent equation that explains the bond variable is omitted by Walras' Law, the bond variable does not drop out of the model. If government debt is important in the economy, a variable representing it should appear in the model. That is where the GBR comes in.

The GBR says that total government expenditure for purchases and for transfer payments must be financed by some combination of taxes, borrowing from the central bank (that is, issuing high powered money), borrowing from others, and depleting stocks of foreign assets such as gold and foreign exchange reserves. This means that the authorities cannot independently choose the values of government purchases, transfers, taxes, high powered money, government debt held outside the central bank, and foreign assets. At least one of these policy variables will be chosen endogenously by the economy to satisfy the GBR, when the rest of them have been chosen exogenously.

Analysis of models containing the GBR has shown that the path of the economy, following a policy change, will depend upon which of the policy variables is allowed to adjust endogenously. The stability of the path may also depend on this choice. Several authors have obtained results suggesting that in simple models the adjustment path may be unstable if government debt is the endogenous variable. See, for example, Tobin – Buiter (1976) and Christ (1978, 1979).

In an open-economy model, there is at least one more endogenous policy variable: under fixed exchange rates the balance of payments will be endogenous, whereas under flexible exchange rates the exchange rate will be endogenous. And foreign holdings of government debt should be accounted for.

The GBR can be expressed in an equation. Let g stand for real government purchases, tr for real transfers other than interest, B for government debt (assumed to be perpetuities) held outside the central bank, r_1 for the interest rate on that debt, P for the price level, tx for real tax receipts, F for government and central bank holdings of gold and foreign exchange expressed in domestic currency, r^* for the interest rate on such foreign assets, H for the high powered money stock, and D for the derivative with respect to time. Then the GBR says spending equals sources of finance, thus:

$$g + tr + r_1 \frac{B}{P} = tx + r^* \frac{F}{P} + \frac{DH + DB - DF}{P}. \tag{1}$$

Here DH, DB, and DF are to be understood as flows, taking account of asset quantity changes but not changes in asset prices.[1] It will be convenient to write t = taxes less net debt interest less other transfers, thus:

$$t = tx + r^* \frac{F}{P} - tr - r_1 \frac{B}{P}. \tag{2}$$

Then the GBR can be written as

$$g = t + \frac{DH + DB - DF}{P}. \tag{3}$$

IV.   Some Data Regarding the GBR in Japan

Tables 3, 4, and 5 show data for three definitions of the government budget deficit for Japan, together with the three major components of its financing. In each table, the three components are the increase in the high powered money stock held outside the government and the Bank of Japan, the increase in government debt held outside the Bank of Japan, and the decrease in gold and net foreign assets held by the government and the Bank of Japan.

The three definitions of the government deficit are as follows. In Table 3 the central government sector is as defined by the flow of funds accounts of the Bank of Japan. In Tables 4 and 5 the government sectors are as defined by the Economic Planning Agency in the System of National Accounts, Table 4 being for the central government only, and Table 5 for the general government sector including central

1.   Of course the price of H does not change—it is always 1. But the price of a perpetuity that yields 1 yen per year is $1/r_1$, and it changes when r_1 changes. Denote the number of such perpetuities by b and their value by b/r_1. Then the change in value, $D(b/r_1)$, is $(Db)/r_1 - (b/r^2_1)Dr_1$. The expression DB in the text denotes $(Db)/r_1$, excluding the capital gain $-(b/r^2_1)Dr_1$. The symbol B in the text stands for b/r_1.

and local government and the social security system. In each table, the definitions of all the variables correspond to the chosen definition of the government sector.

I have been unable to find quarterly data for government deficits defined as I wish to define them (namely, the decrease in financial net worth of a government sector, where government sectors are defined as in the System of National Accounts, and their deficits are measured by the transactions flows in their asset and liability accounts). Also, I have been unable to find annual data for such variables extending back before 1970. (The Bank of Japan prepares quarterly data for the flow of funds starting in 1955, but I prefer the national accounting data because the national accounting definitions of the government sectors correspond better to the distinction between public and private goods.) The national accounting data for fiscal years 1970

Table 3   Financing of Japan's Central Government Deficit
(Flow of Funds Data)

F.Y.	Deficit	DH	DB	−DF
1965	−63.4	363.8	−321.2	−106.0
1966	209.8	324.4	−168.6	54.0
1967	176.3	585.8	−480.7	71.2
1968	−277.0	552.6	−219.5	−610.1
1969	−438.8	921.3	−951.9	−408.2
1970	−1156.0	759.6	−914.6	−1001.0
1971	−693.6	802.3	2434.2	−3930.1
1972	−776.4	2239.2	−726.0	−2289.6
1973	−2090.9	2388.9	−6745.9	2266.1
1974	193.9	1747.8	−1709.4	155.5
1975	4375.1	526.4	3971.9	−123.2
1976	5517.1	1532.3	4682.3	−697.5
1977	7999.0	1114.5	10090.8	−3206.3
1978	10244.8	1702.6	9293.2	−751.0
1979	9609.6	2421.5	5453.0	1735.1
1980	8869.6	364.3	12583.7	−4078.4
1981	10197.1	633.0	8255.2	1308.9
1982	10279.6	1749.0	9718.6	−1188.0
1983	11207.8	1410.3	10028.5	−231.0
1984	9231.4	1116.9	8346.6	−232.1

Source: See the Appendix
Units: Billion yen per year

Table 4 Financing of Japan's Central Government Deficit
(SNA Data)

F.Y.	Deficit	DH	DB	−DF	RESIDUAL
1970	−244.9	744.2	−29.3	−626.2	−333.6
1971	399.4	901.5	3868.1	−3875.1	−495.1
1972	1054.4	2376.3	798.0	−352.6	−1767.3
1973	−124.5	2406.3	−4852.6	1333.9	987.9
1974	2426.4	1867.5	32.0	−196.3	723.2
1975	6222.1	687.4	5638.8	−21.0	−83.1
1976	7536.6	1574.5	6556.5	−752.9	158.5
1977	10079.4	1286.5	12149.5	−2696.1	−660.5
1978	12566.6	1071.1	11364.9	380.8	−250.2
1979	12186.5	3877.3	6561.3	2376.7	−628.9
1980	13203.2	−692.6	15688.5	−3104.0	1311.3
1981	14242.6	780.7	12266.6	405.9	789.5
1982	14234.8	1667.2	13561.2	545.4	−1539.0
1983	13723.1	838.8	13438.4	−408.2	−145.9
1984	12245.4	1887.4	12155.3	−263.6	−1533.7

Table 5 Financing of Japan's General Government Deficit
(SNA Data)

F.Y.	Deficit	DH	DB	−DF	RESIDUAL
1970	−1638.7	739.0	−1391.8	−626.2	−359.7
1971	−1004.7	890.4	2462.0	−3875.1	−482.0
1972	−374.8	2303.0	−471.0	−353.0	−1853.8
1973	−1423.6	2353.1	−6049.0	1333.7	938.6
1974	66.9	1760.6	−2186.8	−196.5	689.6
1975	5246.8	586.0	4782.6	−21.9	−99.9
1976	5968.5	1598.5	4974.1	−754.4	150.3
1977	7757.0	1246.9	9905.7	−2699.5	−696.1
1978	10779.6	1325.5	9313.2	369.0	−228.1
1979	9369.6	2709.8	5091.1	2370.9	−802.2
1980	10295.9	229.2	11899.3	−3110.6	1278.0
1981	10182.9	755.4	8121.3	388.2	918.0
1982	9711.4	1753.1	8970.4	526.0	−1538.1
1983	9545.8	1097.3	9057.7	−424.6	−184.6
1984	8123.5	1372.7	8680.3	−293.8	−1635.7

Source: See the Appendix
Units: Billion yen per year

through 1984 are all from the Economic Planning Agency, either directly from their published reports on National Accounts (1985, 1986), or indirectly by way of the master file of data maintained on the computers of the Bank of Japan. For more detail, see the Appendix.

For the purpose of studying the GBR, it seems preferable to consider the central government rather than general government because only the central government creates high powered money by borrowing from the Bank of Japan. Therefore Table 4 is the preferable one. However, because there may be some interest in the role of general government, Table 5 is presented as well.

Figure 4 shows the deficits according to each definition. Figures 5, 6, and 7 show the deficits and their financing, as percentages of GNP, for each of the three definitions. All show that the budget had small deficits (or even surpluses) through 1974, and that the deficit/GNP ratio rose rapidly beginning in 1975, reaching a peak in 1978, and declining somewhat thereafter. All also show that the ratio of newly issued high powered money to GNP reached a peak of around 2% in 1972, which was about the time of the inflationary surge, and has been kept fairly steady at modest levels (generally under 1%) since 1975. The main source of financing of the large deficits has been the sale of government debt to investors outside the Bank of Japan, that is, increases in B.

V.   The Relation of Deficits to the Equilibrium Rate of Inflation

The nominal deficit is financed by issuing high powered money and debt and by spending foreign exchange reserves:

$$\text{nominal deficit} = DH + DB - DF = H\left(\frac{DH}{H} + \frac{DB}{B}\frac{B}{H} - \frac{DF}{F}\frac{F}{H}\right). \tag{4}$$

The inflation rate is related to the growth rate DH/H of the high powered money stock, through the growth rates of real output and of the velocity of H. That is, the inflation rate $\frac{DP}{P}$ is given by

$$\frac{DH}{H} + \frac{DV_H}{V_H} = \frac{DP}{P} + \frac{Dy}{y} \tag{5}$$

where V_H is the velocity of the high powered money stock H and y is real output. Hence, Equation (4) indicates that deficits do not necessarily cause inflation if they are financed mainly by depleting foreign exchange reserves and issuing debt. But these two methods, alone or together, cannot finance a large deficit indefinitely. The depletion of foreign exchange reserves can continue only until they are used up. And pure debt finance cannot continue indefinitely, as an appendix shows. Hence a

Figure 4   Three Definitions of the Japanese Government Deficit as Percentages of GNP

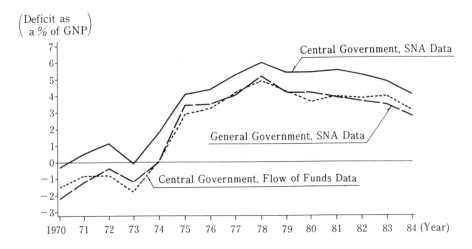

Figure 5   Financing of Japan's Central Government Deficit (Flow of Funds Data)

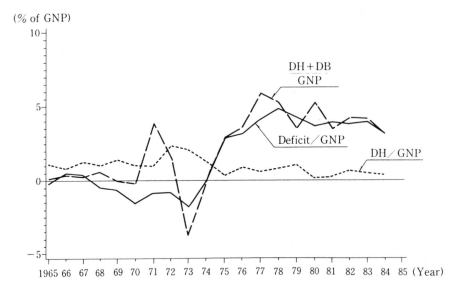

Figure 6   Financing of Japan's Central Government Deficit (SNA Data)

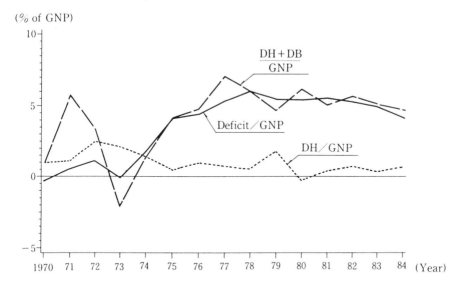

Figure 7   Financing of Japan's General Government Deficit (SNA Data)

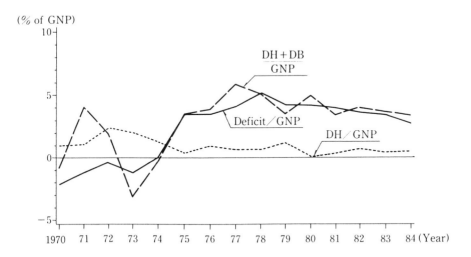

sustainable path with perpetual large budget deficits involves some creation of high powered money.

On a sustainable long-run steady-state balanced-growth equilibrium path, the nominal stocks of high powered money, government debt, and foreign exchange reserves all have the same growth rate. Denote this rate by g_H. Then Equation (4) becomes

$$\text{nominal deficit} = g_H(H + B - F). \tag{6}$$

Dividing by nominal GNP yields

$$\text{deficit/GNP} = g_H(H + B - F)/\text{GNP}. \tag{7}$$

On such an equilibrium path, the ratio $(H + B - F)/\text{GNP}$ is constant. And because the velocity of the high powered money stock is also constant on such a path, the growth rate of H equals the sum of the growth rates of the price level and real output, that is $g_H = g_P + g_y$. Therefore we find that on such an equilibrium path the inflation rate is given by

$$g_P = \frac{\text{deficit}}{\text{GNP}} \; \frac{\text{GNP}}{H+B-F} - g_y. \tag{8}$$

A higher deficit/GNP ratio leads to higher inflation, for a given $\text{GNP}/(H+B-F)$ ratio and a given real growth rate g_y. The $\text{GNP}/(H+B-F)$ ratio can decline for a time, if debt grows faster than GNP, but cannot fall below a certain limit, as we have seen. Furthermore, $\text{GNP}/(H+B-F)$ is likely to increase during inflation, because the velocity of H will increase, and this will worsen the inflation. At present, in Japan, the ratio of GNP to $(H+B-F)$ is about 2.6 when central government data are used, and g_y is about .05 per year. Therefore, if the Japanese economy were to follow a steady state equilibrium path starting now, with those magnitudes, the equilibrium inflation rate would be equal to about 2.6 times the central government's deficit/GNP ratio, minus .05. The following table gives some examples.

Central Government Deficit

GNP	g_H =2.6 (Deficit/GNP)	inflation rate g_P $=g_H - .05$
.01	.026	−.024
.02	.052	.002
.03	.078	.028
.04	.104	.054
.05	.130	.080

These calculations suggest that if inflation is to be prevented in Japan in the long run, it will be necessary to keep the deficit/GNP ratio at a moderate level on the average.

VI. The Definitions of Wealth and Disposable Income

The introduction of government debt into a macroeconomic model requires a careful definition of wealth. Let us suppose that the private sector holds B_P yen's worth of government bonds, and regards them as λB_P yen's worth of net wealth, where λ is a constant between 0 and 1, inclusive. The fraction $1 - \lambda$ represents the extent to which the private sector regards its wealth as diminished by the present value of the future taxes that are required to service the debt. If the private sector fully accounts for these taxes, $\lambda = 0$ and government debt is not regarded as wealth at all. If the private sector ignores these taxes, $\lambda = 1$ and government debt is regarded as wealth at full value.

Now suppose that foreign investors hold an amount B_f of domestic government debt, and that the taxes required to service this foreign-held debt must be paid by the private domestic sector. Then the private sector's wealth will be diminished by $1 - \lambda$ times the foreign-held debt B_f.

Therefore we will define the real wealth of the private sector as the sum of its holdings of real physical capital k, real high powered money H/P, λ times its real holdings of government debt B_p/P, and real net claims against the rest of the world A/P, minus $(1 - \lambda)$ times foreign-held domestic government debt B_f/P, thus:

$$w = k + \frac{H + \lambda B_p - (1 - \lambda)B_f + A}{P} \tag{9}$$

Therefore the change Dw in wealth is given by

$$Dw = DK + \frac{DH + \lambda DB_p - (1 - \lambda)DB_f + DA}{P} + cg \tag{10}$$

where DH, DB_p, DB_f, and DA are nominal flows of assets at the current period's asset prices, and cg, the real capital gain on the holdings of financial assets, is

$$cg = -\frac{H + \lambda B_p - (1 - \lambda)B_f + A}{P^2}DP - \frac{\lambda B_p - (1 - \lambda)B_f}{Pr_1}Dr_1. \tag{11}$$

The two terms in this expression reflect the real capital gains arising from changes in the price level P and the market value of long term bonds due to changes in interest rates Dr_1. An additional term could be included to reflect changes in the value of foreign assets due to changes in the exchange rate.

We will use the national income identity

$$y = c + DK + g + nx \tag{12}$$

where y = real NNP, c = real consumption, and nx = real exports.

Disposable income is the sum of consumption plus additions to wealth. Therefore, using first the expression for Dw and then the national income identity, it can be expressed as

$$yd = c + Dw = c + Dk + \frac{DH + \lambda\, DB_p - (1 - \lambda)DB_f + DA}{P} + cg \qquad (13)$$

$$= y - g - nx + \frac{DH + \lambda\, DB_p - (1 - \lambda)DB_f + DA}{P} + cg.$$

Notice that this expression defines disposable income in terms of the resources remaining after government purchases and net exports are subtracted from income, namely, $y - g - nx$, and after certain adjustments to assets. It does not involve taxes or transfer payments. (We will come back to this expression later, when we discuss a form of the model in which debt and taxes don't matter.) Alternatively, the GBR can be used to express g in terms of taxes and transfers and other variables. (Note that DB in the GBR is equal to $DB_p + DB_f$.) When this is done, the expression $(DA + DF - DB_f)/P - nx$ appears, but it drops out because it is zero by virtue of the balance of payments equation. Then disposable income can be written in terms of taxes less transfers, thus:

$$yd = y - t - \frac{(1 - \lambda)(DB_p + DB_f)}{P} + cg. \qquad (14)$$

If government bonds are regarded as wealth, so that $\lambda = 1$, bonds drop out of this definition of disposable income. And if the price level and the interest rate are constant, cg=0. Then disposable income becomes simply $y - t$, as in simple textbook models.

VII.   A Simple Model of an Open Economy

Consider an open economy containing 4 sectors: the government including the central bank, the private domestic sector, the foreign sector, and a fictitious sector to be called the capital sector, whose liabilities are the physical capital held by the other sectors, and whose assets are the net worths of the other sectors. Consider 5 types of assets: physical capital k, domestic high powered money H, domestic government debt of which B_p is net private domestic holdings and B_f is foreign holdings, foreign-issued debt A, and gold and foreign exchange reserves F. Domestic private debt is assumed to be held only within the domestic private sector, and to be a perfect substitute for domestic government debt, so that the private sector's net holdings of both private and government debt are equal to B_p, its net holdings of government debt alone.

Table 6 shows the intersectoral claims among these 4 sectors. The entries in any column are the assets of the sector named at the top of the column, and the entries in any row are the liabilities of the sector named at the left of the row. Each sector's balance sheet equation is given by equating the total assets at the bottom of its column to the total liabilities at the right of its row. Only 3 of the 4 balance sheet equations are independent, because any one of them can be obtained by appropriate addition or subtraction from the other three. Let us omit the capital sector's balance sheet. Then, after the other equations of the model have been specified, it will turn out that the government's net worth variable appears only in the government's balance sheet equation, and similarly, the foreign sector's net worth variable appears only in that sector's balance sheet equation. Therefore those two equations do not affect the behavior of the rest of the model: they can be set aside and ignored, unless and until one wishes to use them to find the net worths of their two sectors.

Table 6   Nominal Intersectoral Claims, in Yen

assets of liabilities of	private	government and central bank	foreign	capital	total
private	–	$(1-\lambda)(B_p+B_f)$		wP	$(1-\lambda)(B \cdot B_f)$
government and central bank	$H+B_p$	–	B_f	w_gP	$H+B_p+B_f$ $+w_gP$
foreign	A	F	–	w_fP	$A+F+w_fP$
capital	kP	$k'P$		–	$kP+k'P$
total	$H+B_p$ $+A+kP$	$(1-\lambda)(B_p+B_f)$ $+F+k'P$	B_f	$wP+w_gP$ $+w_fP$	$\Sigma \ \Sigma$

The model then has 14 equations. It will be assumed that government debt B_p is the endogenous policy variable in the GBR, and that exchange rates are allowed to float freely so that e is endogenous and F is exogenous.

Then the 14 endogenous variables are

      A = private net holdings of foreign debt, in yen
      B_p = private net holdings of government debt (perpetuities)
      c = private real consumption
      e = exchange rate (yen per unit of foreign currency)
      k = private real physical capital stock
      nx = real net exports

p = price level

r_1 = nominal interest rate on domestic debt (government and private)

r_2 = nominal rate of return on equity (titles to physical capital)

r_3 = real marginal product of capital

t = real taxes less net government interest payments less non-interest transfer payments

w = real private net wealth

y = real national product

yf = real productive capacity

The exogenous variables are

B_f = foreign holdings of domestic government debt (perpetuities)

$(De/e)^e$ = expected rate of growth of the exchange rate

F = government and central bank holdings of gold and foreign exchange, in yen

g = real government purchases of goods and services

H = high powered money stock

k' = government's real physical capital stock

P^* = foreign price level

$(dP/P)^e$ = expected inflation rate

r^* = foreign interest rate

rt = rate of taxes less transfer payments

Different policy choices would lead to different selections of endogenous variables. In particular, the endogenous macroeconomic policy variables might be H or g or a tax rate or a transfer rate instead of B_p. And the endogenous foreign exchange policy variable might be the balance of payments instead of the exchange rate. Indeed, more complex policies can be considered, for example, a rule that says what fraction of a deficit is to be financed by money creation and what fraction by borrowing; or a rule for intervention in the foreign exchange market. Such a rule constitutes an additional equation for the model, and causes an additional policy variable to become endogenous. But for simplicity only one policy choice will be considered here, namely the one corresponding to the above list of endogenous variables.

The equations of the model are displayed in Table 7. Equation 1 is an expectations-adjusted Phillips curve. It says that the inflation rate will be the same as, or less than, or greater than expected, according to whether real output is equal to, or less than, or greater than capacity. Equation 2 says that investment depends on the difference between the real marginal productivity of capital and the expected real rate of return on equity. Equation 3 is the balance of payments equation. It says that the net change in domestic holdings of foreign assets is equal to net exports (which

Table 7   Equations of the Model

Associated Endogenous Variables	Equation Number	Equation	Description
P	1	$\dfrac{DP}{P} = f_1\left[\dfrac{y}{yf}\right] - 1 + \left[\dfrac{DP}{P}\right]^e$	inflation
k	2	$DK = f_2\left[r_3 - r_2 + (DP/P)^e\right]$	investment
A	3	$DA + DF - DB_f = P \cdot nx$	balance of payments
B	4	$g = t + \dfrac{DH + DB_p + DB_f - DF}{P}$	GBR
yf	5	$yf = f_5\,(k + k')$	production function
r_3	6	$r_3 = f_6\,(k + k')$	marginal production of k
w	7	$w = k + \dfrac{H + \lambda B_p - (1-\lambda)B_f + A}{P}$	private wealth
e	8	$\dfrac{A}{P} = f_8\left[y, w, r_1, r_2, e, \left[\dfrac{DP}{P}\right]^e, \left[\dfrac{De}{e}\right]^e\right]$	foreign bond demand
r_2	9	$\dfrac{\lambda B_p}{P} = f_9\left[y, w, r_1, r_2, e, \left[\dfrac{DP}{P}\right]^e, \left[\dfrac{De}{e}\right]^e\right]$	domestic bond demand
r_1	10	$\dfrac{H}{P} = f_{10}\left[y, w, r_1, r_2, e, \left[\dfrac{DP}{P}\right]^e, \left[\dfrac{De}{e}\right]^e\right]$	money demand
c	11	$c = f_{11}\left\{\left[y - g - nx + \dfrac{DH + \lambda DB_p - (1-\lambda)DB_f + DA}{P}\right.\right.$ $-\dfrac{H + \lambda B_p - (1-\lambda)B_f + A}{P^2}\,DP$ $\left.-\dfrac{\lambda B_p - (1-\lambda)B_f}{Pr_1}\,Dr_1\right],$ $\left. r_1, r_2, \left[\dfrac{DP}{P}\right]^e, w\right\}$	consumption
nx	12	$nx = f_{12}\left[y, \dfrac{P}{P^*e}, \dfrac{F + A}{P}\,r^* - \dfrac{B_f r_1}{P}\right]$	net exports
t	13	$t = f_{13}\left[y, \dfrac{r_1(B_p + B_f) - r^*F}{P}, rt\right]$	taxes less transfers
y	14	$y = c + Dk + g + nx$	income identity

include net interest from abroad). Equation 4 is the GBR, which has already been described. Recall that DB in Equation (3) has been replaced by its equivalent, $DB_p + DB_f$, here. Note that these 4 equations are dynamic, that is each of them determines the rate of change of a state variable (P, k, A, or B_p) from one period to the next. We will speak of the past levels of these variables as predetermined.

Equation 5 is the production function. It gives real capacity as a function of the total (private and government) capital stock. It can be thought of as a long-run aggregate supply curve, in the sense that if enough time is allowed or the price level to come to equilibrium, then the quantity of output supplied will be equal to the normal capacity level yf. Equation 6 says that the marginal productivity of capital depends on the total capital stock. Equation 7 is the definition of private wealth, discussed earlier. Equation 8, 9, and 10 are the private portfolio demand equations for real foreign assets, domestic debt, and high powered money. Each depends on income, interest rates, wealth, the exchange rate, and expectations about inflation and changes in the exchange rate. A fourth portfolio demand equation, for physical capital, is dependent upon Equations 7-10, since it can be obtained by subtracting Equations 8, 9, and 10 from Equation 7. Hence this physical capital demand equation has been omitted. (Either Equation 7, 8, 9 or 10 could have been omitted instead, without affecting the model's behavior.) Equation 11 says that consumption depends on disposable income as defined in Equation (13) above, as well as on expected real interest rates and wealth. Equation 12 says that net exports depend on income, the terms of trade, and net interest received from abroad. Equation 13 says that taxes less net government interest and other transfers depend on income, tax-transfer rates, and net government interest payments $(r_1(B_p+B_f)-r^*F)/P$. Equation 14 is the national income identity mentioned above.

It would be possible to endogenize the expected inflation rate and the expected change in the exchange rate, by introducing two more equations. If those two equations were to contain no new variables in adition to those that already appear in Equation 1-14, then most of the analysis that follows would be unaffected.

The static equilibrium form of the model is obtained by setting all time-derivatives equal to zero, that is, the exogenous variables DB_f, DF, and DH, the exogenous expectations $(De/e)^e$, and $(DP/P)^e$, and the endogenous rates of change DP, DK, DA, DB_p, and Dr_1. This means that in static equilibrium output y is equal to capacity yf in Equation 1, the marginal product of capital r_3 is equal to the expected real rate of return on equity $r_2-(DP/P)^e=r_2$ in Equation 2, the current account is balanced in Equation 3, and the budget is balanced in Equation 4.

Of course, it is only for simplicity that equilibrium is defined as having zero growth, zero inflation, and a balanced budget. One could consider a balanced-growth equilibrium with a steady rate of inflation and a continuous budget deficit or surplus, and transform all variables so as to express the model in terms of deviations from such a balanced-growth equilibrium. The resulting transformed model would look very much like Equations 1-14. Christ (1978) gives an example of such a transformation when the equilibrium has zero real growth but steady nominal growth and a constant real budget deficit (that is, steady inflation).

VIII. Recursive Dynamics

A model of this sort generates the time paths of its endogenous variables, given the paths of its exogenous variables, in a two-step recursive manner. The model has two subsets of variables, and two subsets of equations. The dynamic variables are the ones whose rates of change from period t-1 to period t are determined by dynamic equations, given the values of all variables for period t-1. The static variables are the ones whose levels at time t are determined by static equations, given the levels of the dynamic variables for period t. The dynamic equations are a subset of the equations, containing time derivatives of the dynamic variables. There should be as many equations in this subset as there are dynamic variables. The remaining equations will be called the static equations (even though they may contain some time derivatives).

Consider first a simple case in which the static equations don't contain any time derivatives. Then the model may be expressed in terms of vector equations, as follows:

$$F(y_{1,t-1}, y_{2,t-1}, Dy_{1t}, x_t) = 0 \text{ (dynamic equations)} \tag{15}$$
$$y_{1t} = y_{1,t-1} + Dy_{1t} \text{ (updating equations)} \tag{16}$$
$$G(y_{1t}, y_{2t}, x_t) = 0 \text{ (static equations)} \tag{17}$$

Earlier lagged variables may be included, but are not shown. Here y_1 is a vector of n dynamic endogenous variables, y_2 is a vector of m static endogenous variables, x is a vector exogenous variables, and F and G are vector functions of order n and m respectively. The first vector equation (15) represents the dynamic part of the model, and the third vector equation (17) represents the static part. At the beginning of period t, the levels of all variables for period t-1 have been predetermined. The values for period t are generated as follows. The n dynamic equations (15) involving F are solved or Dy_{1t}, the change in y_1 from period t-1 to period t. Then y_1 for period t is obtained from Equation (16) by adding to the level for period t-1 the change so obtained. Then the m static quations (17) involving G are solved for y_2 to obtain its value for period t. Then the cycle repeats for the next period, t+1, and so on.

In a more general case some time derivatives of dynamic variables appear in the static equations. For example, P, k, A, and B_p are the dynamic variables in the model discussed earlier, Equations 1-4 are the dynamic equations, and Equations 5-14 are the static equations. Observe from Table 7 (to be described in the next section) that DP, Dk, DA, and DB_p appear in the static equations 11 and 14. In such a case, the recursive dynamic process described just above works in almost the same way as before, with one exception: Replace the Dy_1 that appears in the static equations by a function of y_1, y_2, and x, which is obtained by solving the dynamic equations involving F for Dy_1. Then the static part no longer contains any dynamic variables, and the recursive dynamic process can proceed as before. (Note that although Equation 11 contains Dr_1, Equation 11 is not a dynamic equation, and r_1 is not a dynamic variable: its level at time t is determined by Equations 5-14, given the values of the dynamic variables P, k, A, and B_p for period t, and the. lagged value of r_1 (and perhaps other variables) from period t-1.)

In the 14-equation model presented above, the process works as follows. At the start of period t, all variables for period t-1 are predetermined. Given these predetermined variables, the dynamic equations 1-4 determine the changes DP, Dk, DA, and DB_p between periods t-1 and t. These are added to the old levels of P, k, A, and B_p to get the new levels for period t. Then the static equations 5-14 determine the values of the remaining 10 endogenous variables for period t, given the now predetermined levels of P, k, A, and B_p for period t. Then the cycle repeats for later periods.

IX.   The Causal Structure of the Model

In order to make it easy to visualize the structure of the model, it is useful to construct a table showing which endogenous variables appear in each equation. This is done twice, once for the dynamic version of the model in Table 8 and once for the static equilibrium version in Table 9. It is convenient to associate each endogenous variable with one of the equations in which it appears (there is typically more than one way to do this, unless the model is fully recursive). The variable so associated with each equation is shown by an x in the variable's column and the equation's row in Tables 8 and 9. Other endogenous variables appearing in an equation are shown by circles in the appropriate columns in that equation's row.

Consider first Table 8, for the dynamic version of the model.[2] Each of its first 4 rows has only a single entry in the first 4 columns corresponding to the 4 dynamic variables. This means that each of the first 4 equations can be regarded as a single-equation model that determines one dynamic variable, in terms of values of static variables and levels of the dynamic variables. Further inspection of the next 3 rows shows that each of them has only a single entry in the first 14 columns. This means that each of the 3 equations 5, 6, and 7 can be regarded as a single-equation model determining one variable in terms of exogenous variables and the levels of state variables. The 3 variables so determined are yf, r_3, and w.

Inspection of the last 7 rows of Table 8 does not obviously reveal whether the last 7 equations are fully simultaneous or not. McElroy (1978) gives a simple method for determining the causal structure of a model. It reveals that 6 of these 7 equations

---

2.   Table 8 does not have a column for Dr_1, because Dr_{1t} has been replaced by $r_{1t} - r_{1,t-1}$. Thus r_1 is treated like the other static variables.

Table 8   Endogenous Variables in the Dynamic Version of the Model

Equation	Dynamic				Static										Predetermined Variables			
	DP	Dk	DA	DBp	yf	r_3	w	e	r_2	r_1	c	nx	t	y	p	k	A	B_p
1 inflation	X				O									O	O			
2 investment		X				O			O									
3 balance of payments			X									O			O			
4 GBR				X									O		O			
5 production function					X											O		
6 marginal production of k						X										O		
7 private wealth							X								O	O	O	O
8 foreign bonds demand							O	X	O	O				O	O		O	O
9 domestic bonds demand			O				O	O	X	O				O	O		O	O
10 money demand							O	O	O	X				O	O			O
11 consumption	O							O			X			O	O		O	
12 net exports								O				X		O	O		O	
13 taxes-transfers										O			X	O				
14 income identity		O									O	O		X				

Table 9   Endogenous Variables in the Equilibrium Version of the Model

	Equation	y	r_2	nx	t	yf	r_3	k	A	B_p	r_1	w	e	P	c
1	inflation	X				O									
2	investment		X				O								
3	balance of payments			X											
4	GBR				X										
5	production function					X		O							
6	marginal production of k						X	O							
7	private wealth							X	O	O		O		O	
8	foreign bonds	O	O						X		O	O	O	O	
9	domestic bonds	O	O							X	O	O	O	O	
10	money	O	O								X	O	O	O	
11	consumption	O	O								O	X			O
12	net exports	O		O				O					X	O	
13	taxes-transfers	O			O					O	O			X	
14	income identity	O		O											X

(all except Equation 13) are fully simultaneous, determining the 6 variables e, r_2, r_1, c, nx, and y. Then Equation 13 determines t, given the other variables.

Hence the model is not fully simultaneous, but has 9 causal segments, as follows:

1–4: Equations 1-4 are from separate segments, which determine respectively DP, dk, DB_p, and DA, given the values of variables from the previous period.

5–7: Equations 5, 6, and 7 are three separate segments, which determine respectively, yf, r_3, and w, given the new levels of P,k, A, and B_p that have been determined by adding to their previous levels their first differences obtained from Equations 1-4.

8: Equations 8-12 and 14 are a simultaneous segment that determines the 6 endogenous variables e, r_1, r_2, c, nx, and y, given the values of the 7 variables that have been determined by Equations 1-7.

9: Equation 13 is a one-equation segment that determines t, given the values of the other already-determined variables.

The same method can be applied to Table 9 to find the causal structure of the equilibrium version of the model. Equation 3 (the balance of payments) is a complete one-equation model that implies nx = 0. Equation 4 (the balanced-budget GBR) is a complete one-equation model that determines taxes less transfers t. The remaining 12 equations are a simultaneous system, which does not decompose into causal segments.

X. The Reduction of the Model to Two Static and Four Dynamic Equations

It is useful to reduce the static subset of equations algebraically to two equations, a long-run aggregate supply curve and an aggregate demand curve (AS and AD). The AS curve is Equation 5, giving the level of productive capacity as a function of the real capital stock of the economy. The AD curve gives the level of real GNP demanded in terms of exogenous variables and the endogenous levels of dynamic variables that have been predetermined by the dynamic equations. One of these predetermined variables is the price level P; it is the one that is usually plotted against output y in a graph of the AD curve. The AD curve is obtained in two steps. First, substitute Equations 1-4 for DP,Dk, DA, and DB_p wherever they appear in Equations 6-14 (that is, in Equations 11 and 14). Second, by repeated substitution, eliminate from this new version of Equations 6-14 all static variables except y, obtaining the AD equation which expresses y in terms of predetermined variables. The result, ignoring lags that may appear, and supposing at expectations have been endogenized as described in VII, is

$$y = f(P,k,A/P,B_p/P,B_f/P,H/P,F/P;g,rt,k',r^*,P^*) \qquad (18)$$

The semicolon separates exogenous variables (which are listed after it) from predetermined endogenous variables. The reason that B_f/P,l H/P and F/P are endogenous is that, while B_f and H and F are exogenous, P is endogenous. This equation can be called partially reduced-form equation, based on the static equations 6-14. It contains only one static variable, y. It is not a reduced form equation of the whole model, because it contains current values of the dynamic endogenous variables P, k, A, and B_p which have been predetermined by the previous operation of the dynamic part of the model. It is identified, since all its explanatory variables are predetermined.

Note that this equation contains more variables than the celebrated St. Louis equation, which has sometimes been regarded as a reduced form equation. See Anderson – Carlson (1970).

Suppose that now, in Equations 1-4, the level of each static variable (other than real output and capacity) is replaced by its partially reduced-form solution in terms of exogenous and predetermined variables from Equations 5-14. Then the model has been reduced to 6 equations in 6 endogenous variables, P, k, A, B_p, y, and yf. Its operation can be thought of as follows. Given the previous period's levels of all variables, the four dynamic equations determine the current period's changes DP, Dk, DA, and DB_p. The new levels of P, k, A, and B_p are obtained by adding the changes to the old levels. Then the AS and AD curves determine current real output and capacity in terms of the current exogenous variables and the current levels of P, k, A, and B_p. Then the cycle repeats.

XI.   The Reduced Form of a Dynamic Model

One can consider two kinds of reduced form for a dynamic model. One express-es the current period's endogenous variables in terms of their previous values and exogenous variables. This is in effect a system of difference or differential equations. To find the explicit path of each variable as a function of time, one needs to find the solution of these difference or differential equations. Such a solution requires that the path of each exogenous variable be specified as a function of time (in a purely static model the function of time that emerges for this purpose is a constant).

The second kind of reduced form of a dynamic model comes from the static equilibrium form of the model. It gives the static equilibrium values of all endoge-nous variables in the model, as functions of the exogenous variables.

XII.   How the Model Changes If Government Bonds Are Not Net Wealth

Suppose that the private sector does not regard government bonds as part of its wealth, that is, $\lambda = 0$. Then B_p disappears from Equations 7,9, and 11, and appears in the model only in the GBR equation 4 which determines DB, and in the tax-transfer equation 13. Now suppose that all taxes and transfer payments are of the lump-sum type, so that they have no allocative effects. Note that in Equation 11 (the consumption equation) disposable income is expressed in terms of government purchases g instead of taxes less transfers t. Therefore t, like B_p, appears only in Equations 4 and 13. It is determined by Equation 13 in lump-sum fashion. However, foreign-held debt B_f does not disappear.

Therefore the 12 equations excluding 4 and 13 are a complete subsystem that determines all endogenous variables except t and B_p. This illustrates the point made by Barro (1974, 1976), namely, that if government bonds are not wealth, and if taxes and transfers are lump-sum, and if it is certain that debt charges will be covered by future taxes, then the only macroeconomic policy variables that matter are govern-ment purchases and the money supply; once they are chosen, it makes no difference whether the remaining government expenditures are financed by taxes now, or by borrowing from the market now and taxes later. Interest rates, investment, capacity, real output, and prices are determined with no dependence whatever upon taxes or upon market borrowing. In such a model, the values of t and B_p are of no consequ-ence. Their values can be obtained from Equations 4 and 13 if desired, but nothing in the economy is affected by them. In such a case, the AD equation (18) would not contain variables for B_p or tax-transfer rates.

Therefore a test of the Ricardian equivalence proposition could be based on whether or not the coefficients of B_p and taxes in the aggregate demand equation are zero. If they are, the Ricardian proposition is supported.[3,4]

If debt and taxes do not influence the other variables in any way, it would mean that the government could cut its taxes to zero, and perpetually finance all its expenditures by issuing debt, without any change in the money stock, prices, interest rates, or any other variable besides debt and taxes. As indicated in V, the interest burden of the debt would then grow to exceed the taxing capacity of the economy, and hence such a policy could not be sustained.

XIII. Conclusion

Japan has had rather large budget deficits since 1975, sometimes as high as 5% of GNP. As the government budget restraint shows, deficits need not lead to inflation in the short run. Indeed, Japan has an enviable record of price stability in the last decade, because the deficits were not financed to an excessive degree by issuing money. But large persistent deficits entail inflation on a sustainable balanced-growth equilibrium path. A macroeconomic model containing the government budget restraint can be helpful in understanding the effects of different methods of financing the government budget.

3. Estimates of several versions of the aggregate demand equation (18) were attempted, without success. Data on a consistent basis were available only annually and only for 1970-1984, as noted in the text. Lagged variables were required in order to begin to obtain good fits and some significant coefficients, but then the number of degrees of freedom became very small: only 1 or 2. And when approximate data for 1969 (constructed by assuming zero values for some small unavailable components) were included in the sample, the results were drastically changed. I conclude that the available sample is so small, relative to the length of the lags required to represent the economy's adjustment process, that there are not enough degrees of freedom to yield credible estimates of an aggregate demand equation such as Equation (18).

4. Hirschhorn (1984) shows that a positive correlation between government debt and output does not imply that government debt is wealth, if individuals have imperfect information about future debt issue. This is because the unanticipated part of the debt issue will lead to an increase in output even if government debt is not wealth.

DATA APPENDIX

I.   General Comments Regarding the Data

Data are for fiscal years. Fiscal year t ends on March 31 of calendar year t + 1.

Where the same letter is used both in upper case and lower case form, such as Y and y, upper case denotes current dollars and lower case denotes constant dollars in calendar year 1980 prices.

Unless otherwise stated, the units for flows are billions of yen per year; the units of stocks are billions of yen; price deflators have the value 1.00 in calendar year 1980.

Three definitions of the government sector are used in what follows. One is central government as defined in the Flow of Funds accounts; it is used in IV of this Appendix. The other two are central government and general government as defined in the National Accounts; they are used in III.A and III.B of this Appendix.

II.   Data from the Master File of the Bank of Japan

Y = nominal GNP.

y = real GNP.

P = GNP deflator.

H = high powered money stock outside the central government (as defined by the Flow of Funds accounts) and the Bank of Japan, year end.

M_1 = narrow money stock, year-end.

$M_2 + CD$ = broad money stock, year-end.

CCA = capital consumption allowances.

$GDCF$ = gross domestic capital formation.

$gdcf$ = real gross domestic capital formation.

Dk = real net domestic capital formation, estimated by $(GDCF - CCA)/(GDCF/gdcf)$

k = real capital stock, computed by cumulating Dk starting from a benchmark value of zero at the end of 1964. (Because of the zero benchmark, the intercept of any linear equation containing k will be in error, but the slopes will not.)

m = money multiplier = (monetary aggregate)/H in Table 2.

V = velocity of circulation = Y/(monetary aggregate) in Table 2.

III.   Data from EPA Reports on National Accounts (1985, 1986)

The sources given here are for the 1980-1984 data obtained from EPA (1986), but those for 1970-1979 from EPA (1985) are similar because the formats of the two reports are similar.

Each of the variables defined in this section is computed twice, once for each of two National-Accounts definitions of the consolidated Bank-of-Japan-plus-government sector. One definition is the Bank of Japan plus the central government (including nonprofit institutions controlled by government (jigyodan)), and the other is the Bank of Japan plus general government. The EPA National Accounts tables contain columns for the sectors and subsectors needed for this purpose.

A.   Current Transactions Data from EPA (1986), Part 1 Flow, [3] Supporting Tables, Table 6 Current and Capital Transactions by the Subsectors of General Government, pp. 228-231

G = government purchases of goods and services = line 12 (final consumption expenditure) + line 28 (gross capital formation).

INT = government net interest payments = line 13 (interest paid) − line 1 (interest received).

TX = tax receipts = line 11 (current receipts) − line 1 (interest receipts) − lines $(8 + 9 + 10)$ (current transfers received).

TR = net transfers paid (other than interest) = line 22 (current disbursements) − line 12 (final consumption expenditure) − line 13 (interest paid) − (lines $8 + 9 + 10$) (current transfers received) − (lines $25 + 26$) (capital transfers received).

TXR = taxes less non-interests transfer payments = $TX − TR$.

T = taxes less all transfer payments = $TX − TR − INT = TXR − INT$.

$DEF(NF)$ = government deficit based on nonfinancial transactions = $G − T −$ consumption of fixed capital + net land purchases = (-1) times (line 30).

g = real government purchases = G/P.

$rtxr$ = average rate of tax less non-interest transfers = TXR/Y.

rt = average rate of tax less all transfers = T/Y.

B.   Financial Transactions Data from Part 1 Flow, [3] Supporting Tables, Table 21 Financial Tfransactions by Subsectors, pp. 262-271 and 294-298

Each quantity defined in this section is obtained from the sum of increases in certain liability items minus the sum of increases in the same asset items or the relevant sectors in Table 21.

DH = increase in high powered money outside the Bank of Japan and the government = line 2(1) (currency) + line 2(3) (deposits at the Bank of Japan) + line 2(4) (government current deposits).

$DB = DB_p + DB_f$ = increase in government debt outside the Bank of Japan =

lines 3(1) + 3(3) + 3(4) (time deposits + trust + negotiable CD's) + lines 4 through 10 (short term securities + long term bonds + corporate shares + loans + life insurance + transfers from general government + trade credits) + lines 11(1) + 11(2) + 11(3) (deposits in Trust Fund Bureau + investments by government + nonlife insurance) + line 2(2) (deposits on demand). (The last item, deposits on demand, does not strictly belong in any of the categories defined here, but it is so small that rather than define a separate category for it I have simply included it in DB.)

DF = increase in foreign exchange and gold held by the government and Bank of Japan = (−1) times (lines 11(5) through 11(9)) (foreign direct investments + foreign trade credits + foreign loans + foreign securities + other foreign claims and debts) + (liabilities in lines 1 + 11(4) for the rest-of-the-world column) (gold and SDR's and other foreign exchange reserves, which are shown only in total in the rest-of-the-world column, not separately in the government and Bank of Japan columns).

RESIDUAL = line 11(10) (others).

Note that lines 1, 3(2), and 11(4) for the Bank of Japan, for central government, and for general government have not been assigned to any of the foregoing variables; however, this does not matter since their published values are always zero for those sectors.

DEF(F) = government deficit based on financial transactions = (−1) times (last line, giving the increase in financial assets minus liabilities). [This item is also equal to (−1) times (line 31 of Table 6).]

Note that DEF(F) is equal to DH + DB − DF + RESIDUAL, in Tables 6 and 7.

DA = increase in private sector holdings of claims against the rest of the world = − DF − increase in foreign sector's financial net worth = − DF − (last entry in rest-of-the-world column of Table 21). This makes use of the balance sheet of the rest-of-the-world sector.

IV.   Data from Flow of Funds Accounts

These data are for the consolidated Bank of Japan and central government sector as defined in the Flow of Funds accounts and presented in Bank of Japan (1982). Units are 100 million yen.

Each variable defined below is obtained from the sum of increases in certain liability items minus the sum of increases in the same asset items for the two sectors in question. Because some items are not shown separately, it is necessary to get their values from other columns of line e in the same table, as explained below.

DH = increase in high powered money= lines A + B (deposits with the Bank of

Japan + currency).

DB = DB_p + DB_f = increase in government debt held outside the Bank of Japan = lines I + S + U + V + Z (securities + Bank of Japan loans + bills + loans + deposits with Trust Fund Bureau) − (line e for public financial institutions and for public corporations and local authorities) (equity advanced by central government to those two sectors).

DF = increase in the Bank of Japan and central government holdings of gold and foreign exchange reserves = (−1) times (lines d + e) (other foreign claims and debts + others) + (−1) times (line e for public financial institutions and for public corporations and local authorities) (equity advanced by central government to those two sectors).

DEF(F of F) = central government deficit from Flow of Funds accounts = (−1) times (line f) (financial surplus).

Note that DEF(F of F) is equal to DH + DB − DF, in Table 5.

REFERENCES

Anderson, Leonall and Carlson, Keith, "A Monetarist Model for Economic Stabilization," Federal Reserve Bank of St. Louis *Review,* 52 April 1970, 7-15.

Bank of Japan, *Flow of Funds Accounts in Japan 1975-1981,* 1982 and earlier and later related releases (in Japanese and English).

Barro, Robert, "Are Government Bonds Net Wealth?" *Journal of Political Economy,* 82 December 1974, 1095-1117.

————, "Reply to Feldstein and Buchanan," *Journal of Political Economy,* 84 April 1976, 343-349.

Christ, Carl F., "Some Dynamic Theory of Macroeconomic Policy Effects on Income and Prices under the Government Budget Restraint," *Journal of Monetary Economics,* 4 January 1978, 45-70.

————, "On Fiscal and Monetary Policies and the Government Budget Restraint," *American Economic Review,* 69 September 1979, 526-538.

Economic Planning Agency, *Comparison of Japanese and English Item-name of Annual Report on National Accounts, 1979.* (This small book, in Japanese and English, is indispensable to those who read English but not Japanese and who wish to use the national accounts of Japan.)

————, *A System of National Accounts in Japan (Definitions-Concepts-Sources-Methods),* 1980. (This small book in English, is very helpful for understanding the Japanese national accounts.)

————, *Report on Revised National Accounts on the basis of 1980,* 1985, (2 volumes, in Japanese).

————, *Annual Report on National Accounts,* 1986 (in Japanese).

Hirschhorn, Eric, "Rational Expectations and the Effects of Government Debt," *Journal of Monetary Economics,* 14 July 1984, 55-70.

McElroy, Frederick W., "A Simple Method of Causal Ordering," *International Economic Review,* 19 February 1978, 1-23.

Tobin, James and Buiter, Willem H., "Long-Run Effects of Fiscal and Monetary Policy on Aggregate Demand," in Jerome L. Stein edited, *Monetarism,* Amsterdam, 1976, 273-309.

APPENDIX II

On the Impossibility of Perpetual Pure Debt Finance of Deficits

To see why pure debt finance of continuous government deficits cannot go on indefinitely, consider the following. Let real national income grow at the constant rate q, so that $y_t = y_0(1 + q)^t$. Suppose that there is no government debt and no deficit until the beginning of period 0, at which time the government borrows an amount d_0, and uses it to finance a deficit of d_0 in period 0. Suppose that in each subsequent period the government's deficit other than for interest payments is $d_t = d_0(1 + q)^t$, that is, the non-interest deficit is a constant fraction d_0/y_0 of national income. Suppose that at the beginning of each period the government borrows enough to finance that period's non-interest deficit, plus enough to pay the interest on its outstanding debt at the constant rate r. Then the debt outstanding at the beginning of periods 0, 1, 2, and t is as follows:

$$b_0 = d_0 \qquad b_1 = d_0(1 + q) + b_0(1 + r) = b_0(2 + q + r)$$
$$b_2 = d_0(1 + q)^2 + b_1(1 + r) = b_0(1 + q)^2 + b_0(2 + q + r)(1 + r)$$
$$b_t = d_0(1 + q)^t + b_{t-1}(1 + r)$$

Inspection shows that the debt always grows at a rate that exceeds the economy's growth rate q, and exceeds the interest rate r. Note that if the interest rate exceeds the economy's growth rate, $r > q$, then the term $b_{t-1}(1 + r)$ will eventually dominate, and the debt's growth rate will approach r from above. If $q > r$, the term $d_0(1 + q)^t$ will eventually dominate, and the debt's growth rate will approach q from above. If $r = q$, we easily see that

$$b_0 = d_0 \qquad b_1 = d_0(1 + r) + b_0(1 + r) = 2b_0(1 + r)$$
$$b_2 = d_0(1 + r)^2 + 2b_0(1 + r)(1 + r) = 3b_0(1 + r)^2$$
$$b_t = d_0(1 + r)^t + tb_0(1 + r)^{t-1}(1 + r) = (t + 1)b_0(1 + r)^t$$

In this case the debt's instantaneous growth rate is $r + 1/(1 + t)$, which approaches r from above.

We can now show that if the interest rate equals or exceeds the economy's growth rate, $r \geq q$, the path just described is not sustainable. We do so by showing that it would require the ratio of government debt interest divided by national income, rb/y, to grow without limit. But this cannot happen, because no government would be able to find lenders willing to lend amounts so large that the entire national income would be insufficient to cover the annual interest due.

Consider first the case where $r > q$. Then, as noted above, the debt always grows at a rate that approaches r from above, and since $r > q$, the ratio of the debt interest to income grows without limit.

Consider now the case where $r = q$. Then the ratio of debt interest to inicome is

$$\frac{rb_t}{y_t} = \frac{r(t + 1)b_0(1 + r)^t}{y_0(1 + r)^t} = r(t + 1)\frac{b_0}{y_0}.$$

This ratio grows without limit, even though the debt's growth rate approaches r.

What of the case where $r < q$, the interest rate is less than the economy's growth rate? This can be ruled out if the intertemporal allocation of resources has been chosen optimally. The argument is as follows. The interest rate is the marginal product of capital. Phelp's Golden Rule of Economic Growth shows that in the neoclassical growth model, if the capital/labor ratio is so large that the marginal product of capital exceeds the growth rate, consumption per person can be increased and maintained at a permanently higher level by reducing the capital stock per person until the marginal product of capital becomes equal to the growth rate.

This completes the argument that pure debt finance of continuous government deficits cannot go on indefinitely. It has assumed that the non-interest deficit is a constant fraction of national income. If the non-interest deficit is a declining fraction of national income, the argument is almost as strong, but not quite. Consider the case where the deficit is constant at d_0 per year, instead of growing in proportion to national income as above. Then the debt at the beginning of each year is

$$b_0 = d_0 \qquad b_1 = d_0 + b_0(1 + r) = b_0(2 + r)$$
$$b_2 = d_0 + b_1(1 + r) = b_0 + b_0(2 + r)(1 + r)$$
$$b_t = d_0 + b_{t-1}(1 + r) = b_0[(1 + r)^{t+1} - 1]/r.$$

The general result given by the latter expression can be verified by mathematical induction. The instantaneous growth rate of the debt is $r(1 + r)^{t+1}/[(1 + r)^{t+1} - 1]$, which always exceeds r, but approaches r from above. The ratio rb/y, debt interest divided by national income, is

$$\frac{rb_t}{y_t} = \frac{b_0[(1 + r)^{t+1} - 1]}{y_0(1 + q)^t}$$

if $r > q$, this ratio grows without limit and so the path is not sustainable. However, in the borderline case where $r = q$, this ratio is always less than $(1 + r)b_0/y_0$, but approaches $(1 + r)b_0/y_0$ from below. Hence if $r = q$, but not if $r > q$, debt financing can be used indefinitely to cover a deficit that decreases geometrically as a proportion of national income.

Finally, consider the case where there is a non-interest deficit for only a single period, $d_t = 0$ when $t = 0$; thereafter, $d_t = 0$ and additional debt finance is used only to cover the interest on the outstanding debt. Then the debt at the start of year t is $b_t = d_0(1 + r)^t$. Then, as in the preceding case, the path is sustainable if $r = q$ but not if $r > q$.

PART IV

MONETARY ECONOMICS AND MONETARY POLICY

[15]

RULES VS. DISCRETION IN MONETARY POLICY
Carl Christ

Introduction

In this paper I will take the phrase "stable money" to mean a monetary regime that insures zero inflation on the average over long periods, small variations (if any) in the price level over short periods, and either no effect or (better) a stabilizing effect on fluctuations in real output and employment during business cycles. In retrospect, it appears that economic policy in the United States came closer to this ideal during the immediate postwar period, from about 1948 to 1960, than at any time since.

A major problem since 1960, in my view, is that too often a short-term policy objective has been pursued, to the neglect of its long-term consequences. A conspicuous and unfortunate example is the expansionary policy that was followed from about 1961 into the 1970s. It yielded short-term results that seemed very good while unemployment was low in the 1960s, but in the longer term it yielded the inflation of the 1970s, and the low unemployment proved to be temporary.

One fundamental conclusion about inflation is abundantly clear from the experience of many countries in the years since the start of World War I: No nation can maintain a rapid inflation for an extended period of time without a correspondingly rapid increase in its money stock. And conversely, no nation can avoid rapid inflation over an extended period if it permits continuous rapid growth of its money

Cato Journal, Vol. 3, No. 1 (Spring 1983). Copyright © Cato Institute. All rights reserved.

The author is Abram G. Hutzler Professor of Political Economy, The Johns Hopkins University, Baltimore, Md. 21218.

The author expresses appreciation to James Buchanan, Masahiro Kawai, Louis Maccini, and Jurg Niehans for their helpful comments on an earlier draft. He also wishes to thank David Lenze for his indispensable help with the word-processing program used in preparing this paper.

CATO JOURNAL

stock. There is not complete consensus about which comes first when inflation starts, the rise in prices or the rise in the money stock. But a continued rapid rise in either is a necessary and sufficient condition for a continued rapid rise in the other.

There is a second conclusion that is less well established than the foregoing one, but I believe that it is coming to be accepted by an increasing number of economists. It is this: When there is a significant change in the growth rate of the money stock, the first effect is a *temporary* change in real output and employment in the same direction, and the later effect is a change in the inflation rate in the same direction.

These conclusions suggest that in our search for stable money, we should adopt monetary policies that involve slow growth of the money stock on the average over long periods, so as to avoid inflation, and that involve only small and gradual changes in the rate of growth of the money stock over short periods, so as to avoid creating or exacerbating business cycles. They also suggest that we cannot, and hence should not try to, permanently reduce the long-run average unemployment rate by monetary policy. (For a thoughtful statement of a partially different view, see Tobin 1980.)

Monetary policy has been delegated to the Federal Reserve by the Congress, pursuant to Article I.8 in the Constitution that gives the Congress authority to coin money and regulate its value. It is important to remember, however, that monetary policy and fiscal policy interact. The Congress and the executive branch determine fiscal policy through tax rates and expenditure programs, which (together with the response of the economy) determine the federal budget deficit or surplus. The deficit (or surplus) is financed essentially by increasing (or decreasing) the sum of the monetary base plus private holdings of federal debt. Thus the deficit is essentially equal to the sum of the increases in the base and in private holdings of federal debt. The Federal Reserve directly controls the base. When the deficit is large, as in recent years, the Fed is faced with the difficult choice of whether or not to help finance the deficit. No matter which choice the Fed makes, there is trouble for the economy. If the Fed finances a large share of the deficit, the monetary base rises rapidly, which leads to inflation. If the Fed finances little or none of the deficit, the Treasury must sell large quantities of debt to the private sector. This leads to a high real interest rate, which crowds out private capital formation.

An Optimum Policy Rule

In principle, one could derive an optimum policy rule by maximizing an objective function (defined over a time horizon of a number of years) with respect to the policy variables, subject to the structure of the economy. But in practice, there are several difficulties.

First, an appropriate objective function has not been agreed on. It is determined and changed through the political process. Presumably, however, there is general agreement that positive value should be assigned to a stable price level, to a low rate of unemployment, and to increasingly efficient production.

Second, the structure of the economy is not perfectly known, to say the least. In particular, the demand for money function is not known with certainty. The survey by Judd and Scadding (1982) gives a good account of contemporary estimates of the money demand function, particularly of the apparent deterioration of the quality of its fit after about 1972.

Third, monetary policy variables (with which this paper is mainly concerned) are not the only policy variables that ought to enter into the kind of optimization procedure mentioned earlier. Hence the monetary authorities alone, even if they were omniscient, could not successfully carry out the complete optimization described above.

A Constant Monetary Growth Rate Rule?

In my view, no constant monetary growth rate rule could be optimal if we knew enough to perform a complete optimization. A constant moderate growth rate for the monetary base would hardly have been good policy between 1929 and 1933. During that period the base grew by one fifth, but M1 fell by one third because of a large decline in the money multiplier (see Appendix Table 1). The velocity of the base has been increasing at a varying rate over the past three decades, as shown in Appendix Table 3, which suggests that a constant growth rate for the base would not have been the best policy.

The velocity of M1 has also increased at a varying rate over the past three decades, as shown in Table 3. Hence a constant growth rate of M1 would not have been likely to lead to perfect price stability. It should be noted, however, that had there been a steady increase in M1 or in the base at a modest rate such as two or three percent a year, we would not have had the inflation of the 1960s and 1970s; and the velocities of M1 and the base would have been more nearly constant than they actually were. This means that constant monetary growth would not have been as bad as the actual velocities of the base and M1 in Table 3 suggest.

A constant growth rate for M2 looks as though it would have been a fairly good policy for the period from 1959 through 1981, since the velocity of M2 was nearly constant over this period (see Table 3).

CATO JOURNAL

This suggests that if M2 had been made to grow at a constant rate of, say, three percent a year over the period, nominal GNP might have been expected to grow at about the same rate, which would imply approximately zero inflation for the period. However, two caveats are in order. First, there is no guarantee that the constancy of the velocity of M2 would have been unaffected by a policy of making M2 grow at a steady three percent a year. Second, even leaving that problem aside, it is likely that the nearly constant velocity of M2 was an accident, due to the cancellation of opposite influences, and that this velocity cannot be relied upon to remain as nearly constant in the next two decades as it was in the past two.

As shown in Table 3, the velocity of M3 declined between 1959 and 1981. Thus there is a progression in the velocity behavior of the three M's: M1's velocity rose, M2's velocity was roughly constant, and M3's velocity fell. This behavior is consistent with the fact that over the period interest rates on assets included in M2 and especially in M3 (but not in M1) rose dramatically, which would be expected to lead to substitution away from M1 toward M2 and M3, and away from M2 toward M3. The Divisia indexes of these M's, proposed by William Barnett (1980) and now computed monthly by Paul Spindt and Clifton Wilson of the Federal Reserve Board staff, are a promising attempt to construct quantity indexes of the monetary aggregates, using as weights the degree of "moneyness" of each type of asset. The idea is that an asset, such as currency, that pays zero interest must be held exclusively for the monetary services it renders, while a high-yielding asset such as a long-term bond presumably provides little or no monetary services to its owner. Hence Divisia indexes give zero weight to the highest-yielding asset available, on the presumption that it provides no monetary services, and give to each other asset a weight corresponding to the difference between its interest yield and the highest available yield. At present, while the interest rates on many assets are still controlled by federal regulation, the technique has flaws. But when deregulation of all interest rates is complete, and borrowers and lenders have fully adjusted, Divisia indexes may be expected to respond negatively to interest-rate changes in a more predictable and regular manner than do M1, M2, and M3. Indeed, Barnett (1980) reports that this is true even now, before interest-rate deregulation is complete.

Interest Rate Rules

In practice, an interest rate rule is going to be worse than a monetary growth rule. This is because in practice it is very difficult, one

RULES VS. DISCRETION

might as well say impossible, to gauge correctly the target interest rate that is required from week to week in order to achieve desired results. The reason for this difficulty is that the long-run and short-run effects upon interest rates, when monetary growth rates are changed, are often in opposite directions. For example, putting aside expectational changes for a moment, when monetary growth rates are raised, the initial effect is to lower interest rates as an excess supply of money in nominal terms is created. But after the more rapid monetary growth rate has generated more rapid inflation, and the economy has adjusted to that inflation by reducing real money holdings and by bidding up nominal interest rates so that they include an expected inflation premium, then nominal interest rates are higher than they were in the first place. The result is that merely by looking at the level of nominal interest rates, one cannot tell whether monetary growth is too high or too low. A high nominal interest rate may be the short-run result of a recent reduction in the money stock or its growth rate; or it may be the long-run result of an increase in monetary growth that began some years earlier. When monetary growth rates are allowed to vary from quarter to quarter or year to year, it is not possible to calculate the interest-rate path that would be required to bring inflation under control. We simply do not have sufficient knowledge of the dynamic pattern of response of interest rates to monetary changes and other changes in the economy. This difficulty is compounded by the attempts of bond traders to anticipate future responses by the Fed to current changes in money stocks.

It is my view that the high nominal interest rates of the 1970s resulted mainly from the Fed's previous attempts to keep rates artificially low. By supplying additional base money (either by open market purchases or by permitting loans through the discount window at a below-market rate) when market rates threatened to exceed the unnaturally low target levels, the Fed permitted the monetary base to grow too fast. Inflation and higher nominal interest rates followed. A comparison of the FOMC's target ranges for the monetary growth rates and the federal funds rate, on the one hand, with the actual behavior of these quantities, on the other hand, suggests that this is the case. Surges in monetary growth often occurred when the federal funds rate went above, or threatened to go above, the upper limit of its target range. Poole (1982) has found the same pattern for the period since October 1979, when the Fed announced it would henceforth pay more attention to monetary growth rates than to interest rates.

Beginning in 1981 when large tax cuts were enacted without corresponding cuts in aggregate real federal expenditures, the prospect of very large federal deficits may have contributed to the unusually high and variable real interest rates. Some ex post real interest rates are shown in Appendix Table 4.

The Transition to Monetary Deregulation

The combination of interest-rate ceilings and inflation has caused profound changes in monetary markets, including the invention and proliferation of the money-market funds. The ceilings have been with us for many years, but they did not start to bite until inflation led to increases in the market-clearing levels of nominal interest rates in the 1960s. The Depository Institutions Deregulation and Monetary Control Act of 1980 and subsequent legislative accelerations of the deregulation process have created considerable debate about the proper definitions for the monetary aggregates, and uncertainty about the meaning of their behavior. This uncertainty will persist until the deregulation process is completed and market participants have adjusted to it fully. The process is likely to require another two or three years.

Ex post real interest rates have varied much more than usual in the past few years, as can be seen in Table 4. I conjecture that this is because of the increased uncertainty concerning the inflation rate that has accompanied the large changes in the inflation rate. If the path of the inflation rate had been correctly foreseen by most borrowers and lenders, it is likely that nominal interest rates would have incorporated a correct inflation premium, and that the ex post real interest rate would not have varied as much. (Of course it is the ex ante real interest rate, based on expected rather than actual inflation, that influences investment. It varies across persons and is much harder to measure than the ex post real rate.)

For the two years after the new monetary control procedures were announced in October 1979, the annual growth rates of the base and of M1 were about two percentage points lower than in the two years before. This is a change in the right direction. (The growth rate of M2 rose about half a point.) However, the standard deviation of the quarterly time series of annual growth rates of all three aggregates approximately trebled (see Appendix Table 5). This confirms the by now well-known fact that the variability of the growth rates of the monetary aggregates increased substantially after the new control procedures were announced. Interest rates also became more variable, as expected. Whether the new procedures were responsible for all of this increase in variability is an unsettled matter thus far. It is at least possible that the uncertainty surrounding the deregulation process has made some contribution to it.

Events of late 1982 have made it difficult to decide what is the most appropriate action for the Fed to take. The Fed accurately predicted that M1 would grow more rapidly than the other aggregates toward the end of the year, as the all-saver certificates matured in quantity beginning in October and depositors "parked" substantial amounts of these maturing funds in checkable deposits while waiting to see the terms on which banks would offer the newly permitted money market accounts in December and super-NOW accounts in January. Indeed, the growth rate of M1 accelerated greatly, reaching 22 percent, at an annual rate, in October and 18 percent in November, and slackening to nine percent in December. The growth rate of the base showed no significant change through November, but accelerated to 12 percent in December. M2 showed no significant acceleration through October, but an acceleration to 12 percent in November, with a retreat to nine percent in December. (See Appendix Table 6.)

Thus very different actions would have been required in late 1982 to keep the growth rate of M1 constant, as compared with keeping the growth rates of the base and M2 constant. Because the economy is still adjusting to monetary deregulation, I believe that the wiser choice was made—namely, to maintain the growth rate of the base approximately constant, rather than to suppress temporary rapid growth of M1. But if the Fed allows the rapid growth of M1 to persist and the growth rates of M2 and the base to accelerate, as computed from the money stock levels reached in the fourth quarter of 1982, we risk losing all the headway we have made, at such high cost, against inflation.

Policy Recommendations for More Precise Monetary Control

Three rather simple changes in Fed procedures would contribute to improved ability to make the monetary aggregates come close to their target values. One, which is already in the process of being adopted, is the return to contemporaneous reserve accounting. Admittedly, such a return will be inconvenient for small banks. But it will mean that when the Fed changes the monetary base in any week, the response of M1 and M2 will be prompter and more precise than under two-week lagged reserve accounting.

The second change would be to peg the discount rate to the previous week's 90-day Treasury bill rate, at a level of say one percentage point higher. This would insure that the Fed would always be available as a lender of last resort, at a rate sufficiently high that banks would take advantage of it only when threatened by a critical shortage of liquidity. When inflation is finally brought down to zero, the differential between the discount rate and the Treasury bill rate could be reduced perhaps to half a percentage point or less.

The third change would be to discontinue the practice of announcing target ranges for the federal funds rate, and use targets only for the monetary aggregates. The last two changes would make it clear that the Fed was no longer going to try to calculate and achieve the proper interest rate week by week, a task that we have seen cannot be carried out successfully in the present or likely future state of knowledge. It would mean actually adopting the change that was announced in October 1979 but has not yet been actually adopted, namely, that of shifting attention from interest rates to money stocks.

Policy Recommendations for Stable Money

Suppose it is agreed that no one yet knows how to write a monetary policy rule that is optimal, and that, a fortiori, no constant monetary growth rate rule is optimal. (The reason for the latter is that from time to time events occur that disturb the velocity, or the money multiplier, or both, of one or more of the monetary aggregates. Or events occur that disturb the growth rate of real GNP.) Under such circumstances, what kind of monetary policy gives the best prospect of leading to stable money? I do not believe we know the full answer to this question.

My judgment is that we would have been better served over the last 23 years by a strictly constant growth rate of the monetary base, or of M1, or of M2, at some modest rate such as three percent a year, than we were by the policies that we actually adopted. We would certainly not have had the inflation that has plagued us in the 1970s. And we would not have had the procyclical behavior of the money stock, rising rapidly in booms, and less rapidly, or even declining, in recessions.

Nevertheless, until economic research gives us better knowledge of the structure of the economy and of the effects of monetary policy changes, it is advisable to give the monetary authorities some discretion to try to deal with the kinds of events mentioned above, so as to try to ameliorate the vicissitudes of the business cycle and of liquidity crises. But this discretion must be strictly circumscribed, in order that it not be used to create or permit inflation as was done in the 1960s and 1970s.

RULES VS. DISCRETION

What combination of discretion and monetary growth rate rule would be suitable? The question has two parts, the long-range part dealing with the proper policy to follow once the inflation rate has been brought down to zero, and the immediate part dealing with the proper policy to achieve the transition from our present state to a state of zero inflation. Again, I do not think we know the full answers, although we do know that rapid growth of the money stock should not be permitted, that declines in the money stock should be avoided, and that rapid and substantial changes in the growth rate of the money stock should also be avoided. With this in mind, I shall attempt to formulate a combination of discretion and a monetary growth rate rule that could be serviceable if discretion were wisely used. (Of course, if we could be certain that discretion would always be wisely used, there would be no point in circumscribing it. But the experience of the past two decades makes it clear that discretion is not always wisely used.)

Let me begin with the long-range part of the problem, which is the easier part. Recall that it deals with a situation where the inflation rate has already been brought down to zero. We can take it for granted that by the time this happens, the Deregulation Act will have taken full effect and markets will have completed their adjustment to it. The growth rate of real output has averaged about three percent a year for many decades (though it has slowed recently). Hence we may take three percent as an estimate of its average growth rate for the next decade or so. The velocity of M1 has grown at an average rate of about three percent a year since 1948, very likely in large part because nominal interest rates were rising during the whole period. Hence we may take one percent a year as an estimate, at zero inflation, of the average growth rate of the velocity of transactions balances (that is, currency plus checkable deposits) over the succeeding decade or so. This means that to insure a zero average inflation rate, the required average growth rate of transactions balances should be about 3 − 1 = 2 percent a year. Of course, if the difference between the growth rates of real output and velocity turns out to be different from two percent a year, then the appropriate average growth rate for transactions balances will need to be adjusted accordingly. Such an adjustment, if required, is not likely to be large or sudden, and therefore no serious harm will be done.

So much for the *average* growth rate of transactions balances. What kind of discretion should the monetary authorities have to vary this growth rate from its average, in the short run and in the long run? Short-run variations might be desirable in order to dampen business cycles. For example, it might be desirable to make the money stock

CATO JOURNAL

grow slightly faster than its average rate during recession, so as to counteract the spending decline and slightly slower than its average rate during boom, to dampen the excess-demand pressure. (The Fed has typically used its short-run discretion in the opposite way in the past.) I suggest that the authorities be given discretion to allow the annual growth rate of transactions balances in each calendar quarter to vary by, at most, plus or minus two percent from the average—that is, within the range from zero to four percent.

Erratic changes in the growth rate of the money stock should be avoided. I therefore suggest that discretionary changes in the growth rate of transactions balances be limited to algebraic changes (at an annual rate) of two percent in any calendar quarter, and two percent in any calendar year. This would mean that if the long-run growth rate of real income/velocity is two percent, the *average* growth rate of the money stock would be confined to between zero and four percent a year over long periods and would not change rapidly or substantially.

Now let us consider the more difficult part of the problem, namely, how to combine discretion and a monetary growth rate rule for the purpose of getting from where we are now to a zero inflation rate, so that the long-range policy just described can be put into effect. Should the transition be made suddenly or gradually? I prefer gradualism. As Friedman and Schwartz (1963) have pointed out, abrupt reductions in the growth rate of the money stock have historically been followed in most cases by recessions. Hence I have advocated (1978, 1979) that the growth rate of the money stock be reduced very gradually, at about one-half to one percent a year, for several years until the inflation rate comes down to zero. Let a gradual adjustment speed of one percent a year be adopted. This policy could be carried out if the Federal Reserve were required to make the monetary base grow at a rate between five and nine percent in 1983, and then between four and eight percent in 1984, three and seven percent in 1985, and so on until the inflation rate reaches zero. Thereafter the long-range rule discussed above could be put into effect. An adjustment speed of one-half percent a year would work similarly, but more slowly.

The experience in the United States since the reduction of two percentage points in the growth rates of the monetary base and M1 in October 1979 (see Appendix, Table 5) does not contradict the Friedman-Schwartz finding mentioned above: We are having the most severe recession since World War II. Of course there are other contributing factors. But historical experience suggests that a more gradual reduction of monetary growth would have had a lower cost in terms of forgone output and increased unemployment. And there is no doubt that it could be successful at bringing the inflation rate down to zero.

Why was the monetary growth rate increased, beginning in the 1960s? Arthur Burns, in his lecture entitled "The Anguish of Central Banking" (1979), delivered after the completion of his service as Federal Reserve Board chairman, gave a very frank answer to this question:

> Viewed in the abstract, the Federal Reserve System had the power to abort the inflation at its incipient stage fifteen years ago or at any later point, and it has the power to end it today. At any time within that period, it could have restricted the money supply and created sufficient strains in financial and industrial markets to terminate the inflation with little delay. It did not do so because the Federal Reserve was itself caught up in the philosophical and political currents that were transforming American life and culture.

He then referred to the Full Employment Act of 1946, which imposes on the federal government the responsibility "to promote maximum employment, production, and purchasing power" but does not include price stability among the goals to be promoted.

The removal of the gold reserve requirement against member bank reserves and Federal Reserve notes, in two steps in 1965 and 1968, made possible the subsequent monetary expansion. At the time, I was in favor of removing the gold-reserve requirement, because I believe (and still believe) that such a requirement can at times interfere with a prudent expansion of the money stock. I also believed (which I can no longer believe because of the excessive monetary expansion that followed the removal of the gold-reserve requirement) that monetary authorities could be relied upon to use unfettered discretion in a non-inflationary manner. The gold standard certainly has severe problems of its own, but the persistence of substantial inflation is not one of them.

Before concluding, I would like to direct attention to a quite different type of proposal for achieving stable money. It is found in the last chapter of Jurg Niehans's book, *The Theory of Money* (1978), entitled "The Art of Central Banking." Niehans proposes that the monetary policy of the central bank be divided into three functions. He describes them by imagining that they are assigned to three separate departments.

The price department is initially assigned the entire security portfolio of the central bank, and is given a single responsibility: to assure that the inflation rate remains at or near zero (say, between − 1 and + 1 percent) on the average over the long run. It is free to engage in any operation it regards as necessary to reach this objective.

The output department is initially assigned a portfolio of zero, and is given a single responsibility: to reduce the fluctuations of output and employment in the Keynesian short run. It is free to buy government securities on the open market, or to borrow securities from the price department and sell them on the open market, in any amount, provided that it brings its portfolio back to zero at some time within the next five years. Whenever its portfolio reaches zero again, be it after two months or four or five years, a new five-year period begins. Since the output department, while being free to attempt to counteract short-run fluctuations, is required to undo any action it takes at some point not more than five years later, it is unlikely to disturb the success of the price department.

The liquidity department is also initially assigned a portfolio of zero, and is given a single responsibility: to prevent critical fluctuations in bank liquidity from day to day and week to week. It too is free to buy or sell securities on the open market in any amount, but unlike the output department it must return its portfolio to zero some time within the next six months. Since it must reverse its actions after roughly one quarter, it is unlikely to interfere with the operations of the price or output departments.

Niehans adds that his scheme is a crude one, and that more ingenious and intellectually satisfying schemes could be invented, but that this crude device seems to be good enough to convey his basic idea. Though it is quite different in technique from my proposal, I believe it springs from the same desire to limit the central bank's freedom to create or permit inflation, while leaving some leeway for reducing the severity of business cycles and for serving as a lender of last resort.

APPENDIX TABLE 1
MONETARY STOCKS AND RATIOS, 1929–1933
(Stocks are for December, Seasonally Adjusted)

Year 1 Source	Y 2 *	H 3 *	VH 4 2/3	R 5 3-7	VR 6 2/5	C 7 *	VC 8 2/7	D 9 *	VD 10 2/9	M1 11 7+9*	V1 12 2/11	M1/H 13 11/3
						Levels						
1929	103.4	7.0	14.8	3.2	32.3	3.8	27.2	22.6	4.6	26.4	3.9	3.8
1930	70.7	7.1	12.8	3.3	27.5	3.8	23.9	21.1	4.3	24.9	3.6	3.5
1931	76.1	7.7	9.9	3.1	24.5	4.6	16.5	17.3	4.4	21.9	3.5	2.8
1932	58.3	8.0	7.3	3.2	18.2	4.8	12.1	15.5	3.8	20.3	2.9	2.5
1933	55.8	8.3	6.7	3.5	15.9	4.8	11.6	14.9	3.7	19.8	2.8	2.4
					Growth Rates, Annual Average (percent)							
1929–33	−14.3	4.4	−18.0	2.3	−16.2	6.0	−19.2	−9.9	−5.3	−6.9	−8.0	−10.9

*See note on sources.

APPENDIX TABLE 2

MONETARY STOCKS AND NOMINAL GNP SINCE 1948

(Stocks are for December, Seasonally Adjusted)

Year 1	Y 2	HF 3	HS 4	C 5	R 6	M1 7	M2 8	M3 9	D1 10	D2 11	D3 12
Source	*	*	*	*	4–5	*	*	*	*	*	*
					Levels						
1948h	260	—	37.2	25.8	11.4	111.5	147.6	147.6	—	—	—
1959h	488	44.3	45.2	28.9	16.3	141.2	297.1	298.3	—	—	—
1961	525	45.7	46.8	29.6	17.2	146.7	334.4	338.3	—	—	—
1969h	944	67.9	70.0	46.1	23.9	205.9	588.6	611.4	1.025	1.028	1.018
1971	1078	77.1	80.0	52.6	27.4	231.0	711.1	771.1	1.147	1.210	1.223
1973h	1326	90.3	93.4	61.6	31.8	266.4	859.8	977.9	1.323	1.435	1.483
1975	1549	104.5	109.1	73.8	35.3	291.8	1024	1163	1.456	1.670	1.696
1979h	2414	142.5	150.3	106.1	44.2	390.5	1525	1776	1.939	2.246	2.303
1980	2626	155.0	162.5	116.1	46.4	415.6	1669	1965	2.093	2.367	2.431
1981	2938	162.7	169.9	123.1	46.8	440.9	1823	2188	2.384	2.499	2.592
1982	3058	—	183.4	132.6	50.8	478.5	1999	2404	—	—	—
			Growth Rates, Annual Average		(percent)						
1948–79	7.5	—	4.6	4.7	4.5	4.1	7.8	8.4	—	—	—
1948–59	5.9	—	1.8	1.0	3.3	2.2	6.6	6.6	—	—	—
1959–69	6.8	4.4	4.5	4.8	3.9	3.8	7.1	7.4	—	—	—
1969–79	9.8	7.7	7.9	8.7	6.3	6.6	10.0	11.3	6.6	8.1	8.5
1979–80	8.8	8.8	8.1	9.4	5.0	6.4	9.4	10.6	7.9	5.4	5.6
1980–81	11.9	5.0	4.6	6.0	.9	6.1	9.2	11.3	13.9	5.6	6.6
1981–82	4.1	—	7.9	7.7	8.5	8.5	9.7	9.9	—	—	—

*See note on sources.

APPENDIX TABLE 3

MONEY VELOCITIES AND MULTIPLIERS SINCE 1948
(Based on Data from Table 2)

Year	VHS	VC	VR	VM1	VM2	VM3	VD1	VD2	VD3	M1 HS	M2 HS	D1 HS	D2 HS
	2	3	4	5	6	7	8*	9*	10*	11	12	13**	14**
Source in Table 2	2/4	2/5	2/6	2/7	2/8	2/9	2/10	2/11	2/12	7/4	8/4	10/4	11/4
						Levels							
1948h	7.0	10.1	22.8	2.33	1.76	1.76	—	—	—	3.00	3.97	—	—
1959h	10.8	16.9	29.9	3.46	1.64	1.64	—	—	—	3.12	6.57	—	—
1961	11.2	17.7	30.5	3.58	1.57	1.55	—	—	—	3.13	7.15	—	—
1969h	13.5	20.5	39.5	4.58	1.60	1.54	.92	.92	.93	2.94	8.41	1.46	1.47
1971	13.5	20.5	39.3	4.67	1.52	1.40	.94	.89	.88	2.89	8.89	1.43	1.51
1973h	14.2	21.5	41.7	4.98	1.54	1.36	1.00	.92	.89	2.85	9.21	1.42	1.54
1975	14.2	21.0	43.9	5.31	1.51	1.33	1.06	.93	.91	2.67	9.39	1.33	1.53
1979h	16.1	22.8	54.6	6.18	1.58	1.36	1.24	1.07	1.05	2.60	10.2	1.29	1.49
1980	16.2	22.6	56.6	6.32	1.57	1.34	1.25	1.11	1.08	2.56	10.3	1.29	1.46
1981	17.3	23.9	62.8	6.66	1.61	1.34	1.23	1.18	1.13	2.60	10.7	1.40	1.47
1982	16.7	23.1	60.2	6.39	1.53	1.27	—	—	—	2.61	10.9	—	—

Continued overleaf

APPENDIX TABLE 3 (cont.)

Year	VHS	VC	VR	VM1	VM2	VM3	VD1	VD2	VD3	M1 HS	M2 HS	D1 HS	D2 HS
1	2	3	4	5	6	7	8*	9*	10*	11	12	13**	14**
Source in Table 2	2/4	2/5	2/6	2/7	2/8	2/9	2/10	2/11	2/12	7/4	8/4	10/4	11/4
						Growth Rates, Annual Averages							
						(percent)							
1948–79	2.7	2.7	2.9	3.2	–.3	–.8	—	—	—	–.5	3.1	—	—
1948–59	4.0	4.8	2.5	3.7	–.6	–.6	—	—	—	.4	4.7	—	—
1959–69	2.3	1.9	2.8	2.8	–.2	–.6	—	—	—	–.6	2.5	—	—
1969–79	1.8	1.1	3.3	3.0	–.1	–1.2	3.0	1.5	1.2	–1.2	1.9	–1.2	.1
1979–80	.6	–.9	3.7	2.3	–.6	–1.5	.8	3.7	2.9	–1.5	1.0	.0	–2.0
1980–81	6.8	5.8	11.0	5.4	2.5	.0	–1.6	6.3	4.6	1.6	3.9	8.5	.7
1981–82	–3.5	–3.3	–4.1	–4.1	–5.0	–5.2	—	—	—	0.4	1.9	—	—

* Columns 8, 9, and 10 have been divided by 1000.
**Columns 13 and 14 have been multiplied by 100.

APPENDIX TABLE 4
EX POST REAL YIELD ON 90-DAY TREASURY BILLS

Year 1 Source	Nominal r 2 *	Inflation Rate 3 *	Real r 4 2–3
1948	1.0	6.9	−5.9
49	1.1	− .9	2.0
1950	1.2	2.1	− .9
51	1.6	6.6	−5.0
52	1.8	1.4	.4
53	1.9	1.6	.3
54	1.0	1.2	− .2
1955	1.8	2.2	− .4
56	2.7	3.2	− .5
57	3.3	3.4	− .1
58	1.8	1.7	.1
59	3.4	2.4	1.0
1960	2.9	1.6	1.3
61	2.4	.9	1.5
62	2.8	1.8	1.0
63	3.2	1.5	1.7
64	3.5	1.5	2.0
1965	4.0	2.2	1.8
66	4.9	3.2	1.7
67	4.3	3.0	1.3
68	5.3	4.4	.9
69	6.7	5.1	1.6
1970	6.5	5.4	1.1
71	4.3	5.0	− .7
72	4.1	4.2	− .1
73	7.0	5.7	1.3
74	7.9	8.7	− .8
1975	5.8	9.3	−3.5
76	5.0	5.2	− .2
77	5.3	5.8	− .5
78	7.2	7.4	− .2
79	10.0	8.6	1.5
1980	11.5	9.3	2.5
81	14.1	9.4	5.0
82	10.7	6.0	4.7

*See note on sources.

APPENDIX TABLE 5

MEANS AND STANDARD DEVIATIONS OF QUARTERLY DATA FOR MONETARY GROWTH
(Growth at Annual Percentage Rates)

Period	HS		M1		M2	
	Mean	Std. Dev.	Mean	Std. Dev.	Mean	Std. Dev.
1	2	3	4	5	6	7
Before Oct. 1979						
8 quarters 1977³–1979³	8.7	1.0	8.4	1.6	8.8	1.2
1 quarter 1979³–1979⁴	8.2	—	4.6	—	5.8	—
After Oct. 1979						
8 quarters 1979⁴–1981⁴	6.3	2.8	6.3	5.8	9.4	3.0
12 quarters 1979⁴–1982⁴	6.8	2.5	7.1	5.9	9.5	2.4

SOURCE: *Monetary Trends*, Federal Reserve Bank of St. Louis.

APPENDIX TABLE 6

RECENT SHORT-PERIOD GROWTH OF MONETARY AGGREGATES, 1982–83
(Growth at Annual Percentage Rates)

Month or Week	H Monthly		M1 Monthly		M2 Monthly	
1	Level 2	Growth 3	Level 4	Growth 5	Level 6	Growth 7
January 1982	171.6	12.7	448.6	23.1	1841	13.0
February	173.2	11.8	447.3	-3.4	1848	4.5
March	173.7	3.5	448.3	2.7	1865	11.8
April	175.1	10.1	452.4	11.5	1881	10.4
May	176.6	10.8	451.5	-2.4	1898	11.3
June	177.9	9.2	451.4	-.3	1908	6.8
July	178.0	.7	451.3	-.3	1923	10.2
August	179.3	9.1	455.2	10.9	1946	15.3
September	179.9	4.1	460.5	14.9	1954	5.1
October	181.0	7.6	468.4	22.6	1968	8.5
November	181.7	4.7	475.0	18.3	1987	12.2
December 1982	183.4	11.8	478.6	9.5	2002	9.4

SOURCE: *Monetary Trends*, Federal Reserve Bank of St. Louis.

Note on Sources for Data in Tables

Table 1:

Col. 2: Y = nominal GNP, $billion per year, from U.S. Bureau of Economic Analysis, *National Income and Product Accounts of the U.S. 1929–74*, p. 324.

Col. 3: H = high-powered money, $billion, from Friedman and Schwartz (1963), pp. 803-4.

Cols. 7, 9, and 11, $billion, from Friedman and Schwartz (1963), pp. 712–14:

C = currency held by the public.

D = demand deposits in commercial banks.

M1 = C + D.

Table 2:

Col. 1: h = business cycle high or peak.

Col. 2: Y = nominal GNP, $billion per year, from *Economic Report of the President,* 1983, p. 1963.

Cols. 3 and 4: monetary base, adjusted for changes in reserve requirements:

HF is from the Banking Section of the Federal Reserve Board.

HS is from releases of the Federal Reserve Bank of St. Louis. The 1948 figure is from that bank's *Review,* July, 1977, p. 24. Later figures are from *Monetary Trends* and a supplement thereto dated 10/14/81.

Cols. 5, 7, 8 and 9 are from the *Economic Report of the President.* The 1948 figures are from 1972, p. 256; the others are from 1983, pp. 233–4.

C = currency outside banks.

M1 = C + checkable deposits + travelers' checks.

M2 = M1 + savings and small time deposits + overnight RP's and Eurodollars + balances at non-institutional money market funds.

M3 = M2 + large time deposits + term RP's + balances at institution-only money market funds.

Cols. 10, 11, and 12 are from the monthly release, "Recent Behavior of the Divisia Monetary Aggregates" by Paul Spindt and Clifton Wilson of the Division of Research and Statistics of the Federal Reserve Board.

D1, D2, D3 = Divisia indexes of M1, M2, M3.

J4 G1054$$TB7   06-13-83 16-16-53

Note on Sources (cont.)
Table 4:

Cols. 2 and 3 are from *Economic Report of the President,* 1983, pp.
169 and 240.
r = 90-day Treasury bill rate (p. 240).
inflation rate = annual percentage change in the GNP deflator (p. 169).

References

Barnett, William A. "Economic Monetary Aggregates." *Journal of Econo-
metrics* 14 (Summer 1980): 11–48.
Burns, Arthur F. *The Anguish of Central Banking: The 1979 Par Jacobsson
Lecture.* Washington, D.C.: International Monetary Fund, 1979.
Christ, Carl F. *Review of Monetary Policy in 1977.* Hearing before the Sub-
committee on Domestic Monetary Policy of the Committee on Banking,
Finance and Urban Affairs, House of Representatives, 95th Congress, Sec-
ond Session, January 30, 1978, pp. 4–24 and 42–54, esp. p. 49.
Christ, Carl F. *The 1979 Economic Report of the President.* Hearings before
the Joint Economic Committee, 96th Congress, First Session, February 6,
1979, pp. 189–204 and 213–230, esp. pp. 192 and 197.
Friedman, Milton, and Anna J. Schwartz. *A Monetary History of the United
States 1867–1960.* Princeton, N.J.: Princeton University Press for the National
Bureau of Economic Research, 1963.
Judd, John P., and Scadding, John L. "The Search for a Stable Money Demand
Function," *Journal of Economic Literature* 20 (September 1982): 993–
1023.
Niehans, Jurg. *The Theory of Money.* Baltimore: The Johns Hopkins Press,
1978.
Poole, William. "Federal Reserve Operating Procedures," *Journal of Money,
Credit, and Banking* 14 (November 1982, Part 2): 575–596.
Tobin, James. *Asset Accumulation and Economic Activity: The 1978 Yrjo
Jahnsson Lectures.* Oxford and Chicago: Basil Blackwell and University of
Chicago Press, 1980.

16

9   When is Free Banking More Stable Than Regulated Banking?

Carl F. Christ*

1. INTRODUCTION

This paper presents a model of an open economy with free banking, and asks what features of free banking permit its advocates to say that it is more stable than regulated banking, both with respect to inflation and with respect to bank runs, failures and panics.

Free banking has been the subject of several studies in recent years. Lawrence White (1984) reports that during a period of free banking in Scotland, from 1716 to 1845, there were few bank runs and failures,[1] no bank panics, and no losses to banknote holders or bank depositors. George Selgin (1988) argues that free banking is more stable than regulated banking.

White defines free banking as the absence of political restrictions on the business of issuing private banknotes and deposits, both convertible into full-bodied coin on demand. Selgin's definition is broader: he considers private banknotes and deposits convertible into a high-powered money that may be either a commodity money (such as gold), or a frozen stock of fiat paper money, or a mixture of both. He assumes no reserve requirements, no rules against branch banking, no other government regulations and no central bank.

I shall adopt the latter definition, except that for more generality I shall allow for the possible existence of a central bank that has no power to regulate the creation or behavior of banks, but has the power to create and destroy high-powered money (in the form of paper currency and bank reserve deposits) by offering to buy and sell other assets in exchange for it. This power may or may not be limited, as for example, by a requirement that the central bank stand ready to redeem for gold, on demand, any high-powered money that it has created, or that the central bank keep the high-powered money stock, or its growth rate, within prescribed bounds.[2]

185

Selgin assumes that in a mature free banking system the public desires to hold deposits and banknotes issued by private banks, but no high-powered money. This very strong assumption rules out a major source of cyclical instability in a fractional reserve banking system, that is, changes in the public's desired ratio of high-powered money to private-bank money. Thus it rules out the major cause of bank runs and bank panics, which have occurred in the past when the public lost confidence in the solvency of banks and demanded to convert its holding of private-bank money (deposits or banknotes) into high-powered money (gold or central-bank money). Also, Selgin assumes a closed economy, and treats the high-powered money stock, real income, and monetary velocity as exogenous.

This paper proposes a model of free banking in which these assumptions are relaxed. That is, the public is assumed to want to hold some high-powered money as well as some bank deposits and banknotes, in proportions that may vary from time to time. An open economy is considered, first on the assumption that the free-banking economy maintains a flexible exchange rate with the rest of the world, and later on the assumption that the exchange rate is fixed. The velocity of money is treated as an endogenous variable, dependent on the interest rate. Real income is assumed to fluctuate around a full-employment level (which itself is assumed constant, but steady growth of full-employment income could be handled easily). And the high-powered money stock can change in response to central-bank actions (if any) and international transactions.

The model proposed here is very similar to Don Patinkin's model in which banks hold reserves of high-powered money and the public holds bank deposits and high-powered money. See his *Money Interest and Prices*, second edition (1965), sections XII.5–6, especially pp. 299–301. In Patinkin's model, as here, the nominal money stock and the price level are endogenous, and depend on the banks' reserve ratio and on the ratio of the public's holdings of high-powered money to bank liabilities. The main differences are that in this paper there is a foreign sector, the possibility of inflation is allowed for in a simple way, the demand for bank reserves is modeled endogenously, and, as in free banking, banks issue private banknotes which are held by the public along with bank deposits and high-powered money.

Private banknotes and deposits are considered as perfect substitutes throughout, since under free banking a change in their proportions has no major consequences either for their holders or for the banks that issue them.[3] For simplicity, gold and central-bank paper money will be considered as perfect substitutes during most of the discussion, but the consequences of a change in the public's and banks' desired ratios of gold to central-bank money will be considered toward the end, in Section 6.

The demand for bank reserves is modeled in the following way. A bank holds reserves in order to be able to meet demands for the conversion of its deposits and notes into high-powered money. These demands can come either from other banks that present checks and notes for redemption in the clearing process, or from nonbank depositors and note-holders. It is assumed that high-powered money flows into and out of banks in a series of statistically independent transactions in which deposits are made, checks are cleared or cashed for high-powered money, and banknotes are exchanged for high-powered money, either by other banks in the clearing process or by the public. In equilibrium the probability distribution of the real size of these positive and negative high-powered-money transactions at banks has a mean of zero; its standard deviation is exogenous and equal to s base-year dollars. The representative bank experiences n such transactions per day. Hence the representative bank's real net reserve flows per day will have a mean of zero and a standard deviation of $\sqrt{ns}$. For *nominal* reserve flows the mean will be zero and the standard deviation will be $\sqrt{ns}P$, where P is the price level. The representative bank wants its reserves in equilibrium to be proportional to this standard deviation, with a proportionality factor q representing its degree of risk-avoidance. (Note that according to this view, a bank does not first determine a desired reserve ratio and then adjust reserves to achieve that ratio; rather, it determines its desired level of total reserves directly.) Thus, in equilibrium, the aggregate demand for nominal reserves by all banks will be $qb\sqrt{ns}P$, where b is the number of banks.[4]

The representative bank's equilibrium nominal reserve demand will therefore change proportionally if there is any change in its degree of risk avoidance, q, or in the standard deviation of the real size of its reserve transactions, s, or in the square root of the number of its daily reserve transactions, $\sqrt{n}$, or in the price level, P. We will see later that if the public increases its desired ratio of high-powered money to bank money, this will result in a reduced equilibrium demand for bank reserves, operating through a reduction in the price level.

When a bank finds that its actual reserves fall below the equilibrium demand level, it may believe that the decline is a temporary random fluctuation, and it may then either take no action, or borrow from another bank, while waiting for reserves to come back to the normal level. However, if the bank believes that the decline in its reserves is not a temporary random fluctuation, but is the result of some permanent change, then it will reduce its outstanding loans or sell some securities so as to obtain more reserves.

This paper's assumption that reserve transactions at banks are statistically independent with zero mean is satisfactory most of the time, but during a bank run, when a contagious fear has caused depositors and note-holders to lose confidence in a bank and to withdraw deposits and/or redeem banknotes in exchange for high-powered money, it may be more realistic to assume that reserve transactions are positively serially correlated. However, under this paper's assumption of statistically independent reserve transactions, the contraction of bank liabilities and of the money supply that occurs during bank runs can be explained in terms of an exogenous increase in the public's desired ratio of high-powered money to bank money.

The main results of this paper may be briefly previewed as follows. First, the model presented here shows how the price level, the money stock, and money income respond to changes in important factors such as risk avoidance, shocks to private behavior, and the determinants of the high-powered money stock. None of these results are surprising. They apply equally well, whether banks can issue private banknotes or not. Second, therefore, the question of whether banks should be allowed to issue private banknotes is not, in itself, an important question. Private note issue is neither necessary nor sufficient for reducing the cyclical instability that fractional-reserve banking systems exhibit when the public loses confidence in the banking system and wants to convert banknotes and bank deposits into high-powered money. The feature of free banking, or indeed of regulated banking, that would eliminate inflation is a limitation of the power of the central bank and the government to create paper money rapidly. The features that would reduce cyclical instability will be discussed later, in Section 8.

The paper is organised as follows. Section 2 gives a list of notation. Section 3 presents Model 1, for the case of a flexible exchange rate. Section 4 gives the equilibrium responses of the price level, the money stock and related variables, to several exogenous variables under a flexible exchange rate. Section 5 presents Model 2, a much simpler model inspired by Selgin's treatment of free banking. Section 6 discusses the consequences if banks and the public have preferences about their holdings of gold relative to central-bank money. Section 7 describes and analyses Model 3, for the case of a fixed exchange rate. Section 8 is a summary and conclusion. An appendix displays the balance sheets of the four sectors considered, and several identities that underlie the models.

2.   NOTATION

All variables are in domestic currency in nominal terms (call it dollars), unless otherwise stated. A subscript indicates the sector that owns the asset in question: b for banks, c for the central bank, p for the public, and f for the foreign sector. The notation En1 or En3 or En1,3 preceding a variable's symbol means that the variable is endogenous in Model 1, in Model 3, or in both. If nothing precedes a variable's symbol, the variable is exogenous throughout. An asterisk (*) indicates a variable that does not appear explicitly in Model 1, but that appears in the discussion (possibly in the appendix).

Variables

	B	Bank borrowings from the central bank
	b	Number of banks (dimensionless)
*	C_b, C_p	Central-bank currency and deposits held by banks, by the public
En1,3	D	Private banknotes *plus* deposits
En1	e	Foreign exchange rate (dollars per unit of foreign currency)
	F_c, F_p	Foreign paper (currency and debt) held by the central bank, by the public
	G	Gold (world stock)
*	G_b, G_c, G_f, G_p	Gold held by the four sectors
En1,3	H	High-powered money
En1,3	H_p	High-powered money held by the public
En1,3	i	Real interest rate (per year)
	K_f, K_p	Physical capital
*	L	Bank loans
En1,3	M	Money stock $= G_p + C_p + D$
*	m	Money multiplier $= M/H$ (dimensionless)
	n	Number of high-powered-money transactions at the representative bank (per day)

En3	NFA	Net foreign assets held domestically
En3	NX	Net exports ($ per year)
En1,3	P	Price level ($ per base-year dollar)
	P_f	Foreign price level (foreign currency per unit of real value)
	π^*	Expected inflation rate (per year)
En1,3	q	Bank risk-avoidance index (days)
En1,3	R	Bank reserves (desired and actual)
*	r	Bank reserve ratio = R/D (dimensionless)
	s	Standard deviation of size distribution of real high-powered money transactions at the representative bank (base-year dollars)
En1,3	σ	Standard deviation of size distribution of nominal daily reserve flow at the representative bank ($ per day)
En1,3	V	Income velocity of money (per year)
*	W_f, W_p	Net worth of the foreign sector, of the public
En1,3	y	Real income (base-year dollars per year)
	y^*	Normal full-employment capacity output (base-year dollars per year).

Functions: $i, q, rho, V, x.$

Behaviour parameters: $\beta, \gamma, c, c' = c/(c+1), i_0, q_0, V_0, x_0.$

3.   MODEL 1: A FLEXIBLE EXCHANGE RATE

Four sectors are considered: the domestic public, the domestic banks, the domestic central bank (if there is one), and the rest of the world. The balance sheets of the four sectors are shown in the appendix. There is no government sector, except for the possible existence of a central bank. The absence of a government does not hamper the discussion of a free banking system. The central bank can deal in private debt *vis-à-vis* the private banks, which, in turn, can do the same *vis-à-vis* the public.

For simplicity it is assumed that the only internationally-held assets are gold and foreign-issued paper (currency or securities), but a negative foreign-asset position of the home country can be represented by negative values of its holdings of foreign paper.

Most of the discussion will deal with the case of a flexible exchange rate. The equations of Model 1, representing this case, are as follows. Explanations of the equations follow.

$$H = NFA - F_p + B \qquad \text{High-powered money supply} \qquad (1)$$

$$H = R + H_p \qquad \text{Components of high-powered money} \qquad (2)$$

$$\sigma = \sqrt{ns}P \qquad \text{Standard deviation of daily reserve flows at the representative bank} \qquad (3)$$

$$R = qb\sigma \qquad \text{Equilibrium between actual and desired bank reserves} \qquad (4)$$

$$MV = Py \qquad \text{Equation of exchange} \qquad (5)$$

$$M = D + H_p \qquad \text{Components of money stock} \qquad (6)$$

$$H_p/D = c \qquad \text{Equilibrium between the public's actual and desired ratios of high-powered money to private-bank money} \qquad (7)$$

$$\Delta P/P = \\ \rho[(y/y^*) - 1] + \pi^* \qquad \text{Expectations-adjusted Phillips curve} \qquad (8)$$

$$i = i(y) + i_0 \qquad \text{IS curve} \qquad (9)$$

$$V = V(i + \pi^*) + V_0 \qquad \text{LM curve} \qquad (10)$$

$$q = q(i + \pi^*) + q_0 \qquad \text{Banks' risk-avoidance level} \qquad (11)$$

$$0 = x(P/P_f e, y) + x_0 \qquad \text{Zero foreign capital outflow} \qquad (12)$$

Equation (1) determines the domestic high-powered money supply as the sum of the domestic economy's net foreign assets NFA *minus* the public's net holdings of foreign paper, F_p, *plus* the central bank's holdings of domestic debt, B. It is derived from other identities in the appendix.

Equation (2) says that the domestic high-powered money stock, H, consists of bank reserves, R, and the public's holdings, H_p.

Equation (3) says that the standard deviation, σ, of daily net nominal reserve flows at the representative bank is equal to the product of the standard deviation, s, of the real size distribution of high-powered money transactions at banks *times* the square root $\sqrt{n}$ of the number of such transactions per day *times* the price level, P, as explained above in the introduction.

Equation (4) says that in equilibrium the actual aggregate amount of bank reserves, R, equals the amount desired by banks, $qb\sigma$, as explained above in the introduction.

Equation (5) is the equation of exchange, which equates two expressions for aggregate money income, the money stock, M, *times* its income velocity, V, and the price level, P, *times* real income, y.

Equation (6) says that the money stock, M, consists of bank money, D (deposits and/or private bank notes) *plus* the amount of high-powered money, H_p, held by the public.

Equation (7) says that in equilibrium the public's actual ratio of high-powered money to private-bank money, H_p/D, is equal to their desired ratio, c.

Equation (8) says that the actual inflation rate, $\Delta P/P$, is equal to the expected rate, π^*, *plus* an increasing function, ρ, of the excess of actual real income, y, over the normal capacity level, y^*. Although the expected inflation rate is treated as exogenous, note that no equilibrium makes sense in this model unless the expected inflation rate is equal to the growth rate of the money stock. For simplicity we shall usually assume that the expected inflation rate is zero.

Equation (9) says that the real interest rate, i, is a decreasing function of real income, y, *plus* a shock, i_0. It is the IS curve.

Equation (10) says that the income velocity of money, V, is an increasing function of the nominal interest rate, $i + \pi^*$, *plus* a shock, V_0. It is the LM curve, that is, the demand for money.

Equation (11) says that banks' level of risk-avoidance, q, is a decreasing function of the nominal interest rate, $i + \pi^*$, *plus* a shock, q_0.

Equation (12) says that net capital outflows (that is, net exports) are a decreasing function of the real exchange rate, $P/P_f e$, and real income, y, *plus* a shock, x_0, and that they are zero in equilibrium. Later, when fixed exchange rates are considered, this equation will be modified to permit an international capital flow, which will be equal to the trade balance.

The endogenous variables (arranged in a nonunique order so that the i-th one appears in the i-th equation, $i = 1, \ldots, 12$) are: $H, R, P, \sigma, M, D, H_p, y, i, V, q,$ and e.

In this flexible exchange rate model, equation (1) by itself determines the high-powered money stock, H, because it contains no other endogenous variable. Thus the high-powered money stock can be considered effectively exogenous in equations (2)–(12). However, remember that it is influenced by past capital flows which have determined $NFA - F_p$, and by central-bank holdings of private debt, B.

This model is dynamic because of equation (8), which describes the change in the price level for each period, given the levels of all other variables inherited from the previous period. Once the new price level for a period has been determined, as the sum of the previous price level *plus* the change determined by (8), the rest of the endogenous variables are determined for that period by the static equations that form the rest of the model. Then, for the next period, the change in P is again determined by (8), and the cycle repeats indefinitely. The root of the difference equation for P is negative at equilibrium, so that the equilibrium is locally stable.

This dynamic model is partly recursive. The causal (and chronological) ordering is as follows. As noted above, equation (1) by itself determines the high-powered money stock. Given the price level from (8), equation (4) determines σ, the standard deviation of reserve flows at the typical bank. Then the eight equations (2)–(3), (5)–(8) and (9)–(11) are a fully simultaneous subset that determines the eight variables R, q, M, D, y, V, i, H_p, as is easily shown by the method of McElroy (1978). Equation (12) determines the flexible exchange rate by itself, once equations (1)–(11) have determined all the other endogenous variables.

When the inflation rate has reached equilibrium, equation (8) implies that real income, y, has reached the normal capacity level, y^*. Thus, in equilibrium, real income and the high-powered money can both be regarded as effectively exogenous. The rest of the equilibrium version of the model is also partly recursive. The causal (but this time not the chronological) ordering is as follows. Given real income, equation (9) determines the interest rate. Given the interest rate, equation (10) determines velocity and equation (11) determines banks' risk-avoidance level. Then the six equations (2)–(7) are a fully simultaneous subset, determining the six variables $R, q, \sigma, M, D,$ and

H_p. Again, equation (12) determines the exchange rate, once all other variables are determined.

Similarly, once equations (1)–(11) have determined the values of the high-powered money stock, H, reserves, R, and the money stock, M, in either the dynamic or the equilibrium version of the model, the values of the reserve ratio, r, and the money multiplier, m, can easily be obtained from their definitions, as follows:

$$r = R/D \qquad \text{reserve ratio} \qquad\qquad (13)$$

$$m = M/H \qquad \text{money multiplier} \qquad\qquad (14)$$

Note that from equations (14), (2) and (6), the money multiplier can be written in the familiar way, as follows:

$$m = (1 + c)/(r + c) \qquad\qquad (15)$$

The solutions of the equilibrium version of the model for real income, the interest rate, velocity and banks' risk-avoidance are as follows:

$$y = y^* \qquad\qquad (16)$$

$$i = i(y^*) \qquad\qquad (17)$$

$$V = V[i(y^*)] \qquad\qquad (18)$$

$$q = q[i(y^*)] \qquad\qquad (19)$$

The four preceding variables, and H from equation (1), are in effect exogenous to equations (2)–(7). The simultaneous solution of (2)–(7) yields the following expression for the price level, in terms of H, y, V, q, and other exogenous variables:

$$P = \frac{V(1 + c)H}{V(1 + c)qb\sqrt{ns} + cy} = \frac{VH}{Vqb\sqrt{ns} + c'y} \qquad\qquad (20)$$

where c' is defined as the public's preferred ratio of high-powered money to its total money stock, that is,

$$c' = \frac{H_p}{M} = \frac{H_P}{D + H_p} = \frac{cD}{D + cD} = \frac{c}{1 + c} \tag{21}$$

The price level is proportional to the high-powered money stock, as shown by (20). The solutions for the remaining endogenous variables (except for the exchange rate, e) are all proportional to P (and hence also to H), thus:

$$\sigma = \sqrt{ns}P \tag{22}$$

$$R = qb\sqrt{ns}P \tag{23}$$

$$M = (y/V)P \tag{24}$$

$$H_p = c'M = (c'y/V)P \tag{25}$$

$$D = \left[\frac{1}{(1 + c)}\right]M = \left[\frac{y}{V(1 + c)}\right]P \tag{26}$$

The equilibrium value of the exchange rate is obtained by solving equation (12).

4.   THE EFFECTS OF EXOGENOUS CHANGES ON ENDOGENOUS VARIABLES IN MODEL 1

The effects of exogenous changes on the equilibrium values of endogenous variables can be obtained in the usual way by differentiating the model and solving the resulting linear system algebraically, or, equivalently, by differentiating the solutions (16)–(26). When this is done, the determinant that appears in the denominators is, of course, the same as the denominator of (20); for brevity it will be denoted by Δ. Thus:

$$\Delta = V(1 + c)qb\sqrt{ns} + cy > 0 \tag{27}$$

Here are a few of the derivatives for the price level:

$$\partial P/\partial y = \frac{-V(1 + c)\sigma bi_y q_i - c(P - MV_i i_y)}{\Delta} < 0 \tag{28}$$

$$\partial P/\partial q_0 = \frac{-V(1+c)\sigma b}{\Delta} < 0 \qquad (29)$$

$$\partial P/\partial c = \frac{-VD}{\Delta} < 0 \qquad (30)$$

The signs of the foregoing effects (and others) are derived from the signs of the derivatives of the behaviour functions, which are as follows:

Positive signs: ρ', V_i , x_e

Negative signs: i_y, q_i, x_p, x_y

It is no surprise that in this model the price level is proportional to the high-powered money stock H, as is clear from equation (20). A rise in real income y reduces the price level, because the attendant fall in the interest rate in (17) makes velocity fall in (18) and banks' risk avoidance rise in (19), all of which reduce P in (28). Note that from (20) the decline in the price level is great enough so that money income Py declines as a result of a rise in real income. A rise in banks' risk-avoidance parameter q_0 reduces the price level, as in (29), because it doesn't affect y, i, or V in (16)–(18), but it raises q in (11), and hence it raises bank reserves and contracts the money stock. A rise in c, the public's preferred ratio of high-powered money to bank-issued money, reduces the price level, as in (30), by reducing the money multiplier and contracting the money stock, as in bank panics.

Table 9.1 summarises the algebraic signs of the equilibrium effects of several exogenous variables upon several interesting endogenous variables. The H column shows that an increase in the high-powered money stock causes increases in all other monetary aggregates, in the price level, P, and in money income, Py; this is a straightforward quantity-theory result.

The c column shows that an increase in the public's preferred ratio of high-powered money to bank money causes a reduction in the price level and in all monetary aggregates except the public's holdings of high-powered money, H_p (which increases); this is the same type of monetary contraction that occurs at present in fractional reserve banking systems that prohibit the issue of private banknotes.

The q_0 column shows that an upward shift in banks' risk avoidance level causes declines in the price level and in all monetary aggregates except bank reserves, R (which rise); this type of contraction (like the preceding one) occurs no matter whether private banknotes are permitted or not.

As the V_0 column shows, a downward shift in money demand (an increase in velocity) causes an increase in the price level and hence in bank reserves, and decreases the public's money holdings; these asset changes are unfamiliar in standard textbook treatments – they arise from the increase of bank reserves in proportion to the price level, which requires a decline in the public's holdings of high-powered money since the total high-powered money stock is fixed.

The i_0 column shows that an upward shift in aggregate demand increases the price level and money income, and has ambiguous effects on the monetary aggregates (see the footnotes to Table 9.1).

The y^* column shows that an increase in productive capacity of the economy decreases the price level through the equation of exchange, and has ambiguous effects on the monetary aggregates (again, see the footnotes to Table 9.1).

The n and s columns show that increases in either the number or the average size of reserve transactions at banks reduce the price level and all monetary aggregates except bank reserves (which rise).

Table 9.1 Signs of effects on equilibrium values of endogenous variables when selected exogenous variables are increased in a free banking system like Model 1 for a flexible exchange rate ($+$, $-$, or 0 for no change)

Endogenous variable	Exogenous variable(s) that is (are) increased							
	H	c	q_0	V_0	i_0	y^*	s	n
Price level, P	+	–	–	+	+	–	–	–
Money, M	+	–	–	–	$-^b$	$+^a$	–	–
Private-bank money, D	+	–	–	–	$-^b$	$+^a$	–	–
Public's high-powered money, H_p	+	+	–	–	$-^b$	$+^a$	–	–
Bank reserves, R	+	–	+	+	$+^b$	$-^a$	+	+
Money income, Py	+	–	–	+	+		–	–
Reserve ratio, r			+	+	$+^b$	$-^a$	+	+
Money multiplier, m	–	–	–	–	$-^b$	$+^a$	–	–

[a] True if V is more interest-elastic than q.
[b] True if and only if V is more interest-elastic than q.

5.   MODEL 2: A MUCH SIMPLER MODEL

It is interesting to compare these results with those of a much simpler model from Christ (1989), devised, in the process of reviewing Selgin's book, for the purpose of analyzing his treatment of free banking. In this simpler model the economy is closed; velocity, real income, and the high-powered money stock are exogenous; and because the public wants to hold no high-powered money, the stock of it is equal to bank reserves, $c = 0$, and the money stock consists only of private bank notes and deposits. Model 2 has three equations, namely, equations (3)–(5) above:

$$\sigma = \sqrt{nsP} \tag{3}$$

$$R = qb\sigma \tag{4}$$

$$MV = Py \tag{5}$$

This is a fully recursive model. The first link in the causal chain is the equilibrium condition (4), which determines the standard deviation, σ, of reserve flows at the typical bank, given R. The second link is equation (3), which determines the price level given σ. The last link is equation (5), which determines the money stock, given P. This simple model can be solved recursively for the equilibrium values of the endogenous variables, with the following results:

$$\sigma = R/(qb) \tag{31}$$

$$P = R/(qb\sqrt{ns}) \tag{32}$$

$$M = Ry/(qb\sqrt{ns}V) \tag{33}$$

$$MV = Py = Ry/(qb\sqrt{ns}) \tag{34}$$

These solutions are special cases of the solutions to Model 1 given above.

Table 9.2 summarises the equilibrium responses of the price level, the money stock, and money income to a doubling of the high-powered money stock, R, banks' risk-aversion, q, velocity, V, real income, y, and the absolute real size (s) and number (n) of high-powered money transactions at banks. The H column shows that P, M, and money income are all proportional to the high-powered money stock, H. The q column shows that they are all inversely proportional to the amount of reserves banks want to hold against a given probability distribution of reserve flows.

The V column shows that if velocity doubles, the money stock is halved, so that the price level and money income are not affected. The y column shows that if real income is doubled with no change in the absolute size or number of cash and clearing transactions at banks, the price level is unaffected, but the money stock and money income are doubled.

The s column shows that if the absolute size of real transactions at banks is doubled with no change in their number or in real income, P, M, and money income are all halved. The n column shows that if the number of transactions at banks is doubled, with no changes in their real size or in real income, P, M, and money income are all reduced by the factor $\sqrt{2}$.

The $y\&s$ column shows that if real income is doubled and this is accompanied by a doubling of the absolute size of real transactions at banks, the price level is halved but M and money income are not affected. The $y\&n$ column shows that if the doubling of real income is accompanied by a doubling of the number of transactions at banks with no change in their absolute size, the price level is reduced by the factor $\sqrt{2}$, and M and money income are increased by the same factor.

Typically, as an economy grows, both population and per capita real income grow, and hence as real income, y, increases, both the number (n) and the absolute real size (s) of cash and clearing transactions can be expected to increase. Hence, in a simple free banking system corresponding to Model 2, if velocity does not change much, the result

Table 9.2   Factors by which equilibrium values of endogenous variables are multiplied when selected exogenous variables are doubled in a simplified free banking system like Model 2 for a closed economy

Endogenous variable	Exogenous variable(s) that is(are) increased							
	H	q	V	y	s	n	$y\&s$	$y\&n$
Price level, P	2	1/2	1	1	1/2	$1/\sqrt{2}$	1/2	$1/\sqrt{2}$
Money, M	2	1/2	1/2	2	1/2	$1/\sqrt{2}$	1	$2\sqrt{2}$
Money income, Py	2	1/2	1	2	1/2	$1/\sqrt{2}$	1	$\sqrt{2}$

of economic growth is likely to lie between the last two columns of Table 9.2, that is, the price level is likely to fall slightly faster than half the growth rate of aggregate real income, y, and the money stock and money income are likely to rise slightly slower than half the growth rate of y.

Most of the proportional results in Table 9.2 for the very simple Model 2 are qualitatively similar to those in Table 9.1 for Model 1, but some are not. In particular, in Model 2, unlike Model 1, neither money demand (velocity) nor real income has any effect on the price level. This can be seen by comparing the two solutions for the price level in the two models, given in equations (20) and (32) above. The two solutions become identical if the public wants to hold no high-powered money, that is, if $c = 0$.

6.   WHAT IF GOLD AND CENTRAL-BANK MONEY ARE IMPERFECT SUBSTITUTES?

So far it has been assumed that banks and the public regard gold and central-bank money as perfect substitutes. This presupposes that central-bank money is convertible into gold. Now suppose that convertibility is maintained, but each sector has a preferred ratio between the two assets. Then we append the following four equations to Model 1:

$$R = G_b + C_b \qquad \text{Components of bank reserves} \qquad (35)$$

$$G_b = \beta C_b \qquad \text{Banks' preferred gold ratio} \qquad (36)$$

$$H_p = G_p + C_p \qquad \text{Components of the public's } H_p \qquad (37)$$

$$G_p = \gamma C_p \qquad \text{Public's preferred gold ratio} \qquad (38)$$

where β and γ are behaviour parameters of the banks and the public. These equations determine the four new endogenous variables, namely, the holdings of gold and fiat money by the banks and the public, once reserves, R, and the public's holdings of high-powered money, H_p, have been determined by Model 1.

The solutions discussed above for Model 1 still hold as before, *provided* that the high-powered money stock does not change. But this proviso is unlikely to remain true. For suppose that the banks and/or the public becomes less confident about the safety of central-bank money. Then they will redeem some of it for gold. This will not, by itself, reduce the high-powered money stock, but it will reduce both the stock of central-bank money and the central bank's gold reserve ratio, which is $G_c/(C_b + C_p)$. If this ratio falls below some desired level, the central bank will seek to raise it again. The only way it can do so is to sell some of its paper assets for gold.[5] This *will* reduce the high-powered money stock, as shown by equations (46) and (47) in the appendix. Thus a monetary contraction can be caused by a loss of confidence in central-bank money relative to gold, or indeed by anything that induces the public or the banks to raise their ratios of gold to central-bank money, or by anything that reduces the central bank's gold reserve below its desired level.

Of course, if the central bank's gold reserve becomes depleted, there is an alternative possible outcome, not dealt with in this model: the suspension of the convertibility of central-bank money into gold. In this case, inflation becomes a serious possibility, as the experience of the US and many other countries has shown.

7.   MODEL 3: A FIXED EXCHANGE RATE

We now turn to the case of a fixed exchange rate. Suppose that all countries are on the gold standard, and that units of currency are chosen so that the exchange rate is equal to 1. Several modifications need to be made in Model 1 to deal with this case. First, disturbances to international trade will now be reflected in capital flows, rather than in variations of the exchange rate. Hence equation (12), which equates net capital outflow to zero, must be modified. Denote net exports by NX, and rewrite (12) as

$$NX = x(P/P_f, y) + x_0 \qquad (12')$$

When $NX = 0$ and $e = 1$, (12') is equivalent to (12).

Second, the identity that equates net exports to net capital outflows is now needed:

$$NX = \Delta NFA \qquad (39)$$

Finally, because net exports are a component of national expenditures, which enters the *IS* curve, (9) must be revised thus:

$$i = i(y, P/P_f) + i_0 \tag{9'}$$

The result of revising Model 1 by appending the identity (48) and replacing (12) and (9) by (12') and (9') will be called Model 3. Its thirteen endogenous variables include all those in Model 1 except for the exchange rate, e, and two others: net exports, NX, and net foreign assets, NFA.

Model 3 is also dynamic. As in Model 1, equation (8) determines the change in the price level. Apart from that, the rest of Model 3 is a fully simultaneous system.

In the equilibrium version of Model 3, as in Model 1, equation (8) implies that output is equal to its normal level. Apart from that, the rest of the equilibrium version of Model 3 is also fully simultaneous. The system is so nonlinear that the solutions cannot be written explicitly (except for $y = y^*$). However, the effects of exogenous changes upon equilibrium values of the endogenous variables can be obtained by differentiating the model and solving the resulting linear system algebraically, as before. The determinant that appears in the denominators of the solution is

$$\Delta' = V(1 + c)[b(q\sqrt{ns} + \sigma i_p q_i) - x_p] + c(y - MV_i i_p) > 0 \tag{40}$$

Some of the solutions for the price level are:

$$\frac{\partial P}{\partial y} = \frac{-V(1 + c)(b\sigma i_y q_i - x_y) - c(P - MV_i i_y)}{\Delta'} < 0 \tag{41}$$

$$\frac{\partial P}{\partial q_0} = \frac{-V(1 + c)b\sigma}{\Delta'} < 0 \tag{42}$$

$$\frac{\partial P}{\partial c} = \frac{-VD}{\Delta'} < 0 \tag{43}$$

Table 9.3 summarises the signs of the effects of exogenous factors on several interesting endogenous variables. For example, an increase in central bank credit, B, increases the high-powered money stock, H, and all other monetary aggregates, as well as the price level. As in Table 9.1, which is for flexible exchange rates, an increase in the public's desired ratio, c, of high-powered money to bank money does not affect the high-powered money stock, but reduces the price level and all monetary aggregates except the public's holdings of high-powered money, H_p (which increases). With one exception, the effects of an increase in banks' risk-avoidance, q_0, are in the same direction as in Table 9.1, that is, there are declines in the price level and in all monetary aggregates except bank reserves, R (which increase); the exception is that now the high-powered money stock is increased, because the price decline generates an export surplus which raises the foreign component of the monetary base. With one exception, the effects of a downward shift in money demand (an increase in V_0) are in the same direction as in Table 9.1, that is, an increase in the price level and hence in bank reserves, and decreases in private money holdings; the exception is that the high-powered money stock declines, because the price increases generate a trade deficit which reduces the foreign component of the monetary base. The effects of increases in aggregate demand, i_0, full-employment income, y^*, and the size (s) and number (n) of reserve transactions, are all in the same direction as in Table 9.1, except that their effects on the high-powered money stock are opposite to their effects on the price level, because of the effect of the price level on net exports.

If the public and/or the banks have preferences concerning gold versus central-bank money, the consequences for Model 3 are similar

Table 9.3   Signs of effects on equilibrium values of endogenous variables when selected exogenous variables are increased in a free banking system like Model 3 for a fixed exchange rate ($+$, $-$, or 0 for no change)

Endogenous variable	Exogenous variable(s) that is (are) increased							
	B	c	q_0	V_0	i_0	y^*	s	n
High-powered money, H	+	0	+	–	–		+	+
Price level, P	+	–	–	+	+	–	–	–
Money, M	+	–	–	–	$-^a$	$+^a$	–	–
Private-bank money, D	+	–	–	–	$-^a$	$+^a$	–	–
Public's high-powered money, H_p	+	+	–	–	$-^a$	$+^a$	–	–
Bank reserves, R	+	–	+	+	$+^a$		+	+
Money income, Py	+	–	–	+	+		–	–
Reserve ratio, r			+	+	$+^a$		+	+
Money multiplier, m	–	–					–	–

^{a} True if V is more interest-elastic than q.

to those for Model 1, except that, as is well known, the domestic money supply is more sensitive to foreign disturbances under fixed exchange rates than under flexible rates.

8. CONCLUSION

In this paper we have considered free banking, defined essentially as a system in which private banks can issue not only deposits but also paper banknotes convertible into gold or other high-powered money. We have studied the effects upon the price level, the money stock, money income, and related variables in a free banking system when there are changes in important explanatory variables such as the full employment level of real income, the public's desired ratio of high-powered money to bank money, the risk-avoidance level of banks, the size and number of high-powered money transactions at banks, and, in cases where it is effectively exogenous, the high-powered money stock. The results, as shown in Tables 9.1 and 9.3, differ somewhat between Models 1 and 3, depending on whether exchange rates are flexible or fixed. The principal differences between the two models' results have been noted in the preceding section.

We can now assess two advantages that have sometimes been claimed for free banking, namely, that it avoids bank runs, failures, and panics that are due to changes in the public's preferred ratio of currency to deposits, and that it avoids inflation. In fact, neither of these advantages is found in free banking systems where the public prefers to hold some of its money in high-powered form, and where there is a central bank that can buy and sell private assets in return for central-bank money without restraint.

Bank runs, failures, and panics occur when the public loses confidence in a bank or banks, and wants to get rid of substantial amounts of its holdings of bank money in return for high-powered money. Let us suppose that banks are freed of regulation and are allowed to issue paper banknotes as well as deposits. There is no reason to believe that the public will thereby acquire such confidence in the banking system that it will never want to hold any high-powered money. And there is no reason to believe that the public will cease to find, from time to time, that its confidence in one or more banks has waned to the point where it wants to exchange some of its holdings of private banknotes and deposits for high-powered money. The danger of bank runs, failures and panics under free banking is shown by the negative effect of increases in the public's desired ratio, c, of high-powered money to bank money, displayed in Tables 9.1 and 9.3.

The experience in Scotland in the 18th and 19th centuries, described by White, strongly suggests that the danger of bank runs, failures and panics would be reduced if there were no constraints on branch banking, so that the typical bank would operate nationwide and have many branches, and if bank stockholders bore unlimited liability, so that depositors and note-holders would know that stockholders were responsible for losses. However, the likelihood of instituting unlimited stockholder liability is remote.

The existence of a lender of last resort can help to reduce bank runs, failures and panics, as shown by the experience of certain countries at certain times, when central banks fulfilled this function in a responsible manner. One of the arguments in favour of establishing a lender of last resort under a gold standard is that private banks and the public will feel safe in holding smaller gold reserves than they would without such a lender, thus saving real resource costs.

When central banks have the power to create fiat high-powered money at will, and do so too rapidly, the result is inflation. This is true whether or not private banks are prohibited from issuing paper banknotes and whether or not they are subjected to reserve requirements.

To answer the question posed in the title of this paper: First, if free banking is resistant to inflation, it will be because of the convertibility of bank money into gold, or into some other form of high-powered money that cannot be arbitrarily increased by a central bank or a government, and not because of the existence of private banknotes. Secondly, if free banking is more resistant to bank runs, failures and panics than the present US banking system, it will not be primarily because of the right to issue private banknotes.

Appendix: Balance Sheets and Other Identities

The balance sheets of the four sectors are tabulated below, with assets in the left column and liabilities in the right column. In some cases, some of the items in these balance sheets will be zero.

Banks

R = Reserves	D = Deposits and banknotes
= G_b gold and C_b fiat currency	B = Borrowings at central bank
L = Loans	

Central Bank

G_c = Gold	$C_b + C_p$ = Central bank deposits and
B = Borrowings by banks	fiat currency
F_c = Foreign paper	

Public

H_p = High-powered money	L = Loans
= G_p gold and C_p fiat currency	W_p = Net worth
D = Deposits and banknotes	
F_p = Foreign paper	
K_p = Physical capital	

Foreign Sector

G_f = Gold	$F_c + F_p$ = Foreign paper
K_f = Physical capital	W_f = Net worth

As noted in Section 3 above, this picture abstracts from government, except for the possible existence of a central bank, and for simplicity it is assumed that the only internationally-held assets are gold and foreign-issued paper (currency or securities).

The four balance-sheet equations of these four sectors are functionally independent of each other. The assets of each of these sectors are liabilities of the other three sectors, and *vice versa*, except for the physical assets (gold and physical capital) and the net worths, which are not. One can think of a fifth sector, whose assets are the net worths and whose liabilities are the physical assets. This fifth sector's balance-sheet equation is obtained by aggregating the other four, and hence is functionally dependent on the other four by Walras' law. The only balance-sheet equation we shall need to use is that for the central bank.

Eleven functionally independent identities are used in the discussion. They are presented below. All but the last three have appeared above in the text.

$H = R + H_p$	Components of high-powered money	(2)
$MV = Py$	Equation of exchange	(5)
$M = H_p + D$	Components of money stock	(6)
$r = R/D$	Banks' reserve ratio	(13)
$m = M/H$	Money multiplier	(14)
$R = G_b + C_b$	Components of bank reserves	(35)
$H_p = G_p + C_p$	Components of the public's H	(37)
$NX = \Delta NFA$	Balance of trade	(39)
$\sum G_i = G(i = b, c, f, p)$	Components of the world gold stock	(44)
$NFA = G_b + G_c + G_p + F_c + F_p$	Components of net foreign assets	(45)
$G_c + B + F_c = C_b + C_p$	Central bank balance sheet	(46)

Equations (2), (35), (37) and (46) imply that the high-powered money stock is the sum of domestically-held gold *plus* the central bank's holding of domestic debt and foreign paper, thus:

$$H = G_b + G_p + G_c + F_c + B \tag{47}$$

In an open economy, (45) and (47) imply that the high-powered money stock is the economy's net foreign assets *minus* the public's holdings of foreign paper *plus* the central bank's holdings of domestic debt, which is equation (1), thus:

$$H = NFA - F_p + B \tag{1}$$

References

Baltensperger, Ernst (1974) "The Precautionary Demand for Reserves", *American Economic Review*, 64 (March): 205–10.
—— (1980) "Alternative Approaches to the Theory of the Banking Firm", *Journal of Monetary Economics*, 6 (January): 1–37.
Black, Fischer (1970) "Banking and Interest Rates in a World without Money", *Journal of Bank Research*, 1 (Autumn): 9–20.
Christ, Carl F. (1957) "Patinkin on Money, Interest and Prices", *Journal of Political Economy*, 65 (August): 347–54.

—— (1989) "On Free Banking: Essay Review of *The Theory of Free Banking* by George Selgin", *Market Process*, 7 (Spring): 5–10.

Edgeworth, Francis Ysidro (1888) "The Mathematical Theory of Banking", *Journal of the Royal Statistical Association*, 51 (March): 113–27.

Fama, Eugene (1980) "Banking in the Theory of Finance", *Journal of Monetary Economics*, 6 (February): 39–57.

Greenfield, Robert, and Leland Yeager (1983) "A Laissez-Faire Approach to Monetary Stability", *Journal of Money, Credit and Banking*, 15 (August): 302–15.

Hall, Robert E. (1982) "Explorations in the Gold Standard and Related Policies for Stabilizing the Dollar", in Robert E. Hall (ed.), *Inflation*, Chicago: University of Chicago Press for the National Bureau of Economic Research, pp. 111–22.

McCallum, Bennett (1985) "Bank Deregulation, Accounting Systems of Exchange, and the Unit of Account: A Critical Review", in Karl Brunner and Allan Meltzer (eds.), *Carnegie–Rochester Conference Series on Public Policy*, 23 (Autumn): 13–45.

McElroy, F. W. (1978) "A Simple Method of Causal Ordering", *International Economic Review*, 19 (February): 1–23.

Orr, Daniel, and W. G. Mellon (1961) "Stochastic Reserve Losses and Expansion of Bank Credit", *American Economic Review*, 51 (September): 614–23. See also errata in volume 53 (September 1963): 745.

Patinkin, D. (1956, 1965, 1989) *Money, Interest, and Prices*, Evanston, Ill.: Row Peterson, 1956; New York: Harper and Row, 1965; 2nd ed. Abridged, with a new introduction. Cambridge, Mass.: MIT Press, 1989.

Selgin, George A. (1988) *The Theory of Free Banking: Money Supply under Competitive Note Issue*, Totowa, NJ: Rowman and Littlefield.

White, Lawrence H. (1984) *Free Banking in Britain: Theory, Experience, and Debate, 1800–1845*, New York: Cambridge University Press.

Notes

* It is a great honour to be invited to take part in this conference in celebration of the work of Don Patinkin. I am indebted to him for stimulating my interest in monetary economics beginning many years ago, and for his contributions ever since, especially his classic book, *Money, Interest, and Prices* (1956, 1965, 1989), which I reviewed (1957). I am grateful to David Bizer, Louis Maccini, Allan Meltzer, Hugh Rose and George Selgin for helpful discussions concerning the topic of this paper, and to Stanley Fischer for constructive suggestions on an earlier draft.

1. White (1984) reports that 109 Scottish banks were chartered between 1716 and 1845, and that by 1845, 36 of them "had failed or been wound up", 12 had disappeared for unknown reasons, 11 had disappeared without apparent failure, 30 had merged into other banks, and 20 were still operating independently. I leave it to the reader to judge whether this indicates that there were few bank failures during that time. White also

reports that in 1984, three of the original Scottish banks were still operating, and still issuing private bank notes.

2. Two points should be noted here. First, by assuming convertibility into high-powered money, I am ruling out the possibility that free banks might compete with each other in defining the nature of the claims they will permit depositors and banknote-holders to assert. Second, since this paper is concerned chiefly with privately-issued convertible banknotes, it does not deal with the recent work of Black (1970), Fama (1980), Hall (1982) and Greenfield and Yeager (1983) on accounting systems of exchange and the definition of the unit of account in terms of a standard commodity bundle. See McCallum (1985) for a critical review of this work.

3. Note that the high powered money and private bank deposits are *not* perfect substitutes. Hence if private bank notes are prohibited, a change in the public's desired currency/deposit ratio does have a major consequence, namely, a change in the money multiplier. Note also that one difference between private banknotes and deposits is that a person who is offered a private bank note needs to be concerned only about the soundness of the issuing bank, and not also about the soundness of the person offering payment. Private bank notes are rather like certified checks in this respect. This difference is not crucial for present purposes.

4. This view of bank reserve demand goes back to Edgeworth (1888), and has been used by Orr and Mellon (1961) and Baltensperger (1974; 1980).

5. Here I am supposing that foreign holdings of gold are exogenous, so that the domestic central bank can sell paper assets for gold only to the domestic private sector.

PART V

REFLECTIONS ON
ECONOMIC MODELLING
AND ON ECONOMIC POLICY

17

Essays in Honor of Karl A. Fox
Tej K. Kaul and Jati K. Sengupta (Editors)
©Elsevier Science Publishers B.V., 1991

Pitfalls in Macroeconomic Model Building

Carl F. Christ

Department of Economics
The Johns Hopkins University,
Baltimore, MD 21218, U.S.A.

1. Introduction

Many and varied are the inconsistent, incomplete, or inappropriate macro-economic models I have encountered in refereeing papers for journals and reading first drafts for students. But certain types of difficulties occur repeatedly. These pages offer a number of steps designed to detect such difficulties and to assist in correcting them. The order in which the steps should be carried out is not graven in stone: it should no doubt be varied somewhat from case to case. Three different models are presented and used to illustrate the proposed steps.

2. Some Helpful Steps In Model Building

2.1. Decide the Purpose of the Model

A clear decision about the model's purpose is helpful in choosing many of the features to include (or exclude).

The work underlying this paper was supported in part by a grant from the National Science Foundation. The views expressed are those of the author and not necessarily those of the Foundation. Helpful comments on earlier drafts were made by Joe Amoako-Tuffour, Stephen Blough, Paul Boothe, John Iton, Louis Maccini, David Majerus, Hugh Rose, David Ryan, and Naoyuki Yoshino.

2.2. Decide How Many Sectors to Include

ls a foreign sector needed? A government sector? If the latter, is is satisfactory to consolidate the central bank with the treasury, or does the model's purpose require two separate sectors? Presumably there will be a private sector if the model is meant to apply to a private-enterprise economy. If so, will the private banking system be a separate sector, or will it be consolidated with the private nonbank sector? (Or with the central bank?) If the model is to include any saving or investment or capital stock, a fictitious capital-account sector is implied: it holds other sectors' net worth as its assets, carries the capital stock as its liability, receives saving as its revenue, and pays for investment as its expenditure.

2.3. State Any Assumptions that Underlie the Model

Such assumptions may deal with stochastic disturbances (e.g., they may be assumed to have zero means and to be statistically independent of certain quantities). Or they may deal with systematic economic variables (e.g., the net worth of the banking system is often assumed to be negligible so that it can be ignored, or business saving is often assumed to be zero, or expectations may be assumed to be rational, etc.). Careful attention to assumptions is very important, in order to assure that the model says what its builder intends it to say, no more and no less.

2.4. Make Two Intersectoral Tables, One for Claims (Stocks) and One for Flows

Each table should have a row and a column for each sector, and a "total" row and a "total" column. Let the table of claims be organized so that any entry is an asset of the sector in whose column it appears, and a liability of the sector in whose row it appears. Then the total of each sector's assets appears at the foot of its column, and the total of its liabilities and net worth appears at the end of its row.

A 3-sector, 2-asset example appears below, in which the price level is assumed constant and equal to 1, and the government sector holds no assets. There is no foreign sector in this example. The asset and liability variables are:

$k =$ physical capital net of depreciation
$m =$ money stock
$w_p =$ private sector net worth
$w_g =$ government sector net worth

Table I is the table of claims. The balance sheet equation for each sector can be read off from the totals in its column and row, thus:

sector	assets	= liabilities
private	$m + k$	$= w_p$
government	0	$= m + w_g$
capital	$w_p + w_g$	$= k$

(Government debt could easily be introduced if desired; it behaves like m here.) Notice that any of the three balance sheets can be derived from the sum of the other two. This is true in general, that is, when there are n sectors, only $n - 1$ of the n balance sheet equations are functionally independent.

In this economy, suppose that only the private sector produces output and invests in physical capital. The revenue and expenditure variables are:

$g =$ government purchases of goods and services

$i =$ net investment

$s =$ net saving

$t =$ government tax revenue

Table II is the table of flows, assuming a balanced government budget. The revenue = expenditure statements can be read off from the totals in each column and row, thus:

sector	revenue	= expenditure
private	$g + i$	$= t + s$
government	t	$= g$
capital	s	$= i$

Notice that any of the three revenue = expenditure statements can be derived from the sum of the other two. This too is true in general. Only $n - 1$ of the n flow equalities are functionally independent.

Notice that consumption, c, does not appear explicitly, because it is both a revenue and an expenditure item for the private sector; it has been canceled out from both sides of the private sector's equation. Income, y, is defined by the equation

$$y = c + i + g$$

Table I: Intersectoral claims.

Assets of Liabilities of	private sector	government	capital account	total liabilities
private sector	—		w_p	w_p
government	m	—	w_g	$m + w_g$
capital account	k	—	—	k
total assets	$m + k$	0	$w_p + w_g$	$m + k + w_p + w_g$

Table II: Intersectoral flows.

Revenues of Expenditures of	private sector	government	capital account	total expenditures
private sector	—	t	s	$t + s$
government	g	—		g
capital account	i		—	i
total revenues	$g + i$	t	s	$g + i + t + s$

Observe that when the time derivative of each balance sheet equation is taken, the resulting equations are the revenue = expenditure statements (bear in mind that because of the balanced budget, $\Delta m = g - t = s - i = 0$).

When a model with asset/liability and revenue/expenditure accounts is built, constructing two tables like Tables I and II is an aid to clear thinking about the model.

2.5. Formulate the Equations of the Model

As we have seen, some of the equations may be accounting identities for stocks, some for flows. Besides these any additional definitional relations should be included — such as $i = \Delta k$, investment equals change in capital stock. And behavior equations for the model's agents should be included. Each equation should have a carefully stated economic meaning. If possible, it is desirable to relate each behavior equation to optimizing behavior on the part of economic agents.

It may be necessary to reformulate the equations later, if it turns out after subsequent thought that they are incomplete, or inconsistent, or un-satisfactory in some other way. (Much of this paper is directed to the process of formulating the equations properly in the light of the model's purpose).

2.6. Check that the Equations are Functionally Independent

If any set of a model's equations are functionally dependent, one or more of the dependent set can be dropped without altering the behavior of the model. We have seen examples of this above, regarding the balance-sheet equations and the revenue = expenditure equations. The same can arise with behavior equations.

Suppose a model says that disposable income y_d is allocated between consumption and saving, thus:

$$c = \alpha + \beta y_d \qquad \text{consumption}$$

$$s = \gamma + \delta y_d \qquad \text{saving}$$

$$c + s = y_d \qquad \text{accounting identity}$$

These three equations are functionally dependent, for the first two must add up to the third no matter what the value of disposable income y_d. Hence we must have $\alpha + \gamma = 0$ and $\beta + \delta = 1$. Hence the second equation says

$$s = -\alpha + (1 - \beta)y_d$$

Thus any of the three equations can be derived from the other two. The choice of which one to drop is arbitrary: the behavior of the model's vari-ables is not affected by the choice. The model may be easier to understand if one drops either the consumption equation or the saving equation, and explicitly retains the accounting identity, which the data must satisfy.

In larger models, where the functional dependence of equations may be less obvious to the eye than in the preceding case, it can be ascertained from the Jacobian determinant of the system. If the Jacobian is zero, the equations are either inconsistent or functionally dependent. If it is not zero, they are functionally independent. In the preceding three-equation example, after rewriting the three equations so that each is expressed as $f_i(c, s, y_d) = 0$, where $i = 1, 2, 3$, the Jacobian is

$$J = \frac{\partial(f_1, f_2, f_3)}{\partial(c, s, y_d)} = \begin{vmatrix} 1 & 0 & -\beta \\ 0 & 1 & -\delta \\ 1 & 1 & -1 \end{vmatrix} = \begin{vmatrix} 1 & 0 & -\beta \\ 0 & 1 & -(1-\beta) \\ 1 & 1 & -1 \end{vmatrix} = 0$$

A similar example arises with asset demands. Suppose the demands for money m and for bonds b depend on income y, interest rate r, and f which is itself the sum of money and bonds:

$$m = \alpha + \beta y + \gamma r + \delta f \qquad \text{money}$$

$$b = \epsilon + \eta y + \theta r + \lambda f \qquad \text{bonds}$$

$$m + b = f \qquad\qquad \text{accounting identity}$$

Again the third equation must be the sum of the first two, regardless of the values of income, the interest rate, and financial assets. Hence we must have $\alpha + \epsilon = 0$, $\beta + \eta = 0$, $\gamma + \theta = 0$, and $\delta + \lambda = 1$. Hence

$$b = -\alpha - \beta y - \gamma r + (1 - \delta)f$$

Any of the three equations can be dropped because it can be derived from the other two. One can condense the two independent equations to one, and eliminate the variable f, by substituting $m + b$ for f in the money equation:

$$m = \frac{\alpha}{1-\delta} + \frac{\beta}{1-\delta} + \frac{\gamma}{1-\delta}r - \frac{\delta}{1-\delta}b$$

This example applies the precepts given in Brainard and Tobin (1968).

Note that when an equation is dropped because of its functional dependence on other equations, no variables drop out of the system. In particular, dropping the bond equation by appealing to Walras' law does not remove the bond variable from the system.

2.7. List All Endogenous Variables in the Model, and all Exogenous Variables

A list of all variables is very helpful to the reader, and even to the writer. The classification of variables as endogenous or exogenous should make economic sense. For example, a long-run monetary policy model under flexible exchange rates (or for a closed economy) can hardly treat the price level as exogenous, though this might be acceptable for a small open economy with fixed exchange rates, or for a very short-run model. Variables representing expectations of current or future variables can be regarded as exogenous (not very realistically), or can be replaced by adaptive-expectations functions or other functions of observable past or current variables, or can be assumed to be rational.

If the model is linear (or if it is to be linearized for purposes of analysis), the number of endogenous variables should be equal to the number of functionally independent equations. (It is possible to devise complete and consistent nonlinear equation systems in which the number of variables differs from the number of independent equations.)

2.8. *Consider Whether to Condense the Model by Substitution*

Often one has a choice to make about whether or not to eliminate one or more endogenous variables, and an equal number of equations, by substitution. For example, consider a supply-and-demand model as follows, where p is price, q is quantity sold, and q^d and q^s are quantities demanded and supplied respectively:

$$q^d = D(p)$$
$$q^s = S(p)$$
$$q^d = q^s$$
$$q = q^s$$

One can eliminate q^d and q^s by substitution, obtaining a 2-equation model:

$$q = D(p)$$
$$q = S(p)$$

Or one can go further and eliminate q also, obtaining a one-equation model:

$$D(p) = S(p)$$

It is a matter of taste whether to use the 4-equation, a 3-equation, the 2-equation, or the one-equation version. A good rule is: eliminate variables and equations when the effect is to remove unnecessary clutter, but not

when it hides important features. The 4-equation version is rather unnec-
essarily cluttered. The one-equation version is an implicit reduced form
equation for p and does not explicitly indicate how to find the quantity
sold. Hence the 2-equation version might be preferred.

Note that if a model is condensed by substitution of one or more equations into others, the only variables eliminated are endogenous variables.

2.9. Make a Table Showing Which Variables Appear in Each Equation, and Examine its Causal Structure

Such a table can conveniently be made by assigning one row to each equation, and one column to each variable. Then an entry (such as an X) in
any cell indicates that the variable in that column appears in the equation
in that row. A table like this is helpful in ensuring that variables have been
properly classified as endogenous or exogenous, in checking that there are
the same number of endogenous variables as there are functionally independent equations, and in discovering the causal structure of the model.

By "causal structure" is meant the manner in which the set of equations
of the model can be decomposed into several segments (if at all), such that
each segment determines the values of a subset of one or more endogenous
variables, given the values of certain other variables. If there is a segment
(smaller than the full model) that determines the values of a proper subset of the endogenous variables, given only the values of exogenous and
predetermined variables, this segment is causally prior to the rest of the
model. That is, it can be treated as a complete system without reference
to the rest of the model. Then the rest of the model is a second segment
that determines the values of the remaining endogenous variables, given
the values of exogenous and predetermined variables, and possibly given
the values of one or more other endogenous variables that are determined
in the causally prior segment. The second segment is causally posterior
to (i.e., causally dependent on) the prior segment. (Note that there are
two different kinds of dependence, causal and functional.) In that case the
variables determined by the prior segment can be regarded as exogenous
to the posterior segment, and the model has a recursive structure. (An
exception to this statement occurs if there are stochastic disturbances in
both segments, and the disturbances in one segment are not statistically
independent of those in the other).

In some models there is a causal hierarchy of three or more segments,
each one prior to those that are closer to the end of the causal hierarchy

(or to put it in another but equivalent way, each segment is posterior to those that are closer to the beginning of the causal hierarchy).

If each of two segments is causally prior to the other, then the two segments are causally unrelated to each other. In that case they can be thought of as two separate submodels. (The above-mentioned exception applies here too.)

If it is impossible to decompose the model causally in any way, then its causal structure has only one segment; the model is fully simultaneous.

Examples of such tables are given below, and each table is used to explore the causal structure of its model.

2.10. Obtain the Causal Structure of the Model by the McElroy Method

If the model is too complex to permit the discovery of its causal structure by inspection of the table proposed above, the method of McElroy (1978) can be used. It is easy to apply, using only pencil and paper, to most models of less than 50 equations. Unfortunately, in many models it will indicate that a particular causal segment can be broken down into subsegments, and that the subsegments so obtained (and their causal substructure) will depend on the arbitrary choice that is made about which dependent equation(s) to drop. The behavior of a model's variables, as pointed out in item 6 above, does not depend on this arbitrary choice. Therefore any conclusions about causal structure are illusory if they are not invariant to this choice. Examples of the method's use, and of its hazards and their avoidance, are provided below.

When the causal structure has been determined, it is illuminating to remake the table proposed in the preceeding section, putting the equations of prior segments first, and the equations of posterior segments last, and putting the endogenous variables first, in their order of causation. This helps to call attention to the causal structure.

2.11. Make a Diagram that Illustrates the Flow of Causality

A simple diagram can be made that illustrates whether the model is causally segmentable, and if so, what the segments are and how they are related. Such diagrams are shown for each of the examples given below.

2.12. Verify that the Number of Price Variables in the Model Corresponds to the Number of Goods (Allowing for the Numeraire)

If the model has two goods, money and one other, and if money is the numeraire, the model should contain one price, for the other good. If there are markets for n goods including money, there should be $n - 1$ prices. If some of the goods are assets, their yields may appear in place of their prices.

2.13. If the Model is Dynamic, Verify that its Static Equations (if any) and its Dynamic Equations Work Together Properly

The static equations (if any) should determine the values of the static variables for given levels and rates of change of the dynamic variables. And the dynamic equations should determine the rates of change of the dynamic variables given their levels and the values of the static variables.

This is illustrated below in example 2, which is a dynamic model.

2.14. If the Model is Dynamic, Determine Whether it is Stable or Not

For linear differential-equation systems, as is well known, a necessary and sufficient condition for stability is that the real parts of all characteristic roots be negative. For a linear difference-equation system, a necessary condition is that all characteristic roots have absolute values less than 1. For nonlinear systems the conditions are more complex. See, for example, Gandolfo (1987) and Pontryagin (1962).

2.15. Prepare for Econometric Estimation and Testing

The focus of this paper is on model building, not on econometric estimation and testing. However, in specifying a model that is to be used for empirical work, it is important to pay attention to econometric considerations. Only a few will be mentioned here. For example, are appropriate data available? Are the equations identified? Does the model, or a suitable transformation of it, have stationary stochastic processes? Are estimation methods available that have small expected loss functions, or at least that yield estimators with desirable asymptotic properties such as consistency?

3. Example 1: A Simple Income-Consumption Model

Consider the simple model that explains real income y, consumption c, and real government tax revenue t, given real government purchase of goods and service g and real net investment i:

$$c = \alpha + \beta(y - t) \qquad \text{consumption function} \qquad (1)$$

$$y = c + i + g \qquad \text{income} = \text{expenditure} \qquad (2)$$

$$t = g \qquad \text{balanced budget} \qquad (3)$$

The purpose of this model is to describe how aggregate demand determines income when there is plenty of productive capacity, and a fixed price level.

There are four sectors: households (which consume and save), firms (which produce), government (which taxes households and buys output), and the capital-account sector (which receives saving and makes investment expenditures). Assume that the capital stock is owned by households and leased to firms. Assume that firms have no assets or liabilities. Assume that the government budget is balanced.

The full version of the model includes some accounting identities in addition to (1) and (2). The variables in the full version are as follows: Endogenous variables (there are 7):

$$c = \text{real consumption}$$

$$k = \text{real capital stock}$$

$$s = \text{real net saving}$$

$$t = \text{real tax revenue}$$

$$w_g = \text{real net worth of government}$$

$$w_h = \text{real net worth of households}$$

$$y = \text{real net national product and income}$$

Exogenous variables:

$$b = \text{government bonds}$$

$$g = \text{real government purchases}$$

$$i = \text{real net investment}$$

$$m = \text{money stock}$$

Tables III and IV show the intersectoral flows and claims.

Observe that again the time derivatives of the balance sheet equations are consistent with the revenue = expenditure equations (bearing in mind that because of the balanced budget, $\dot{m} + \dot{b} = g - t = s - i = 0$).

The set of all equations in the full model is given below, including some redundant functionally dependent equations. Next to each of seven independent equation is given the symbol for an endogenous variable that can be associated with that equation. (The reason why no variable is given next to the other equations will be explained later.)

Associated Endogenous Variable	Equation	Interpretation	Eq. No
c	$c = \alpha + \beta(y - t)$	consumption behavior	(1)
y	$c + i + g = y$	firms' revenue = expense	(2)
t	$t = g$	government's revenue = expense	(3)
s	$y = c + s + t$	households' revenue = expense	(4)
–	$s = i$	capital account's revenue = expense	(5)
–	$s + t = i + g$	from (2) and (4)	(6)
–	$s = -\alpha + (1 - \beta)(y - t)$	saving behavior	(7)
k	$k - k_{-1} = i$	relation of Δk to i	(8)
w_g	$0 = m + b + w_g$	government's balance sheet	(9)
w_h	$w_h + w_g = k$	capital account's balance sheet	(10)
–	$m + b + k = w_h$	households' balance sheet	(11)

The four flow identities (2), (3), (4), and (5) are obtained from Table III. They are functionally dependent, that is, any one of them can be deduced from the other three. Another way to see this is to equate the sum of all revenues in the flows table to the sum of all expenses, obtaining the tautology:

$$y + c + i + g + t + s = c + s + t + y + g + i \qquad (12)$$

Now subtract any three of the four flow identities from (12), and the fourth one is the result. Hence any one of the four is redundant and can be dropped without changing the content of the model. We will drop (5) provisionally.

Similarly the four balance sheet identities are obtained from Table IV, and they are functionally dependent. The sum of all assets in the claims

Table III: Intersectoral flows in example 1.

Revenue of Expense of	households	firms	government	capital account	total expense
households	—	c	t	s	$c + t + s$
firms	y	—			y
government		g	—		g
capital account		i		—	i
total revenue	y	$c + g + i$	$t\cdot$	s	$\Sigma\Sigma$

Table IV: Intersectoral claims in example 1.

Assets of Liabilities of	households	firms	government	capital account	total liabilities
households	—			w_h	w_h
firms		—			0
government	$m + b$		—	w_g	$m + b + w_g$
capital account	k			—	k
total assets	$m + b + k$	0	0	$w_h + w_g$	$\Sigma\Sigma$

table equals the sum of all liabilities, thus:

$$m + b + k + w_h + w_g = w_h + m + b + w_g + k \qquad (13)$$

The balance sheet of firms contains no asset or liabilities (the table of claims shows that it says $0 = 0$). Subtracting any two of (9), (10), and (11) from (13) yields the third. Hence one of the three is redundant and we can drop it without changing the content of the model. We will drop (11) provisionally.

There are two more sets of dependent equations among equations (1)–(11). Equation (6) is obtainable as the sum of (2) and (4); we will drop (6) provisionally. And equation (7) is obtainable from (1) and (4); we will drop (7) provisionally.

Thus, after dropping equations (5), (6), (7), and (11), we have retained seven independent equations: (1)–(4) and (8)–(10). This complete model determines the seven endogenous variables listed above. The reason that equations (5)–(7) and (11) do not have any endogenous variable shown next to them in the above list of equations is that they can be deduced from the seven retained equations, and hence cannot determine any variables that are not already determined by those seven.

Table V shows which variables appear in each of the eleven equations. An X or an $\otimes$ in a particular row and column means that the variable listed at the head of the column appears in the equation listed at the left of that row. Thus, the row for equation (1) shows that c, y, and t appear in equation (1), and so on. The $\otimes$'s show the variables that are associated with certain equations in the original model (1)–(11) above. The order of the variables and equations in Table V has been chosen so that if the to-be-dropped equations (5)–(7) and (11) are ignored, the $\otimes$'s appear on the main diagonal of the table. The order has also been chosen to illuminate the model's causal structure, as follows. First, notice that equations (1)–(7) contain only 4 endogenous variables — c, y, t, and s — and only 4 independent equations. (Recall that equations (1)–(7) contain 3 dependent subsets: (2)–(5); (2), (4), and (6); and (1), (4), and (7).) Hence equations (1)–(7) (or any subset of them that contains 4 independent equations) are a causally prior segment of the model, determining c, y, t, and s with no reliance on the rest of the model. Notice also that equation (8) contains only a single current endogenous variable, k, which does not appear in equations (1)–(7). Hence (8) is causally unrelated to equations (1)–(7), because it is both causally prior and causally posterior to them. Notice further that equations (9), (10) and (11) contain only two independent equations, and three endogenous variables: k, w_g, and w_h, none of which appear in equations (1)–(7). Note that k is determined by (8), and hence is exogenous in (9)–(11). Thus we see that (9)–(11) (or any two of them) are a segment that determines w_g and w_h, causally posterior to (8). We also see that (8)–(11) is a segment causally unrelated to (1)–(7).

A diagram depicting this causal structure is in Figure 1. The diagram is constructed as follows. The flow of causality goes from left to right. Exogenous variables are arrayed in a column at the left. (Lagged endogenous variables are also shown at the left, but in dynamically complex models this may complicate the diagram considerably). Each causally prior set of equations is represented by a compound path that leads from left to right, beginning with those exogenous variables appearing in the set, and ending with arrowheads pointing to the endogenous variables determined by the set, which are arrayed in a second column. The equation numbers involved are shown as a label for the compound path. Then each causal segment (if any) which is dependent on a prior first segment is similarly shown, with

Table V: Causal structure for example 1.

Equation		current endogenous						lag	exogenous			
		flow					stock					
	c	y	t	s	k	w_g	w_h	k_{-1}	g	i	m	b
1. consumption	⊘	x	x									
2. $y = c + i + g$	x	⊘							x	x		
3. $t = g$			⊘						x			
4. $y = c + s + t$	x	x	x	⊘								
5. $s = i$				x						x		
6. $s + t = i + g$			x	x					x	x		
7. saving		x	x	x								
8. $k = k_{-1} + i$					⊘			x		x		
9. gov't.						⊘					x	x
10. cap. acc't.					x	x	⊘					
11. households					x		x				x	x

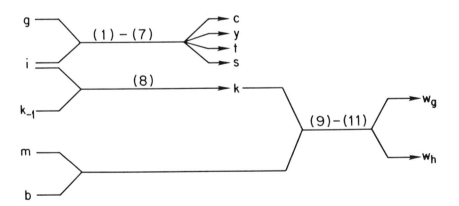

Figure 1: Flow of causality for example 1. Source: Table V.

the variables that it determines being arrayed in a third column, still further to the right. Thus the flow of causation can be followed from left to right. The diagram shows that equations (1)–(7) and (8)–(11) are causally unrelated segments, and that (8) is causally prior to (9)–(11).

This is almost all that can be said unequivocally about the causal structure of equations (1)–(11). When one considers a segment obtained by dropping 3 functionally dependent equations from (1)–(7), it is indeed possible to break it into two or more causal subsegments. But unfortunately, the question of which of the 4 variables c, y, t, and s are causally prior, and which are causally posterior, has different answers, depending on which 3 dependent equations are dropped before the segmentability is examined. This can be easily seen by considering two of the possible decisions about which dependent equations to drop.

First, suppose that equations (5), (6), and (7) are dropped, as we provisionally decided to do earlier. Then, from Table V, or from McElroy's method, one can see that the independent equations (1)–(4) have three segments. The prior segment is (3) which alone determine t because the budget is balanced. The next segment is (1) and (2) which determines c and y simultaneously, given t. The posterior segment is (4), which determines s, given c, y, and t. Here the causal order of the variables is first t, then c and y, and finally s.

Now suppose that equations (1), (2), and (3) are dropped instead. Then Table V or McElroy's method shows that the independent equations (4)–(7) have 4 segments. The prior segment is (5) which determines s. The next segment is (6) which determines t, given s. The next is (7) which determines y, given t and s. The posterior segment is (4) which determines c, given y, t, and s. Thus the causal order of the variables here is quite different: first s, then t, then y, and finally c.

This shows that the causal ordering among the 4 variables c, y, t, and s within equations (1)–(7) is not invariant to an arbitrary decision that has no effect on the values of the variables determined by the model, namely, the decision about which 3 dependent equations to drop.

Regarding causal structure, the most meaningful statements are those that are invariant to arbitrary decisions about which dependent equations to drop. In Example 1, the causal structure illustrated in Figure 1 is invariant to such arbitrary decisions, and hence is a meaningful property of the model.

Note that the 3 dependent equations (9)–(11) also yield different causal structures, depending on which one is dropped. Table V shows that if (10) is dropped, w_g and w_h are causally unrelated, if (9) or (11) is dropped one of them is causally posterior to the other. This causal structure is not invariant.

Finally, note that the original model of equations (1)–(3) completely determines the values of the endogenous flow variables c, y, and t, given the exogenous variables g and i. This can be seen from Table V. These equations are in the 11-equation model; they remain after a process of dropping equations that are causally unrelated to them or posterior to them, and also dropping equations that are functionally dependent on them. In this simple example it is of course easy to see that equations (1)–(3) are a complete consistent model of 3 independent equations, even without using the tables of intersectoral claims and flows and the table and diagram of causal structure. The tables and diagram are presented for this case because it is easy to illustrate how they work here, and because such tables and diagrams are useful for analyzing models that are more complex.

4. Example 2: A Simple Government-Budget-Restraint Model

Consider the following dynamic model, adapted from Christ (1978, 1979). Its purpose is to analyze the effects of monetary and fiscal policy on the price level and on fluctuations of real output about a fixed natural rate of real output, when the authorities choose one policy variable to be determined endogenously and fix the other policy variables exogenously. The endogenous policy variable is one of the following set: nominal privately held government debt B, high powered money H, real government purchases of goods and services g, the marginal tax-transfer rate u, or nominal autonomous taxes less transfers V. The exogenous variables are four of the five just-named policy variables, investment i, and the expected inflation rate π. The equations are (in real terms):

(1) $\dot{k} = i$	capital growth
(2) $\dot{P}/P = \rho(y/x - 1) + \pi$	inflation adjustment
(3) $g = t + \dot{H}/P + \dot{B}/rP$	gov't budget restraint
(4) $x = \phi(k)$	capacity
(5) $c = \alpha_0 + \alpha_1(y - t) + \alpha_2/r + \alpha_3 H/P + \alpha_4 B/rP + \alpha_5 \pi$	consumption
(6) $y = c + i + g$	income identity
(7) $t = uy + V/P + (u - 1)B/P$	tax-transfer
(8) $H/P = \mu_0 + \mu_1 y + \mu_2/r + \mu_3(H/P + B/rP)$	money demand

There are four sectors: households (which consume), firms (which produce), the government including the central bank (which issues money and spends and collects taxes and borrows), and the capital-account sector. Assume that the entire physical capital stock is owned by households and leased to firms. Firms have no assets or liabilities.

The variables in the full version of this model are as follows: Endogenous variables (11):

$$c = \text{real consumption}$$

$$k = \text{real capital stock}$$

$$P = \text{price level}$$

$$r = \text{nominal interest rate}$$

$$s = \text{private saving}$$

$$t = \text{real taxes less transfers}$$

$$W_h = \text{nominal net worth of household sector}$$

$$W_g = \text{nominal net worth of government sector}$$

$$x = \text{real capacity output}$$

$$y = \text{real income and output}$$

one of the policy variables listed below:

Policy variables (5):

$B =$ nominal government interest paid to private sector, equal to number of perpetual bonds each paying \$1 per year.

$g =$ real government purchases of goods and services

$H =$ nominal high powered money stook

$u =$ marginal tax-transfer rate

$V =$ nominal autonomous taxes less transfers

Exogenous variables (6):

four of the policy variables listed above

$$i = \text{real net investment}$$

$$n = \text{expected rate of inflation}$$

Table VI: Real intersectoral flows in example 2.

Revenue of Expense of	households	firms	government	capital account	total expense
households	—	c	t	s	$c+t+s$
firms	y	—			y
government		g	—		g
capital account		i	$\frac{\dot{H}}{P}+\frac{\dot{B}}{rP}$	—	$i+\frac{\dot{H}}{P}+\frac{\dot{B}}{rP}$
total revenue	y	$c+g+i$	$t+\frac{\dot{H}}{P}+\frac{\dot{B}}{rP}$	s	$\Sigma\Sigma$

Table VII: Nominal intersectoral claims in example 2.

Assets of Liabilities of	households	firms	government	capital account	total liabilities
households	—			W_h	W_h
firms		—			0
government	$H+\frac{B}{r}$		—	W_g	$H+\frac{B}{r}+W_g$
capital account	Pk			—	Pk
total assets	$H+\frac{B}{r}+Pk$	0	0	W_h+W_g	$\Sigma\Sigma$

Tables VI and VII show the intersectoral flows and claims.

The set of all equations in the full model is given below. Next to each of eleven functionally indepenndent equations is given the symbol for an endogenous variable that can be associated with that equation. The other equations have no associated variable because they can be deduced from the 11 functionally independent equations as we shall see, and hence cannot determine any additional variables.

The four flow identities (3), (6), (10), and (11) are functionally dependent: any three imply the remaining one. Hence we provisionally omit (11) from the model without affecting its content. Similarly we omit (16), because the four stock identities are also functionally dependent: (14), (15), (16), and the balance sheet of the firms which says $0 = 0$. The identity (12) can be dropped since it is implied by (6) and (10). And the saving function (13) can be dropped since it is implied by (5) and (10). The bond demand equation (9) can also be omitted, because it is equivalent to (8),

Eq. No	Endog. Varbl.	Equation	Interpretation
(1)	$\dot{k}$	$\dot{k} = i$	capital growth
(2)	$\dot{P}$	$\dot{P}/P = \rho(y/x - 1) + \pi$	inflation adjustment
(3)	policy	$g = t + \dot{H}/P + \dot{B}/rP$	gov't expense = revenue
(4)	x	$x = \phi(k)$	real capacity
(5)	c	$c = \alpha_0 + \alpha_1(y - t) + \alpha_2/r$ $+\alpha_3 H/P + \alpha_4 B/rP + \alpha_5\pi$	consumption
(6)	y	$c + i + g = y$	firms' revenue = expense
(7)	t	$t = uy + V/P + (u - 1)B/P$	taxes less transfers
(8)	r	$\frac{H}{P} = \mu_0 + \mu_1 y + \mu_2/r$ $+\mu_3(H/P + B/rP)$	money demand
(9)	–	$\frac{B}{rP} = \nu_0 + \nu_1 y + \nu_2/r$ $+\nu_3(H/P + B/rP)$	bond demand
(10)	s	$y = c + t + s$	household rev. = expense
(11)	–	$s = i + \dot{H}/P + \dot{B}/rP$	cap. acct. rev. = exp.
(12)	–	$s + t = i + g$	from (6) and (10)
(13)	–	$s = -\alpha_0 + (1 - \alpha_1)(y - t) - \alpha_2/r$ $-\alpha_3 H/P - \alpha_4 B/rP - \alpha_5\pi$	saving
(14)	W_g	$W_g = -H - B/r$	gov't balance sheet
(15)	W_h	$W_h + W_g = Pk$	cap. acct. balance sheet
(16)	–	$W_h = H + B/r + Pk$	household balance sheet

with $\nu_0 = -\mu_0$, $\nu_1 = -\mu_1$, $\nu_2 = -\mu_2$, and $\nu_3 = 1 - \mu_3$.

Thus after dropping equations (9), (11)–(13), and (16), we have a model with eleven endogenous variables listed above, and the eleven independent equations (1)–(8), (10), (14), and (15).

Table VIII shows which variables appear in each equation for the case in which the high powered money tock H is the endogenous policy variable. The X and $\otimes$ entries in the table have the same meanings that were previously described for Table V in example 1.

Note that in Table VIII, $\dot{k}$, $\dot{P}$, and $\dot{H}$ have been classified as current endogenous, while k, P, and H have been classified as predetermined. This is consistent with the treatment that would be appropriate if a discrete-time version of the model were used, with the first differences Δk, ΔP, and ΔH being used in place of the time derivatives $\dot{k}$, $\dot{P}$, and $\dot{H}$, and with lagged levels k_{-1}, P_{-1}, H_{-1} and being used in (1)–(3) in place of k, P, and H. In a continuous-time model such as (1)–(16), an analogous treatment applies.

Table VIII: Causal structure for example 2 when high powered money H is endogenous.

equation	dynamic endog.			static endogenous								predetermined			exogenous						
	$\dot{k}$	$\dot{P}$	$\dot{H}$	x	c	y	t	r	s	W_g	W_h	k	P	H	$\dot{B}$	B	g	μ	V	i	π
1. $k = i$	⊘			×																×	
2. inflation		⊘				×							×								×
3. gov. budget			⊘				×	×					×		×		×				
4. capacity				⊘								×									
5. consumption					⊘	×	×	×					×	×		×				×	×
6. $y = c + i + g$					×	⊘											×	×	×		
7. tax-transfer						×	⊘											×			
8. money demand						×		⊘					×	×		×					
9. bond demand						×		×					×	×		×					
10. $y = c + s + t$					×	×			⊘												
11. $s = i +$ def.			×				×	×	×						×					×	
12. $s + t = i + g$							×	×	×								×			×	
13. saving						×	×	×	×				×	×		×					×
14. gov.										⊘				×		×					
15. capital										×	⊘	×	×	×							
16. households											×	×	×	×		×					

Equations (1)–(3) are three dynamic equations, causally unrelated to each other, in three time derivatives $\dot{k}$, $\dot{P}$, and $\dot{H}$, and they determine these rates of change for given values of the static variables y, t, r, and x and the predetermined level of P and the values of exogenous variables. Then, an infinitesimal time interval dt later, each new predetermined level is given by the sum of the old level plus the increment, for example, $P(t + dt) = P(t) + \dot{P}dt$. Equations (4)–(16) are static equations: they contain no time derivatives (except for (11) which contains $\dot{H}$, but we can think of $\dot{H}$ in (11) as being replaced by an equivalent function of static endogenous variables from (3)). Equations (4)–(16) determine the eight variables x, c, y, t, r, s, W_g, and W_h for given predetermined levels k, P, and H. Then the cycle repeats in a recursive manner, alternating between the dynamic equations (1)–(3) and the static equations (4)–(16). A continuous time path of all eleven endogenous variables in (1)–(16) is generated in this way. For more details on this process see Gandolfo (1981) and Wymer (1972). In some models the number of dynamic equations is not the same as the number of dynamic variables. For such cases Pontryagin (1962), Section 11, pp. 67–76, gives a general treatment, which covers the substitution of (3) for $\dot{H}$ in (11) that was mentioned just above.

Table VIII shows, further, that the static equations (4)–(16) can be broken into three causal segments. Equation (4) is causally unrelated to (5)–(16); it determines capacity x, given the predetermined capital stock k. Equations (5)–(13) are causally prior to (14)–(16), and determine c, y, t, r, and s, given the predetermined variables P and H and exogenous variables. Then (14)–(16) are causally posterior to (5)–(13), and determine W_g and W_h, given the interest rate r, and the predetermined levels of k, P and H.

Thus the causal structure of Example 2 is as shown in in Figure 2 when the high powered money stock H is endogenous.

The segment (5)–(13) can be further broken into causally prior and posterior subsegments but the membership of these subsegments depends on the arbitrary choice as to which four dependent equations are dropped from (5)–(13). Therefore causal structure within the set of equations (5)–(13) is not an invariant property of the model. The same is true of causal structure within the set of equations (14)–(16).

What if a different policy variable had been chosen as endogenous instead of H as above? Then Table VIII and Figure 2 would have to be revised. For example, suppose g were chosen as endogenous and B and H were exogenously held constant ($\dot{B} = \dot{H} = 0$), and $\pi = 0$. Then there would be only two dynamic equations (1) and (2) instead of three. It is easy to verify that then (1) and (2) are two separate one-equation dynamic

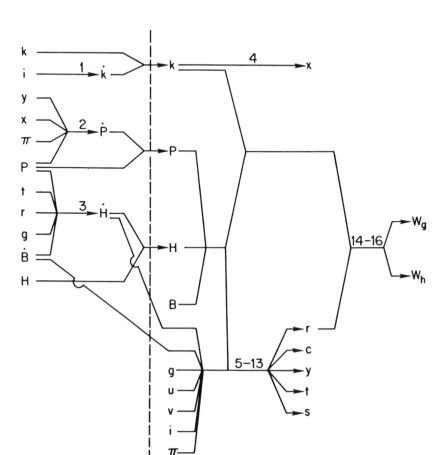

Figure 2: Flow of causality for example 2 when high powered
money H is endogenous. Source: Table VIII.

segments determining $\dot{k}$ and $\dot{P}$ for given y, x, and P; (4) is a one-equation
static segment determining x given k; (3) and (5)–(13) are a static segment
determining c, y, t, r, s, and g for given level of P; and (14)–(16) are as
before, a static segment determining W_g and W_h given k, P, and r.

The same method can also be aplied to the static equilibrium form of

Table IX: Causal structure for the static equilibrium version of example 2 when high powered money H is endogenous.

equation		endogenous										exogenous				
	r	y	t	r	c	P	H	s	W_g	W_h	k	B	g	u	V
4. capacity	⊘										×				
2. $y = $ cap'y	×	⊘													
3. bal. budg.			⊘										×		
5. consumption		×	×	⊘	×	×	×					×		×	
6. $y = c + g$		×			⊘								×		
7. tax-transfer		×	×			⊘								×	
8. money demand		×		×		×	⊘					×			×
9. bond demand		×		×		×	×					×			×
10. $y = c + s + t$		×	×		×			⊘							
11. $s = $ deficit			×					×							
12. $s + t = g$			×					×					×		
13. saving		×	×	×		×	×	×				×			
14. gov.				×		×	×		⊘			×			
15. capital									×	⊘	×				
16. households				×		×	×			×	×	×			

the model, obtained by setting all time derivatives in (1)–(16) equal to zero and $\pi = 0$. Then i and $\dot{k}$ must be zero, and so equation (1) degenerates to $0 = 0$ and k can be taken to be exogenous. Since $\dot{P} = 0$, (2) reduces to $y = x$, output equals capacity. And since $\dot{H} = \dot{B} = 0$, (3) reduces to $t = g$, a balanced budget. Then (11) or (12) implies that $s = i$, which means that $s = 0$.

A given static equilibrium position can be obtained with any choice as to which policy variable is endogenous, but the causal structure will depend on this choice. Suppose again that H is endogenous. Then Table IX shows the causal structure for the static equilibrium of Example 2. Figure 3 illustrates the logical (not chronological) flow of causality in the static equilibrium form of this model. Predetermined endogenous variables have not been shown because they do not differ from the equilibrium values. Exogenous variables are in the left-hand column.

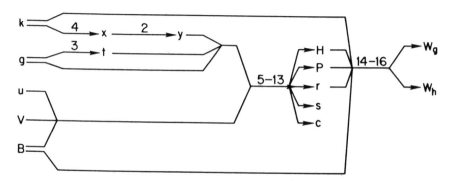

Figure 3: Flow of causality for the static equilibrium version of example 2 when high powered money H is endogenous. Source: Table IX.

5. Example 3: A Simple Rational Expectations Model

Consider the following simple model designed to show the effects of systematic and unsystematic monetary policy upon real output and the price level, in the presence of rational expectations about future prices. The government's budget restraint and its debt are neglected. The model is adapted from Sargent and Wallace (1975). Notation is as follows:

$A_t p_{t+1} =$ subjective expected log price level (endogenous; will temporarily be treated as exogenous)

$E_t p_{t+1} =$ objective expected log price level
(Both expectations are for the price level at time $t + 1$, and are formed at time t, based on information known at time t)

$m =$ log of money supply (endogenous)

$p =$ log of price level (endogenous)

$r =$ nominal interest rate (endogenous)

$y =$ log of real output (endogenous)

$\bar{y} =$ log of normal output (exogenous)

$Z =$ other exogenous variables (including fiscal stimulus)

$t =$ time (t is written as a subscript; p_{-1} means p_{t-1})

$\theta_t =$ information known at end of period t (predetermined at time $t + 1$)

$\epsilon, \mu, \eta, U =$ random disturbances, mutually and serially independent, with zero means

$\gamma, b, c, d =$ parameters

The 5 equations are:

$y_t - \gamma p_t$	$= \bar{y}_t - \gamma A_{t-1} p_t + U_t$	aggregate supply	(1)
$y_t - c p_t - c r_t$	$= \bar{y}_t - c A_t p_{t+1} + d Z_t + \epsilon_t$	IS curve	(2)
$y_t + p_t + b r_t - m_t$	$= \eta_t$	LM curve	(3)
m_t	$= v_m m_{t-1} + v_\eta \eta_{t-1} + v_\epsilon \epsilon_{t-1}$		(4)
	$\quad + v_U U_{t-1} + v_{\bar{y}} \bar{y}_{t-1}$		
	$\quad + v_Z Z_{t-1} + \mu_t$	monetary policy	
$A_t p_{t+1}$	$= E_t p_{t+1}$	rational expectations	(5)

The aggregate supply equation is the Lucas supply curve. The IS equation shows how output demand, y_t, depends on normal output $\bar{y}_t$, the expected *real* interest rate (r_t minus the expected inflation rate, $A_t p_{t+1} - p_t$), and exogenous factors Z_t such as fiscal stimulus variables. It can be derived from a consumption equation, an investment equation, and the income-equals-expenditure identity. Thus the model is in a partially reduced form, because the consumption and investment variables have been eliminated by substitution. The LM equation is similar to the usual one: real money demand $m_t - p_t$ depends on income y_t and the *nominal* interest rate r_t. The monetary policy equation says that the authorities set the money supply m as a systematic function of last period's values of the money supply, capacity $\bar{y}$, fiscal variables Z, and the model's disturbances, plus a current error term.

The rational expectations hypothesis assumes that subjective expectations of price are exactly equal to the objective mathematical expectations of price based on knowledge of all preceding values for all variables and disturbances and of the true model of the economy and the true values of its parameters. That is, the subjective expectation $A_t p_{t+1}$ is equal to $E(p_{t+1}|\theta_t)$, where θ_t includes all values of all variables and all disturbances for period t and earlier, and also the true model and the true values of its parameters, and where $E(p_{t+1}|\theta_t)$ stands for the conditional expectation of p_{t+1}, given all the information in θ at the end of period t. It is abbreviated by the symbol $E_t p_{t+1}$. Thus the equation that describes the formation of rational expectations is (5).

If one were to analyze Example 3 the way Examples 1 and 2 were analyzed, one would present the tables of intersectoral claims and flows, and the associated identities (including functionally dependent ones). One would also present the investment and consumption equations that underlie the IS equation, and other functionally dependent equations such as the savings equation. This would yield a model with more equations than endogenous variables, but of course the number of functionally independent equations would be the same as the number of endogenous variables. Then one could use a table similar to Tables V, VIII, and IX to analyze this model. We omit these steps here, because they have already been illustrated in Examples 1 and 2, and because our main interest here is the treatment of expectations. Accordingly, we will analyze the 5 functionally independent equations (1)–(5) in the 5 endogenous variables m, r, y, p, and subjective price expectations. This means that we have omitted the causally posterior stock equations, and we have already made the decision as to which of the causally dependent (and hence redundant) flow equations to drop.

To analyze the behavior of an expectations model, it is useful first to consider the model as if expectations were exogenous. In that case, we have equations (1)–(4) which determine y, p, r, and m. Table X and Figure 4 show the causal structure of the these equations. This model has two segments. Equation (4) is causally prior to the others. It determines the money supply m_t in terms of lagged variables only. Thus m_t is predetermined in equations (1)–(3) since disturbances are serially indenpendent. Equations (1)–(3) are a fully simultaneous segment determining y_t, p_t, and r_t. (Temporarily treating expectations as exogenous, as in Table X, is applicable to any type of expectations model, not only to rational expectations models.)

Of course, Table X does not give a complete picture of the causal struc-

Table X: Causal structure of example 3 if expectations are exogenous.

Eq.	current endogenous				lagged endog	exogenous						disturbances	
	y	p	r	m	m_{-1}	$A_{-1}p$	Ap_{+1}	$\bar{y}$	$\bar{Z}$	$\bar{y}_{-1}$	$\bar{Z}_{-1}$	current	lagged
1	⊗	X				X		X				X	
2	X	⊗	X				X	X	X			X	
3	X	X	⊗	X					X			X	
4				⊗	X					X	X	X	X

Table XI: Causal structure of rationally expected equations in example 3.

Eq.	current endogenous				predetermined						
	$E_{t-1}y_t$	$E_{t-1}p_t$	$E_{t-1}r_t$	$E_{t-1}m_t$	$E_{t-1}p_{t+1}$	$E_{t-1}\bar{y}_t$	$E_{t-1}Z_t$	lagged values of			
								m	$\bar{y}$	Z	dists
6	⊗										
7	X	⊗	X		X	X					
8	X	X	⊗	X		X	X				
9				⊗				X	X	X	X

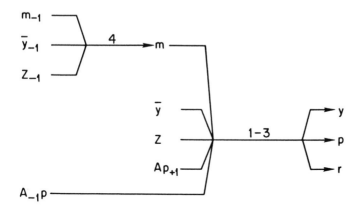

Figure 4: Flow of causality in example 3 when expectations are exogenous. Source: Table X.

ture of the entire rational expectations model, because it does not include the rational expectations equation (5). It will not do simply to add another row to Table X in an attempt to represent equation (5), because (5) is not like the other equations of the model: it does not state a purely algebraic relation between endogenous and exogenous variables. Rather, it calls for the application of the mathematical expectation operator E. Let us therefore use (5) to replace $A_{t-1}p_t$ and $A_t p_{t+1}$ by $E_{t-1}p_t$ and $E_t p_{t+1}$ respectively, and then take the mathematical expectation of each of the equations (1)–(3) conditional on information available as of time $t-1$. The result, after canceling $\gamma E_{t-1}p_t$ from both sides of (6), is:

$$E_{t-1}y_t = E_{t-1}\bar{y}_t \qquad (6)$$

$$E_{t-1}y_t - cE_{t-1}p_t - cE_{t-1}r_t = E_{t-1}\bar{y}_t - cE_{t-1}p_{t+1} + dE_{t-1}Z_t \qquad (7)$$

$$E_{t-1}y_t + E_{t-1}p_t + bE_{t-1}r_t - E_{t-1}m_t = 0 \qquad (8)$$

$$E_{t-1}m_t = v_m m_{t-1} + v_\eta \eta_{t-1} + v_\epsilon \epsilon_{t-1} + v_U U_{t-1} + v_{\bar{y}}\bar{y}_{t-1} + v_Z Z_{t-1} \qquad (9)$$

The term $E_{t-1}p_{t+1}$ arises in (7) after taking the expectation of $E_t p_{t+1}$ because that is the best estimate, at time $t-1$, of what will be expected at time t for p_{t+1}. All the variables on the left sides of (6)–(9) will now be regarded as endogenous. All those on the right sides will be regarded as predetermined. This is obvious enough for the expectations of $\bar{y}_t$ and Z_t (which themselves are predetermined and hence must be forecast for time t in some way other than (6)–(9)), and for lagged variables. It may seem strange to regard $E_{t-1}p_{t+1}$ as predetermined, because it is the expectation of price at a time further in the future than p_t whose expectation at time $t - 1$ is endogenous. A justification for doing so will be given later, when the forward-looking solution rather than the backward-looking solution of a difference equation is adopted. Table XI and Figure 5 give the causal structure of (6)–(9). Equation (6) is a causally prior segment that determines $E_{t-1}y_t$, and equation (9) is also a causally prior segment, causally unrelated to (6), that determines $E_{t-1}m_t$. Then (7) and (8) are a causally posterior segment that simultaneously determines $E_{t-1}p_t$ and $E_{t-1}r_t$, given the values of $E_{t-1}y_t$ and $E_{t-1}m_t$. (The causal structure within the set of four equations (6)–(9) is invariant to arbitrary decisions about which dependent equations to drop.)

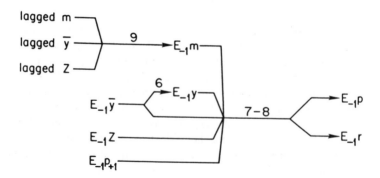

Figure 5: Flow of causality in example 3 when rational expectations are used. Source: Table XI.

In order to handle the presence of the expectations of both p_t and p_{t+1} in (7), we can use (6) and (8) to eliminate the expectations of y_t and r_t from (7). The result, after collecting terms, is

$$E_{t-1}p_t = \frac{b}{b-1}E_{t-1}p_{t+1} + \frac{1}{1-b}E_{t-1}m_t$$

$$- \frac{1}{1-b}E_{t-1}\bar{y}_t + \frac{db}{c(1-b)}E_{t-1}Z_t \qquad (10)$$

This is an important result. Recall that we got it by first taking the expectations of (1)–(3) as of time $t-1$, to get (6)–(8), and then solving for (expected current) price. In the rational expectations literature those two steps are often put in the opposite order: first solve for the endogenous variables, to get the so-called quasi-reduced form, and then take expectations. The result (10) is the same either way.

Notice that (10) is a difference equation in $E_{t-1}p$, containing expectations of p_t and p_{t+1}. Usually, in studying a difference equation, one regards it as explaining the later variable as a function of the earlier variable. If that were done with (10), its coefficient would be $(b-1)/b$, which is >1 since $b<0$. The conventional backward-looking solution is thus unstable. However, in studying rational expectations, it makes sense to look at the equation the other way around, as in (10), which says that what we expect at time $t-1$ about p_t depends on what we expect at the same time about p_{t+1}. The forward-looking solution of this equation can be obtained by iterative substitution, and is stable because its coefficient $b/(b-1)$ is positive but less than 1. The solution is

$$E_{t-1}p_t = \frac{1}{1-b} \sum_0^\infty \left(\frac{b}{b-1} \right)^j E_{t-1}m_{t+j}$$

$$- \frac{1}{1-b} \sum_0^\infty \left(\frac{b}{b-1} \right)^j E_{t-1}\bar{y}_{t+j}$$

$$+ \frac{db}{c(1-b)} \sum_0^\infty \left(\frac{b}{b-1} \right)^j E_{t-1}Z_{t+j} \qquad (11)$$

where it has been assumed that as $j \to \infty$ the limit of $[b/(b-1)]^j E_{t-1}p_{t+j}$ is zero, i.e., that the expected growth (if any) of future prices is not fast enough to match or overpower the rate of convergence of the solution.

Suppose the system's parameters are known. Then the solution (11) can be computed if one can form expectations about future values, from now to the infinite future, of the exogenous variables $\bar{y}$ and Z. (The expectations $E_{t-1}m_{t+j}$ for the infinite future, which are also needed for (11), can be obtained from the values in period $t-1$ of m, $\bar{y}$, Z, and the disturbances, and the expectations $E_{t-1}\bar{y}_{t+j}$ and $E_{t-1}Z_{t+j}$; this can be seen by applying the expectations operator E_{t-1} successively to equation (4) for periods t, $t+1, t+2, \ldots$.) In some cases the expectations of $\bar{y}_{t+j}$ and Z_{t+j} are gotten from ARIMA models, and in some from other exogenous sources such as news about impending events. The solution (11) can then be substituted for price expectations in the original model (1)–(4). The result is a new system of "structural" equations ("structural" is enclosed in quotation marks because, as noted earlier, the IS equation (2) is not structural but is a partially reduced form equation). This system determines y_t, p_t, r_t, and m_t in terms of current and previous-period disturbances and exogenous variables, and expectations of the values of the exogenous variables for the infinite future. The causal structure table for this model would resemble Table X and Figure 4 except that in place of $A_{t-1}p_t$ and $A_t p_{t+1}$ there would be functions, obtained from (11), of expectations of the exogenous variables for the infinite future. This "structural" system can be solved algebraically for the actual values of y_t, p_t, r_t, and m_t. This solution is the reduced form of the complete rational expectations model. (The so-called quasi-reduced form, mentioned earlier, takes expectations as exogenous, and therefore is not the reduced form of the entire rational expectations model (1)–(5).)

Observed that we have considered three different "structural" equation systems in Example 3. The first is the original system (1)–(5). Equations (1)–(4) relate the actual current values of the four endogenous variables y, p, r, and m to each other and to price expectations, given certain predetermined variables. Their causal structure is displayed in Table X and Figure 4. Equation (5) states the rational expectations hypothesis. The second system is (6)–(9), which is the mathematical expectation of (1)–(4) using the rational expectations hypothesis (5). Its causal structure is displayed in Table XI and Figure 5. It relates the expectations of y, p, r, and m to each other and to predetermined variables. The third system, not explicitly shown, is obtained when price expectations in the original system (1)–(4) are replaced by the solution for the rational expectation of prices, from (11). It relates the actual current values of the endogenous variables y, p, r, and m to the lagged money stock, current and lagged values of exogenous variables and disturbances, and expectations (held at the end of last period) about exogenous variables for the current period and the infinite future. Its reduced form can be used to show the familiar result of rational expectations models, namely, that unanticipated changes in the money supply affect prices but not output.

References

Brainard W., and J. Tobin (1968): "Pitfalls in Financial Model Building", *American Economic Review* 58: 99–122.

Christ C.F. (1978): "Some Dynamic Theory of Macroeconomic Policy Effects on Income and Prices under the Government Budget Restraint", *Journal of Monetary Economics* 4: 45–70.

Christ C.F. (1979): "On Fiscal and Monetary Policies and the Government Budget Restraint", *American Economic Review* 69: 526–538.

Gandolfo G. (1981): *Qualitative Analysis and Econometric Estimation of Continuous Time Dynamic Models*. Amsterdam: North-Holland.

Gandolfo G. (1987): "Stability", in: John Eatwell, Murray Milgate, and Peter Newman, eds., *The New Palgrave: A Dictionary of Economics*. London: Macmillan and New York: Stockton, 4: 461–464.

McElroy F.W. (1978): "A Simple Method of Causal Ordering", *International Economic Review* 19: 1–23.

Pontryagin L.S. (1962): *Ordinary Differential Equations*. Reading, Mass., Addition-Wesley.

Sargent T.J., and N. Wallace (1975): "'Rational' Expectations, the Optimal Monetary Instrument, and the Optimal Monetary Supply Rule", *Journal of Political Economy* 83: 241–254.

Wymer C.R. (1972): "Econometric Estimation of Stochastic Differential Equation Systems", *Econometrica* 40: 565–577.

18

2

ECONOMICS AND PUBLIC POLICY

CARL F. CHRIST

Economics is the study of behavior that seeks the highest possible level of human satisfaction when the available resources are limited. Satisfaction can come from goods and services, or from intangible things such as the feeling that one is treating others fairly, or conditions in the workplace, or anything that people care about.

Some people think that economists care only about money. I have heard an unkind critic say that an economist is someone who would sell his grandmother to the highest bidder. This is quite wrong. An economist, or at least a good economist, would not sell his grandmother to the highest bidder unless the highest bid was enough to compensate him for the loss of his grandmother. Most of us hold some things so dear that we would not sell them for any imaginable price. Economics is not confined to money and material things, but can take into account whatever people care about, including grandmothers.

One of the most important ideas in economics is that of *opportunity costs*. The opportunity cost of anything you do is the most valuable thing you could have done instead. For example, the opportunity cost of your reading this chapter is the best alternative use of your time. Similarly, the opportunity cost of a public policy is the best thing that could have been done instead with the resources that the policy would require. You can see that it is unwise to choose a policy whose value is less than its opportunity cost.

This chapter was originally presented as a lecture at a Howard University symposium entitled "Economics: Its Place in Our Times." Howard University has graciously consented to its publication here.

The opportunity cost idea is a simple but powerful one. It is built into the structure of economic theory, which is a very highly developed and technical body of analysis. One chapter cannot make people experts in economic theory. What I hope this chapter can do is to give some under-standing of the kinds of things economics can and cannot do for public policy, and offer some examples.

The seven main topics I shall discuss are as follows:

1. The distinction between positive and normative statements.
2. The distinction between policies aimed at economic efficiency and those aimed at fairness or equity.
3. Remarks on economic efficiency.
4. The existence of many ways to achieve economic efficiency, all of which have different interpersonal distributions of well-being.
5. The difficulty of designing policies that promote both fairness and economic efficiency.
6. Some hazards in economic policy-making.
7. Some personal policy recommendations.

The first main topic is the distinction between *positive* and *normative* statements—that is, between statements about what actually happens in the world and statements about what should be done. A familiar example in engineering involves the building of bridges. Engineers know that a dozen more bridges could be built across the Chesapeake Bay, with the capacity to carry certain loads, withstand 200-mile-an-hour winds, and so forth, at such-and-such a cost. That's a positive statement. To say that a dozen more bridges should be built is a normative statement.

It isn't possible to make good normative recommendations without good positive knowledge. Nor is it possible to make normative recommendations on the basis of positive knowledge alone: some scale of values is needed.

The economist, as a scientist, is confined to positive statements. Economics as a science conveys no authority to make normative statements. The econ-omist is a citizen, however, and as a citizen, can offer normative statements, just as any citizen can. These normative statements are based in part on the goals or values of the speaker. It is helpful to keep in mind which of an economist's statements arise from positive science alone, and which ones are based in part on value judgments.

Normative statements in economics (or anywhere else) are by nature controversial, because there are differences of opinion about goals. This is why issues of public policy are settled in the political arena, not the scientific arena.

Everyone knows that economists often disagree among themselves. You've heard the gag that if all the economists in the world were laid end to end, they would not reach a conclusion. More often than not, the disagreement among economists is not about positive economics, but about normative economics.

For example, economists generally agree that if a mandatory price ceiling is imposed on the price of a product, at a point below the uncontrolled price, the result will be a shortage of that product. They sometimes disagree about whether such a price ceiling should be imposed.

Similarly, economists generally agree that if the growth rate of the money supply is increased substantially and kept at the new high rate for several years, the first result will be a decline in unemployment and a rise in output, both of which will fade away. And the long-run result will be an increase in the rate of inflation, which will last as long as the high growth rate of the money stock lasts. But they may disagree about whether the growth rate of the money stock should be increased or not.

Positive economics is by nature amenable to progress through research. Disagreements about positive economics can in principle be settled by appeal to evidence and to reason. Of course, not all such disagreements have been settled yet. But research has already settled many of them and will surely be able to settle many more.

Imagine a discussion about the normative question of whether the Federal Reserve should cut the growth rate of the supply of money to 3% a year starting tomorrow and hold it there forever. Most economists agree that the sudden adoption of this policy would stop inflation permanently and induce a temporary recession. But we do not know whether the recession is more likely to last two years or six. Progress in answering the positive question of how long the adjustment takes can help to bring agreement on the normative question of what policy to follow.

Issues of economic policy are normative, but in order to settle them wisely we need good positive economics.

My second main point is to distinguish between policies aimed at economic efficiency and policies aimed at fairness or equity. An analogy often used here is the distinction between the size of a pie and the distribution of the pie. It would seem that no one could object to policies that increase the size of the national pie. But in fact it often happens that there are powerful objections to policies that increase economic efficiency. The analogy of the size versus the distribution of the pie is far too simple. It conceals the guts of the concept of economic efficiency, which does not depend simply on how much output is produced.

To understand this, we turn to the third main point, remarks on economic efficiency. Here we need to use one of the main ideas in modern economics, which is Vilfredo Pareto's concept of an optimum allocation of resources. It is easier if we first define a *Pareto improvement* in the allocation of resources. A Pareto improvement is a change that makes at least one person better off without making anyone worse off. And a *Pareto optimum* is a situation in which all possible Pareto improvements have already been made, so that no further Pareto improvement is possible. If the status quo is a Pareto optimum, it means that there is no way to make anyone better off without at the same time making someone else worse off. Economists use the terms "economic efficiency" and "Pareto optimum" interchangeably, and I will do so here.

To attain a Pareto optimum, it is necessary to attain technical efficiency, but that's not enough. To illustrate, imagine an economy with only one person, Robinson Crusoe on his island (economists love Robinson Crusoe, for the simplicity of his situation). And suppose there are just three goods, fruit, fish, and leisure. Imagine that Crusoe has studied the technical possibilities and found that he can spend each half day either foraging for fruit, fishing, or at leisure. Thus, he can have each day any one of the following menus:

- A whole day of leisure, no fruit, and no fish.
- A half day of leisure, and either a half day's haul of fruit and no fish, or a half day's haul of fish and no fruit.
- No leisure, and one of these three choices: a whole day's haul of fruit and no fish, or a whole day's haul of fish and no fruit, or a half day's haul of each.

Suppose that whatever time he allocates to work is spent in a technically efficient way, that is, he gets the most possible fruit or fish from each half day devoted to it.

The crucial property of a technically efficient situation is that to obtain more of one good, be it fruit or fish or leisure, one must give up some of another (or else use more resources). In a technically inefficient situation, one can get more of some good without giving up anything, just by reorganizing production.

We have described Crusoe's technically efficient possibilities. But some of them are not economically efficient. Suppose that Crusoe hates fish, but likes fruit. Then he would be foolish to spend any time fishing, even though it is possible to fish all the time in a technically efficient way. It would be a Pareto improvement for him to switch from fish to fruit. This could be done by transferring resources (Crusoe's time) from one technically efficient use (fishing) to another (foraging).

This simple example illustrates that in order to achieve economic efficiency (a Pareto optimum), it isn't enough to achieve technical efficiency. It is necessary also to take into account the preferences of the actors, and to allocate resources among technically efficient activities in such a way as to exhaust all the possibilities for Pareto improvements. The same point carries over to economies having two people, or many people.

The idea is that for economic efficiency, the economy must shift resources toward those things whose value exceeds their opportunity cost, and must keep shifting until the excess is reduced to zero through the operation of the law of diminishing returns.

In principle the attainment of mere technical efficiency is a simple matter. All one needs is complete technical and engineering information. The catch is that many of our decisions concern investment projects whose returns will come (if at all) only in the distant future. And it is difficult to get complete technical engineering information now about what the possibilities will be in the future.

There is a very important theorem about Pareto optima. It might be called the "invisible hand" theorem, after Adam Smith, who states an imperfect version of it. It says that under suitable conditions, the allocation of resources that results from the operation of a private-property economy with voluntary production and exchange will be a Pareto optimum. It is based on the idea that when people decide what voluntary production and exchange to engage in, they consider what will make them better off.

An important contribution of Gerald Debreu, who was awarded the Nobel Prize for Economic Science in 1983, was to formulate this theorem in careful terms and give a mathematical proof of it. The theorem suggests one way to improve economic efficiency: first select policies that will create the "suitable conditions" under which a private-property voluntary economy leads to a Pareto optimum, and then establish a private-property voluntary economy and let it work without further policy interference. This is a brief and oversimple description of the policy position of many of the best laissez-faire economists. An example is the argument of James Buchanan and Gordon Tullock in their book *The Calculus of Consent*.

To understand it, we need to look at the "suitable conditions" of the invisible hand theorem. They include the following:

1. Every person in the market is so small, relative to the market, that his or her individual actions do not influence the price of anything. Or at least every person acts as if that were true. (General Motors and Toyota violate this condition to some extent in the auto market. Saudi Arabia does in the crude oil market.)

2. Every person has complete information about his or her tastes, about technological possibilities, and about the characteristics and prices of all goods. (This assumption is not completely satisfied for future technology and future goods).

3. Every individual action, or voluntary agreement, affects only the actors involved. That is, nobody is benefited or harmed by actions to which he or she is not a party. (Dirty smokestacks violate this condition. So does a person who builds a flood-control dam on his property that also protects the property of others further downstream.)

Clearly these conditions are not exactly met in real life. For some purposes, they are good approximations of the truth. For others, one or more of them is far from the truth. For each of them, policies have been adopted in the attempt to make the real world conform more closely to them. Consider antitrust policy. It is intended to keep one or a few large firms from exerting monopoly power in any market. Consider truth-in-lending and truth-in-labeling laws. They are designed to inform people as to the true prices and character of the products they are offered. Consider laws that impose fines for discharging harmful substances into the environment. They are attempts to make polluters bear the cost that they impose on others, and hence give incentives to reduce pollution to the point where the damage it does is smaller than the cost of completely eliminating the last bit of pollution.

Clearly it is not possible to enact a set of policies that will make the real world conform exactly to the conditions under which a private-property laissez-faire economy would lead to an optimum allocation of resources. But even if it were possible, and even if it had already been done, this would not settle all policy problems. To see why, let us go on to the next main topic.

The fourth topic is the fact that there is not just one Pareto optimum allocation of resources, there is an infinite number of them. The Pareto optimum that we get from laissez-faire depends on the interpersonal distribution of productive resources that we start with. For example, if you owned all of the Texas oil fields and I owned none, any optimum generated by laissez-faire would produce large amounts of goods that you prefer, and would deliver them to you, but would not produce much for me. On the other hand, if I owned all the Texas oil fields and you owned none, any optimum generated by laissez-faire would produce for me large amounts of goods that I prefer, and not much for you. Thus, the optimum allocations differ in the distribution of well-being among persons. This must be so, by the definition of an optimum. The only way someone can be made better off, if the allocation of resources is already optimal, is by making someone else worse off, that is, by changing the interpersonal distribution of well-being.

Therefore the question of economic efficiency is conceptually separate from the question of fairness of the interpersonal distribution of well-being. One can imagine many different economically efficient allocations, each with a different distribution of well-being among persons. And one can imagine many different distributions of well-being, each of which can be economically efficient or inefficient.

The concept of economic efficiency, that is, of a Pareto optimum, is attractive because it says any reallocation that benefits someone without harming anyone is a move toward an optimum and is therefore desirable. Only a dog in the manger would object to that. But notice that this principle is completely silent on the question of whether the distribution of well-being underlying an optimum should be changed or not. Indeed, the concept of optimum resource allocation is essentially a conservative one, because it directs attention away from the question of whether or not the existing distribution of well-being should be changed. But this question is one of the most pressing perennial policy questions.

This brings us to the fifth main topic, the relation between fairness and efficiency. People feel very strongly about fairness and unfairness. Revolutions are sometimes made over this issue. Have you noticed that people feel especially aggrieved if they lose something that they regarded as their own property, much more so than if they lose the possibility of gaining something that they did not already own?

Though economic efficiency and fairness are conceptually separable, they are intimately tied together because most changes in the economy affect both economic efficiency and the distribution of well-being. Most policies do not constitute Pareto improvements. In fact it is quite difficult to find policies that are Pareto improvements. How many policies can you think of that benefit someone without harming anyone? The abolition of a price ceiling moves the economy closer to a Pareto optimum, but it harms the people who were previously receiving the goods at the ceiling price. The curbing of a monopolist's power over price brings the economy closer to a perfectly competitive equilibrium, but it harms the monopolist. The publication of information about where there are vacancies in the labor markets brings the economy closer to a competitive optimum, but the few who already knew where to find the vacancies lose the advantage that was bestowed on them by their exclusive knowledge.

It is not even true that most technological progress constitutes Pareto improvement. There is nearly always someone who is adversely affected by any policy, or by any technological improvement. The proverbial buggy whip manufacturers suffered from the invention of the automobile. The makers of slide rules have lost from the development of the electronic calculator. And so on.

The connection between fairness and economic efficiency operates in the other direction as well. That is, policies aimed at changing the distribution of well-being in the name of greater fairness almost always reduce economic efficiency. Examples abound.

During the oil embargo of 1973–74, oil products became very scarce at the pre-embargo price. Under a free market policy, the price of oil products would have risen in the United States, as it did in Europe, and the higher price would have cleared the market, so that anyone who wanted to pay the going price could readily be served, as occurred in Europe. In this country, many people felt that if the price were permitted to rise, undeserved profits (unfair profits) would be reaped by those companies who happened to have large inventories of oil products. Hence, price ceilings were imposed, and were defended on the grounds of fairness. Economic efficiency suffered, for many of us spent a valuable resource, our own time, waiting in line for gasoline when we could have been producing something useful.

The minimum wage provides another example. Some people support the minimum wage law on the ground that it redistributes income from employers (who are thought to be mainly in the upper income groups) to the lowest-paid workers. It is true that the minimum wage law raises the wages of those workers who would otherwise be earning less than the minimum, provided that they remain employed. However, it also has the effect of pushing some of those workers into unemployment. It does this by making it illegal for employers who want help at $6,700 a year, and workers who want jobs at $6,700 a year, to get together and make a deal to that effect. Thus, it prevents a Pareto improvement from occurring.

Import quotas are another example. An import quota limits the amount of a commodity that can be brought into the country that imposes the quota. Import quotas are often advocated on the grounds that they protect domestic firms and workers from "unfair" foreign competition. They do permit domestic producers to sell more goods at higher prices. But of course that means domestic consumers must pay more for the protected product. Further, quotas depress the price received by domestic producers of whatever goods would have been exported to pay for the extra imports that would have come in without the quota. Thus, both domestic producers of exportable goods and domestic consumers suffer from an import quota. In fact, economic theory shows that if those who gain from the quota were to pay enough to the losers to compensate them for their loss, the gainers would be worse off than they would have been without the quota. Thus, the imposition of a quota, together with the compensation of the losers by the gainers, would be a Pareto retrogression: some people would be made worse off while nobody would be made better off.

These are but three of countless cases in which policies aimed at improving fairness create situations that are economically inefficient. This situation is very common. I believe that the greatest single problem of economic engineering is to devise policies, when fairness is an important issue, that do not impede economic efficiency. It is essentially impossible to solve this problem completely. The best we can do, if we want to redistribute wealth or income, is to choose policies that involve as small a departure from economic efficiency as possible.

Why is this? Economic theory tells us that if any policy is adopted that redistributes wealth from rich to poor, then those people who are considering productive activity that might increase their wealth will know that if they succeed, the policy will take away some of their wealth and transfer it to the poor. Hence, they will see that the reward they can expect from their productive activity is less than it would be without the redistributive policy. Hence, if they respond at all, they can be expected to devote less effort to productive activity than they would without the redistributive policy.

Further, those who have little wealth will know that if they do not try to increase their wealth by productive activity, the policy will transfer some wealth to them. Hence, they will see that the net reward of productive activity is less than it would be without the policy. Hence, if they respond at all, they can be expected to devote less resources to productive activity than they would without the redistributive policy.

This is not an argument against policies to redistribute wealth. It is an argument about positive economics, not normative economics. Indeed, as will soon become clear, I favor certain types of redistributive policies.

Positive economics offers no solution to the problem of what redistributive policies should be adopted. Kenneth Arrow, in his famous book *Social Choice and Individual Values*, set out to derive a social preference ordering of states of the world that would be based on individual preference orderings and would have certain desirable properties, but he ended up proving that it could not be done. Many economists and philosophers and others have written about the problem, in each case bringing some normative considerations into play. John Rawls in *A Theory of Justice* and Robert Nozick in *Anarchy State and Utopia* have taken radically different positions. Rawls argues in favor of an innovative concept of egalitarianism. Nozick argues that the state has no right to interfere in anyone's private use of his own property so long as he does not forcibly restrain others. Bruce Ackerman in *Social Justice in the Liberal State* takes a view closer to Rawls than to Nozick.

In thinking about policies designed to increase equality, it is useful to distinguish between two kinds of equality, equality of opportunity and equality of outcomes. In a static world where nothing changed, the distinction would not be necessary, for the two would be the same. But in our changing world, they are not the same. It is not uncommon for two people with the same opportunities to do quite different things with them. Either concept of equality alone, carried to the extreme, appears to be unacceptable in modern societies.

Complete equality of outcomes, applied to income, would imply transferring income away from any above-average-income person to a below-average-income person. In effect this would amount to a 100% tax on all income above the average. Its incentive effects would be extremely detrimental to productive activity. No society has such a policy.

Complete equality of opportunity, with no concern for outcomes, would amount to an initially equal distribution of resources in each new generation of people, followed by laissez-faire. This would soon result in an unequal distribution of income. No modern society has a policy of complete laissez-faire, and none enforce a completely equal initial distribution of resources.

Most societies pay some attention to both kinds of equality. Public education contributes to equality of opportunity. So do progressive estate and inheritance taxes. The progressive income tax contributes to equality of outcomes.

The sixth main topic is hazards in economic policy-making. This topic is an outgrowth of the previous one, namely, the relation between fairness and economic efficiency.

One of the chief hazards in economic policy-making is that private or special interests often try to capture public policy and turn it to their own advantage. George Stigler once wrote that public regulation is a commodity obtained by an industry and used for its benefit. This has certainly been true of some industries at some times. One thinks of the railroads and the Interstate Commerce Commission, and of the airlines and the Civil Aeronautics Board. One also thinks of the oil companies and the federal import quotas during the pre-OPEC era, when Arab oil cost pennies a barrel to produce and domestic oil cost dollars a barrel. We would have been better off as a nation to have had no quota and to have imported more cheap OPEC oil in those years and preserved our own oil reserves in the ground.

Anthony Downs has written an interesting book, *An Economic Theory of Democracy*. His theory says that elected officials like to hold office and try to be reelected. Pressure groups are effective in elections, because they organize their members to make their views known to officials, provide campaign contributions, and bring out the vote. Most pressure groups deal with the interests of some producing group, rather than a consumer group, because most people have more to gain or lose by a policy that affects their livelihood than by a policy that affects a product on which they spend only a fraction of their income. Because of the prevalence of producer-oriented pressure groups, many of our statutes have the effect of favoring particular producer interests.

Winston Churchill said that democracy is the worst form of government, excepting only all the other forms that have been tried. One of the main virtues of democracy, in my view, is that whenever a special interest group obtains for itself privileges so egregious that the rest of the population notice it and want to put a stop to it, there is a peaceful way to do it: Vote the ins out.

A second hazard in policy-making is the all too common failure to understand what the effects of a proposed policy will be. This often arises when the long-term effects of a policy are different from the short-term effects. Unfortunately we often pay more attention to the short-term effects than to the long-term ones, and live to regret it. This may be due in part to the fact that we have elections every two years for the House of Representatives and every four years for the presidency. It is surely tempting for a politician to do something that will look good now and that won't turn sour until after the end of his term in office.

One example is provided by the rapid expansion of the money stock that was begun in the 1960s. The short-run effects were wonderful. Unemployment fell. Real output and income rose. The inflation rate hardly rose at all until the late sixties. But then favorable effects on employment and output and income proved to be temporary short-run effects. The long-run effect was a higher rate of inflation. Research in macroeconomics in the past 20 years confirms that this is what happened in many countries in Europe, as well as in Canada and Japan. And it confirms the long-known fact that continued rapid growth of the money stock is a surefire recipe for inflation.

Our difficulty now is that we have to choose between continuing the inflation, which has its disadvantages, and stopping the inflation, which also has its disadvantages. The chief disadvantage of continuing the inflation is the result of two things. First, the experience of many countries shows that if inflation is permitted, it is virtually impossible to maintain it at a constant rate. Second, inflation at a fluctuating rate is very detrimental to long-term planning by both public and private agents, and to stability of employment, output, and income. On the other hand, the chief disadvantage of stopping the inflation is that the required reduction in the growth rate of the money stock has the unhappy side effect of a temporary short-run decline in employment, output, and income. I have advocated reducing the average growth rate of the money stock gradually, from its present rate (about 9% for the past year) to about 8% this year, 7% next year, 6% the next year, and so on, until it reaches the noninflationary rate of about 4% per year, in the belief that a gradual reduction would not create much of a recession, if any. But the effect of gradual versus sudden reduction in the growth of the money stock is not a topic on which we have much reliable positive knowledge.

Another example, which may have helped to elect Ronald Reagan president, is that the budgetary cost of a policy sometimes turns out to be far greater than expected. This problem is especially likely to occur with so-called entitlement programs, such as social security, unemployment compensation, and welfare. Why? Because when such a program is adopted, there is usually no budgetary ceiling. Rather, eligibility conditions are set down, and anyone meeting them is entitled to certain specified benefits. This hazard has been encountered by many countries, not only the United States. Such programs were adopted to fill a clearly perceived need. Perhaps it is possible to continue them, and still keep their cost within limits that are acceptable to the body politic, by adopting the technique that a family would use in adversity. That is, a budgetary ceiling could be set, and all eligible persons could receive the specific benefits, as long as the budgetary ceiling is not reached. But when the ceiling is reached, every eligible person's benefits would be proportionately reduced every time an additional person became eligible.

The seventh and last topic consists of some personal policy recommendations. If you have followed my argument so far, you will understand that I cannot hope to use the results of positive economic science alone to persuade you to agree with these recommendations. I can hope to use positive economics to indicate the effects that can be expected from the adoption of various policies. You will then apply your own values to these effects in order to decide what policies you support. If we agree about what the effects of the policies are, and also about values, then we will agree about the policy recommendations.

The values on which my recommendations are based are that economic efficiency is a good thing, that equality of opportunity is a good thing, and that great inequality of outcomes is a bad thing. The positive economic knowledge I have described indicates clearly that one cannot achieve the extreme in all of these realms at once. They conflict with each other to some extent.

With this preamble, it is almost tautological that the resulting policy recommendations fall into three broad categories. One, seek economic efficiency, within limits. Two, seek equalization of opportunity, within limits. Three, seek equalization of outcomes, again within limits. This doesn't mean much unless the limits are specified. The best way to specify those limits is to get down to cases.

Consider first policies for promoting economic efficiency. For the most part they are aimed at trying to make the economy more like the idealized competitive economy in which voluntary private transactions make Pareto improvements, so that the economy approaches a Pareto optimum. But I don't support complete laissez-faire.

One efficiency-promoting policy is antitrust policy, designed to prevent any private agent or group from monopolizing any important resource. Positive economics contains a theorem saying that a monopolist prevents the achievement of a Pareto optimum, by preventing a deal from being made between customers who want to buy a product at a certain price and resource-owners who are willing to supply the required resources even at a lower price. The theorem also says that the gain made by the monopolist in so doing, if it were all paid as compensation to those who lose by being prevented from making a mutually beneficial deal, would not be enough to compensate the losers for their loss. That is why we say that monopoly entails a misallocation of resources. This is another way of saying that monopoly entails economic inefficiency.

A second policy to promote economic efficiency is to "internalize externalities." What does this phrase mean? An example may help. Consider the buyer of electricity on the one hand, and on the other hand, the utility company that burns coal to produce electricity and spills dirty smoke on its neighbors. In such a case, the buyer of electricity uses more of it than he would in the corresponding Pareto optimum, because he is not paying the cost of the damage done by the dirty smoke. The price he pays for electricity is too cheap. If the utility were required to compensate those who suffer from the dirty smoke, then it would incorporate the cost of that compensation into its calculations and would charge a higher price. In that case, when the electricity buyer and the utility made a mutually beneficial private deal for the sale of electricity, they would not be harming anyone else, and so their private deal would be a Pareto improvement.

This is called internalizing the external cost that the smoke would impose on the utility's neighbors in the absence of any policy. The term is an apt one, for it suggests the shifting of costs away from people who are not a party to a contract (that is, who are external to it), on to the people who make the contract (that is, who are internal to it). It is easy to describe in principle. It is not so easy to carry out in practice, for it requires at least approximate knowledge of who the people are who lose from the externality, and how much they lose.

The same principle of internalizing externalities can be applied to benefits as well as to costs. Consider a person who is considering whether to build a flood-control dam on his property, which will benefit not only himself but also people downstream. Suppose the benefit to him is worth $2 million, and the benefit to people downstream is also worth $2 million, for a total of $4 million. Suppose the dam costs $3 million. Then he will not build it if he has to bear the whole cost himself, for the $3 million cost exceeds his $2 million benefit. But if the gainers downstream could be induced or made to pay half of the cost, then the project would be a Pareto improvement. For centuries, the community taxing power has been used to make everyone pay a share of the cost of a project whose total benefits exceed its cost, when no private person will undertake it because his private benefits are less than the cost. This can be defended on the grounds that it is internalizing an external benefit, and thus facilitating Pareto improvements.

A third recommendation aimed at economic efficiency is to avoid those redistributive policies that have the most pernicious effects on resource allocation. These include quotas that limit imports, exports, and outputs. Also price controls, whether ceilings or floors. Not quite so bad are excise taxes on specific goods, including import tariffs, and subsidies.

The redistributive measures that impede economic efficiency the least are progressive taxes on income, on consumption, and on estates and inheritances. Even they have some detrimental effects on economic efficiency, especially if the marginal rate of tax is very high. These effects operate by shifting the balance of incentive toward leisure (which is not taxed) and away from production of things for sale (which is taxed).

A progressive consumption tax would be similar to a progressive income tax in most respects. One main difference—quite important—is that the consumption tax taxes saving only once, when the income yielded by past savings is consumed, whereas the income tax taxes saving twice, once when the saving occurs, and again when the income yielded by past savings is received. Some advocates of faster growth through greater saving and investment favor the consumption tax over the income tax for this reason.

American death and gift tax rates, which have recently been reduced, probably have relatively little adverse effect on economic efficiency.

To sum up about policies for economic efficiency: the limits I would place on such policies are those imposed by a moderately progressive tax system. This willing departure from economic efficiency is motivated by a concern for fairness, to which I now turn.

Some equalization of opportunity is desirable, in my view, as contrasted with complete laissez-faire. That is the aim of the second type of policy recommendation I support. Universal public education can be seen as a policy of this type. When it works as it is supposed to, it gives each young person tools for improving life, personal and political as well as economic. The breaking down of barriers to entry into particular industries or professions is another example of this type of policy. Unfortunately, all too often, public policy erects barriers to entry rather than breaking them down. Some of these barriers are justified on the grounds that they protect the public against practitioners who are incompetent, such as in the licensing of physicians, attorneys, airline pilots, electricians, and the like. But sometimes legal barriers act primarily to protect the incumbents in an industry from competition. Civil rights legislation also comes under the heading of increasing equality of opportunity. And progressive death taxes have a similar effect, by lessening the extreme differences of inherited wealth that would occur under pure laissez-faire.

Some equalization of outcomes is desirable too, in my view, as compared with laissez-faire. Against this view it is sometimes argued that if two people start out in the world with the same abilities and opportunities, but one works hard and saves much while the other works little and saves nothing, then the resulting difference in wealth and in property income is perfectly justified. It is hard to disagree with this, and I don't. I would be quite happy to leave untaxed any income differences that arose from this source alone. The difficulty is that it's not possible to determine exactly how much of each person's income and wealth came from hard work and thrift, and how much from luck. Don't forget that luck includes the kind of ability one is born with. Hence, I favor a moderately progressive income tax (or consumption tax if you prefer), as a way of diminishing the gross inequalities of income that would occur under laissez-faire. I believe this is quite fair as concerns those income differences that do arise from luck, though I concede it isn't quite fair as concerns those differences that arise from hard work and thrift. However, in my view, luck accounts for more income variation than do hard work and thrift.

Economic efficiency is like the goose that lays the golden eggs. There will always be controversies over how to distribute the golden eggs. In dealing with those controversies, we will be best served if we choose policies that give much scope, rather than little scope, for economic efficiency.

REFERENCES

My thinking on these matters owes a considerable debt to the excellent book, *An Essay on the Nature and Significance of Economic Science*, by Lionel Robbins.

Ackerman, Bruce. *Social Justice in the Liberal State*. New Haven: Yale University Press, 1980.

Arrow, Kenneth J. *Social Choice and Individual Values*. New York: John Wiley and Sons, 1951. Reprint. New Haven: Yale University Press, 1963.

Buchanan, James M., and Gordon Tullock. *The Calculus of Consent*. Ann Arbor: University of Michigan Press, 1962.

Downs, Anthony. *An Economic Theory of Democracy*. New York: Harper and Bros., 1957.

Nozick, Robert. *Anarchy, State and Utopia*. New York: Basic Books, 1974.

Rawls, John. *A Theory of Justice*. Cambridge: Belknap Press of Harvard University Press, 1971.

Robbins, Lionel. *An Essay on the Nature and Significance of Economic Science*. 2d ed. London: Macmillan, 1935.

List of publications of Carl F. Christ

Books

1. *Econometric Models and Methods* (New York, Wiley, 1966), pp. 705 + xxiii. Japanese translation, 1973, Spanish translation, 1974.

2. *Notes on Western Macroeconomics* (a volume in the series of *Lecture Notes of Foreign Economists* in the Chinese University Development Project II), with Chinese translation by Zhang Jun and others. (Shanghai, Fudan University press, 1992), pp. 171 (Chinese) + 219 (English).

3. *Simultaneous Equations Estimation*, edited with an introduction by Carl F. Christ (Aldershot, England, Edward Elgar, 1994), pp. 534 + xxii.

Papers and articles

1. 'A Test of an Econometric Model for the United States, 1921–1947', in Universities–National Bureau Committee, *Conference on Business Cycles* (New York, National Bureau of Economic Research, 1951), pp. 35–107, 123–6. Reprinted as Cowles Commission Paper, new series, no. 49, 1952.

2. 'History of the Cowles Commission 1932–52', in *Economic Theory and Measurement: A Twenty Year Research Report* (Chicago, Cowles Commission for Research in Economics, 1952), pp. 3–65. See also item 32a below.

3. 'A Review of Input–Output Analysis', in Conference on Research in Income and Wealth, *Input–Output Analysis: An Appraisal* (*Studies in Income and Wealth*, Vol. 18) (Princeton, Princeton University Press for National Bureau of Economic Research, 1955), pp. 137–69.

4. 'Aggregate Econometric Models', *American Economic Review* **46** (No. 3, June, 1956), pp. 385–408. Reprinted in American Economic Association *Readings in Business Cycles* (Homewood, Illinois, Irwin, 1965), pp. 307–33.

5. 'On Econometric Models of the U.S. Economy', in Milton Gilbert and Richard Stone (eds), *Income and Wealth*, Series VI (London, Bowes and Bowes for International Association for Research in Income and Wealth, 1957), pp. 1–23.

6. 'Patinkin on Money, Interest, and Prices', *Journal of Political Economy* **65** (No. 4, August, 1957), pp. 347–54.

7. 'Resource Allocation, Economic Stabilization, and Public Policy Toward Prices', in US Congress, Joint Economic Committee, *The Relationship of Prices to Economic Stability and Growth: Compendium*, (Washington, US Government Printing Office, 1958), pp. 345–60.

8. 'Free Enterprise vs. Government Control: A Theoretical Economic Analysis' (in Japanese translation), *Sekai Keizai* (World Economy), February, 1960, pp. 19–32.

9. 'Simultaneous Equation Estimation: Any Verdict Yet?', *Econometrica* **28** (No. 4, October, 1960), pp. 835–45.

10. 'On the Report of the Commission on Money and Credit', *Review of Economics and Statistics* **44** (No. 4, November, 1962), pp. 418–27.

11. 'Interest Rates and "Portfolio Selection" among Liquid Assets in the United States', in Carl F. Christ and others, *Measurement in Economics: Studies in Mathematical Economics and Econometrics in Memory of Yehuda Grunfeld* (Stanford, Stanford University Press, 1963), pp. 201–18.

12. 'Econometrics and Model-Building', *Annals of the American Academy of Political and Social Science* **370** (March, 1967), pp. 164–75.

13. 'A Short-Run Aggregate-Demand Model of the Interdependence and Effects of Monetary and Fiscal Policies with Keynesian and Classical Interest Elasticities', *American Economic Review* **57** (No. 2, May, 1967), pp. 434–43.

14. 'Econometrics in Economics: Some Achievements and Challenges', *Australian Economic Papers* **6** (No. 9, December, 1967), pp. 155–70.

15. 'A Simple Macroeconomic Model with a Government Budget Restraint', *Journal of Political Economy* **76** (No. 1, January/February, 1968), pp. 53–67.

16. 'Econometric Models, Aggregate', in *International Encyclopedia of the Social Sciences* (New York, Macmillan and Free Press, 1968), Vol. 4, pp. 344–50. See also item 26a below.

17. 'Monetary and Fiscal Policy in Macroeconomic Models', in *The Economic Outlook for 1969* (Ann Arbor, University of Michigan Department of Economics, 1969), pp. 93–112.

18. 'A Model of Monetary and Fiscal Policy Effects on the Money Stock, Price Level, and Real Output', *Journal of Money, Credit, and Banking* **1** (No. 4, November, 1969), pp. 683–705.

19. 'Cash or Credit', in *Family Life Education Series* (Baltimore, Baltimore Urban League, 1970), 32 pp.

20. 'Econometric Models of the Financial Sector', *Journal of Money, Credit, and Banking* **3** (No. 2, May, 1971), pp. 419–49.

21. 'Econometrics and Model Building, 1967–1972', *Annals of the American Academy of Political and Social Science* **403** (September, 1972), pp. 153–62.

22. 'Monetary and Fiscal Influences on U.S. Money Income, 1891–1970', *Journal of Money, Credit, and Banking* **5** (No. 1, February, 1973), pp. 279–300.

23. 'The 1973 Report of the President's Council of Economic Advisers: A Review', *American Economic Review* **63** (No. 4, September, 1973), pp. 512–26.

24. 'Judging the Performance of Econometric Models of the U.S. Economy', *International Economic Review* **16** (No. 1, February, 1975), pp. 54–74. Reprinted in Lawrence R. Klein and Edwin Burmeister (eds), *Econometric Model Performance: Comparative Simulation Studies on the U.S. Economy* (Philadelphia, University of Pennsylvania Press, 1976), pp. 322–42.

25. 'An Evaluation of the Economic Policy Proposals of the Joint Economic Committee of the 92nd and 93rd Congresses', in Karl Brunner and Allan H. Meltzer (eds), *Institutions, Policies, and Economic Performance* (Vol. 4 in the *Carnegie–Rochester Conference Series on Public Policy*, a supplementary series to the *Journal of Monetary Economics*), (Amsterdam, North–Holland Publishing Co., 1976), pp. 15–49. See also item 33a below.

26. 'Some Dynamic Theory of Macroeconomic Policy Effects on Income and

Prices under the Government Budget Restraint', *Journal of Monetary Economics* **4** (No. 1, January, 1978), pp. 45–70.

26a. 'Econometric Models, Aggregate', in *International Encyclopedia of Statistics* (New York, Free Press, 1978), Vol. 1, pp. 181–8. A reprint of item 16 above, with Postscript and additional references.

27. 'The Economic Policy Proposals of the Joint Economic Committee of the 94th and 95th U.S. Congresses, 1975 through September 1978', *Journal of Monetary Economics* **5** (No. 3, July, 1979), pp. 375–95.

28. 'On Fiscal and Monetary Policies and the Government Budget Restraint', *American Economic Review* **69** (No. 4, September, 1979), pp. 526–38.

29. 'Regression When Each of Two Variables Is Dependent Some of the Time', in Lawrence R. Klein *et al.* (eds), *Quantitative Economics and Development* (New York, Academic Press, 1980), pp. 115–22.

30. 'Changes in the Financing of the Federal Debt and their Impact on the U.S. Economy, 1948–90', in U.S. Congress, Joint Economic Committee, *Special Study on Economic Change, Vol. 6, Federal Finance: The Pursuit of American Goals* (Washington, U.S.G.P.O., December 23, 1980), pp. 93–185.

31. (with Alan A. Walters), 'The Mythology of Tax Cuts', *Policy Review* **16** (Spring, 1981), pp. 73–86.

32. 'Analysis of Stability in Macroeconomic Models with a Government Budget Restraint', *Revista de Econometria* **2** (No. 1, April, 1982), pp. 5–27.

32a. 'The Founding of the Econometric Society and Econometrica', *Econometrica* **51** (No. 1, January, 1983), pp. 3–6. Reprinted from pp. 5–12 of item 2 above.

33. 'Rules vs. Discretion in Monetary Policy', *CATO Journal* **3** (No. 1, Spring, 1983), pp. 121–41.

33a. 'An Evaluation of the Economic Policy Proposals of the Joint Economic Committee of the 92nd and 93rd Congresses', in Karl Brunner and Allan H. Meltzer (eds), *Theory, Policy, Institutions: Papers from the Carnegie–Rochester Conferences on Public Policy* (Amsterdam, North–Holland Publishing Co., 1983), pp. 349–83. A reprint of item 25 above.

34. 'Early Progress in Estimating Quantitative Economic Relationships in America', *American Economic Review* **75** (No. 6, December, 1985), pp. 39–52.

35. 'Unemployment and Macroeconomics', in Thomas M. Gannon (ed.), *The Catholic Challenge to the American Economy* (New York, Macmillan, 1987), pp. 116–27.

36. 'The Financing of the Government Budget in Japan and Its Relation to Macroeconomic Variables, Appendix II', *Bank of Japan Monetary and Economic Studies* **5** (May, 1987), pp. 1–32.

37. 'On Free Banking: Essay Review of *The Theory of Free Banking* by George Selgin', *Market Process* **7** (Spring, 1989), pp. 5–10.

38. 'A Philosophy of Life', *The American Economist* **34** (Spring, 1990), pp. 33–9.

39. 'Economics and Public Policy', in Shripad Pendse (ed.), *Perspectives on an Economic Future: Forms, Reforms, and Evaluations (Contributions in*

Economics and Economic History, No. 116) (New York, Greenwood Press, 1991), pp. 15–29.

40. 'Pitfalls in Macroeconomic Model Building', in Tej K. Kaul and Jati K. Sengupta (eds), *Economic Models, Estimation, and Socioeconomic Systems: Essays in Honor of Karl A. Fox (Contributions to Economic Analysis*, No. 186) (Amsterdam, North–Holland, and New York, Elsevier, 1991), pp. 257–89.

41. 'Decomposition of the Expected Squared Error of Forecast from a Linear Forecasting Equation', *Indian Economic Review* **27** (Special Number in memory of Sukhamoy Chakravarty, 1992, but published in 1994), pp. 325–8.

42. 'When Is Free Banking More Stable Than Regulated Banking?', in Haim Barkai, Stanley Fischer and Nissan Liviatan (eds), *Monetary Theory and Thought: Essays in Honour of Don Patinkin* (London, Macmillan Press, 1993), pp. 185–209.

43. 'Assessing Applied Econometric Results', *Federal Reserve Bank of St. Louis Review* **75** (No. 2, March/April 1993), pp. 71–94.

44. 'The Cowles Commission's Contributions to Econometrics at Chicago, 1939–1955', *Journal of Economic Literature* **32** (No. 1, March, 1994), pp. 30–59.

Other publications: discussions, comments, reviews, abstracts, hearings, notes, etc.

1. Review of *Variability in Recognizing Scientific Inquiry: An Analysis of High School Science Textbooks* by Richard H. Lampkin, *Etc.: A Review of General Semantics* **7** (No. 1, Autumn, 1949), pp. 54–6.

2. Discussion of 'Productivity in the Airframe Industry', by Herman Bergman. Presented at Chicago meeting of Econometric Society, December, 1950. Abstract in *Econometrica* **19** (No. 3, July, 1951), pp. 329–30.

3. Comment on 'Business Cycle Analysis and Public Policy', by Arthur Smithies, in Universities–National Bureau Committee, *Conference on Business Cycles* (New York, National Bureau of Economic Research, 1951), pp. 420–22.

4. Review of *The Role of Measurement in Economics* by Richard Stone, *American Economic Review* **41** (No. 5, December, 1951), pp. 953–5.

5. Review of *The Problem of Summation in Economic Science* by Goran Nyblen, *Journal of Political Economy* **60** (No. 4, August, 1952), p. 365.

6. 'What Kind of Data for Econometrics?', Presented at East Lansing meeting of Econometric Society, September, 1952. Abstract in *Econometrica* **21** (No. 2, April, 1953), pp. 338–9.

7. Discussion of 'The Development of the Concepts of Mechanism and Model in Physical Science and Economic Thought', by Gregor Sebba, *American Economic Review* **43** (No. 2, May, 1953), pp. 271–4.

8. Review of *Econometrics* by Gerhard Tintner, *Journal of Political Economy* **61** (No. 3, June, 1953), pp. 262–3.

9. 'Pitfalls in Econometrics'. Presented at Washington meeting of Econometric Society, December, 1953. Abstract in *Econometrica* **22** (No. 4, October, 1954), pp. 521–2.

10. Review of *Post Keynesian Economics* edited by Kenneth K. Kurihara, *Political Science Quarterly* **70** (No. 3, September, 1955), pp. 436–9.

11. Review of *Mathematical Economics* by R.G.D. Allen, *Journal of Farm Economics* **40** (No. 4, November, 1958), pp. 971–4.

12. *Relationship of Prices to Economic Stability and Growth, Hearings*. US Congress, Joint Economic Committee, May 12–22, 1958 (Washington, US Government Printing Office, 1958), pp. 247–8, 252–84.

13. *Employment, Growth and Price Levels, Hearings.* Part 8, US Congress, Joint Economic Committee, September 28–October 2, 1959 (Washington, US Government Printing Office, 1959), pp. 2483–5, 2503–13.

14. Comment on 'On the Design of Consistent Output and Input Indexes for Productivity Measurement' by Irving Siegel, in Conference on Research in Income and Wealth, *Output, Input, and Productivity Measurement (Studies in Income and Wealth*, Vol. 25) (Princeton, Princeton University Press for National Bureau of Economic Research, 1961), pp. 41–6.

15. Review of *Economic Forecasts and Policy* by H. Theil, *Econometrica* **30** (No. 1, January, 1962), pp. 209–10.

16. Comment on 'Money and Business Cycles' by Milton Friedman and Anna J. Schwarz, *Review of Economics and Statistics* **45** (No. 1, February, 1963), pp. 154–5.

17. Discussion of three papers on empirical investment functions by Robert Eisner, Dale Jorgenson, and Edwin Kuh, *American Economic Review* **53** (No. 2, May 1963), pp. 269–70.

18. (with Michael Kolodny) 'Efficiency, Economics and Engineering', *The [Johns Hopkins] Vector* **18** (January, 1964), pp. 16, 26, 28.

19. Comment on 'A Forecast Determination of National Product, Employment, and Price Level in Canada from an Econometric Model' by T.M. Brown, in Conference on Research in Income and Wealth, *Models of Income Determination (Studies in Income and Wealth*, Vol. 28) (Princeton, Princeton University Press for National Bureau of Economic Research, 1964), pp. 86–92.

20. Review of *Academic Encounter: The American University in Japan and Korea* by Martin Bronfenbrenner, *Journal of Political Economy* **72** (No. 2, April, 1964), pp. 207–8.

21. Review of *The New Science of Economics* by George Soule, Baltimore Sunday *Sun* (10 May 1964).

22. Discussion of 'A Structural Approach to the Impact of Monetary Policy' by R.L. Teigen, *Journal of Finance* **19** (No. 2, May, 1964, Part 1), pp. 309–10.

23. 'National Product', in *A Dictionary of the Social Sciences*, edited by Julius Gould and William L. Kolb (Glencoe, Illinois, The Free Press, 1964), pp. 453–5.

24. 'Elasticity', in *A Dictionary of the Social Sciences*, edited by Julius Gould and William L. Kolb (Glencoe, Illinois, The Free Press, 1964), pp. 232–3.

25. Review of *Capital Formation in Japan 1867–1940* by Henry Rosovsky, *Journal of Political Economy* **72** (No. 6, December, 1964), pp. 622–3.

26.   Review of *Econometric Theory* by Arthur Goldberger, *Journal of Farm Economics* **47** (No. 1, February, 1965), pp. 156–8.

27.   Discussion of 'Pitfalls in Financial Model Building' by William C. Brainard and James Tobin, *American Economic Review* **58** (No. 2, May, 1968), pp. 150–54.

28.   *Standards for Guiding Monetary Action, Hearings.* US Congress, Joint Economic Committee, May 8–16, 1968 (Washington, US Government Printing Office, 1968), pp. 77–83, 101–18.

29.   Review of *Input–Output Economics* by Wassily Leontief, *Journal of Political Economy* **76** (No. 6, November/December, 1968), pp. 1247–9.

30.   Review of *Topics in Regression Analysis* by Arthur Goldberger, *Journal of Economic Literature* **7** (No. 1, March, 1969), p. 100.

31.   Discussion of three papers on price determination by Lawrence R. Klein, Albert A. Hirsch, and George deMenil and Jared J. Enzler, in Otto Eckstein (ed.), *The Econometrics of Price Determination: Conference* (Washington, US Board of Governors of the Federal Reserve System, 1972), pp. 325–32.

32.   'Nixonomics vs. McGovernomics', *Johns Hopkins Magazine* (Fall, 1972), pp. 10–13.

33.   Discussion of 'Is Verification Possible? The Evaluation of Large Econometric Models' by Harold T. Shapiro, *American Journal of Agricultural Economics* **55** (No. 2, May, 1973), pp. 271–3.

34.   Letter on the US oil problem, *Congressional Record* (8 March 1974), pp. S3190–91.

35.   Discussion of 'Econometric Studies of Health Economics' by Martin S. Feldstein, in M.D. Intriligator and D.A. Kendrick (eds), *Frontiers of Quantitative Economics*, Vol. II (*Contributions to Economic Analysis*, Vol. 87) (Amsterdam, North–Holland and New York, American Elsevier, 1974), pp. 434–6.

36.   *Monetary Policy Oversight, Hearings.* US Senate, Committee on Banking, Housing, and Urban Affairs, Feb. 25–6, 1975 (Washington, US Government Printing Office, 1975). Written Statement to the Committee, pp. 150–51.

37.   *First Meeting on the Conduct of Monetary Policy, Hearings.* US Senate, Committee on Banking, Housing, and Urban Affairs, April 29–30 and May 1, 1975 (Washington, US Government Printing Office, 1975), pp. 76–80, 101–15, and 135–61.

38.   Discussion of 'Segregation on a Continuous Variable' by Thomas G. Schelling and 'A Model of Attitude Change' by Frank L. Adelman and Irma Adelman, in Joel Bergsman and Howard L. Wiener (eds), *Urban Problems and Public Policy Choices* (New York, Praeger, 1975), pp. 118–20.

39.   *Controlling Inflation, Hearings.* US Senate, Committee on the Budget, February 26, 1976 (Washington, US Government Printing Office, 1976), pp. 77–80, 83–99.

40.   Discussion of 'Inside the Monetarist Black Box' by Jerome Stein, in Jerome Stein (ed.), *Monetarism* (*Studies in Monetary Economics*, Vol. I) (Amsterdam, North–Holland, 1976), pp. 233–40.

41. 'A Modest Proposal', in Jerome Stein (ed.), *Monetarism (Studies in Monetary Economics*, Vol. I) (Amsterdam, North–Holland, 1976), p. 337.

42. 'On Economic Policies', *The [Johns Hopkins] News Letter* (15 October 1976), p.3.

43. 'Karl Brunner at the Cowles Commission: A Reminiscence', *Journal of Money, Credit, and Banking* 9 (No. 1, February, 1977, Part 2), pp. 245–6.

44. 'Stop Rocking the Boat, or The Misery Index and How to Deflate It', *Johns Hopkins Magazine* 28, No. 6 (November, 1977), pp. 21–5.

45. *Review of Monetary Policy in 1977, Hearings.* US House of Representatives, Subcommittee on Domestic Monetary Policy of the Committee on Banking, Finance and Urban Affairs, January 30, 1978 (Washington, US Government Printing Office, 1978), pp. 4–24 and 42–54, together with replies to questions posed by the Subcommittee Chairman, pp. 76–8 and 100–101.

46. *The 1979 Economic Report of the President, Hearings.* US Congress, Joint Economic Committee, February 6, 1979 (Washington, US Government Printing Office, 1979), pp. 189–204, 213–30.

47. Comment on 'Statistical Analysis of Econometric Models' by Arnold Zellner, *Journal of the American Statistical Association* 74 (No. 367, September, 1979), pp. 645–6.

48. *Budget Policy Outlook for Fiscal Year 1981, Hearings.* US House of Representatives, Committee on the Budget, 26 February 1981 (Washington, US Government Printing Office, 1981) pp. 570–82.

49. (with Louis J. Maccini), 'What's Wrong with the Economic Plan', Baltimore *Sun* (26 March 1981), page A–23.

50. (with Alan A. Walters), 'Reply' (to comments by Paul Craig Roberts and by Alan Reynolds on No. 31 in Section II above, 'The Mythology of Tax Cuts'), *Policy Review* 17 (Summer, 1981), pp. 5–7.

51. (with Louis J. Maccini), 'Deficits: The Truth', Baltimore *Sun* (10 March 1982), page A–11.

52. Comment on 'How Much Is Owed by the Federal Government?' by Rudolph G. Penner, in Karl Brunner and Allan Meltzer (eds), *Monetary Regimes and Protectionism* (Vol. 16 in the *Carnegie–Rochester Conference Series on Public Policy*), (Amsterdam, North–Holland Publishing Co., 1982), pp. 257–64.

53. (with Louis J. Maccini) 'The Course Ahead', Baltimore *Sun* (5 April 1983), p. A–7.

54. Comments on 'Structural Econometric Modeling and Time Series Analysis: An Integrated Approach' by Franz C. Palm, in Arnold Zellner (ed.), *Applied Time Series Analysis of Economic Data* (Economic Research Report ER–5, US Bureau of the Census, Washington, USGPO, 1983), pp. 234–6.

55. (with Louis J. Maccini) 'What's the Matter with Deficits?', Baltimore *Sun* (29 March 1984), p. A–11.

56. Comment on 'Forecasting by Extrapolation: Conclusions from 25 Years of Research' by J. Scott Armstrong, *Interfaces* 14 (No. 6, November–December 1984), pp. 62–3.

57. (with Louis J. Maccini) 'To Avert the Crisis', Baltimore *Sun* (May 15, 1985).

58. Review of *Advanced Econometrics: A Bridge to the Literature* by Edward Greenberg and Charles E. Webster, Jr., *Journal of the American Statistical Association* **80** (No. 391, September, 1985), pp. 781–3.

59. 'Accuracy of Forecasting as a Measure of Economic Uncertainty' (a discussion of 'Some Evidence on the Comparative Uncertainty Experienced under Different Monetary Regimes' by Allan H. Meltzer), in Colin D. Campbell and William R. Dougan (eds), *Alternate Monetary Regimes* (Baltimore, Johns Hopkins University Press, 1986), pp. 154–60.

60. 'Government Budget Restraint', in John Eatwell, Peter Newman, and Murray Milgate (eds), *The New Palgrave* (New York, Stockton, 1987), Vol. 2, pp. 554–6.

61. (with Leonid Hurwicz) 'Tjalling Charles Koopmans', in John Eatwell, Peter Newman, and Murray Milgate (eds), *The New Palgrave* (New York, Stockton, 1987), Vol. 3, pp. 62–7.

62. Review of *The History of Statistics: The Measurement of Uncertainty before 1990* by Stephen Stigler, *Journal of Economic Literature* **25** (No. 4, December, 1987), pp. 1859–60.

63. *Zero Inflation, Hearing.* US House of Representatives, Subcommittee on Banking, Finance, and Urban Affairs, Part 3, February 22, 1990 (Washington, US Government Printing Office, 1990), pp. 2–6, 1–33, 35–44.

64. 'Teaching Economics in China', in Richard T. Gill (ed.), *The National Economists Club Reader* (Bristlecone Books, Mountain View, California, 1991), pp. 62–3.

65. 'U.S. Demographics and Saving: Predictions of Three Saving Models. A Comment', in Allan H. Meltzer and Charles I. Plosser (eds), *Carnegie–Rochester Conference Series on Public Policy*, Vol. 34 (Amsterdam, North–Holland, 1991), p. 163.

66. 'Hopkins economist dies' (an obituary for Bela Balassa), *Johns Hopkins Magazine* **43** (August, 1991), p. 15.

67. 'Policy undertakings by the seven "summit" countries: ascertaining the degree of compliance. A comment', in Allan H. Meltzer and Charles I. Plosser (eds), *Carnegie–Rochester Conference Series on Public Policy*, Vol. 35 (Amsterdam, North–Holland, 1991), pp. 309–13.

68. 'In Memoriam: Bela Belassa (1928–1991)', *Journal of Comparative Economics* **15** (No. 4, December, 1991), pp. 577–81.

69. Review of *A History of Macroeconometric Model Building* by Ronald Bodkin, Lawrence R. Klein, and Kanta Marwah, *Journal of the History of Economic Thought* **14** (No. 1, Spring, 1992), pp. 110–12.

70. Review of *The Formation of Econometrics* by Qin Duo, *Economica* **62** (No. 246, May, 1995), pp. 273–4.

Name index

Aberthaw 170
Abramovitz, Moses 66
Ackerman, Bruce 500, 506
Adams, F. Gerard 205
Ahlbrecht, Jonathan 211
Albach, Horst 322
Allen, Roy G.D. 19, 30, 38, 72–3, 78
Allen, Stephen G. 45, 49, 59, 95–6, 106
Almon, Shirley 273, 275, 278
Amemiya, Takeshi 98, 106
Amoako-Tuffour, Joe 459
Andersen, Leonall C. 194, 205, 219, 276, 278–9, 399, 406
Anderson, R.L. 39
Anderson, Theodore W. 29, 37, 39, 63, 80, 82, 94, 96–9, 106, 113, 123, 134, 146, 183
Ando, Albert 197, 204–5
Andrews, Jr., William H. 39–40, 96, 108
Archibald, G.C. 237, 247
Arrow, Kenneth 29, 58–9, 63–5, 81, 500, 506
Asako, Kazumi 375

Balbach, Ted 11
Baltensperger, Ernst 454, 456
Barnett, William 414, 441
Barro, Robert 378, 406
Bartky, Walter 26
Basmann, Robert 96, 99, 102, 105–6
Bayes, Thomas 220
Bean, Louis 19
Becker, Gary 85, 107
Beckmann, Martin J. 45
Belcher, Donald R. 9
Bell, Laird 20
Benini, Rodolfo 68, 77
Bergstrom, A.R. 374
Bizer, David 455
Black, Fischer 454, 456
Blinder, Alan S. 284–6, 299, 301, 309, 315, 317–20, 322
Blough, Stephen 80, 211, 459
Boddy, Francis 64
Boissevain, Charles H. 7
Boorstein, E. 41
Boothe, Paul 459
Borts, George 50, 96, 106

Bowley, Arthur L. 10
Box, George E.P. 73, 98, 102, 106, 194, 216
Brainard, William C. 464, 490
Bronfenbrenner, Jean 59, 92, 106, 113, 148, 183
Brown, Tillman Merritt 63, 64, 188, 205
Brownlee, Oswald H. 237
Brumberg, Richard E. 95, 106
Brunner, Karl 237, 284–6, 303, 309, 315, 322, 455
Bucci, Gabriella 66
Buchanan, James 406, 411, 496, 506
Buiter, Willem H. 310, 315, 318–20, 322, 381, 406
Burke, P.E. 246, 261
Burns, Arthur F. 85, 104, 106, 353, 374, 421, 431

Cagan, Phillip D. 246
Canning, John B. 12
Carlson, Keith 194, 205, 349, 406
Cassels, John M. 74, 77
Cassio 35
Chapman, Edward N. 17, 21
Charnes, A. 65
Chernoff, Herman 29, 82, 94, 98, 106, 113, 160, 167
Christ, Carl F. 45, 49, 80, 90, 95–7, 104, 106–8, 219, 222, 232–4, 245–6, 249, 251, 261, 264–5, 268, 276, 278, 284–5, 290, 309, 320, 322, 381, 394, 406, 431, 445, 454–5, 475, 491
Churchill, Winston 501
Clark, John Bates 69
Clifford, W.K. 21
Cobb, Charles W. 69, 77, 83, 85, 98, 106, 140, 142
Cochrane, Donald 167, 184
Coen, Robert M. 190–94, 197–201, 204, 206
Cooper, Gershon 39
Cooper, W.W. 65
Copeland, Morris 246
Courakis, A.S. 232
Cournot, Augustin 19, 66, 69, 71, 78
Cowles, Alfred 3–4, 7–15, 17–18, 20, 22–3, 25–6, 41, 44, 46, 80, 81, 106

Economists of the Twentieth Century

Monetarism and Macroeconomic
Policy
Thomas Mayer

Studies in Fiscal Federalism
Wallace E. Oates

The World Economy in Perspective
Essays in International Trade and European
Integration
Herbert Giersch

Towards a New Economics
Critical Essays on Ecology, Distribution and
Other Themes
Kenneth E. Boulding

Studies in Positive and Normative
Economics
Martin J. Bailey

The Collected Essays of Richard E.
Quandt (2 volumes)
Richard E. Quandt

International Trade Theory and Policy
Selected Essays of W. Max Corden
W. Max Corden

Organization and Technology in Capitalist
Development
William Lazonick

Studies in Human Capital
Collected Essays of Jacob Mincer, Volume 1
Jacob Mincer

Studies in Labor Supply
Collected Essays of Jacob Mincer, Volume 2
Jacob Mincer

Macroeconomics and Economic Policy
The Selected Essays of Assar Lindbeck,
Volume I
Assar Lindbeck

The Welfare State
The Selected Essays of Assar Lindbeck,
Volume II
Assar Lindbeck

Classical Economics, Public Expenditure
and Growth
Walter Eltis

Money, Interest Rates and Inflation
Frederic S. Mishkin

The Public Choice Approach to Politics
Dennis C. Mueller

The Liberal Economic Order
Volume I Essays on International Economics
Volume II Money, Cycles and Related Themes
Gottfried Haberler
Edited by Anthony Y.C. Koo

Economic Growth and Business Cycles
Prices and the Process of Cyclical Development
Paolo Sylos Labini

International Adjustment, Money and
Trade
Theory and Measurement for Economic Policy,
Volume I
Herbert G. Grubel

International Capital and Service Flows
Theory and Measurement for Economic Policy,
Volume II
Herbert G. Grubel

Unintended Effects of Government
Policies
Theory and Measurement for Economic Policy,
Volume III
Herbert G. Grubel

The Economics of Competitive Enterprise
Selected Essays of P.W.S. Andrews
*Edited by Frederic S. Lee
and Peter E. Earl*

The Repressed Economy
Causes, Consequences, Reform
Deepak Lal

Economic Theory and Market Socialism
Selected Essays of Oskar Lange
Edited by Tadeusz Kowalik

Trade, Development and Political
Economy
Selected Essays of Ronald Findlay
Ronald Findlay

General Equilibrium Theory
The Collected Essays of Takashi Negishi,
Volume I
Takashi Negishi

The History of Economics
The Collected Essays of Takashi Negishi,
Volume II
Takashi Negishi

Studies in Econometric Theory
The Collected Essays of Takeshi Amemiya
Takeshi Amemiya

Exchange Rates and the Monetary System
Selected Essays of Peter B. Kenen
Peter B. Kenen

Econometric Methods and Applications
(2 volumes)
G.S. Maddala

National Accounting and Economic
Theory
The Collected Papers of Dan Usher, Volume I
Dan Usher

Welfare Economics and Public Finance
The Collected Papers of Dan Usher, Volume II
Dan Usher

Economic Theory and Capitalist Society
The Selected Essays of Shigeto Tsuru, Volume I
Shigeto Tsuru

Methodology, Money and the Firm
The Collected Essays of D.P. O'Brien
(2 volumes)
D.P. O'Brien

Economic Theory and Financial Policy
The Selected Essays of Jacques J. Polak
(2 volumes)
Jacques J. Polak

Sturdy Econometrics
Edward E. Leamer

The Emergence of Economic Ideas
Essays in the History of Economics
Nathan Rosenberg

Productivity Change, Public Goods and
Transaction Costs
Essays at the Boundaries of Microeconomics
Yoram Barzel

Reflections on Economic Development
The Selected Essays of Michael P. Todaro
Michael P. Todaro

The Economic Development of Modern
Japan
The Selected Essays of Shigeto Tsuru,
Volume II
Shigeto Tsuru

Money, Credit and Policy
Allan H. Meltzer

Macroeconomics and Monetary Theory
The Selected Essays of Meghnad Desai,
Volume I
Meghnad Desai

Poverty, Famine and Economic
Development
The Selected Essays of Meghnad Desai,
Volume II
Meghnad Desai

Explaining the Economic Performance
of Nations
Essays in Time and Space
Angus Maddison

Economic Doctrine and Method
Selected Papers of R.W. Clower
Robert W. Clower

Economic Theory and Reality
Selected Essays on their Disparities and
Reconciliation
Tibor Scitovsky

Doing Economic Research
Essays on the Applied Methodology of
Economics
Thomas Mayer

Institutions and Development Strategies
The Selected Essays of Irma Adelman,
Volume I
Irma Adelman

Dynamics and Income Distribution
The Selected Essays of Irma Adelman,
Volume II
Irma Adelman

The Economics of Growth and
Development
Selected Essays of A.P. Thirlwall
A.P. Thirlwall

Theoretical and Applied Econometrics
The Selected Papers of Phoebus J. Dhrymes
Phoebus J. Dhrymes

Innovation, Technology and the Economy
The Selected Essays of Edwin Mansfield
(2 volumes)
Edwin Mansfield

Economic Theory and Policy in Context
The Selected Essays of R.D. Collison Black
R.D. Collison Black

Location Economics
Theoretical Underpinnings and Applications
Melvin L. Greenhut

Spatial Microeconomics
Theoretical Underpinnings and Applications
Melvin L. Greenhut

Capitalism, Socialism and Post-
Keynesianism
Selected Essays of G.C. Harcourt
G.C. Harcourt

Time Series Analysis and
Macroeconometric Modelling
The Collected Papers of Kenneth F. Wallis
Kenneth F. Wallis

Foundations of Modern Econometrics
The Selected Essays of Ragnar Frisch
(2 volumes)
Edited by Olav Bjerkholt

Growth, the Environment and the
Distribution of Incomes
Essays by a Sceptical Optimist
Wilfred Beckerman

The Economics of Environmental
Regulation
Wallace E. Oates

Econometrics, Macroeconomics and
Economic Policy
Selected Papers of Carl F. Christ
Carl F. Christ

Economic Analysis and Political Ideology
The Selected Essays of Karl Brunner,
Volume One
Edited by Thomas Lys